Appraising Residences & Income Properties

Henry S. Harrison

MAI, RM, SRPA, ASA, IFAS, CSA, CERA, DREI

Published by the H Squared Company
315 Whitney Avenue, New Haven, CT 06511
(203) 562-3159

ACKNOWLEDGMENTS

All the house style pictures in this book are by artist Joseph Jaqua. The other illustrations are by Peter A. Farbach. All the artwork and Illustrations are the property of Henry S. Harrison. They were first published In his book Rouses: *The Illustrated Guide to Construction, Design and Systems* published by the Realtors National Marketing Institute of the National Association of Realtors, Chicago, IL, 1973. All rights reserved.

No reproductions are permitted without written permission.

A portion of the material in this book is taken from **Appraising the Single Family Residence,** written by the author and the late Dr. George F. Bloom, and published by the American Institute of Real Estate Appraisers. This material, as well as other material appearing In every chapter of this text, is based on **The Appraisal of Real Estate,** published by The Appraisal Institute, Chicago, Illinois, which is considered by the author to be the definitive reference work on the subject of real estate appraising. All of this material is copyrighted by The Appraisal Institute. The author sincerely appreciates The Appraisal Institute's permission to use this copyrighted material.

Published by the H Squared Company
315 Whitney Avenue
New Haven, Connecticut 06511
(203) 562-3159

© 1989-2004 *The H Squared Company*
All rights reserved. First published 1989
Printed in the United States of America
Library of Congress Catalog Number 89-83459

First Printing	1989
Second Printing	1990
Third Printing	1991
Forth Printing	1991
Fifth Printing	1992
Sixth Printing	1992
Seventh Printing	1993
Eight Printing	1993
Ninth Printing	1993
Tenth Printing	1995
Eleventh Printing	1996
Twelfth Printing	1997
Thirteenth Printing	1999
MILLENNIUM EDITION	
Fourteenth Printing	2000
Fifteenth Printing	2001
Sixteenth Printing	2002
Seventeenth Printing	2003
Eighteenth Printing	2004

Harrison, Henry S.
Appraising Residences and Income Properties

ISBN 0-927054-00-0 pbk

FOREWORD

Real Estate Appraisers enjoy a unique position of trust in the real estate profession and in the whole community. They help people buy homes, Investment properties and many other kinds of real estate. They help lenders determine the suitability of property being offered as loan security, estimate value for insurance purposes, help the courts set condemnation awards, settle estates and establish property tax rates just to mention a few of the hundreds of reasons why their estimates of the *value* of real estate are required.

My goal in writing this book and keeping it updated annually is to help students learn about real estate appraising by presenting the materials in a straight-forward easy-to-understand manner.

This printing of **Appraising Residences and Income Properties** incorporates some of the sections of the *Uniform Standards of Professional Appraisal Practice* (Standards 1-3) which pertain to real estate appraising. All appraisers are required to take an additional course that just covers the USPAP.

It would have been impossible to write this book without a lot of help and encouragement. My wife and partner in business, Ruth Lambert, acted as first edition editor, proofreader and major supporter of this project. She and my children H Alex, Kate, Eve, Julie and my grandchildren Nina, Ruby, Joseph and Zev always give up time which would have been theirs each time I write or update a book.

Jacqueline Koral supervised the original editing, typesetting and printing. Original type was set by Naomi Corso. Graphic designer, Josephine Craig, was in charge of the artwork. I would especially like to thank Ed Petka and Pete DePasquale who spent man hours proofreading the text and Tom Heath, an appraisal instructor from Massachusetts who made many excellent suggestions for corrections. Also, many thanks to Maura Glanakos and David Highnote, Production Managers, and Kelley Gill, Production Assistant, for their work in updating some of the new printing.

The model appraisal was developed by Barbara Kaye, my former appraisal associate, who became a bank Vice President, Additional photographs were taken by Richard Chamberlin, Sr. Even my late father, Dr. J.M. Harrison (at the time age 94) sent material for the model appraisal from Florida and this Is the third book in which my father-in-law, Dr. Joseph M. Lambert's bell curve drawing has appeared.

The beautiful cover was designed by graphic artist Lauri Wirta using the house drawings of Joseph Jaqua.

Because this book has become widely used on the West Coast, we have added additional pictures of California houses and other material applicable to appraising properties in the western United States.

I am looking forward to meeting many of you sometime in the future at my seminars and at our booths at the various conventions we attend. I hope this book Is just the first step in your appraisal education.

I wrote this book in 1989. This is the 18th printing and you are joining over 100,000 other students who have used this book.

H^2

In memory of my mother

HELEN S. HARRISON

She never doubted I could do anything
I wanted to, even write books.

and

Dr. George F. Bloom, MAI, SRPA
Professor of Real Estate, Indiana University

His words from our book *Appraising The Single Family Residence*

"The close relationship that this project necessitated between the authors has produced an even closer friendship. Many hours spent together have produced not only a tangible product but a distinct camaraderie, compassion and total respect for each other. May it last forever."

If a man does not keep pace with his companions,
perhaps it is because he hears a different drummer.
Let him step to the music which he hears,
however measured or far away.

Thoreau: Walden XVIII

All of the house style pictures used to illustrate this book were taken from my first book, Houses The Illustrated Guide to Construction Design and Systems, published by the Realtors National Marketing Institute of the National Association of Realtors. In this book a full page is devoted to each of the 58 house styles. Below is a typical page illustrating the "Octagon House". It is my favorite style because it is 100% American. Its inventor, Orsen Squire Fowler was the Dr. Rubens of the 1800's. His popular books expounded his theory that living in an octagon house improved the occupants health and sex life (similar to the recent pyramid house theory). As a result of his books and lectures, over 10,000 octagon houses were built around 1850, in all 50 states.

Nineteenth Century American

OCTAGON HOUSE (Octagon - 704)

Key Distinguishing Characteristics

The most distinguishing characteristic of this style is the octagonal shape.

Other Distinguishing Characteristics

Stone, wood or concrete walls
Flat roofs
Chimney or beleveder in the center
Variety of window and door types used

History

Most of these houses were built around 1850. They were a result of an idea put forth by Orson Squire Fowler, a popular author of the time who wrote about love, marital happiness, sex and phrenology. In several of his popular books he expounded the theory of a happy life in an octagon-shaped house. He thought that this design made for good interior circulation, heating and lighting. Octagon houses were built throughout the U.S. and several hundred are still lived in today. The house was explained in detail in his book, *A Home for All, or the Gravel Wall and Octagon Mode of Building, New, Cheap, Convenient, Superior and Adapted to Rich and Poor.*

CONTENTS

*The entire text of this book and the Student Workbook
can be found on the enclosed CD-ROM.*

1 The Appraisal Profession
Uniform Standards of Professional Appraisal Practice

TYPES OF RESIDENTIAL APPRAISAL ASSIGNMENTS

Real estate appraisals are generally made by staff appraisers in the organizations requiring such appraisals or by fee appraisers, who are independent contractors. Almost anyone the appraiser meets can be a potential source of business. The list of those seeking the services of a real estate appraiser includes:

--**Buyers and sellers of homes.** Appraisers assist them in setting listing and offering prices and in making final decisions to complete a sale or purchase.

--**Lending institutions** such as savings and loan associations, savings banks, commercial banks, credit unions, insurance companies, pension funds and investment trusts. Appraisers estimate the market value of residences being accepted as loan security. The trust departments of these organizations use appraisers for estate planning and estate disposal. Real estate departments use appraisers to help manage and plan their activities.

--**Investors.** Appraisers help them acquire and dispose of real estate investments.

--**Architects.** Appraisers help judge the economic feasibility of proposed projects as well as site selection and acquisitions.

--**Builders and developers.** Appraisers help them to make site acquisitions, develop sites to highest and best use, test the feasibility of projects, obtain mortgages and equity financing, attract investors and assist in the sale of projects.

--**Lawyers.** Appraisers are often hired on behalf of clients. Lawyers also recommend appraisers to help divide property between disputing heirs, partners or clients. They use appraisers for condemnation cases, tax appeals, estate planning and disposal of estates and a variety of other uses.

--**Tenants.** Appraisers help them estimate fair rental. In condemnation proceedings, tenants need appraisers to estimate their leasehold value (leasehold interests are those of the lessee, tenant or renter).

--**Insurers and the insured.** Appraisers estimate the insurable value of property to aid in determining the proper amount of insurance. Appraisers also play an important role in claims adjustments.

--**Accountants**. Appraisers are hired for clients to help estimate the value of assets and to establish rates of depreciation.

--**Business corporations.** Appraisers help acquire and dispose of residential property, assist in the transfer of employees, evaluate real estate assets, develop real estate programs and plan real estate activities.

--**Non-profit organizations.** Appraisers assist in purchase decisions and value the organization's holdings.

--**Government agencies at Federal, state and local levels.** These are all large users of appraisals. Some Federal agencies that use appraisals are the Veterans Administration, Federal Housing Administration, Federal Home Loan Mortgage Corporation, General Services Administration, Internal Revenue Service, Post Office Department, and Farm Home Administration. States condemn and purchase residential land for schools and other government buildings, parks, open space programs and wetlands. Local governments depend on appraisers in the process of acquiring property for schools and other government buildings. Redevelopment programs require appraisers for both acquisition and reuse programs. Ad valorem (property) taxes are based on real estate assessments (appraisals).

--**Public Utility companies.** Appraisers are needed for the acquisition of rights-of-way for utility wires, pipelines and other real estate acquisitions.

The list of users of residential appraisals is almost endless, and the need for appraisers appears to be constantly increasing. The field presents good opportunities for those who are willing to acquire the necessary skills to serve the public as professionals.

THE DEFINITION OF AN APPRAISAL

There is no standard accepted definition of the word **appraisal** or **real estate appraisal.** However, most of the accepted definitions incorporate the following seven principles:

1. An appraisal is an opinion of value.
2. The opinion must be appropriately supported with general and specific data.
3. It must be as of a specific date.
4. The value estimated must be defined.
5. The property being appraised must be adequately and accurately described.
6. The person making the appraisal must be qualified by reason of adequate education and experience.
7. The person making the appraisal must be unbiased and have no undisclosed interest in the property.

An appraisal is an appropriately supported objective and unbiased opinion of the value, as of a specific date, of an adequately and accurately described property, made by a qualified person who has no undisclosed interest in the property.

An appraisal may include such complicated considerations as various interests, equities, historic and future values and other conditions which are present. It may be based on assumed conditions, provided they are clearly stated and there is a reasonable probability that the assumptions will take place some time in the near future.

PURPOSE AND USE OF AN APPRAISAL

The fundamental purpose of an appraisal is to estimate some kind of value. The need for an appraisal of market value may arise from many situations, including:

1) Transfer of ownership.
2) Financing and credit.
3) Just compensation in condemnation (eminent domain) proceedings.
4) As a basis for taxation.
5) To establish rental schedules and lease provisions.
6) Feasibility analysis.

In addition to the need for estimating market value, appraisals are also made to estimate:

1) Insurable value.
2) Going-concern value.
3) Liquidation value.
4) Assessed value (which may be a percentage of market value).

Although the list does not include all the needs for appraisals, it does indicate the broad scope of the professional appraiser's typical activities.

THE IMPORTANCE OF THE APPRAISER

The appraiser is frequently regarded by lenders and the public as the expert in evaluating a neighborhood's strengths and weaknesses. Accordingly, the appraiser must exercise this responsibility with care and be certain that a considered judgment about a community's trend is supportable by objective facts. Emotional arguments or advocacy must never affect the professional appraiser's presentation of demonstrable facts.

GROWTH OF PROFESSIONALISM IN REAL ESTATE APPRAISING

A profession is, by definition, a vocation that involves primarily intellectual activities and requires high levels of technical competence, individual responsibility and personal integrity. Historically, the first professionals were physicians and surgeons, professors, lawyers, accountants, engineers and the clergy. Today, a professional is a member of an organized vital vocation or activity in which the membership is highly competent, thoroughly honest and devoted to the ideal of performing a service to the maximum of their capacity, regardless of compensation. A professional has a responsibility to help make the world a better place in which to live.

Appraisers have aspired to professional status in the eyes of the public and the rest of the real estate field for many years. Today, appraisals written by appraisers who have achieved some level of professionally-recognized expertise usually receive greater acceptance than those prepared by the non-professional.

The need for professional real estate appraisers came into focus with the collapse of real estate values during the depression of the 1930's. Prior to that time, real estate appraising as a vocation had been unstructured and little educational material was available, although as early as 1929, the National Association of Real Estate Boards had a publication called Standards of Appraisal Practice. To the early appraiser, market price was the equivalent of market value.

PROFESSIONAL ORGANIZATIONS AND DESIGNATIONS

Some lenders formerly would only use appraisers who have designations from certain appraisal organizations. They believed that such a designated appraiser would be automatically qualified. This practice is now prohibited by federal law for any federally related appraisal.

Unfortunately, not all designations are the same. There are at least 30 national appraisal organizations which award designations to their members.

The American Institute of Real Estate Appraisers (which awards the RM and MAI designations) and the Society of Real Estate Appraisers (which awards the SRA, SRPA and the SREA designations) have existed since before World War II. Both have a long history of rigid standards for awarding their designations. To earn any of these designations, an appraiser must have taken several courses, have years of proven experience, produced demonstration appraisals and passed several examinations. On January 1, 1991 the A.I.R.E.A. and the Society officially merged into The Appraisal Institute.

There are also some good appraisers who, for various reasons, have decided not to apply for any designation. Lenders who refuse to consider appraisers who do not have designations may be eliminating some well-qualified appraisers who are capable of doing their work.

WHAT APPRAISERS HAVE TO SELL

An appraiser basically has five things to sell a client:

A. Adequate knowledge
B. Experience
C. Integrity
D. Objectivity
E. Uncompromised willingness to do the work on a timely basis for a mutually agreed upon fee

ADEQUATE KNOWLEDGE

A qualified appraiser should have had a good general education, taken a variety of appraisal courses and seminars, and be keeping current with continuing education in the field.

In a profession as complex as real estate appraising, most lenders feel that a minimum of a high school education is required. The Appraisal Institute now requires a college degree for their designations. However, this is a recent requirement and many of their older members are not college graduates.

Unfortunately, there are appraisers in the field who have never even taken a basic appraisal course. Others have only been to a few one-day seminars. Why lenders accept work from these appraisers is hard to understand. At a bare minimum, every appraiser should have taken a basic appraisal course given by an accredited educational institution or national appraisal organization.

Since the appraisal profession and appraisal requirements are changing all the time, it is necessary that the appraiser keep up with current appraisal practice. Many feel the best way to insure this is to require appraisers to attend continuing education courses and/or seminars on a regular basis. However, it should be kept in mind that it is possible for an appraiser to keep current by reading the available appraisal journals and other appraisal publications.

EXPERIENCE

There is an old saying that nothing is a substitute for experience. This is not what a new appraiser wants to hear. The reality is that appraising is still not a science but rather an art. Often, when it comes to making adjustments, rating the neighborhood and/or the improvements and reconciling differences throughout the appraisal, the appraiser must rely primarily upon judgment.

Since no one is born with experience, a substitute has to be found for the new appraiser. Appraisal experience can be obtained by working as an appraiser, lender, contractor or Realtor. At least some of the required experience should be obtained by actually making residential appraisals.

It is appropriate for an inexperienced appraiser to work with a seasoned appraiser who reviews their work and jointly assumes responsibility for it by signing the appraisal report as the review appraiser. It is a good policy to require that the review appraiser, who jointly signs the appraisal, also inspect the interior of the subject property when the primary appraiser is very inexperienced, when the value of the house is high, when the house is old, or when the property has some significant atypical characteristics. Many people feel that at least two years experience is a minimum requirement for an appraiser to be able to sign an appraisal without supervisory review.

INTEGRITY

There are a variety of ways a client can check on the integrity of an appraiser. The most common is by checking personal, general business and professional references. Others include talking with other appraisers. The participation of the appraiser in community activities and in their professional association are other indicators of their reputation in the community and their standing among peers.

OBJECTIVITY

The appraiser signs a certificate with each appraisal saying that they have no present or future contemplated interest in the property being appraised. This includes making appraisals for friends and relatives.

Unfortunately, clients are sometimes their own worst enemy when it comes to appraiser objectivity. It does not take long for an appraiser to figure out whether a client is primarily interested in making loans regardless of the value of the loan security or whether they are primarily interested in obtaining the true value of the property in order to protect their loan portfolio.

The amount of pressure that some clients put on appraisers is well documented. Many people feel such pressure is a primary cause of poor appraisals. It is up to the clients to communicate to the appraiser how they really feel. If they want true value estimates, they must make it clear to the appraiser that the assignments and payments they receive in the future will not be in jeopardy if they produce appraisals where the appraised value is less than the contract price of the pending loan application.

UNCOMPROMISED WILLINGNESS TO DO WORK ON A TIMELY BASIS FOR A MUTUALLY AGREED UPON FEE

The final step in selecting appraisers is finding those who are willing and able to do the client's work on a timely basis for a mutually agreed upon fee. The client should investigate the appraiser's capacity to produce work. If the appraiser has a one, two or three person operation, the amount of work they can turn out is limited. Usually the appraiser has other clients who also want their work done on a timely basis.

The best arrangement is when the client and appraiser agree upon the approximate number of appraisals that will be ordered in any given period of time. Unfortunately, clients cannot always control the number of appraisals they need and when they get busy, may give appraisers more work than they can handle. It seems to be a pattern that in the Spring when business traditionally picks up, appraisers become swamped and get behind in their work.

Clients have different policies on how they pay appraisers. Some large lenders have a published fee schedule. Appraisers must decide whether they are willing to accept the offered fee in order to get assignments from the lender. Other lenders negotiate fee schedules with each appraiser, taking into consideration the appraiser's knowledge, experience and the length of time they have been working together. Clients should recognize that some appraisal assignments require substantially more work than others. Often the fee will be adjusted to reflect the extra work required to make an appraisal of a high value home, waterfront property, historic property, contemporary house and other houses with significant atypical characteristics.

PROFESSIONAL CONDUCT

The essence of our civilization is that people acknowledge the limited right of society to control the activities of individuals for the benefit of the public. In addition, many people conduct their own activities at a higher level than is required by the law or by their fellow humans.

There are several levels of conduct. The first deals with the laws that apply to all people. In the United States, there are Federal, state and local laws. Everyone is required to obey these laws. It makes little difference if one agrees or disagrees with them. If someone does not obey a law, society has the right to punish the lawbreaker. (Of course, not all laws are enforced uniformly and many of the people who break laws are not necessarily caught or punished.)

The second level of conduct consists of the laws that apply to certain groups of people. These are laws and rules that regulate special activities such as those of lawyers and doctors. Often one has to obtain a license or permit to participate in such activities. For example, in the real estate field, one must have a license to sell or rent real estate for compensation. Real estate brokers are subject to special laws that control their activities. Other common examples at this level are the laws pertaining to driving automobiles, building houses, practicing medicine, or running a store. Such regulatory laws apply only when one voluntarily engages in a special activity controlled by the legislation or regulation which applies. In all states, real estate appraising will fall into this category of control.

The third level consists of *The Uniform Standards of Professional Appraisal Practice* and the various codes of ethics that have been developed by the professional organizations to control the activities of their members. The members of the organization agree to be governed by its code of ethics as one of the conditions of membership. The organization itself develops and enforces the code of ethics. Violators may be disciplined in a variety of ways. The maximum penalty usually is expulsion from the group. The American Medical Association, the American Bar Association, the National Association of Realtors as well as many other organizations have such codes governing the conduct of their members with the public, their clients and among their own members.

The fourth level encompasses the personal rules people set for themselves to control their own lives according to their personal (and religious) beliefs. Many everyday decisions people make about their professional activities and conduct fall outside the scope of the three preceding levels of conduct. The decision regarding how to act must be made by the individual based on personal standards of conduct. The rewards for functioning at this higher level are personal satisfaction and approval by one's family and peers. The punishment is from one's own conscience and disapproval by others.

UNIFORM STANDARDS OF PROFESSIONAL APPRAISAL PRACTICE
The Appraisal Standards Board of the Appraisal Foundation - Effective   1/1/03
(This material is for teaching purposes only. Footnotes have been eliminated and some sections condensed)

PREAMBLE

The purpose of these Standards is to establish requirements for professional appraisal practice, which includes appraisal, appraisal review, and appraisal consulting, as defined. The intent of these Standards is to promote and maintain a high level of public trust in professional appraisal practice.

These Standards are for appraisers and users of appraisal services. To maintain a high level of professional practice, appraisers observe these Standards. However, these Standards do not in themselves establish which individuals or assignments must comply; neither The Appraisal Foundation nor its Appraisal Standards Board is a government entity with the power to make, judge, or enforce law. Individuals comply with these Standards either by choice or by requirement placed upon them or upon the service they provide, by law, regulation, or agreement with the client or intended users.

It is essential that professional appraisers develop and communicate their analyses, opinions, and conclusions to intended users of their services in a manner that is meaningful and not misleading. These *Uniform Standards of Professional Appraisal Practice* (USPAP) reflect the current standards of the appraisal profession.

The importance of the role of the appraiser places ethical obligations on those who serve in this capacity. These Standards include explanatory <u>Comments</u> and begin with an ETHICS RULE setting forth the requirements for integrity, impartiality, objectivity, independent judgment, and ethical conduct. In addition, these Standards include a COMPETENCY RULE that places an immediate responsibility on the appraiser prior to acceptance of an assignment as well as during the performance of an assignment. DEFINITIONS applicable to these Standards are also included. The Standards contain binding requirements, as well as specific requirements to which the DEPARTURE RULE may apply under certain conditions. The DEPARTURE RULE does not apply to the PREAMBLE, ETHICS RULE, COMPETENCY RULE, JURISDICTIONAL EXCEPTION RULE, SUPPLEMENTAL STANDARDS RULE, or DEFINITIONS Section.

These Standards deal with the procedures to be followed in performing an appraisal, appraisal review, or appraisal consulting service and the manner in which an appraisal, appraisal review, or appraisal consulting service is communicated. STANDARDS 1 and 2 establish requirements for the development and communication of a real property appraisal. STANDARD 3 establishes requirements for reviewing a real or personal property appraisal and reporting on that review. STANDARDS 4 and 5 establish requirements for the development and communication of various real property appraisal consulting functions by an appraiser. STANDARD 6 establishes requirements for the development and reporting of mass appraisals of a universe of properties for ad valorem tax purposes or any other intended use. STANDARDS 7 and 8 establish requirements for developing and communicating personal property appraisals. STANDARDS 9 and 10 establish requirements for developing and communicating business appraisals.

These Standards include Statements on Appraisal Standards issued by the Appraisal Standards Board for the purpose of clarification, interpretation, explanation, or elaboration of a Standard or a Standards Rule.

> <u>Comment:</u> Comments are an integral part of the Uniform Standards and are extensions of the Rules, Definitions, and Standards Rules. Comments provide interpretation from the Appraisal Standards Board concerning the background or application of certain Rules, Definitions, or Standards Rules. Comments also establish the context of certain requirements and the conditions that apply only in specific situations or type of assignments.

To promote and preserve the public trust inherent in professional appraisal practice, an appraiser must observe the highest standards of professional ethics. This ETHICS RULE is divided into four sections: Conduct, Management, Confidentiality, and Record Keeping. The first three sections apply to all appraisal practice, and all four sections apply to appraisal practice performed under Standards 1 through 10.

> Comment: This rule specifies the personal obligations and responsibilities of the individual appraiser. However, it should also be noted that groups and organizations engaged in appraisal practice share the same ethical obligations.

Compliance with these standards is required when either the service or the appraiser is obligated by law or regulation, or by agreement with the client or intended users, to comply. Compliance is also required when an individual, by choice, represents that he or she is performing the service as an appraiser.

An appraiser must not misrepresent his or her role when providing valuation services that are outside of appraisal practice.

> Comment: Honesty, impartiality, and professional competency are required of all appraisers under these *Uniform Standards of Professional Appraisal Practice* (USPAP). To document recognition and acceptance of his or her USPAP-related responsibilities in communicating an appraisal, appraisal review, or appraisal consulting assignment completed under USPAP, an appraiser is required to certify compliance with these Standards. (See Standards Rules 2-3, 3-3, *5-3*, 6-8, 8-3, and 10-3.)

Conduct

An appraiser must perform assignments ethically and competently, in accordance with USPAP and any supplemental standards agreed to by the appraiser in accepting the assignment. An appraiser must not engage in criminal conduct. An appraiser must perform assignments with impartiality, objectivity, and independence, and without accommodation of personal interests.

In appraisal practice, an appraiser must not perform as an advocate for any party or issue.

> Comment: An appraiser may be an advocate only in support of his or her assignment results. Advocacy in any other form in appraisal practice is a violation of the ETHICS RULE.

An appraiser must not accept an assignment that includes the reporting of predetermined opinions and conclusions.

An appraiser must not communicate assignment results in a misleading or fraudulent manner. An appraiser must not use or communicate a misleading or fraudulent report or knowingly permit an employee or other person to communicate a misleading or fraudulent report.

An appraiser must not use or rely on unsupported conclusions relating to characteristics such as race, color, religion, national origin, gender, marital status, familial status, age, receipt of public assistance income, handicap, or an unsupported conclusion that homogeneity of such characteristics is necessary to maximize value.

> Comment: An individual appraiser employed by a group or organization that conducts itself in a manner that does not conform to these standards should take steps that are appropriate under the circumstances to ensure compliance with the standards.

MANAGEMENT

The payment of undisclosed fees, commissions, or things of value in connection with the procurement of an assignment is unethical.

> Comment: Disclosure of fees, commissions, or things of value connected to the procurement of an assignment must appear in the certification of the written report and in any transmittal letter in which conclusions are stated. In groups or organizations engaged in appraisal practice, intra company payments to employees for business development are not considered to be unethical. Competency, rather than financial incentives, should be the primary basis for awarding an assignment.

It is unethical for an appraiser to accept compensation for performing an assignment when the assignment results are contingent upon:

1. the reporting of a predetermined result (e.g., opinion of value);

2. a direction in assignment results that favors the cause of the client;

3. the amount of a value opinion;

4. the attainment of a stipulated result; or

5. the occurrence of a subsequent event directly related to the appraiser's opinions and specific to the assignment's purpose.

Advertising for or soliciting assignments in a manner that is false, misleading, or exaggerated is unethical.

> Comment: In groups or organizations engaged in appraisal practice, decisions concerning finder or referral fees, contingent compensation, and advertising may not be the responsibility of an individual appraiser, but for a particular assignment, it is the responsibility of the individual appraiser to ascertain that there has been no breach of ethics, that the assignment is prepared in accordance with these Standards, and that the report can be properly certified when required by Standards Rules 2-3, 3-2, 5-3, 6-8, 8-3, or 10-3.

Confidentiality

An appraiser must protect the confidential nature of the appraiser-client relationship.

An appraiser must act in good faith with regard to the legitimate interests of the client in the use of confidential information and in the communication of assignment results.

An appraiser must not disclose confidential information or assignment results prepared for a client to anyone other than the client and persons specifically authorized by the client; state enforcement agencies and such third parties as may be authorized by due process of law; and a duly authorized professional peer review committee. It is unethical for a member of a duly authorized professional peer review committee to disclose confidential information presented to the committee.*

> Comment: When all confidential elements of confidential information are removed through redaction or the process of aggregation, client authorization is not required for the disclosure of the remaining information, as modified.

Record Keeping

An appraiser must prepare a workfile for each appraisal, appraisal review, or appraisal consulting assignment. The workfile must include the name of the client and the identity, by name or type, of any other intended users; true copies of any written reports, documented on any type of media; summaries of any oral reports or testimony, or a transcript of testimony, including the appraiser's signed and dated certification; and all other data, information, and documentation necessary to support the appraiser's opinions and conclusions and to show compliance with this rule and all other applicable Standards, or references to the location(s) of such other documentation.

An appraiser must retain the workfile for a period of at least five (5) years after preparation or at least two (2) years after final disposition of any judicial proceeding in which testimony was given, whichever period expires last, and have custody of his or her workfile, or make appropriate workfile retention, access, and retrieval arrangements with the party having custody of the workfile.

> Comment: A workfile preserves evidence of the appraiser's consideration of all applicable data and statements required by USPAP and other information as may be required to support the appraiser's opinions, conclusions, and recommendations. For example, the content of a workfile for a Complete Appraisal must reflect consideration of all USPAP requirements applicable to the specific Complete Appraisal assignment. However, the content of a workfile for a Limited Appraisal need only reflect consideration of the USPAP requirements from which there have been no departure and that are required by the specific Limited Appraisal assignment.

A photocopy or an electronic copy of the entire actual written appraisal, appraisal review, or consulting report sent or delivered to a client satisfies the requirement of a true copy. As an example, a photocopy or electronic copy of the Self-Contained Appraisal Report, Summary Appraisal Report, or Restricted Use Appraisal Report actually issued by an appraiser for a real property Complete Appraisal or Limited Appraisal assignment satisfies the true copy requirement for that assignment.

Care should be exercised in the selection of the form, style, and type of medium for written records, which may be handwritten and informal, to ensure that they are retrievable by the appraiser throughout the prescribed record retention period.

A workfile must be in existence prior to and contemporaneous with the issuance of a written or oral report. A written summary of an oral report must be added to the workfile within a reasonable time after the issuance of the oral report.

A workfile must be made available by the appraiser when required by state enforcement agencies or due process of law. In addition, a workfile in support of a Restricted Use Appraisal Report must be available for inspection by the client in accordance with the <u>Comment</u> to Standards Rules 2-2(c)(ix), 8-2(c)(ix), and 1O-2(b)(ix).

COMPETENCY RULE

Prior to accepting an assignment or entering into an agreement to perform any assignment, an appraiser must properly identify the problem to be addressed and have the knowledge and experience to complete the assignment competently; or alternatively, must:

1. disclose the lack of knowledge and/or experience to the client before accepting the assignment;

2. take all steps necessary or appropriate to complete the assignment competently; and

3. describe the lack of knowledge and/or experience and the steps taken to complete the assignment competently in the report.

> Comment: Competency applies to factors such as, but not limited to, an appraiser's familiarity with a specific type of property, a market, a geographic area, or an analytical method. If such a factor is necessary for an appraiser to develop credible assignment results, the appraiser is responsible for having the competency to address that factor or for following the steps outlined above to satisfy this COMPETENCY RULE.

> The background and experience of appraisers varies widely, and a lack of knowledge or experience can lead to inaccurate or inappropriate appraisal practice. The COMPETENCY RULE requires an appraiser to have both the knowledge and the experience required to perform a specific appraisal service competently.

If an appraiser is offered the opportunity to perform an appraisal service but lacks the necessary knowledge or experience to complete it competently, the appraiser must disclose his or her lack of knowledge or experience to the client before accepting the assignment and then take the necessary or appropriate steps to complete the appraisal service competently. This may be accomplished in various ways, including, but not limited to, personal study by the appraiser, association with an appraiser reasonably believed to have the necessary knowledge or experience, or retention of others who possess the required knowledge or experience.

In an assignment where geographic competency is necessary, an appraiser preparing an appraisal in an unfamiliar location must spend sufficient time to understand the nuances of the local market and the supply and demand factors relating to the specific property type and the location involved. Such understanding will not be imparted solely from a consideration of specific data such as demographics, costs, sales, and rentals. The necessary understanding of local market conditions provides the bridge between a sale and a comparable sale or a rental and a comparable rental. If an appraiser is not in a position to spend the necessary amount of time in a market area to obtain this understanding, affiliation with a qualified local appraiser may be the appropriate response to ensure development of credible assignment results.

Although this rule requires an appraiser to identify the problem and disclose any deficiency in competence prior to accepting an assignment, facts or conditions uncovered during the course of an assignment could cause an appraiser to discover that he or she lacks the required knowledge or experience to complete the assignment competently. At the point of such discovery, the appraiser is obligated to notify the client and comply with items 2 and 3 of the rule.

DEPARTURE RULE

This rule permits exceptions from sections of the Uniform Standards that are classified as specific requirements rather than binding requirements. The burden of proof is on the appraiser to decide before accepting an assignment and invoking this rule that the scope of work applied will result in opinions or conclusions that are credible. The burden of disclosure is also on the appraiser to report any departures from specific requirements.

An appraiser may enter into an agreement to perform an assignment in which the scope of work is less than, or different from, the work that would otherwise be required by the specific requirements, provided that prior to entering into such an agreement:

1. the appraiser has determined that the appraisal process to be performed is not so limited that the results of the assignment are no longer credible;

2. the appraiser has advised the client that the assignment calls for something less than, or different from, the work required by the specific requirements and that the report will clearly identify and explain the departure(s); and

3. the client has agreed that the performance of a limited appraisal service would be appropriate, given the intended use.

Comment: Not all specific requirements are *applicable* to every assignment. When a specific requirement is *not applicable* to a given assignment, the specific requirement is irrelevant and therefore no departure is needed.

A specific requirement is *applicable* when:

*   it addresses factors or conditions that are present in the given assignment, or

*   it addresses analysis that is typical practice in such an assignment.

A specific requirement is *not applicable* when:

*   it addresses factors or conditions that are not present in the given assignment, or

*   it addresses analysis that is not typical practice in such an assignment, or

*   it addresses analysis that would not provide meaningful results in the given assignment.

Of those specific requirements that are *applicable* to a given assignment, some may be *necessary* in order to result in opinions or conclusions that are credible. When a specific requirement is *necessary* to a given assignment, departure is not permitted.

Departure is permitted from those specific requirements that are *applicable* to a given assignment but *not necessary* in order to result in opinions or conclusions that are credible.

A specific requirement is considered to be both *applicable* and *necessary* when:

• it addresses factors or conditions that are present in the given assignment, or

• it addresses analysis that is typical practice in such an assignment, and

• lack of consideration for those factors, conditions, or analyses would significantly affect the credibility of the results.

Typical practice for a given assignment is measured by:

• the expectations of the participants in the market for appraisal services, and

• what an appraiser's peers' actions would be in performing the same or a similar assignment.

If an appraiser enters into an agreement to perform an appraisal service that calls for something less than, or different from, the work that would otherwise be required by the specific requirements, Standards Rules 2-2(a)(xi), 2-2(b)(xi), 2-2(c)(xi), 8-2(a)(xi), 8-2(b)(xi), 8-2(c)(xi), IO-2(a)(x), and 1 O-2(b)(x) require that the report clearly identify and explain departure(s) from the specific requirements.

Departure from the following development and reporting rules is not permitted: Standards Rules 1-1, 1-2, 1-5, 2-1, 2-2, 2-3, 3-1, 3-2, 4-1, 4-2, 5-*1*, 5-2, 5-3, 6-1, 6-3, 6-6, 6-7, 6-8, 7-1, 7-2, *7-5*, 8-1,8-2, 8-3, 9-1, 9-2, 9-3, 9-5, 10-1, 10-2, and 10-3. This restriction on departure is reiterated throughout the document with the reminder: "This Standards Rule contains binding requirements from which departure is not permitted."

The DEPARTURE RULE does not apply to the PREAMBLE, ETHICS RULE, COMPETENCY RULE, JURISDICTIONAL EXCEPTION RULE, SUPPLEMENTAL STANDARDS RULE, or DEFINITIONS section.

JURISDICTIONAL EXCEPTION RULE

If any part of these standards is contrary to the law or public policy of any jurisdiction, only that part shall be void and of no force or effect in that jurisdiction.

Comment: The purpose of the JURISDICTIONAL EXCEPTION RULE is strictly limited to providing a saving or severability clause intended to preserve the balance of USPAP if one or more of its parts are determined to be contrary to law or public policy of a jurisdiction. By logical extension, there can be no violation of USPAP by an appraiser disregarding, with proper disclosure, only the part or parts of USPAP that are void and of no force and effect in a particular assignment by operation of legal authority. It is misleading for an appraiser to disregard a part or parts of USPAP as void and of no force and effect in a particular assignment without identifying in the appraiser's report the part or parts disregarded and the legal authority justifying this action.

As used in the JURISDICTIONAL EXCEPTION RULE, law means a body of rules with binding legal force established by controlling governmental authority. This broad meaning includes, without limitation, the federal and state constitutions; legislative and court-made law; and administrative rules, regulations, and ordinances. Public policy refers to more or less well-defined moral and ethical standards of conduct, currently and generally accepted by the community as a whole, and recognized by the courts with the aid of statutes, judicial precedents, and other similar available evidence. Jurisdiction refers to the legal authority to legislate, apply, or interpret law in any form at the federal, state, and local levels of government.

SUPPLEMENTAL STANDARDS RULE

These Uniform Standards provide the common basis for all appraisal practice. Supplemental standards applicable to assignments prepared for specific purposes or property types may be issued (i.e., published) by public agencies and certain client groups, such as regulatory agencies, eminent domain authorities, asset managers, and financial institutions. An appraiser and client must ascertain whether any such published supplemental standards in addition to these Uniform Standards apply to the assignment being considered.

> **Comment:** The purpose of the SUPPLEMENTAL STANDARDS RULE is to provide a reasonable means to augment USPAP with requirements issued by client groups, governmental entities, and/or professional appraisal organizations that add to the requirements set forth by USPAP.
>
> Supplemental standards cannot diminish the purpose, intent, or content of the requirements of USPAP.
>
> By certifying conformity with USPAP for an assignment in which an appraiser satisfied a professional appraisal organization's ethics or practice standard not in USPAP, the appraiser acknowledges that this supplemental standard adds to but does not diminish the purpose, intent, or content of USPAP.
>
> Upon agreeing to perform an assignment that includes acceptable supplemental standards, an appraiser is obligated to competently satisfy those supplemental standards, as well as applicable USPAP requirements.
>
> An appraiser who represents that an assignment is or will be completed in compliance with agreed upon supplemental standards and who then knowingly fails to comply with those supplemental standards violates the ETHICS RULE, or who then inadvertently fails to comply with those supplemental standards violates the COMPETENCY RULE. (See the ETHICS RULE and the COMPETENCY RULE.)

STANDARD 1   REAL PROPERTY APPRAISAL DEVELOPMENT

In developing a real property appraisal, an appraiser must identify the problem to be solved and the scope of work necessary to solve the problem, and correctly complete research and analysis necessary to produce a credible appraisal.

> Comment: STANDARD 1 is directed toward the substantive aspects of developing a competent appraisal of real property. The requirements set forth in STANDARD 1 follow the appraisal development process in the order of topics addressed and can be used by appraisers and the users of appraisal services as a convenient checklist.

Standards Rule 1-1 (This Standards Rule contains binding requirements from which departure is not permitted.)

In developing a real property appraisal, an appraiser must:

(a)   be aware of, understand, and correctly employ those recognized methods and techniques that are necessary to produce a credible appraisal;

> Comment: This rule recognizes that the principle of change continues to affect the manner in which appraisers perform appraisal services. Changes and developments in the real estate field have a substantial impact on the appraisal profession. Important changes in the cost and manner of constructing and marketing commercial, industrial, and residential real estate as well as changes in the legal framework in which real property rights and interests are created, conveyed, and mortgaged have resulted in corresponding changes in appraisal theory and practice. Social change has also had an effect on appraisal theory and practice. To keep abreast of these changes and developments, the appraisal profession is constantly reviewing and revising appraisal methods and techniques and devising new methods and techniques to meet new circumstances. For this reason, it is not sufficient for appraisers to simply maintain the skills and the knowledge they possess when they become appraisers. Each appraiser must continuously improve his or her skills to remain proficient in real property appraisal.

(b)   **not commit a substantial error of omission or commission that significantly affects an appraisal; and**

Comment: In performing appraisal services, an appraiser must be certain that the gathering of factual information is conducted in a manner that is sufficiently diligent, given the scope of work as identified according to Standards Rule 1-2(f), to ensure that the data that would have a material or significant effect on the resulting opinions or conclusions are identified and, where necessary, analyzed. Further, an appraiser must use sufficient care in analyzing such data to avoid errors that would significantly affect his or her opinions and conclusions.

(c)   **not render appraisal services in a careless or negligent manner, such as by making a series of errors that, although individually might not significantly affect the results of an appraisal, in the aggregate affect the credibility of those results.**

Comment: Perfection is impossible to attain, and competence does not require perfection. However, an appraiser must not render appraisal services in a careless or negligent manner. This rule requires an appraiser to use due diligence and due care. The fact that the carelessness or negligence of an appraiser has not caused an error that significantly affects his or her opinions or conclusions and thereby seriously harms an intended user does not excuse such carelessness or negligence.

Standards Rule 1-2 (This Standards Rule contains binding requirements from which departure is not permitted.)

In developing a real property appraisal, an appraiser must:

(a)   **identify the client and other intended users;**

(b)   **identify the intended use of the appraiser's opinions and conclusions;**

Comment: Identification of the intended use is necessary for the appraiser and the client to decide:

- the appropriate scope of work to be completed, and
- the level of information to be provided in communicating the appraisal.

An appraiser must not allow a client's objectives or intended use to cause an analysis to be biased.

(c)   **identify the purpose of the assignment, including the type and definition of the value to be developed, and, if the value opinion to be developed is a market value, ascertain whether the value is to be the most probable price:**

(i)   **in terms of cash; or**

(ii)   **in terms of financial arrangements equivalent to cash; or**

(iii)   **in other precisely defined terms; and**

(iv)   **if the opinion of value is to be based on non-market financing or financing with unusual conditions or incentives, the terms of such financing must be clearly identified and the appraiser's opinion of their contributions to or negative influence on value must be developed by analysis of relevant market data;**

Comment: When the purpose of an assignment is to develop an opinion of market value, the appraiser must also develop an opinion of reasonable exposure time linked to the value opinion.

(d)   **identify the effective date of the appraiser's opinions and conclusions;**

(e)   **identify the characteristics of the property that are relevant to the purpose and intended use of the appraisal, including:**

(i)   **its location and physical, legal, and economic attributes;**

(ii)   **the real property interest to be valued;**

(iii)   **any personal property, trade fixtures, or intangible items that are not real property but are included in the appraisal;**

(iv)   **any known easements, restrictions, encumbrances, leases, reservations, covenants, contracts, declarations, special assessments, ordinances, or other items of a similar nature; and**

(v)   **whether the subject property is a fractional interest, physical segment or partial holding**

Comment on (i)-(v) If the necessary subject property information is not available because of assignment conditions that limit research opportunity (such as conditions that preclude an onsite inspection or the gathering of information from reliable third-party sources), an appraiser *must:*

- obtain the necessary information before proceeding, or

- where possible, in compliance with Standards Rule 1-2(g), use an extraordinary assumption about such information.

An appraiser may use any combination of a property inspection and documents, such as a physical legal description, address, map reference, copy of a survey or map, property sketch, or photographs, to identify the relevant characteristics of the subject property. Identification of the real property interest appraised can be based on a review of copies or summaries of title descriptions or other documents that set forth any known encumbrances. The information used by an appraiser to identify the property characteristics must be from sources the appraiser reasonably believes are reliable.

An appraiser is not required to value the whole when the subject of the appraisal is a fractional interest, a physical segment, or a partial holding.

(f) identify the scope of work necessary to complete the assignment;

Comment: The scope of work is acceptable when it is consistent with:

- the expectations of participants in the market for the same or similar appraisal services; and

- what the appraiser's peers actions would be in performing the same or a similar assignment in compliance with USPAP.

An appraiser must have sound reasons in support of the scope-of-work decision and must be prepared to support the decision to exclude any information or procedure that would appear to be relevant to the client, an intended user, or the appraiser's peers in the same or a similar assignment.

An appraiser must not allow assignment conditions or other factors to limit the extent of research or analysis to such a degree that the resulting opinions and conclusions developed in an assignment are not credible in the context of the intended use of the appraisal.

(g) identify any extraordinary assumptions necessary in the assignment; and

Comment: An extraordinary assumption may be used in an assignment only if:

- it is required to properly develop credible opinions and conclusions;

- the appraiser has a reasonable basis for the extraordinary assumption;

- use of the extraordinary assumption results in a credible analysis; and

- the appraiser complies with the disclosure requirements set forth in USPAP for extraordinary assumptions.

(h) identify any hypothetical conditions necessary in the assignment.

Comment: A hypothetical condition may be used in an assignment only if:

- use of the hypothetical condition is clearly required for legal purposes, for purposes of reasonable analysis, or for purposes of comparison;

- use of the hypothetical condition results in a credible analysis; and
- the appraiser complies with the disclosure requirements set forth in USPAP for hypothetical conditions.

Standards Rule 1-3 (This Standards Rule contains specific requirements from which departure is permitted. See the DEPARTURE RULE.)

When the value opinion to be developed is a market value, and given the scope of work identified in accordance with Standards Rule 1-2(f), an appraiser must:

(a)   identify and analyze the effect on use and value of existing land use regulations, reasonably probable modifications of such land use regulations, economic demand, the physical adaptability of the real estate, and market area trends; and

Comment: An appraiser must avoid making an unsupported assumption or premise about market area trends, effective age, and remaining life.

(b)   develop an opinion of the highest and best use of the real estate.

Comment: An appraiser must analyze the relevant legal, physical, and economic factors to the extent necessary to support the appraiser's highest and best use conclusion(s). The appraiser must recognize that land is appraised as though vacant and available for development to its highest and best use, and that the appraisal of improvements is based on their actual contribution to the site.

Standards Rule 1-4 (This Standards Rule contains specific requirements from which departure is permitted. See DEPARTURE RULE.)

In developing a real property appraisal, an appraiser must collect, verify, and analyze all information applicable to the appraisal problem, given the scope of work identified in accordance with Standards Rule 1-2(f).

(a)   When a sales comparison approach is applicable, an appraiser must analyze such comparable sales data as are available to indicate a value conclusion.

(b)   When a cost approach is applicable, an appraiser must:

(i)   develop an opinion of site value by an appropriate appraisal method or technique;

(ii)   analyze such comparable cost data as are available to estimate the cost new of the improvements (if any); and

(iii)   analyze such comparable data as are available to estimate the difference between the cost new and the present worth of the improvements (accrued depreciation).

(c)   When an income approach is applicable, an appraiser must:

(i)   analyze such comparable rental data as are available to estimate the market rentalof the property;

(ii)   analyze such comparable operating expense data as are available to estimate the operating expenses of the property;

(iii)   analyze such comparable data as are available to estimate rates of capitalizationand/or rates of discount; and

(iv)   base projections of future rent and expenses on reasonably clear and appropriate evidence.

Comment: An appraiser must, in developing income and expense statements and cash flow projections, weigh historical information and trends, current supply and demand factors affecting such trends, and anticipated events such as competition from developments under construction.

(d)   When developing an opinion of the value of a leased fee estate or a lease-hold estate, an appraiser must analyze the effect on value, if any, of the terms and conditions of the lease(s).

(e)   An appraiser must analyze the effect on value, if any, of the assemblage of the various estates or component parts of a property and refrain from valuing the whole solely by adding together the individual values of the various estates or component parts.

Comment: Although the value of the whole may be equal to the sum of the separate estates or parts, it also may be greater than or less than the sum of such estates or parts. Therefore, the value of the whole must be tested by reference to appropriate data and supported by an appropriate analysis of such data.

A similar procedure must be followed when the value of the whole has been established and the appraiser seeks to value a part. The value of any such part must be tested by reference to appropriate data and supported by an appropriate analysis of such data.

(f)   An appraiser must analyze the effect on value, if any, of anticipated public or private improvements, located on or off the site, to the extent that market actions reflect such anticipated improvements as of the effective appraisal date.

(g)   An appraiser must analyze the effect on value of any personal property, trade fixtures, or intangible items that are not real property but are included in the appraisal.

Comment: Competency in personal property appraisal (see STANDARD 7) or business valuation (see STANDARD 9) may be required when it is necessary to allocate the overall value to the property components. A separate valuation, developed in compliance with the Standard pertinent to the type of property involved, is required when the value of a nonrealty item or combination of such items is significant to the overall value.

(h)   When appraising proposed improvements, an appraiser must examine and have available for future examination:

(i)   plans, specifications, or other documentation sufficient to identify the scope and character of the proposed improvements;

(ii)   evidence indicating the probable time of completion of the proposed improvements; and

(iii)   reasonably clear and appropriate evidence supporting development costs, anticipated earnings, occupancy projections, and the anticipated competition at the time of completion.

Comment: Development of a value opinion for a subject property with proposed improvements as of a current date involves the use of the hypothetical condition that the described improvements have been completed as of the date of value when, in fact, they have not.

The evidence required to be examined and maintained may include such items as contractors' estimates relating to cost and the time required to complete construction, market and feasibility studies; operating cost data, and the history of recently completed similar developments. The appraisal may require a complete feasibility analysis.

STANDARD 2 REAL PROPERTY APPRAISAL REPORTING

In reporting the results of a real property appraisal, an appraiser must communicate each analysis, opinion, and conclusion in a manner that is not misleading.

Comment: STANDARD 2 addresses the content and level of information required in a report that communicates the results of a real property appraisal.

STANDARD 2 does not dictate the form, format, or style of real property appraisal reports. The form, format, and style of a report are functions of the needs of users and appraisers. The substantive content of a report determines its compliance.

Standards Rule 2-1 (This Standards Rule contains binding requirements from which departure is not permitted.)

Each written or oral real property appraisal report must:

(a)   clearly and accurately set forth the appraisal in a manner that will not be misleading;

(b)   contain sufficient information to enable the intended users of the appraisal to understand the report properly; and

(c)   clearly and accurately disclose any extraordinary assumption, hypothetical condition, or limiting condition that directly affects the appraisal and indicate its impact on value.

Comment: Examples of extraordinary assumptions or hypothetical conditions might include items such as the execution of a pending lease agreement, atypical financing, a known but not yet quantified environmental issue, or completion of onsite or offsite improvements. In a written report the disclosure is required in conjunction with statements of each opinion or conclusion that is affected.

Standards Rule 2-2 (This Standards Rule contains binding requirements from which departure is not permitted.)

Each written real property appraisal report must be prepared under one of the following three options and prominently state which option is used: Self-Contained Appraisal Report, Summary Appraisal Report, or Restricted Use Appraisal Report.

Comment: When the intended users include parties other than the client, either a Self-Contained Appraisal Report or a Summary Appraisal Report must be provided. When the intended users do not include parties other than the client, a Restricted Use Appraisal Report may be provided.

The essential difference among these three options is in the content and level of information provided.

An appraiser must use care when characterizing the type of report and level of information communicated upon completion of an assignment. An appraiser may use any other label in addition to, but not in place of, the label set forth in this Standard for the type of report provided.

The report content and level of information requirements set forth in the Standard are minimums for each type of report. An appraiser must supplement a report form when necessary to ensure that any intended user of the appraisal is not misled and that the report complies with the applicable content requirements set forth in this Standards Rule.

A party receiving a copy of a Self-Contained Appraisal Report, Summary Appraisal Report, or Restricted Use Appraisal Report in order to satisfy disclosure requirements does not become an intended user of the appraisal unless the client identifies such party as an intended user as part of the assignment.

The content of a Self-Contained Appraisal Report must be consistent with the intended use of the appraisal and, at a minimum:

(i)   state the identity of the client and any intended users, by name or type;

Comment: An appraiser must use care when identifying the client to ensure a clear understanding and to avoid violations of the Confidentiality section of the ETHICS RULE. In those rare instances when the client wishes to remain anonymous, an appraiser must still document the identity of the client in the workfile but may omit the client's identity in the report.

Intended users of the report might include parties such as lenders, employees of government agencies, partners of a client, and a client's attorney and accountant.

(ii)   state the intended use of the appraisal;

(iii)   describe information sufficient to identify the real estate involved in the appraisal, including the physical and economic property characteristics relevant to the assignment;

Comment: The real estate involved in the appraisal can be specified, for example, by a legal description, address, map reference, copy of a survey or map, property sketch and/or photographs or the like. The information can include a property sketch and photographs in addition to written comments about the legal, physical, and economic attributes of the real estate relevant to the purpose and intended use of the appraisal.

(iv)   state the real property interest appraised;

Comment: The statement of the real property rights being appraised must be substantiated, as needed, by copies or summaries of title descriptions or other documents that set forth any known encumbrances.

(v)   state the purpose of the appraisal, including the type and definition of value and its source;

Comment: Stating the definition of value requires the definition itself, an appropriate reference to the source of the definition, and any comments needed to clearly indicate to the reader how the definition is being applied.

When the purpose of the assignment is to develop an opinion of a market value, state whether the opinion of value is:

- in terms of cash or of financing terms equivalent to cash, or

- based on non-market financing or financing with unusual conditions or incentives.

When an opinion of a market value is not in terms of cash or based on financing terms equivalent to cash, summarize the terms of such financing and explain their contributions to or negative influence on value.

(vi)   state the effective date of the appraisal and the date of the report;

Comment: The effective date of the appraisal establishes the context for the value opinion, while the date of the report indicates whether the perspective of the appraiser on the market or property use conditions as of the effective date of the appraisal was prospective, current, or retrospective.

Reiteration of the date of the report and the effective date of the appraisal at various stages of the report in tandem is important for the clear understanding of the reader whenever market or property use conditions on the date of the report are different from such conditions on the effective date of the appraisal.

(vii)   describe sufficient information to disclose to the client and any intended users of the appraisal the scope of work used to develop the appraisal;

Comment: This requirement is to ensure that the client and intended users whose expected reliance on an appraisal may be affected by the extent of the appraiser's investigation are properly informed and are not misled as to the scope of work. The appraiser has the burden of proof to support the scope of work decision and the level of information included in a report.

When any portion of the work involves significant real property appraisal assistance, the appraiser must describe the extent of that assistance. The signing appraiser must also state the name(s) of those providing the significant real property appraisal assistance in the certification, in accordance with SR 2-3.

(viii) state all assumptions, hypothetical conditions, and limiting conditions that affected the analyses, opinions, and conclusions;

Comment: Typical or ordinary assumptions and limiting conditions may be grouped together in an identified section of the report. An extraordinary assumption or hypothetical condition must be disclosed in conjunction with statements of each opinion or conclusion that was affected.

(ix) describe the information analyzed, the appraisal procedures followed, and the reasoning that supports the analyses, opinions, and conclusions;

Comment: The appraiser must be certain the information provided is sufficient for the client and intended users to adequately understand the rationale for the opinion and conclusions.

When the purpose of an assignment is to develop an opinion of market value, a summary of the results of analyzing the information required in Standards Rule 1-5 is required. If such information was unobtainable, a statement on the efforts undertaken by the appraiser to obtain the information is required. If such information is irrelevant, a statement acknowledging the existence of the information and citing its lack of relevance is required.

(x) state the use of the real estate existing as of the date if value and the use of real estate reflected in the appraisal; and, when the purpose of the assignment is market value, describe the support and rationale for the appraiser's opinion of the highest and best use of the real estate;

Comment: The report must contain the appraiser's opinion as to the highest and best use of the real estate, unless an opinion as to highest and best use is unnecessary for example, as in insurance valuation or "value in use" appraisals. If the purpose of the assignment is a market value, the appraiser's support and rationale for the opinion of highest and best use is required. The appraiser's reasoning in support of the opinion must be provided in the depth and detail required by its significance to the appraisal.

(xi) state and explain any permitted departures from specific requirements of STANDARD 1 and the reason for excluding any of the usual valuation approaches; and

Comment: A Self-Contained Appraisal Report must include sufficient information to indicate that the appraiser complied with the requirements of STANDARD 1, including any permitted departures from the specific requirements. The amount of detail required will vary with the significance of the information to the appraisal.

When the DEPARTURE RULE is invoked, the assignment is deemed to be a Limited Appraisal. Use of the term "Limited Appraisal" makes clear that the assignment involved something less than or different from the work that could have and would have been completed if departure had not been invoked. The report of a Limited Appraisal must contain a prominent section that clearly identifies the extent of the appraisal process performed and the departures taken.

The reliability of the results of a Complete Appraisal or a Limited Appraisal developed under STANDARD 1 is not affected by the type of report prepared under STANDARD 2. The extent of the appraisal process performed under STANDARD 1 is the basis for the reliability of the value conclusion.

(xii) include a signed certification in accordance with Standards Rule 2-3.

(b)   The content of a Summary Appraisal Report must be consistent with the intended use of the appraisal and, at a minimum:

Comment: The essential difference between the Self-Contained Appraisal Report and the Summary Appraisal Report is the level of detail of presentation.

(i)   state the identity of the client and any intended users, by name or type;

Comment: An appraiser must use care when identifying the client to ensure a clear understanding and to avoid violations of the Confidentiality section of the ETHICS RULE. In those rare instances when the client wishes to remain anonymous, an appraiser must still document the identity of the client in the workfile but may omit the client's identity in the report.

Intended users of the report might include parties such as lenders, employees of government agencies, partners of a client, and a client's attorney and accountant.

(ii)   state the intended use of the appraisal

(iii)   summarize information sufficient to identify the real estate involved in the appraisal,
including the physical and economic property characteristics relevant to the assignment;

Comment: The real estate involved in the appraisal can be specified, for example, by a legal description, address, map reference, copy of a survey or map, property sketch, and/or photographs or the like. The summarized information can include a property sketch and photographs in addition to written Comments about the legal, physical, and economic attributes of the real estate relevant to the purpose and intended use of the appraisal.

(iv)   state the real property interest appraised;

Comment: The statement of the real property rights being appraised must be substantiated, as needed, by copies or summaries of title descriptions or other documents that set forth any known encumbrances.

(v)   state the purpose of the appraisal, including the type and definition of value and its source;

Comment: Stating the definition of value requires the definition itself, an appropriate reference to the source of the definition, and any comments needed to clearly indicate to the reader how the definition is being applied.

When the purpose of the assignment is to develop an opinion of a market value, state whether the opinion of value is:

- in terms of cash or of financing terms equivalent to cash, or

- based on non-market financing or financing with unusual conditions or incentives.

When an opinion of a market value is not in terms of cash or based on financing terms equivalent to cash, summarize the terms of such financing and explain their contributions to or negative influence on value.

(vi)   state the effective date of the appraisal and the date of the report;

Comment: The effective date of the appraisal establishes the context for the value opinion, while the date of the report indicates whether the perspective of the appraiser on the market or property use conditions as of the effective date of the appraisal was prospective, current, or retrospective.

Reiteration of the date of the report and the effective date of the appraisal at various stages of the report in tandem is important for the clear understanding of the reader whenever market or property use conditions on the date of the report are different from such conditions on the effective date of the appraisal.

(vii) **summarize sufficient information to disclose to the client and any intended users of the appraisal the scope of work used to develop the appraisal;**

Comment: This requirement is to ensure that the client and intended users whose expected reliance on an appraisal may be affected by the extent of the appraiser's investigation are properly informed and are not misled as to the scope of work. The appraiser has the burden of proof to support the scope of work decision and the level of information included in a report.

When any portion of the work involves significant real property appraisal assistance, the appraiser must summarize the extent of that assistance. The signing appraiser must also state the name(s) of those providing the significant real property appraisal assistance in the certification, in accordance with SR 2-3.

(viii) **state all assumptions, hypothetical conditions, and limiting conditions that affected the analyses, opinions, and conclusions;**

Comment: Typical or ordinary assumptions and limiting conditions may be grouped together in an identified section of the report. An extraordinary assumption or hypothetical condition must be disclosed in conjunction with statements of each opinion or conclusion that was affected.

(ix) **summarize the information analyzed, the appraisal procedures followed, and the reasoning that supports the analyses, opinions, and conclusions;**

Comment: The appraiser must be certain that the information provided is sufficient for the client and intended users to adequately understand the rationale for the opinion and conclusions.

When the purpose of an assignment is to develop an opinion of market value, a summary of the results of analyzing the information required in Standards Rule 1-5 is required. If such information was unobtainable, a statement on the efforts undertaken by the appraiser to obtain the information is required. If such information is irrelevant, a statement acknowledging the existence of the information and citing its lack of relevance is required.

(x) **state the use of the real estate existing as of the date of value and the use of the real estate reflected in the appraisal; and, when the purpose of the assignment is market value, summarize the support and rationale for the appraiser's opinion of the highest and best use of the real estate;**

Comment: The report must contain the appraiser's opinion as to the highest and best use of the real estate, unless an opinion as to highest and best use is unnecessary for example, as in insurance valuation or "value in use" appraisals. If the purpose of the assignment is a market value, a summary of the appraiser's support and rationale for the opinion of highest and best use is required. The appraiser's reasoning in support of the opinion must be provided in the depth and detail required by its significance to the appraisal.

(xi) **state and explain any permitted departures from specific requirements of STANDARD 1 and the reason for excluding any of the usual valuation approaches; and**

Comment: A Summary Appraisal Report must include sufficient information to indicate that the appraiser complied with the requirements of STANDARD 1, including any permitted departures from the specific requirements. The amount of detail required will vary with the significance of the information to the appraisal.

When the DEPARTURE RULE is invoked, the assignment is deemed to be a Limited Appraisal. Use of the term "Limited Appraisal" makes clear that the assignment involved something less than or different from the work that could have and would have been completed if departure had not been invoked. The report of a Limited Appraisal must contain a prominent section that clearly identifies the extent of the appraisal process performed and the departures taken.

The reliability of the results of a Complete Appraisal or a Limited Appraisal developed under STANDARD 1 is not affected by the type of report prepared under STANDARD 2. The extent of the appraisal process performed under STANDARD 1 is the basis for the reliability of the value conclusion.

(xii)   include a signed certification in accordance with Standards Rule 2-3.

The content of a Restricted Use Appraisal Report must be consistent with the intended use of the appraisal and, at a minimum:

(c)

(i)   **state the identity of the client, by name or type;**

Comment: An appraiser must use care when identifying the client to ensure a clear understanding and to avoid violations of the Confidentiality section of the ETHICS RULE. In those rare instances when the client wishes to remain anonymous, an appraiser must still document the identity of the client in the workfile but may omit the client's identity in the report.

(ii)   **state the intended use of the appraisal;**

Comment: The intended use of the appraisal must be consistent with the limitation on use of the Restricted Use Appraisal Report option in this Standards Rule (i.e., client use only).

(iii) **state information sufficient to identify the real estate involved in the appraisal;**

Comment: The real estate involved in the appraisal can be specified, for example, by a legal description, address, map reference, copy of a survey or map, property sketch, and/or photographs or the like.

(iv)   **state the real property interest appraised;**

(v)   **state the purpose of the appraisal, including the type of value, and refer to the definition of value pertinent to the purpose of the assignment;**

(vi)   **state the effective date of the appraisal and the date of the report**

Comment: The effective date of the appraisal establishes the context for the value opinion, while the date of the report indicates whether the perspective of the appraiser on the market or property use conditions as of the effective date of the appraisal was prospective, current, or retrospective.

(vii)   **state the extent of the process of collecting, confirming, and reporting data or refer to an assignment agreement retained in the appraiser's workfile that describes the scope of work to be performed;**

Comment: When any portion of the work involves significant real property appraisal assistance, the appraiser must state the extent of that assistance. The signing appraiser must also state the name(s) of those providing the significant real property appraisal assistance in the certification, in accordance with SR 2-3.

(viii)   **state all assumptions, hypothetical conditions, and limiting conditions that affect the analyses, opinions, and conclusions;**

Comment: Typical or ordinary assumptions and limiting conditions may be grouped together in an identified section of the report. An extraordinary assumption or hypothetical condition must be disclosed in conjunction with statements of each opinion or conclusion that was affected.

(ix)   **state the appraisal procedures followed, state the value opinion(s) and conclusion(s) reached, and reference the workfile;**

Comment: An appraiser must maintain a specific, coherent workfile in support of a Restricted Use Appraisal Report. The contents of the workfile must be sufficient for the appraiser to produce a Summary Appraisal Report. The file must be available for inspection by the client (or the client's representatives, such as those engaged to complete an appraisal review), state enforcement agencies, such third parties as may be authorized by due process of law, and a duly authorized professional peer review committee. The review of a Restricted Use Appraisal Report in compliance with STANDARD 3 is not possible without the reviewer having benefit of the information retained in the workfile.

When the purpose of the assignment is to develop an opinion of market value, information analyzed in compliance with Standards Rule 1-5 is significant information that must be disclosed in a Restricted Use Appraisal Report. If such information was unobtainable, a statement on the efforts undertaken by the appraiser to obtain the information is required. If such information is irrelevant, a statement acknowledging the existence of the information and citing its lack of relevance is required.

(x)   **state the use of the real estate existing as of the date of value and the use of the real estate reflected in the appraisal; and, when the purpose of the assignment is a market value, state   the appraiser's opinion of the highest and best use of the real estate;**

Comment: The report must contain a statement of the property uses both as is and as reflected in the appraisal and include the appraiser's opinion as to the highest and best use of the real estate, unless an opinion as to highest and best use is unnecessary—for example, insurance valuation or "value in use" appraisals. If an opinion of highest and best use is required, the appraiser's reasoning in support of the opinion must be stated in the depth and detail required by its significance to the appraisal or documented in the workfile and referenced in the report.

(xi)   **state and explain any permitted departures from applicable specific requirements of STANDARD 1; state the exclusion of any of the usual valuation approaches; and state a prominent use restriction that limits use of the report to the client and warns that the appraiser's opinions and conclusions set forth in the report cannot be understood properly without additional information in the appraiser's workfile; and**

Comment: When the DEPARTURE RULE is invoked, the assignment is deemed to be a Limited Appraisal. Use of the term "Limited Appraisal" makes it clear that the assignment involved something less than or different from the work that could have and would have been completed if departure had not been invoked. The report of a Limited Appraisal must contain a prominent section that clearly identifies the extent of the appraisal process performed and the departures taken.

The Restricted Use Appraisal Report is for client use only. Before entering into an agreement, the appraiser should establish with the client the situations where this type of report is to be used and should ensure that the client understands the restricted utility of the Restricted Use Appraisal Report.

(xii) include a signed certification in accordance with Standards Rule 2-3.

Standards Rule 2-3 **(This Standards Rule contains binding requirements from which departure is not permitted.)**

Each written real property appraisal report must contain a signed certification that is similar in content to the following form:

I certify that, to the best of my knowledge and belief:

— **the statements of fact contained in this report are true and correct.**

— **the reported analyses, opinions, and conclusions are limited only by the reported assumptions and limiting conditions and are my personal, impartial, and unbiased professional analyses, opinions, and conclusions.**

— **I have no (or the specified) present or prospective interest in the property that is the subject of this report and no (or the specified) personal interest with respect to the parties involved.**

— **I have no bias with respect to the property that is the subject of this report or to the parties involved with this assignment.**

— **my engagement in this assignment was not contingent upon developing or reporting predetermined results.**

— my compensation for completing this assignment is not contingent upon the development or reporting of a predetermined value or direction in value that favors he cause of the client, the amount of the value opinion, the attainment of a stipulated result, or the occurrence of a subsequent event directly related to the intended use of this appraisal.

— my analyses, opinions, and conclusions were developed, and this report has been prepared, in conformity with the *Uniform Standards of Professional Appraisal Practice.*

— I have (or have not) made a personal inspection of the property that is the subject of this report. (If more than one person signs this certification, the certification must clearly specify which individuals did and which individuals did not make a personal inspection of the appraised property.)

— no one provided significant real property appraisal assistance to the person signing this certification. (If there are exceptions, the name of each individual providing significant real property appraisal assistance must be stated.)

Comment: A signed certification is an integral part of the appraisal report. An appraiser, who signs any part of the appraisal report, including a letter of transmittal, must also sign this certification.

Any appraiser(s) who signs a certification accepts full responsibility for all elements of the certification, for the assignment results, and for the contents of the appraisal report.

When a signing appraiser(s) has relied on work done by others who do not sign the certification, the signing appraiser is responsible for the decision to rely on their work. The signing appraiser(s) is required to have a reasonable basis for believing that those individuals performing the work are competent and that their work is credible.

The names of individuals providing significant real property appraisal assistance who do not sign a certification must be stated in the certification. It is not required that the description of their assistance be contained in the certification, but disclosure of their assistance is required in accordance with SR 2-2(a), (b), or (c)(vii), as applicable.

Standards Rule 2-4 (This Standards Rule contains specific requirements from which departure is permitted. See DEPARTURE RULE.)

An oral real property appraisal report must, at a minimum, address the substantive matters set forth in Standards Rule 2-2(b).

Comment: Testimony of an appraiser concerning his or her analyses, opinions, and conclusions is an oral report in which the appraiser must comply with the requirements of this Standards Rule.

See the Record Keeping section of the ETHICS RULE for corresponding requirements.

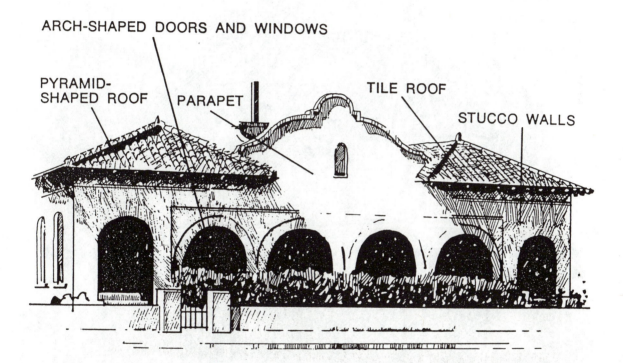

LOOKS LIKE OLD MISSION CHURCH

ARCH-SHAPED DOORS AND WINDOWS

PYRAMID-
SHAPED ROOF

PARAPET

TILE ROOF

STUCCO WALLS

Nineteenth Century American

MISSION (Mission - 717)

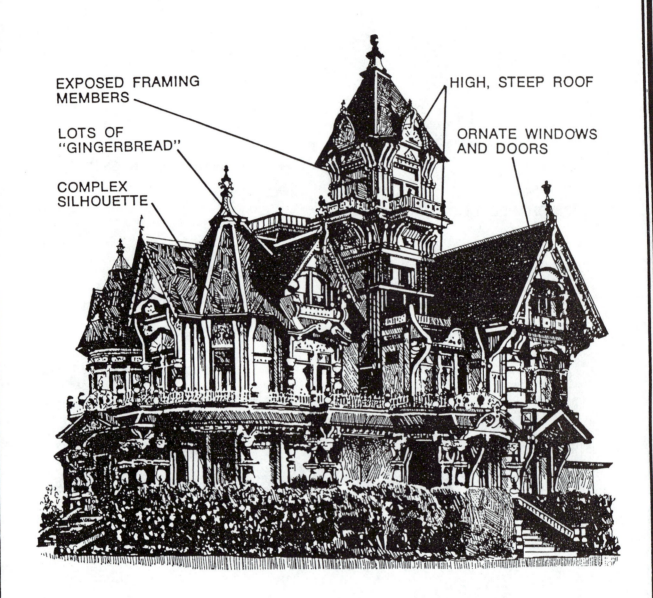

EXPOSED FRAMING MEMBERS

LOTS OF "GINGERBREAD"

COMPLEX SILHOUETTE

HIGH, STEEP ROOF

ORNATE WINDOWS AND DOORS

Nineteenth Century American

STICK STYLE OR CARPENTER GOTHIC
(Stick or C Goth - 708)

2 The Nature of Real Property and Value

Real property has economic value and significance only as it satisfies the needs and desires of human beings. The utilization of and the collective desire for real property gives it value. Although land acquires value when it is desired and has a feasible use, the value assigned to a parcel of real estate is not limited to the individual whose desires create it. Reflections of that value have significance for everyone whose welfare might be affected by its utilization. Before value can be discussed, however, the nature of real property must be understood.

The economic thinkers of the eighteenth and nineteenth centuries first developed the modern value theories. They identified the four agents of production known as land, capital, coordination and land. They examined the relationships between these basic factors to explain the basic factors that create value and supply and demand. There were two basic schools of economic thinking. The Mercantilists who believed that wealth was a source of national power and that wealth consisted of gold in the national treasury. The Physiocrats did not agree that bullion was wealth. They believed that agricultural production was the primary source of wealth.

Land has been the subject of human study throughout recorded history because it is essential to human existence. This study is divided into various disciplines including geography, law, sociology and economics. Each discipline studies land in a different way and has developed different concepts of land.

The appraiser's concept of land includes the concepts of all the other disciplines. By understanding these concepts, a foundation is laid to form the background against which appraisal activities are conducted.

Value is the principal subject of inquiry in a residential appraisal. In order to estimate the value of any property, it is first necessary to understand value theory. This theory includes anticipation, change, supply and demand, substitution, balance and externalities. Other theories the appraiser needs to understand are highest and best use, the forces that influence real property values (social, economic, government and environmental), and the factors of value (utility, scarcity, desire and effective purchase power). Such comprehension provides the foundation for a competent appraisal and an analysis of events and motivations that affect residential property value.

CONCEPTS OF LAND AND REAL ESTATE

GEOGRAPHIC CONCEPT OF REAL ESTATE

Geography focuses on describing the physical elements of land and the distribution and activities of people who use it. It recognizes the diverse physical characteristics and the significance of the combination of these characteristics in a particular area.

Land is affected by a number of processes. Ongoing physical and chemical processes modify the land's surface; biological processes affect the distribution of all life forms; and socioeconomic processes direct human habitation and activity on the land. Together, these processes influence land capability and, therefore, land use.

Land may be used for many purposes, including agriculture, commerce, industry, residence, and recreation. Land-use decisions are influenced by climate, topography, and the distribution of natural resources, population centers, and conditions, population pressures, technological practices, and cultural influences. The degree of influence of each of these varies, depending on the geographic area.

These subjects of geographic study are particularly significant for appraisers. The importance of the land's physical characteristics - climate, geology, soils, water, and vegetation - is obvious. Just as important are the distribution of people and their facilities, as are services and the movement of goods and people. With its emphasis on such matters as resources and resource bases, industrial location, and actual and potential markets, the geographic concept of land forms much of the background knowledge about land that is required in any real estate appraisal.

LEGAL CONCEPT OF REAL ESTATE

The original legal concept of real estate is more comprehensive than is generally realized. By definition it

> ...includes not only the ground, or soil, but everything that is attached to the earth, whether by course of nature, as trees and herbage, or by...(society), as houses and other buildings. It includes not only the surface of the earth, but everything under it and over it. Thus, in legal theory, a tract of land consists not only of the portion on the surface of the earth, but is an inverted pyramid having its tip or apex at the center of the earth, extending outward through the surface of the earth at the boundary lines of the tract, and continuing on upward to the heavens.[2]

This, theoretically, is full and complete ownership. However, acts passed by Congress in 1926 and 1938 give the United States complete sovereignty over the air space above the nation. In general, the courts have held that an owner can control only as much air space above the land as can be reasonably utilized, depending upon its location, zoning and other factors governing the use of the property.

A variety of terms describe land and the structures thereon, either natural or synthetic.

---

[2]Robert Kratovil, **Real Estate Law,** 6th Ed. (Englewood Cliffs, NJ: Prentice-Hall, Inc., 1974), p. 5.

Definition of Terms

-- Real Estate. The physical land and appurtenances, including structures affixed thereon. In some states, by statute, this term is synonymous with real property.

-- Property. Synonymous with rights as used in the bundle of rights. It includes the rights to future benefits by ownership or possession of economic goods.

    a. **Real property.** The interests, benefits and rights inherent in the ownership of the physical real estate. It is the bundle of rights with which such ownership is endowed. This term does not include personal property.

    b. **Personal property.** Movable items, those not permanently fixed to and part of real estate.

        In deciding whether an item is personal property or real estate, four factors must be considered: (1) the manner in which it is annexed, (2) the intention of the party responsible for the annexation (i.e., to leave it permanently or to remove it at some time), (3) the purpose for which the premises are used, and (4) the cost of the item. With some exceptions, items remain personal property if they can be removed easily and without damage to the real estate or the item itself.

-- Chattel. A legal term referring to any property other than a freehold or fee estate in real estate. Chattels are treated as personal property but are divided into two subcategories:

    a. Chattels real include all interest in real estate not constituting a freehold or fee estate in land, including leasehold estates and other interests issuing out of or annexed to real estate.

    b. Chattels personal are all movable things.

-- Fixtures. Tangible items that previously were personal property and have been attached to or installed on land or in a structure in such a way as to become a part of the real estate.

Thus, real estate, real property, personal property, chattels and fixtures are different and precise concepts. The distinctions between them are significant and the appraiser must have a thorough understanding of them.

The chief characteristics of real estate are its immobility and tangibility. Real estate is land and all things of a permanent and substantial nature affixed thereto, whether by nature or people. Real property, however, embraces in its broadest sense the tangible elements of real estate plus the intangible attributes that are the rights of ownership. The appraiser is concerned with real property, since the estimate of value made in an appraisal is of the rights and benefits to be derived from the ownership and/or use of real estate.

The major characteristic of personal property is its mobility. Furniture and furnishings, machinery, mortgages and securities of every type comprise personal property.

Chattel is a legal concept referring to non-ownership interests in real estate or personal property.

Because the distinction between real estate and personal property is not always evident and because it is important in the evaluation of real estate, appraisers should be familiar with the law of fixtures as it applies in their area. In the case of controversial items, the appraiser may abide by local custom; however, the appraisal report should clearly state the distinction.

SOCIAL CONCEPT OF REAL ESTATE

As physical characteristics and legal limitations increasingly affect land use, many different groups in society become concerned with how land is used and how rights are distributed. Because the supply of land is fixed, the demand for land in modern American society causes pressure for its more intensive use. Conflicts often arise between groups whose views on proper use of the land differ. Certain people believe that land is a resource to be shared by all. They want to preserve the land's scenic beauty and important ecological functions. Other persons view land primarily as a marketable commodity and believe that society is best served by private, unrestricted ownership. The fact that land is both a resource and a commodity prevents clear-cut solutions to these group conflicts.[3]

Both groups have won support for their beliefs. As a resource, land is protected for the good of society. Because land is also a marketable commodity, its ownership, use, and disposal are regulated so that unjust infringement on individual rights is precluded.

The government's right to regulate "the manner in which (a citizen) shall own his own property when such regulation becomes necessary for the public good" was established in 1876 by the U.S. Supreme Court, which repeated the words of England's Lord Chief Justice Hale: "When private property is 'affected with a public interest,' it ceases to be juris privati only." [4]

Even earlier, land ownership had been recognized as fundamental to America's institutions. John Adams wrote, "If the multitude is possessed of real estate, the multitude will take care of the liberty, virtue, and interest of the multitude in all acts of government." [5]

The restrictions that society may fix in the public interest include building restrictions, zoning and building ordinances, development and subdivision regulations, and environmental controls. The latter include provisions to prohibit the pollution of air and water through dumping wastes, emitting dirt and chemicals, and causing excessive noise. Concern for preserving the natural state has made possible certain regulations that protect wetlands, beaches and navigable waters.

---

[3] Richard N. L. Andrews, *Land in America* (Lexington, MA: D.C. Heath and Company, 1979), p. ix
[4] Andrews, **Op cit.**, p. 31.
[5] Andrews, **Op cit.**, p. 31.

ECONOMIC CONCEPT OF REAL ESTATE

Land is a physical substance imbued with ownership rights that can be legally limited for the good of society. Further, land is a major source of wealth. In economic terms, wealth is measured in relation to money value or exchange value. Land and its products are of economic value only as they are converted into goods or services that are useful to, desired and paid for by, consumers. The economic concept of land as a source of wealth and object of value is central to appraisal knowledge and inquiry.

APPRAISER'S CONCEPT OF REAL ESTATE

The geographic, legal, social, and economic concepts of land all are germane to the real estate appraiser's concept of land. Land, as defined legally to include everything attached to it, constitutes real estate. The appraiser studies the value of physical real estate and its accompanying ownership rights. The potential uses of land are influenced by geographic, legal, social, and economic considerations. These considerations form the background against which appraisal activities are conducted.

RIGHTS AND INTERESTS

The rights and interests in real estate can be divided into public rights and private rights. Public rights are included in the bundle of rights. Private rights may be classified further as (1) undivided fractional interests or (2) divisions based on physical separation.

PUBLIC RIGHTS

Bundle of Rights Theory

The bundle of rights theory holds that the ownership of real property may be compared to a bundle of sticks wherein each stick represents a distinct and separate right or privilege of ownership. These rights, inherent in ownership of real property and guaranteed by law but subject to certain limitations and restrictions, include:

1. The right to occupy and to use real property.

2. The right to sell it in whole or in part.

3. The right to bequeath it,.

4. The right to lease it.

5. The right to transfer by contract for specified periods of time the benefits to be derived by occupancy and use ("beneficial interests").

6. The right to do nothing at all with it.

FIG. 2-1 BUNDLE OF RIGHTS

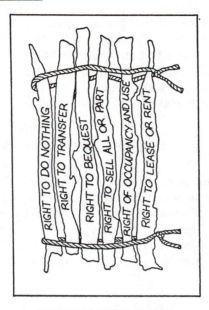

BUNDLE OF RIGHTS THEORY

-- Ad valorem taxation.   The right of the state to levy and collect a tax varying with the assessed value of the property. It is a compulsory contribution exacted from all owners of real estate for the general support of the state and for the maintenance of public services. Also included are special assessments that may be levied against certain real estate benefiting from public improvements, usually to offset directly the cost of such improvements.

-- Eminent domain. The right reserved by government to force an involuntary conveyance or taking of title to private land through the process of condemnation for public benefit, provided just compensation is paid. The concept of what constitutes public benefit has been extended to quasi-government or public bodies such as housing authorities and public utilities.

-- Police power.   The right to regulate property to promote the safety, health, morals and general welfare of the community via zoning ordinances, building codes, traffic regulations and other restrictions such as fair housing laws.

-- Escheat.   The reversion to the state of property ownership if the owner dies without a will and with no known legal heirs.

PRIVATE RIGHTS

In addition to the controls and restrictions imposed by the four powers of government, provisions may be inserted into deeds by which properties are transferred that further restrict property uses. Through private deed restrictions, owners can limit property uses, establish building restrictions, regulate land coverage, and control property in other ways.

Such restrictions may apply to one property or to an entire area. Deed restrictions can be enforced by the original owners, subsequent owners or other affected individuals or organizations. Where restrictions include conditions upon which the deed is given, a reversionary clause may provide that the property revert to the seller if violations can be proved.

Federal, state and local fair housing laws guarantee persons the right to buy, sell, lease, hold and convey property without being subjected to discrimination on the basis of race, color, religion, sex or national origin. These laws have nullified private deed restrictions which limit occupancy on racial, ethnic or religious grounds. They also prohibit all types of discrimination in housing and rental transactions so that equal housing opportunity is now often regarded as one of the basic property rights.

Estates

Several estates exist which affect the holding of title to the real estate. They include:

-- **Absolute fee simple** title to real property is the most complete degree of ownership but some restrictions and reservations are included. It does not guarantee the unrestricted exercise of the entire bundle of rights. These rights and privileges are limited by four powers of government:

-- **A freehold estate,** which is not common in the United States, is the ownership of real estate for some indeterminate duration such as life of the owner.

-- **Ownership in Severalty.** Estates held by one person, in contrast to joint estates that are held by more than one person, are ownership in severalty.

-- **Life Estates.** Titles conveyed for the life of a specified person are called life estates. The life estate can create a reversion to the grantor upon the life tenant's death or it can go to a remainderman as a third party grantee.

-- **Statutory Estates.** These estates are created by law and include dower, a wife's rights in her husband's real property; courtesy, a husband's rights in his wife's real property and community property where each spouse gains 1/2 interest in the marital property.

Undivided Interests

Division of earnings or productivity occurs when ownership is in undivided interests such as either tenancy-in-common or joint tenancy. Co-ownership, also called concurrent ownership in real estate, has several different forms.   The rights of the co-owners and their creditors vary depending on the type of co-ownership.

Some co-ownerships are formed to control the transfer from one owner to the other upon the death of one of them. Others permit the pooling of resources by several individuals to buy real estate that no one of them could afford individually.

Co-ownership can result even without the co-owners intending to be co-owners. They can result from inheriting real estate from one who dies intestate. It may also occur when tenancy by a husband and wife is converted upon divorce to a tenancy in common.   The dollar value of such interests is usually less than the numerical percentage of the portion of ownership, particularly where the ownership is less than a 50% in the property. Some examples of co-ownership are:

-- Joint Tenancy.   Joint tenancy never happens by accident. A clearly expressed intent to create a joint tenancy plus time, title, possession, and interest must exist before a joint tenancy with the right of survivorship can arise.   The right of survivorship which exists under a true joint tenancy is one of its most important features. Upon the death of one joint tenant, the entire interest passes to the surviving tenant(s).

-- Tenancy by the Entireties. This is the most common form of co-ownership or concurrent ownership and arises from any conveyance to a man and woman who are husband and wife at the time of the conveyance.   Termination of tenancy by entireties can be achieved by sale only if both the husband and wife consent to the sale. Termination can also occur upon the death of either the husband or the wife and the survivor succeeds to the total interest held by the entireties.   Finally, in the event of a divorce by the tenants of the entirety, the real estate is subsequently held by them as tenants in common.

-- Community Property.   Community property acquired by a husband and wife during marriage is owned in equal, undivided interests no matter how much each spouse contributed to the acquisition.

-- Tenancy in Common. The creation of a tenancy in common frequently occurs through dying without a will and leaving several descendants.   It also happens in the case of a divorce in which no definite arrangements were made in connection with real estate held by the husband and wife during the marriage.   It can also happen for investment purposes where tenants in common may purchase unequal shares.

-- Land Trusts.   Title is held by a trustee, usually a bank or trust company, for the benefit of the fractional owners.

-- General and Limited Partnerships.   Limited partners share proportionately in the net earnings and other benefits and depreciation but have no voice in the management decisions or individual responsibility.   General partners are usually the persons who develop the partnership, retain special benefits, including the right of management decisions, and are solely liable for all obligations.

-- Condominium Ownership.   A condominium is a form of ownership which involves a separation of property into individual ownership elements and common elements.   A condominium is established by a declaration or master deed.   Each owner of a unit receives a unit deed and finances the unit with an individual mortgage and their share of the common charges.   The individual condominium unit is that portion of the condominium which is for the exclusive use and possession of the owner.

A Homeowner's Association is responsible for the governance of the condominium and maintenance of the common areas.   Common elements are those portions of the community property owned pro-rata on an undivided basis by the owners of the individual units. State statutes which permit the creation of the condominium form of real property ownership are called *Horizontal Property Acts*.   They permit ownership of a specified horizontal layer of airspace as opposed to the traditional vertical method of ownership from the earth below to the sky above.

FIG. 2-2 TYPES OF OWNERSHIP (COOPERATIVE & CONDOMINIUM)

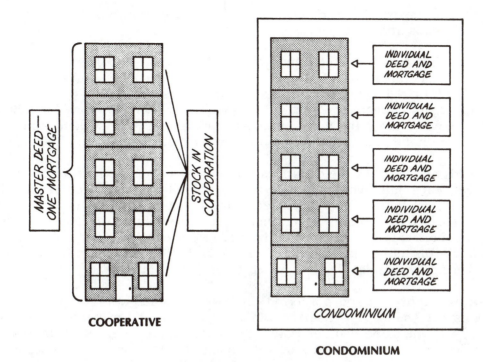

COOPERATIVE

CONDOMINIUM

CONDOMINIUM

-- **Cooperative Ownership.** Cooperative ownership is a form of ownership in which a corporation is established to hold title to the entire property. It is usually financed with a blanket mortgage on the entire property. Each stockholder is given a proprietary lease on a unit, subject to certain conditions and obligations as to its use, sub-leasing and sale. Usually the lease or sale is subject to the approval of a board of directors of the cooperative. A subscription agreement is signed by a person wishing to occupy a unit for stock in a corporation which holds title or the occupancy agreement is given to the party in return for the purchase of the stock. The obligations of the tenant include payment of a proportional share of the expenses incurred by the corporation for maintenance, property taxes and debt service.

-- **Corporate Ownership.** Stock ownership in a property that has been incorporated results in corporate ownership. One of the disadvantages of real estate corporate ownership is that depreciation for income tax purposes cannot always be passed through directly to the owner of the corporate stock. Income received by the stockholders of a corporation is often subject to double taxation.

-- **Timeshares.** Fractional interests created by timesharing have been marketed extensively in recent years. Timesharing is the sale of limited ownership interests in residential apartments or hotel rooms.

-- **Equity syndications.** Another popular financial division of property interests is the equity syndication. A syndication is a private or public partnership that pools funds for the acquisition and development of real estate projects. Syndications, sometimes referred to as partnerships, are established when an individual or group purchases interests in real estate for the purpose of transferring those interests to a limited partnership. The limited partnership interests are then sold to investors.

Physical Division

The second category of fractional ownership or interest is a division of the physical use of the property.

-- Horizontal and Vertical Subdivision. Horizontal subdivision is the description of the surface area boundaries of a property. Vertical subdivision refers to the division of air rights and subsurface rights. Subsurface rights in the form of oil or mineral rights are commonly leased or sold. Their exclusion may have little effect on surface land values if the terms of conveyance protect the surface from interference. Subsurface rights may also involve underground pipes and cable lines.

-- Air Rights. Within the distances normally encompassed above or below the land surface, real estate ownership may be considered to be between vertical boundaries above and below the site. This means that a 100-by-100 foot parcel of land is not a square surface but a cube. Accordingly, this cube may be divided not only vertically, but also horizontally, as in the individual layers of the cake. The useful height or depth of this cube (number of stories) is limited only by the practicalities of engineering, economics (highest and best use) and zoning.

-- Water Rights. Land bordering on flowing bodies of water such as rivers and streams has the right to use the water along with the owners of other contiguous portions of the same body of water. Such rights are referred to as riparian rights. Land bordering on large bodies of water such as a lake or a sea carries with it littoral rights which allows the owners use and enjoyment of a body of water.

-- Mineral Rights. Like air and other rights, mineral rights may be owned, sold, bought and transferred to another party for profit. The estimation of value of each right is becoming a more common appraisal assignment.

-- Profits. Profits are the right to take part of the soil or produce of the land of another.

-- License. A license is a personal right given by contract to go onto the land of another. A license does not encumber the title to real property.

-- Easement. A non-possessing interest held by one person in the land of another person whereby the first person is accorded partial use of such land for a specific purpose. Easements are created to allow access to property whether it be from public or private land. An easement may be vertical and/or horizontal, such as underground utility lines. Where an easement is granted to allow specific access to or through a property, it may be called a right-of-way.

-- Liens. An owner may give a claim on his property to another to secure a debt. Such liens fall into the category of either voluntary or involuntary. Voluntary liens are given freely by the property owner, an example of which is a mortgage lien. Involuntary liens are created by operation of law, examples of which are mechanic liens, property tax liens and judgment liens.

-- Transferable Development Rights (TDRs) emerged in the real estate industry during the 1970s. A transferable development right is a development right that cannot be used by the landowner but can be sold to landowners in another location. Some TDRs are used to preserve property for agricultural production, open space or historic buildings.

Lease Interests

Lease interests are another type of partial interest in real estate, which can be divided into two types.

-- **Leased Fees.**   An owner may lease real estate, relinquishing the right of occupancy but retaining the title to the fee, subject to the lease, including the recovery of use at the expiration of the lease, known as the reversionary rights.   The value of a leased fee interest is profoundly affected by its length and terms, which may cover a wide range of provisions agreed upon between the parties.

-- **Leasehold or Possessory Interest.**   That portion of the rights including occupancy that is transferred from the owner of the fee to a tenant. This is usually done by a lease, permit, license, concession or other type of contract.   It is the opposite of the leased fee.   The value of possessory interests usually refers to the value of the interest leased (i.e., the value of the use and occupancy of the property for the lease term, known as a leasehold interest).

Knowing exactly which rights are under consideration is fundamental in appraising. Precise definition is customarily a matter of documentation.   In the absence of such definition, it may be necessary to obtain a legal opinion.   The appraiser, however, should be generally familiar with the broad range of property rights, their more common characteristics, and the usual manner in which they are utilized and transferred.

ECONOMIC PRINCIPLES

The basic economic principles are defined, explained, and illustrated in this section, with emphasis on their impact upon real property value.   This section begins with the traditional agents of production and surplus productivity.   Next the broad principle of supply and demand is discussed, followed by more specific real estate principles: anticipation, balance, change, competition and excess profit, conformity, contribution, externalities and substitution.

The last to be discussed, highest and best use, is the most fundamental principle in understanding real property value.   Estimating highest and best use has been described by many appraisers as the most critical step in the total appraisal process. Some steps of the process may be more technical, others may lead more directly to the value conclusion, but none is more basic or fundamental than the concept of highest and best use.

FOUR AGENTS OF PRODUCTION

Economic theory holds that for any good or service to be produced, expenditures must be made for the agents of production: land, labor, capital, and coordination.

Definitions

-- **Land** refers to the earth and all its resources, which include water, fish, game, woods, and minerals in their natural state. Land provides the basic space and the raw materials needed for all production.

-- **Labor** is the work required to obtain and process natural resources, to shape them into salable products, and to transport these products to a location where buyers will purchase them. Management and highly skilled labor such as that provided by an engineer or architect are *not* included in this category.

-- **Capital** refers to the money committed to the creation and operation of an enterprise apart from the money needed for the other three agents of production. Materials, tools, machinery, warehouses, and buildings, which are the physical parts of the enterprise and not part of the natural land, represent forms of invested capital.

-- **Coordination** refers to the knowledge, skill, business acumen, managerial talent, and entrepreneurial ability that are typically required to provide beneficial items efficiently. Successful production of some items requires more or less coordination, but all items require this agent of production in some degree.

Because a limited amount of each of these agents is available in any one area at any one time, production costs are largely shaped by competition in the local market. There is competition for land in real estate markets; for labor in employment markets; for capital in financial markets; and for coordination in markets for trained professionals, skilled entrepreneurs, and effective business managers. Naturally, local markets are often influenced by the broader markets for these agents and by external economic conditions. Therefore, for example, residential appraisers must follow trends that affect local construction costs to analyze supply and understand the data used in the cost approach.

SURPLUS PRODUCTIVITY

Surplus productivity is defined as the net income remaining after the four agents of production have been paid. It may be attributed to the land in its present use. Surplus productivity is dependent upon the principles of balance and increasing and decreasing returns and the proper apportionment of the four agents of production.

SUPPLY AND DEMAND

The principle of supply and demand involves the interrelationship of the desire for a commodity and its scarcity. Demand for a commodity is created by its utility (ability to satisfy a need) and its scarcity and is limited by the financial ability of people to purchase it. The greater the supply of a commodity, the lower its price will tend to be. There is a point, at least theoretically, at which supply and demand are in balance. At this point, market value tends to reflect the cost of production or replacement. As the supply increases or demand decreases, the price in the market decreases. Recently this market phenomenon has been called a soft market.

Abstract demand is unlimited because people continually desire more goods. But effective demand is limited in the economic sense by the purchasing power of the participants in the market. Because demand is closely related to desire, both advertising and education can greatly influence demand.

Among the factors affecting supply and demand for housing are population changes, purchasing power, and price levels. The supply of housing, for example, is controlled in part by rentals and sales prices and the relationship these bear to the temper of the market. A certain combination of factors must be present in the housing market to stimulate additions to the housing supply. There must be a shortage in the supply of units, a strong demand for housing, and effective purchasing power to satisfy the demand at the rentals and sales prices offered, which in turn must be high enough to encourage builders to construct new units. If demand is very strong and purchasing power is increasing faster than the ability of the supply to satisfy the increased need, rentals and sale prices for available units rise (inflation results when demand exceeds supply). When increased rentals or sales prices continue to find a ready market, more builders enter the scene, accelerating the pace of additions to the supply. Should this result in an excess of units, prices fall (deflation results when supply exceeds demand).

Other factors influencing the real estate market are the cost of labor, taxation of property, the money supply and the cost of financing, rent controls, zoning and other government regulations.

The following principles operate within the structure of the market. Market activity is composed of supply and demand; the interaction of the two is expressed as a price. To understand the influence of the market on prices (as well as on values and costs), the appraiser must understand and apply the concept of micro- and macro-economics. Micro-economics is the study of the individual property in the market. Macro-economics is the study of the industry; in real estate appraising it applies to all the properties of a certain type and their activity in the market.

Obviously a substantial difference exists between the study of an individual residence in its market and the analysis of all such residences as a segment of the market. The basic principles that follow are applicable to both micro and macro situations although the application and interpretation may vary.

Although all of these relationships and reactions are stated definitely, there may be exceptions (called "phenomena"); furthermore, these are indicated as "tendencies," that is, "the price tends to increase," etc.

ANTICIPATION

Value is created by the expectation of benefits to be derived in the future. The future, not the past, is important in deriving estimates of value. The primary use of past experience is in its significance in forecasting possible future trends and conditions.

Value may be defined as the present worth of the rights to all prospective future benefits, tangible and intangible, accruing to the ownership of real estate. In most cases the quantity, quality and duration of future benefits may be estimated in the light of past experience as disclosed by analysis of the property being appraised and comparable properties.

An illustration of changing attitudes and wants on the part of a segment of the residential market is found in the reactions during the energy crunch in 1974 and 1975. Some consumers in the market altered their desires for housing, from larger to smaller units within closer proximity to employment and schools, with more attention to the costs to heat and cool the structure. Such a significant change in a major part of the market must be considered by the professional appraiser in his or her analysis.

Recent sales prices of comparable houses indicate the attitudes of informed buyers and investors in the market concerning the present value of the anticipated benefits of ownership of a particular property. However, the market value of an individual property is not necessarily established by past selling price or by the cost to create it.

BALANCE

Maximum value is achieved when the agents of production are in economic balance. The value of a property depends on the balance of these four:

1. Land (rents).
2. Labor (wages).
3. Capital (the investment in buildings and equipment).
4. Coordination (management or entrepreneurial contribution).

The classical economists, especially David Ricardo, recognized the importance of the agents of production. They are used today to help explain the principle of balance and the residual nature of the value of the land.

There is a theoretical point of equilibrium in each property that will produce the greatest net return. An imbalance exists when a building represents an under-improvement or overimprovement in relation to its site; one also is present when the cost and amount of special services to the occupants are inadequate or excessive when related to the character of the building or neighborhood. These conditions illustrate the principle of balance, affirming that a disadvantage or loss in value attends any excess or deficiency in the contribution of the four agents of production.

The use of goods and services resulting from these agents produces gross income. Gross income is first applied to labor, capital, coordination and finally to land.

The principle of balance is applied in the process of estimating highest and best use in appraisal practice. Thus the proper apportionment of the agents of production is essential if maximum net return is to be produced and maximum land value developed. Because land has last claim on the gross income produced by the proper apportionment of the four agents, the land value is residual.

The natural operation of the market is towards balance. This concept applies to individual productive units as well as to all units in a market. It is difficult to alter the relationship between the units of production in an existing building, although it might be accomplished by a renovation program, refinancing or new ownership. New units added to the market use the experience of existing units to maximize their chances of reaching balance.

Three sub-elements of the principle of balance are contribution, increasing and decreasing returns and surplus productivity, each involving the agents of production.

CHANGE

Change is constantly occurring; in real estate. It affects individual properties, neighborhoods and cities. Change can evolve so slowly that it is almost indiscernible. The appraiser must be sensitive to subtle as well as obvious indications of change. The future, not the past, is of primary importance in the valuation of real estate.

The appraiser's concern is with the market's view of transition. Recognition must be made of the social, economic, governmental and environmental forces at work and their present and future effect on the market value of single family residences.

Individual properties, districts, neighborhoods and entire communities often follow a four-phase life span:

-- **Growth.** A period during which there are gains in public favor and acceptance.

-- **Stability.** A period of equilibrium without marked gains or losses.

-- **Decline.** A period of diminishing demand and acceptance.

-- **Renewal.** A period of rejuvenation and rebirth of market demand.

In the market the basis of the value of a property is neither the price paid for it in the past nor the cost of its creation, but rather the prospective amenities and uses that buyers and sellers believe it will provide for them in the future. The actions of the market (sales) reflect informed buyers' opinions of the probable future benefits of ownership. The attitude of the market towards property in a specific neighborhood reflects the probable future trend of that neighborhood. For example, following World War II, more ranch-style houses were built than two-story houses. Buyers in the market developed a preference for one-story houses, reducing the demand for two-story houses.

COMPETITION AND EXCESS PROFIT

NORMAL PROFIT

Profit tends to breed competition and excess profit tends to encourage ruinous competition. Profit is defined as that portion of the net income produced by real property over and above the costs of labor, capital, coordination and land (the agents of production).

Profit as applied to real property is not the same as profit obtained from the operation of a business. Normal business profit is the monetary incentive and reward for capital investment. The yield on real property investments also is the monetary incentive for investment in land and buildings. But profit, as it is considered by the appraiser, is the prospective net income remaining after operating costs and adequate returns on land and building(s) have been satisfied. In other words, it is what remains after providing for the agents of production. *yes ALL FOUR Agents*

Competition is one of the most familiar and easily recognized forces present at all levels of economic activity. Reasonable competition stimulates further creative contribution, but in excess it can destroy profits. A lack of competition, such as created by a monopolistic situation, must be recognized by the appraiser as being outside the realm of market value definition and consider it accordingly in his or her analysis. The appraiser not only recognizes competition in normal situations but also perceives those situations in which it is excessive and, if unchecked, may undermine value. Competition is a product of supply and demand; a proper study of the highest and best use of a property includes current supply and demand factors.

CONFORMITY

Maximum value is realized when a reasonable degree of architectural homogeneity exists and land uses are compatible. Conformity in use is usually a highly desirable feature of real property since it tends to create and maintain value; and maximum value affords the owner maximum return. Reasonable homogeneity implies reasonable similarity; it does not mean monotonous uniformity. Generally, the most satisfactory use of land is realized when it conforms to the standards governing the area in which it is located.

The standards of conformity are subject to the principle of change. For example, racial homogeneity was once considered a sign of social conformity and neighborhood stability. Conversely, racial integration was once considered a sign of social non-conformity and neighborhood decline. Social perceptions and attitudes have changed. The notion that racial or ethnic homogeneity is a requirement for maximum value is without empirical support. Many strong and stable neighborhoods are composed of residents of varied and diverse racial, religious and cultural backgrounds.

Other signs of change may be observed in architectural design and urban planning. The trend toward multipurpose urban structures and a deliberate mixing of land uses reflects an increasing awareness of the interdependence of land uses to maximize utility and value.

The elements of conformity are not preconceived standards of development but have evolved as cities have grown and land uses have multiplied. Homeowners have recognized the advantages of living in neighborhoods designed and developed to provide facilities or amenities which add to the benefits of ownership, and they have protected those assets by maintaining conformity through zoning.

CONTRIBUTION

The principle of contribution (also known as the principle of marginal productivity) is the principle of increasing and decreasing returns applied to a portion or portions of real property. It affirms that the value of any individual agent in production depends on how much it contributes to value by its presence or detracts by its absence. An example of this principle in the appraisal of residential properties is the valuation of lots of varying depths. The appraiser must estimate the value, if any, that additional depth contributes to a parcel over and above the value of lots of standard depth in the area. If the lot is of less than standard depth, its value would reflect a loss of contribution attributable to the missing piece.

This principle has practical application in estimating the degree of overimprovement, underimprovement, or misplaced improvement in highest and best use analysis.

-- Increasing and Decreasing Returns. Larger amounts of the agents of production produce a greater net income up to a point at which the maximum value has been developed. Any additional expenditures will not produce a return commensurate with such investment. The fertilization of farmland affords a simple example of this principle. Up to a certain point, increasing use of fertilizer results in a greater crop yield. Beyond that point, it will not produce an additional return sufficient to warrant the additional cost.

It is frequently necessary to determine the character and size of the structural improvements that will enable the land to produce the greatest net yield. To ascertain this point, hypothetical combinations of probable income and expenses and capital requirements for improvements of various types and sizes should be analyzed. Different combinations may represent higher or lower probable yields.

The process of developing hypothetical improvements to determine that combination of the agents of production providing the greatest yield illustrates the principle of increasing and decreasing returns.

EXTERNALITIES

The principle of externalities is that external economics result from goods, products, or conditions that have a positive or negative effect on people other than those who produce or own the goods or products, or who create the conditions. For example, an external economy occurs when one group of ticket purchasers for a concert pays a price higher than the cost of its seats so that others may attend at a lower, subsidized price. When external economics affect great numbers of people, the product or service will probably be provided by government. Bridges, highways, police and fire protection, and other commonly needed services are provided more cheaply per user through common purchase by the government than through separate purchase by each individual.

External economics occur when costs or inconveniences are imposed on other people by an individual or a firm. For example, a person who litters imposes the cleanup costs on other people. A business firm that erects an unattractive sign imposes the cost of offensive visual sensations on people who see the sign.

Real estate is affected by externalities more than any other type of economic good, service, or commodity. Its physical immobility subjects it to many types of external influences. Such influences emanate from all levels - international, national, regional, community, and neighborhood. The influences may be as broad as international currency and gold prices or as narrow as a neighbor's standard of maintenance. An appraiser should be knowledgeable about, and analyze the impact of, all such influences on a parcel of real estate.

At the international and national levels, such influences as international trade policy, manufacturing efficiency, interest rates, and socioeconomic priorities affect real estate values greatly. For example, the combination of these influences caused many U.S. real estate values in the early 1980's to fall or to increase less rapidly than in previous years. Foreign imports tended to make U.S. manufacturing operations and equipment less efficient than certain foreign counterparts. High interest rates tended to depress home buying and industrial expansion.

Moreover, a lesser emphasis on homeownership as a national priority resulted in competition for credit. Borrowers who wanted to buy a home had to compete with government and industry.

At the regional level, real estate values during these years prospered better in some areas than in others. Generally, the population migration to the Sunbelt tended to enhance values there at the expense of older, northern regions, where values tended to stabilize or decline. Industrial areas with manufacturing operations most susceptible to foreign competition suffered more than areas less reliant on such industries.

At the community and neighborhood levels, property values are affected by local laws, local government policies and administration, property taxes, economic growth, and social attitudes. Different trends in property values often are noted among communities in the same state or region and among neighborhoods in the same community.

An appraiser should be familiar with such externalities and be able to assess their impact on individual property values.

SUBSTITUTION

When several commodities or services with substantially the same utility or benefit are available, the one with the lowest price attracts the greatest demand and widest distribution. The importance and application of this principle can be found in many segments of the economy. In real estate, for example, if two homes offer approximately the same advantages, the prospective buyer will select the one with the lower price.

The principle of substitution is found in each of the three approaches to value:

-- **Sales Comparison Approach.** When there are alternate choices of like or similar residences, market value tends to be set at the price of acquiring an equally desirable substitute property, assuming that no costly delay is encountered in making the substitution.

-- **Cost Approach.** No rational person will pay more for a property than that amount for which one can obtain, by purchase of a site and construction of a building without undue delay, a property of equal desirability and utility.

-- **Income Approach.** Value tends to be set by the effective investment necessary to acquire, without undue delay, a comparable substitute income property offering an equally desirable net income return.

The principle of substitution is the basis for these premises:

1. The market value of property tends to match the value indicated by the actions of informed buyers in the market for comparable real estate having similar physical and locational characteristics.

2. The cost of producing, through new construction, an equally desirable substitute property may set the upper limit of value, if new construction can be completed in a reasonable period of time.

3. The value of a property tends to be related to its competitive position among alternative investment choices producing the same net income.

HIGHEST AND BEST USE

Fundamental to the concept of value is the theory of highest, best and most profitable use. Highest and best use is defined as: the reasonable and probable use that will support the highest present value, as defined, as of the effective date of the appraisal. It is also defined as: the use, from among reasonably probable and legal alternative uses, found to be physically possible, appropriately supported and financially feasible and which results in highest land value.

This definition applies specifically to the highest and best use of land. Where a site has existing improvements, the highest and best use of the site <u>as if vacant</u> may be different from the existing use. The existing use will continue, however, unless and until land value in its highest and best use exceeds the total value of the property in its current use.

Implied in the definition of highest and best use is the concept that, in addition to the maximization of profit for the property owner, consideration must also be given to the effect on the community environment and to the overall community development goals. Also implied is that the determination of highest and best use results from the appraiser's judgment and analytical skill--that is, that the use determined from analysis represents opinion, not a fact. In appraisal practice, the concept of highest and best use represents the premise on which value is based. In the context for most probable selling price (market value), another appropriate term to reflect highest and best use would be most probable use.

The most profitable likely use cannot always be interpreted in terms of money. Net return sometimes takes the form of amenities, usually more applicable to houses than other kinds of properties.

Deed restriction, zoning and government regulations may not conform to current market requirements, and thus the site may remain undeveloped to its highest and best use. If the site has more valuable use potential then allowed by law, and if there is a reasonable probability that a change in use will be permitted, its value will be affected to the extent that a buyer or seller might recognize this potential, after giving due consideration to the expense involved in the change.

FORCES THAT INFLUENCE REAL PROPERTY VALUE

The value of all real property--including residential property--is created, maintained, modified or destroyed by the interplay of four great forces that affect human behavior.

1. **P**hysical or environmental forces.
2. **E**conomic activities and trends.
3. **G**overnment regulations and actions.
4. **S**ocial ideals and standards.

These dynamic forces set the pattern for the variables affecting real estate market values. Combined, they are the essence of cause and effect that influences every parcel of real estate on earth and directly affects both the demand and the supply side of the market.

PHYSICAL OR ENVIRONMENTAL FORCES

Physical or environmental forces created by either nature or society encompass:

1. Natural resources.
2. Climate and topography.
3. Characteristics of soil and subsoil to support improvements.
4. Soil fertility.
5. Mineral resources.
6. Flood control and soil conservation.
7. Technological advances affecting land use.

ECONOMIC ACTIVITIES AND TRENDS

Economic forces, including the resources and efforts of society to achieve its social goals, are made up of factors such as:

1. Gross national product.
2. Economic trends and activity.
3. Employment trends and wage levels.
4. Availability of money and credit.
5. Price levels, interest rates and tax burdens.
6. All other factors having an effect upon purchasing power.

GOVERNMENT REGULATIONS AND ACTIONS

Forces created by government regulations and activities include:

1. Zoning laws.
2. Building codes.
3. Environmental regulations.
4. Police and fire regulations.
5. Rent controls, national defense measures, special-use permits, and credit controls.
6. Government-sponsored housing and guaranteed mortgage loans.
7. Monetary policies, including all forms of taxation, that affect the free use of real estate.

SOCIAL IDEALS AND STANDARDS

When these forces are closely examined, it becomes apparent that they are composed of many complex factors that are constantly changing. A partial list of social forces includes:

1. Population growth, decline or stability.
2. Shifts in population density.
3. Changes in family size.
4. Geographical distribution of social groups.
5. Attitudes toward education and social activities.
6. Attitudes toward architectural design and utility.
7. Factors emerging from human social instincts, ideals, moral codes, likes and dislikes.

Because all these factors affect cost, price and value, their impact--whether direct or indirect--must be considered in estimating the cost, the probable price or the value of real property. These four forces and the factors comprising them constitute the basic raw material for making an appraisal of value. Any decision on or action about the market value of real estate is based upon an appraisal, whether it is a formal narrative written report or a verbal estimate of value.

Students of real property valuation are prone to attempt to categorize a factor specifically and concisely under one of the four forces. Often, however, a factor may appear in two or more of the classifications. The reason for itemizing the four major forces is to assist both beginning and experienced appraisers in making a comprehensive analysis of all possible factors and conditions that may affect a real estate decision.   To assist in classifying activities and trends in the most appropriate categories, greatest emphasis is given to the force from which the factor tends to stem. For example, the impact of population statistics is typically classified under social forces but the appraiser recognizes that it may be expressed in terms of economic impact as well.

The conclusions drawn from all the forces must be expressed in terms of dollars, but this does not justify the inclusion of all activities under the economic force. Another example of potential conflict in classifying has to do with natural resources. As illustrated so dramatically in the energy crisis, a shortage of fuel is typically expressed economically although the matter is originally and primarily classified as a physical and environmental force.

TYPES OF VALUE

Because the term value has many possible interpretations, its meaning for the appraisal of real property must be precise. Value has been defined as the quantity of one thing that can be obtained in exchange for another or the ratio of exchange of one commodity for another. Money is the common denominator by which real property value is usually measured.

An appraisal of value is based on an interpretation by the appraiser of facts and value indications processed and reconciled to produce an estimate as of a specific date. Because the term *appraised value* is too general, the type of value must be precisely defined in the appraisal report. The value most commonly sought in an appraisal is market value, although there are other types of value that may be considered depending on the use for which the client requires the appraisal and the nature of the valuation problem being solved. Obviously, the reliability of an appraised value depends on the basic competence and integrity of the appraiser and on the skill with which pertinent data is processed.

The emphasis in appraising is on the relationship between a thing desired and the potential purchaser or consumer. The idea that need alone is responsible for the creation of value would imply that value is a characteristic inherent in the object itself. If this concept were true, bread would be intrinsically valuable because it is needed to satisfy hunger. But hunger is limited. Therefore, if bread were produced in excess of the need to satisfy all normal hunger, its value would decrease. The value of any object is not intrinsic but depends upon the relationship between supply and demand.

An object also cannot have value unless it has utility--that is, unless it is able to satisfy the desire for possession; but utility is relative to the satisfaction gained from the object. For example, bread has great utility to a hungry person but much less to one who is not hungry.

Although utility is basic to value, utility alone does not establish value. Scarcity also must be present before significant value exists. For example, air is highly useful but because it is usually so plentiful it has little value. No object, including a parcel of real estate, can have value unless it possesses in some degree the two factors of utility and scarcity.

Yet, utility and scarcity do not by themselves create value. The another necessary element for an object to have value (as defined by the appraiser) is purchasing power--the ability of the individual to participate in the market in order to satisfy the desire to possess. For example, if no one has the purchasing power (money) to buy bread, bread becomes valueless.

The appraiser's interpretation of value can be summarized as follows:

1. Value is not a characteristic inherent in real property itself but depends on the desires of people. It varies from person to person and from time to time, as individual wants vary.

2. An object (real property) cannot have value unless it has utility. Usefulness arouses desire for possession and has the power to give satisfaction.

3. An object (real property) must also be relatively scarce to have value.

4. The desire of a purchaser who has the purchasing power to buy must be aroused for the object to have value.

Unlike rapidly consumed goods, the benefits of real property are realized over a much longer period. Land and its improvements usually have a useful life extending over decades. The value of real property, consequently, is equal to the present value of the future benefits forthcoming from the property.

Estimating the market value of the highest and best use is the paramount problem in the valuation of real estate. Any such estimate must take into consideration the social, economic, government and environmental forces that may influence the property's highest and best use. A clear understanding of current and future conditions and the perception to recognize the forces that modify and affect these conditions are essential.

In considering these factors, the professional appraiser should never lose sight of the fact that what must really be interpreted are the reactions of typical users and investors. Appraisers do not make value; they interpret it, chiefly from market evidence. The appraiser must sift through large quantities of data to select those that have the greatest significance relative to market value.

DISTINCTIONS AMONG VALUE, PRICE, AND COST

Appraisers make important distinctions among the terms value, price and cost. By traditional definition, value and price are equal only under conditions of a perfect market. Value, as applied to real estate, represents an expected price that should result under specific conditions.   Price, commonly referred to as a sale or transaction price, is an accomplished fact. A price represents what a particular purchaser agreed to pay and a particular seller agreed to accept under the particular circumstances surrounding their transaction.

Presumptions requisite for market value - rational behavior by buyer and seller and no undue duress or pressure - are not implicit in any actual sales price. Neither is there a presumption that the transaction was typical in the market.

Without making an appraisal, an appraiser does not know whether a price actually paid or received represented the property's value. Although actual prices can provide strong evidence of market value, the appraiser must analyze specific transaction prices carefully before reaching a market value conclusion.

Cost, as used in appraisal procedures, applies to production, not exchange, and is not synonymous with either value or price. Cost is the total dollar expenditure for labor, materials, legal services, architectural design, financing, taxes during construction, interest, contractor's overhead and profit, and entrepreneurial overhead and profit. Cost is either a retrospective fact or a current estimate. It may or may not have a direct relationship to the utility (present or future) of the property created. Consider, for instance, the classic example of the luxury hotel built in an unpopular location. The hotel might cost much to build but have little value because of the lack of business.

Appraisal procedures provide the means to refine conclusions about whether the cost to construct a property equals the property's market value. Such market conditions as oversupply, undersupply, or poor design cause market values to fall below the current cost of duplicate development.

Cost will equal market value if the new building represents the highest and best use of the land as though vacant; that is, if there is no accrued depreciation. Value can exceed cost only to the extent that buyers are willing to avoid the delay of constructing a duplicate property.

VALUE DEFINITIONS FOR REAL PROPERTY APPRAISAL

By far the majority of residential appraisal assignments are to estimate the market value of the residence. However, appraisers receive a wide variety of other assignments for many different purposes. It is therefore necessary that many types of value be understood.

MARKET VALUE

Market value, or value-in-exchange, is relative. It implies a comparison of available alternative economic goods from which the potential purchaser may make a choice; it also reflects the interaction of buyers, sellers and investors.

Most real estate appraisal assignments involve estimates of market value. Numerous definitions of market value have been devised over the years by professional organizations, government bodies and the courts. These definitions are subject to frequent change, and appraisers performing services that may be subject to litigation are cautioned to seek the exact definition of market value which is accepted in the jurisdiction in which the services are performed. A widely accepted definition of market value required for federally related appraisals by FIRREA is: [1]

"The most probable price which a property should bring in a competitive and open market under all conditions requisite to a fair sale, the buyer and seller each acting prudently, and knowledgeably, and assuming the price is not affected by undue stimulus. Implicit in this definition is the consummation of a sale as of a specified date and the passing of title from seller to buyer under conditions whereby:

---

[1]Federal Register, Vol 55, No.251, December 31, 1990, Washington, D.C.

1. Buyer and seller are typically motivated.

2. Both parties are well informed or well advised, and acting in what they consider their best interests.

3. A reasonable time is allowed for exposure in the open market.

4. Payment is made in terms of cash in United States dollars or in terms of financial arrangements comparable thereto; and

5. The price represents the normal consideration for the property sold unaffected by special or creative financing or sales concessions granted by anyone associated with the sale.

Substitution of another currency for *United States dollars* in the fourth condition is appropriate in countries or in reports addressed to clients from other countries."

Because of varied decisions in different legal jurisdictions, there is no "universal" definition of market value. Each definition carries its own parameters and presumptions.

Obviously, different definitions of market value can result in different value estimates, and appraisers should be careful to state the definition they use in an appraisal.[2]

Market value, or value in exchange, is the purpose of most valuations. A market value estimate reflects the appraiser's interpretation of the actions of buyers and sellers in the marketplace.

OTHER VALUES IN RESIDENTIAL APPRAISAL

In the process of solving an appraisal problem, one of the earliest decisions that must be made is the kind of value applicable to the situation, i.e., value-in-use or value-in-exchange. The decision is based on the problem to be solved. If it is a question of the most probable selling price, then the appraiser is committed to value-in-exchange. If the problem is related to a proposed renovation program, then the most likely kind of value may be value-in-use to the owner.

A financial institution considering a mortgage wants to know the likely selling price of the property. Therefore, the market value (value-in-exchange) is the appropriate kind of value. Assessed value historically has been based on costs rather than market prices which tends to relate such values to *use* rather than *market values*. In recent years, however, there has been a trend to relate assessed values to the market rather than solely to costs to reproduce or replace.

VALUE-IN-USE

Use value is the value or importance of an object to a particular owner who may have no intention of exposing it on the open market. Value-in-use has been defined as the

---

[2]See Halbert C. Smith, *Value Concepts as a Source of Disparity Among Appraisals*, The Appraisal Journal, April 1977. pp. 203-09.

value of an economic good to its owner-user based on its productivity (in the form of income, utility or amenity).

Value-in-use does not necessarily represent market value, unless there are a significant number of buyer-users active in the market place who are willing and able to pursue the commodity or service.

INVESTMENT VALUE

Closely related to use value is investment value. As employed in appraisal assignments, investment value is the value of an investment to a particular investor based on his or her investment requirements. In contrast to market value, investment value is value to an individual, rather than value in the marketplace.

Investment value is the subjective relationship between a particular investor and a given investment. When measured in dollars, it is the highest price an investor will pay for an investment in view of its perceived capacity to satisfy a desire, need, or investment goal. In colloquial use, investment value may refer to the "reasoned value" of a given investment from the viewpoint of a typical, rather than actual, investor. In appraisals that estimate investment value, specific investment criteria must be known.

Investment value appraisals are fairly common when the appraiser is employed by a potential purchaser of an existing investment or income-producing property, or by a developer of a new property.

INSURABLE VALUE

Insurable value is based on the concept of replacement and/or reproduction cost of physical items subject to lose from hazards. Insurable value designates the amount of insurance that may or should be carried on destructible portions of a property to indemnify the owner in the event of loss.

LIQUIDATION VALUE

Liquidation value is a price that an owner is compelled to accept when the property must be sold with less-than-reasonable market exposure.

ASSESSED VALUE

Assessed value is a value based on a uniform schedule for tax rolls in ad valorem taxation. The schedule may not conform to market value, but usually has some relation to a market value base.

SUMMARY

Real estate has economic value and significance only as it satisfies the needs and desires of human beings. Land has been studied throughout history and these studies have included geography, law, sociology and economics. An appraiser must understand all of these concepts as a required background for their appraisal activities.

Interests in real estate are shared between the government and the property owner. The rights of the property owner may be further limited by restrictions inserted into deeds by prior owners. The rights of the property owner are described as a "bundle of rights".

Division of earnings or productivity occurs when ownership is an undivided fractional interest such as tenancy-in-common or joint tenancy. Another category of fractional ownership or interest is a division of the physical use of the property. When the property is leased, the interest is divided between the owner and the tenant. The appraiser must be familiar with how these rights are divided.

The value of land depends on its usefulness, including all of its improvements and appurtenant rights. Real property is distinct from personal property and chattels. Title is limited by the four great powers of government and frequently by private restrictions and agreements as well. There are many facets to the term value, but the real estate appraiser is customarily interested in estimating market value (value-in-exchange). The legal definition of market value becomes most significant when an assignment will involve litigation where precise, legally accepted definitions are required.

Several fundamental economic principles provide the basis for analyzing the action of the real estate market, which are of particular interest to the real estate appraiser.

FOUR AGENTS OF PRODUCTION

Economic theory holds that for any good or service to be produced, expenditures must be made for the agents of production: land, labor, capital, and coordination.

SURPLUS PRODUCTIVITY

three other?

After the four agents of production are paid for, what ever value is left is attributable to the land.

SUPPLY AND DEMAND

1. Utility and scarcity combined create demand, which is the desire for possession.

2. Demand is effective only when supported by purchasing power.

3. Value is increased if supply is reduced or demand increased.

ANTICIPATION

1. Value is the present worth of the rights to all prospective future benefits accruing to ownership and use of real property.

2. Recent sales prices of comparable properties indicate the market value of such rights and benefits.

BALANCE

1. The value of a property depends on the balance of the four agents of production: labor, capital, coordination, and land.

CHANGE

1. Change is constantly occurring.

2. Cities, neighborhoods and individual properties undergo the process of change.

3. The effect of prospective changes is reflected in the market.

4. Change is fundamentally the law of cause and effect.

COMPETITION AND EXCESS PROFIT

1. Excess profit breed ruinous competition.

CONFORMITY

1. Conformity is the result of a reasonable degree of architectural homogeneity and compatible land uses.

2. The standards of conformity have changed over the years reflecting changes in market attitudes, social trends, economic conditions and public policy.

3. The highest and best land use is generally realized under circumstances of harmony or conformity.

4. The principal purpose of zoning regulation and private restriction is to maintain conformity.

CONTRIBUTION

1. The principle of contribution deals with increasing and decreasing return applied to a portion or portions of an improvement.

2. The value of an item in production is measured by its contribution to the net return of the enterprise.

3. Application of this principle is basic to any feasibility study or remodeling or modernization program and in the valuation of lots of varying depths.

EXTERNALITIES

The principle externalities is that goods, products or conditions produced by one group of people can have an effect on many other people besides the ones who produce them.

SUBSTITUTION

1. The value of a property tends to be indicated by the value of an equally desirable substitute property.

2. The value of a property tends to coincide with the value indicated by the actions of informed buyers in the market for comparable properties.

3.   Disadvantage attends any excess or deficiency in the supply of the agents of production.

4.   Equilibrium (balance) in character, amount and location of essential uses of real estate creates and maintains value.

5.   The principle of contribution is related to surplus productivity in that the value of an individual agent of production depends upon how much it adds to or detracts from the income because of its presence.

HIGHEST AND BEST USE

1.   Highest and best use is that which, at the time of appraisal, is the most profitable, likely use of a property. It may also be defined as the available use and program of future utilization that produces the highest present land value.

2.   Existing use may not conform to highest and best use.

3.   Highest and best use may comprise a combination of profitable interim (transition) uses and a deferred, more profitable potential use.

4.   Highest and best use may be limited by zoning or deed restrictions

5.   Improvements must add to the value of the land to have value attributed to them.

6.   The principle of increasing and decreasing returns affirms the proper apportionment of land and improvement to achieve maximum land value.

7.   Balance and consistent use are important collateral considerations in the selection of highest and best use.

FORCES THAT INFLUENCE REAL PROPERTY VALUES

A value is created, maintained, modified or destroyed by the interplay of four great forces that affect human behavior (social, economic, government and physical or environmental). The appraiser expresses conclusions based on these forces in dollars of property value.

THE FACTORS OF VALUE

The meaning of value must be precise in the valuation process. Money is the common denominator by which real property value is measured. Real estate does not have value unless it has utility and scarcity.

DISTINCTIONS AMONG MARKET VALUE, PRICE AND COST

1. Price is the historic amount paid for something.

2. Cost is the total dollar expenditure for labor, materials, legal services, architectural design, etc.

3. Value is the expected price a property should bring under a specific set of assumptions.

VALUE DEFINITIONS FOR REAL PROPERTY VALUATION

Most residential appraisals are to estimate market value which must be defined as part of the report.

Market Value

It is the most probable price in terms of money which a property should bring in a competitive and open market under all conditions requisite to a fair sale. All full definitions expand and clarify this concept.

Other Values in Residential Appraisal

Besides market value the residential appraiser is called upon to estimate value-in-use, investment value, insurable value, assessed value and other special values.

LARGE GLASS WINDOWS AND DOORS

LARGE OVERHANGING EAVES

Post World War II American

SOLAR HOUSE (Solar - 904)

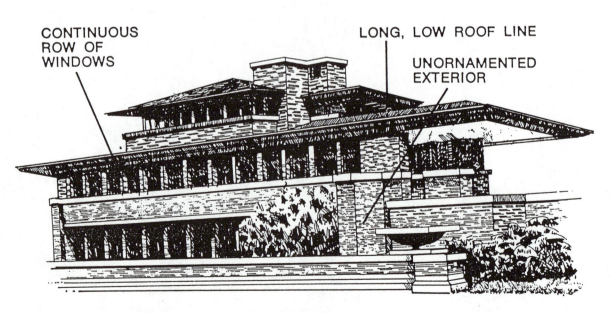

CONTINUOUS ROW OF WINDOWS

LONG, LOW ROOF LINE

UNORNAMENTED EXTERIOR

Early Twentieth Century American

PRAIRIE HOUSE (Prairie - 801)

3 Valuation Process

For over 50 years, the appraisal profession has been working to perfect a process for estimating the value of real estate. The process is not stagnant--it improves as time goes on. Appraisers who feel they have an improvement to the process are invited to write an article for one of the appraisal journals published by the professional organizations. If the improvement gains acceptance, the next edition of the **APPRAISAL OF REAL ESTATE**[1] incorporates the change. (Most appraisers consider this to be the definitive work on real estate appraising.) However, there are many other texts covering different real estate appraising specialties.

The purpose of a professional appraisal is to help the client make a decision. For example, an appraisal helps a Lender decide if a property is adequate security for a proposed loan. Other purposes are to help a buyer or seller decide how much to buy or sell a house for, how much to insure a house for, its value for estate or tax purposes, etc.

The appraisal process, as it is described in this textbook, has been simplified. The author has kept in mind that the reader will be a new appraiser possibly with limited formal appraisal training.

THE VALUATION PROCESS

DEFINITION OF THE PROBLEM
    Identification of the Real Estate
    Identification of the Property Rights to be Valued
    Date of Value Estimate
    Use of the Appraisal
    Definition of Value
    Other Limiting Conditions

PRELIMINARY SURVEY AND APPRAISAL PLAN
    Data Needed
    Data Sources
    Personnel Needed
    Time Schedule & Flow Chart
    Fee Proposal and Contract

---

[1]*Appraisal of Real Estate*, 10th Edition, Appraisal Institute, Chicago, IL 1992.

DATA COLLECTION AND ANALYSIS - GENERAL DATA
Economic
   Market Analysis
   Financial
   Economic Base
   Trends
Locational
   Region
   Community
   Neighborhood

DATA COLLECTION AND ANALYSIS - SPECIFIC DATA
Appraised Property
   Title & Record Data
   Relationship of Site to Land Pattern
   Physical Characteristics of the Site and Improvements
Comparative Properties
   Sales
   Listings
   Costs
   Rentals

HIGHEST AND BEST USE
Highest and Best Use as Though Vacant
Highest and Best Use as Improved

SITE VALUE ESTIMATE
Purpose of Separate Site Valuation
Procedures for Estimating Value
         Sales Comparison Approach
         Allocation Procedure
         Extraction Method
         Subdivision Development
         Land Residual Technique
         Ground Rent Capitalization
      Sales Comparison Approach
         Elements of Comparison
               Financing Terms
               Conditions of Sale
               Market Conditions
               Location
               Physical Characteristics
               Income Characteristics
         Techniques for Making Adjustments
      The Allocation Procedure
      Extraction Method
      Capitalization of Ground Rental
      Land Residual Technique
   Reconciliation of Adjusted Site Sales Prices

APPLICATION OF THE THREE APPROACHES
Cost Approach
Sales Comparison
Income

**RECONCILIATION OF VALUE INDICATIONS INTO
A FINAL ESTIMATE OF DEFINED VALUE**

APPRAISAL REPORT

It is helpful for many appraisers and students to see the Valuation Process in the form of a flow chart:

FIG. 3-1 THE VALUATION PROCESS

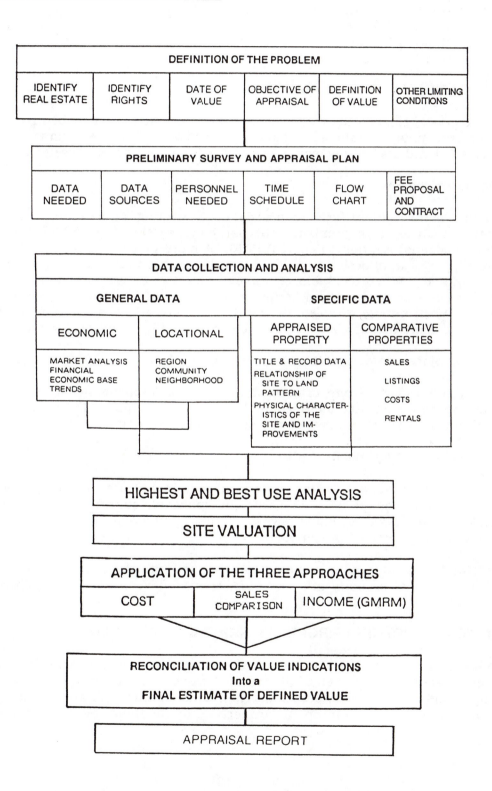

DEFINITION OF THE PROBLEM

The first step in an appraisal is to define the problem to be solved. There are six major steps in the definition of the problem.

      1 . Identification of the Real Estate
         a) Site
         b) Improvements
         c) Personal Property
      2 . Identification of the Property Rights to be Valued
      3 . Date of Value Estimate
      4 . Use of the Appraisal
      5 . Definition of Value
      6 . Other Limiting Conditions

IDENTIFICATION OF THE REAL ESTATE

It must be crystal clear to the reader of an appraisal exactly what is being appraised. The appraisal must contain an accurate description of the real estate (Site and Improvements) and also any personal property included in the appraised value.

Identification of the Site

A property is first identified by means of a mailing address or other short description such as a lot number. This is shown in the "Subject" section of the Uniform Residential Appraisal Report (URAR). A more precise identification, such as that provided by a legal description which can be copied from the deed or mortgage, is also required. When available, a survey helps to precisely identify a property. Whether or not a complete legal description is needed in the appraisal is a matter of judgment. When a more complete description is included, it is attached as part of the addenda. More details about the site follow in the "Specific Data" section.

Identification of the Improvements

A required and important part of every appraisal is a complete, accurate description of all of the improvements included in the appraised value. More details about improvement identification follow in the specific data section.

Identification of the Personal Property

The statutes vary from state to state as to what is personal property and what is real estate. Appraisers should be familiar with the applicable statutes in the areas where they make appraisals. One cannot always tell just by physical inspection what is real estate and what is personal property.

In residential appraising, some typical items that fall into the gray area between real estate and personal property are carpeting, drapes, T.V. antennas, appliances and lighting fixtures.

IDENTIFICATION OF THE PROPERTY RIGHTS TO BE VALUED

An appraisal of real property is not directly a valuation of the physical land and improvements; it is a valuation of the rights of ownership. A specific appraisal may require a value estimate of all property rights, while another will analyze only limited rights in property. Ownership of property may be held by an individual, a partnership, a corporation or a group of heirs. When ownership is vested in more than one interest, each may hold an equal or unequal share.

The property rights or interests to be appraised may be fractional interests such as air rights over a specified property, subsurface rights, an easement, a right-of-way or fee simple subject to an easement. Because the value of real property is not limited to its physical components, the appraiser cannot define the problem precisely until fully aware of which property rights are involved. Without this knowledge, the appraiser may produce an estimate of value that is irrelevant to the problem. A clear conception of the rights being appraised will also help the appraiser evaluate the complexity of the problem and the amount of work it will require.

DATE OF VALUE ESTIMATE

An appraisal must be a value estimate as of a specific date. The value of a property may change from day to day. For example, the sudden announcement of some event that affects all of the market will have a significant effect on the value of property. Typical announcements which affect the value of property are the expansion or contraction of business activities which are major sources of employment in the area. Other announcements that may suddenly affect value are the additions or relocation of roads and highways or anything else in the close vicinity of the property.

Sudden changes in the physical condition of the property by fire, the environment or man-made additions, demolitions or alterations all affect the property value.

When the date of the appraisal is the same date as the date of last inspection, no assumptions about the future or past are needed. On the other hand, when the date of the appraisal is either before or after the date of last inspection, the appraisal must contain statements that express the assumptions the appraiser made about the property on the date of the appraisal.

It is very customary for an appraisal to be as of some date in the past. The appraiser then makes assumptions about the condition of the property and the site as of that date and uses data that reflect values as of the date of the appraisal.

Appraisals that attempt to estimate the value of the property in the future tend to be speculative. Special care must be taken by the appraiser to fully report all of the assumptions that were made (or not made) about the property, the neighborhood, the community and region, the economy (both locally and nationally), and other unknown information about the future. Most appraisals of future value tend to be highly speculative in nature, in spite of the care appraisers use to tell what assumptions were made.

USE OF THE APPRAISAL

The objective of most appraisals is to estimate the value of a property as of a specific date. Market value is by far the most common value that is estimated by appraisers, but there are other kinds of value estimates such as insurable value, investment value, partial interest value, etc. that are becoming a more significant proportion of the assignments available to appraisers.

It is helpful for the appraiser to know the purpose of the appraisal so that the report will provide the reader with all of the information required to make a decision. When the appraisal is made for mortgage lending purposes, the appraiser must know if it should comply with Freddie Mac, Fannie Mae, HUD/FHA, VA, or FmHA requirements. Each of these organizations have their own special appraisal requirements.

DEFINITION OF VALUE

In all cases, it is necessary that the appraisal include a clear statement as to what value is being estimated. Appraisals that are made for loan purposes base their Value Estimate on "Market Value". The current accepted definition of "Market Value" is either attached to each appraisal or a copy is filed by the appraiser with the client and is referred to in the appraisal. Below is that portion of form FHLMC #439-FNMA #1004B which has the Freddie Mac - Fannie Mae accepted "Market Value" definition.

"DEFINITION OF MARKET VALUE: The most probable price which a property should bring in a competitive and open market under all conditions requisite to a fair sale, the buyer and seller, each acting prudently, knowledgeably and assuming the price is not affected by undue stimulus. Implicit in this definition is the consummation of a sale as of specified date and the passing of title from seller to buyer under conditions whereby: (1) buyer and seller are typically motivated; (2) both parties are well informed or well advised, and each acting in what he considers his own best interest; (3) a reasonable time is allowed for exposure in the open market; (4) payment is made in terms of cash in U.S. dollars or in terms of financial arrangements comparable thereto; and (5) the price represents the normal consideration for the property sold unaffected by special or creative financing or sales concessions* granted by anyone associated with the sale.

*Adjustments to the comparables must be made for special or creative financing or sales concessions. No adjustments are necessary for those costs which are normally paid by sellers as a result of tradition or law in a market area; these costs are readily identifiable since the seller pays these costs in virtually all sales transactions. Special or creative financing adjustments can be made to the comparable property by comparisons to financing terms offered by a third party institutional lender that is not already involved in the property or transaction. Any adjustment should not be calculated on a mechanical dollar for dollar cost of the financing or concession but the dollar amount of any adjustment should approximate the market's reaction to the financing or concessions based on the appraiser's judgment."

OTHER LIMITING CONDITIONS

For the appraiser's and client's protection, it is often important to add additional limiting conditions. The following are eight which might be appropriate.[1]

1. Any value estimates provided in the report apply to the entire property, and any portion or division of the total into fractional interests will invalidate the value estimate, unless such portion or division of interests has been set forth in the report.

2. Only preliminary plans and specifications were available in the preparation of this appraisal; the analysis, therefore, is subject to a review of the final plans and specifications when available.

---

[1]*Appraisal of Real Estate*, 10th Edition, .Appraisal Institute, Chicago, IL 1992.

3 . Any proposed improvements are assumed to have been completed unless otherwise stipulated; any construction is assumed to conform with the building plans referenced in the report.

4 . The appraiser assumes that the reader or user of this report has been provided with copies of available building plans and all leases and amendments, if any, encumbering the property.

5 . No legal description or survey was furnished so the appraiser utilized the county tax plat to ascertain the physical dimensions and acreage of the property. Should a survey prove these characteristics inaccurate, it may be necessary for this appraisal to be adjusted.

6 . The forecasts, projections, or operating estimates contained herein are based upon current market conditions, anticipated short-term supply and demand factors, and a continued stable economy. These forecasts are, therefore, subject to changes in future conditions.

7 . This report should be considered a limited analysis in that the appraiser did not perform all of the requirements for an appraisal as set forth in the Uniform Standards of Professional Appraisal Practice.

8 . This limited assignment is not an appraisal, in that a value estimate of the subject property has not been provided.

PRELIMINARY SURVEY AND APPRAISAL PLAN

The second step of the Valuation Process is the Preliminary Survey and Appraisal Plan. There are six steps:

> 1 . Decide which data is needed.
>
> 2 . Identify the sources of the needed data.
>
> 3 . Determine what personnel are needed.
>
> 4 . Make a time schedule.
>
> 5 . Make a flow chart.
>
> 6 . Present a fee proposal, agree upon a fee and sign a contract.

DATA NEEDED

The type of data required for an appraisal consists of General Data about the market and location and Specific Data about the property being appraised and the comparative properties.

General data is divided into the broad categories of social, economic, governmental and environmental factors that affect the value of the property. There are a variety of ways to organize the General Data. The most common way is to break the data down into Regional, State, Community, and Neighborhood sections.

An advantage of this system is that once the data is assembled and organized it can be used for other appraisals in the same region, state, community or neighborhood. In some areas, two of the classifications may be combined. For example, the state and regional data are often the same. When the community is small, it may contain only one neighborhood.

The collection of Specific Data is probably the most difficult part of making appraisals. This is especially true when the property is located in a territory that is unfamiliar to the appraiser. Specific data collection about the site and the improvements is described in more detail elsewhere in this textbook.

DATA SOURCES

An appraiser should maintain a reliable data collection and storage system. A large bank of market data should be accumulated in the appraiser's own files and should be organized to serve the appraiser's needs most effectively. Only some of the data will be immediately pertinent; the remainder is collected, filed, and cross-indexed for future use. Sales information usually is collected and recorded on standardized sheets. Many appraisers are using computers for data storage, retrieval and analysis.

PERSONNEL NEEDED

A simple appraisal made in a one-person shop requires only one individual.

The most common configuration of an appraisal company consists of the designated appraiser, who is usually the owner or manager, and an assistant who helps gather data and completes on their own, with supervision, the less complex assignments. A clerical support person is available to staff the office, answer the phone, and do most of the typing, computer entry, filing and billing.

Whether an office is like this typical small office or a large facility, a decision should be made for each assignment about how the work will be divided among the available personnel.

TIME SCHEDULE

The timely production of appraisals is essential to the successful management of an appraisal practice. In many areas, the competition for single family appraisal business requires delivery of the finished work within a few days of receiving the assignment.

A planned schedule of how the work will be performed is a good management tool. This helps the staff begin with a clear understanding of the exact nature of the work to be done by each person, which will go a great way to expedite the efficient completion of an assignment.

FLOW CHART

A commonly used device to keep track of the work in an appraisal office is a flow chart. This can be as simple as a calendar on which are marked the dates when portions of the appraisal are due. Another common type of flow chart is a metal board on which magnetic holders are displayed indicating the steps of the appraisal and when they are due. Larger offices often have computerized flow charts that help them keep track of the status of each job in progress.

FEE PROPOSAL AND CONTRACT

Some large lenders determine how much they will pay for an appraisal and the appraisers only decide if they can afford to do the work for the fee being offered.

Many other clients require the appraiser to quote a fee or a fee range in advance of a commitment to proceed with an appraisal assignment.

The relationship some appraisers have with select regular clients is so well established that these clients permit the appraiser to proceed with an assignment without having previously agreed upon a fee.

The fee an appraiser may charge for the services performed depends on the reputation of the appraiser. Appraisers who, in the view of their clients, have an established reputation for experience and sound judgment command higher fees than those appraisers who do not have the same well-established reputations.

Finally, since appraisers are professionals, competent work is required regardless of the fee. An inadequate fee is not considered a valid excuse for inadequate work, since a professional is obliged to perform competent work regardless of the fee charged. Therefore, the appraiser should be careful to correctly estimate the scope of work an assignment will require, so that a reasonable fee can be charged.

When an assignment is done for a regular client such as a lending institution, mortgage broker, mortgage banker or relocation company, the appraiser often elects to work without a contract. However, even in these situations, a contract or letter of authorization is desirable if it can be obtained. Personnel in large institutions often change jobs; what is authorized and understood by one employee may be objectionable to their replacement.

When making appraisals for the public or their representative, it is very desirable for the appraiser to have a contract that reflects what work will be done, when it will be completed and how and when the appraiser will be paid. It is also customary in many areas for the appraiser to receive a retainer.

DATA COLLECTION AND ANALYSIS - GENERAL DATA

ECONOMIC

Appraisers should consider all the significant social, economic, governmental, and environmental influences that affect property values in their region.

This information is gathered from general and specialized publications including national and local newspapers, financial magazines and real estate appraisal publications. Analysis of current economic conditions such as interest rates, effective purchasing power, construction costs, and availability of financing is included here.

LOCATIONAL

Background data deals with the locational and economic forces outside the appraised property that influence its value. This includes information about the region, community and neighborhood such a population characteristics, price levels, employment opportunities, economic base analysis, etc.

DATA COLLECTION AND ANALYSIS - SPECIFIC DATA - APPRAISED PROPERTY

Specific data pertaining to the appraised property includes title and record data, the relationship of the site to general land patterns, a description and analysis of the physical characteristics of the property, and highest and best use analysis.

TITLE AND RECORD DATA

Pertinent title data may include the identity of the owners, type of ownership, existing easements and encroachments, zoning regulations affecting the property, assessed value and taxation, and deed or other restriction.

RELATIONSHIP OF SITE TO LAND PATTERN

Descriptive data includes a complete evaluation of the site. Site features such as size, shape, topography, lot and building orientation, utilities and relationship to the existing land-use pattern are also analyzed here.

CHARACTERISTICS OF THE SITE AND IMPROVEMENTS

Legal Description

A parcel of land consists of any piece of land that can be identified by a common description in one ownership. A special characteristic of real estate is that every parcel is unique. The best identification of a parcel is a legal description and a survey, which eliminates all confusion because it specifically identifies and locates a parcel of real estate.

The three methods used in the United States to legally describe land are the Metes and Bounds System, the Rectangular Survey System, and the Lot and Block System.

--Metes and Bounds. This is a system that measures and identifies the property by describing the property boundaries. It began in the 1600's in the original 13 colonies where it is still used today. It describes the property's boundaries in terms of reference points.

A metes and bounds description starts at an identified point of beginning (POB). This POB is often described in relationship to some other established point on an adjoining survey. The description then moves clockwise through several other intermediate reference points until finally returning to the POB.

Metes are descriptions of the direction of movement from the POB to each reference point. The direction is the "Course" and is described in degrees, minutes and seconds of angle from north or south.

Bounds are the lines between the points. To describe a bound, it is necessary to know its length in terms of feet and inches and the angle from the point at which it starts to the point at which it ends. Courses are described in degrees, minutes and seconds of angle from north or south.

In addition to being the primary method of describing real property in 21 states, the metes and bounds system is often used as a corollary system in other states.

-- Rectangular Survey. The U.S. Rectangular Survey System references townships, sections, ranges and acres. It was established in 1785 and also known as the Government Survey System. It is the principal survey system used west of the Mississippi River.

The system is based on reference points established by the U.S. government, from which true east-west and north-south lines run; these are called base lines and principal meridians. Each meridian has a unique name and is crossed by its own base line.

The land is then divided by north-south range lines, six miles apart and east-west township lines, also six miles apart. Each square thus created is called a township and contains 36 square miles.

Townships are further divided into 36 sections. Each standard section is one square mile and contains 640 acres. Sections are further divided into quarter sections and fractions of quarter sections.

-- Lot and Block System. This is a system used by developers who sub-divide parcels of land into small lots. It is based on a map or survey which is filed in the land records showing the location of the lots, together with identifying numbers.

Other Descriptive Information

The description of the site should also include information about the type of ownership. The property may be in fee simple ownership, Planned Unit Development (PUD), De Minimis PUD, condominium, cooperative or some unique form of fractional ownership. (FNMA & FHLMC permit use of the URAR for single family residences in fee simple ownership, on leased land or when there is a De Minimis PUD. It is not permitted for multi-family residences or ones that are Planned Unit Developments, or cooperative or condominium ownership.)

The appraiser should check for any outstanding apparent rights that may affect the value such as surface or subsurface rights, easements, restrictions, air rights, water rights, mineral rights, obligations for unique lateral support, easements for common walls, etc. The appraiser is not responsible for reporting rights that are not apparent.

The description also includes information about the applicable zoning regulations and other environmental regulations that affect the use of the property. It is the responsibility of the appraiser to determine and report whether the improvements are a non-conforming (legal or illegal) use.

Assessment and Taxes

How a property is taxed affects its value. Real estate taxes are based on ad valorem assessments. At a minimum, the appraisal should report the current taxes. If they are not typical, the appraisal should compare them with typical taxes and estimate the effect of atypical taxes on the value.

Physical Characteristics of the Site

The important physical characteristics to be described consist of the size and shape, corner influence, plottage, excess land, topography, utilities, site improvements, location and environment.

--Size and Shape. The description of the site includes a description of its size and shape. Included in this description are the site dimensions, street frontage, width, depth and any advantages or disadvantages caused by the physical characteristics. Special attention is given to any characteristics that are atypical. Deviations in size and shape may have a substantial effect on the values of some sites. In other instances, these deviations have little effect.

The size of the site should be described in the unit customary for such land use in the area of the appraised property. Acreage is often the unit used for large tracts of land. Smaller parcels are often described in square footage, although acreage is sometimes used even for small residential parcels.

Frontage is usually described separately. It usually is the frontage that abuts the street. Sometimes the frontage is that portion of the site that abuts a stream, lake or a body of water.

The effect on a property of being bordered by two or more streets varies with different types of properties and locations. The appraiser must determine whether the local market considers a corner location favorable or unfavorable.

The advantage of a corner site is that it may have utility not possessed by inside properties. Often, a more flexible building layout is possible. Houses on corner sites often can have their garages more conveniently located. Corner sites also have their disadvantages. The cost of off-site improvements is higher. For residential properties, the assessment is often higher, too. There is a lack of privacy and the requirement for additional sidewalks and other site improvements increases the overall cost of the site.

-- Plottage. In a given market there usually is an optimum site size for each of the various permitted uses. When two or more parcels are combined together under a single ownership in such a way that their result is a plot closer to the optimum size, there is a value increment obtained from the combining of two smaller parcels. If the combined parcels have a greater unit value than they did separately, plottage value results.

-- Excess Land. It is not uncommon to find that the amount of land involved in the parcel being appraised is greater than that necessary to serve the existing improvements. If it is located in such a way that it is impossible to sever or use it in the future, it probably adds little or no value to the overall property. On the other hand, if the excess land can be used for other purposes, either now or in the future, or it permits expansion of the existing facility, it may add significant value to the property being appraised.

-- Topography. The topography of the land should be part of the site description. The topographical description should include information about the contour, grades, drainage, soil conditions, view and general physical usability of the land.

Utilities

This description should include mention of all the utilities and services that are available to the site. Typical facilities are storm and sanitary sewers, water, gas, electricity and telephone service.

The neighborhood description should include all of those utilities available to the neighborhood. Special mention should be made of any utilities available in the neighborhood which are not utilized by the site being appraised. If there is a potential of connecting these unused utilities to the site, an estimate of this cost should be part of the appraisal.

When the cost of utilities is either more advantageous or more burdensome than the typical cost of utilities in the market, it will affect the value of the property.

Site Improvements

The first part of this description is that of off-site improvements and an analysis of their effect on the value of the property. This description includes the quality, condition and adequacy of sewers, curbs, access to utility hook-ups and the potential of these items being available in the future. On-site improvements include landscaping, fences and walls, curbs, gutters, walks, on-site roads and a wide variety of other man-made site improvements.

The location of any existing buildings on the site should also be described. It is very helpful to the reader when the appraiser makes a plot plan which shows all the buildings in relationship to the lot lines.

Location

The location of the site within the neighborhood is an appropriate part of the site description. This description includes information about the access to and from the property, parking, and the size and condition of the streets and highways that bring vehicular traffic to the site.

Residential sites are influenced by the ease with which residents can go to and from work, school, shopping, recreation, places of worship, etc. Public transportation for residents and workers also affects the value of the site.

Environment and Pollution

When there are unique environmental influences or evidence of pollution that affect a particular site, they should be included in the site description. Such influences include unusual wind exposure, exposure to the sun, and inland and tidal wetland use restrictions. Sometimes the development of adjoining properties has an advantageous effect on the value of the site being improved. Examples are adjoining attractive buildings, compatible commercial buildings and a favorable industrial park environment.

PHYSICAL CHARACTERISTICS OF THE IMPROVEMENTS

General Description

All appraisal forms provide room for a general description of the improvements. A mandatory important part is an accurate and adequate description of the property including the improvements.

For appraisal purposes the appraiser estimates both the actual age of the house and its effective age. The actual age is the chronological age. The effective age is how old a house appears to be, based on its design and condition. A property of typical design and average condition will have an effective age approximately the same as its actual age. When a house is modernized or renovated and well-cared-for, its effective age will be less that its actual age. A house in poor condition will have an effective age greater than its actual age.

The description of the improvements can be organized as follows for many improvements. (Unique improvements require special descriptions).

1 . Site improvements.
2 . Relationship of the improvements to the site.
3 . General description and classification of improvements.
4 . Exterior.
5 . Interior.
6 . Mechanical systems and equipment.
7 . Items requiring immediate repair.
8 . Deferred maintenance items.
9 . Overall condition of improvements.
10 . Design and layout (functional utility).
11 . Renovation: rehabilitation, modernization, and remodeling.

DATA COLLECTION AND ANALYSIS - SPECIFIC DATA - COMPARATIVE PROPERTIES

SALES AND LISTINGS

Sufficient specific data is collected about the sales and listings in the market to apply the Sales Comparison Approach. The Sales Comparison Approach chapter provides details about how to collect and analyze sales and listing data.

COSTS

To process the Cost Approach the appraiser collects information on what it would cost to reproduce the subject property on the date of the appraisal. Information on how this data is collected and analyzed is presented in the Cost Approach chapter of this text.

RENTALS

To process both the Income Capitalization Approach and the Income GMRM Approach, it is necessary to obtain information about rentals in the subject's market.

This data is used to estimate the market rent of the subject property and also to develop a Gross Monthly Rent Multiplier (GMRM).

ANALYSIS OF HIGHEST AND BEST USE

Two separate highest and best use analyses are made. Some appraisers think this is the most important part of the appraisal process.

HIGHEST AND BEST USE AS THOUGH VACANT

Analyzing the highest and best use of the site as though vacant serves two functions. First, it helps the appraiser identify comparable properties. The comparable properties' highest and best use of the site as though vacant should be similar to that of the subject property.

The second reason to analyze the property's highest and best use as though vacant is to identify the use that would produce maximum income to the site after proper income is allocated to the improvements. In the cost approach and some income capitalization techniques, a separate value estimate of the site is required. Estimating the site's highest and best use as though vacant is a necessary part of deriving a site value estimate.

HIGHEST AND BEST USE AS IMPROVED

There are also two reasons to analyze the highest and best use of the property as improved. The first is to help identify comparable properties. Comparable improved properties should have the same or similar highest and best uses as the improved subject property.

The second reason to analyze the highest and best use of the property as improved is to decide whether the improvements should be demolished, renovated, or retained in their present condition. They should be retained as long as they have some value and the return from the property exceeds the return that would be realized by a new use, after deducting the costs of demolishing the old building and constructing a new one. Identification of the existing property's most profitable use is crucial to this determination.

SITE VALUE ESTIMATE

PURPOSE OF SEPARATE SITE VALUATION

It has been argued that once the site is improved with a house, a separate site valuation is difficult, if not impossible and unnecessary. The claim is that only a total property valuation is possible in such cases and that the two units are inseparable. In spite of the theoretical merits of this argument, however, many practical reasons exist for making separate site valuations even when the property is already improved.

Separate site valuations are required by statute in most states for ad valorem (real estate) tax purposes. The assessed value is almost universally split between the land (or site) and the improvements. Special assessments for public improvements, such as streets, water lines, sewers, etc., are often based on their estimated effect on land or site values. Income tax preparation also requires that the cost of a property be split between the improvements and the site. The first step of the Cost Approach is to estimate a separate market value for the site. Separate site value estimates are also commonly used for establishing condemnation awards, adjusting casualty losses, deciding whether to raze existing improvements to use the site for new structures and establishing site rentals. FNMA, FHLMC, VA and HUD/FHA all require separate site valuations.

PROCEDURES FOR ESTIMATING VALUE

Six basic procedures for estimating the market value of individual sites are:

1 . Sales Comparison Approach
2 . Allocation Procedure
3 . Extraction Method
4 . Subdivision Development
5 . Land Residual Technique
6 . Capitalization of Ground Rental

Sales Comparison Approach

The Sales Comparison Approach is based on comparing and contrasting pertinent data on comparable sites that have actually sold, with data about the site being appraised. It is the most popular and practical site valuation procedure. The appraiser may also consider offering and listing prices and other market information, but primary attention is given to actual sales of like sites, consummated under typical market conditions, as close to the date of the appraisal as possible. Sellers may offer a property at any price they choose, and potential purchasers may bid any price they like, but the actual selling price of a site (a figure acceptable to both buyer and seller) best reflects market conditions.

Market value is intended to describe the result of the interaction of buyers and sellers operating in an open market, all parties being knowledgeable, willing and able. Thus, having exposed the real estate in the open market for a reasonable period of time, the result is an agreed upon price that is recognized as market value. The Sales Comparison Approach results in the development of market values of sites by converting sales prices (and sometimes other evidence) into market value for the site being appraised.

The process of comparing the property being appraised with others in the market always involves two components - elements of comparison and units of comparison. To better organize the comparison process, a standard format is recommended.

-- Elements of Comparison

Appraisers use six elements of comparison when considering the comparability of like sites. They are:

1 . Financing Terms
2 . Conditions of Sale
3 . Market Conditions (Time)
4 . Location
5 . Physical Characteristics
6 . Income Characteristics

Professional appraisers generally accept that these six elements encompass every possible consideration necessary to extract market value from market prices.

--Techniques for Making Adjustments

There are a variety of techniques for making adjustments. For example, a site being appraised is considered to be $500 better than Comparable Site A because of physical terrain. If Comparable Site A sold for $6,000 the adjustments would be made as follows: The comparable is poorer than the site being appraised, therefore a plus $500 adjustment is required, giving an indicated value of the subject site of $6,500 ($6,000 + $500).

Now consider the situation in which the property being appraised is poorer than the comparable. The comparable lot sold for $7,500 and is served by a sanitary sewer; the lot being appraised is not served by a sanitary sewer. The market indicates a preference in the amount of $750 for sanitary sewer. Therefore, the comparable site is superior and a minus $750 adjustment is made. The indicated market value of the site being appraised is $6,750 ($7,500 - $750).

The Allocation Procedure

A relationship exists between the application of the agents of production and the market value of a site. This is confirmed by the application of the principles of balance, contribution, surplus productivity and increasing and decreasing returns. Therefore, site value can be estimated by allocating the total sales price of a comparable between its two utilitarian and productive parts--the lot and the improvements. The appraiser determines what portion of a property's sales price typically may be allocated between the lot and the improvements, estimating the market value of the house and other improvements first. The balance (residual) is then allocated to the site. The National Association of Home Builders reports that land which was about 11% of the cost of a new home after World War II represents nearly 30% of the cost today.

Statistics from the U.S. Census Bureau demonstrate the relationship between the sales price and site value of residential properties. The statistics are presented as a national and regional average. The older the improvements, the higher the ratio of land value to total value. The typical ratio can be affected by a site of unusual size or characteristics and by building costs.

To estimate the value of unimproved property in an area where vacant land sales are lacking, the appraiser can allocate from the total sales price of a comparative property that part which could reasonably be assigned a building value. The remainder, except for intangibles, is the site value.

For example, assume that a property with a 1,500 square foot house sold for $190,000 the appraiser estimates the value of the house at $100 per square foot, or $150,000. The remainder of $40,000 is the residual value of the site, assuming that the house represents typical or highest and best land use and that no extraneous considerations were involved in the transaction.

The advantage of this procedure is that a sense of proportion is retained. If a neighborhood is typically improved with certain types of properties that can justify only a certain land value, the typical vacant lot probably will not be improved to a higher and better use. Where no vacant site sales are available, this method does afford an indication of site value. However, the results may sometimes be inconclusive and need collateral confirmation.

Extraction Method

The extraction method also involves an analysis of improved properties where the improvements contribute only a small percentage of the total property value.. The contribution of the improvements is estimated and deducted from the total sales price of the comparable sale to arrive at a comparable sales price attributable to the land.

Subdivision Development Method

The subdivision method can be used when the highest and best use of the land is for a subdivision. The first step is to estimate the total number of lots that will be obtained from the proposed subdivision. Next, the total estimated sale price is estimated. From this is deducted all the costs of development and marketing (1. Development costs for grading, clearing, paving, waste disposal, utility services, design and engineering. 2. Management and supervision. 3. Contractors overhead and profit. 4. Sales expenses. 5. Taxes. 6. Developer's entrepreneurial profit.) The figure that results is the estimated value of the site.

Capitalization of Ground Rental

The ground rental attributable to a property can be capitalized into an indication of the value of a site. This procedure is useful when comparable rents, rates, and other factors can be developed from an analysis of sales of leased land.

Land Residual Technique

In the land residual technique, the site is assumed to be improved to its highest and best use, and the net operating income attributable to the site is capitalized by the land capitalization rate into an indication of land value. This technique works best on commercial and industrial sites.

RECONCILIATION OF ADJUSTED SITE SALES PRICES

The next step is to reconcile all the adjusted comparable sales prices into an indicated value of the site being appraised. Use of a simple arithmetic average of value indications is not acceptable appraisal practice. Averaging small groups of numbers produces a meaningless measure of central tendency, which may or may not reflect actual market value. The accepted procedure is to review each sale and judge its comparability to the property being appraised. The final value is based on all the information available to the appraiser, with greater weight given to particular comparables for well-explained reasons.

APPLICATION OF THE THREE APPROACHES

The fifth step of the Valuation Process is the Application of the Three Approaches traditionally used by appraisers to estimate the value of a property.

The Uniform Standards of Professional Appraisal Practice require that the appraiser attempt to use all three approaches to estimate the value of each property appraised.

However, it is recognized that this is not always possible simply because there may be insufficient data available. When an appraiser elects not to use one or two of the three approaches to value, the reasons for their elimination should be part of the appraisal report.

The three traditional approaches to value are:

1. Cost Approach
2. Sales Comparison Approach
3. Income (Gross Monthly Rent Multiplier, or Income Capitalization) Approach

COST APPROACH

The Cost Approach provides the appraiser with the opportunity to make an additional estimate of the value of the property. This value estimate is arrived at by using different data than that used for the Sales Comparison Approach and the Income Approach.

The Cost Approach starts with an estimate of the value of the site and site improvements. (This first step is required by FNMA and FHLMC even when the Cost Approach is not used to estimate the value of the improvements. Site Valuation is covered separately in this textbook).

Historically, the Cost Approach was often the only approach used by appraisers for many appraisals. After World War II, it fell out of favor and some states prohibit it for condemnation cases. Many relocation companies also discourage appraisers from using it for relocation appraisals.

Experienced appraisers know that, when correctly used, the Cost Approach is a valuable technique. They feel more confident when they are able to make two or three independent estimates that tend to confirm each other than when their value estimate is based solely on the Sales Comparison Approach.

Unfortunately, some appraisers misuse this approach by backing into the numbers to make them agree with the Sales Comparison Approach.

The Cost Approach is most appropriate when the site value is well substantiated, when the improvements are new or nearly new and when they are the highest and best use and do not suffer from substantial amounts of depreciation.

To estimate the value of a property using the Cost Approach, the appraiser selects the information that will be required from data gathered when the property was inspected.

STEPS OF THE COST APPROACH

The data is processed following the 5 steps described below:

1. Estimate the value of the site and site improvements (this technique is described elsewhere in this text).

2 . Estimate the Reproduction Cost of the improvements (some appraisers use Replacement Cost). When Replacement Cost is used, it should be noted in the comments section).

3 . Estimate the amount of depreciation from all causes and categorize it into the three major types of depreciation: Physical Deterioration, Functional Obsolescence and External Obsolescence.

4 . Deduct the total estimated depreciation from the reproduction or replacement cost of the improvements to derive the amount of value the improvements contribute to the property.

5 . Add together the value of the site, the value contributed by the site improvements and landscaping, and the cost of all the improvements less the applicable depreciation.

ESTIMATING THE REPRODUCTION COST OF THE IMPROVEMENTS

The reproduction cost of the improvements is estimated as of the date of the appraisal (not when they were constructed).

Reproduction cost is an appraisal term for the cost to reproduce an exact replica of the improvements at current costs using the same materials and the same design as the original structure.

Replacement cost is the cost of creating a residence having the same or equivalent utility, using currently available material and current design. When replacement cost is used some of the depreciation that exists is automatically accounted for.

Methods of Cost Estimating

There are a variety of ways for appraisers to estimate the cost of the property being appraised.

-- Square Foot Method

The comparative method is widely used by residential appraisers. It is a simple, practical approach to cost estimating, based on unit figures applicable to the gross living area of the house. It involves a comparison of the known costs of similar houses which have been reduced to units per square foot of gross living area. In applying this method, the number of square feet of gross living area in the house being appraised is first computed.

The cost of known similar houses is obtained from local builders, lenders or from a cost service.

-- Building Cost Estimates

A building cost estimate is a detailed breakdown of all the costs that make up a house item by item. This is similar to what a builder prepares when estimating what it will cost to build a house.

These cost estimates are usually prepared by professional cost estimators, builders or cost services.

DEPRECIATION

A simple definition of depreciation is "the difference between the cost of an improvement on the date of the appraisal and the value of the improvement."

Depreciation begins upon construction of the improvements; they immediately begin to age physically and to suffer from functional obsolescence in their design. Negative environmental forces cause immediate external obsolescence.

When the improvements are constructed, their economic life begins. During this period, they should contribute value to the property. If they are the "perfect improvement", the amount of value they contribute would be their total cost. Since few, if any, perfect improvements are constructed, a difference exists between their total cost and their value, which represents some form of depreciation. At the point when an improvement cannot be profitably utilized, or when it no longer contributes to the value of the property, it is at the end of its economic life and depreciation has reached 100%.

Generally, if the house is of average condition and design and conforms to the other houses in a neighborhood that is not subject to unusual economic influences, its effective age and chronological age will be about the same. If the house has had better than average maintenance, rehabilitation or modernization, its effective age probably will be less than its chronological age. If it is in poorer condition than typical houses of the same age or has not been modernized or rehabilitated as other similar houses in the neighborhood, or if some off-site economic or environmental factor is negatively affecting the value, the effective age will be greater than the chronological age.

Techniques for Estimating Accrued Depreciation

Accrued depreciation may be estimated directly through observation and analysis of the components of depreciation affecting the property or through use of a formula based on physical or economic age-life factors. It may also be estimated indirectly by use of the income or market data approaches.

Three techniques are used by appraisers to measure depreciation:

1 . The abstraction or market method extracts depreciation directly from the market.

2 . The age-life method is accomplished by estimating the typical economic life of the improvements and their effective age.

3 . The breakdown method separates charges on the basis of origin of cause of the loss (physical deterioration, curable and incurable; functional obsolescence, curable and incurable; and external obsolescence). Each component is estimated separately, using the engineering method or observation techniques.

TYPES OF DEPRECIATION

Depreciation is traditionally divided into three separate components:

1 . Physical Deterioration
2 . Functional Obsolescence
3 . External Obsolescence (economic)

Physical deterioration and functional obsolescence may be further broken down into curable and incurable types. External obsolescence is rarely curable.

Physical Deterioration - Curable

These are all the items of maintenance that a prudent owner would accomplish on the date of appraisal to maximize the profit (or minimize the loss) if the property were sold. Items of normal maintenance usually fall into this category, including paint touch-ups and minor carpentry, plumbing and electrical repairs (leaking faucets, squeaking or tight doors and windows, etc.). Interior and exterior painting and redecorating may also be included.

The measure of physical deterioration -curable is the cost to cure. Many appraisal clients require that an itemized list of the curable items be part of the report together with an estimate of the cost to cure.

Physical Deterioration - Incurable

As soon as a house is constructed, it begins to age and suffer from wear and tear. Physical deterioration -incurable is based on the physical life of the components of the house. The total physical life of the house would equal its total economic life if no other forms of depreciation were present. One of the practical problems in estimating the percentage of physical deterioration-incurable is estimating the physical life of the components. There is a tendency to assign too much depreciation to physical deterioration-incurable by using estimates of 50 to 100 years for items such as footings, foundations, framing, wall and ceiling covering, etc. Some of these items may last hundreds of years.

Functional Obsolescence - Curable

Most functional obsolescence-curable in residential properties is caused by some kind of deficiency. Typical items that fall into this category are kitchens that need new counters, cabinets, fixtures and floor coverings; inadequate electrical service and hot water systems; and need for an additional bath or powder room where adequate space exists. Again, the test is whether the value added by correcting the obsolescence is greater than the cost to cure as indicated in the market.

The measure of functional obsolescence-curable is the difference between what it would cost on the date of the appraisal to reproduce the house with the curable items included and to reproduce the house on the same date without it. Only the excess cost of adding the item to the existing structure over the cost of incorporating the item as part of a total house construction process represents the measure of accrued depreciation.

Functional Obsolescence - Incurable

These items can be divided into two categories: loss in value caused by a deficiency or by an excess or superadequacy.

Deficiencies are caused by exterior or interior design that does not meet current market expectations. The amount of functional obsolescence to be deducted is the difference between the cost of the missing item, less all other forms of depreciation, and the value loss indicated by the market.

The second type of incurable functional obsolescence is caused by superadequacy. Probably only a small percentage of houses exist that do not have some such obsolescence. The number of superadequacies tends to increase as a house gets older and the occupants improve it with features suited to their individual living style. Superadequacies are not only improvements made after construction but also anything initially built into a house that does not add value at least equal to its cost. For example, a builder elects to install in a new house an intercom system, central air conditioning, stainless steel kitchen sink and vinyl kitchen floor, the cost of which might total $10,000. If they only add $4,000 value to the house, the lost $6,000 would be functional obsolescence-superadequacy, assuming no other forms of depreciation.

Another example is a master bedroom, 16 by 18 feet, which cost $1,000 more to build than a bedroom 14 by 16 feet. If the extra size only adds $300 value, the lost $700 is functional obsolescence.

External Obsolescence

Also called locational, economic or environmental obsolescence by some appraisers, it is the loss of value caused by factors outside the property's boundaries. It is unique to real estate, caused by its fixed location. The value of a property is directly affected by the neighborhood, community and region in which it is located. In analyzing the location and environment of the property, the appraiser must consider governmental actions, economic forces, employment, transportation, recreation, educational services, taxes, etc.

Consideration must also be given to factors in the immediate vicinity that detract from value. Unattractive natural features such as swamps, polluted waterways, and obstructed views are examples of items that will detract from value. Poorly maintained non-conforming houses, numerous houses for sale, increasing ratio of rented houses, and uncollected junk in yards are all indications of possible external obsolescence. Although facilities such as fire stations, schools, stores, restaurants, hospitals and gas stations are nice to have in the neighborhood, if they are too close to the subject property, they detract from its value. Nearby industry, highways and airports may be another type of nuisance, especially if they are unattractive, noisy or smoke-and-odor-emitting. External obsolescence can also be caused by factors that affect the supply or demand for houses competitive with the one being appraised, such as an unusual number of houses for sale.

The list of factors causing external obsolescence is almost endless and the appraiser should carefully search for and evaluate anything off the property that may detract from the value of the property.

SUMMARY

When used correctly, the Cost Approach provides the appraiser with an excellent way to confirm the values estimated by the other approaches to value.

To be useful, it must include a supported site value estimate, an accurate estimate of the reproduction cost of the improvements plus a complete estimate of all forms of depreciation that affect the property.

Only in rare instances can the Cost Approach be used alone to estimate the value of a residential property. There are usually comparable sales available even for unique residences. On the other hand the Cost Approach often is the only applicable approach for the valuation of special purpose, governmental and institutional properties.

SALES COMPARISON APPROACH

The Sales Comparison Approach involves making a direct comparison between the property being appraised and other properties that have been sold (or listed for sale).

When carefully collected, analyzed, verified and reconciled, market data usually provides the best indication of market value for a property. The price that a typical buyer pays is often the result of a shopping process, in which many properties being offered for sale have been examined and evaluated. Buyers often base their value conclusions primarily on properties that are being offered for sale. Appraisers use this information plus information about properties that have sold and rented.[1]

Individual sales often deviate from the market norm because of individual motivations, knowledge and/or conditions of sale, but in sufficient numbers, they tend to reflect market patterns. When information is available on a sufficient number of comparable sales, offerings and listings in the current market, the resulting pattern is the best indication of market value.

STEPS OF THE SALES COMPARISON APPROACH

The appraiser follows these five steps:

1 . Finds comparable sales, listings, and offerings.

2 . Verifies each sale including selling price, terms, motivation, and its bona fide nature.

3 . Analyzes each comparable property and compares it to the property being appraised as to time of sale, location, physical characteristics and conditions of sale.

4 . Makes the necessary adjustments to compensate for any dissimilarities noted between the comparables and the property being appraised. The adjustments are derived by comparing comparables with each other whenever possible.

5 . Derives an indicated value for the property being appraised by comparison with the adjusted selling price of the comparables.

Data Sources

The accuracy of the value estimated by the Sales Comparison Analysis depends heavily upon the quantity and quality of data about the comparable sales and listings collected and analyzed by the appraiser. This data is collected from a variety of sources, the most common of which are the following:

---

[1]George Bloom and Henry S. Harrison, *Appraising the Single Family Residence*, American Institute of Real Estate Appraisers, Chicago, IL 1978.

Multiple Listing Services
Tax Transfer Records
Assessment Records
Atlases and Survey Maps
Government and Private Mortgage Insurers
Mortgage Loan Records
Title Companies
SREA Market Data Center
Deed Records
Realtors, Appraisers, Managers and Bankers
Published News
Commercial Publications
General Circulation Newspapers
Public Records

Verification of Sales Data

The reliability of comparable data is greatly increased if the Comparable Sale or Listing is inspected and verified. The verification process provides the appraiser with an opportunity to explore the motivating forces involved in the sale, such as:

1 . Were both Buyer and Seller acting without financial pressure?

2 . Was the sale an "arms-length" transaction or were the parties related in some way?

3 . Were both the Buyer and Seller knowledgeable about the residence and the market in which the sale took place?

4 . Did the Seller have a reasonable time to sell and the Buyer a reasonable time to buy?

5 . Was the financing typical of the market, or was there a purchase money mortgage, second mortgage, assumed mortgage or some other unusual financing?

6 . Did the Seller pay any closing costs, financing cost or other fees normally paid by the Buyer?

7 . Did change of possession of the residence take place at the time of the closing or was deferred occupancy part of the transaction?

8 . Was any personal property included in the sales price (furniture, above-ground pools, boats, automobiles, sports equipment, etc.)?

9 . Was the sales price determined in the past (option, unrecorded sales contract, etc.) when the market was different?

10 . Was there any special government program involving a subsidy, attractive financing terms, or guarantee of payment?

These are only some of the possible special conditions that might make the reported sales price different from the current Market Value. Only by verifying the sales data can the appraiser become knowledgeable about existing special conditions.

Analyzing and Comparing the Data

Comparison of sales, offers and listings provides a basis for estimating the market value of the property being appraised. When comparable properties are similar to the property being appraised, have sold very recently, and have few if any physical, locational and conditions of sale adjustments, such information is helpful to the appraiser in reaching a market value figure. On most assignments, however, the appraiser recognizes substantial differences between the appraised property and the comparable sales. The appraiser must adjust the comparable sales to reflect these differences.

Adjusting the Comparables

Once all of the elements of comparison between the comparable sales and the property being appraised are described in the appraisal report, they must be analyzed and adjustments must be made to reflect the dollar or percentage value of the dissimilarities noted.

--Matched Pairs of Sales

In the past, many adjustments were based on nothing more than educated guesses. Good appraisal practice requires that adjustments be supported with data from the market. The best technique is to extract the amount of the adjustment from the market by utilization of "matched pairs". This is often the only acceptable technique to many sophisticated purchasers of appraisals. It involves the selection of two sales in the market, one having the item for which the adjustment is sought, and the other without it. The theory behind this technique is that if this is the only difference between the two sales, the difference in sales price can be attributed to the item. Although generally reliable where only one difference is present, the technique may be less reliable where there are several differences.

--Regression Analysis

In recent years, attention has been drawn to methods of analyzing market data through use of regression analysis and other mathematical techniques. Step-wise multiple regression routines, like more traditional methods, are based upon the concept that certain identifiable characteristics of residential markets (called independent variables) may each be studied for their individual and joint contributions to value. Unlike traditional methods, the mathematics of this method of analyzing comparables sales are complex and it generally requires more powerful computer equipment.

A major contribution of these newer techniques has been to focus attention on the adjustment process in sales analyses. Where more than one set of matched pairs is used to extract adjustment factors, the possibility of "doubling up" on adjustments exists. This is due to the interdependence or interaction of many comparison elements (often referred to as their "co-linearity"). Traditional comparison methods have generally overlooked these relationships and do not provide a means for measuring interdependence of data.

For example, if adjustments are made for both square footage of living area and number of bedrooms, either variable is likely to already include some consideration of the other. Regression techniques (particularly step-wise) can serve to reduce this problem and provide a means of measuring where significant interdependence is present.

--Cost-New Less Depreciation

Another commonly used indirect technique for adjusting the comparables is to estimate the cost new, less depreciation, of the item for which adjustment is needed. The accuracy of this technique depends on the relationship of the cost-less-depreciation estimates and value differences in terms of market recognition. Depreciation is especially difficult to estimate, because the market may recognize only a small portion of the cost, and substantial functional and external obsolescence may have to be deducted to obtain the actual value contributed by a specific item.

Reconciliation of Direct Sales Comparison Analysis

After the best comparable sales have been selected and adjusted to give an indicated value of the appraised property, the indications must be reconciled to produce a final estimate of value via the market data approach. It is not acceptable appraisal practice to use a simple arithmetic mean of the value indications. Averaging small groups of numbers produces a meaningless measure of central tendency, which may or may not reflect actual market value.

The accepted procedure is to review each sale and judge its comparability to the property being appraised. Generally, the fewer and smaller the adjustments used on a comparable sale to produce the indicated value estimate, the more weight the sale is given in the final reconciliation. However, consideration should also be given to the basis for the adjustments.

Comparison Rating Grid

In the Sales Comparison Analysis each comparable property is adjusted to indicate the value of the residence being appraised. The information about the Subject Property and the Comparable Sales is displayed on a rating grid together with the adjustments.

SUMMARY

In spite of its many limitations, the Sales Comparison Approach is generally considered the most applicable one in residential appraising, since it reflects most directly the actions of buyers and sellers in the market.

In order to obtain all of the information needed to use a comparable sale, the appraiser should inspect each comparable property and verify the nature of the sale with either the buyer, seller or broker. These are the people who can tell the appraiser about the conditions of sale and the actual physical condition of the property at the time of sale.

New techniques using more sales are available as alternatives to the above techniques. They do not depend upon adjustments based on limited market information but rather on statistical treatment of many comparable sales.

When the market data approach is based upon a sufficient number of carefully chosen sales similar to or adjustable to the appraised property, the value indication is usually persuasive.

INCOME CAPITALIZATION APPROACH

In the income capitalization approach, appraisers measure the present value of the future benefits of property ownership. Income streams and values of property upon resale (reversion) are capitalized (converted) into a present, lump-sum value. Basic to this approach are the formulas:

Income ÷ Rate = Value
Income x Factor = Value

The income capitalization approach, like the cost and sales comparison approaches, requires extensive market research. Specific areas that an appraiser investigates for this approach are the property's gross income expectancy from rents and other income, the expected reduction in gross income from lack of full occupancy and collection loss, the expected annual operating expenses, the pattern and duration of the property's income stream, and the anticipated value of the resale or other real property interest reversions. When accurate income and expense estimates are established, the income streams are converted into present value by the process of capitalization. The rates or factors used for capitalization are derived by the investigation of acceptable rates of return for similar properties.

Research and analysis of data for the income capitalization approach are conducted against a background of supply and demand relationships. This background provides information in trends and market anticipation that must be verified for data analysis by the income capitalization approach.

The investor in an apartment building, for example, anticipates an acceptable return on the investment in addition to return of the invested funds. The level of return necessary to attract investment capital fluctuates with changes in the money market, tax laws and with the levels of return available from alternative investments. The appraiser must be alert to changing investor requirements as revealed by demands in the current market for investment properties, and to changes in the more volatile money markets that may indicate a forthcoming trend.

INCOME APPROACH GROSS MONTHLY RENT MULTIPLIER (GMRM)

The use of the income approach in valuing residential real estate is based on the assumption that value is related to the economic rent (income) that the real estate can be expected to earn. This approach has its greatest application in areas where there is a substantial rental market. In neighborhoods that are predominantly owner-occupied, rental data may be too scarce to permit the use of this approach.

When sufficient data is available, the appraiser follows these steps to derive a value indication:

1 . Develops an applicable multiplier.
   a. Finds houses that have recently sold in the neighborhood that are comparable and were rented at the time of sale.
   b. Divides the sales price of each comparable by the monthly rental to derive a monthly rent multiplier, known as a Gross Monthly Rent Multiplier (GMRM).

    c. Reconciles the multipliers developed in "Step b." to obtain a single multiplier or range of multipliers applicable to the appraised property. This is not an average; it is a judgment of comparability and applicability.

2 . Estimates economic rent for the residence being appraised.
    a. Finds comparable rentals in the neighborhood.
    b. Analyzes each comparable rental and compares its features with those of the appraised property.
    c. Estimates the adjustments required to obtain an indicated rental for the property being appraised.
    d. Considers each comparable carefully, with emphasis on the need for adjustments, and formulates an opinion of the market (economic) rent of the appraised house based upon the actual rents of the comparables.

3 . Estimates the value of the residence being appraised.
    a. Multiplies the estimated market rent by the estimated monthly multiplier (or range of multipliers) to obtain an indicated value of the property being appraised via the income approach.

Even if the property being appraised is rented at the time of valuation, it is necessary to consider the market (or economic) rental that would apply if the residence were available for occupancy as of the date of appraisal. The market rent is defined as the rental income a property would command on the open market, as indicated by current rentals being paid for comparable space. This may be the same as the contract rent or it may be more or less than the rent specified in an existing lease. As a lease ages, the contract rental usually differs from market rental. In applying the income approach, therefore, the contract rent cannot be used as the market rent unless the competitive rents in the market substantiate its applicability.

To develop the GMRM, comparables are chosen that have sold recently in the market and were rented at the time of sale. The selling price of each comparable is divided by its gross monthly rental to obtain this factor. For example, if the appraiser finds single family residences in the subject neighborhood selling for $38,500 and renting for $308 per month, the indicated GMRM will be 125 ($38,500 ÷ $308 = 125).

A value for the appraised property is estimated by multiplying the estimated economic rent by the GMRM. For example, if the economic rental of the property has been estimated to be $315 per month, multiplying the GMRM of 125 by $315 gives an indicated value of $39,375.

The final estimate of value based on the value indication of the income approach will be only as good as the market data used to process it. Therefore data used in this method must be carefully sorted and selected for applicability. Care must be taken to verify the comparability of all sales and rentals selected for processing in this approach, and only properties that are comparables in type, age, size, condition and location should be considered.

In using the GMRM to arrive at an indicated value of the property being appraised, taxes, insurance and other operating expenses of comparable properties used are assumed to be similar to those of the appraised property. If this is not the case, the appraiser should eliminate such sales from consideration. The appraiser should inspect both the exterior and interior of all comparable properties to adjust properly for differences. Whenever shortcuts are taken that bypass this step, the possibility of error in the final value judgment is substantially increased.

RECONCILIATION OF VALUE INDICATIONS INTO A FINAL ESTIMATE OF DEFINED VALUE

The sixth step in the valuation process is the reconciliation of the value indications obtained in each of the three approaches to derive an estimate of value for the residence being appraised.

Under no circumstances are these value indications merely averaged. This would be analogous to asking three people for the right time and then averaging their replies. Rather, the appraiser considers the relative applicability of each of the three approaches to the final estimate of defined value and the reliability of the data used in each approach.

In the reconciliation, the appraiser brings together all of the data and indicated values resulting from the three approaches and evaluates them in a logical cause-and-effect analysis which leads to a supportable value conclusion.

In this process, the appraiser must evaluate the sources and reliability of data, choose the approach or approaches that are most applicable to the specific appraisal problem and select from among alternative conclusions or indications of value those that best represent the defined value of the property being appraised.

For example, in the case of a typical single family residence, where the purpose of the appraisal is to estimate market value for mortgage financing, the market data approach would be greatly emphasized. Alternatively, in a highly active rental market, where most residences are tenant-occupied and are owned as income properties, the income approach would certainly be considered more heavily.

The final estimate should be rounded to indicate the degree of accuracy. By rounding to the nearest one hundred dollars the appraiser indicates he or she believes their estimate is accurate to the nearest one hundred dollars. With the data available for most appraisals, it would be difficult to estimate value to a one hundred dollar accuracy and therefore appraisers often round their estimates to the nearest one thousand dollars. For a very expensive property it may be appropriate to round to the nearest five thousand or ten thousand dollars.

REPORT OF DEFINED VALUE

The final step of the Valuation Process is to produce an appraisal report. The report may be verbal, a letter, on a form or a short or long form narrative report.

FORM REPORTS

More and more appraisals are being made on forms. Most single family appraisals are now being made on the URAR form or the ERC form. Freddie Mac and Fannie Mae also have forms that are widely used for Small Income Properties and Condominiums, Planned Unit Developments and Cooperatives. A commercial form has been released by The Appraisal Foundation. It was tested extensively for over two years and is now approved by the Federal Home Loan Bank Board.

LETTER (CERTIFICATE) OR ORAL REPORTS

There are situations where a letter or oral report is required because of the circumstances of the assignment. When a letter or oral report is made, the appraiser must preserve the notes and factual records as well as complete memoranda of each analysis, conclusion and opinion contained in the letter or oral report.

NARRATIVE REPORTS

The appraiser is afforded the best opportunity to support opinions and conclusions and to convince the client of the soundness of the value estimate in a narrative report. Its content and arrangement may vary. A typical report follows the table of contents shown in Fig. 3-3. A complete narrative appraisal report appears as Addenda A to this text. Some other appraisal organizations have their own specific guidelines for the preparation of demonstration appraisals to be used for credit towards their designations.

FIG. 3-2 CONTENTS OF A TYPICAL NARRATIVE APPRAISAL REPORT

Part One - Introduction
    Title Page
    Letter of Transmittal
    Certification
    Table of Contents
    Qualifications of the Appraiser
    Photographs of the Property
    Summary of Salient Facts and Conclusions

Part Two - Premises of the Appraisal
    Underlying Assumptions and Limiting Conditions
    Purpose and Use of Appraisal
    Market Value Definition and Date of Appraisal
    Property Rights Appraised

Part Three - Presentation of Data
    Identification of the Property
    Identification of Non-Realty Items
    Regional Map
    Regional Data
    Community Map
    Community Data
    Neighborhood Boundary Map
    Neighborhood Data
    Zoning Data
    Assessment and Tax Data
    Site Plan
    Site Data
    Description of the Improvements
    History of the Property
    Floor Plans

SUMMARY

The valuation process is the orderly step-by-step procedure an appraiser follows to produce a valid appraisal. It begins with the definition of the problem to be solved and concludes with a report of the solution in the form of an estimate of the defined value that is sought. The purpose of the appraisal process is to provide the outline for making thorough, accurate appraisals in an efficient manner.

Most appraisers would agree that making appraisals is an art, not a science. They would further explain that the profession is constantly trying to make appraising more scientific. A big step toward this goal has been the development of the valuation process. Within this theoretical framework, a concise, logical and clearly supported value conclusion can be presented which meets the needs of clients as well as the standards of the appraisal profession. New techniques using statistical methods to abstract information from the market, such as multiple regression analysis, are also making the appraisal process more scientific.

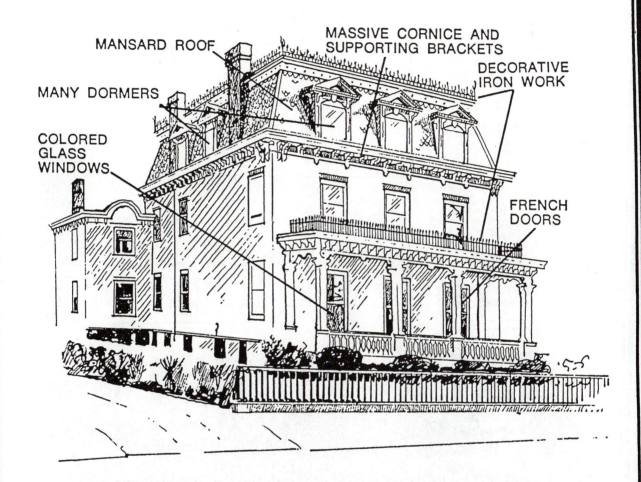

MANSARD ROOF

MANY DORMERS

COLORED GLASS WINDOWS

MASSIVE CORNICE AND SUPPORTING BRACKETS

DECORATIVE IRON WORK

FRENCH DOORS

Nineteenth Century American

AMERICAN MANSARD OR SECOND EMPIRE STYLE
(Mansard or 2nd Emp - 707)

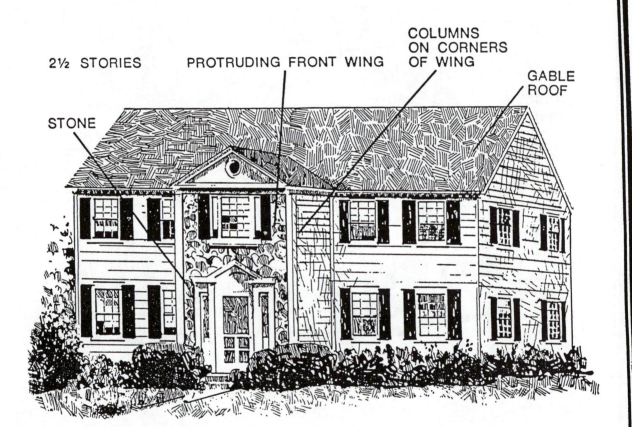

2½ STORIES PROTRUDING FRONT WING

COLUMNS
ON CORNERS
OF WING

GABLE
ROOF

STONE

Colonial American

**FRONT GABLE NEW ENGLAND COLONIAL OR
CHARLESTON COLONIAL OR ENGLISH COLONIAL
(F Gab NE or Charles or Eng Col - 114)**

4 Financing

Interest rates and the availability of mortgage money have a direct effect on the value of residential real estate.

The complex relationship between financing and the valuation of residences is difficult to recognize, explain and understand. Experts agree that there is a relationship between financing and the price, cost or value of residences. They agree that the market reflects this relationship, but acknowledge it is difficult to "tie down". In spite of this difficulty, the influence of financing must be considered in the appraisal process.

Buyers and Sellers are affected by changes in interest rates and the availability of mortgage money. They play a major role in buying decisions. The appraiser must consider how much of an impact special or unusual conditions of finance have on price, cost and value.

Because a residence is fixed in location and has a relatively long life, it makes excellent security for a loan. Because it is high in cost compared to the assets of a typical buyer, the cost of housing ranges from 25% to 50% of a typical family income after taxes.[1] Residences are almost always financed with a long-term loan secured by a mortgage on the property.

THE MORTGAGE INSTRUMENT

Because long-term financing arrangements are necessary in most cases when a residence is purchased, the mortgage instrument has been developed to fit these needs. It is a legal document comprised of two parts--the mortgage and the note. The use of the mortgage instrument has been commonplace in this country for many decades.

The traditional first mortgage is categorized as a conventional mortgage. Non-conventional mortgages are those which are insured or guaranteed by an agency of the Federal government (Federal Housing Administration or Veterans Administration) or a private insurance company. Since the 1930's the FHA has been insuring loans to persons who require assistance because of their lack of financial capacity. The VA provides a similar service to veterans. Both FHA and VA interest rates tend to be lower than rates for conventional loans. They usually have longer terms and a higher loan-to-value ratio.

---

[1]Cost of housing includes mortgage interest and amortization, property taxes and utilities.

Other types of financing include deeds of trust, privately insured and guaranteed loans, cash, second mortgages and contract purchases.

Legal restrictions and requirements applying to a mortgage vary from state to state. Such legal considerations impact on the mortgage instrument and are two-sided: On one side the homeowner is given as much protection and encouragement as possible, and on the other side risk to the lender must be considered. The best examples of this are the foreclosure laws of the various states. A state having foreclosure legislation excessively favorable to the borrower may attract few funds from outside the state. Those states that give the greatest protection to the mortgagee, with short time periods for foreclosure, tend to attract more funds from around the country.

MORTGAGE MONEY SOURCES

The two primary sources of money for purchase of single family homes are the savings deposits of customers in the nation's thrift institutions and the secondary mortgage market [which is dominated by Freddie Mac (Federal Home Loan Mortgage Company) and Fannie Mae (Federal National Mortgage Association)]. The thrift organizations obtain some of their funds from people who save with them. However, a substantial portion of their mortgage money comes from the secondary mortgage market. Lenders package a portfolio of mortgages and sell them to Freddie Mac, Fannie Mae and other organizations in the secondary mortgage market.

Savings and loan associations and mortgage brokerage companies are the leading sources of funds to the residential buyer. Life insurance companies provide some funds, but they tend to look more towards multi-family and other types of income property. Commercial banks provide a limited supply of funds, usually on much shorter terms. Mutual Savings banks (which are similar to S & L's) also are a large source of mortgage money in their limited geographic areas.

FINANCING AND RISK

Lending institutions and mortgage brokers who are the prime originators of mortgage loans, analyze the risk in making residential loans very much like any other investment. The security of the real estate in the mortgage loan gives added incentive to many institutions and individuals to make mortgage loans. However, certain risks are involved, such as delinquencies which result in the need to foreclose. Another risk is that at some point in the future, the loan will be greater than the value of the real estate (the amount for which the real estate can be sold under pressure), thereby resulting in a loss to the financial institution. The high risk of mortgage loans is now receiving a substantial amount of publicity. It is one of the major causes of the failure of many thrift institutions.

In analyzing the relationship of financing to real estate values, it is necessary to consider the mortgage lending system and the risks involved. The quoted interest rate for a mortgage loan is the cost of the money. The annual rates of interest tend to be commensurate with the risk involved in a specific investment.

Interest rates may be different from the actual yield on an investment. The mortgage market has become active on a much broader basis and so the impact of the secondary market (and the national market in some respects) affects the yield which a mortgage may produce. A 10% interest rate on a $50,000 loan pays, on an annual basis, $5,000. If an individual or institution acquires the loan at a discounted price of $45,000, the yield per year would be $5,000 on a $45,000 investment - a rate of 11.11% ($5,000 divided by $45,000), rather than the contract rate of 10%. Conversely if the investor paid $55,000, the yield is reduced to 9.09%.

To compete in the market, it is necessary at times to charge "points" or to use a discount rate. For example, if a loan were to be made in the amount of $100,000 at the going rate of 9%, the lender may feel that rate is inadequate under the circumstances and make one of the following adjustments: The borrower may be asked to pay points--say, four points--which on a $100,000 loan would be $4,000. Another technique is applying a discount rate. By discounting the loan 3%, the amount of money actually advanced at the time of closing is 3% less than the original $100,000; however, the borrower still pays 9% interest on $100,000. In other words, a 9% return would be earned on $100,000 even though only $97,000 was loaned. This increases the yield to the lender, providing compensation for what the lender perceives to be a higher risk or to match yields in other types of investment opportunities.

COMPETITION FOR FUNDS

When there is a shortage of mortgage money or when interest rates are high, the number of potential home buyers decreases. This has an effect on the value of houses. The appraiser therefore is concerned with the amount of money available, and with the interest rate at which loans are being made, the length of the term and the ratio of loan to value. Each of these variables or combinations thereof are critical to the buyer making a decision in the market. The appraiser's first concern, however, is the total amount of investment funds flowing to the single family housing market. As this book goes to press in early 1993, interest rates are going down again very slowly. It is too early to determine what effect this will have on the availability of mortgages.

THE MONEY MARKET

Money is defined as all currency plus all deposits in private checking accounts and "near monies", which include time and savings deposits, savings and loan shares, mutual savings bank deposits and short-term U.S. government securities. All are cash or the equivalent to cash; that is, they are available for expenditure without delay. To understand the competition for investment funds, it is necessary to comprehend to a certain extent the nature of the whole money market.

The amount of money available for borrowing is regulated by the U.S. Treasury Department and the Federal Reserve System. It is their obligation to assist the economy by having adequate money available. Originally the "Fed" was charged with the primary responsibility for the money market. The function of the Federal Reserve System is to foster a flow of credit and money that will facilitate orderly economic growth, a stable dollar, and long-run balance in our international payments. Its original purpose, as expressed by the founders, was to give the country a lasting currency, to provide facilities for discounting commercial paper, and to improve the supervision of banking. As the economy changed, broader objectives were outlined, namely to help counteract inflationary and deflationary movements, and to share in creating conditions favorable to a high level of employment, a stable dollar, growth of the country, and a rising level of consumption.

The mortgage market, which provides the basic supply of funds for residential property, is in direct competition for these funds. At times the mortgage market is not competitive with other users. Then the supply of funds goes down, the cost of money goes up, or both occur. At other times, slow decline in the cost of money takes place without a corresponding reduction in the supply of money. It is hard to accurately predict what effect interest rate changes and mortgage money availability will have on the value of houses in a specific market.

THE SECONDARY MORTGAGE MARKET

The financing of real estate has been facilitated greatly by the development of the secondary mortgage market. Many lending institutions formerly made home loans and held them; now they are able to sell loans in the secondary market and thus secure additional funds for home financing. A number of private investors and institutions purchase home mortgages.

A major influence on the secondary mortgage market is the activity of the Federal National Mortgage Association (FNMA). "Fannie Mae" purchases mortgages from primary mortgage markets, thus increasing liquidity among primary mortgage lenders. It issues long-term debentures and short-term discount notes to raise most of its funds. FNMA programs emphasize insured and guaranteed mortgages.

The Federal Home Loan Mortgage Corporation (FHLMC) known as The Mortgage Corporation or "Freddie Mac" conducts both mortgage purchase and sales programs. Its main emphasis is on conventional mortgages.

The Government National Mortgage Association (GNMA or "Ginnie Mae") is a government organization that gets its funds from the U.S. Treasury. It is specializing in the purchase of mortgages which require extraordinary support.

ADJUSTABLE RATE MORTGAGES (ARMs)

In the past 20 years, interest rates have changed much more rapidly than in the past. Lending institutions with large portfolios of low interest mortgages found themselves in serious financial trouble when the rates of interest they were forced to pay to keep and attract depositors exceeded the yield on their mortgage portfolios.

To prevent a re-occurrence of the problem, an Adjustable Rate Mortgage (ARM) was developed as an alternative mortgage instrument carrying an interest rate that varies with changes in market rates.

Since 1985, the majority of home buyers have financed the purchase of their homes with an ARM. ARMs now account for about 60% of home mortgages being written.

The interest rate on an ARM is indexed to some other interest rate. This means that when the interest rate changes on the indexing instrument the interest rate also changes on the mortgage.

There is an endless variety of ARMs being offered. They have a few common characteristics:

1 . The interest rate on the mortgage changes only once or twice a year (or less often), not every time the interest rate on the index instrument changes.

2 . There is a maximum amount the interest may be increased in any one year (often 2%).

3 . There is a total maximum amount the interest may be increased (often 6%) over the life of the mortgages.

The following are some of the ARM plans that have been approved by Fannie Mae:

1 . One Year Treasury Bills.
2 . One year 11th District Federal Reserve Funds.
3 . Six month 11th District Federal Reserve Funds.
4 . Three Year Treasury Bills.

Other indices which are used are:

5 . National Mortgage Contract Rate.
6 . National Median Cost of Funds to FSLIC - Insured Savings Institutions.
7 . Prime Rate.
8 . London Interbank Offering Rate (LIBOR).
9 . Certificates of Deposit.

OTHER TYPES OF FINANCING

Second Mortgages

In addition to the first mortgage, a second or "junior" mortgage may be used to facilitate the purchase of a residential property. As its name implies, a second mortgage is secondary to the rights of the first mortgagee. It is used in circumstances in which the buyer is unable to arrange for adequate financing based on one mortgage and so requires a second mortgage. This technique provides additional funds and facilitates the purchase of the property when the buyer may not be able to do so otherwise.

Deed of Trust

While the mortgage is a traditional means of financing the purchase of a property, some states provide vehicles to accomplish the same end but with different kinds of legal arrangements. In some western states, a deed of trust, which is similar to a mortgage, is used. It involves a third party who serves as a trustee. Money is borrowed in the same manner as with a mortgage but the trustee holds the title to the property until the borrower meets all obligations at which time the title is conveyed.

Conditional Sales Contract

A relatively common means of financing property is with a conditional sales contract (buying on contract). This device requires the seller to finance the sale of the property to the new buyer. Title does not pass from the seller to the buyer until the buyer has satisfied the contract--that is, paid it off. Quite often terms are different from those available with first mortgages; a conditional sales contract may have a shorter term or provide for a higher ratio of loan-to-value, traditionally at a higher interest rate than a conventional mortgage.

All Cash Purchases

A few buyers provide all cash for the entire purchase of a property. Through the sale of other property or the accumulation of funds in some manner, they are able to purchase property with a lump-sum cash payment. Such financial arrangements quite often expedite the purchase and affect the negotiating ability of the buyer.

Private Mortgage Insurance

A variation of FHA insured loans has been developed by private mortgage insurance companies for conventional mortgages. Such companies typically insure the risk to the lender on the top 10% above the amount traditionally loaned as a conventional mortgage. If an 80% loan-to-value ratio were available, the next 10% (increasing the loan to 90% of value) is insured by the private mortgage company.

Favorable Purchase Money Mortgages

The most common financing market is the conventional first mortgage loan. In the conventional market, if the going loan for a particular community is 13 1/2%, 20 year term with 80% loan-to-value ratio, sales used as comparables should have a similar type of financing. If financing varies by a quarter percent of interest, a few years differences in length or a few percentage points variation in loan-to-value ratio, these would not be considered adequate differences in conditions of sale to require adjustments. In the above example, however, if a comparable were financed (because of special arrangements) at a 10 1/2% rate for 30 years with a 95% loan-to-value ratio, adjustments must be made before it could be used, on the assumption that such special and favorable conditions of financing affected the sales price. Similarly, a buyer required to pay 16 1/2% interest with a maximum term of only 15 years and a 70% loan-to-value ratio would probably have paid less for the property, and an adjustment would have to be made.

FHA and VA Insured Mortgages

FHA-insured and VA-guaranteed loans tend to be in a market by themselves and when such properties are being appraised, comparables should be those with FHA or VA loans. It is quite common today for investors to seek out subdivisions that have been predominantly FHA- or VA-financed. By doing so, financing terms are typically very favorable--sometimes interest rates are one-half or two-thirds of the going conventional rate. The length of the term may be greater and the original loan-to-value ratio may be very competitive with conventional mortgages as of the date of the purchase. These unique financing arrangements have a marked effect on sale prices. To compare the sale of a house having favorable financing arrangements with the sale of a house subject to conventional financing arrangements cannot be justified unless an appropriate adjustment is made. Rather than attempt to make an adjustment for such differences most appraisers feel that it is better appraisal practice to restrict themselves to using comparable sales from a similar market.

TRUTH IN LENDING

The Board of Governors of the Federal Reserve System has been charged by Public Law 90-321 (as amended) Title I to administer the "Truth-In-Lending Act" which applies to almost everyone who loans money to the public for real estate transactions.

The purpose of this law is to educate the borrower about the true cost of the money they borrow.

To implement this act of Congress the Board of Governors of the FHLBB issued Regulation Z which provides rules and tables with which it is possible to calculate the "Annual Percentage Rate (APR)" for any loan.

The APR is made up of all of the following charges paid by the borrower in addition to the interest:

1 . Fees or premiums for title examination, title insurance, or similar purposes.

2 . Fees for preparation of a deed, settlement statement, or other documents.

3 . Escrows for future payments of taxes and insurance.

4 . Fees for notarizing deeds and other documents.

5 . Appraisal fees.

6 . Credit reports.

Lenders are required to advertise the APR of all loans they advertise and advise all borrowers of the APR of each real estate loan they make.

NEW TYPES OF MORTGAGES (GIMMICKS?)

Recently two types of mortgages have been advertised by lenders as being superior to more traditional types of mortgages.

BI-WEEKLY MORTGAGE

A mortgage in which payments are made every two weeks as opposed to the more typical payment once a month. Payments are calculated initially according to the terms of the contract on a monthly basis and then halved. Payments made on a bi-weekly basis in this manner result in the equivalent of thirteen monthly payments per year.

In order to be sure that the payments are made on a timely basis many lenders require that the payment be transferred directly from the borrower's bank account which must be opened in the lender's institution.

There is no doubt that the total dollars of interest paid over the course of a loan is substantially less than on a similar monthly payment loan, as shown in Fig. 4-1.

FIG. 4-1 BI-WEEKLY MORTGAGE SAVINGS

Conventional Monthly Mortgage Payment

Principal Amount	$100,000
Annual Interest Rate	11.5%
Monthly Payment	$1066.43
Term of Mortgage	20 Years

Total Payments over 20 years

Principal	$100,000
Interest	$155,943
Total Payments	$255,943

Mortgage with Bi-weekly payment (1/2 conventional monthly payment)

Principal Amount	$100,000
Annual Interest Rate	11.5%
Bi-weekly Payment	$533.22
Term of Mortgage	15 years 3 months

Total Payments over 15 years 3 months

Principal	$100,000
Interest	$111,155
Total Payments	$211,155

Total Dollar Savings $ 44,787.88
($255,943 - $211,155)

By paying 1/2 the conventional mortgage payment bi-weekly the term of the mortgage is reduced from 20 years to 15 years and 3 months. This results in total dollars of interest saved of $44,787.88.

The reason this happens is that the bank gets the mortgage principal paid back faster and therefore less interest is paid on the remaining balance.

"TEASER" RATE MORTGAGES

This is the nick name given to mortgages where the first 6 month's interest or first year's interest is substantially below market rate. "Teaser Loans" are offered by lenders as an enticement to potential borrowers to apply for their ARM mortgage versus that of the competition.

It is poor underwriting practice to qualify the borrower based on the reduced first year payments.

Michael Smilow, Executive Vice President of Fannie Mae is quoted in the 2/27/89 issue of National Thrift News: "As rates rise, the crazies come out of the woodwork".

He went on to add: "Fannie Mae will buy only those loans that are properly underwritten."

REVERSE AMORTIZATION MORTGAGES

These are mortgages with low monthly payments. They started as a convenience for elderly borrowers who had large equity in their homes but didn't want to sell to realize their equity. Each month, the base amount of the mortgage is increased by the difference between what payment is needed for the mortgage interest and the amount the borrower pays.

CASH EQUIVALENCY

The accepted definitions of Market Value all presume that the value of the subject property will be based on the assumption that it will be purchased by a typical buyer who will finance it with a typical conventional mortgage that is available in the market.

Therefore, whenever a property is sold and financed with some special financing it is assumed that the special financing had an effect (usually upward) on the sales price. When a property was sold with special financing, it usually requires a minus adjustment to reflect the higher price that was received for it as compared to what the sales price would have been if the property had been purchased by a buyer who could not take advantage of the special financing.

There is far from universal agreement between appraisers, underwriters and the secondary mortgage market about how to make so called "cash equivalency" adjustments. All agree that any mathematical formula or method by itself is not sufficient. The appraiser must always try to determine how the market reacts to the special financing which may be different than the raw dollar adjustment indicted by whatever formula is used.

SELLER PAID POINTS

The easiest and least controversial cash equivalency adjustment to make is for seller paid points. Simply put, what points the seller pays are deducted from the sales price to give the cash equivalency price. Even in this situation the appraiser may modify the figure to reflect his or her judgment about how seller paid points actually affected the market value of properties in a specific market at the time of the appraisal.

FIG 4-2 CASH EQUIVALENCY ADJUSTMENT FOR SELLER PAID POINTS

Reported sales price of house (conventional first mortgage $120,000)	$160,000
2 points paid by seller ($120,000 x .02)	$ -2,400
Adjusted sales price of house (may be modified by appraiser to reflect market)	$157,600

Even the simplest adjustment is not universally accepted. The VA and FHA handle points differently. Appraisers who do work for these and other agencies should seek specific instructions about how they want special financing adjustments for seller paid points handled.

LOWER THAN MARKET INTEREST RATES

There are a variety of methods used to estimate the effect below market interest rates on purchase money mortgages has on the value of the property sold subject to the advantageous mortgage.

One method that is used by myself and many other appraisers is to calculate the monthly savings that is enjoyed by the buyer because of the special financing, estimate how long the savings will last assuming that the buyer was a typical buyer and then discount this monthly savings to present value using the current market interest rate. (See Fig. 4-3).

FIG 4-3 ADJUSTMENT FOR DIFFERENCE IN FINANCING

Typical Financing in this market:

$90,000 conventional first mortgage:
11% fixed interest rate
20 year term (monthly payments)
Monthly payment $ 928.97

Special owner provided financing:

$50,000 conventional first mortgage:
11% fixed interest rate
20 year term (monthly payments)
Monthly payment $ 516.09

$40,000 purchase money second mortgage:
9% fixed interest rate
20 year term (monthly payments)
Monthly payment $ 359.89

Total monthly mortgage payments $ 875.98

Monthly Savings: $ 52.99

Present value of monthly savings
discounted at market interest rate of 11%
over typical holding period of 10 years $3,846.80

SUMMARY

There is a strong connection between the availability of mortgage money, interest rates and the value of residential real estate.

Residences have been traditionally financed with long-term mortgages categorized as conventional mortgages and non-conventional mortgages which are insured or guaranteed.

The government, through the Federal Reserve Banking System, attempts to control the economy by changing the interest rate and the reserve requirements of Federal banks.

Risk is an important factor in setting mortgage interest rates. Lenders can make small adjustments to interest rates by also charging a borrower points at the inception of the loan.

Adjustable rate mortgages (ARMs) are now more popular than fixed rate mortgages. Their interest rate is tied to some other financial instrument. Usually, the amount they can change in a year is limited as is their total potential interest change.

Other types of residential purchase financing includes second mortgages, deeds of trust, conditional sales contracts, private mortgages, purchase money mortgages and FHA/VA insured mortgages.

Truth-In-Lending laws require that all lenders who make consumer loans on real estate make known to the borrower the annual percentage rate (APR) of every loan they offer, in person and in their advertising and promotional material.

Several new types of mortgages have recently been introduced by lenders in an attempt to increase their share of the mortgage market. Bi-weekly mortgages, mortgages with low "teaser" rates and mortgages with reverse amortization are being criticized as not being in the public's best interest.

Whenever a property is sold with favorable special financing, the sales price must be split by the appraiser into what was paid for the real estate and what was paid for the special financing. When the property is used as a comparable sale, an adjustment is required to reflect the value of the special financing.

When percentage adjustments are used, special financing and special conditions of sale adjustments are made first.

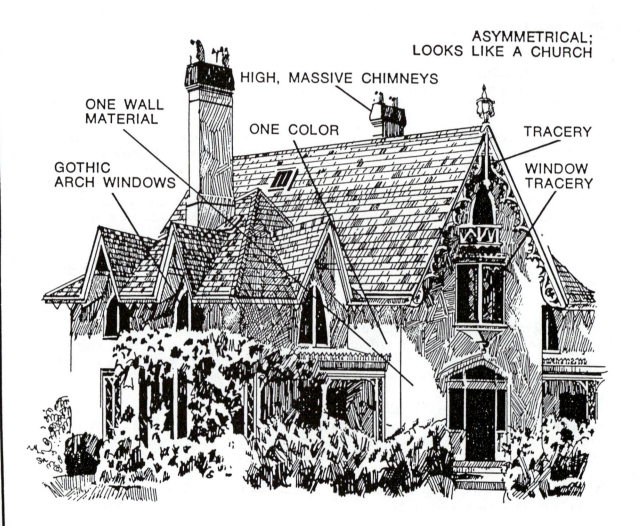

ASYMMETRICAL;
LOOKS LIKE A CHURCH

HIGH, MASSIVE CHIMNEYS

ONE WALL
MATERIAL

ONE COLOR

TRACERY

GOTHIC
ARCH WINDOWS

WINDOW
TRACERY

Nineteenth Century American

EARLY GOTHIC REVIVAL (E Goth - 701)

5 Collection and Analysis of General Data

TYPES OF GENERAL DATA

General data useful to appraisers can be divided into items of information that help them understand the influence of the four forces originating outside a property and their effect on the value of the property. These forces are social, economic, government and environmental. It is different from specific data which includes details about the property being appraised, comparable sales and rental properties, and relevant local market characteristics.

General data is classified as primary or secondary. Primary data includes original elements of information generated by an appraiser or some other group or agency. An example of primary data an appraiser can gather is the number of vacant houses and apartments in the neighborhood of the property being appraised.

Primary data becomes secondary data when it is published and available to the public for general use.

Macro data comprises information on aggregate phenomena, such as total employment at the national, regional and local levels; national and regional income or product growth or decline; interest rates; or the balance of trade. Macro data is typically general data obtained from secondary sources.

Micro data is more specific data. The supply of new apartment units in the community, the vacancy rates in a housing sub market, the number of local households in the $25,000 to $49,999 income bracket, and the comparable sale properties used in the sales comparison approach are all examples of micro data. Micro data may be obtained from a primary source, such as a sample of vacant units taken from the local apartment market, or from a secondary source, such as the number of persons employed locally in manufacturing, as reported in the United States Census of Population.

USES OF GENERAL DATA

General data is essential in valuation because it (1) provides a background against which to place specific properties being appraised; (2) supplies information from which possible trends affecting land values can be inferred and figures for appraisal calculations within the three approaches can be derived; and (3) forms a basis for judgments about highest and best use, reconciliation of value indications within the three approaches, and the final estimate of defined value.

An appraiser should have an understanding of all elements that contribute to the market price and market value of all types of real estate. An awareness of social, economic, government, and environmental trends allows an appraiser to interpret specific market phenomena.

In estimating value using sales or cost data, an appraiser uses prices and costs that have been determined in the market, which are the products of the interaction of all value determinants. Similarly, the income capitalization approach to value requires estimation of market-determined rents, interest rates, capitalization rates, and financing terms. When the methodology of the income capitalization approach requires an appraiser to make explicit forecasts of future income or reversion value at the end of an assumed investment holding period, these forecasts are conditioned by judgments concerning the effects of the basic determinants of value embodied in general data.

An appraiser also may do a quantitative analysis in which he or she reports the level, changes, and trends in general data; then applies the quantitative data to the problem under consideration; and finally shows the relative importance of the data trends. For example, the comparison of two local economies among markets for various types of real estate, or the analysis of comparable sales data from a given market, requires consideration of relative trends and cross-sectional differences in the variables appropriate to the problem.

The significance of a 2% population increase in one city depends on the population increases in other cities. The demand for apartments must be considered relative to the demand for detached single family houses. The selection of comparable properties depends on their competitiveness and substitutability relative to the subject property.

SOURCES OF SECONDARY DATA

Today there is an almost unlimited supply of data covering the items outlined in this chapter and the following chapter. Although good unbiased data pertaining to local communities can be difficult to find, it usually is available. Government agencies at all levels and the Federal Reserve System and its district banks around the country are excellent sources of economic data. The Federal Home Loan Bank System, which is closely related to the real estate industry, is also widely known for its economic research with application to local and state areas. Some states have computerized retrieval systems that provide printouts listing historical and current economic, social and governmental data.

Many private organizations also serve as clearing houses for such statistics. Some real estate appraisers and consultants make a practice of collecting pertinent statistical data; such a procedure is costly and justifiable only if kept current. A thorough analysis cannot depend on technique alone; it depends heavily upon sound information.

METROPOLITAN AREA ECONOMIC ANALYSIS

The economic environment of a residential property and the market of which it is a part are of vital concern to the appraiser. A close relationship exists between the economic analysis of a metropolitan area and the analysis of its residential market.

The principal characteristic of real estate is its fixity of location. Although an oversimplification, it is true that real property is either the benefactor or the victim of its surroundings. Most real estate can be no better than that of which it is a part.

One major limiting factor affecting the market value of real estate is the economic potential of the community in which it is located. Any reasonably qualified analyst recognizes that the marketability of real estate depends heavily upon the economic potential of its community. Just as a close relationship exists between economic development and income producing properties, such as office buildings or retail stores, there is also a high correlation between the economic potential of the community and the marketability of residential property. This chapter deals with the steps in analyzing the economic base and its impact on the market value of residential property.

DEFINITION OF METROPOLITAN AREA ECONOMIC ANALYSIS

Metropolitan area economic analysis has many other names. It frequently is referred to as economic base analysis, regional and local economic analysis, and input-output analysis; the term little economies[1] is a more descriptive name because it refers to the economic health of an area and its ability to bring in income from outside the area. It can be compared to international trade situations where countries seek to establish favorable balances of trade. For example, if the United States sells more to Canada than Canada sells to the United States, the balance of trade will be in favor of the United States - that is, gold or the equivalent will flow into the United States, thereby enhancing its economic growth.

It is simple to apply this same concept to the economic area of a local community or metropolitan area. Compare and contrast the growth potential of a particular metropolitan area with other metropolitan areas of similar characteristics, size and physical location. In which community is it most desirable to live? Which community has the greatest growth potential? Which has the greatest protection against unfavorable economic developments? Obviously, the one that rates highest on each of these three questions, is the one that has the most favorable future.

IDENTIFICATION OF A METROPOLITAN AREA

The boundaries of a metropolitan area must be identified before one can analyze such an area. Most simply, it is a geographic area that is contiguous and operates as one unit. It may cross state boundaries, such as the greater Louisville area or the greater St. Louis area. Quite often it encompasses several counties. It may be the Standard Metropolitan Statistical Area (SMSA) as defined by Bureau of the Census. Recent directives from agencies of the federal government delineate certain economic communities; thus, statistical data is most readily available for these standardized areas. Because substantial data is necessary to analyze the potential of a specific area, it is good practice to follow defined areas and regions.

---

[1]Committee for Economic Development, 1958.

GROWTH OF CITIES

To understand the importance of metropolitan area economic analyses, one must understand why cities exist at all and why they grow in a particular location.

Humans are social beings. Historically, they came together for defense and self-protection or to facilitate trade among themselves and outsiders or for religious motives. Usually a combination of reasons brought people together into communities. Problems have developed where many people are clustered together, but these have been offset by the advantages of such groupings.

Why did people gather at a particular geographic point to develop a community? One obvious reason was location on established trade routes or other points of transportation access such as rivers. The specific points along such routes may have been established for convenience -- for example, a day's travel distance from an established point -- or related to access to raw materials and natural resources, such as a waterfall or other source of energy, and to those who were going to be served by the products being developed. Added to these reasons is a catalytic force that has played a greater part in recent community growth -- a favorable climate. The greatest growth in the United States in the latter half of this century has been in warmer, more moderate climates.

ECONOMIC BASE ANALYSIS

Appraisers are concerned primarily with the economic potential of a community as it affects the market value of the property they are appraising. They must look at the economic potential of a community compared to competitive communities.

Real estate markets depend on growth or the expectation of growth. Although there may be short-run market conditions that are favorable without growth, such circumstances are rare. The market for residential properties depends heavily on families and their economic capacity to purchase homes, which depends on their jobs and the competitive position of such jobs. If the average family income within a specific community is higher than the national or state average, the potential for purchase or construction of homes in that community is greater than in other communities.

It may be helpful to understand the relationship between residential values and the community's economic future by pointing out that certain areas in the United States are recognized for their special economic conditions, both good and bad. Much publicity has been given to Appalachia and its economic problems. The federal government has conducted special programs for this geographic area.

Certain sections of the northeast United States are experiencing marginal economic growth because their major industries have moved to other sections of the country or have become obsolete.

In contrast, some geographic areas are undergoing great physical and economic growth. The sun belt has had spectacular growth in the last two decades. Parts of Florida and California, as well as sections in other southwestern states, have had spectacular population growth. Along with such growth, however, there must be sound economic development. Population increase alone does not imply substantially sound economic growth; there must be a correspondingly strong economic base to ensure that the community can support itself and be competitive with others. Overdependence on one industry, such as oil in the Southwest, can bring about rapid destabilization of the real estate market in such areas when the economics of that industry change.

BASIC AND NON-BASIC EMPLOYMENT

Because the economic potential of a community is dependent on its ability to produce income, metropolitan area economic analysis deals to a great extent with gathering and analyzing employment data. It involves the collection of statistics regarding the total basic employment within the community plus similar statistics for non-basic employment.

Basic employment is the type of employment that attracts dollars from consumers and others outside the metropolitan area being analyzed. This kind of employment is, by definition, the basis for the level of the economy in the area. Non-basic employment generates its income from within the community. Lawyers, doctors and service employees, such as the supermarket clerk or city sanitation worker are included in this category. A community cannot thrive without these people and if they are insufficient in number to satisfy the needs of those in basic employment, the latter will become dissatisfied and less productive. Ideally, there must be both basic and non-basic employment in proper proportion to maximize the prosperity of the whole community.

There is no consistent standard ratio of basic to non-basic employment within an economic community. Such relationships are derived locally and vary in accordance with the income level and nature of the basic employment. If the basic employees are primarily white-collar research and scientific personnel with extremely high levels of income, they will probably require more services; a ratio of two basic to one service employee might be appropriate. In other communities, where basic employees have lower income levels, a ratio of three basic to one service employee might be entirely satisfactory. Certain special kinds of communities occasionally have a ratio of one to one. The ratio itself is not important in the analysis of the level and potential of economic activity; however, it does affect the general social and economic climate in terms of the subjective analysis of the community as a good or less satisfactory place to live.

Data on basic employment is collected on an historical as well as a current basis and divided into three major categories; industry; specialty, such as government and recreation; and trade, including retail, wholesale, finance and transportation. These categories are intended to include all types of basic employment and are considered to be the most critical in the estimation of the economic growth of the community being analyzed. They are rated according to predicted employment trends, diversification, and cyclical fluctuation. The importance of diversification in basic employment and the need for types of basic employment that are not subject to cyclical fluctuation have long been recognized.

--**Industry.** This basic employment category, also called manufacturing, includes all components of fabrication, assembly, manufacturing and extractive activities. Industry is the truly essential, critical and fundamental area of employment for most communities, although there are some communities, such as Washington D. C., that have virtually no industry. Most communities, however, rely on industrial employment to carry the future of their economy. Accordingly, this analysis is made first and typically is given the greatest weight in the conclusion.

--Specialty. This category includes non-industrial types of employment, such as government service, education and recreation. For purposes of this analysis, local government employees are not included. Only those whose salaries are paid by outside sources, such as a federal court in the community which attracts its income from outside that community, are considered. The fire department is paid from local tax revenue and therefore is not considered base employment. Likewise, education is limited to those institutions that attract most of their operating revenue from outside the economic area, such as a state university or a private college. Local elementary, junior and senior high schools are excluded as basic employment.

Recreation communities, such as Miami Beach, Florida or Scottsdale, Arizona, base their employment on providing tourist and retirement services and facilities. In such communities, the waiter employed in a hotel catering to out-of-town people is a basic employee, but the busboy in a restaurant catering primarily to local citizens is a non-basic employee.

--Trade. This category includes positions in retailing, wholesaling, finance and transportation that exist to serve users outside the economic community. A regional shopping center that attracts those outside the community as well as consumers inside the community, is partially a basic employer. Major banks serving the entire state or region obviously attract some of their revenue from outside the local economic community. The headquarters of a national bus service or moving company would be primarily a basic employer.

QUALITY RATING

The procedure for rating the three categories of employment is to look at them individually in light of three quality rating requirements: predicted employment trends, diversification and cyclical fluctuation.

Briefly, the predictable trend for employment opportunities requires the analyst to project the relative position of the types of industry in the local community in competition with other communities and the nation. If the results of the comparison show that the community is in the middle range of all other communities and with national figures, a different kind of future will be forecast than if it is in the top 10% of all communities. In one respect, this technique is similar to the use of GNP for the national compared to a specific community's gross product.

Estimating the predicted employment trend requires the analyst to project soundly and objectively the growth patterns (decline or increased stability of employment) in each of the factories and other types of industry supporting the local economic base. Such an analysis is not to be a Chamber of Commerce projection which, by its nature, tends to be optimistic. To be useful for the appraiser, it must be done thoroughly, carefully and with insight.

The second area of quality rating is diversification. Obviously, if one industrial firm hires 50% of all those employed in industry, the risk to the community is greater if a negative trend develops in this organization (or the industry it represents) than if a major employer hires only 15% of all industrial employees. If the latter plant should be moved, shut down or cut employment by half, the community would not suffer so severely.

The third quality rating deals with cyclical fluctuation. Evaluation of this factor is based on how business in the community will fare in the event of recession or depression. Few types of business are recession or depression proof. The staple food industry tends to be least affected by recession or depression but high-priced luxury goods tend to drop off in sales the minute the consumer has less money.

This step requires a judgment as to how businesses will rate in the event of adverse conditions. If there is a tendency for overall stability and resistance to such cyclical phenomena, the quality rating would be high. If the majority of the firms can be subject to rapid cutbacks in production or services in the event of unfavorable economic changes, the quality rating would be low.

Industrial, specialty and trade categories of employment are evaluated on the three quality ratings in comparison with the nation and other communities. There may be a tendency for much wider variation in the specialty category, which should be recognized and adjusted for.

The final ratings in each of the three categories of employment are totaled to reach a figure applicable to all categories of employment. Such a figure is of value only when it is compared to a rating of competitive communities.

LOCAL RESOURCES

In analyzing the economic potential of a community, consideration is given to its primary physical and human resources. Obviously, a complete and thorough supply of data regarding the people who make up an economic area is essential. Also, information is required regarding its energy sources and physical resources such as mineral and other types of natural resources. Favorable weather and climate conditions may be considered a resource especially in dealing with the recreational potential of a community. Unfavorable factors such as smog, odors, polluted waters or unusual weather conditions obviously are considered a disadvantage. Capital resources or access to capital is affected by the attitudes of bankers, investors, and other financial sources.

FUTURE ECONOMIC ACTIVITY

Economic base analysis is not merely a collection of data; it is developed so that the analyst can project the economic potential of a defined area. It is useless to collect a mass of data and perform a thorough statistical analysis and then fail to draw clear, concise conclusions regarding the future of the economic entity. This latter step is vital in the analysis of the economic potential of a metropolitan area. Concise and definitive projections regarding the competitive position of the community, compared to other communities and the nation as a whole, are essential. If such projections are not made, there is no validity or justification for the economic base analysis.

Economic base analysis is not the only technique used in predicting the economic future of an area. An input/output analysis has been developed by urban economists to rate the economics of a community on an income and expense basis. It may be further analyzed in terms similar to a profit and loss statement. Urban economists have also developed a regional accounting system that compares one part of a region or area with other parts to see which has competitive advantages. A third type of analysis is referred to as a balance of payments, which is basically a study to reveal historical, current, and future projected capacity for the favorable balance of trade in one economic community compared to the world, the nation, and other economic areas. All economic analysis techniques, however, are projections or estimates of the future. The appraiser must recognize that all prognostications about the future must be used wisely and cautiously.

SUMMARY

The whole process of rating the economic base of a community and its future is an attempt to produce an honest and critical analysis. In no way can all subjectivity be removed, of course, but the analyst would be subject to criticism if too many personal likes, dislikes or prejudices are used in developing the ratings.

The process is also a way to measure more scientifically the degree of competitiveness among the "little economies" (economic communities). It adds a degree of reliability to the appraiser's conclusions regarding the community in which the residential property being appraised is located. Communities do vary widely. There are great ones, good ones and some marginal ones. The appraisal process must recognize the impact of the community. The marketability of residential property will be affected accordingly.

General data consists of data about the four forces originating outside a property and what effect they have on the value of the property being appraised. They are known as the social, economic, governmental and environmental forces.

General data is divided into primary data which is original data collected by the appraiser or other groups and agencies. When it becomes published and available to the public it becomes secondary data.

Another way to classify data is Macro data comprised of information on aggregate phenomena and Micro data which are more specific observations.

General data is essential to the valuation estimate. It provides needed background information about trends that affect property value and form a basis for judgments about highest and best use, reconciliation and final value estimates.

A parcel of real estate reflects what surrounds it: the community of which it is a part; the state, district or region; and, of course, its general location within the nation. The economic potential of the community can be analyzed in a logical and orderly manner. This type of rating emphasizes the future economic potential of the community, not its past or present status. The future is paramount in such analyses.

To analyze a metropolitan area, it must be properly identified and its boundaries located. Typically, it is wise to choose an established type of community for which statistics are readily available, such as an SMSA.

Metropolitan area economic analysis requires identification of local resources, establishment of data sources and development of clear and careful estimates regarding the future economic potential of the area.

6 Residential Real Estate Markets

The market value of a parcel of real estate cannot be estimated without first under-standing its relationship to the real estate market. The appraiser must be familiar with the structure of the market and how it functions, its peculiarities and idio-syncrasies, and its degree of effectiveness. In estimating the market value of a single family residence or a small residential income property, the appraiser must have full knowledge of the market in which it is being offered; without this knowledge the estimate may be inaccurate and unreliable.

To obtain this background, the appraiser may use detailed market analyses prepared by experts in that field. The purpose of this chapter is to provide the appraiser with a broad background to facilitate an understanding of market analysis. It is not intended to provide complete instructions on the techniques of making such an analysis. This chapter examines the real estate market, discusses its special economic characteristics and analyzes the relationship of the market and market value estimates.

THE MARKET PLACE

All transactions, purchases, sales, leases, exchanges and like activities occur in a market. The marketplace may be a specific location where business is transacted (e.g., the New York Stock Exchange) or it may refer to the activity of negotiating toward agreement between parties. The real estate market has no central exchange to facilitate its activities of buying and selling; therefore, when reference is made to the real estate market, it refers to the activities of the market.

The major factors in the activity of all markets are demand, supply and price. Demand and supply are causal factors; price is the result or effect of the interaction of the other two, the pressures or lack of activity.

From a brief and general description of the forces operating in the real estate market and the functions they perform, the competitive process may seem to bring about smooth adjustments among supply, demand and prices. This is not necessarily the case. Competition is the main regulative force but the actual operation of the real estate market is far from perfect.

The real estate market is subject to many outside influences such as seasonal activity peaks, general and local economic activity, the availability of financing and government regulations. At any given time these factors can combine to create a buyers' or a sellers' market. When supply is greater than demand, prices tend to fall, making it a buyers' market. When demand exceeds supply, prices tend to rise, creating a sellers' market.

CRITERIA OF AN EFFECTIVE MARKET

Any open and free market has a tendency to move toward a point of equilibrium--that is, a point at which supply equals demand. This basic economic principle is clearly understandable because when prices fall, activity on the demand side of the market tends to increase, which results in increased purchases and lowered supply. As demand increases beyond existing supply, prices tend to rise, thereby automatically encouraging suppliers to produce more goods or services for the market. Because of the inefficiencies of most markets, an oversupply can develop, in which case prices drop again and the cycle starts over again.

These statements about the market are generalized and oversimplified. Most markets are more formal and efficient than real estate markets, so special effort must be made to understand the real estate market. The reason the real estate market does not match other product markets in efficiency is that the real estate market does not possess features essential for maximum efficiency, including:

1 . Central marketplace.
2 . Standardized product, movable and requiring little care or protection.
3 . Non-seasonal and non-cyclical activity.
4 . Simplicity of financing.
5 . Minimal legal requirements and restrictions.
6 . Free, open market not supervised or regulated by governments.

The real estate market has improved in efficiency over the last two decades because of the contribution of brokers, appraisers, lawyers, title companies, financial institutions, and government agencies; however, it still has not reached the efficiency of most other markets.

Certain restrictions are placed on the real estate market that impair its open and effective functioning. To understand these restrictions, one needs to know the criteria of an effective market. Competition can operate more easily if the goods involved are durable and can bear long carriage and if they can be standardized, graded, and bought and sold from samples. Furthermore, a market requires good organization, preferably with a central exchange that is easily accessible to all and where offers to buy and sell can be cleared with a minimum of difficulty. The more buyers and sellers know about the forces bearing on the market, the more effective market competition becomes. Buyers and sellers must be free from compulsion (for example, where some single group dominates the market) if competition is to be effective. Financing must not be difficult or time consuming; and a minimum of legal requirements and few, if any government regulations or restrictions can exist.

In a model competitive market, both buyers and sellers are numerous and they are seen as bidding against each other until a price is reached that is agreeable to both parties. The action of any single buyer or seller in this model has only an infinitesimal effect on the market as a whole; but the interactions of all operators taken together create changes in supply, demand, and price. All that any individual buyer can do is buy or not buy, or buy greater or smaller quantities, as prices change. Likewise, an individual seller can choose to sell, not sell, sell more or sell less. A producer can produce, not produce, or produce different amounts. The quantities supplied will thus be changed and this will affect price.

The real estate market ranks comparatively low in effectiveness among various types of markets, and it differs in several ways from the model of a competitive market outlined above. In general, real estate cannot be standardized, graded, or bought and sold from samples. Also, real estate transactions involve a variety of legal rights that may differ from property to property, and every transfer of real property involves many legal formalities and much documentation. Financing may be a severe restriction on the free action of the market.

In some real estate markets a single buyer may have a significant effect due to the relative "thinness" of the market, such as that for unimproved land. This is similar to the over-the-counter securities market where stocks are traded in limited volume.

ECONOMIC CHARACTERISTICS OF THE SINGLE FAMILY RESIDENCE

To understand the operation of the single family residential market, the appraiser must first appreciate the special economic characteristics of the single family residence. Real estate is different from most economic goods, in terms of its size, the manner in which it is used and the way in which it is marketed. Four special economic characteristics of single family residences make them distinct and separate from most other economic goods: fixity of location, long life, large economic units, and the interdependence of public and private property. These four characteristics affect the reaction of buyers and sellers in the marketplace.

FIXITY OF LOCATION

Land stays where it is; it is location in itself. Added to this is the lack of mobility of the dwellings that are built upon the sites. (Even today's "mobile home" is not truly mobile). Because of fixity of location, each residential property is unique; no two properties can possibly be identical because the site for each is different. Two models of a manufactured home may be built by the same builder with exactly the same interiors and exteriors, but both houses cannot sit on the same lot. The total package may differ in that one may be located on an inside lot and the other on a corner lot. The market will recognize this difference.

The second aspect of fixity of location is that the surroundings of each residence have a direct impact on the marketability and livability of such a residence. This is referred to as "neighborhood impact." A single family residence located in a neighborhood in which all the other houses are much older and in poorer condition will be looked upon by buyers in a different light from the same residence in a neighborhood of its approximate age and in good condition. Other factors on neighborhood are discussed in the next chapter.

The third feature of fixity of location is that by its very nature the markets are more limited. Buyers or users must come to the product; the product cannot be moved to the buyers. Therefore, existing inventories of houses must depend on the market that is active in the community or can be attracted to it. To fully appreciate the operation of the residential market, this pertinent point must be remembered.

The fourth special feature of fixity of location deals with the legal distinctions applicable to real property. Real property has more special legal complications, limitations and provisions than virtually all other types of economic goods. An automobile, for instance, is conveyed from one owner to another by the simple registration certificate. A real estate transaction may involve many title complications and resultant recording requirements. While these may be looked upon as a handicap, the intention is protection for the owners rather than a limitation. The additional complications of legal arrangements obviously affect the marketability or the operation of exchanges in the market.

LONG LIFE

Although land itself, the surface of the earth, is enduring, the buildings built upon it will not last forever. However, in terms of other economic goods, a house has a long life. Most houses are useful for 30 to 50 years. Some are still being lived in after 200 years. Most types of houses have an economic life of many decades .

Long duration and physical existence mean that once constructed, the product will remain in inventory (on the market) for a long time. It is not quickly consumed like other products. Once the product is added to inventory, it will be a factor in a specific locational market for a long time. Furthermore, it takes a reasonably long period of time to add new units to a specific market. Six months is probably a minimum period for the most efficient home builder; two years or longer may be required under certain circumstances.

LARGE ECONOMIC UNITS

The median sale price of a residential unit in the United States now has exceeded the $100,000 range. Not many people make such a purchase frequently. Rather, it may be once in a lifetime. In most cases, special financing arrangements are necessary so that the buyer can afford the purchase. This requirement complicates the marketing of the product. While much progress has been made in streamlining the financing process, it still is a time-consuming factor and in some cases, prevents a buyer in the market from becoming an effective bargainer. Obviously, such a matter must be weighed in analyzing the demand aspects of the residential market.

INTERDEPENDENCE OF PRIVATE AND PUBLIC PROPERTY

The fourth economic characteristic of single family residences is the interdependence of private and public property. No matter how well built or architecturally attractive it may be, a house's usability depends upon its accessibility. Because of fixity of location, the residence must be reached by public access. It must have street and/or sidewalk access. Many other types of dependence on the public sector are needed to make a house livable. Most houses depend heavily on public utilities--sanitary sewer, water, gas, electricity and telephone. Public transportation is an important factor in many kinds of living units. The close relationship of schools, public recreation areas and other public activities either enhances or detracts from the marketability of a home.

The four special characteristics outlined above must be related to the economic characteristics of the real estate market. The housing unit is a product in the market. The market is made up of buyers interested in such a product and sellers desirous of selling their commodities. The interaction of the market is directly affected by the special characteristics of the product. The following section analyzes the special economic characteristics of the residential real estate market for small income properties.

ECONOMIC CHARACTERISTICS OF THE SMALL RESIDENTIAL INCOME PROPERTY

The market for small residential income properties operates differently than the market for single family residences. The typical buyer of a single family residence is primarily looking for a place to live with their family. Studies show that the buyers tend to be divided into two broad groups, those who move from one community to another usually because of the requirements of their employment or retirement and those who move within the same region because they wish to upgrade their standard of living by moving into a more desirable neighborhood and/or a better home.

In contrast buyers of small residential income properties do so primarily for investment and potential tax savings purposes. Some also elect to live in their investment properties but they tend to place more emphasis on the quality of the property as an investment than as a residence.

FIXITY OF LOCATION

A distinguishing characteristic of all real estate is its fixity and its permanent location. Small income property investors are usually concerned more with the impact of location on the quality of the investment than on the direct quality of life offered by living in the property. Many owner-occupants of multiple family dwellings will live in neighborhoods they perceive to be less desirable than what they would choose if they were to purchase a single family residence.

The second factor of fixity of location is that the surrounding of each residence is very important. Many buyers of single family residences prefer to select homes that conform with the rest of the neighborhood (the principle of conformity appears to be less important in urban settings than it was in the past in suburban neighborhoods). By contrast, often the best small income investment properties are located in single family neighborhoods where they do not conform to the surrounding homes.

The third feature of fixity of location is that by its very nature the markets are more limited. Buyers of investment properties tend to consider properties over a larger geographic area than the typical single family home buyer would consider.

The fourth feature of fixity of location deals with the legal distinctions applicable to real property. Small income properties have all the special legal complications, limitations and provisions of single family homes plus the additional ones caused by the landlord/tenant relationship such as leases, rental commissions, management contracts, evictions, etc. Many people choose not to buy real estate as an investment because they do not wish to become involved in the many complications of real estate ownership.

LARGE ECONOMIC UNITS

Few small income producing properties are purchased for all cash. In most cases, special financing arrangements are necessary. More favorable financing has a significant impact on the investment. Buyers often seek lower down payments, lower interest rates, longer mortgage terms, etc. While there are many sources of financing for residential income properties, they usually are more limited than the sources of single family mortgages in the same market.

INTERDEPENDENCE OF PRIVATE AND PUBLIC PROPERTY

Small residential income properties are also dependent upon accessibility. A much smaller segment of rental tenants are willing to live in isolated areas than are single family home owners. Therefore, multiple family dwellings tend to be located in areas where there is good access to transportation leading to shopping areas and work places. Because the density of multiple family housing tends to be higher than single family housing in the same community, they are more dependent on public utilities, especially public water and sewers.

ECONOMIC CHARACTERISTICS OF THE MARKET

The following is a partial list of factors that influence the operation of the residential real estate market:

1 . The uniqueness of each parcel of real estate.

2 . Local restrictive factors, such as taxes, zoning regulations, rent controls, availability of services, environmental controls.

3 . The general economic climate and outlook.

4 . The lack of mechanisms for selling short.

5 . The variability of improvements. Lack of standardization may create desirable features or hidden defects.

6 . Long lease periods, causing some properties to be removed from the market for a length of time.

7 . Uninformed buyers and sellers.

8 . Buyers limited to those who are able to take advantage of bargains or the necessities of the seller.

9 . Financing terms, which influence prices.

10. Possibility of legal complications in the exchange. Agreements must be in writing to be legally enforceable.

11 . Title, which must be clear and transferable.

12 . Sentimental attachment on the part of the seller, creating an unwillingness to sell for the market value.

MARKET VARIATIONS

Real estate markets can be classified according to types of properties, scope, and whether transfers are permanent (sales) or temporary (rentals, leases). The rental and sales markets are not mutually exclusive because they form parts of a larger whole, but the rental market is not characterized by the wide variations that occur in the permanent transfer of properties. The rental market is similar in nature to a consumer goods market and the sale market to a producer goods market. Usually variations in market activity in consumer goods are not so marked as those in producer goods.

The rental market does, however, influence selling prices and the rate of construction. In a sellers' market, prices may move high enough to stimulate new construction. If more new buildings are constructed than can be absorbed at prices characteristic of a sellers' market, a long period of time may be required for absorption to take place, creating a buyers' market as oversupply lowers prices.

DEMAND PRESSURES

An increase in rents and selling prices is normally the result of an increase in the demand for space, although an inflationary trend may result in across-the-board higher prices. In the short-run, demand conditions are of greater importance than those of supply. The basic element in demand is purchasing power, which includes income and the terms and availability of financing. When an increase in demand occurs, an expansion of activity usually follows. Expansion of economic opportunities usually is necessary to attract people or to increase their incomes. Similarly, a loss of such opportunities tends to depress the real estate market.

An increase in population growth does not cause real estate activity to increase substantially unless there is a simultaneous increase in purchasing power on the part of the newcomers. Likewise, the lack of population growth does not necessarily prevent an expansion from occurring if incomes advance and financing terms are liberal.

INFLEXIBLE SUPPLY

Wide variations in real estate activity can be explained in terms of the relative inflexibility of the supply of space. People may be willing to live in more crowded conditions for a variety of reasons although they are usually unwilling to do so when incomes increase. Under depressed economic conditions, new construction tends to decrease because it will not pay to build at the existing low sales prices.

As the population expands in number and in purchasing power, the large supply of vacant units typical of depressed periods tends to be rapidly absorbed. When the percentage of vacant units reaches a low figure, prices begin to rise. Hence, the rate of profit is increased, and it becomes profitable for builders to construct new units again.

MARKET EXPANSION

In the early stages of economic expansion, construction of single family houses tends to dominate because many are constructed for consumers with incomes sufficient to make down payments, even if the houses would not command rents sufficient to yield a normal monetary return on their costs. Similarly, business firms may expand plants or stores. As expansion progresses, however, it becomes profitable to construct apartment buildings, business blocks, industrial structures, shopping centers and office buildings that are financed primarily for return on investment.

A period of construction usually begins with a period of easy credit. During such a period it may be quite easy to finance projects of various types. As new buildings absorb vacant land and subdivision activity gathers momentum, a land boom may result if the pressure to build continues to increase. Large areas may be added to the supply of land available to a community. As outward movement from the city center occurs, the available area increases in a manner comparable to the square of the radius of a circle.

Expenditures for public improvements tend to increase at the same time that the volume of building and subdividing gains momentum. The nature of this type of expansion does not allow it to be done piece by piece or in small quantities. A sewer trunk line, for example, may open many thousands of acres to development.

MARKET CONTRACTION

In as much as the market does not operate "in balance," there tends to be a teeter-totter effect. Eventually, supply will begin to exceed demand. It becomes difficult to transfer properties and the sources of credit begin to tighten up, which results in delinquencies.

This decline in demand and increase in foreclosures signals a period of economic decline. Many sectors of the real estate market may still maintain a peak level of activity because a marked decline in rents has not yet been experienced. Operating expenses may increase, however, and further foreclosures are likely to take place. The fact that real estate is financed more on a debt than an equity basis probably helps to intensify the variations that occur. Thus, those who finance real estate may unsuspectingly make or break the market.

If foreclosures continue to increase as credit tightens, the entire market is affected. Prices fall and land values decline. Just as net rentals rise more rapidly than gross rentals in the early period of expansion, they fall more rapidly because of the fixed charges involved. Hence profits are wiped out and market activity falls to low levels.

A recession in the real estate market is intensified during a simultaneous general recession. As incomes drop, vacancies increase and rents decline. Foreclosures increase rapidly, first in leased properties (apartment and office buildings), as rents decline faster than operating expenses. If a long recession ensues, foreclosures extend to single family residences and owner-occupied business properties. As a result, real estate prices are forced down.

A large volume of foreclosures is characteristic of a depressed real estate market. Following the foreclosure process, properties are refinanced. The financial wreckage is cleared away to make way for a new period of expansion, which usually results from some special impetus to increase demand for real estate.

ANALYSIS OF THE REAL ESTATE MARKET

PURPOSE OF MARKET ANALYSIS

The objective of the analysis governs the pattern it takes, the information employed and the degree of detail used. Because each market analysis is individual and unique, the priority and emphasis assigned to the topics of consideration may vary.

The first step is to state the objective: what is the purpose of the analysis? An analysis may be used for many reasons, such as to learn what has happened in a specific market in the past, to conclude what market conditions prevail currently or to project market activity in the future. It may seek to answer whether a builder should start a new project or a lender should risk financing single family residences.

The problems involved in making market analyses generally fall into two major categories: (1) those pertaining to short-run objectives and (2) those pertaining to long-run objectives. For example, a builder may be concerned with the immediate marketability of his houses; a lender may be concerned with property stability over the next 30 years.

Defining the purpose of the analysis helps to determine which of these two considerations should be given the most weight, the sector of the market that should be emphasized, and the appropriate intensity with which the market should be studied. In defining the purpose of the market analysis, the particular market segment under discussion must be isolated and identified. The whole market, or general climate, affects the segmented markets within it. These segments may be defined by geographical location, type, age, or value range of the properties.

MAJOR TOPICS OF ANALYSIS

The main topics in the analysis of residential markets are supply factors, demand factors or a combination of both.

--Supply Factors. The first item under this heading is an inventory of the existing stock of all housing units in the defined market area. The Census Bureau's statistics on housing is the primary source of this data, which is updated at regular intervals.

Next under supply factors are new construction volume and costs, including:

1. Recent building rate--new housing starts.

2. Conditions in the building industry as they relate to construction costs-- availability and price of the agents of production.

3. Actual and potential changes in building technology and how they might affect construction costs.

4. Relationship of construction costs to sales prices.

5. Cost of improving raw land and supply available.

Among sources of information will be the Bureau of the Census, Bureau of Labor Statistics, city and county building departments and planning commissions, real estate boards and builders' groups.

The third supply factor is the vacancy rate, one of the important indicators of real estate market conditions and trends. A high vacancy rate results in lowered prices and rents, even when demand is high. Normal vacancy for single family homes is usually less than 5% and for apartments, slightly over 5%. Business units may run somewhat higher. These are general guidelines that may vary from place to place. If the supply of vacant units exceeds a normal percentage, the market is oversupplied and/or short in demand. Competition may force prices and rents downward, followed by a decrease in new construction. When the vacancy rate declines, rents and prices increase, and optimistic entrepreneurs begin the process of adding more units to the market.

Vacancy information may be obtained from local real estate boards, the post office, local public utility companies and property managers. Vacancy rates for different market segments should be computed separately because one part of the market may have a shortage of space while another has a surplus.

--Demand Factors. First under this heading is general population change (past, present and predictable future trends), including:

1 . Changes in population numbers--current population.

2 . Changes in population distribution.

3 . Ratios of different population segments--for example, ratio between elementary school enrollment and population, net migration figures, marriage and divorce rates.

Again, sources of information include the Census Bureau, utility companies (the current population can be estimated by multiplying the present number of electric or water meters by the ratio of population to number of meters at the time of the last census), local chamber of commerce, county offices, school districts and visitors' bureau.

Changes in preferences and taste are an important demand factor. Within any real estate market, the shifts that occur in the preference and tastes of the consumer may be difficult to identify or evaluate. Many real estate professionals rely on their own experience and observation to guide them, almost intuitively, with respect to such changes. Surveys may not reveal basic shifts in preference, especially for goods that are unfamiliar to consumers, even though once available consumers may flock to buy. Preference and taste are highly subjective and therefore very difficult to quantify and predict.

Any change in market prices or rents that persists for a year or more is a strong market trend indicator. Of special importance is the range between the listing and actual sales price, compared property by property. Similarly, the difference between the rental rate asked and finally paid is a reflection of the strength of the market. The length of time to dispose of properties on the market also indicates its strength. When long periods are required to dispose of property, the market is weakening, assuming, of course, that prices have been set at a reasonably competitive level.

Variations in market activity are reflected in the number of real estate transfers. The county record office can supply figures on the number of deeds, mortgages and foreclosures recorded. Studies of this data covering fairly long periods of time are desirable. This data may be related to population trends, vacancy ratios, prices, rents, cost indices and the volume of construction. Such relationships provide a good indication of the present position of the market with regard to past periods. This overall perspective should allow an accurate prediction for future market activity.

-- Combined Supply and Demand Factors. Business conditions, employment and income and financing conditions all fall within this category.

Estimates of general business trends usually precede the analysis of a specific real estate market. Local markets follow national economic trends to the degree that they represent a typical cross-section of the economy. The appraiser must note whether local conditions follow closely or deviate significantly from general trends.

The most important factors to consider when studying local business conditions are employment and income data. Sources for this type of information include local Chambers of Commerce, state employment services, local employers and monthly business reviews published by certain universities and financial institutions. These reports give information on local business activities, including retail sales activity, real estate transfers, new housing starts, and electricity production.

Recent changes in employment or income have a vital influence on all phases of local real estate market activity. Of special significance are potential developments likely to strengthen or diminish the demand for specific types of properties. Such developments must be related directly to the specific market problem under discussion. If local incomes are good and income prospects favorable, the real estate market is likely to be active (unless there has already been a great surge of building and a large unused inventory). Even though no new residents are attracted to the area, higher incomes mean an increase in the demand for housing. Heavier spending leads to greater demand for commercial property. Thus, demand for real estate can rise in a locality even though there has been no major increase in population. Similarly, demand falls with a decline in incomes, even if there has been no loss of population.

It is important in analyzing real estate markets to know what sections of the city are occupied by high, middle or low income families. For cities of 50,000 population or more, data is available on a census tract basis, including the average monthly rent and average value of owner-occupied houses, which gives indications of income ranges in the area. The terms and availability of financing are also primary factors in determining the strength or weakness of demand for real estate. When financing is readily available at attractive interest rates, the demand for property is strengthened. A tight interest market tends to limit demand for real estate. Financing conditions vary not only from region to region but also from one real estate market to another. The availability of funds for the real estate market is dependent on the yield an investor can anticipate from his investment. For instance, if the bond market is offering a higher return on invested funds than the mortgage market, funds are diverted away from the real estate market. Information regarding the real estate finance market can be obtained from many different sources including publications of The Federal Reserve System, The Federal Home Loan Bank Board, or from financial newspapers, lending institutions, magazines and journals.

RELATIVE PRICES AND RELATIONSHIPS

Of major importance in market analysis are relative prices. For example, construction costs may be rising but if rents, selling prices and incomes are rising proportionately, further construction is likely to continue. An upward or downward trend in prices and rents may cause buyers, investors and property users to expect still further changes in the same direction and accentuate the trend that has been developing.

An increase in funds available for real estate investment, resulting in more favorable financing terms, may stimulate market activity even though no other basic changes have occurred. The effect of rising incomes may be limited if the price of all goods and services, including real estate, is also increasing. In other words, real income, rather than monetary income, is the primary consideration.

Real estate resources are in competition with other goods and services for a portion of the consumer's income. The real estate market is not isolated from other markets; it is an integral part of the entire economic system. Real estate market changes must always be considered in relation to other developments in the local or national economy.

HOUSING MARKET ANALYSIS

The factors discussed above refer to all types of real estate markets. In making an analysis of the single family residential market, the following factors are considered in detail.

HOUSING DEMAND

Expanding economic opportunities will encourage growth and stimulate the demand for housing. Rising incomes, even without expansion of employment, may also lead to heavier housing demand. Thus economic base and similar types of analyses are often helpful in housing market studies.

In analysis of housing demand, income must be related to house prices. As a rule, families cannot afford to pay more than two to three times their annual income for housing. Consequently, a good housing market analysis requires information on the income distribution of the families in the area. Data of this type is available by census tract in metropolitan regions and for cities, towns and counties. Census reports also indicate the number of owner-occupied and rental units by price in rent brackets.

Closely related to income, cost and price factors, are financing considerations. If financing is available on easy terms, demand may be maintained even though incomes are not advancing. Conversely, if financing terms are not favorable, housing demand may reduce rapidly even though incomes are steady or advancing. Changes in the terms of financing may have an even greater impact on the market than changes in incomes because of the large proportion of borrowed funds that go into most purchases of single family residences.

HOUSING SUPPLY

The supply of new dwelling units can be estimated on the basis of new building permits and the number of water or electric meters added. Data of this type can be broken down by districts and related to base periods such as those for which census information is available.

A long period of strong building activity may point towards a weakening market, especially if vacancies are increasing and new houses are selling slowly. Also, construction costs must be studied in relationship to current prices to determine whether it is profitable to continue high volumes of construction activity.

Efficiency of building and low sale prices stimulate demand. Larger builders, both those with large-scale, on-site operations and prefabricators, have been able to stimulate demand in this way. However, whenever market prices fall below the cost of construction, regardless of scale or methods used, few new housing starts are initiated.

Fashion in design or style may reflect changing tastes and preferences of consumers, thus affecting demand.

SUMMARY

All real estate transactions take place in the real estate market, a term that refers to the activity of the transactions, not to a specific marketplace. An appraiser must gain a thorough understanding of the real estate market before being able to accurately estimate the market value of any parcel of real estate.

Competition from both supply and demand must exist to create an effective market. Demand in excess of supply creates a sellers' market; supply in excess of demand creates a buyers' market.

The restrictions on the open and effective functioning of the real estate market are caused by the uniqueness of each different parcel of real estate and the involvement of legal rights in each transaction. The economic characteristics particularly applicable to the single family residence are: (1) fixity of location; (2) long life; (3) large economic units, and (4) interdependence of private and public property.

Factors that influence market operation are generally dependent upon supply, demand, price, legal procedures and complications, subjective values of both buyers and sellers and the overall economic climate.

The objective of any market analysis influences how it is conducted and what information or data is used in the analysis. Major topics for analysis can be divided into supply factors, demand factors or a combination of both. The analysis of a housing market involves applying factors that are pertinent to the residential sector of the real estate market.

GABLE ROOF

1½ STORIES

SHINGLES

CENTRAL
ENTRANCE

Colonial American

CAPE COD COLONIAL (Cape Cod - 104)

7 Neighborhood Analysis

Every property is an integral part of its neighborhood and its community. Its market value is very substantially affected by the neighborhood in which the house is located. Therefore, the primary purpose of neighborhood analysis is to identify the geographic area which is subject to the same influences as the property being appraised. Prices paid for comparable properties in the defined area theoretically reflect the positive and negative influences of that particular neighborhood. Two houses with similar physical characteristics may have significantly different market values, due to location in different neighborhoods.

In the appraisal process, neighborhood analysis provides background for valuation. Information that has no bearing on value is irrelevant and may mislead the reader who can rightfully assume everything in the appraisal report is related to the appraisal process and the final estimate of value. Incorrect use of neighborhood analysis can lead to double counting and false conclusions.

Assume, for example, that after complete neighborhood analysis, the appraiser delineates the neighborhood and obtains an indication of value based on recent prices received for similar properties in the same neighborhood. In such a case, it would be incorrect to adjust value for neighborhood influences because these influences must be assumed to be reflected in the observed market prices.

The depth of analysis varies according to the need but a neighborhood must be defined in terms of some common characteristics and trends in order to interpret market evidence fairly. The appraiser should avoid reliance on the racial, religious or ethnic characteristics of the residents. Racial and other ethnic factors are not reliable predictors of value trends and use of such factors by the appraiser in neighborhood analysis can be misleading. People's reactions and preferences are so diverse and variable that they are not readily quantifiable in the course of the appraisal process.

Consideration of observable neighborhood conditions and trends is an important aspect of neighborhood analysis and typically includes observation of factors that enhance or detract from property values.

OBJECTIVITY IN NEIGHBORHOOD ANALYSIS

Objectivity is essential in identifying and discussing these conditions, trends or factors. For instance, general reference to a presumed "pride of ownership" (or lack thereof) may be too vague and too subjective to be indicative of an actual contribution to or detraction from property values. The presence of special amenities or detrimental conditions should be noted and described clearly and carefully.

The appraiser's findings with respect to neighborhood conditions and the effects of these conditions on property values are considered by buyers, sellers, brokers, lenders, courts, arbiters, public officials and other decision-makers or advisors. Because of this broad influence, the appraiser is often called upon to provide specific evidence of neighborhood conditions and trends and to elaborate the findings in a written appraisal report. The use of photographs and detailed field notes enables the appraiser to recall important evidence and verify the facts considered in the analysis.

The appraiser should avoid generalization with respect to the desirability of particular types of neighborhoods. Older urban neighborhoods, as well as newer suburban subdivisions, can attract a wide range of residents. Neighborhood trends do not necessarily depend upon the age of the neighborhood or the income of neighborhood residents.

NEIGHBORHOODS

What constitutes neighborhood is difficult to describe precisely.[1] In fact its meaning has been changing. Neighborhoods previously were defined as a segment of a community that gave a noticeable impression of unity. This unity might have been based on similar uses of the properties within the neighborhood such as mostly industrial plants, retail stores or multiple or single family housing. It also might have been a unity of structural appearance such as mostly colonial or contemporary style buildings. It sometimes was a unity based on the economic, religious, racial or ethnic status of most of the residents of the neighborhood. For example, some neighborhoods would be occupied predominantly by workers from a local industry or by persons of a particular national origin, race or religion.

Neighborhoods that can be described on these basis are becoming less common. Often industrial, commercial and residential uses all exist in the same neighborhood. Likewise, people with a variety of economic, ethnic, racial and religious backgrounds now often live compatibly together in the same neighborhood.

The criteria for neighborhood analysis are clearly changing, reflecting changes on our social structures and attitudes. Obsolete standards of conformity have no place in modern neighborhood analysis. Broad federal and state Fair Housing laws have made discrimination on the basis of racial, religious or ethnic factors unlawful in the sale, rental and financing of housing. These laws, and changing social norms, have contributed to the establishment and maintenance of many stable, integrated residential areas.

Today a neighborhood tends to be any separately identifiable cohesive area within a community with some commonality of interest shared by its occupants. Some neighborhoods may have recognizable natural or man-made boundaries. Neighborhoods sometimes have their own names, such as Old Town or Pigeon Hills, but frequently neighborhoods of this size actually consist of many sub-neighborhoods with different characteristics. A neighborhood may be as large as an entire community, or as small as a one-or two-block area.

---

[1]An intriguing description.of Dr. Robert O. Harvey is "a neighborhood is the area around a lot to a point where changes in land use have no direct effect on the value of the lot." AREA Course Instructors' Manual, Real Estate Certification Program, Indiana University, Revised Edition, August 1977.

BOUNDARIES

The first step in the study of a neighborhood is to identify its boundaries. Sometimes these are natural physical barriers such as lakes, rivers, streams, cliffs, swamps and valleys. They also can be highways, main traffic arteries, railroad tracks, canals and other man-made boundaries. The boundary of a residential neighborhood may also be a change of land use to commercial, industrial, institutional or public park. Some boundaries are clearly defined, while others are more difficult to identify precisely.

1. **Inspection of the area's physical characteristics.** An appraiser should drive around to develop a sense of the area, particularly the degree of similarity in land uses, types of structures, architectural styles, maintenance and upkeep. On a map of the area, an appraiser should note points where these characteristics show perceptible changes and should note any physical barriers, such as major streets, hills, rivers, and railroads, that coincide with such changes.

2. **Drawing preliminary boundaries on a map.** An appraiser should draw lines that connect the points where physical characteristics change. The appraiser should identify the streets, hills, rivers, railroads, and so forth, that coincide with or that are near the shifts in physical characteristics.

3. **Testing preliminary boundaries against socioeconomic characteristics of the area's population.** If possible, an appraiser should obtain accurate data concerning the ages, occupations, incomes and educational levels of the neighborhood occupants. Such data is collected every 10 years by the Bureau of the Census, U.S. Department of Commerce. U.S. Census of Population data that pertain to population and housing characteristics, employment, and earnings are also available.

Reliable data may also be available from local chambers of commerce, universities, and research organizations. In unusual cases, the appraiser may also consider sampling the population of the area to obtain an indication of the relevant characteristics.

The appraiser may informally interview neighborhood occupants, business persons, brokers, and community representatives to determine their perceptions about how far the neighborhood extends.

CHANGE

The analysis of the neighborhood continues with a description of the properties within the neighborhood. In addition to single family housing, a typical residential neighborhood may contain multi-family dwellings, retail stores, service establishments, schools, churches, theaters, municipal buildings, health institutions and sometimes industrial and commercial buildings.

Part of this analysis is the consideration of discernible patterns of urban growth that will influence the neighborhood. Careful analysis can reveal the general trends in the surrounding community area and the patterns of growth, decay and renewal that will affect the neighborhood.

Few neighborhoods are fixed in character. Most are dynamic in nature and are changing at various rates of speed. What is happening in one neighborhood in a community often affects other neighborhoods in the same and nearby communities. As new neighborhoods in a community are developed, they compete with existing neighborhoods. An added supply of new homes also tends to induce shifts from old to new. New neighborhoods may have the advantage of new housing stock. Older neighborhoods may have the advantage of closer location to places of work. Community historic significance, and access to parks, recreational facilities and shopping also affect the competitive position of a neighborhood. All these things being equal, a new house usually has an advantage over an older one.

STAGES OF A NEIGHBORHOOD

Neighborhoods are established when new buildings are constructed together with streets, utilities and other services. Sometimes a new neighborhood is established where an old neighborhood existed. This transition is most common where a residential neighborhood changes into a commercial or industrial neighborhood. With the help of urban renewal, an industrial or commercial neighborhood can be changed into a residential neighborhood.

The first stage of a new residential neighborhood is the growth period. This growth period may last for a year or so, or it may spread over many years. It may continue until all the available land is used or it may stop when the demand for new houses diminishes or when acceptable financing is not available. If the neighborhood is successfully developed, there will be active building. New construction will attract new inhabitants and usually the neighborhood gains public recognition and favor.

When the growth period ends, the neighborhood enters a period of relative equilibrium. Changes rarely stop completely but in this stabilizing period they may slow down considerably. New construction may continue on a limited basis as demand increases or financing terms improve and make building profitable. The period of stability is characterized by the lack of marked gains or losses. Many neighborhoods are stable for long periods of time. There is no preset life expectancy for a neighborhood and decline is not imminent in all older neighborhoods. The period of decline starts when the neighborhood is less able to compete with other neighborhoods. During this period, prices may have to be lowered to attract buyers to the neighborhood. Among the characteristics of a declining neighborhood are properties in a poor state of maintenance, conversions to more intensive uses and a lack of enforcement of building codes and zoning regulations.

The period of decline may end when the neighborhood changes to another land use and a new neighborhood is developed or when it moves into a renewal period. This may be caused by a change in one or more of the economic, social, physical or governmental forces. For example, expansion of commercial activities in the community may increase the demand for housing in the neighborhood.

Neighborhood rejuvenation can also be the result of organized community activities such as redevelopment programs, organized rebuilding and historical renovation. The rebirth of an older neighborhood is often caused by a combination of these factors, some of which are a result of planning and outside aid and some simply because of changing preferences and lifestyles.

After the rebirth of an older neighborhood the life cycle may be repeated in which a period of stability and eventually a period of decline may occur unless, again, a change in the forces that affect desirability and marketability takes place.[2]

EVIDENCE OF CHANGE

An appraiser often detects neighborhood change, or transition, by variations within the neighborhood. For example, a neighborhood in which some homes are well maintained and others are not, may indicate that the neighborhood is in the process of decline or of revitalization. The introduction of different uses, such as rooming houses or offices, into a single family residential neighborhood indicates a possible change. These new uses may indicate potential increases or decreases in neighborhood property values.

The changes in one neighborhood are usually influenced by changes occurring in others and in the larger area of influence. In any relatively stable city, for example, the rapid growth of one neighborhood or district may adversely affect a competitive neighborhood or district. A city's growth may reach the point where accessibility to the center from the more remote districts is difficult. In such instances, the establishment of new, competing business centers may better serve the needs of the outlying neighborhoods. Thus, commercial sub-centers come into being; the city's pattern becomes complex.

Gentrification and Displacement

A relatively recent neighborhood phenomenon is called gentrification, whereby middle and upper-income families and single persons purchase properties and renovate or rehabilitate them. Gentrification appears to be the result of an increase of smaller families and single persons in metropolitan areas who enjoy living in proximity to urban activities.

When gentrification occurs, existing residents often become displaced. The existing residents are often lower-income families, who moved into certain older neighborhoods in various cities when middle and upper-income residents either left or did not move in because they found the neighborhoods unappealing and unattractive. Often two or more households would occupy what was formerly a single family residence. Some neighborhoods became blighted.

ANALYSIS OF VALUE-INFLUENCE FORCES

To understand these life cycles and how neighborhoods change involves under-standing the relevant physical, social, economic and governmental factors that affect value. The following is an outline of these factors, together with their various consid-erations. After the outline, each of the considerations is developed in more detail.

---

[2]There are many interpretations regarding the cycles in residential neighborhoods. An interesting concept is presented in a report entitled, "The Dynamics of Neighborhood Change," prepared by Public Affairs Counseling, a division of Real Estate Research Corporation, San Francisco, for HUD, under Contract #H-2151R, dated December, 1975.

PHYSICAL OR ENVIRONMENTAL

1 . Location within the Community.
2 . Barriers and Boundaries.
3 . Topography.
4 . Soil, Drainage and Climate.
5 . Services and Utilities.
6 . Proximity to Supporting Facilities.
7 . Street Patterns.
8 . Pattern of Land Use.
9 . Conformity of Structure.
10 . Appearance.
11 . Special Amenities.
12 . Nuisances and Hazards.
13 . Age and Condition of Residences and Other Improvements.

ECONOMIC

1 . Relation to Community Growth.
2 . Economic Profile of Residents.
3 . New Construction and Vacant Land.
4 . Turnover and Vacancy.

GOVERNMENTAL

1 . Taxation and Special Assessments.
2 . Public and Private Restrictions.
3 . Schools.
4 . Planning and Subdivision Regulations.

SOCIAL

1 . Population Characteristics.
2 . Community and Neighborhood Associations.
3 . Crime Level.

PHYSICAL OR ENVIRONMENTAL FACTORS

These factors cover conditions of the natural and man-made environment that physically define and limit the neighborhood.

-- Location within the Community. The location of a neighborhood in relation to the larger community is important. A neighborhood adjacent to the central business district, for example, may benefit from the convenience of local shopping and municipal services, or it may suffer from exposure to a high crime rate and heavy traffic. Locations in the direction of growth may benefit, but those away from growth may suffer.

-- Barriers and Boundaries. Both natural and man-made boundaries can effectively protect and define a neighborhood. These boundaries frequently help to reinforce the neighborhood identity, particularly when they are prominent landmarks such as a large park, super highway or river. Explicit boundaries are usually a favorable characteristic.

-- Topography. Like barriers and boundaries, topography may be natural or man-made conditions of terrain. Typically, the desirability of various topography depends upon the nature of the residential development. For large-lot, high-value properties, hillside or wooded sites are often at a premium; tract developers, however, usually seek a level area or plateau which is more conducive to subdivision construction. Proximity to a lake, river, swamp or salt marsh may constitute a topographical advantage or disadvantage. Good topography can contribute protection from wind, fog or flood as well as provide an attractive view. The preferred topography is a rolling terrain at a slightly higher elevation than surrounding neighborhoods. Values tend to rise with the elevation of the land in many areas. Values are penalized where the land is very flat or excessively rugged without reasonable access.

-- Soil, Drainage and Climate. The natural quality of the soil directly affects the cost to build and the value of residences in the neighborhood. Its bearing quality, ability to support landscaping and lawns, and the absorption rate for water disposal must be considered.

Drainage of surface water and neighborhood susceptibility to flooding also affect values. Flood maps are now available for many communities and the appraisal report should indicate if the neighborhood and residence being appraised are subject to flooding. Even in neighborhoods not subject to flooding, the disposal of storm water is an important consideration. Sometimes because of proximity to water, mountains or other natural conditions, a neighborhood has a different climate than nearby neighborhoods which affects its competitive position, either positively or negatively.

-- Services and Utilities. The availability of services and utilities such as electricity, city water, sanitary sewers and natural gas affect the relative desirability of a neighborhood. Large price differentials for obtaining these services would also be detrimental to values.

-- Proximity to Support Facilities. In analyzing a neighborhood, an appraiser must consider the proximity of and accessibility to major support facilities, such as public transportation, places of worship, schools, shopping areas, recreational facilities and centers of employment. Some people prefer to live within reasonable walking distance of convenience stores and service establishments, yet such support facilities should not inflict a commercial atmosphere on a residential neighborhood. Convenient access to these facilities often adds to the desirability of a neighborhood and to the values of homes in the area.

-- Street Patterns. Streets are an important man-made physical element which can affect value. They are the entrances and exits of a neighborhood. The physical plan of a neighborhood is strongly influenced by its street pattern. The attractiveness of individual settings depends on the effective use of natural contours, wooded areas, ponds and other features. Contemporary planned neighborhoods make use of curving streets, cul-de-sacs with generous turn-around space and circular drives. These act as deterrents to through traffic, which can be a hazard in older neighborhoods. Where well-planned streets reduce such traffic hazards, they make a neighborhood more aesthetically attractive, and help to preserve the communication and unity of the area.

Ideally, expressways and boulevards should be outside the immediate residential neighborhood but should offer easy access from local streets. Traffic within the neighborhood should move easily and slowly.

-- Patterns of Land Use. The pattern of land use within a neighborhood often helps an appraiser estimate the stage in the life cycle of that neighborhood. A stable neighborhood has clearly defined areas for various uses, well-buffered areas between uses, and respect for zoning and deed restrictions which helps maintain neighborhood integrity.

-- Conformity of Structure. The character of a neighborhood is partially set by its "average" house. The class of ownership, structural nature of the house and its architectural style, combined with its age and condition are physical considerations that have an important impact on the desirability of the neighborhood. Widely diverse styles and levels of care often indicate a transitional period within a neighborhood.

-- Appearance. Maintenance of individual homes and their architectural compatibility influence the general appearance of a neighborhood. Landscaping, plantings and open space preservation also directly affect the appearance of a neighborhood. Neatly kept yards and houses as well as community areas reflect on-going care by owners and residents.

-- Special Amenities. In neighborhood analysis, the consideration of amenities is of major importance. People tend to live in the best housing they can afford, and a major factor in higher priced housing is amenity value. The homebuyer in the lowest income group purchases "shelter level" housing--that is, the bare necessities exclusive of most amenities. The more prosperous can afford to pay for the availability of external amenities such as parks, beaches, pools, tennis courts, country clubs and libraries. Amenities strongly improve a neighborhood's competitive position in attracting new residents.

-- Nuisances and Hazards. Noise, traffic congestion, smoke and other nuisances directly affect the desirability of a neighborhood. Tolerance of nuisances and hazards tends to be inversely related to the income level of the residents. Values of properties tend to be higher in neighborhoods that have higher standards of public health, comfort and safety. A nearby factory complex or the flight path of an adjacent airport usually have a marked negative affect on the property values in a residential neighborhood. Effective barriers against such disturbances tend to create a premium.

-- Age and Condition of Improvements. The age and condition of all residences in a neighborhood can affect the marketability of a house located in that neighborhood. Age alone may not be an indication; however, buildings do wear out even with good maintenance or become obsolete and therefore less marketable, or their location in relation to community growth may cause economic obsolescence. Regardless of age, delayed building maintenance may cause rapid loss of marketability in a residence. Several neglected houses in a neighborhood may not cause the entire neighborhood to decline in attractiveness, but as the percentage of neglected houses increases, there is a tendency for the entire neighborhood to follow the same pattern. The presence of community and neighborhood associations (which will be discussed further in the following section) often spurs maintenance and repair programs, thereby preserving market value and preventing decline among residences in the neighborhood.

ECONOMIC CONSIDERATIONS

These are factors that are the result of economic forces affecting a neighborhood.

-- Relation to Community Growth. Property values in a neighborhood are directly affected by the growth pattern of the surrounding community. Houses in the path of an expanding community are usually marketable and tend to increase in value. Other neighborhoods less accessible to newly developing community centers or places of employment may be less desirable.

-- Economic Profile of Residents. The income and employment profile of the residents of a neighborhood, and the corresponding price levels and rents these support are important economic parameters in the analysis of a neighborhood. The type, stability and location of employment have a strong impact on the value of residential property, since employment determines to a large degree the ability of individuals to purchase or rent in a particular area. Income levels tend to set a value range for a neighborhood. The influence of neighborhood is often obvious; a superior house will be penalized for its location in a neighborhood that does not support its value.

Changes in purchasing power result in changes in property values. Therefore, substantial change affecting the available income of people living in the area as well as of those who constitute the market for property in the neighborhood must be considered. A downward trend in available income for shelter usually previews a dip in property values.

-- New Construction and Vacant Land. Vacant land suitable for the construction of additional houses within a neighborhood may exist simply because the owners, for personal reasons, do not wish to develop or sell the land. It may forecast additional future construction activity or indicate a lack of effective demand.

If only a few vacant lots remain in a neighborhood, residential construction on them usually will not substantially affect values in the neighborhood. However, if they are zoned non-residential, or if variances are granted permitting non-residential construction, the non-conforming uses may have an adverse effect on the surrounding properties.

Proposed construction for the larger parcels of vacant land may substantially affect values in the neighborhood. Available information about proposed future development of these parcels is an integral part of the neighborhood analysis.

-- Turnover and Vacancy. The rate and duration of vacancies is another statistical indicator of the economic health of a neighborhood. Some turnover of properties within a neighborhood is usually a sign of a healthy market. At the same time, a neighborhood that is stable and attractive continues to hold a majority of its residents. High rates on long-term vacancy may signal decline or the necessity of changes in use. A large number of "For Sale" signs may be a warning that the neighborhood is experiencing a downturn in stability. Reviewing newspaper ads offering available rentals and sale units helps the appraiser estimate the strength of housing demand and the extent of the supply.

GOVERNMENTAL FACTORS

These are based on the activities of government, including taxation, restrictions, schools, planning and building regulations.

-- Taxation and Special Assessments. Neighborhoods are competitive with one another and the level of taxation can be an important deciding factor for potential residents. Taxation is often a significant variable in making comparisons from one neighborhood to another. Special assessments should be directly related to the extra services or advantages they provide, such as a private beach association or extra fire protection. When special assessments become high compared to other houses in the market, they may seriously reduce the value of the highly taxed house. An unpaid special assessment lien will often reduce the value of the house by approximately the amount of the lien. This value reduction may be offset by the enhancement that results from the special improvement or service that is the basis of the special assessment.

-- Public and Private Restrictions. Zoning regulations and building codes are important guardians of stability for a neighborhood. They provide legal protection against adverse influences, nuisances and hazards. When special exceptions or variances are easily obtained without consideration for their effect on surrounding properties, the value of all houses in the neighborhood may be decreased. A breakdown in the enforcement of existing zoning and building regulations may also cause a decrease in value. Such violations often start with illegal signs, uses for businesses and conversion to higher density use than permitted by zoning.

Deed restrictions can protect properties from the negative impact of incompatible uses; breakdown of their enforcement may lead to lower values. Some deed restrictions written years ago, however, may be obsolete or unenforceable. For example, deed restrictions setting the minimum cost of construction may be meaningless based on today's costs. The courts have ruled that deed restrictions based on race, religion, or national origin are not enforceable. Generally, any deed restriction that is against the public interest is not enforceable.

-- Schools. Educational facilities may be a strong attraction for prospective homebuyers. Families may be attracted to a neighborhood, at least in part, by its schools. Schools are of immediate interest to all families with children. Even homeowners with no children may consider the availability of educational facilities when purchasing a house, because future buyers of their home may have children. Neighborhood schools may be of less importance where children are bussed to schools outside the area.

-- Planning and Subdivision Regulations. Planning for the future development of a community is an important task of government. Such planning should include protection of the integrity and character of existing neighborhoods, while providing for anticipated future uses of undeveloped areas. Poor planning for recreational facilities, schools, service areas, and other needs of residents may lead to neighborhood disintegration.

Requirements imposed on developers and subdividers influence the types and quality of basic services available to homeowners in the neighborhood and have a strong affect on the value of existing structures. The protection of open space areas such as wetlands will act as a deterrent to developers who may attempt to sacrifice the character of a neighborhood in order to build the maximum number of units.

SOCIAL FACTORS

Social factors include population characteristics, community and neighborhood organizations and crime level.

-- Population Characteristics. Population trends and characteristics indicated by U.S. Census figures or statistics compiled by local agencies are important tools in estimating the trend of a neighborhood.

It was once common practice by some appraisers to examine the racial composition of a neighborhood in an effort to detect signs of change which were assumed to be indications of a trend toward lower values. Such an approach is now regarded as misdirected. This evolution in appraisal practice reflects a corresponding evolution in social attitudes and public policy. The old applications of the principle of racial or ethnic conformity have no place in current neighborhood analysis techniques. Changing social standards supported by broad federal and state Fair Housing laws have made it possible for the racial or ethnic composition of a neighborhood to change without values decreasing. They have also encouraged the establishment and maintenance of many stable, integrated residential areas. There is no factual support for the outdated assumption that racial or ethnic homogeneity is a requirement for maximum value.

Changing social standards and lifestyles now support a growing preference on the part of many people for social heterogeneity in their neighborhoods. In these areas, traditional social groupings are changing to reflect these social preferences. Analysis based on traditional, outdated social groupings has no relevance in current appraisal process. Some of the most desirable and dynamic urban neighborhoods reflect extremely wide diversity in all parameters, from income level to racial or ethic make-up.

-- Community and Neighborhood Associations. A wide variety of community and neighborhood associations exist. Some are legal entities formed by the original developers of an area, with membership including all the owners within defined boundaries. Many of these organizations were started before World War II, often in coastal communities, around lakes or in other recreational areas. The developer would deed the beach, lakefront or other desirable natural area to the association, which in turn would maintain and control it for the benefit of its members.

Associations were also formed to maintain and guard exclusive subdivisions having common grounds, parks, courts and limited access. In addition to maintenance of common facilities, a major function of the association was to hire guards to keep uninvited guests off the association property. Some of the typical functions of this type of homeowners' association were:

1 .   Maintaining commonly owned land, beaches, courts, pools, club house and golf course.

2 .   Collecting rubbish and garbage, removing snow, and sweeping streets.

3 .   Providing and maintaining sewer disposal systems and water supply systems.

4 . Providing police and fire protection.

5 . Providing lifeguards on beaches, waterfronts and pools.

These groups often tried to exercise considerable control by enforcing private convenants and restrictions that gave them the right to approve the transfer of title or rental of property and to approve the style and size of any new buildings. They were also empowered to (1) establish an annual charge to be paid by the association members; (2) put a lien on the property of owners who did not pay their charges; (3) borrow money on behalf of the members; and (4) buy and sell property.

After World War II, the planned unit development became popular. Common land was deeded by the developer of a PUD to the local community. When the community accepted the common land, it incurred a financial obligation to maintain it and also lost tax revenue on it. Because of these reasons and also because the land became usable by the whole community, many communities refused to accept such common land. Developers then formed private homeowners' associations to accept the land and maintain it. They found this was a good way to provide recreational facilities and often constructed swimming pools, tennis courts and golf courses on the common land as an added inducement to potential purchasers.

Other types of neighborhood organizations have been formed on a voluntary basis by the residents in a neighborhood or segment of a neighborhood (for example, a block association). The purposes of these organizations are usually neighborhood preservation and enhancement, social interaction among the residents, and political lobbying efforts to prevent zoning changes the community believes to be detrimental to the neighborhood. Such groups also maintain contact with community officials to obtain services, facilities and improvements within the neighborhood. They may also become involved in political activities, supporting local candidates and parties. Neighborhood improvement projects with the members doing all or some of the work themselves, social gatherings, block parties, fairs, parades, etc., are sponsored by such community groups. Membership is voluntary and usually open to everyone within the neighborhood.

Some associations have little or no effect on the value of property; they have limited functions, few activities and low dues or assessments. Other associations have a substantial impact on the value of property in their areas. Often they define a whole neighborhood. Houses that are in the association may have higher values than nearby houses that are not in the association. These associations usually control important recreational facilities and/or provide substantial needed services, security and other amenities.

The appraiser must investigate such associations to determine the facilities or services provided and the additional costs to individual property owners. When these services appear to be substantial or their cost is high, it is usually best to select comparables from within the association. It is often difficult to make a location adjustment to reflect the difference in value between houses in the association and those outside. (The subject of adjustments is covered in detail in later chapters.)

-- Crime Level. Unfortunately, the crime level in many communities and neighborhoods continues to increase and so the appraiser must consider the impact of crime level as part of the neighborhood analysis. When a neighborhood obtains the reputation of having an excessively high crime rate, some residents may leave and potential new residents are discouraged from buying homes there. Increased street lighting and police protection as well as vigilance on the part of residents in reporting suspicious activities to the police may help reduce the crime rate.

NEIGHBORHOOD STABILITY

The stability of a neighborhood is largely determined by the reasons why its residents (residential, commercial and industrial) want to live and work in the neighborhood. Occupants are attracted to and choose to remain in a locale for its status, physical environment, services, affordability, convenience and a variety of other reasons that are particular to a specific neighborhood.

When making a neighborhood analysis, the appraiser attempts to identify the social, economic, governmental, environmental and other influences that attract people and businesses to the neighborhood.

The identification and description of these influences is not simple. Some characteristics have greater influence than others. Also, as these characteristics change, the desirability of the neighborhood to its population may change.

When considering the relative importance of these characteristics, the appraiser should be aware that they tend to overlap. Thus, in the final analysis, it is how the subject neighborhood compares to other competing neighborhoods which matters the most. All of these factors have a bearing on the relative price levels of the sites in different competing neighborhoods.

To project the future stability of a neighborhood, the appraiser must first consider the current characteristics and then consider how these will change in the future. The introduction of land uses change within a neighborhood may have a significant effect on the stability of the neighborhood. For example, the building of a highway in or near the neighborhood may decrease its desirability as a residential neighborhood and increase its desirability as a commercial neighborhood.

URBAN ECONOMIC RELATIONSHIPS

The relationship of a neighborhood to the rest of the urban community is measured in both distance and time. This is known as the linkage of a neighborhood to the origins and destinations of the people and businesses in the neighborhood. In residential neighborhoods, this linkage is primarily to where people go to work, shop and for recreation. For commercial neighborhoods, it is how potential customers get to the neighborhood. For industrial neighborhoods it is how the workers get to work, how the industries get their raw materials and how they ship their finished products to their markets.

To analyze the impact of the linkage of a neighborhood, the appraiser should identify important linkages and measure their time distances by the most commonly used types of transportation. The most suitable transportation often depends on the preferences and needs of the residents in the neighborhood.

Existing and projected future linkages should be analyzed and judged in terms of how well they serve the typical resident. Much consideration should be given to transportation by automobile and trucks because these are important types of transportation for almost every neighborhood. However, in some areas, especially around larger metropolitan cities, public transportation is especially important because it is difficult to drive and park in the city.

Many industrial neighborhoods have developed around water, rail and highway transportation. Any projected change in their availability may have a significant effect on the continued desirability of the neighborhood to its current occupants.

When the appraiser reconciles the Neighborhood Analysis section of the report, the reconciliation should contain the appraiser opinion of how the Urban Economic Relationship of the neighborhood will effect the value of properties in the neighborhood.

SOURCES OF NEIGHBORHOOD DATA

Much neighborhood data must be gathered in the field through close observation and analysis of existing conditions. However, other sources of information are needed for population statistics, income and employment profiles and vacancy information. In addition to census data, local utility companies and community-level government organizations frequently have pertinent data available. Other sources include real estate brokers, lending institutions, appraisers and the residents of a neighborhood.

NEIGHBORHOOD ANALYSIS IN FORM REPORTS

Certain organizations and business firms have developed their own appraisal forms. The forms often contain sections in which the appraiser rates and summarizes various elements believed to enhance or detract from value. Probably the most widely used are the FHLMC and FNMA forms for appraisals of properties for which these agencies may later purchase the mortgage.

Note that the neighborhood section of the FNMA-FHLMC form contains a number of items with boxes at their left. By checking the appropriate boxes, an appraiser describes and rates a neighborhood. Although the form includes a number of considerations, it does not afford as complete or thorough an analysis as a narrative report. It is usually adequate and the FNMA-FHLMC form provides space for additional comments. It does not contain specific provision for an analysis other than that applicable for the subject neighborhood. Appraisers are obligated to extend the neighborhood analysis beyond the guidelines of the form whenever appropriate.

APARTMENT DISTRICTS

In large cities, an apartment district usually covers an extensive area. In smaller cities, the district may be dispersed or limited in size. Apartment design may be multi-story, garden, row or townhouse. Units may be privately owned as cooperatives or condominiums.

Although apartment districts differ somewhat from single family residential areas, they are subject to many similar influences. Thus, an appraiser can outline the characteristics and amenities that affect an apartment district in a manner similar to that applied to a single family residential neighborhood, but with a change of emphasis. In an apartment district, desirability and value may be influenced by:

1. Access to work places.
2. Transportation service.
3. Access to shopping centers and cultural facilities.
4. School facilities.
5. Neighborhood reputation.
6. Residential atmosphere, neighborhood appearance, and protection against unwanted commercial and industrial intrusion.
7. Proximity to parks, lakes, rivers, or other natural features.
8. Supply of vacant apartment sites that are likely to be built up, with the potential effect of making present accommodations either more or less desirable.
9. Parking for tenants and guests.
10. Economic status of tenants.
11. Vacancy and tenant turnover rate.

Such characteristics and other pertinent data form the background for an appraiser's study of rental housing property. In certain cities, statistics are available concerning the supply of apartments, vacancy, and rent levels. When statistics are not available, an appraiser gathers data from primary research.

SUMMARY

An appraiser's description and opinion of a neighborhood are an important part of an appraisal report. This places a special responsibility upon the appraiser to be objective. The analysis of a neighborhood starts with a description of the area and the properties it contains. It also describes the growth pattern around it.

A neighborhood today tends to be any separately identifiable area of a community, usually having recognizable natural or man-made boundaries. Sometimes neighborhoods are clearly defined and other times they are difficult to precisely identify. The old concepts of unity and conformity no longer apply.

Most neighborhoods are changing at various rates. What happens in one neighborhood affects surrounding neighborhoods. An added supply of new houses tends to induce a shift from older houses to the new ones. However, other factors such as location, community facilities, educational facilities and parks also influence the rate of shift.

Neighborhoods go through life cycles that start when the neighborhood is developed. This is called the growth period. When construction slows down or stops, a period of stability follows. This period ends either because the housing stock deteriorates or changes occur in the economic, social, physical and governmental forces that affect the neighborhood. Decline may cease when these forces change again or when there is an organized effort to rejuvenate the neighborhood. This renewal period is comparable to the original growth period. The life cycle is then repeated with another period of stability and a delayed period of decline. If the period of decline is not reversed, the neighborhood will come to the end of its economic life and usually will change to another use.

To understand neighborhood cycles, one must understand the relevant physical, social, governmental and economic forces that affect value. Information about the neighborhood and the factors that make up the four great forces must be gathered in the field by close observation and interviewing of information sources and local residents. This information is reconciled to determine what effect the neighborhood has on the value of the house being appraised. It must always be objective, supported by facts and based on current social standards.

Most data about a neighborhood is gathered by the appraiser based on observations and interviews. Published data is useful but must be carefully used as it often pertains to areas larger than the neighborhood in which the property being appraised lies.

Many residential appraisal reports are now being made on forms which limit the appraiser's ability to report completely on a neighborhood. Additional space in the form of addenda should be used by the appraiser to provide for complete reporting.

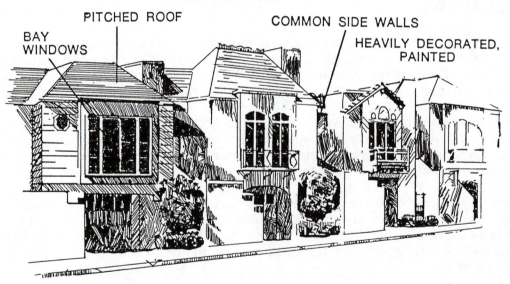

Nineteenth Century American

WESTERN ROW HOUSE OR WESTERN TOWNHOUSE
(West Row - 714)

8 Residential Site Description and Analysis

According to tradition, when an appraiser is asked to name the three most important factors affecting value, the answer is: "Location, location, location." More specifically, the answer might be stated: "Community location, neighborhood location and site location."

Because of the fixed nature of real estate, location contributes more than any other single factor to wide variations in value among similar improvements. Therefore, good appraisal practice requires that the exact location of the subject property be clearly and definitively established. An accurate description of the legal boundaries and a detailed review of the physical features are combined with a thorough analysis of the site's location in the neighborhood and community.

LAND AND SITE DESCRIPTION

In the specialized vocabulary of the real estate professional, land and site are not synonymous. "Land" means the surface of the earth, which is unimproved by man, plus a wedge-shaped subsurface piece that theoretically extends to the center of the globe and air rights extending upward to the sky. In practice, the use of air rights is limited in the United States by an act of Congress, which holds that navigable air space is public domain. In some areas of the country, subsurface mineral rights are owned by the government or someone other than the owner of the rest of the fee. All natural resources in their original state are also considered to be part of the land, including mineral deposits, fossil fuels, wildlife and timber. In the appraiser's definition, everything that is natural and within the property boundaries is part of the land.

"Site" is the land plus improvements that make it ready for use, including streets, sewer systems and utility connections.

Many appraisers include such items as the cost of clearing the site, grading and landscaping, drainage, water and sewer connections (or septic systems), electric and gas service, private access streets, alleys, drives and sidewalks as part of the site analysis. Occasionally, local custom dictates that some of these items be treated as building improvements rather than site improvements. It is important in making an appraisal to indicate this distinction clearly and treat the comparable market data in a consistent manner. Proper appraisal terminology states that "improvements to the site" are those described above and that "improvements on the site" are house, garage and other out buildings.

LEGAL DESCRIPTIONS

Every appraisal must describe the property so that it is easily and accurately identified and cannot be confused with any other. The best way to establish the exact location of a property is to incorporate a deed description and survey into the appraisal. In addition, a location map showing the site in relation to the surrounding neighborhood should be provided. A reliable way to identify the property is by street name and number if the parcel is within the limits of a defined community. Rural areas also have improved identification systems.

Often the appraiser decides that the use of street address numbers does not provide the required positive identification of the property. In such cases, an accurate legal description of the property must be obtained from the deed, mortgage or other land record sources in the community. Legal descriptions found in these documents are prepared in one or a combination of four ways: (1) lot and block; (2) metes and bounds; (3) geodetic survey; and (4) government survey system.

--Lot and Block System. This system, derived from the rectangular survey system, applies in most urban communities. It originated in the manner in which these communities grew. The early developers had their tracts surveyed and platted in rectangular blocks and lots. Each was numbered and the numbers were entered on a plat map. Copies of the plat were filed in the local government record office for permanent reference. Identification by use of lot and block numbers is usually sufficient in subdivisions where each lot is clearly distinguished from its neighbors. An example of this system is shown in Figure 8-1.

FIG. 8-1 LOT AND BLOCK SYSTEM

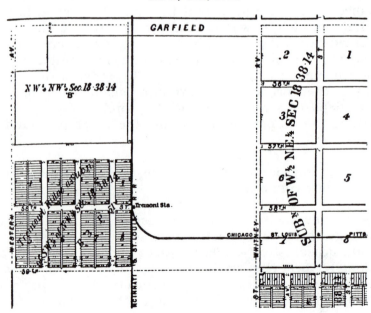

Sec. 18, T. 38, R. 14.

--Metes and Bound System. Originally used in colonial America, this system identified property by delineating its boundaries in terms of a series of directions and distances, starting at a fixed point. (Typical points referred to in old deeds are large trees, rocks, streams, etc., which, in some cases, have become difficult, if not impossible, to positively locate). Each boundary line is described in succession, using a compass bearing and distance, until the entire parcel has been enclosed; for example, "Starting at the old oak tree known as Grand Dad's Oak, South 63 degrees 35 minutes for a distance of 185 feet..."(see figure 8-2).

FIG. 8-2 METES AND BOUNDS SYSTEM

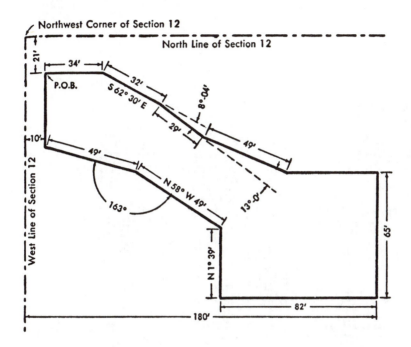

--Geodetic Survey. A land survey that was initiated to identify tracts of land owned by the Federal government gradually has been extended throughout the nation. These survey maps are prepared by the United States Geological Survey Division, Department of the Interior. They show, among other things, height contours, latitude and longitude, existing rivers and streams, buildings and railroads. They are available on various scales by named quadrangles. The skeleton of this survey is a network of "benchmarks," which cover the entire country, each of which is located by its latitude and longitude.

--Government Survey System. This system was also developed during colonial times; it provides for a unit of land approximately 24 miles square, bounded by base lines running east and west and meridians extending north and south. Because of the curvature of the earth, the north boundary of the square is slightly shorter than the south. The 24-mile square unit is divided into areas six miles square, called townships. A "tier" is an east/west row of townships between two parallels of latitude six miles apart. Ranges and tiers are assigned numbers from principal meridians and base lines. A township is divided into 36 sections, each one mile square. The sections are numbered consecutively, beginning with the northeast corner and continuing, east to west and west to east, down to Section 36 in the southeast corner.

Discrepancies pertaining to the north boundary, and others due to errors in measurement or alignment, are allowed for in the most westerly half mile of the township (see Fig. 8-3).

FIG. 8-3a GOVERNMENT SURVEY SYSTEM

**Public Land Survey
Systems of the
United States**

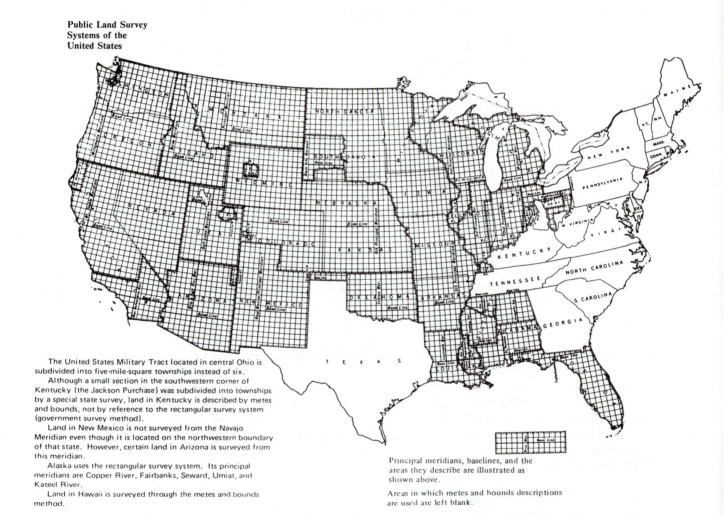

The United States Military Tract located in central Ohio is subdivided into five-mile-square townships instead of six.

Although a small section in the southwestern corner of Kentucky (the Jackson Purchase) was subdivided into townships by a special state survey, land in Kentucky is described by metes and bounds, not by reference to the rectangular survey system (government survey method).

Land in New Mexico is not surveyed from the Navajo Meridian even though it is located on the northwestern boundary of that state. However, certain land in Arizona is surveyed from this meridian.

Alaska uses the rectangular survey system. Its principal meridians are Copper River, Fairbanks, Seward, Umiat, and Kateel River.

Land in Hawaii is surveyed through the metes and bounds method.

Principal meridians, baselines, and the areas they describe are illustrated as shown above.

Areas in which metes and bounds descriptions are used are left blank.

FIG. 8-3b   GOVERNMENT SURVEY SYSTEM

FIG. 7-4: Government Survey System

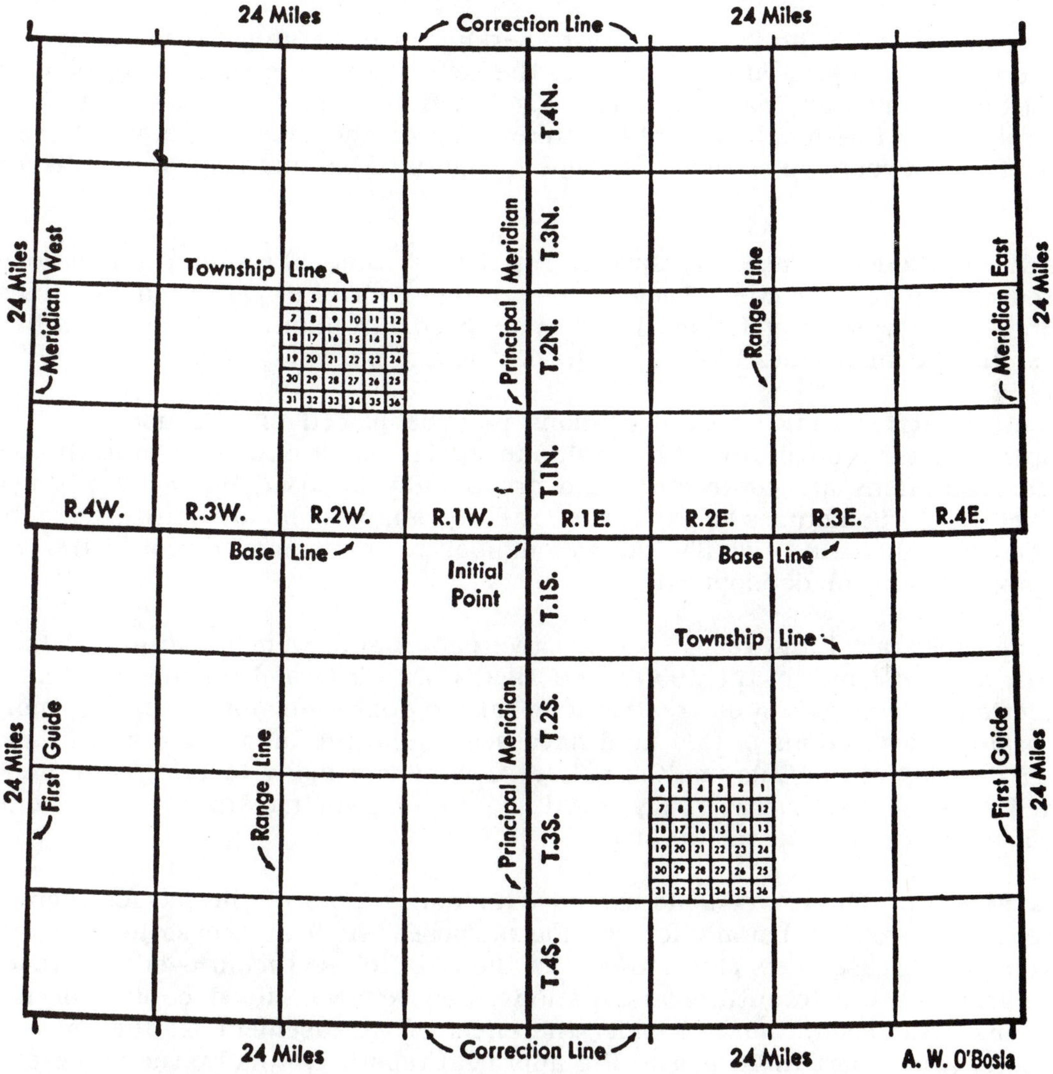

SOURCE: John S. Hoag, *Fundamentals of Land Measurement* (Chicago: Chicago Title Insurance Company).

OTHER TITLE AND RECORD DATA

Ownership information plus data relating to taxes, special assessments, zoning, easements and other restrictions are covered in this section.

OWNERSHIP INFORMATION

A property's legal owner and type of ownership can be ascertained from public records, which are maintained by a county clerk and recorder. Local title or abstract companies may also provide the information.

The most common form of property ownership is ownership in "fee simple". If a property is not appraised in fee simple, the elements of title that are to be excluded must be indicated and carefully analyzed. When an appraiser is asked to estimate the value of a fractional ownership interest, he or she must understand the exact type of legal ownership so that the property rights to be appraised will be accurately defined.

--Building Codes. These are specific restrictions that, like zoning regulations, are based on the police power. They provide design control of permitted buildings and delineate the types of materials that may be used. In addition to a general building code, many communities have separate electric and plumbing codes.

--Deed Restrictions. These limitations may be placed on the use of land by a property owner and will run with the title to the land as it passes on to future owners. Deed restrictions are contractual and are usually imposed by the deeds used to convey title. Sometimes deed restrictions are imposed on an entire tract by the developer of the land. Usually, the goal of such restrictions is to protect the value of all properties in the development.

At one time, racial and religious restrictive convenants were not unusual in single family subdivisions. In the 1930's and 1940's, the Federal Housing Administration sometimes required such restrictions as a condition for granting mortgage insurance. Restrictions of this kind have been unlawful for many years, following a 1948 decision of the Supreme Court, and now violate many federal, state and local Fair Housing laws. Occasionally, deeds containing such restrictive covenants still surface but they are not enforceable.

--Easements. These are rights extended to non-owners of the fee for ingress and egress over property usually for specific purposes, such as access to a roadway or beach. Other easements give non-owners the right to use the air over the property or subsurface rights for utility installations, soil removal, flood control or mineral deposits. Appraisers must consider the effect of an easement on the value of the property and report this effect in the appraisal report. Normally, the value estimate includes the assumption that the property is free and clear of all easements. If this is not the case, the appraiser must take special care to evaluate and report the nature and effect of any easements so that the report will not be misleading.

--Encroachments. Two types of encroachments exist. Either the improvement may extend over the property line onto abutting properties or the improvements on abutting properties may encroach onto the subject site. The appraiser is not expected to make a survey to determine if there are any encroachments. Normally, a statement in the "limiting conditions" section of the report declares that the assumption is that there are no encroachments. However, as with easements, if an encroachment is evident, it must be reported in the appraisal and care must be taken not to mislead a potential user of the appraisal as to the effect of such encroachment.

--Party Wall Agreements.   A party wall exists when improvements are so erected that one common wall is used by two abutting property owners. Many party walls exist without any written agreement. When such an agreement is part of a deed, the appraiser should ascertain whether it imposes any unusual requirements upon the owner of the property being appraised and include this in the report.

--Environmental Restrictions.   Controls on land use are becoming more common and more important to appraisers. Like zoning regulations, they appear to be based on the police power of government, although some of the laws are still being tested in the courts. Appraisers must be familiar with current environmental developments that affect value, including wetland controls, flood hazard area designations and other land use restrictions.

--Riparian Rights.   These deal with the rights of owners whose land abuts a body of water (lake, river, stream, ocean) with respect to the use of the water. These rights may include the right to construct piers, boathouses and other improvements over the water or may be for use of the body of water for fishing and recreational purposes or for irrigation. Riparian rights may have a substantial effect upon the value of the land and must be carefully considered where they apply.

-- Zoning.   Zoning is part of the police power of the government. Zoning gives the public the right to control the uses of private property for the benefit of the entire community.   Zoning as it is known today did not exist during the 19th century, which was the major development period for most American cities. As a result of this lack of control and planning, cities developed with congested streets, overcrowd buildings, poor light and air, and a mixture of uses, each negatively affecting the others. From this disorganization came the deteriorated commercial areas, slums and urban blight of today. Uncontrolled social pressures increased the population density still further, resulting in the construction of large apartment houses that were built to the boundaries of their lots. People with enough money fled the cities into newly developing suburbs. As city redevelopment continues, this trend has reversed. During the 1970s and 1980s there was trend to move back into the cities.

In the early 1900's, Los Angeles and Boston passed laws that controlled the use of land. In 1916, New York City passed the first truly comprehensive zoning law. Included in it were use districts, control of building heights and area coverage regulations. Shortly thereafter other cities passed zoning ordinances that stood up against many court challenges. By the middle of the 1920's the constitutionality of zoning laws, based upon the government's right to use its police power to regulate private property, was well established in legal precedent.

The zoning regulations of the 1920's were primarily concerned with height regulations and front, side and rear yard requirements, to ensure that the population had adequate light and air. By the late 1920's, zoning regulations began to emphasize the separation of residential neighborhoods from commercial and industrial uses. Also, high density apartments were segregated from low density single family areas.

Since World War II a new thrust in city zoning has occurred. These newer zoning regulations emphasize direct control of development and design in an effort to prevent further spread of urban congestion and decay. Zoning often restricts the use of a site that would be physically possible and economically feasible. In such cases, a change in zoning to permit such uses would change the highest and best use of the site. The highest and best use must always be a use that is legally permitted (see Chapter 9), but an appraiser must be alert to potential zoning changes. If there is a reasonable probability that the applicable zoning may be changed in the near future, the appraiser must consider how the market will react. Care must be taken not to anticipate changes that are only speculative. Residential properties are often bought and sold subject to the success of an application for zone change, such as from residential to more intensive apartment use or from residential to industrial or business use. The potential re-zoning of nearby property may have a substantial effect on the value of the property being appraised.

Some suburban communities have attempted to use zoning as a method of preventing further growth, which is accomplished by increasing the minimum lot requirements to sizes greater than necessary for orderly growth. Other requirements making it economically impossible to develop vacant land have been imposed in some areas, but growing social and legal pressures are being applied to stop the use of punitive (or "exclusionary") zoning to restrict community growth.

Ideally, zoning should be used to regulate and promote orderly and consistent development but should not be used to stop expansion. Good zoning fosters sound values, sufficient municipal services such as schools and parks and a climate of orderly growth without the stagnation of highly restrictive regulation.

A new type of zoning classification increasing in popularity is the planned unit development (PUD). Residences are grouped in clusters, with part of the land dedicated to open space for use by everyone. Ownership in the common land may be held by an owners' association or by the community. In its most advanced form, the PUD can actually be an entire city, where some of the non-residential land is reserved for commercial and industrial development as well as recreational and open space use.

Not every community has resorted to zoning to control its development. There are vast areas of the country that are not governed by zoning regulations. Many of these areas are rural or sparsely populated. However, one of the best anti–zoning arguments in the country is the metropolitan center of Houston, Texas. Without zoning, Houston has developed into one of our most modern, exciting cities. The citizens of Houston have voted several times to remain an unzoned community.

The key to Houston's orderly development has been the use of deed restrictions and the enforcement of a rigid building code that includes control of density. By a special act of the Texas legislature, the enforcement of deed restrictions is the responsibility of the city attorney rather than the individual property owner. Deed restrictions are also enforced by the local lending institutions, which refuse to loan money for purposes that violate deed restrictions. In addition, Houston's civic clubs help enforce and police deed restrictions. There are problems, of course. Federal funds for urban renewal were withheld for a time, and in many areas the mixture of uses has caused severe losses in value for adjoining properties. Older residential areas tend to be hastened through the last phase of their life cycle. Still, advocates of non-zoning make a strong case that land values and land uses should depend on the natural highest and best use of property, and not on the misguided whims or outright self-interest of local political appointees.

Any reasonable probability of a zoning change must be considered. If the highest and best use of a site requires a zoning change, an appraiser investigates the probability of such a change. An appraiser may obtain pertinent information by interviewing planning and zoning staff or elected officials. An appraiser may also consult a study of patterns of zoning changes to draw conclusions about the likelihood of a change in a particular instance. If a highest and best use recommendation relies on the probability of a zoning change, that probability must be supported by three elements. These are physical practicality, economic feasibility, and political probability.

ASSESSMENT AND TAXES

Traditionally, a substantial portion of the funds needed by a community to provide services to its citizens is raised by taxes levied on real estate, based on the value of the property, hence the term "ad valorem" taxation.

Taxes are intended to pay for services that make ownership more desirable, but net benefit is obviously decreased when taxes are out of proportion for those benefits. Therefore, the appraiser compares the tax status (assessed values, tax rates, and tax burdens) of the appraised site with that of competitive or comparable sites. In some communities the assessed value of land for tax purposes bears a reasonable relation to market value, particularly when a recent reassessment has been made; but in other communities the assessed value does not have a realistic relation to value.

The first step the appraiser takes in considering taxation is to report the actual assessment and tax rate of the community as it applies to the appraised property. The assessment is often divided between the land and the improvements. Sometimes the site improvements are assessed separately. There may be a single tax rate or a series of separate tax rates to provide segregated funding for education, utilities, etc.

Usually the assessment is supposed to represent some percentage of market value. In communities with efficient assessors and frequent revaluations there is a good relationship between assessments and values. In many communities, however, where the assessor is unqualified, understaffed or not motivated, or where revaluations are infrequent, there may be little relationship between assessments and market values.

Two long-standing traditions exist in the assessment and taxation process. One is that assessments are often a percentage of market value; the second is that the tax rate is expressed in mills rather than as a percentage of assessment. A mill is a tenth of a cent. The "mill rate" is the number of dollars per thousand dollars of assessed value. For example:

Assessment	$1.00
Mill Rate	100 ($1.00 x .100)
Taxes	$ .10
Assessment	$1,000
Mill Rate	90
Taxes	$90

This system is confusing to both the public and the appraiser because it is difficult to readily compare the taxes in one community with those in another. For example, a lot that has a value of $8,000 might be assessed at 70% in one community with a tax rate of 40 mills. Taxes would be calculated as follows:

Market Value	$8,000
Assessment ratio	70% (.70 x $8,000 = $5,600)
Assessment	$5,600
Tax rate	40 Mills
Taxes	$ 224 (.040 x $5,600)

A similar lot valued at $8,000 in another community might be assessed at 35% with a tax rate of 80 mills.

Market Value	$8,000
Assessment ratio	35% (.35 x $8,000 = $2,800)
Assessment	$2,800
Tax rate	80 Mills
Taxes	$ 224 (.080 x $2,800)

In some states, tax rates are expressed in terms of dollars per $100 of assessed value. The above example for this system is:

Assessment	$2,800
Tax rate	$8.00
Taxes	$ 224 (28 x 8)

Widely varying assessment ratios and mill rates can produce the same tax burden on a property, depending on their combined influence. However, far too often a community's supposed assessment ratio (for example, 60% of market value) is actually not in effect. Although legally set at 60%, the actual relationship of the assessed value to market value may be markedly different among similar properties or among different classifications of property.

The second step the appraiser takes is to compare the tax burden on the appraised property to that on competitive properties both in the subject community and in competing communities. One way to accomplish this is to compare the dollars of taxes directly with the market value. This is done by dividing the actual dollar amount of the tax burden on a property by the market value of the property, to give an "effective rate" of taxes.

Market Value $8,000

Taxes $ 224

Tax rate   .028 or 2.8% ($224 ÷ $8,000)

By using this direct comparison method, the appraiser determines how consistent the taxes are within a community are and also how taxation in one community compares with that of competitive communities.

Unit-foot depth and corner premium tables are often used to establish uniformity between assessments in valuations made by assessors for tax purposes. The purpose of such tables is to express equivalent values for one foot of frontage applicable to sites of varying depth. The standard area of land represented has one foot of frontage in a uniform lot width, and a specified depth. For a lot of any stated type or location, a standard depth is established. (It originally was fixed in most localities at 100 feet). For example, if the adopted standard depth is 100 feet, a lot 50 by 100 feet worth $2,175 would have unit-front-foot value of $43.50. Another lot, 50 feet wide and 150 feet deep, might be worth $2,500, or $50 per front foot, with the same unit-front-foot value of $43.50--that is, it would be equivalent in value to $43.50 per front foot for a depth of 100 feet, multiplied by a depth factor of 115%. The percentages are designed to provide a uniform system of measuring the additional value that accrues because of added depth.

One of the first depth rules was the 4-3-2-1 rule which described a system where the front quarter of a lot contributed 40% of the value; the second quarter, 30%; the third quarter, 20%; and the fourth quarter, 10%. Because this left too wide a margin for assessment purposes, the deficiency usually has been overcome by the establishment of more specific depth tables expressed in percentages for every foot, or at least for every 10 feet of depth, to reflect the conditions applicable in a certain locality or for certain types of property (residential, business, industrial, commercial).

Similarly, corner influence (premium) tables have been developed for "ad valorem" tax purposes, to establish the amount by which the market value per unit foot of an inside lot is increased for a lot with a corner location. Such tables are also related to the localities and types of land for which they are prepared.

Appraisers should exercise extreme caution in using any standard depth or corner influence (premium) table. The use of such tables is a major cause of non-uniform assessments. To apply a table established for one neighborhood or community to another area is not good appraisal practice. The only depth tables that might be useful would be those specifically constructed for the community and neighborhood in which the appraised property is located. Assessors are required in some communities to use them to provide equalizations.

SPECIAL ASSESSMENTS

These are levied by a specific district taxing authority for a definite period of time, usually for a public improvement such as sewers, street paving, sidewalk construction, etc. Usually the assessment is based on the benefits derived by the property from the improvement, rather than the cost of providing the improvement to a specific property. For example, it might cost $3,000 to provide sewers for one lot and $1,000 to provide sewers for another lot in the same project area. The amount of the special assessment, however, may well be equal, based on the assumption that the lots would be equally enhanced in value.

When a property is sold subject to a special assessment, adjustment must be made if comparable properties are not subject to the same special assessment. When a property is subject to special assessments that are greater than the value of the benefits derived, the property is reduced in value by the special assessment burden.

PHYSICAL CHARACTERISTICS

Every appraisal must contain an accurate, physical description of the site being appraised. Although much of the data can be obtained easily, some of it may prove to be more difficult to find or be totally unavailable. The appraisal report must state the assumptions that have been made about the nature of the property or site in the absence of precise information. For example, in the case of an unimproved lot, a soil test is usually desirable. In the absence of such a test, the appraiser should carefully point out that assumptions have been made as to the physical characteristics of the soil, and that the value estimate as given may be substantially different if these assumptions do not reflect the actual conditions of the site.

SIZE AND SHAPE

--Width and Frontage. Although width and frontage are often used synonymously, they have two distinct meanings. Width is the distance between the side lines of a lot. When a lot is irregular in shape, the term "average width" is often used. Another important measurement is width at the building line. Many zoning regulations specify a minimum width at this point, which is required in order to permit the use of the site for construction of a particular type of improvement. "Frontage" refers to the length of boundaries that abut a thoroughfare or access way. In the valuation of residential lots, "front feet" are often used as units of comparison, but the importance of frontage appears to vary from one location to another. Care must be exercised in using front footage as the unit of comparison for residential lots. Once a lot meets the standard size acceptable in the neighborhood, excess frontage does not always add proportionately to the value of the lot.

--Depth. Depth is always considered together with the width and frontage of a lot. Most residential neighborhoods have a standard acceptable lot depth so that lots with less depth sell for less, and lots with excess depth sell at a premium. The penalty or premium paid for depth consideration, however, is rarely directly proportionate to the actual footage involved.

The problem of varying and disproportionate increases or decreases in value relative to changes in depth may be analyzed by constructing a table to reflect these value changes. These depth tables are popular with assessors and other mass appraisers who staunchly defend their use, claiming that the tables can be constructed and adjusted to work in different neighborhoods. Theoretically, this may be possible; nevertheless, depth tables have been so widely misused and misunderstood that most professional appraisers avoid using them altogether, unless absolutely convinced that a particular table truly applies to the neighborhood of the property being appraised. Some rules do apply to many residential lots, which the appraiser should know about when considering the influence of depth:

1. As the depth of a lot decreases from that of the typical lot in the neighborhood, its value per front foot decreases, but its value per square foot or per acre increases.

2. As the depth of a lot increases beyond that of the typical lot in the neighborhood, the value per front foot increases, but its value per square foot or per acre decreases.

--**Shape.** The shape of a lot affects the value of the lot differently from one neighborhood to another. In some areas, irregularity of shape may decrease value; in other areas, as long as the lot is suitable for a house, little difference appears to exist between the value of regularly and irregularly shaped lots. If the irregular lot shape results in increased construction costs, however, it would probably decrease the value of the lot. The value of irregularly shaped parcels is usually indicated in dollars per square foot of area or in dollars per acre.

--**Size.** If value were directly related only to size, the unit of comparison (such as square feet or acre) for lot values would always be value per square foot or value per acre. However, frontage, width, depth and shape interplay with size to affect value.

PLOTTAGE

"Plottage value" is the increase in unit value resulting from improved utility when small plots are combined to form a larger one. To accommodate a substantial building development, small plots may be assembled, often from different owners. This procedure usually entails extra costs, and key parcels may need to be purchased for more than their individual land value, either because they are already improved or because of a negotiating disadvantage.

After assembly, the project must support the excess costs of the land in addition to other capital costs involved. It is not the cost of assembly that creates plottage value. Size itself is no guarantee of a plottage increment in value. For plottage value to be realized, there must be the potential of a higher and more profitable use. Otherwise, the whole could not be worth more than the sum of its parts, as is the case with plottage.

The area of a lot can also be divided into its effective area and its excess land. Usually the excess land (particularly if it cannot be used) is worth substantially less per unit of measurement than that part of the lot within the effective (usable) area.

CORNER INFLUENCE

--**Corner and Cul-de-Sac Influences.** Historically, because a corner location provides more light and air and may afford more prominence on a particular street, it was thought to have more value. However, a corner lot also has less privacy and often is taxed at a higher rate. It also may be subjected to more noise and more passing traffic. The appraiser must make a judgment, based on the specific lot and its market, if a corner location adds or detracts from the value when the property is compared with other lots in the neighborhood. Lots located at the end of dead-end streets that have cul-de-sacs for turnarounds also may have different values from similar lots without the cul-de-sac influence. Again, no universal rule applies, and the appraiser must look to the market for evidence of the effects of a specific location on value.

--Contour and Topography. Probably the most desirable residential lot is one that slopes up gently from the street to where the house is located, and then slopes downward steeply enough so that there can be a walkout basement door leading directly to the rear yard recreation area. Again, what is true for one neighborhood is not necessarily the case for other areas. Sites tend to have lower value if they are costly to improve because of extreme topographical conditions. A lot higher or lower than the abutting street level may create additional costs to correct poor drainage, erosion, or accessibility problems. Frequently, however, difficult conditions are offset by advantages recognized in the market, such as a scenic view or extra privacy. Another factor to be considered is the amount of site work required to make the site buildable. If there is bedrock, excess excavation costs may be incurred. In some cases a site may require fill, or it may have excess fill that can be sold.

SURFACE AND SUBSOIL

--Surface Soil. In many areas the soil's ability to support a lawn and landscaping is an important factor in the marketability of the property. An appraiser should note whether the soil appears to be suitable and typical of the surrounding neighborhood. When appraising a new subdivision, the appraiser should determine if the natural surface soil (topsoil) will be replaced at the end of the construction process or whether it is being stripped during site preparation. A trend today among developers is to disturb as little as possible the natural growth and topsoil during the building process. A naturally sandy or rocky soil may require the extra expense of purchased topsoil to support future lawns and landscaping.

--Subsoil. The character of subsoil definitely affects the cost of preparing a site for building; it can also influence the design of the structure that can be erected on the site. If bedrock must be blasted, or if the soil is unstable, the cost of improvements is increased. Soil conditions are usually determined by an engineering study of the bearing quality of the soil and its suitability for foundations. Extra expense is incurred for foundation walls and the sinking of pilings if a site must be filled in. Underground tunnels can present a hazard in mining districts. The appraiser must include a consideration of such possibilities in a thorough site analysis.

LANDSCAPING

--Value of Landscaping. Natural trees and shrubs are usually considered part of the land itself. Landscaping is treated separately by most appraisers as a site improvement. Lawns, shrubbery, gardens and plantings in general improve the appearance and desirability of residential properties. However, because plantings are a matter of individual taste and will deteriorate rapidly without good care, typical buyers are inclined to discount the cost of replacing such plantings especially if they are very elaborate. Although such improvements are usually regarded as an asset, their contribution to the value of a property will vary with location and character.

DRAINAGE

--Surface and Storm Water Disposal. Some method must be provided to drain the site of surface and storm water. It may be a simple swale that channels the water off the surface of the lot to the street or into some natural drainage. When the lot is level or slopes away from the water disposal area, storm sewers must be constructed. In some areas, the leaders or downspouts that collect rain falling on the house may be connected into the storm water disposal pipes. When a house has a basement, footing drains are needed to carry the water from under the basement to prevent leaks from developing. When the house is built on a slope, special care must be taken to keep the surface water away from the sides of the house.

UTILITIES

--**Water.** Every house requires an adequate supply of water of acceptable quality. Water can be obtained from a municipal or private company or from a well. Common sense and the FHA Minimum Property Standards require that when a public water supply is available, it should be used. Some houses still obtain water directly from rivers, streams, lakes and even rain water collected from the roof and stored in tanks. None of these systems is considered satisfactory, since they will not consistently supply an adequate quantity of safe water. When water is supplied by a public or publicly regulated company, the appraiser usually need only check on its availability at the site, including whether there is sufficient pressure. When the water is supplied by a smaller, unregulated company, this must be reported and the dependability of the supply must be analyzed. Wells, either artesian or shallow, should be capable of delivering sustained flow of five gallons per minute. The water should meet the standard bacteriological and chemical requirements of the local health authorities.

When appraising vacant land not on a public water supply, appraiser should check surrounding properties where wells have been dug to determine the probability of an adequate water supply being found for the property being appraised.

--**Sewers.** Few will argue the substantial advantage of being connected to a municipal sewer system. It is estimated, however, that almost 50 million people in 15 million homes depend on septic systems for their waste disposal and that 25% of new houses being constructed do not connect to municipal systems. If no public sewer exists, a percolation test must be made to determine if the soil can absorb the runoff from a septic system.

--**Installation of Public Utilities to the Site.** Included in the value of a site is the cost of bringing water, electricity, gas, telephone, and storm and sanitary sewers to the site. A recent addition to this list is cable television. The site may have additional value because of the availability of these utilities even if they are not connected to the subject house. It is not unusual to find a house still using a well or septic system even where public water and sanitary sewers are available.

ACCESS

--**Streets and Alleys.** A site cannot be used unless there is some type of usable access. It may be a right-of-way over abutting property or a private driveway or street. Access may also take the form of a public street or alley. When access is not by public street, special attention should be given to who maintains the street and if lending institutions servicing the neighborhood will make mortgages on houses without public access.

--**Street Improvements.** The description of a site should also include information about street improvements, such as the width of the street, how it is paved, and the condition of the pavement. In some areas, lenders require substantial details about private streets when they represent the only access to a property. Also reported are details about the sidewalks, curbs, gutters and street lighting.

SITE IMPROVEMENTS

--Other site improvements. In addition to utility connections, which are sometimes classified as site improvements, a variety of other site improvements are typically found on an improved residential lot. These include fences, walls, sidewalks and driveways, pools and patios, tennis courts and other recreational facilities. These all must be described in the appraisal report, and an analysis must be made as to their contribution to the value of the property.

VIEW'S AFFECT ON VALUE

--The view enjoyed from a property may substantially affect its value. Lots in the same neighborhood identical in all respects except location and orientation, have markedly different values which are directly attributable to the effect of superior views. The most popular views are of water, mountains and valleys. Conversely, a poor view reduces value.

HAZARDS AND NUISANCES

--Hazards. Sometimes hazards exist in the neighborhood that reduce the value of a property. The most common hazard is heavy traffic, and the market will definitely recognize and penalize this problem. The awareness of flood hazards has become quite important in many parts of the country now that most lenders cannot issue a mortgage in a flood hazard area without flood insurance. An appraiser must learn whether the site is in an identified flood hazard area, and if so, if flood insurance is available and at what cost. The effect on value must also be considered and reported in the appraisal. Other hazards that should be investigated include potential slides, earthquakes, dangerous ravines and bodies of water, or any unusual fire danger.

--Nuisances. A variety of services contribute to the value of a site when they are in the neighborhood but detract from value when they are too close. For example, a fire house, public school, stores, restaurants, hospital, medical offices and gas stations are desirable nearby but not immediately adjacent to residential property. Industries, large commercial buildings and offices, noisy highways, utility poles and high tension wires, motels and hotels, funeral parlors and vacant houses all generally detract from property values when they are located in a residential neighborhood.

ENVIRONMENT

--Climatic or Meteorological Conditions. Generally, climate affects the whole region or community and should be reported and analyzed in that section of the appraisal report. Sometimes these conditions specifically affect the value of the site being appraised. In some regions there may be an increase in the value of lots that face a certain direction. For example, if prevailing winds are consistent, lots may be favorably or adversely affected by their relation to the direction of the wind.

EXCESS LAND

The portion of land area that provides a typical land-to-building ratio with the existing improvements may be considered an economic unit. Excess land is the portion of a property that is not necessary to serve existing improvements. Assuming that the excess land is marketable or has value for future use, its market value as vacant land constitutes an addition to the estimated value of the economic entity. Therefore, excess land is typically valued separately.

RELATIONSHIP TO SURROUNDINGS

Because the location of a site is fixed, its surroundings have a significant effect on value. Much of this location effect has been covered in the region, community and neighborhood analysis. To be considered here is the relationship of the specific site to its immediate environment.

CONSIDERATIONS

--Use of Nearby Lots. The use of the immediately adjacent lots is of great importance to the value of a property. The principle of conformity states that to obtain maximum value, the improvements of the property being appraised should reasonably conform to those on surrounding lots. For example, if neighboring lots are improved with medium-value, colonial-style, multi-story houses, the appraiser might seriously question the appropriateness of plans for construction of a high-priced, extremely contemporary, split-level on the site being appraised. However, it is not always necessary to conform to obtain maximum value.

--Orientation of Improvements. Again, the principle of conformity applies in the orientation of the improvements. If the abutting houses are set back 75 feet from the street and face out towards it, it will probably be difficult to orient the house on the subject lot differently, even if such orientation (such as with the living/social zones facing towards the rear yard) would seem preferable.

--Abutting and Nearby Streets and Traffic Flow. Abutting and nearby streets may be in the older grid pattern or the newer style of dead-end or limited-access streets. Some streets in a neighborhood will become thoroughfares and suffer from heavy traffic flow. Access by a back alley or a special service road may add to or detract from value, depending on the market.

--Public Transportation. The value of a residential lot is affected by the availability of public transportation. Most important is the availability of such transportation to places of work and shopping, and to recreational areas. Changes in the availability of public transportation can affect the value of property. New systems, such as San Francisco's BART rapid transit system, increase values in the area but deteriorating systems tend to decrease values. The quality and quantity of public highways leading from the property being appraised to places of work, shopping and recreation also have an effect on property values.

--Access by Car. Automobile access to work, shopping and recreation areas substantially affects value. Lots that slope steeply upward towards the street are less desirable than level lots or lots that slope downwards. It is dangerous to have to back into traffic or be forced to enter on a curve or hill where visibility from oncoming cars is limited and the market will penalize a site for these problems.

--Safety of Children from Traffic. The sheer volume of traffic is not the only safety consideration of parents with smaller children. Traffic and speed controls and sidewalks from the site to places such as schools and parks are also important factors. Another important point is the availability of places away from the streets for children to play.

ECONOMIC FACTORS

Many economic factors have already been discussed in the regional, community and neighborhood analyses. Some economic factors apply specifically to the individual site under appraisal rather than to larger areas.

CONSIDERATIONS

--Prices of nearby lots. The price of nearby lots offered for sale has at least a short-term effect on the value of a site. The principle of substitution would limit the price paid for the lot being appraised to that paid for similar lots in the neighborhood at least until the supply was exhausted.

--Tax burden compared to competitive lots. If assessments are not uniform, lots with excessive tax burdens are depressed in value, at least temporarily, by the excess levy. The reverse would also be true; lots that are under assessed might be expected to bring a premium.

--Utility costs. If location necessitates incurring extra costs to bring utilities to a site, the market may recognize a parallel decrease in the value of the lot.

--Service costs. Some lots are not eligible for municipal services such as garbage collection because they are not on public streets. These services must be purchased privately, which would decrease the value of the site, if competitive sites had such municipal services.

SUMMARY

The site data and analysis portion of the appraisal should first positively identify and describe the property being appraised. A deed description and survey, together with a neighborhood and community map, is the ideal way. Other shortcut methods are acceptable only if the property being appraised is positively identified.

Data is gathered and organized into four categories: (1) title and record data; (2) on-site physical characteristics; (3) relationship to surroundings; and (4) economic factors.

All of the data is carefully considered and analyzed in relation to the appraised site. Relevant material is reconciled and processed for use in the highest and best use analysis, which forms the basis of the appraisal.

GRAY
LEDGE
STONE
WALLS

UNSUPPORTED HOOD
OVER FRONT DOOR

PENT ROOF

2½ STORIES

CLAPBOARD ON
ADDITIONS

Colonial American

**PENNSYLVANIA DUTCH COLONIAL OR
PENNSYLVANIA GERMAN FARM HOUSE** (Penn Dut - 110)

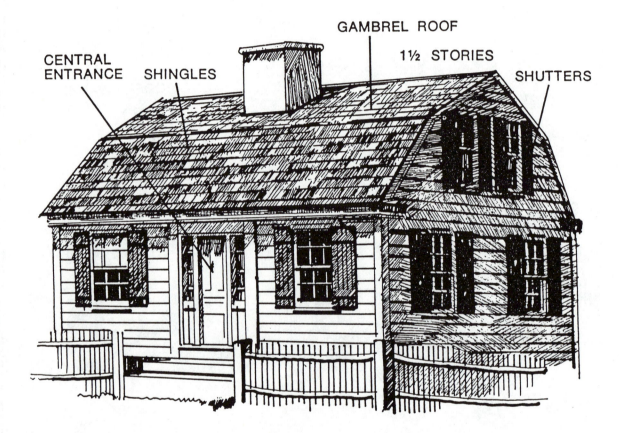

CENTRAL ENTRANCE   SHINGLES   GAMBREL ROOF   1½ STORIES   SHUTTERS

Colonial American

CAPE ANN COLONIAL (Cape Ann - 105)

9 Highest and Best Use

This chapter discusses that highest and best use analysis of the two major elements of a residential property - the site and the improvements thereon. Appraisal theory has long supported the concept of the highest and best use of the site. Only relatively recently has the concept been developed of the highest and best use of improvements on the site - the house, apartment or other major buildings as improved.

For a site to have value, it must have utility and be in demand. In highest and best use analysis, the appraiser considers that use, among all options that most fully develops a site's potential utility. Highest and best use analysis forms the base on which the appraiser builds the three traditional approaches to value.

DEFINITION

Highest and best use is defined as that reasonable and probable use that will support the highest present value, as defined, as of the effective date of the appraisal. Alternatively, it is "that use, from among reasonable, probable and legal alternative uses, found to be physically possible, appropriately supported, financially feasible, and which results in highest land value." Simply stated, the highest and best use of a site is "the perfect improvement that can be constructed on the site which will produce the maximum rate of return on the capital invested."[1]

The second definition applies specifically to the highest and best use of land or sites as though vacant. When a site contains improvements, the highest and best use may be determined to be different from the existing use. The existing use will continue unless and until land value in its highest and best use exceeds the value of the entire property in its existing use plus the cost to remove the improvements.

The determination of highest and best use takes into account the contribution of a specific use to community development goals as well as the benefits to individual property owners. The determination of highest and best use results from the appraiser's judgment and analytical skill - that is, that the use determined from analysis represents an opinion, not a fact. In appraisal practice, highest and best use is the premise upon which value is based. In the context of most probable selling price (market value), another term for highest and best use would be "most probable use." In the context of investment value, an alternative term would be "most profitable use."

---

[1] Henry S. Harrison, *The Residential Appraiser*, Highest and Best Use Analysis of a Single Family House, The Real Estate Appraiser, March/April, 1975, pp. 48-49.

The definitions of highest and best use indicate that there are two types of highest and best use. The first type is highest and best use of land or a site <u>as though vacant.</u> The second is highest and best use of a property <u>as improved.</u> Each type requires a separate analysis. Moreover, in each case, the existing use may or may not be different from the site's highest and best use.

Any determination of highest and best use includes identifying the motivations of probable purchasers. These motivations are based on perceptions of the benefits that accrue to property ownership. Different motivations influence highest and best use and are significant to an appraiser's conclusions about the highest and best uses of any parcel of real estate.

When potential buyers contemplate purchasing real estate for personal use or occupancy, their principal motivations are such user benefits as enjoyment, prestige, or security. Such motivations are particularly evident in the purchase of residential properties. User benefits also apply to commercial and industrial property ownership. Benefits to the owner-occupant include assured occupancy, low management costs, control and potential enhancement as well as future value.

The benefits of investment properties that are not owner-occupied relate to net income potential and to eventual resale or refinancing. The highest and best use decision for investment property is often influenced by tax implications and inflation-hedge aspects of the existing or proposed improvements. Determination of the type and intensity of the improvements which will be the highest and best use of an investor's land requires an "after-tax return" analysis of all reasonable alternatives.

Land or improved property that has resale profit as its principal potential benefit is purely speculative land. The price such land commands in the market reflects the real motivation of the typical purchaser -- speculation.

Highest and best use analysis is always done in two steps. First the site is analyzed as if vacant and the second step is to analyze the property as improved.

HIGHEST AND BEST USE OF LAND OR A SITE AS THOUGH VACANT

For purposes of this analysis, it is assumed that the site has no building improvement. In other words, the problem the appraiser solves is if the site was vacant, what would the best potential use of the site be? What improvements would return the maximum in terms of money and amenities? The appraiser should describe the type of building or buildings and other improvements (if any) which should be constructed on the land if it were vacant.

Not every parcel of land (even those already improved) are economically ready to be developed. In fact, the majority of vacant land falls into this category. In these cases, the correct conclusion is that the highest and best use is to leave the parcel vacant until some time in the future, when it may become economically feasible to develop.

If the conclusion is that the site is economically feasible to develop, the appraiser must conclude which type of improvement with which characteristics should be constructed.

The prevailing use on the site may not be the highest and best use. The land may be suitable for a much higher (more intense) use than the existing use. For instance, the highest and best use of the land as though vacant may be a 10-story office building, whereas the current office building contains only three stories.

HIGHEST AND BEST USE OF PROPERTY AS IMPROVED

The appraiser considers the use that should be made of the property as it exists. Should the 100 year old home be maintained as it is, renovated, expanded, partly demolished, or any combination of these? Or should it be replaced with a use different in type or intensity?

In this context, the use that maximizes the investment property's net operating income (NOI) on a long-term basis is its highest and best use. For uses that require no capital expenditures for remodeling, the net operating incomes estimated for various uses can be compared directly. However, for uses that would require capital expenditures to convert the structure from its existing use to another use, a rate of return must be calculated for the total investment in the property, including capital expenditures. This rate of return can then be compared with rates of return for uses that do not require capital expenditures.

An appraiser's conclusions regarding highest and best use for owner-occupied properties also reflect consideration of rehabilitation or modernization that is consistent with owner-occupant motivations. For example, highest and best use conclusions for a luxury residence would include the amount and type of rehabilitation required for maximum enjoyment of the property.

PURPOSE OF HIGHEST AND BEST USE ANALYSIS

The purpose of highest and best use analysis is different for each type of highest and best use. An appraiser should clearly separate the two types in the appraisal analysis. An appraiser's report should clearly identify, explain and justify the purpose and conclusion for each type. The value of land is always estimated as though vacant. For land that is, in fact, vacant, the reasoning is obvious: an appraiser values the land as it exists. For land that is not vacant, land value is dependent on the uses to which it can be put. Therefore, highest and best use of land, as though vacant, must be considered in relation to a variety of uses, including its existing and all potential future uses.

There also are two reasons for analyzing the highest and best use of a property as improved. The first is to identify the use of property that is expected to produce the highest overall return per dollar of invested capital. The second reason is to help in identifying comparable properties.

RELATION TO ECONOMIC THEORY

Although modern economists have rejected the idea that land or real estate is less entitled to a return than other agents in production, the residual analysis implied by classical economic theory still prevails in highest and best use analysis. Even though land may be as entitled to a return as the other agents in production, buildings can be changed while the essential characteristics of sites cannot. This means that the income potential of any particular site is dependent on the use decision. From an overall or economic, point of view, the fact that one site can be substituted for another means that their returns are established in the general market for sites. For a particular site, however, land value is a function of the income that remains after improvement costs are compensated.

Highest and best use of land as though vacant is an old concept. Highest and best use of a property as improved is a much newer concept. It has evolved since the 1960s to answer two important questions that the older concept does not address. How should the property as improved be used? Should the existing improvement be continued in use, or should it be demolished and a new improvement constructed. The older concept of highest and best use of land as though vacant addresses only the question of how the land should be used if it were vacant; it is primarily a tool for land valuation.

ELEMENTS IN HIGHEST AND BEST USE ANALYSIS

To estimate the highest and best use of a site, the appraiser utilizes four tests. The projected use must meet all four of these tests:

1. Legally permitted.
2. Physically possible.
3. Economically feasible.
4. Most profitable.

Each potential use of a property is considered by the appraiser in terms of these four tests. If a proposed use fails to meet any of the tests, it is discarded and another use is reviewed. The highest and best use meets all four tests.

LEGALLY PERMITTED

Each use must be tested first to see if it is legally permitted on the site. Public legal restrictions consist of zoning regulations, building codes, environmental regulations and other applicable ordinances. Private restrictions are limitations that run with the land and are passed from owner to owner. Generally, they are imposed by the developer of the tract who attempts to preserve the value of the entire development by restricting what can be done with individual lots. Easements, encroachments, party wall agreements and the like also restrict the development of a site.

A gasoline station, for example, may appear to be the highest and best use for a level corner lot at the intersection of two major traffic arteries. The appraiser cannot consider this to be the highest and best use of this site unless it is legally permitted by the zoning regulations currently in effect or there is a high degree of probability that existing zoning can be changed within the near future to permit such development.

Occasionally a site is clearly not being utilized to its highest and best use, not because of any lack of market demand or physical suitability, but solely due to legal restrictions. Since the land is usually zoned according to a political/social scheme, rather than an economic one, zoning frequently does not conform to current market requirements. In such cases, the land remains economically under-utilized until the prescribed limitations are lifted. When the land manifests more valuable potential use than allowed by law and if there is reasonable probability that a change in use will be permitted at some point in the near future, this must be considered by the appraiser.

In such a situation, the appraiser must be extremely careful that the value estimate is not speculative, but rather that the market would widely recognize the strong possibility of a zoning change and that a high degree of probability exists that the zoning can be changed within the very near future.

PHYSICALLY POSSIBLE (SUITABLE)

The use of a site must be physically possible. Uses might be limited by the physical characteristics of a site, such as size, frontage, topography, soil and subsoil conditions and climate conditions. Despite the need for single-family residential housing, an area of severe terrain with poor subsoil characteristics cannot be considered appropriate for such development. For example, sites along earthquake fault lines in California are not considered safe for house construction. Flood plains are also considered unsuitable for house construction. A corridor in the Palm Springs, California, area is considered undesirable because prevailing winds from the coast carry smog and fog.

ECONOMICALLY FEASIBLE

A realistic assessment of market demand for a proposed use is a critical factor. For example, acreage may be available that is zoned for single family residential use of a certain concentration, served by all utilities and with good proximity and access; however, similar subdivisions already in the market have remained unsold for some time. There is no need for the addition of such lots and so even though the property meets the first two tests, it fails economic feasibility.

Thus, market demand acts to create highest and best use. In reviewing alternative uses, the appraiser must consider the demand for each use and the other available competitive land suitable for that use, which constitutes the supply. These factors must be weighed in the economic analysis. All physically possible and legal uses that fail to meet the test of economic feasibility are discarded. The remaining uses produce some net return to the property.

MOST PROFITABLE

The fourth test is essentially a test for maximum return. The appraiser is seeking the most profitable among all legally permitted, physically suitable, and economically feasible uses.

Because change is constantly occurring, the existing use of land is often no longer the highest and best use. If the land alone has a higher value under an alternate physically suitable, legally permitted use than the whole property as currently improved and utilized, the proposed use becomes the highest and best use. The existing improvement is at the end of its economic life but it still will be the highest and best use during the transition period.

For example:

Market value of site zoned for commercial use (highest and best use, as if vacant)	$230,000
Market value of property as currently improved for residential use	$200,000
Contribution of improvement	None

The highest and best use of this property is no longer the existing use, except during the transition period.

TESTING HIGHEST AND BEST USE

To test highest and best use for the land as though vacant or for a property as improved, an appraiser analyzes all logical, feasible alternatives. Usually, the appraiser can reduce the number of such alternatives to three or four uses. Alternative uses must first meet the tests for physical possibility and legal permissibility. The number of uses meeting the first two tests can then be analyzed logically to limit the number of financially feasible alternatives that must be analyzed. For example, a market analysis might indicate need for a large office building in a community. However, if the site being analyzed is surrounded by modern single-family residential developments, a large multi-story office building probably would not be logical even if legally permitted. Similarly, development of housing for the elderly might be permissible for a site, but if most residents of the area are under 40 years old, such development might not be logical and probably would not satisfy the criterion of financial feasibility.

TESTING HIGHEST AND BEST USE OF LAND AS THOUGH VACANT

The following examples illustrate the testing of highest and best use for land as though vacant.

Example #1: Single Family Residence

Once the decision has been made that single family residential use is the highest and best use of a property, the appraiser must describe the "perfect" improvement that should be built on the site. Such a house would take advantage of all the factors analyzed in the community, neighborhood and site sections of the appraisal report. Also considered are the structural type and architectural style of this "ideal" house, its size, number of rooms, layout, quality of construction, kinds of material, mechanical systems and special features.

The principle of conformity tends to set the size, price range and other characteristics of the ideal improvement since houses that are similar to others in the neighborhood will normally have the highest ratio of value to cost. Once the house size has been determined, the structure type should be considered. Generally, single family houses can be classified into one of eight major types. These include 1-story; 1-1/2 story; 2-story; 2-1/2 story; 3 - or more stories; bi-level or split-entry (raised ranch) houses, split-levels and mansions. Two-and three-story houses were popular before 1900 but are not as common today as the split-entry or one-story house.

Once the ideal size and type of house have been chosen, the architectural style should be decided. The neighborhood may call for a traditional colonial look, or one of the popular French or English styles, with special window treatments and exposed half-timbering. In Santa Fe, New Mexico, modern homes in some neighborhoods conform to the highest and best use only if they are built in the accepted pueblo or adobe style. In general, good design produces maximum value, regardless of whether the structural configuration or architectural style of a house is traditional or contemporary.

The next step in highest and best use analysis is to consider the market preferences for interior design. The number of bedrooms, baths and types and sizes of various auxiliary rooms in the ideal improvement vary greatly from neighborhood to neighborhood.

By completing this type of detailed improvement analysis, the appraiser describes the perfect improvement that should be constructed on the site, if it were vacant. If the appraisal is of a piece of unimproved residential land, this would conclude the highest and best use analysis.

Once these decisions have been made the appraiser might finally have to decide how big a house to build. The cost to construct the proposed house is as follows:

> 2,000 Sq. ft. version $48.00 per Sq. ft. $ 96,000
> 2,250 Sq. ft. version $46.00 per Sq. ft. $103,500
> 2,500 Sq. ft. version $44.00 per Sq. ft. $110,000

The value of the site is estimated to be $35,000.

It is estimated that the sale prices of the houses will be as follows:

> 2,000 Sq. ft. version $140,000
> 2,250 Sq. ft. version $155,000
> 2,500 Sq. ft. version $160,000

The calculations to test which proposed house is the highest and best use are:

	2,000 Sq. ft. House	2,250 Sq. ft. House	2,500 Sq. ft. House
Market Value	$140,000	$155,000	$160,000
Cost to Construct	- 96,000	-103,500	-110,000
Site Value	- 35,000	- 35,000	- 35,000
Anticipated Profit	$ 9,000	$ 16,500	$ 15,000

It appears that the 2,250 Sq. ft. house is the highest and best use among the alternatives considered. By constructing the 2,250 Sq. ft. house, the maximum potential profit can be realized. Both the bigger and small houses will potentially produce less profit.

Another consideration the appraiser must take into account is whether the total profit on the investment is high enough to warrant the risk that is incurred whenever one builds new houses on speculation. In this example, the builder must invest $138,500 ($35,000 site plus $103,500 construction costs) to earn $16,500. This is a return on the investment of 11.9% ($16,500 ÷ $138,500). If higher rates of return are available with similar risks then the proposed development is not the highest and best use.

Example #2: Small Income Property

Unlike the first example, where the highest and best use is a single family house and the site value is known, highest and best use here is an income producing property, the value of the site is unknown. Often the purpose of conducting the highest and best use analysis is to estimate the land value. Thus, various permitted uses must be tested to determine which will produce the most <u>residual income</u> after deducting income allocated to improvements for total NOI under each use.

In this example, there is a half acre site zoned residential, multiple family. It is located in a neighborhood with an active rental market. Investigation of the rental market develops the following comparable rental data:

    600 Sq. ft. 1 Bedroom apartments rent for $500 per month
    800 Sq. ft. 2 Bedroom apartments rent for $650 per month
  1100 Sq. ft. 3 Bedroom apartments rent for $725 per month

It will cost the following to construct the buildings:

    600 Sq. ft. 1 Bedroom apartment $45 per Sq. ft.
    800 Sq. ft. 2 Bedroom apartment $40 per Sq. ft.
  1100 Sq. ft. 3 Bedroom apartment $35 per Sq. ft.

In this market, it is estimated that all expenses (fixed, operating and reserves) are 40% of gross rental income. There is enough parking on the site for 12 cars. Zoning requires one space per bedroom. The following are three configurations to be tested to determine which is the highest and best use. The appraiser reduces the choices to some logical alternatives and then assembles data on construction costs, market rates of return and income that can be expected for each alternative use, along with the market capitalization rate for the improvements.

	12 One Bedroom Apartments	6 Two Bedroom Apartments	4 Three Bedroom Apartments
Cost to Construct	$324,000 (600 Sq. ft. x $45 per Sq. ft. x 12 apartments)	$192,000 (800 Sq. ft. x $40 per Sq. ft x 6 apartments)	$154,000 (1100 Sq. ft. x $35 per Sq. ft. x 4 apartments)
Gross Income Potential	$72,000 (500 per month x 12 months x 12 apartments)	$46,800 (650 per month x 12 months x 6 apartments)	$ 34,800 (725 per month x 12 months x 4 apartments)
Estimated Expenses	- 28,800 ($72,000 x 40%)	- 18,720 ($46,800 x 40%)	- 13,920 ($34,800 x 40%)
NOI	$ 43,200	$ 28,080	$ 20,880
Return to Improvements (12%)	- 38,880	- 23,040	- 18,480
Return to Land	$ 4,320	$ 5,040	$ 2,400
Indicated Land Value (at 10%)	$ 43,200	$ 50,400	$ 24,000

According to this analysis, it appears that the 6 two bedroom apartment development is the highest and best use (it is possible that a mixed use building would produce a higher rate of return to the land. With the use of a computer program such as Lotus 1-2-3, all of the possible combinations could easily be tested).

In addition, the calculations indicate that highest and best use is not determined by any single item, such as cost, size, total income, or rate of return. Highest and best use is the relationship among these items that determines the income remaining to the land after the other agents in production contained in the building are allocated their market-determined value.

These items are compensated before land. The tendency is for rents to be lower and expenses to be higher in an older building than in a new building. Thus, the older building would not be replicated on the site if it were vacant. It is only in the case of a new or nearly new building that the residual income to land would be maximized.

TESTING HIGHEST AND BEST USE OF A PROPERTY AS IMPROVED

An analysis of the property as improved should be made to determine if its current use is the highest and best use, or if alternate uses would produce a greater rate of return. When an alternate use produces a higher NOI, it does not automatically mean that this use will produce a higher value. The element of risk must also be considered. Some-times an alternate use can be accomplished with little or no capital expenditures. Others may require substantial expenditures such as rehabilitation or remodeling.

Example #3: No Capital Expenditures

In a college town, many of the property owners are converting their multiple family units from unfurnished apartments rented with one and two year leases to furnished apartments rented to students on an eight month lease. Usually these apartments remain vacant for the balance of the year. Furniture is rented from a local store for $1,200 per year per apartment which assumes the risk of loss or damage to the furniture. Expenses run about 40% of gross income. The vacancy and collection loss is estimated to be 5% for the unfurnished apartments and 10% for the furnished apartments. The six apartments in the building being appraised now rent for $400 per month which is estimated to be their market rent. It is estimated that the market rent of the apartments rented furnished to students will be $800 per month. The calculations for the highest and best use are as follows:

	6 Unfurnished apartments 12 month rentals	6 Furnished apartments 8 month rentals
Gross Income	$28,800 ($400 per month x 12 months x 6 units)	$38,400 ($800 per month x 8 months x 6 units)
Vacancy & Collection Loss	$1,440 (5% Gross Income)	$3,840 (10% Gross Income)
Effective Gross Income	$27,360	$34,560
Furniture Rental	-0-	- 7,200

Operating Expenses	-$11,520 <u>(28,800 x 40%)</u>	-$15,360 <u>(38,400 x 40%)</u>
Net Operating Income	$15,840	$12,000

Thus, it appears from these calculations, that the highest and best use of the property as improved is to continue to rent it as unfurnished apartments.

Example #4: Capital Expenditure Required

A four-family house, each unit with two bedrooms, is located in an area recently re-zoned for high-density multiple dwellings. The owner wants to add a wing to the house. The architect has suggested two plans that meet the new zoning requirement. Plan A will create four additional two bedroom units. Plan B will create six additional one bedroom units. Estimates from local builders indicate that plan A could be constructed for $150,000 and that addition B would cost $200,000.

The property "as is" has an appraised value of $160,000. Vacancy and collection losses are estimated to be 5% in this neighborhood for both one bedroom and two bedroom units. Operating expenses including reserves are 40% of effective gross income. Two bedroom units rent for $550 per month and one bedroom units for $400 per month. The calculations for the highest and best use are as follows:

	Present Use	Addition A	Addition B
	4 Family House	4 Family House and 4 two-bedroom <u>apartment addition</u>	4 Family House and 6 one-bedroom <u>apartment addition</u>
Gross Income	$ 26,400	$ 26,400	$ 26,400
Existing House	($550 per month x 12 months x 4 units)		
Proposed Addition	N/A	26,400 ($550 per month x 12 months x 4 units)	28,800 ($400 per month x 12 months x 6 units)
Potential Gross Income	$ 26,400	$ 52,800	$ 55,200
Vacancy & Collection Losses (5%)	<u>-1,320</u>	<u>-2,640</u>	<u>-2,760</u>
Effective Gross Income	$ 25,080	$ 50,160	$ 52,440
Expenses (40%)	<u>-10,032</u>	<u>-20,064</u>	<u>-20,976</u>
Net Operating Income	$ 15,048	$ 30,096	$ 31,464
Capital Invested, 4 Family House	$160,000	$160,000	$160,000

Addition	N/A	150,000	200,000
Total Investment	$160,000	$310,000 (RD)	$360,000 (RD)
Return on Investment	9.40%	9.71%	8.74%

Thus, it appears from these calculations that the highest and best use of the property as improved, is to build the four, two bedroom apartment addition.

TYPICAL HIGHEST AND BEST USE STATEMENTS

All appraisal reports should contain summary statements that describe the analyses and conclusions for highest and best use of land or a site as though vacant, or of a property as improved, or both if a separate land valuation is included. When the highest and best use conclusion is the primary objective of an evaluation report, the income and return calculations and reasoning should be included. If the conclusion of the highest and best use of an improved property is different from the existing use, similar justification should be included in a market value appraisal report. Whenever the highest and best use conclusions are based on application of techniques to discover the highest and best use among two or more potential uses, the full analysis is included.

In appraisals in which land value is estimated separately, it is appropriate to discuss in the report the highest and best use of the land as though vacant as well as the highest and best use of the property as improved. When land value is not estimated separately and a condition of the appraisal is continued use of the property as improved, the appraiser typically discusses only the highest and best use of the property as improved.

Each parcel of real estate may have one highest and best use of the land or site as though vacant and a different highest and best use of the property as improved. In cases in which an appraiser comments on both highest and best use of the land as though vacant and the property as improved, each highest and best use must be identified separately in the highest and best use section of the appraisal report. First, the highest and best use of the land or site is presented, along with a statement that the determination was made under the theoretical presumption that the land is vacant and available for development. Second, the highest and best use of the property as improved is given, along with a statement that the determination was made according to the future potential of the land and improvements as existing.

If the land is already improved to its highest and best use, the two statements may be combined. But the report should state specifically that the determination is the same for both the land as though vacant and the property as improved, or that the land is improved to its highest and best use.

The report also should identify the highest and best uses, both vacant and improved, of the comparable sales. If the improved comparables have different highest and best uses of the land if theoretically vacant and of the improved property as existing, this must also be explained. The difference could affect value, especially in the sales comparison approach.

The following examples, two for a single family residence and two for an income-producing property, illustrate highest and best use statements. Obviously, the actual statements for any particular appraisal would be tailored to the situation.

Example #5: Single Family Residence - Highest and Best Use of Land as Though Vacant

This type of highest and best use is employed to estimate the value of land separately from improvements. It recognizes that any significant elements of accrued depreciation would not be replicated if the land were vacant and a new building were constructed on the site. It is also helpful in identifying comparable properties, which is why it is used in this appraisal.

The existing structure is not the highest and best use of the land as though vacant. The house was constructed approximately 10 years ago and contains measurable elements of physical deterioration and functional obsolescence, as do most structures after they are two or three years old.

If the site were vacant, a new single family residence would be its highest and best use. The new house would be more architecturally compatible with other houses in the neighborhood. It would contain approximately 2,000 square feet and would include three bedrooms and two baths. The living room would be larger. The house would have more electrical outlets. All elements of physical deterioration would be eliminated.

Example #6: Single Family Residence - Highest and Best Use of Property as Improved

This type of highest and best use recognizes that existing improvements should be continued in use until it becomes financially advantageous to demolish the structure and build a new one or to remodel the existing one. The existing use of the property as a single family residence is its highest and best use of the property as improved. No other use of the property would be so beneficial or profitable.

The existing structure is well maintained and is in good repair. It has an effective age of about 8 years and a remaining economic life of approximately 50. The structure fits well in the neighborhood, which is zoned for single family residential occupancy only. The structure was designed as a single family residence, and no other use would be legally or financially feasible.

Example #7: Income-Producing Property - Highest and Best Use of Land as Though Vacant

The existing structure is not the highest and best use of the land as though vacant. This type of highest and best use recognizes that any significant elements of accrued depreciation would not be replicated if the site were vacant and a new building were constructed. The income allocated to the land under highest and best use is capitalized to estimate the value of the land separately from the improvements. (At this point, an appraiser might state: This valuation procedure is shown in the section entitled Land Valuation.)

If the site were vacant, a new apartment building would be its highest and best use. It would contain 12 apartments, the maximum number permitted by zoning for this site. Each apartment will contain a living room, dining room, kitchen, bathroom, lavatory and two bedrooms.

Each apartment will be 1,025 sq. ft.   The building will be cement block construction with brick veneer exterior walls, frame subfloors, and flat, built-up roof. The building will be two stories with 6 apartments on each floor. It will be set in the middle of the site allowing for an attractive front yard, parking on both sides for 30 cars and a rear yard with recreational facilities for children.   All physical deterioration would be eliminated in a new building, and its functional layout and design would be consistent with modern apartments of this type.

Example #8: Income-Producing Property - Highest and Best Use of Property as Improved

The existing use of the property as rental units should be eliminated and the building should be converted into 10 condominium dwelling units.   The property currently contains 10 apartments that have a high vacancy rate during the past five years. The units require renovation and remodeling to remain competitive in the local housing market.   However, the amount of money necessary to make these renovations and remodeling will make the property uneconomical to maintain as rental units as the rent that would be required is above what can be obtained for this type of property in this market.

The following calculations show the existing capital investment and additional capital investment required for the existing use and for conversion into condominiums.   It shows the return estimated for the current use and the profit anticipated from a condominium conversion.

Type of Use	Present Use	Proposed Conversion
	10 Rental Units	10 Condominiums
Present Capital Investment	$300,000	$300,000
Renovation and Modernization	+$250,000	+$325,000
Total Capital Investment	$550,000	$625,000
Net Operating Income	$40,000	N/A
Overall Return	7.3%	N/A
Selling Costs & Legal Expenses	30,000	75,000
Total Investment	$580,000	$700,000
Estimated Selling Price	$485,000	$800,000 (10 units @ $80,000)
Profit (Loss)	($ 95,000)	$100,000

The figures indicate that continuing the use of the property as rental units would not produce a satisfactory return on the investment, with the needed renovation and remodeling costs. The investment produces 7.3% in a market that expects at least 10% for this type of property. Conversion into a condominium project would produce an estimated $100,000 profit which is considered satisfactory, for this type of project.

SPECIAL SITUATIONS IN HIGHEST AND BEST USE ANALYSIS

The basic premises of highest and best use analysis that have been discussed in the preceding pages are fundamental to all studies of the uses to which vacant land and sites or improved properties may be put. However, unique considerations in identifying and testing highest and best uses are necessitated by single use properties, interim uses, legally nonconforming uses, nonhighest and best uses, multiple uses, special purpose uses, speculative uses, and excess land. The special requirements for highest and best use analysis, in each of these situations, are discussed in the following sections.

SINGLE-USE SITUATIONS

The highest and best uses of land or sites as though vacant and properties as improved are generally consistent with and similar to surrounding uses. For example, single family residential use is usually not appropriate in an industrial neighborhood. Nevertheless, highest and best use may be an unusual or even a unique use. For example, demand may be adequate to support one large multi-story office building in a community, but inadequate to support more than one. A special purpose property, such as a museum, may be unique and highly beneficial to the site but not justifiable for surrounding land uses or comparable properties. The land value will be based on its highest and best use.

INTERIM USES

Often the appraisal is of an existing house that has not reached, but appears to be reaching, the end of its economic life. It may be an older house, in an established neighborhood of older homes, conforming substantially to the houses in the neighborhood. As with the analysis of the site as if vacant, the appraiser must determine what the perfect improvement for the site is. However, the appraisal must consider utilization of the existing improvements to obtain the maximum profit. If there is a house on the site, the appraiser must estimate what can be done to make it the most profitable use of the site. Any improvement that will add more value than the cost to produce it should be considered in the analysis. These improvements might range from simple repairs to major remodeling, modernization or rehabilitation.

An existing use may be nearing the end of its economic life but still be the highest and best use of the site at this point in time. If the existing house still contributes to the overall value of the total property, it continues to have utility. For example:

Market value of property as currently improved for residential use $26,000

Market value of a site zoned for commercial use (highest and best
use, as if vacant)   23,000

Contribution of the structure $ 3,000

Although the highest and best use of this property as if vacant is different from the existing use, the old residential structure continues to add to the total value of the property. Thus, the existing residential use is the best use of the site for the remaining economic life of the structure.

Frequently, a site is improved with a building that is at the extreme end of its economic life. Such use is often an *interim use*, a temporary use of the property, until, the time when the ultimate highest and best use can be attained. A downtown property utilized as a residence may not appear to be the highest and best use of the land but it may still contribute enough additional income to the owner to justify its continuation as a tax payer while plans and financing arrangements are completed for more profitable development in the future. In an area where demand has not created an active market, an interim use may be necessary to hold the property until a more favorable market response is noted. A parcel of land suitable for a residential subdivision, for example, may be marginally farmed, until such time as the residential housing market will support the cost of its conversion to several new building lots.

LEGAL NON-CONFORMING USES[2]

A legal non-conforming use is a use that was lawfully established and maintained, but no longer conforms to the use regulations of the zone where it is located. This kind of use frequently results from subsequent zoning or a change in the zoning ordinances. Zoning changes may create underimproved or overimproved properties. A single-family residence located in an area that is subsequently zoned for commercial use is an underimprovement. In this case, the residence will most likely be removed so that the site can be improved to its highest and best use, or the house will be considered an interim use until converted to commercial use.

Non-conforming, overimproved property results when zoning changes reduce the permitted intensity of property use. For example, an old country store may be included in a neighborhood that is zoned for low-density residential use. Non-conforming uses may also result from changes in the permitted density of development and changes in development standards that affect features such as landscaping, parking, setbacks, and access. Zoning ordinances vary with the jurisdiction; they usually permit a pre-existing use to continue, but prohibit expansion or major alterations that support the non-conforming use. When the non-conforming use is discontinued or terminated, it usually cannot be re-established.

When valuing land with a legal non-conforming use, an appraiser must recognize that the current use may be producing more income, and thus have more value, than the property could produce with a conforming use. It may also produce more income and have a higher value than comparable properties that conform to the zoning. Therefore, to estimate the value of a non-conforming property by comparing it with similar, competitive properties in the sales comparison approach, the appraiser should make an adjustment to reflect the higher intensity of use allowed for the subject property.

In most non-conforming use situations, the property value estimate reflects the non-conforming use. Land value, however, is based on the legally permissible use, assuming that the land is vacant and its value can be deducted from the total property value. The remaining value reflects the contribution of the existing improvements and possible bonus for non-conforming use. The appraiser may find it helpful to allocate value separately to the non-conforming improvements and the bonus created by the non-conforming use.

---

[2]*Appraising Real Estate,* 9th Edition, American Institute of Real Estate Appraisers, Chicago, IL 1988.

Usually, any bonus resulting from a non-conforming improvement and use is directly related to the existing improvements. Therefore, the extra income or benefit should be capitalized over a time period that is consistent with the economic life of those improvements.

Often, legal non-conforming uses that correspond to the highest and best use of the property as improved are easily recognizable. Sometimes, however, it is not clear whether an existing non-conforming use is the site's highest and best use. The question can only be answered by carefully analyzing the income produced by the non-conforming use and the incomes that would be produced by alternative uses if the property were brought into conformity with existing regulations. Some jurisdictions specify a time period for phasing out legal non-conforming uses. In most jurisdictions, a non-conforming use must be eliminated if the property suffers major damage.

Uses That Are Not Highest and Best

The theory of consistent use is basic to appraisal practice and highest and best use analysis. A property nearing transition to a new use cannot be valued on the basis of one use for land and another for improvements. The improvements must add to the value of the land in order to have value attributed to them.

The land is always valued first, and as if vacant. If the buildings existing on the site add to the value of the overall property, even if their presence restricts it to a less intensive use, the existing use continues to be (potentially) the highest and best use. Only when no value may be attributed to such improvements or they represent a negative value (burden) to the property, does an alternative use become the highest and best use.

An illustration of the violation of the consistent use theory in valuing a site is shown in the following example. A turn-of-the-century house is located on a corner lot, where both main thoroughfares are moving to nonresidential uses. Recent rezoning permits business use and the corner being considered is classified to permit the construction of a gasoline service station. The house (converted to apartments) is still being used.

An uninformed appraiser learns from the market that such corners have been selling as service station sites for $70,000. Then, in violation of the consistent use theory, the appraiser adds to site value a value for the existing building of $30,000 for a total of $100,000. The correct consideration is to accept the $70,000 for the site "as if vacant." To make it vacant, demolition costs of $5,000 are estimated. The market value of the site in its highest and best use, therefore, is $65,000 ($70,000 - $5,000).

Multiple Uses

Highest and best use often includes more than one use for a parcel of land or for a building. A larger tract of land may be suitable for a planned unit development, with a shopping center in front, condominium units around a golf course and single family residential sites on the remaining portions of the land. Industrial parks often have sites for retail stores in front and warehouse and light manufacturing structures in the rear. Farms often have family homes, storage areas for crops and equipment, and facilities for raising animals and crops.

Moreover, the same land may serve multiple functions. Lands for timber or pasture may also provide space for hunting, recreation and mineral exploration. Land that serves as a right-of-way for power lines can double as open space or a park.

Buildings can have multiple uses. A hotel may contain a restaurant, a bar, and retail shops as well as guest rooms. A multi-story building may contain offices, apartments, and retail stores. An office building may contain retail stores and a restaurant, as well as offices. A single family, owner-occupied home may contain an apartment upstairs, or a professional office.

An appraiser can often estimate the contributory value of each use on a multiple use site or in a multiple use building. For example, if the market value of a timber tract that can be leased for hunting is compared on a unit basis with another timber tract that cannot, the difference should be the value of the hunting rights. In oil-producing areas, a common problem for appraisers is to segregate the value of mineral rights from the value of other uses of the land. Certain properties may have mineral rights value; others may not. In all such appraisals, an appraiser must make sure that the sum of the values of the separate uses does not exceed the value of the total property.

SPECIAL PURPOSE USES

Special purpose properties are appropriate for one use or for a very limited number of uses. Thus, an appraiser may encounter practical problems of specifying the highest and best uses of such properties. The highest and best use of a special purpose property as improved is probably its current use. For example, the highest and best use of a plant currently used for heavy manufacturing is usually to continue in heavy manufacturing. The highest and best use of a grain elevator probably is to continue as a grain elevator.

In certain cases, if the existing uses of special purpose properties are physically or functionally obsolete and no alternative uses are feasible, the highest and best use of the property as improved may be scrap or salvage.

Sometimes an appraiser needs to make two appraisals of the same special purpose property: one on the basis that a purchaser could be found who would use the property for its existing use, and the other on the basis that a purchaser would use the property for an alternate purpose. This type of analysis may be required because the owner of a large, special purpose property decides to abandon the property to consolidate operations. In such cases, it is usually not possible to determine, in advance, whether a purchaser can be found who has a need for the special purpose features of the improvements.

SPECULATIVE USES

Land that is held primarily for future sale may be regarded as speculative land. The purchaser or owner may believe that the value of the land will appreciate, but there may be considerable risk that the expected appreciation will not occur within the time the speculator intends to hold the land. Nevertheless, the current value of the land is a function of its future highest and best use. In such cases, an appraiser should discuss potential future highest and best uses. The exact future highest and best use may not be predictable, but often the future type of highest and best use (such as a shopping center or industrial park) is known or predictable because of zoning or surrounding land use patterns. In addition, there may be several potential highest and best uses, such as single family or multifamily residential developments. Appraisers usually cannot identify future highest and best uses with much specificity, but they can discuss logical alternatives and general levels of projected incomes and expenses.

As noted previously, interim uses may be the current highest and best uses of properties, for which highest and best uses are expected to change in the foreseeable future. Such properties may derive the greatest value contribution from the future highest and best use. Nevertheless, the interim use may also contribute to present value.

EXCESS LAND

Many parcels of land are too large for their principal highest and best uses. Land, in addition to that which is necessary to accommodate a site's highest and best use, is called excess land. Such parcels may have, in effect, two highest and best uses; the primary highest and best use and the highest and best use of the remaining, or excess land. In many cases, the highest and best use of excess land is for open space, or non-development. In other cases, the highest and best use may be for some less intensive use. In any event, an appraiser should treat parcels having excess land as two separate parcels. The land that supports the site's primary highest and best use usually has a higher unit value than the excess land, which is valued separately.

Land that is required to support the primary use, such as a parking lot for an office building or a playground for a school, is not excess land. Only land beyond the normal needs of a particular use, as determined in the market, can be considered excess land. Some atypically large sites cannot be considered as having excess land because the acreage that is beyond the normal needs of the particular use cannot be separately used. For instance, the overly large lot in an area that is 100% built up or a site that cannot be divided because of the location of its buildings are not considered to have excess land. An appraiser should clearly identify any land that is considered excess and indicate a separate unit value. The appraiser should then add the value of the excess land to the value of the primary parcel to obtain the value of the entire parcel.

SUMMARY

To determine highest and best use, the appraiser first analyzes the site as if vacant and determines what the perfect improvement for such a site would be. Four tests are applied to the proposed uses. Only the use that meets all four tests (legally permitted physically possible, economically feasible and most profitable) is the highest and best use.

Next the appraiser analyzes the property as improved. If the value of the site and its improvements, maintained in its present use, is less than the value of the site if vacant and available for alternative use, the present improvements are no longer the highest and best use. If the present improvement, in its existing program of utilization, produces a higher value for the property than if the site were vacant, the current use is potentially the highest and best use.

The appraiser must analyze the existing improvements to see what rehabilitation, modernization or remodeling is needed to produce the maximum profit (see Chapter

10). The improvements, when renovated, would be the highest and best use of the property, "as improved."

Finally, several special situations may necessitate unique considerations when identifying and testing highest and best use. These include single use situations, interim uses, legal non-conforming uses, uses that are not highest and best, multiple uses, special purpose uses, speculative uses and excess land.

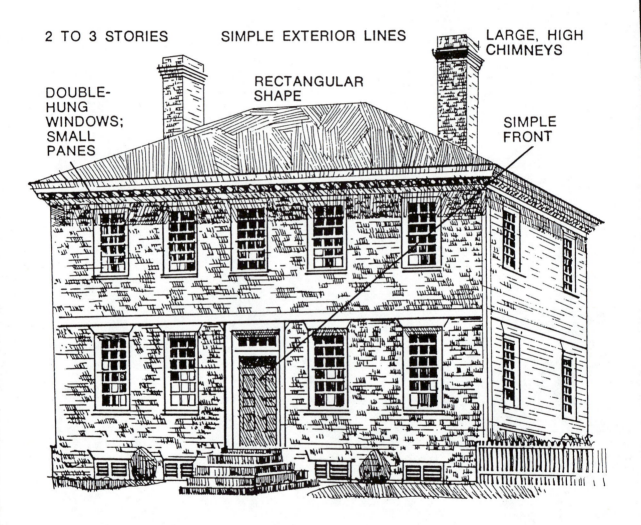

2 TO 3 STORIES

SIMPLE EXTERIOR LINES

LARGE, HIGH CHIMNEYS

DOUBLE-HUNG WINDOWS; SMALL PANES

RECTANGULAR SHAPE

SIMPLE FRONT

English

WILLIAMSBURG GEORGIAN OR EARLY GEORGIAN
(Williams or E Georg - 204)

10 Site Valuation

PURPOSE OF SEPARATE SITE VALUATION

It has been argued that once the site is improved with a structure, a separate site valuation is difficult, if not impossible and unnecessary. The claim is that only a total property valuation is possible in such cases and that the two units are inseparable. In spite of the theoretical merits of this argument, there are many practical reasons for making separate site valuations even when the property is already improved.

Separate site valuations are required by statute in most states for "ad valorem" (real estate) tax purposes. The assessed value is almost universally split between the land (or site) and the improvements. Special assessments for public improvements, such as streets, water lines, and sewers are often based on their estimated effect on land or site values. Income tax preparation also requires that the cost of a property be split between the improvements and the site. The first step of the cost approach is to estimate a separate market value of the site. Separate site value estimates are also commonly used for establishing condemnation awards, adjusting casualty losses, deciding whether to raze existing improvements to free the site for a new use, or establishing site rentals.

There is no single accepted manner in which to organize and present the necessary site valuation data; however, the following example lists the four categories of material in the order they would normally be collected.

1 . Title and record data.
2 . On-site physical characteristics.
3 . Relationship to surroundings.
4 . Economic factors.

SOURCES OF DATA

The sources of market data are varied. They differ by community and the character and location of specific properties. The most direct and thorough approach is to interview the parties involved in the transaction -- the seller, buyer, and broker. By talking directly to individuals, the appraiser can gain information about conditions surrounding the sale that may have influenced the transaction. A good deal of information may be revealed in the recorded instruments of conveyance and other public records on file with the local record office. Such records may identify the buyer, seller, mortgagee and trust deed holder and provide an accurate and complete legal description. Other data, such as sales price, encumbrances and approximate date of sale are also available. In some circumstances, deed restrictions and other limitations on the use of the property are found as part of these records.

Often real estate professionals other than appraisers can provide valuable background material as well as market data. Bankers, savings and loan executives, real estate brokers and mortgage bankers may be able to provide a clear picture of local real estate market activity and can contribute information reflecting the conditions surrounding specific sales which have been chosen for use in the direct sales comparison approach.

A large number of publications and professional information services are available, which serve as another excellent data source. Multiple listing systems (MLS), for example, usually contain records of all the activities of members in a local real estate board. Valid information on listings, offers and final sales prices is available from most MLS services. Certain government agencies (FHA, VA) maintain records of the prices, conditions, sizes and other pertinent information about the housing stock and sales in their jurisdiction.

PROCEDURES FOR ESTIMATING VALUE

Five basic procedures for estimating market value of individual residential sites are:

> 1. Sales Comparison Approach.
> 2. The Allocation Procedure.
> 3. Extraction Method.
> 4. Capitalization of Ground Rental.
> 5. Land Residual Technique.
> 6. Subdivision Development

SALES COMPARISON APPROACH

The Sales Comparison Approach is based on comparing and contrasting pertinent data on comparable sites that have actually sold with the site being appraised. It is the most popular and practical site valuation procedure. The appraiser may also consider offering and listing prices and other market information, but primary attention is given to actual sales of like sites, consummated under typical market conditions as close to the date of the appraisal as possible. Sellers may offer a property at any price they choose, and potential purchasers may bid any price they like; but the actual selling price of a site (a figure acceptable to both buyer and seller) best reflects market conditions.

Market value is intended to describe the results of the interaction of buyers and sellers operating in an open market, all parties being knowledgeable, willing and able. Thus, having exposed the real estate in the open market for a reasonable period of time, the result is an agreed-upon price that is recognized as market value.

The Sales Comparison Approach results in the development of market values of sites by converting sales prices for comparable sites (and sometimes other evidence) into market value for the site being appraised.

Appraisers are cautioned to consider and, if possible, adjust for any unusual pressures present in sales being used as market data. Obviously, the threat of foreclosure, the need to sell or buy rapidly or changes in local zoning regulations resulting in different potential uses all have a strong effect on selling price. Also, prices paid by federal or local governments usually are not acceptable as open market transactions because of the possibility that compulsion was involved, which eliminates the willing buyer-willing seller concept.

CLASSIFICATION AND ANALYSIS OF DATA

All pertinent market data regarding comparables should be organized so that it can be retrieved quickly in a format that promotes easy and accurate comparison with the residential lot being appraised. To qualify as an acceptable comparable sale, the details of each transaction must be verified. Hearsay evidence is not sufficient since the bona fide nature of each comparable must be clearly established. The use of key-sort record cards is a practical and efficient technique. A more expensive method is the computer which provides instant and comprehensive recall of all stored facts. Many professional appraisal organizations are moving toward the development and use of elaborate computer systems.

The process of comparing the property being appraised with others in the market always involves two components - elements of comparison and units of comparison. A standard format is recommended to better organize the comparison process.

ELEMENTS OF COMPARISON

Appraisers use six elements of comparison when considering the comparability of sites. These are:

1 . Financing Terms.
2 . Conditions of Sale.
3 . Market Conditions (Time).
4 . Location.
5 . Physical Characteristics.
6 . Income Characteristics.

Financing Terms

The sale prices of similar properties may differ because financing arrangements vary. If conventional financing is typical for the type of site in question, comparables with 100% financing, conditional sales contracts or other than conventional financing, require special analysis and judgment. If such special conditions produce a price different from that which would have been paid with conventional financing, an adjustment must be made. The conditions of financing, which include the amount of interest charged, the length of the mortgage and the ratio of loan to value, must be analyzed for every sale. When there are substantial differences between the comparables and the property being appraised, either a percentage or dollar adjustment must be made. This must be extracted from the market and requires thorough and complete analysis of the circumstances involved.

Conditions of Sale

This element of comparison is probably the most difficult to extract from the market and to make adjustment for. It refers to the circumstances under which both buyer and seller make their decisions to purchase and sell a specific residential site. By definition, market value requires a willing, informed and able purchaser and a willing and informed seller. Quite often, however, and probably more frequently than is generally realized, there are more than normal compulsions to buy or sell. An obvious situation of unusual pressure is bankruptcy.

The conditions of sale element is often difficult to prove in the market. Even if certain conditions are recognized, it may be difficult to apply an appropriate or justifiable dollar or percentage adjustment for the differences between the property being appraised and the comparable in the market. Some professional appraisers feel strongly that if the conditions of sale are different from those applying to the property being appraised, the comparable should not be used. Others feel that if reasonable adjustments can be made for conditions of sale, it is permissible to use the comparable to reach an indication of the market value of the subject site.

Market Conditions (Time)

The process of comparing the date of the appraisal with the date of sale of the comparables recognizes that market conditions do change from time to time. This process determines if the comparable sale took place under the same or similar market conditions. Sometimes market conditions remain relatively stable for a year or more; at other times they may change within a three- to six-month period, or even less.[1] The interaction of demand and supply affects prices; if one or the other or both change, prices adjust accordingly. In either a sellers' market or a buyers' market, price changes occur. This is the type of phenomenon that the appraiser must investigate, identify and compensate for.

Judgments regarding the element of time of sale are made by a close study of market conditions at the time of the appraisal, compared and contrasted with those at the time of the sale of the comparable. If the comparable was sold in a market similar to that prevailing at the time of the appraisal, no adjustment need be made. If, however, the appraiser recognizes that market conditions varied considerably between the two dates, an adjustment must be made.

The simplest example is that of a residential site which sold one year ago in an open market situation after a reasonable listing period. Then, for justifiable reasons, it sold again just two months ago for $1,200 more than the earlier price. This illustrates a singular example of the change in the market between two time periods, as expressed by the difference in two sales prices. It also illustrates the kind of process the appraiser must apply to identify dollar or percentage adjustments between markets. An intimate knowledge of the market is necessary to establish the amount of the adjustment. Continuous collection and storing of such data are essential to help appraisers reach defensible conclusions.

Location

The fourth element of comparison is that of location. Much emphasis has already been made of the importance of neighborhood influence on marketability of sites.

---

[1] In the process of analyzing the differences in the market from the time of the appraisal to the time of the sale, strange phenomena may be encountered. One may tend to think that market prices and costs are even and steady in their change -- that is, going up 4% per year, or remaining the same throughout the year, or declining 2% per year. This, however, may not be realistic. Markets are known for their erratic activity in short periods of time; such activity may be cyclical, seasonal or a combination of both. There may be short periods of time in an annual market period that will have very erratic activity, but the average for the whole year would not identify them. For example, average increase for the last calendar year may be 6%; however, closer scrutiny reveals that all of this was experienced in the last quarter of the year. Use of sales data from the first three quarters would have to be adjusted accordingly. Thus the monthly average increase is not 1/2% nor is each quarterly average increase 1-1/2%.

Chapter 6 outlined in detail the physical, social, economic, and governmental factors to be considered in analyzing neighborhoods.

If a comparable site is in the same neighborhood as the appraised site, then there is a likelihood that no neighborhood adjustment would be made. In rare instances, if it were on the edge of a neighborhood and subject to either some beneficial or undesirable elements, neither of which affected the site being appraised, an adjustment would be made. If the neighborhood has been properly identified, it is unlikely that differences in schools, parks, and other kinds of important neighborhood considerations will be found.

In the event that a site being considered as a comparable is located in a different neighborhood from the property being appraised, a more thorough analysis must be made of possible differences between the two neighborhoods. Two separate neighborhoods may be very similar in all respects and no adjustments will need to be made. On the other hand, if there are major differences between the two neighborhoods, appropriate adjustments must be calculated.

For example, the neighborhood of the appraised site may be served by excellent schools in close proximity to the site. In contrast, the comparable may be located in a neighborhood with less desirable schools much farther away. The market typically would recognize both factors and pay accordingly. To estimate the difference in price for these two variations, the matched pair system can be used. That is, the comparable in a different neighborhood is compared with an identical site that has sold in the subject's neighborhood. If the former has a lower sale price, this is an indication of the difference the market recognizes in the two neighborhoods because of the school situation.

Many other kinds of neighborhood differences, such as variations in deed restrictions, zoning and building codes must be considered and if they are recognized by the market, an adjustment must be made.

Physical Characteristics

In this comparison process only major physical similarities and differences are identified and considered. A physical inspection of each comparable is desirable. The appraiser must be reasonably well-informed about the basic soil conditions and physical characteristics of the comparable sites so that justifiable adjustments can be made between them and the property being appraised.

If a great number of physical differences exist between the properties, the sale probably should not be used as a comparable. If there are none or only a few such differences, it may be a justifiable and usable comparable.

The same procedure is followed for determining the amount of adjustment for differences in physical characteristics as for the other elements of comparison. Professional appraisers rely heavily on the local, active market from which to extract dollar (or percentage) adjustments. The "matched pair" technique may be used.

If there are two lots which are comparable in all respects except depth, one lot having 20 extra feet of depth, which sold for $250 more than the other lot, it is reasonable to conclude that the market paid $250 more for the extra depth of 20 feet. Such conclusions, however, should be supported by more than one pair of sales. The greater the number of sales to support dollar (or percentage) adjustment figures, the more convincing the appraiser's conclusions. The market will also consider the situation of a lot with area that does not serve the improvements and becomes excess land.

When necessary, pairs of sales can be used to extract adjustments from the market even when there are two or more differences between the sales. One sale is selected as a base sale and all known differences between it and the other sale are adjusted for. The remaining difference is then attributed to any remaining unadjusted difference between sales.

Among other items to be considered are such things as:

1. Inside lot compared to a corner lot.

2. A rectangular lot compared with an odd-shaped lot (five or six sided).

3. Difference in storm water disposal (One area has no facilities; another is well-drained by storm sewer. The market probably would recognize this difference).

4. Difference between a lot which is flat and relatively easy to build on and one which drops 20 feet below the street level.

Income Characteristics

There are a few markets where there is an active residential land rental market. The largest probably is Hawaii. When sites that are in such a market are analyzed, it is appropriate to make comparisons and adjustments based on the property's income characteristics.

TECHNIQUES OF MAKING ADJUSTMENTS

In the past there have been a variety of techniques for making adjustments. Now the URAR has become universally accepted so most appraisers make adjustments according to the instructions which are printed on the URAR. It states: "The undersigned has recited three recent sales of properties most similar and proximate to subject and has considered these in the market analysis. The description includes a dollar adjustment, reflecting market reaction to those items of significant variation between the subject and comparable properties. If a significant item in the comparable property is superior to, or more favorable than, the subject property, a minus (-) adjustment is made, thus reducing the indicated value of the subject; if a significant item in the comparable is inferior to, or less favorable than, the subject property, a plus (+) adjustment is made, thus increasing the indicated value of the subject."

For example, a lot being appraised is considered to be $500 better than Comparable A because of physical terrain. If Comparable A sold for $6,000, the adjustment would be made as follows: The comparable sale is poorer than the subject lot therefore, a plus adjustment of $500 is made to the comparable sales price of $6,000 giving an indicated value for the lot being appraised of $6,500 ($6,000 + $500). It is necessary to remember that an unfavorable element of the comparable property becomes a plus adjustment in the comparison process.

It is essential to remember that adjustments are being made to the comparable for the justifiable difference between the comparable and the property being appraised. In this manner, the comparable is being made as much like the property being appraised as possible.

SEQUENCE OF ADJUSTMENTS

A sequence for making adjustments is required whenever percentage adjustments are used, either solely or in combination with dollar adjustments. An appraiser obtains intermediate price figures and applies succeeding adjustments to each prior adjusted figure. The sequence, which includes all percentage adjustments, appears below:

Element of Comparison	Adjustment	Adjusted Price
Sale Price		$100,000
Special Financing	- 5%	-5,000
Adjusted Price		$95,000
Special Conditions	+10%	+9,500
Adjusted Price		$104,500
Market Conditions	+10%	+10,450
Adjusted Price		$114,950
Location	+ 5%	+5,745
Physical Characteristics	-10%	-11,495
Indicated Value of Subject Property		$109,200

The first adjustment is for special financing which is applied to the transaction price. The adjustment reduces the price for which the property would have sold under normal market financing.

Next any adjustment for special conditions of sale is made. The appraiser should indicate they have considered conditions of sale even when no adjustment is required by entering a zero in the appropriate place. The resulting adjusted price at this stage in the sequence reflects the amount for which the property would have sold under normal financing and sale conditions.

Next, the appraiser adjusts for market conditions. Presumably, the market conditions adjustment has been derived from properties that sold under normal financing and similar conditions of sale. The adjustment would be distorted if applied to an actual transaction price that includes non-market considerations. The adjustment for market conditions results in a figure that represents what the comparable would sell for at the appraisal date under normal financing and conditions of sale.

Next, the appraiser applies adjustments for location and physical characteristics to the time-adjusted normal price. These adjustments account for the differences between the comparable and the subject property. They are applied to the price of the comparable that would pertain at the date of the appraisal under normal financing terms and sale conditions. After all adjustments are made for locational and physical characteristics, the resulting figure is called the adjusted sale price. It is the price that as realistically and accurately as possible reflects the price for which the comparable property would sell on the date of the appraisal if it were exactly like the subject property. It is thus a value indication for the subject property.

Note in the example on the previous page that if the percentage adjustments were added together and the resulting percentage was applied to the transaction price, the adjusted sales price would be $115,000; that is, +25% -15% = +10%. This procedure would result in an error of almost $800 or almost 1%. Obviously, errors could be larger or smaller in situations in which a sequence is not used.

Although a sequence is not required when only dollar adjustments are made, its use is recommended in all applications of the sales comparison approach.

In deriving and applying adjustments, appraisers should always state the percentage relationship of the subject to the comparable. For example, the appraiser should state that the subject property's location is 10% better than that of the comparable, or that the quality of construction of the subject is 5% inferior to that of the comparable. The price of comparable is known; the price or value of the subject property is not. It is incorrect to state a percentage relationship in terms of the unknown.

UNITS OF COMPARISON

Adjustments for differences between the site being appraised and the comparables may be made in dollars or in percentages. If dollar adjustments are used, they may be based on either the total price of the whole property or on the other units of comparison, such as price per square foot, price per front foot (designated F/F), price per acre or per dwelling unit permitted by zoning on the site. Depending on local custom and practice, units of comparison may be used rather than total price of the whole site. A reference to $100 per F/F for a site is more specific and understandable than $10,000 for the site. It is sometimes easier to make adjustments using units of comparison than the whole price of a lot.

A front-foot unit of comparison can be used appropriately even if the front footage of the site being appraised and that of the comparable are not identical. This system automatically takes care of the difference as long as the two lots have basically the same utility. In circumstances where major frontage differences exist, the square-foot unit of comparison may be preferable. Another unit of comparison for residential lots is an acreage unit for larger estate-type sites.

Percentage as well as dollar adjustments may be used. Like dollar adjustments, percentages may be used to recognize differences in market conditions from one time to another. If it is evident from empirical evidence that single family lot prices increased by 10% from last year to this year, a 10% adjustment is applicable to the lot being appraised in comparison with the sale of a year ago.

RECONCILIATION OF ADJUSTED SITE SALES PRICES

The next step is to reconcile all the adjusted comparable sales prices into an indicated value of the site being appraised. Use of a simple arithmetic average of the value indications is not acceptable appraisal practice. Averaging small groups of numbers produces a meaningless measure of central tendency, which may or may not reflect actual market value. The accepted procedure is to review each sale and judge its comparability to the property being appraised. The final value is based on all the information available to the appraiser.

When a unit of comparison is used, two extra steps are needed. First, the adjusted unit sales prices are reconciled into a single (or range of) adjusted sale prices per unit. Then the number of units in the site being appraised is multiplied by the value (or range of values) per unit to give an indicated value (or range of values) of the site.

For example, assume the indicated value of the site being appraised is $100 per F/F, based on the reconciled adjusted sales prices of comparable sites. If the site being appraised has 75 front feet, its total value is $7,500 (75 F/F x $100 per F/F). If the indicated value of the site was $.10 per square foot and the site has 80,000 square feet, its indicated value is $8,000 ($80,000 sq. ft. x $.10 per sq. ft.).

For both dollar and percentage adjustments, the amount of adjustment should be extracted from the market in a valid manner. In some instances, adjustment amounts may not be available from the market. If so, either a logical judgment must be made regarding the amount of the adjustment or the sale must not be used as a comparable.

THE ALLOCATION PROCEDURE

A relationship exists between the application of the agents of production and the market value of a site. This is confirmed by the application of the principles of balance, contribution, surplus productivity and increasing and decreasing returns. Therefore, site value can be estimated by allocating the total sales price of a comparable between its two utilitarian and productive parts--the lot and the improvements. The appraiser determines what portion of a property's sales price typically may be allocated between the lot and the improvements, estimating the market value of the house and other improvements first. The balance (residual) is allocated to the site.[2]

Statistics shown in the U.S. Census reports demonstrate the relationship between sale price and site value of residential properties. The statistics are presented on a national and regional average. The older the improvements, the higher the ratio of land value to total value. The typical ratio can be affected by a lot of unusual size or characteristics, and by building costs.

To estimate the value of unimproved property in an area where vacant land sales are lacking, the appraiser can allocate from the total sales price of a comparative property the part that could reasonably be assigned as building value. The remainder, except for intangibles, is the site value.

For example, assume that a property with a 1,500 square foot house sold for $175,000. The appraiser estimates the depreciated cost of the house at $100 per square foot, or $100,000. The remainder ($75,000) is the residual price of the site, assuming that the house represents typical or highest and best land use and that no extraneous considerations were involved in the transaction.

EXTRACTION METHOD

The extraction method also involves an analysis of improved properties. The contribution of the improvements is estimated and deducted from the total sales

---

[2]The National Association of Home Builders reports that land cost, which was about 11% of the cost of a new home just after World War II, has risen to 35% today.

price to arrive at a sales price for the land. This technique works best when the contribution of the improvements to the total price is small.

CAPITALIZATION OF GROUND RENTAL

The ground rental attributable to a property can be capitalized into an indication of the value of a site. This procedure is useful when comparable rents, rates, and factors can be developed from an analysis of sales of leased land.

LAND RESIDUAL TECHNIQUE

The land residual technique can be used for both improved and unimproved sites.

When the site is improved the value of the improvements is subtracted from the total value of the property to give an indicated value of the site. This works best when the value of the improvements is a small percentage of the total value of the property.

The value of the property is determined by capitalizing the property's income stream. When the income stream is capitalized it is divided into that which is attributable to the improvements and that which is attributable to the site. The capitalized value of the income attributable to the site indicated the value of the site.

This technique can also be used to estimate the value of unimproved sites. The appraiser decides what is the highest and best use of the site. Then the cost of the projected improvements is estimated

VARIATIONS IN THE PROBLEM: VALUE FACTORS

The same fundamental principles underlie all site valuation procedures; however, the key factors that influence the utility and value of a given site vary with the type of property being appraised. For example, heavy pedestrian traffic would tend to increase value in a retail business site but might lower value in a residential area. The aesthetic considerations and amenities that are important in establishing the value of a residential site might have little relevance to the value of a commercial site.

Value factors differ according to the type of land use. For instance, in a residential area the primary value factors may include convenient location to schools and shopping, amenities available in the neighborhood, or the beauty of the site. In an industrial development, the key value factors may be availability of raw materials, zoning regulation or proximity to transportation. Next the projected NOI for the projected is estimated and divided between the improvements and the site. The income that is attributable to the site is capitalized to indicate the value of the site.

SUBDIVISIONS

Special techniques are used to estimate the value of land that is suitable for subdivision into individual lots.

STEPS OF SUBDIVISION ANALYSIS

Subdivision development analysis consists of five steps.

1. Estimate the size and number of the subdivided lots.

2. Estimate the value of the finished lots by sales comparison.

3. Estimate the development costs, the development schedule, the anticipated selling period, and a reasonable entrepreneurial profit.

4. Subtract all development costs and the entrepreneurial profit from the anticipated gross sales price to derive the net proceeds of sale after development is complete and the individual lots have been sold.

5. Select a discount rate that reflects the risk incurred during the anticipated development and selling period. Discount the net sales proceeds over this period to obtain the present value of the raw land.

Determine the Number and Size of the Lots

All physical, legal, and economic factors must be considered. Legal limitations are imposed by subdivisions and zoning regulations. Projected lots must conform to requirements concerning size, frontage, topography, soil quality, and site improvements such as water facilities, drainage, sewage, and streets and curbs. The physical advantages and disadvantages of the subdivision site can be ascertained with the help of a survey and engineering studies. A reasonable estimate of the size and number of lots can sometimes be deduced from zoning and subdivision ordinances, or from the number of lots created in subdivisions with similar zoning. Most importantly, the size and arrangement of the lots should conform to market standards.

Estimate the Value of the Finished Lots

By analyzing appropriate comparables from existing, competitive subdivisions that have recently been developed, an appraiser can obtain an indication of the value of the finished lots.

Estimate All Development Costs

All costs associated with the development and sale of the improved lots must be calculated. These include the engineering expenses to clear, grade, and finish the land; to build streets, roads, and sidewalks; and to install utilities. There are also carrying charges for taxes, insurance premiums, and inspection fees and expenses for sales commissions and advertising.

The development and selling period must then be projected. The longer a property stays on the market, the greater the costs and risks to the developer.

Estimate the entrepreneurial profit that will be realized by the developer if the project is successful. This is included among the costs to develop the land.

Deduct Development Costs

Subtract from the estimated value of the finished lot all the development costs including interest during the holding period, selling costs and entrepreneurial profit.

Discount Income Stream

The income stream that results from the sale of the lots is discounted to present value.

Select an Appropriate Discount Rate

The income stream from the sale of the lots is discounted to present value. The rate should be high enough to reflect the high risk of land subdivisions.

FIG. 10-1 EXAMPLES OF A SUBDIVISION ANALYSIS

A developer is planning to subdivide an eight-acre tract and develop 32 residential lots. The anticipated gross sales price of the finished lots is $800,000 ($25,000 x 32 lots). The following development and absorption costs will be incurred.

Site development costs for grading, clearing, paving, and curbing; sewage and water lines; and design engineering	$300,000
Management and supervision	20,000
Contractor's overhead and profit	100,000
Sales expenses	30,000
Carrying charges (e.g., taxes, insurance)	20,000
Entrepreneurial profit	60,000
Total Costs	$530,000

It is estimated that the developer will sell on the average of one lot per month and therefore receive $25,000 per month. This is discounted to present value at an interest rate of 12%. The present worth of the income stream of $25,000 per month for 32 months discounted at 12 % is $681,739.74 $680,000 (rounded)

The estimated value of the undeveloped land is $150,000

This is a simplistic method of subdivision analysis.   A better method is it determine on a month to month basis the inflow and outflow of the investment made by the developer taking into consideration how the borrowed funds will be released when the expenses will be paid and in which months the sales will take place.   By discounting the positive and negative monthly cash flows a more accurate estimate of the value of the property may be obtained. The techniques of Yield Capitalization are covered in more detail in the *General Certification Supplement.*

SUMMARY

In theory the supply of land is limited. Actually, the majority of the land in the United States is undeveloped and will remain so for the foreseeable future. What gives land value is its specific utility and demand.

The highest and best use of the land or site determines the crucial value factors for consideration in each individual case.

Of the six procedures for site valuation, the comparative process is basic. If the comparative sale is typical, the appraiser compares it with the site being appraised in terms of time, location, physical characteristics and conditions of sale. Adjustments are made to develop an indicated market value for the site being appraised.

Techniques for making adjustments for differences between the site being appraised and comparables, illustrated in this chapter, show that adequate support from the marketplace is essential in developing such dollar or percentage figures.

Other procedures can be used when comparable sales data are lacking or when circumstances limit their application. However, all of these procedures are derived form the three approaches to value.

The allocation procedure is helpful in existing neighborhoods and as an aid to the comparative process.

The extraction procedure deducts the contribution of the improvements directly from the total property value similar to the allocation procedure.

The value of land can be estimated by capitalizing the ground rent. It requires that both market rent and a capitalization rate be estimated by the appraiser. This procedure is most useful when they land is of a type that is typically leased.

The land residual technique can be used for both improved and unimproved sites. It works best when the value of the improvements is a small percentage of the total value of the property.

The value of the property is determined by capitalizing the property's income stream. When the income stream is capitalized it is divided into that which is attributable to the improvements and that which is attributable to the site. The capitalized value of the income attributable to the site indicated the value of the site.

Subdivision analysis requires special techniques. It is incorrect to base the value of vacant land directly on the value of the projected finished lots without deducting all the costs of subdivision including entrepreneurial profit. The income stream must also be discounted to present value.

CHIMNEYS
AT ENDS

SHINGLE COVERED GABLE ROOF

UNFINISHED LOGS

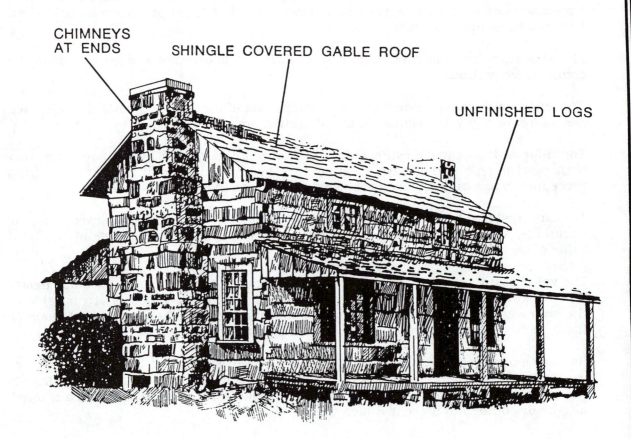

Colonial American

LOG CABIN (Log Cab - 115)

11 Specific Data Collection and Preliminary Analysis

The entire appraisal process is dependent upon the collection and analysis of data from the market. All three approaches to value are really market approaches and depend upon market data.

This chapter presents methods by which Specific Data is collected, screened and analyzed. The final analysis of the data takes place in the improvement description and analysis and in the three approaches to value portions of the appraisal.

Specific Data is the basis of the three approaches to value. The process of extracting relevant material from the vast array of available market data helps an appraiser to develop a perception of the market. The validity of the final estimate of value depends on the extent to which it can be supported by data.

Specific Data is analyzed through the process of comparison. The key to comparison is locating data that provides the information needed to apply the correct techniques in each of the approaches. A number of different data sets may be needed to extract all information pertinent to the appraisal problem. For example, if the subject property is an apartment building of three-bedroom units, the appraiser may be able to base adjustments for time of sale, location and physical characteristics on information from comparable sales of similar apartment buildings. However, it may be necessary to analyze data on competitive properties that have not sold recently to obtain adequate rental rates and expenses for apartment buildings in the area.

INVESTIGATION OF MARKET TRANSACTIONS

A study is made to find those comparable sales and listings whose costs, income and expense information are similar to the property being appraised. Generally, the more current the comparable data and the more similar it is to the property being appraised, the better it will be as an indicator of the value of the property being appraised. Often more sales and listings and other data are considered than are finally used in the appraisal.

COLLECTING DATA

The accuracy of the value indication via the sales comparison approach depends upon the quantity and quality of sales, offerings and listings data for competitive properties.

The selection of the appropriate data first depends upon a detailed description and classification of the subject property's characteristics and components. The information obtained in the land and building analysis help the appraiser select the data to be used in the sales comparison, income and cost approaches.

It is only after a complete analysis of the property being appraised that an appraiser can select the data that is most similar to the subject property.

In selecting market transactions for analysis, an appraiser eliminates transactions that are not pertinent to the specific market for the subject property. For example, when an appraiser considers a 10-year-old single family residence that has three bedrooms, two baths, and 1,800 square feet of livable area, he or she usually eliminates two- and four-bedroom houses if there is sufficient data concerning three-bedroom house sales. The appraiser would also probably ignore the sales of 25- or 30-year-old houses, and possibly the sales of new homes. If sufficient sales remained, sales of houses smaller than 1,600 square feet or larger than 2,000 square feet might be rejected. The first determinant of the data that are ultimately used is the quantity of data that is available.

When comparable sales data in the area is limited, an appraiser may have to extend the data search to adjacent neighborhoods and communities that are similar to that of the subject property. When the selection of data is still limited to an unacceptably narrow sample of current market activity, the appraiser may decide to use sales that are less current and to interview brokers, buyers, sellers, owners, and tenants of similar properties in the area to discover evidence of potential market activity - that is, listings of offers to sell and offers to purchase. These may also be used as comparables if the proper adjustments are made.

An appraiser learns broad information about the market from the pattern of sales. Important information can be revealed by the:

1 . Number of sales.
2 . Period of time covered by the sales.
3 . Availability of property for sale.
4 . Rate of absorption.
5 . Rate of turnover (volume of sales, level of activity).
6 . Characteristics and motivations of buyers and sellers.
7 . Terms and conditions of sale.
8 . Use of property before and after the sale.
9 . Other significant characteristics.

In analyzing available data for the selection of comparable sales, an appraiser begins to form certain conclusions about the general market, the subject property, and the possible relationships between the data and the subject property. The appraiser begins to ascertain market strengths and weaknesses; the probable supply of, demand for, and marketability of properties most similar to the property being appraised; and the variations and characteristics that are likely to have the greatest impact on the value of properties in the market. Thus, an appraiser does not analyze market data in a vacuum. He or she analyzes data against a background of information about the specific area and the specific type of property, as well as the current market.

LOCATION OF SALES DATA

Through a sound collection program, a large bank of market data can be accumulated in the appraiser's own files and organized to serve the appraiser's needs most effectively. Only some of the data may be immediately pertinent; the remainder may be collected, filed and cross indexed for future use. Records should carry the address, a file number, and additional salient information. Sales information is often collected and recorded on a standardized sheet. As the system grows, an indexing system must be devised to facilitate data retrieval. Many offices are using computers for data storage, retrieval and analysis.

--Public records. An appraiser searches public records to acquire a copy of the property deed. Deeds provide important information about the property and the sales transaction. The full names of parties to a transaction and the transaction date are cited on the deed. A legal description of the property is provided, as are the property rights included in the transaction, as well as any outstanding liens on the title.

Occasionally, full names give clues as to unusual motivations for the sale. For example, a sale from John Smith to Mary S. Jones may be a transfer to a daughter, or a sale from John Smith, William Jones, and Harold Long to the SJL Corporation may not be an arms-length transaction.

Statutes in some states require that the consideration paid upon transfer of title be shown on the deed. However, it is not always dependable as a reflection of the sales price because some purchasers deduct the estimated value of personal property (e.g. in motels or apartments) from the true consideration in order to reduce transfer taxes. These personal property values are sometimes inflated, making the recorded consideration for the real property less than the true consideration. Occasionally, the indicated consideration will be overstated in order to obtain a loan higher than actually justifiable, or understated in order to justify a low property tax assessment. Although some states require that the true and actual consideration be reported on the deed, other states allow the consideration to be reported as "$1.00 and other valuable consideration."

Records of the local tax assessor may include property cards for both the subject property and comparables, with land and building sketches, areas, sale prices, and so forth. In some localities, legal or private publishing services issue information about revenue stamps and other pertinent facts about current transfers.

--Real Estate Newspapers. Real estate newspapers concentrate on people making real estate news, major sales and leases and new construction; they often have information about subdivisions, condominiums and other developments that would be difficult to obtain elsewhere.

--Commercial Publications. In some areas, special commercial publications give sales and rental information along with other business news. Although they usually report only the information available from the recorded deeds and leases, they are an excellent source for locating comparable sales.

--General Circulation Newspapers. Daily newspapers often publish information pertaining to real estate transfers as well as proposed developments, zoning changes and other general real estate news. Many weekend papers carry special real estate supplements or sections. The classified advertisements are a good source of information about properties for rent and for sale.

--**Realtors and real estate brokers** provide a good source of data. Especially in areas where other sources are not available, the appraiser may elect to use the files of individual brokers, which are often elaborate and accurate. Brokers are a particularly good source of rental data and information about listings and unsold houses.

--**Sharing sales data is traditional among appraisers**. Working with other professionals saves considerable duplication of effort and increases the quality of everyone's work. Some appraisers charge each other for exchanged sales data. Exchanges of data should not be viewed as a substitute for personal research.

--**Property managers and bankers** often have information about real estate transactions and may give leads to important facts.

--**Multiple Listing Services.** These can be a bountiful source of information because they often require a detailed description of the listed property. There can be pitfalls in using this information however. Adjectives used by brokers and sales people to describe property conditions are sometimes different from those used by appraisers. "Average" to an appraiser should mean a house that is typical of its market, one whose effective age is approximately the same as its actual age (see Chapter 12). A broker or sales person might describe the condition of the same house as "good" or "very good". They may say a substandard house is "fair", and one that is not even habitable may be called "poor". Houses rated by an appraiser as "above average" may be called "like new", "excellent" or "A-1" on the MLS card. Another problem with MLS information is that functional and economic obsolescence is rarely accurately described. Square foot measurements, if shown, may prove to be inaccurate or may not be the gross living area figure used by appraisers. Finally, conditions of sale are rarely indicated. Once the MLS is used to locate a sale, the property should be personally viewed by the appraiser to obtain needed information.

--**Deeds** are a traditional source of sales information but their main contribution is in reflecting the existence of a sale. They usually contain only the address of the property, a legal description (this is part of a good positive identification), names of grantors and grantees, and the date of title transfer (which is sometimes a substantially different date from the actual date of the closing). In some areas, deed records also show the sales price (or have tax stamps affixed, which indicate the sales price) and the terms of the financing, but it is imprudent to rely upon this data alone as comparable sales data.

--**SREA Market Data Center.** The Data Center is an independent nonprofit organization, sponsored by the Society of Real Estate Appraisers. It is a good source of data particularly when it represents a sufficient percentage of the sales in the market. Data is collected on a standardized form (primarily from lending institution appraisers), processed through a central computer and displayed in printouts prepared at regular intervals. Because input is made by appraisers, the description of condition is in appraisal terminology, with at least some functional and economic obsolescence identified. There may be an indication of unusual conditions of sale. This service assists appraisers in identifying potential comparable sales. When a sale is selected, it should be inspected and the data verified by the appraiser.

--**Listing and offers.** Whenever possible, an appraiser should accumulate information on listings of other properties offered for sale. The appraiser can request that his or her name be added to the mailing lists of banks, brokers, and others offering properties for sale. Classified ads also provide information on properties being offered for sale. In addition to providing asking prices, the ads give some measure of the strength or weakness of the local market for a particular type of property. Offers to purchase are also useful information which may be obtained from brokers or managers. Listings are generally higher than the eventual transaction price; offers are generally somewhat lower.

--Government, FHA, VA and Private Mortgage Insurers. The FHA and some private mortgage insurers are good sources of data. Like lending institutions, they often have appraisals in their files for recent sales, which contain good, accurate information.

--Mortgage Loan Records. An excellent source of information, often overlooked by appraisers, are the records of lending institutions. They usually include appraisals of nearly every property for which a loan application has been made. Many lending institutions make this information available to bona fide appraisers.

--Title Companies. Title company data ranges from complete descriptions of houses to information similar to that found on deeds. Even companies that have nothing more than deed information may be helpful, if they file information by street rather than chronologically, as is done in most deed recording offices.

--Assessment Records. A cooperative, knowledgeable assessor with up-to-date records can be a major asset for the appraiser. A good set of assessor's records contains an accurate description of the property. Many assessors, however, inspect properties at intervals of 10 years, and the descriptions may not include recent improvements. Many assessor's measurements are quite accurate. Although they may not use gross living area calculations, their measurements can usually be converted to such figures. Appraisers must resist the temptation, however, to depend on the assessor's description and measurements without personally viewing the property.

--Atlases and Survey Maps. These give data on lot size, relate legal descriptions to street numbers and frequently show building locations and dimensions to scale.

--Transfer Tax Records. Some communities keep separate records of transfer taxes. The main advantage of this information is its accuracy and ease of use, particularly if it is filed by street.

VERIFICATION OF SALES DATA

Each sale used as a comparable in an appraisal report should be personally inspected and the data confirmed with the buyer, seller or broker. The appraiser must be assured that all depreciation has been considered, the measurements are correct and the reported price and terms are accurate.

Verification and inspection processes do more than confirm the accuracy of the data gathered. They also provide for exploration of the motivating forces involved in a sale. Were both buyer and seller acting without financial pressure? Was the sale an "arms-length" transaction, or were the parties related in some way? Were both buyer and seller knowledgeable about the property and market in which the sale took place? Did the seller have reasonable time to sell and the buyer to buy? Were there any special concessions granted by either party? Was financing typical of the market, or was there a purchase money mortgage, second mortgage, assumed mortgage or other unusual situation? Were there any other special sale conditions such as inclusion of personal property in the sale (furniture, above-ground pools, boats, automobiles, sports equipment, etc.)? Was there any special government program involving a subsidy, attractive financing terms or guarantee of payment?

Sometimes an owner sells for less than expected if allowed to continue to occupy the property for a substantial period of time after the transfer of title. Sometimes a sale is the result of an option granted in the past when different market conditions prevailed, resulting in a sales price that may not be typical of the current market. These are only some of the possible conditions that might make the reported sales price different from the market value. Only by personally interviewing the buyer and seller or broker can the appraiser gain knowledge about such conditions.

FILING SALES DATA

A common characteristic among successful appraisers is a filing system where they collect comparable data as it becomes available and store it in an organized manner until such time as they need it for an appraisal assignment. The method of storing this data ranges from index cards to modern computer data banks.

Most of the stored data falls into two broad categories:

1 . Data obtained from published records, MLS services and other sources which provide information about properties which have <u>not</u> been inspected by the appraiser.

2 . Data developed as part of the process of making appraisal reports which contain detailed information about properties that have been inspected.

File Storage System Office

How the data is indexed depends on the type of practice the appraiser has and the volume of data being stored.

An appraiser who specializes in small residential properties and who collects large amounts of data may first divide the data by community and then by type of residential property. An appraiser with less extensive data may elect to put all the residential property together, making the initial division by property category.

One such classification of residential property is as follows:

> Single Family Residences
> Small Income Properties (2 to 12 family)
> Apartments (over 12 families)
> > Garden type
> > High Rise
> Individual Condominium
> Condominium Projects
> Cooperatives
> Mobile Homes
> Timeshare Units
> Residences on Leased Land

Resort and Recreation Houses
Housing for the Elderly
Farm and Ranch Houses
Mansions
Historic Homes
Experimental Houses
Solar Houses

It is appropriate to cross reference data on some properties. For example, a single family solar home would be filed both under single family residences and solar houses.

Appraisers who have practices that include other types of properties would establish similar filing systems for commercial, industrial, agricultural and special purpose properties.

INVESTIGATION OF ADDITIONAL MARKET DATA

The investigation of the market extends beyond the determination of available comparable sale properties. Useful specific data is obtained by investigating properties that are similar to and competitive with the subject property, even though such properties have not sold recently. Information used in applying the cost and income capitalization approaches must often be sought from market sources other than sales. Such information may also be useful in refining adjustments made in the sales comparison approach. In the investigation of general and neighborhood data, an appraiser learns significant information on trends regarding such items as construction costs, lease terms, typical expenses, and vacancy rates. Investigation of these trends provides additional specific data needed to derive value indications through the three approaches.

IMPROVEMENT COST DATA

Several reliable sources for obtaining cost data exist.

--Cost Data File. The use of square foot cost estimates involves assembling, analyzing and cataloging data on actual house costs. An appraiser should have comprehensive current cost information for the types of houses and other improvements, including data on current material and labor costs. A system of grading quality of construction may also be used to refine the data further. This data can often be obtained from local builders, lenders, material suppliers and trade associations.

A file of this kind provides a check against costs of reproducing or replacing an existing residence as well as against known or projected costs for existing or proposed houses of varying grades of construction. It also provides a check against the probable cost of different components of a house.

--Cost Services. Several recognized cost reporting services are also available to the appraiser. Some include illustrations of typical structures and provide adjustments to tailor the standard example to differently shaped or equipped residences. Some provide adjustment for individual cities or areas. Some show cubic foot costs, some square foot costs, and some are designed for unit-in-place information.

--Cost Indices. A cost index service reflecting the relative cost of construction over a period of years is also useful. When the actual cost of a residence constructed some years ago is known, application of the index will indicate the present construction cost (provided the actual cost was a typical figure). For example, assume that a house cost $53,000 to build in January 1955 and that a 1955 cost index from a national service was 284.4 . The April 1977 cost index was 596.3. Based upon this data, in April 1977 the building cost 2.097 times its January 1955 cost (596.3 divided by 284.4), or an indicated cost of $111,141.

INCOME AND EXPENSE DATA

In deriving pertinent income and expense data, an appraiser investigates comparable sales and rentals, as well as information on competitive income-producing properties in the same market. Current gross income estimates should be reviewed in light of average rent levels for several successive years. Vacancy rates, collection losses and operating expenses typical for this type of property help an appraiser to refine the forecasts of income and expenses for an income-producing property.

The published information on property values for several consecutive years suggests the rate of appreciation or depreciation that is evident for various property types. Interviews with owners and tenants in the area can provide lease and expense data. Lenders are a useful source of information on current terms of available financing.

An appraiser attempts to obtain all the income and expense data for income property comparables. These figures should be derived and tabulated in reconstructed operating statement format (see Chapter 18), and filed by property type.

Rental information is often difficult to obtain. Therefore, an appraiser should take every opportunity to add rents to the data plant. Long-term leases are usually a matter of public record. A separate county index of leases may be available, which lists the parties to recorded leases and refers to the volume and page of the recorded lease. Sometimes this information is listed among the deeds and mortgages, but it is normally coded so that a lease may be spotted fairly easily. In certain cities, abstracts of recorded leases are printed by a private publishing service. Classified ads are also a source of rental information. Many appraisers regularly check for advertised rentals and post them to rent comparable cards for a particular property type or area. The final actual rental is usually much closer to the asking rental than is the case for asking prices. Rental data should be filed by property type and area according to the same classifications used for sales data.

The income and expense comparables should be filed chronologically and by property type. They can thus be retrieved easily to help estimate the expenses for a similar type of property. Income and expenses should be converted to units for comparison and analysis. Income may be reported in terms of rent per apartment unit, per room, per hospital bed, per square foot, and so forth. Expenses, such as insurance, taxes, painting, decorating, and other maintenance charges, can be expressed in any of the units of comparison used for income, but they may also by expressed as a percent of the effective gross rent. Any unit comparison must be used consistently throughout the analysis.

The data for a rented property may show the actual vacancy rate and operating expenses as a percentage of the effective gross rent. These data are essential in the valuation of income-producing properties. Other important information includes the age and type of construction and any utilities that are provided by the owner.

CAPITALIZATION RATES

Market capitalization rates are also an essential type of market data. When income, expense, and mortgage data are available for sale properties, these indications may be used to calculate the overall capitalization rate and the equity dividend rate associated with the sale. Whenever possible, an appraiser should derive the overall and equity dividend rates of return, which are indicated by sales of comparable properties, and file the information for future reference. In the sales comparison, these rates would be analyzed according to the similarity of the comparable property's characteristics to those of the subject property.

Overall and equity dividend capitalization rates derived from sales may also be used as bases from which other rates could be derived. Therefore, it is important that appraisers consider these rate indications whenever information on sales is adequate for their derivation.

ORGANIZATION OF DATA

Before undertaking any analysis, an appraiser organizes all specific data accumulated during the market investigation. A spreadsheet that is carefully constructed provides a tabular representation of market data organized into useful and ultimately measurable categories. Depending on the complexity of the information that must be analyzed, an appraiser may have to design several spreadsheets to isolate and study specific data. On the initial spreadsheet, the appraiser lists each characteristic of the subject and comparable properties that can be isolated at that time.

The spreadsheet should include the total sales price for each comparable and the date of each sale, which can be expressed in relation to the date of valuation of the subject property (for example, one month or 16 months ago). The spreadsheet also includes information about financial arrangements and any unusual motivation that resulted in a negotiating advantage for either the buyer or the seller, such as the desire to liquidate for inheritance tax or the desire to acquire a particular property for expansion. Financial arrangements and unusual motivations can significantly influence selling price and thus must be carefully examined.

The spreadsheet often also contains other market data that may be significant for other appraisal assignments. Examples of such data are reproduction costs for building and land improvements, development costs, amount of accrued depreciation, indicated economic life attributed to improvements similar to those on the subject property, rates of return, percent of land value appreciation evident in the area, and average value of commodities produced on or services rendered by properties similar to the one being appraised.

The initial spreadsheet can include all characteristics of the subject and comparable properties, sales transactions, and pertinent market data from sources other than sales. However, an appraiser may decide to use one spreadsheet for comparable sales information and others for information derived from sources other than sales. This tabulation of data allows the appraiser to isolate aspects of both individual sales and the total market that may be significant in the valuation problem.

The isolation of specific data provides an initial indication of the information an appraiser will be able to derive from the collected information, and it identifies variations among properties that may be significant to their value and suitability as comparables.

An analysis of the initial spreadsheet may indicate that certain data is not pertinent and thus will not be useful in the application of the approaches. An appraiser may also find that additional data is required. The analysis may point to the need to create other spreadsheets to include additional information or to isolate data required for specific approaches. Appraisers should view the analysis of data as a developing process and the spreadsheet as a tool that helps advance that process and leads to valid indications of a property's value.

SALES COMPARISON APPROACH: ANALYZING AND COMPARING THE DATA

Comparison of sales, offers and listings provides a basis for estimating the market value of the property being appraised. When comparable properties are similar to the property being appraised; have sold very recently; and have few if any physical, locational and conditions of sale adjustments, such information is helpful to the appraiser in reaching a market value figure. On most assignments, however, the appraiser recognizes substantial differences between the appraised property and the comparable sales. As described in Chapter 14, two analytical tools are used by appraisers: elements of comparison and units of comparison. Each element of comparison (financing terms, conditions of sale, market conditions [time], location, physical characteristics and income characteristics) must be considered; the units of comparison provide a means for making these considerations.

The initial step of the analysis is to determine the appropriate unit of comparison. For a single family house appraisal, it is usually either the total property price including the site and site improvements or the sales price per square foot of gross living area of the house.

Either of the units may also be used when appraising small income properties. Other appropriate units of comparison are price per square foot of total building area (price per square foot of gross living area is usually used only for single family residences), price per bedroom, price per room, price per square foot of livable area and potential or effective gross rent multiplier.

Units of comparison are used in data analysis in all three approaches. In the sales comparison approach, the selling price may be divided by the unit of comparison. In the cost approach, the total cost to construct and the total accrued depreciation are divided by the unit of comparison. In the income capitalization approach, the income and expense items and the net operating income may be similarly divided by the chosen unit of comparison. In all approaches, several different units of comparison may be used, depending on the information the appraiser needs and the focus of the analysis. However, the same unit must be applied to both the subject property and all comparable sales in any single analysis.

Different units of comparison are typically used with different types of property. Comparisons can be made on the basis of the price, cost, income, and expenses per unit, depending on the approach by which the comparable property is being analyzed.

INCOME CAPITALIZATION APPROACH: DATA ANALYSIS

Data from comparable sales, leases, and income and expense statements provide a variety of information that is useful in applying income capitalization approach techniques. Much of the data for this approach is derived from interviews with individuals who are familiar with the subject property or comparable sale properties. An appraiser also interviews owners and managers of similar properties for information on typical rents and other lease terms, vacancy rates, management fees, and other operating expenses.

If all necessary data is not reflected in comparable sales, an appraiser can use data gathered from other market sources. In the income capitalization approach, an appraiser should particularly have market indications of average income and expenses on a unit basis, as well as indications of the various types of relationships between income and value. These trends provide support for the net income and rates that are projected for the subject property.

When the data provides an appraiser with adequate knowledge of the income, expenses, and mortgage associated with each sale, he or she can derive an estimate of the net operating income and equity dividend for each sale property. The overall capitalization rate and equity dividend rate that are reflected in each sale can then be determined by dividing the net operating income by the sale price for the overall capitalization rate and dividing the equity dividend by the equity investment for the equity dividend rate. This data analysis technique provides meaningful information only if an appraiser uses the same income and expense categories to derive net operating incomes from comparable sales and to project the net operating income for the subject property. For example, if an allowance for replacement is made in the expense statement for one comparable property and not in the others, the rate derived by dividing that property's net operating income by its sale price would not be comparable to those derived from other properties.

COST APPROACH: DATA ANALYSIS

The application of the cost approach requires two types of data, plus the information needed to develop the value of the site.

The first is construction cost information which is used to estimate the reproduction cost or replacement cost of the improvements. The best cost data is obtained locally from builders and others who have first hand information about costs in the local area. The problem is that it is difficult to obtain this information in a form that will make it useful.

In developing cost estimates by analyzing data obtained through observation and interviews, an appraiser must ascertain precisely what the reported expenditure represents in relation to the total actual cost of building. Quoted costs for improvements may not reflect the owner's related risk, labor and equipment costs, financial charges, costs of land preparation, engineering cost, or other indirect expenses.

The appraiser must also be aware that cost estimates for reproduction or replacement of improvements as of the appraisal date, which are developed in this type of investigation, may not reflect any profit realized by the current owner because of a change in the property. Of course, final cost estimates should take such profit into consideration if it is evident in the market.

One of the best ways to obtain overall cost data is to extract it directly from the sale of a new residence. This data becomes particularly useful if by interview and analysis, the appraiser is able to obtain a good estimate of site value and developer's profit.

For example, an appraiser locates the sale of a new 10 unit apartment containing 11,000 square feet that sold for $900,000. The developer reports to the appraiser and lender that the profit was a typical 15%. The appraiser develops from good market data that apartment sites in this area are selling for $10,000 per permitted apartment unit and therefore this site has a value of $100,000.

Based on this data, the following analysis provides a good indication of the reproduction cost of apartment houses (including a typical builder's profit).

FIG. 11-1 REPRODUCTION COST BASED ON BUILDER SUPPLIED DATA

Total Sales Price	$900,000
Site Value based on market data	-100,000
Reproduction Cost of the Improvements	$800,000

Reproduction Cost per Units of Comparison

Total Sales Price
Sq. Ft. of Improvements
($800,000 ÷ 11,000 sq. ft.)   = $72.73 per sq. ft.

Number of Apartments
($800,000 ÷ 10 units)   = $80,000 per apartment

SUMMARY

The valuation process divides data selection and collection into general data and specific data. Specific data includes information about the property being appraised and information about comparable sales rentals, costs, expenses and other relevant data. The ability to collect and analyze specific data has a direct bearing on the validity of the final value estimate.

The first step is a detailed description of the property being appraised. It is only after a complete analysis of the subject property that data most relevant to the appraisal of the subject property can be selected from the market.

Some sources of market data are real estate newspapers, commercial publications, general circulation newspapers, Realtors®, property mangers, other appraisers, lenders, multiple listing services, deed records, SREA Market Data Centers, government and private mortgage insurers, mortgage loan records, title companies, assessment records, atlases and survey maps, and tax transfer records.

Improvement cost data can be obtained directly from the market and from published cost services. It can be adjusted for time with the use of cost indices.

The market is also the source of income and expense data used in the Income Approach and to develop capitalization rates.

The data is analyzed and applied to the three approaches to value. In the Direct Sales Comparison Approach it is used to establish the amount of the adjustments needed to compensate for differences between the comparable sales the property being appraised.

For the Cost Approach, it is used to develop the value of the site, the reproduction or replacement cost of the improvements and the amount of depreciation.

Data from the market is used to develop appropriate income and expense estimates and capitalization rates for analysis by income capitalization techniques.

Further analysis of the data takes place in the Improvement Description and Analysis, Sales Comparison Approach, Cost Approach and Income Approach section of the appraisal.

PROJECTING
UPPER STORIES

UNIQUE LOOKING

MULTI-STORY

TURRETS

BAY WINDOWS

BIG CHIMNEYS

VARIETY OF
SURFACE TEXTURES

VARIOUS FORMS
OF WINDOWS

IRREGULAR SHAPE

MANY
SMALL
DETAILS

Nineteenth Century American

QUEEN ANNE (Q Anne - 712)

12 Improvement Description and Analysis

Every appraisal must contain an accurate and adequate description of the improvements. It is also customary to include photographs of the property and a building sketch. This description is based on a physical inspection of the property by the appraiser.

This chapter presents details on residential construction and components to guide the appraiser in making the inspection. The assumption is that the appraiser makes a complete inspection of the exterior and interior of the property. If this is not done, the appraisal report must prominently state that complete inspection was not made by the appraiser and cite the reasons for this omission, and how the information about the property was obtained.

There are a variety of ways to organize a property description and analysis. The following outline works well for many residential properties:

1. Site improvements.
2. Placement of improvements on site.
3. Classification (CTS System).
4. Size of residence.
5. Number of rooms.
6. Car storage.
7. Description of exterior construction.
8. Description of interior construction.
9. Mechanical systems and equipment.
10. Items requiring immediate repair.
11. Deferred maintenance items.
12. Overall condition and age of improvements.
13. Interior design and layout (functional utility).
14. Renovation: rehabilitation, modernization and remodeling.

This chapter also includes information about graphic aides, sketches, photographs and How To Read A House Plan.

SITE IMPROVEMENTS

In the chapter on site data and analysis, it was noted that the term "land" implies no improvements of any kind and that "site" is land plus those improvements which make it ready for use. In the typical appraisal some of these improvements are included as part of the site value and other improvements are valued separately. Because there is no universally accepted way to treat site improvements, the appraiser must be familiar with local customs. The appraisal report must indicate clearly which items are included in the site value and which are treated as site improvements.

The following allocation of improvements between the site value and site improvement is common in many areas:

Improvements Included in the Site Valuation:

Land improvements

1. Clearing.
2. Grading.
3. Draining.
4. Landscaping (often valued separately).
5. Installation of public utilities to the site.
6. Access (streets and alleys).
7. Lighting.
8. Sidewalks and curbs (often valued separately).

Site Improvements Valued Separately:

Site impro

1. Septic system (often included in site valuation).
2. Utility connections.
3. Well (often included in site valuation).
4. Driveways and parking spaces.
5. Patios.
6. Pools and courts.
7. Fences and walls.
8. On-site lights and poles.

BUILDINGS AS IMPROVEMENTS

It is customary on the URAR and other appraisal forms to skip the step of estimating the reproduction cost of the site improvements. Instead the appraiser estimates directly how much they contribute to the value of the property.

PLACEMENT OF IMPROVEMENTS ON SITE

A lot, like a house, should be divided into zones for good planning. There are three zones: the public zone, the private zone and the service zone.

The public zone is the area visible from the street. The service zone consists of sidewalks and driveways plus trash storage and clothes drying areas. The private zone is where the children play, the patio or family porch is located, and the vegetable gardens grow.

As well-designed house takes advantage of the fact that during the summer the sun rises in the northeast, travels in a high arc across the sky and sets in the northwest. In the colder winter months, it rises southeast, travels in a low arc and sets in the southwest. As a result, the south side of the house, when protected by a large roof overhang, will receive much more sun in the winter than in the summer. The opposite is true of the east and west sides of such a house. All other factors being equal, such as street location, topography and view, the best direction in which to face a house is with the broad side containing large windows towards the south.

CLASSIFICATION (CTS SYSTEM)

The Realtors National Marketing Institute of the National Association of Realtors® developed a standard method of describing residences known at the CTS System (Class, Type, Style). This system is described and illustrated in detail in my book *Houses: The Illustrated Guide To Construction, Design and Systems.* The following material and illustrations which describes the CTS System are taken from my book.

Figure 12-1 is a chart that summarizes the CTS System. Figure 12-2 shows illustrations of the most common house types. Next is a brief history of architectural styles in the USA and pictures of the most common styles. In addition to the common national types and styles there are many others found mostly locally in one part of the country or another.

FIG. 12-1 CTS SYSTEM

THE CTS SYSTEM
(CLASS, TYPE, STYLE)
A UNIFORM METHOD FOR DESCRIBING HOUSES

#CODE	DESCRIPTION	ABBREVIATION
	CLASS	
1	One-family, detached	1 FAM D
2	Two-family, detached	2 FAM D
3	Three-family, detached	3 FAM D
4	Four-family, detached	4 FAM D
5	One-family, party wall	1 FAM PW
6	Two-family, party wall	2 FAM PW
7	Three-family, party wall	3 FAM PW
8	Four-family, party wall	4 FAM PW
9	Other	OTHER
	TYPE	
1	One-story	1 STORY
2	One-and-a-half story	1 1/2 STORY
3	Two-story	2 STORY
4	Two-and-a-half story	2 1/2 STORY
5	Three-or-more Stories	3 STORY
6	Bi-level	BI-LEVEL
6	Raised ranch	R RANCH
6	Split entry	SPLT ENT
7	Split-level	SPLT LEV
8	Mansion	MANSION
9	Other	OTHER
	STYLE	
100	COLONIAL AMERICAN	COL AMER
101	Federal	FEDERAL
102	New England Farm House	N E FARM
103	Adams	ADAMS CO
104	Cape Cod	CAPE COD
105	Cape Ann	CAPE ANN
106	Garrison Colonial	GARR CO
101	New England	N E COL
108	Dutch	DUTCH CO
109	Salt Box	SALT BOX
109	Catslide	CATSLIDE
110	Pennsylvania Dutch	PENN DUT
	Pennsylvania German Farm House	GER FARM
111	Classic	CLASSIC
112	Greek Revival	GREEK
113	Southern Colonial	SOUTH CO
114	Front Gable New England	F GAB NE
114	Charleston	CHARLES
114	English Colonial	ENG COL
115	Log Cabin	LOG CAB
200	ENGLISH	ENGLISH
201	Cotswold Cottage	COTSCOT
202	Elizabethan	ELIZ
202	Halt Timber	HALFTIM
203	Tudor	TUDOR
203	Jacobean	JACOBEAN
204	Williamsburg	WILLIAMS
204	Early Georgian	E GEORG
205	Regency	REGENCY
206	Georgian	GEORGE

#CODE	DESCRIPTION	ABBREVIATION
300	FRENCH	FRENCH
301	French Farm House	FR FARM
302	French Provincial	FR PROV
303	French Normandy	FR NORM
304	Creole	CREOLE
304	Louisiana	LOUISIA
304	New Orleans	NEW OR
400	SWISS	SWISS
401	Swiss Chalet	SWISS CH
500	LATIN	LATIN
501	Spanish Villa	SP VILLA
501	Italian Villa	IT VILLA
600	ORIENTAL	ORIENT
601	Japanese	JAPAN
700	19th CENTURY AMERICAN	19th CTY
701	Early Gothic Revival	E GOTH
702	Egyptian Revival	EGYPT
703	Roman Tuscan Mode	RO TUSC
704	Octagon House	OCTAGON
705	High Victorian Gothic	HI GOTH
706	High Victorian Italianate	VIC ITAL
707	American Mansard	MANSARD
707	Second Empire	2nd EMP
708	Stick Style	STICK
708	Carpenter Gothic	C GOTH
709	Eastlake	EAST L
710	Shingle Style	SHINGLE
711	Romanesque	ROMAN
712	Queen Anne	Q ANNE
713	Brownstone	BROWNS
713	Brick Row House	BR ROW
713	Eastern Townhouse	E TOWN
714	Western Row House	WEST ROW
714	Western Townhouse	W TOWN
715	Monterey	MONTEREY
716	Western Stick	W STICK
717	Mission Style	MISSION
800	EARLY 20th CENTURY AMERICAN	EARLY20C
801	Prairie House	PRAIRIE
802	Bungalow	BUNGALOW
803	Pueblo	PUEBLO
	Adobe	ADOBE
804	International Style	INTERNAT
805	California Bungalow	CAL BUNG
806	Shotgun	SHOTGUN
807	Foursquare	F SQUARE
808	Art Deco	A DECO
808	Art Moderne	A MOD
900	POST WORLD WAR II AMER	POST WW2
901	California Ranch	C RANCH
902	Northwestern	NORTH W
902	Pudget Sound	P SOUND
903	Functional Modern	FUN MOD
903	Contemporary	CONTEMP
904	Solar House	SOLAR
905	"A" Frame	A FRAME
906	Mobile Home	MOBILE
907	Plastic House	PLASTIC
909	Contemporary Rustic	C RUSTIC
910	Postmodern	P MODERN

FIG. 12-2a HOUSE TYPES

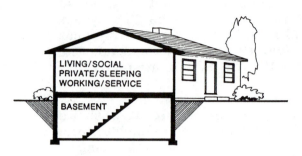

One-Story, Ranch, Rambler (1 Story - 1)

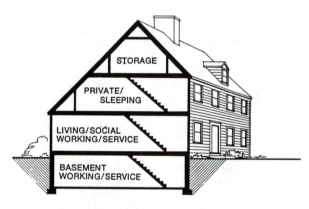

Two and One-Half Story (2½ Story - 4)

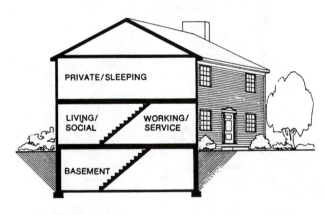

Two-Story (2 Story - 3)

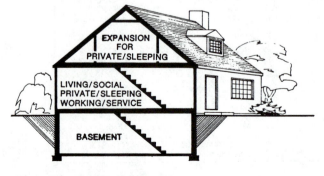

One and One-Half Story (1½ Story - 2)

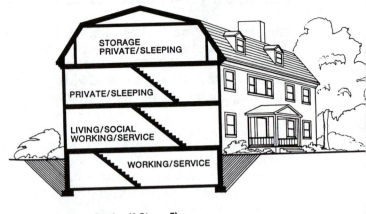

Three or More Stories (3 Story - 5)

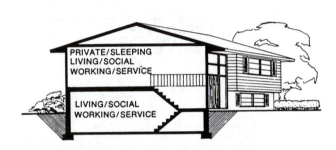

**Bi-Level, Raised Ranch, Split Entry, Split Foyer
(Bi Lev or R Ranch or Splt Ent or Splt Foy-6)**

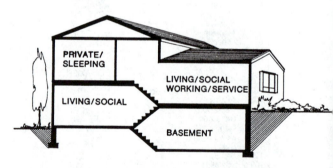

Split Levels — Side To Side, Back To Front, Front To Back (Splt Lev - 7)

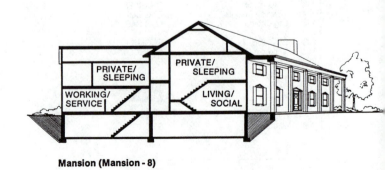

Mansion (Mansion - 8)

FIG. 12-2b HOUSE TYPES

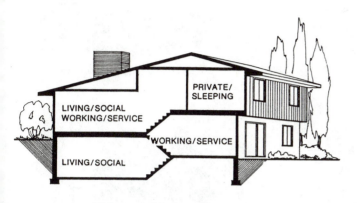

SPLIT LEVEL — BACK TO FRONT

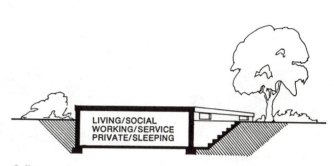

Cellar

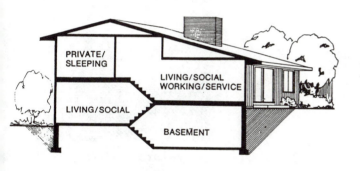

SPLIT LEVEL — FRONT TO BACK

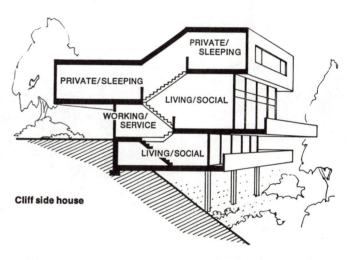

Cliff side house

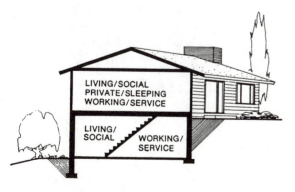

The Hillside Ranch

Townhouse w/Eng. bsmt.

39

FIG. 12-3 HOUSE STYLES - COLONIAL AMERICAN

SOUTHERN COLONIAL

CAPE ANN COLONIAL STYLE

NEW ENGLAND FARM HOUSE STYLE

DUTCH COLONIAL STYLE

ENGLISH COLONIAL STYLE

LOG CABIN

CLASSIC COLONIAL STYLE

GREEK REVIVAL STYLE

GARRISON COLONIAL STYLE

ADAMS COLONIAL STYLE

PENNSYLVANIA DUTCH COLONIAL STYLE

CAPE COD COLONIAL STYLE

NEW ENGLAND COLONIAL STYLE

SALTBOX COLONIAL STYLE

FEDERAL STYLE

FIG. 12-4 HOUSE STYLES - ENGLISH, FRENCH, SWISS, LATIN, ORIENTAL

COTSWOLD COTTAGE

ELIZABETHAN STYLE

MASONRY TUDOR OR JACOBEAN

WILLIAMSBURG GEORGIAN

REGENCY STYLE

GEORGIAN STYLE

FRENCH FARM HOUSE STYLE

FRENCH PROVINCIAL STYLE

CREOLE

SWISS CHALET

SPANISH VILLA STYLE

FRENCH NORMANDY STYLE

JAPANESE HOUSE

ITALIAN STYLE VILLA

ENGLISH TUDOR

FIG. 12-5 HOUSE STYLES - NINETEENTH CENTURY AMERICAN

EARLY GOTHIC REVIVAL STYLE

EGYPTIAN REVIVAL STYLE

ROMAN TUSCAN MODE

OCTAGON HOUSE

HIGH VICTORIAN GOTHIC STYLE

HIGH VICTORIAN ITALIANATE STYLE

CARPENTER GOTHIC STYLE

SHINGLE STYLE

EASTLAKE STYLE

MONTEREY STYLE

QUEEN ANNE STYLE

BROWNSTONE

WESTERN ROW HOUSE

ROMANESQUE STYLE

MISSION STYLE

AMERICAN MANSARD STYLE

WESTERN STICK STYLE

FIG. 12-6 HOUSE STYLES - EARLY TWENTIETH CENTURY AMERICAN, POST WORLD WAR II AMERICAN

PRAIRIE HOUSE

BUNGALOW

PUEBLO STYLE

INTERNATIONAL STYLE

CALIFORNIA BUNGALOW STYLE

PLASTIC HOUSE

CALIFORNIA RANCH STYLE

NORTHWESTERN STYLE

CONTEMPORARY STYLE

"A" FRAME STYLE

SOLAR HOUSE

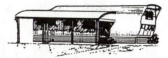

MOBILE HOME

POST MODERN

ART DECO OR ART MODERNE

FOURSQUARE

SHOTGUN

CONTEMPORARY RUSTIC OR
CALIFORNIA CONTEMPORARY

BRIEF HISTORY OF ARCHITECTURAL STYLES

In December, 1620, 102 Pilgrims landed at Plymouth. In spite of cold weather, they immediately started to build their first house. Shortly after it was completed, the house burned down, forcing the Pilgrims to live much of that first winter in holes in the ground that were covered with timbers, canvas and sod.

By the middle 1660's, there were thousands of houses in the Colonies. They ranged in type and style from small wood, thatched roof cottages to large stone, brick and frame houses. Many of these houses were constructed by craftsmen who formerly built houses in the large European cities. With this imported expertise and some imported materials, they were able to construct houses that were equal in quality to those being built in Europe. Many of the colonial styles developed in this early period of our history. At the same time, the fad of copying styles from builders' handbooks and architectural design books was developing. At first, only portions of the exterior designs were taken from the books. Then, whole houses were constructed exactly like their European counterparts, built from designs in the same books.

Different styles developed in different regions of the country. Many of the early colonists copied styles from their homelands. Others copied the classic Gothic, Greek and Roman designs while yet others developed truly indigenous American styles.

SIZE OF THE RESIDENCE

It is only recently that standard methods of measuring residential properties were required by Fannie Mae and Freddie Mac. These standard methods unfortunately are still not used by Realtors® and assessors. Therefore, whenever an appraiser uses size figures supplied by other sources, there is a high probability that had the appraiser measured the property him or her self, a different size figure would result.

SINGLE FAMILY RESIDENCES

The standard method for measuring single family residences is to calculate the Gross Living Area.

Gross Living Area (GLA)

The following are the rules for determining The Gross Living Area (GLA):

1. Measure around the outside of the house above the foundation to determine the GLA per floor.
2. In multi-floor houses count each floor above grade.
3. Include all of the above grade habitable living area.
4. <u>Do not</u> include the basement (even when finished and heated). Do not include any basement area unless it is 100% above grade.
5. Garages are <u>never</u> included in the GLA.
6. Porches are included only when they are heated and finished in a manner similar to the rest of the house.
7. Upper stories are divided into two areas.
   a. Attic – unfinished or having low ceilings (below 5 feet) – <u>does not</u> count in GLA.
   b. Habitable area – finished and heated substantially like the rest of the house with normal ceiling height – <u>is</u> included in GLA.

The Fannie Mae guidelines recognize that these Gross Living Area rules will not work for all houses in all markets. When the appraiser elects to deviate from this system, the appraisal should clearly spell out what system is used.

INDIVIDUAL CONDOMINIUM AND COOPERATIVE UNITS

How to measure a condominium is carefully spelled out by Fannie Mae. Their system seems to be acceptable to Freddie Mac too.

The rules are the same as the Gross Living Area rules with one exception for condominiums, that the **interior perimeter unit dimensions are used** rather than the exterior dimensions.

Only rooms that are 100% above-grade are included regardless of the quality of their finish. **Garages and basements (including those that are partially above-grade) should not be included.**

Fannie Mae says, "However, if the Appraiser needs to deviate from this approach because of the style of the subject property or on any of the comparables, he or she must explain the reasons for the deviation and clearly describe the comparisons that are being made."

Real Estate Valuation Magazine interviewed Mark Simpson, Director of Mortgage Underwriting Standards for Fannie Mae who confirmed that the best way to obtain the necessary interior dimensions for a condominium unit is from their plans which are often available to the Appraiser.

Of course, the plans should be field checked to be sure that they appear to conform with the actual unit being appraised.

SMALL INCOME PROPERTIES (2-12 FAMILIES)

The rules established by Fannie Mae are acceptable to Freddie Mac for measuring Gross Building Area (GBA) and are substantially the same as the rules for calculating Gross Living Area (GLA).

However, some appraisers interpret them to mean that common hallways are not included in the GBA, and that finished living areas below ground maybe included.

APARTMENT BUILDINGS

Most appraisers first calculate the Total Gross Area of the building by measuring around the outside and including everything above grade. They also include living units that are in the basement. They usually do not include unfinished basement area.

Often they also include the measurements of individual units. These are measured the same way as individual condominium or cooperative units.

OTHER TYPES OF BUILDINGS

Commercial, industrial and storage buildings generally are measured around the outside and include all areas of the building, whether they be above or below grade. Since there is no standard measuring system for these types of buildings, the appraiser must describe what was included in the measurements in the appraisal report.

Office buildings in many areas have traditionally been measured in a way that is unique to the area in which it is located. To further complicate the matters, some owners and management companies will take a system used in one area and use it in another location where the local system is different. It is especially important that the appraiser explain what system is used to measure the office building described in the report.

Unique measuring systems also apply to other special purpose buildings. The appraiser must become knowledgeable of these unique systems and accurately describe them in the appraisal report.

HELPFUL HINTS ON HOW TO MEASURE

A house is measured by attaching the end of the tape measure to one exterior corner of the residence, measuring the distance to the next corner, and then repeating this process until all exterior walls have been covered. After noting the measurements on a rough diagram of the house, the appraiser checks to see whether the measurements of parallel sides of the structure are equivalent. This procedure is known as *squaring the house*. The total front building measurements should equal the total rear measurements; the total left-side measurements should equal the total right-side measurements. Minor discrepancies may suggest that the corners of the structure are not perfect right angles; greater discrepancies may be attributable to errors in measuring or rounding inconsistencies.

If there are attachments to the house or the house has an irregular shape, the appraiser sketches the shape of the house and measures each side. Once all the measurements have been verified, the appraiser divides the figure drawn into smaller geometric units, calculates the area of each, and adds the areas together. Areas are not normally considered part of the gross living area, such as attached garages and entry-ways, must be excluded from the calculations. Computer programs are available for calculating areas, but the appraiser must still "square" the property from the measurements.

Current Fannie Mae and Freddie Mac guidelines suggest that the appraiser provide a sketch showing all the dimensions used in the area calculations together with the actual calculations based on these measurements. They should be presented in a format that will permit a reviewer with a calculator to check the appraiser's calculations.

NUMBER OF ROOMS

The HUD/FHA March 1987 guidelines state "room design and count should reflect local custom". Since the reader of the appraisal may not be familiar with local custom, the appraisal should contain information about which rooms are included and excluded from the reported room count.

The HUD/FHA guidelines go on to say, "A dining area built as an L-shape off the kitchen may or may not be a room depending upon the size. A simple test which may be used to determine whether one or two rooms should be counted is to hypothetically insert a wall to separate the two areas which have been built as one. If the residents can utilize the resulting two rooms with the same or more utility and without increased inconvenience, the room should be two. If the existence of the hypothetical wall would result in a lack of utility and increased inconvenience, the room count should be one."

CAR STORAGE

A majority of families owning houses also own two or more cars. Americans like their cars and they like to keep them under cover in garages and in carports. Their desire to do this varies from area to area. In many northern parts of the country any house without a two-car garage is substandard. In parts of the West and South the demand for garages and carports is more flexible and often a one-car carport with an additional parking area for the second or third car is acceptable

The garage that is built to Minimum Property Standards (FHA- MPS) serves only to shelter the car. These standards call for a one-car garage or carport to be 10 feet wide and 20 feet long, measured from the inside of the studs and door to the edge of the opposite wall, stair platform or any obstruction, whichever is the narrowest dimension. To build a garage to these minimum standards is false economy. For only a small additional amount of money, the garage can be built about 3 feet longer and wider. It then becomes a truly functional area of the house. Here is the cheapest and most convenient place to store all of the paraphernalia of outdoor living. If built even bigger, it can house the laundry and drying equipment and also serve as a workshop and a place for the children to play on cold or wet days.

The choice between a carport or a garage is mainly influenced by local custom and climate. Some carports are so elaborate that they cost almost as much as a garage. Others are very simple and consist only of a roof extended from the house supported on a few columns or a simple wall. A carport is a good choice when it fits into the neighborhood and the prime purpose will be to shelter the automobile from the sun and rain. It is also desirable when the house is so located on the site that a garage would tend to block the breeze or appear to crowd the house.

DESCRIPTION OF EXTERIOR CONSTRUCTION

A detailed description of the exterior includes information about the major construction details, including:

1 . Footings and foundation walls.
2 . Framing.
3 . Insulation.
4 . Ventilation.
5 . Exterior wall coverings.
6 . Masonry walls.
7 . Windows.
8 . Storm doors and windows.
9 . Weather-stripping.
10 . Screens.
11 . Gutters and downspouts.
12 . Roofs.
13 . Flashing.
14 . Chimneys.

The condition of these items and any needed repairs or modernization should also be reported in this section of the report.

CONSTRUCTION DETAILS

Footings and Foundation Walls

The objective of the footing is to provide support for the building without excessive differential or overall settlement or movement. It is the perimetric base of concrete on top of which all foundation walls are poured or laid. Block foundations walls must be properly laid and well-mortared, then filled with concrete and made watertight with cement plaster or other waterproofing compounds.

FIG. 12-7 FOOTINGS AND FOUNDATION WALLS

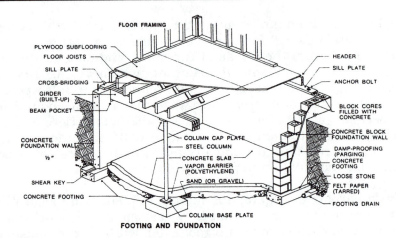

FOOTING AND FOUNDATION

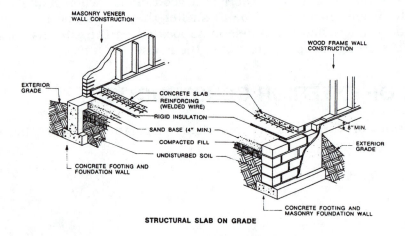

STRUCTURAL SLAB ON GRADE

The three basic design types are slab-on-ground, basement and crawl space. Slabs are constructed by first building footings for support, although some slabs (known as "floating slabs") are built without them. The excavation is then covered with gravel, and a vapor barrier and insulation are installed around the edge. A basement floor is constructed similarly to a slab. Crawl spaces are constructed similarly to basements except that the distance from the floor to the joists is 3 to 4 feet. They provide flooding protection and also a convenient place to run heating ducts, plumbing pipes and wires that must be accessible for repairs.

Framing

Most houses built in the United States are of wood frame construction. This includes many homes that have brick veneer siding. Platform frame construction is the most common type. Balloon framing was popular for multi-story brick veneer houses, but because of poor fire resistance, it does not comply with many building codes. Plank and beam framing was used for barns and colonial houses; it is used today for contemporary designs where the framing members are left exposed (as in exposed beam ceilings). Panelized construction, a new method of framing, is becoming more popular.

Most multi-family buildings are now being constructed of masonry especially in the South and West. It is becoming difficult to construct a frame multi-family building that will comply with the building and fire codes.

It is harder to spot poor construction in a new building. After a building ages, visible defects become more apparent.

Bulging exterior walls can often be detected. Window sills that are not level are a sign of settling, defective framing or original sloppy carpentry. A careful inspection should include opening and closing windows. Sticking windows may be a sign of settling or defects in framing. Doors should be checked, including a look at their bottoms to detect if they have been resawed. Sagging and sloping floors may be detected visually or by putting a marble on the floor and watching if it rolls. Other signs of defective framing include large cracks developing on the outside of the house between the chimney and exterior wall or cracks running outward at an angle from the upper corners of window and door frames.

Cracks in the walls other than these may be cause for concern but in themselves are not conclusive evidence of a serious problem. All buildings settle unless built upon solid rock; it is a rare building that doesn't develop some wall and ceiling cracks. If defects are suspected, professional consultants may be called in to confirm this opinion.

Insulation

Any building without adequate insulation is substandard today. Insulation is as important in warm climates to keep the heat out as it is in cold climates to keep heat in. Prior to World War II, many buildings were constructed without insulation. Many of these homes have since been insulated. Insulation falls into the following five categories: loose, blanket and bat, sprayed-on, foil and wallboard.

The two primary benefits of insulation are fuel economy and occupancy comfort. Its secondary benefits are the reduction of noise transmission and of fire hazard since insulation will impede fire from spreading. The difference between fuel costs for an uninsulated building and for an otherwise identical one with storm windows and doors and good insulation can be 50%. The standard measurement for the effectiveness of insulation is its R value (resistance to heat flow). The higher the R value the better the insulation. Over-the-ceiling or under-the-roof insulation should have an R rating from R-20 to R-24 or higher.

Exterior wall insulation ranges from R-8 to R-11. Floor insulation should be at least R-9 and preferably R-13.

FIG. 12-8 BASIC TYPES OF FRAMING

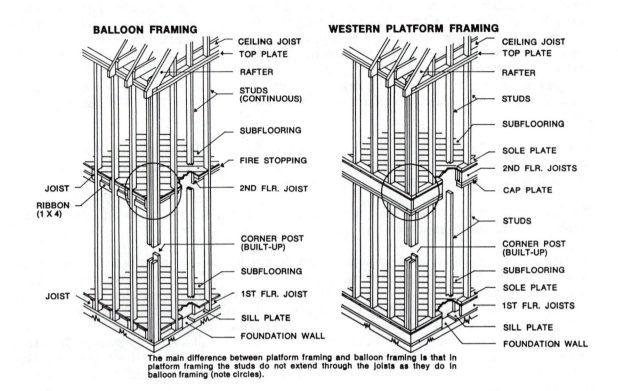

BALLOON FRAMING

- CEILING JOIST
- TOP PLATE
- RAFTER
- STUDS (CONTINUOUS)
- SUBFLOORING
- FIRE STOPPING
- 2ND FLR. JOIST
- JOIST
- RIBBON (1 X 4)
- CORNER POST (BUILT-UP)
- SUBFLOORING
- JOIST
- 1ST FLR. JOIST
- SILL PLATE
- FOUNDATION WALL

WESTERN PLATFORM FRAMING

- CEILING JOIST
- TOP PLATE
- RAFTER
- STUDS
- SUBFLOORING
- SOLE PLATE
- 2ND FLR. JOISTS
- CAP PLATE
- STUDS
- CORNER POST (BUILT-UP)
- SUBFLOORING
- SOLE PLATE
- 1ST FLR. JOISTS
- SILL PLATE
- FOUNDATION WALL

The main difference between platform framing and balloon framing is that in platform framing the studs do not extend through the joists as they do in balloon framing (note circles).

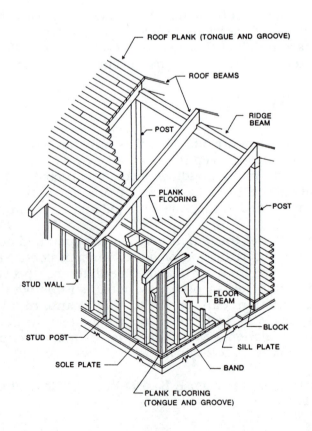

- ROOF PLANK (TONGUE AND GROOVE)
- ROOF BEAMS
- RIDGE BEAM
- POST
- PLANK FLOORING
- POST
- STUD WALL
- FLOOR BEAM
- STUD POST
- BLOCK
- SILL PLATE
- SOLE PLATE
- BAND
- PLANK FLOORING (TONGUE AND GROOVE)

PLANK AND BEAM FRAMING

Ventilation

To prevent water condensation, a flow of air is necessary in the attic, behind the wall covering and through the basement or crawl space. When water condensation collects in unventilated spaces, it promotes rot and decay. This air flow will also reduce attic heat in the summer. Ventilation can be accomplished by providing holes ranging in size from one inch to several feet in diameter; these holes should always be covered with screen to keep out vermin. The use of attic, basement, kitchen and bathroom fans also is part of the ventilation system.

Exterior Wall Covering

The construction of an exterior wall on a frame building starts with the attachment of sheathing to the wall framing studs. Next the sheathing is covered with waterproof sheathing paper (often asphalt-saturated felt). A wide variety of wall finishes and exterior wall covering exists; many buildings have more than one type of siding.

A masonry veneer is built by attaching the masonry (clay or concrete bricks, split blocks or stone) to the sheathing. In buildings with masonry veneer walls, all the structural functions of the walls are performed by the framing and not by the masonry. When the walls are constructed, three-quarters to one-inch air spaces are left between the masonry and the sheathing, and weep holes are installed at the base to let moisture escape.

A variety of other types of siding materials are available, including aluminum, stone, hardboard, gypsum board, fiberglass and metals.

Masonry Walls

Masonry walls are either solid or hollow. Solid masonry walls, if well constructed, are durable and easily maintained. They should be insulated and require a larger foundation than a wood frame wall. Such walls can be either one or two units thick. Single-unit masonry walls are constructed of either two layers of brick, tile or cement block or of a combination of materials, with the higher grade material on the outside and the cheaper unit as the back-up.

Hollow masonry walls have two wall units separated by a two to four-inch air space and bonded together with metal ties for joint reinforcement. These cavity walls are used mainly in northern sections of the United States for protection against severe outside temperature and storms. Masonry bonded walls are similar to cavity walls. Although they are economical to construct, their insulation qualities are inferior to cavity walls and they are used primarily in the Southwest.

Windows

Among window types commonly found are single and double hung windows, casement windows, horizontal sliding (traverse) windows and jalousie windows.

During the inspection, dust streaks or water stains around the windows may be noticed, which can be evidence of leakage. Missing locks and window lifts or counter balance weights also may be discovered.

Weather-stripping

The purpose of weather-stripping on windows and doors is to provide a seal against drafts and dust. A common kind of weather-stripping used today is the "spring tension" type made of bronze, aluminum, rigid vinyl, stainless or galvanized steel or rigid plastic steel. Other types are woven felt, compression sash guides and compression bulbs.

Storm Doors and Windows

These serve as a means of insulation and may provide a fuel savings of between 10% and 20%. Today they are often made of aluminum and permanently installed, together with screens. The wooden type, which are removed and stored during the summer, are becoming obsolete.

Screens

Screens are needed in almost every part of the country. The old-fashioned wood frame is becoming obsolete. Most screens today have aluminum frames and screening material and are combined with storm windows.

Gutters and Downspouts

These provide the means for controlling water run off from the roof to prevent property damage and unsightly exterior wall stains where roof overhangs are not provided. Gutters or eve troughs carry rainwater off the roof to downspouts or leaders. Metal gutters of aluminum, copper or galvanized iron, which are attached with various types of metal hangers, are the most common type of gutter now in use. Built-in gutters are made of metal and set into the deeply notched rafter a short distance up the roof from the eaves. Pole gutters consist of a wooden strip nailed perpendicular to the roof and covered with sheet metal.

Downspouts or leaders are vertical pipes that carry the water from the gutter to the ground and into sewers or dry wells. The junction of the gutter and downspout should be covered with a basket strainer to hold back leaves and twigs.

Roofs

The roof must be constructed to support its own weight, plus that of snow, ice and wind, and also act as a base for the application of the roof finishing materials. The most common systems of roof construction found are trusses, joists and rafters, joists alone, plank and beam roofs and panelized construction.

Roof sheathing provides support for roof loads and a backing for the attachment of roofing materials.

A majority of house roofs consist of shingles and shakes made of wood, asphalt, asbestos, cement, slate or tile. Metal, clay tile and built-up or membrane roofs can also be found. Many multi-family buildings have flat built-up roofing systems. Since the roof covering rarely lasts to the end of the building's economic life, the appraiser carefully observes the roof and reports its condition, age and estimated remaining life.

Water may leak through the roof for a variety of reasons. Asphalt shingle roofs may leak in a high wind if light-grade shingles are used. As these shingles get older, they curl, tear and become pierced with holes. Wood shingles may curl, split, loosen, break and fall off the roof, and asbestos shingles may crack and break. Metal roofs can rust, become bent and pierced with holes. Rolled and built-up roofs may loosen, tear, and become patched and worn through.

--**Flashing.** Flashing is needed whenever a roof is intersected by two different roof slopes, adjoining walls or projections through the surface by chimneys, pipes or vents. Flashing is a process by which metal stripes, impregnated felt or a combination of both are nailed across or under the intersecting point; a waterproofing compound or cement is then applied and finally the roofing or siding materials are applied over the edges to hold the flashing in place permanently.

--**Chimneys.** The efficiency of any heating system (except electric) depends upon the chimney or vent. A good chimney is safe, durable and smoke tight. Defective chimneys and vents may constitute serious fire hazards. A chimney may be a simple flue or an intricate masonry construction consisting of heater flues, ash pits, incinerators, ash chutes, fireplaces and fireplace flues. Whatever its construction, the chimney must be supported by its own concrete footings, which must be designed so that it will not settle faster than the rest of the building. Masonry chimney walls should be eight inches thick when they are exposed, and must be separated from combustible construction. A two-inch air space must extend at least two feet above any part of the roof, roof ridge or parapet wall within 10 feet of the chimney.

The heart of the chimney is the vertical open shaft, called a flue, through which smoke and gas pass to the outside air. A rough surface retards this outward flow of smoke or warm air; a flue lining will overcome this problem. The flue should extend out a few inches above the top of the chimney wall, (which should be capped with concrete, metal, stone or some other noncombustible waterproof material), sloped from the flue to the outside edge.

The furnace and hot water heater are connected to the chimney by a smoke pipe, which, for fire safety, should be at least 10 inches below the floor joists. The joists should be further protected with plaster or a shield of metal or asbestos.

Prefabricated chimneys that are assembled off the premises are now available. Many of these units consist of a flue liner encased in a concrete wall.

FIG. 12-9 ROOF CONSTRUCTION AND COVERING

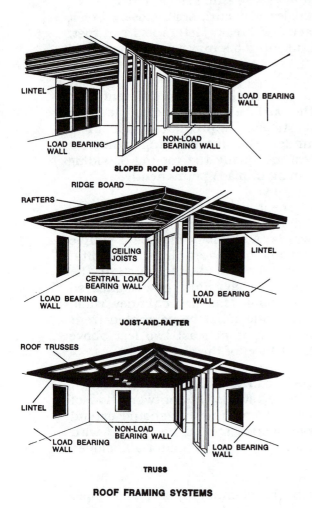

ROOF FRAMING SYSTEMS

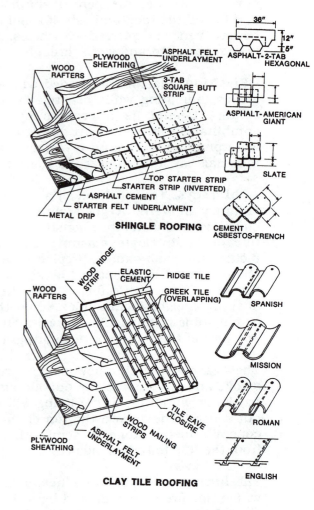

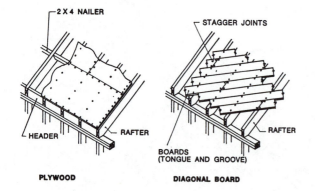

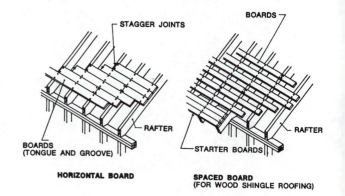

ROOF SHEATHING

DESCRIPTION OF INTERIOR CONSTRUCTION

The description of the interior rooms should provide information about their location, individual size, number of closets, and floor, wall, and ceiling coverings or finishes. Special features should also be described and any needed repairs or modernization should be reported. Typical items included in a description of the general interior construction (exclusive of the mechanical systems and equipment, which are described separately) are:

      1 . Basement construction and finishing.
      2 . Main bearing beam and columns.
      3 . Subflooring.
      4 . Floor covering.
      5 . Interior walls and ceilings.
      6 . Stairs.
      7 . Doors.
      8 . Molding and trim.
      9 . Cabinets.
    10 . Fireplaces.
    11 . Termite protection.

The condition of these items and any needed repairs or modernization should be reported in this section of the report.

CONSTRUCTION DETAILS

--Basement Construction and Finishing. The basic construction of the basement consists of the footings and foundation walls previously described; a basement floor, which usually is poured concrete over a vapor barrier and gravel; and the ceiling, which often is the unfinished underside of the first floor subflooring. Dirt floors are obsolete.

Basements can be finished in a variety of ways. There is a trend to raise the basement part way out of the ground to provide better natural light and ventilation and direct access to the outside. In raised ranch and hillside ranch-type houses the basement often is finished so as to be an integral part of the house.

A main problem with basements is dampness, which may be caused by poor foundation wall construction, excess ground water not properly carried away by ground tiles, poorly fitted windows or hatch, a poorly vented clothes dryer, gutters and downspouts spilling water too near the foundation wall or a rising ground water table. A basement that is wet or damp only part of the year can usually be detected any time by the presence of a powder-white mineral deposit a few inches off the floor. Stains along the lower edge of the walls and columns and on the furnace and hot water heater are indications of excessive dampness, as is mildew odor.

--Main Bearing Beam and Columns. Most buildings are too large for the floor joists to span between the foundation walls. Bearing beams resting on columns are used for support. Steel beams, because of their high strength, can span greater distances than wood beams of the same size. Most beams are supported by wood posts, brick or block piers or metal Lally columns, which are concrete-filled steel cylinders.

--Subflooring and Bridging. Subflooring provides safe support of floor loads without excessive deflection and adequate underlayment for the support and attachment of finish flooring materials. Plywood is the most common material now being used for residential subflooring. Bridging is used to stiffen the joists and prevent them from deflecting sideways.

--Floor Covering. Flooring made of strips of hardwood was the residential standard in many markets for over 50 years. Before that time, planks of hard and soft woods were used.

Carpeting, installed over either finished flooring or subflooring, is rapidly gaining in popularity. Carpeting, however, tends to depreciate very rapidly and often does not add value equal to its cost, especially when it is laid over another floor covering. Ceramic tile is still popular for bathrooms and lavatories, and quarry tile is becoming more common in kitchens.

Concrete slabs may be used for floor covering with no further treatment, painted with special concrete paint or covered with other flooring materials. Resilient tile, glued with special adhesives, must not be installed directly over a board or plank subfloor; a suitable underlayment must first be installed. Terrazzo flooring is made of colored marble chips mixed into cement; it is ground to a smooth surface after being laid.

--Interior Walls and Ceiling. Most interior walls are made of wood studs or metal studs, covered with a variety of materials. The materials most commonly used include plaster, gypsum, plywood, hardboard, fiberboard, ceramic tile and wood paneling.

Gypsum and other wood composition walls are installed directly onto studs or masonry, eliminating the drying time needed for plaster walls. Ceramic tile walls are installed similarly to ceramic tile floors, either by cement plaster or special adhesives.

--Stairs. A well-planned stairway provides safe ascent, adequate headroom and enough space for moving furniture and equipment. A simple check for adequate design includes noting: headroom, width clear between handrails, run, rise, winders, landings, handrail and railings. Railings should be installed around the open sides of all interior stairwells including those in the attic and basement.

--Doors. There are seven basic types of doors: batten, sliding glass, folding, flush solid, flush solid core, flush hollow core, and stile and rail doors. Batten doors, consisting of boards nailed together in various ways, are used where appearance is not important, such as for cellar and shed doors. Flush solid core doors are made with smooth face panels glued to a core that is made of either a composition material, glued-together wood blocks or glued-together wood pieces. Solid doors are often used as exterior doors. Flush hollow core doors are also perfectly flat. They have a core that consists mainly of crossed wooden slats. These doors are light and are used for interior doors. Stile and rail doors consist of a framework of vertical boards (stiles) and horizontal boards (rails). The hanging of doors is difficult. If the door is improperly hung, it will stick. Pre-hung doors are now available.

--Molding and Trim. Molding is made from a variety of hard and soft woods that are cut, planed and sanded into desired shapes. A general rule is; the thicker the molding, and the more intricate the design, the more expensive it is.

--Cabinets. Prior to World War II most cabinets were made of wood. Factory-made metal cabinets are often used today. Drawers, adjustable shelves, back, sides and fronts are of enameled pressed steel sheets. Doors are usually hollow steel.

--Fireplaces. In most American homes a fireplace is an amenity rather than a primary source of heat. There is no rule of thumb as to how much value one adds, and it is a mistake to assume, without market evidence, that it adds value equal to its cost.

Fireplaces are usually constructed of masonry, but metal ones are becoming common. They must be well-designed and constructed to work properly. Many fireplaces allow smoke to back up into the house, especially when it is windy outside. For fire safety, the hearth should extend at least 16 inches from the front and eight inches beyond each side of the opening.

--Termite Protection. The subterranean termite (see Fig. 12-10) is becoming common in most parts of the United States. Termites live in the moist earth, not in wood; they travel from the ground into the wood only to feed. They do not like light and will travel above ground through cracks in masonry foundations, through wood or in mud tunnels they construct on masonry surfaces.

Termite protection is provided by (1) controlling the moisture content of the wood used; (2) providing effective termite barriers and (3) using naturally durable or treated wood. Most appraisers are not qualified to make a complete termite inspection; however, they can make a preliminary examination which should report the following:

1 . Wood that is not at least six inches above ground.
   (Joists, sills and girders should have even more clearance.)

2 . Soft wood that may be termite infested.

3 . Cracks in masonry that could be termite pathways.

4 . Mud termite tubes that are signs of termites.

5 . Insects that appear to be termites.

6 . Termite shields and other special termite protection.

If there is <u>any</u> sign of termites, inspection by a professional termite inspector should be recommended in the appraisal report.

FIG. 12-10 TERMITES AND ANTS

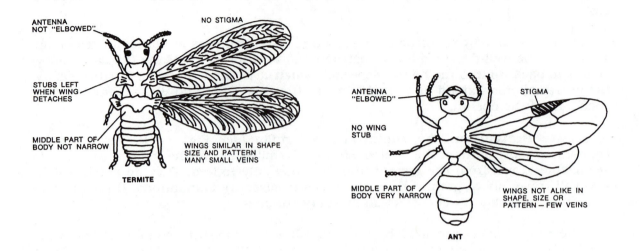

**DIFFERENCES BETWEEN WINGED ADULT
ANTS AND TERMITES**

MECHANICAL SYSTEMS AND EQUIPMENT

A building does not function satisfactorily unless its mechanical systems are in good working order. Each system must be inspected by the appraiser and described in the appraisal report. There is no standard way to categorize the mechanical systems and equipment. The following is a summary of the major systems described in this chapter:

1. Heating system.
2. Cooling system.
3. Plumbing system.
4. Hot water system.
5. Electrical system.
6. Miscellaneous systems.

Heating Systems

Heating systems are based on warm air, water, steam or electricity. Warm (or hot) air heating systems utilize either the natural force of gravity or some type of pressure blower to push heated air through the ducts. Filters can be installed to clean the air and a humidifier is often added to increase the moisture content. All the air systems distribute the heated air into the rooms through registers. Most gravity systems are old and obsolete and ready for replacement; however, gravity floor furnaces are still being installed in small houses. A space heater is another type of low-quality system.

FIG. 12-11a HEATING SYSTEMS

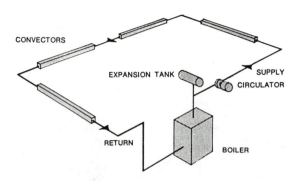

ONE-PIPE SERIES CONNECTED HOT WATER SYSTEM

This system may be identified by looking up at the part of the basement ceiling that is directly under the first floor radiators. In a one-pipe series connected hot water system, one wide-diameter pipe will be seen going in and out of each radiator. There will be no small-diameter feeder pipes.

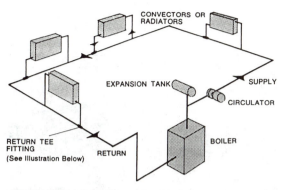

SINGLE PIPE INDIVIDUAL TAKE-OFF HOT WATER SYSTEM

Looking up at the area of the basement ceiling that is directly under the first floor radiators, one wide-diameter pipe will be seen under each radiator. Each of these pipes will be connected to its radiator by two smaller feeder pipes.

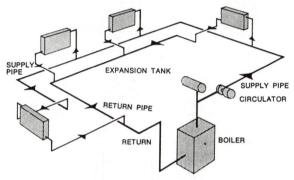

TWO-PIPE REVERSE RETURN HOT WATER SYSTEM

Looking up at the part of the basement ceiling that is directly under the first floor radiators, two wide-diameter pipes will be seen under each radiator. Each will be connected to its radiator by a smaller feeder pipe.

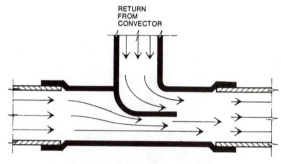

ONE-PIPE RETURN TEE FITTING

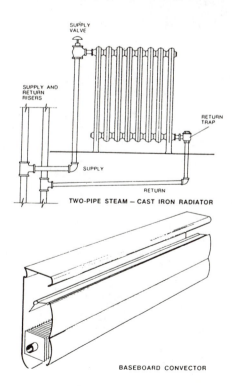

TWO-PIPE STEAM — CAST IRON RADIATOR

BASEBOARD CONVECTOR

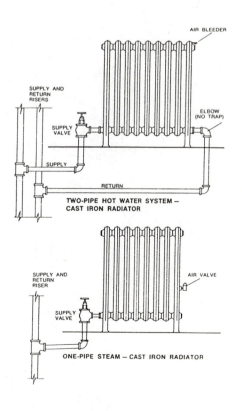

TWO-PIPE HOT WATER SYSTEM — CAST IRON RADIATOR

ONE-PIPE STEAM — CAST IRON RADIATOR

FIG. 12-11b HEATING SYSTEMS

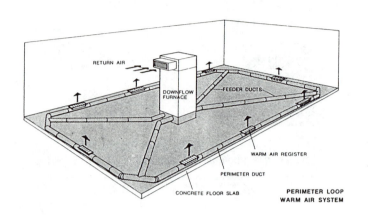

PERIMETER LOOP WARM AIR SYSTEM

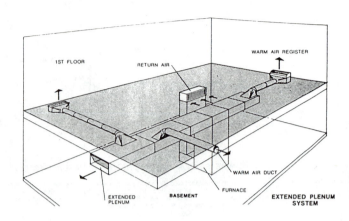

EXTENDED PLENUM SYSTEM

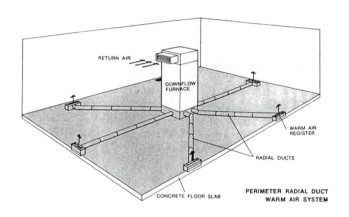

PERIMETER RADIAL DUCT WARM AIR SYSTEM

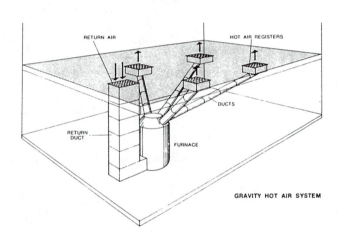

GRAVITY HOT AIR SYSTEM

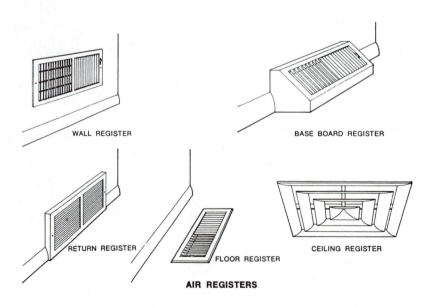

AIR REGISTERS

--**Hot water systems** (also known as hydronic systems) hold heated water in a cast iron or steel boiler. Some old systems depend on gravity to circulate the water through the radiators. Most modern systems use one or more electric circulators to pump the heated water through pipes into either baseboard panels or convectors, radiators or tubes embedded in the floors, walls or ceilings. These units depend on both convection (air being warmed as it passes over the heated metal and then circulated into the room) and radiation (heat waves being transferred directly from the heated metal to the object being heated by radiant energy). There are also combination systems in which the heat is brought to the radiator by warm water. A fan in the radiator blows air over the radiator fins, heating the room by convection.

--**Steam heat** is produced by a furnace that is a boiler with a firebox underneath it. As the water boils, steam is created that is forced by its pressure through pipes into radiators.

--**Electricity** may be considered as either a fuel to heat air or water in a furnace or a source of heat itself. Its use with resistance elements produces heat at the immediate area to be heated. These resistance elements, which convert electricity into heat, are embedded in the floors, walls and ceilings to provide radiant heat. The advantages claimed for electric radiant heat are the lack of visible radiators or grilles and its ability to maintain adequate air humidity levels. Electric heat also provides the advantage of individual room temperature control.

--**Electric heating panels**, also with individual resistance elements, are often used for auxiliary heat.

Type of Fuel

The type of fuel used in any heating system must be considered as world fuel markets and prices change from day to day. Fuel needs and supplies have become a major factor in international economics and politics. Each fuel has its own significant advantages and disadvantages which change from time to time and differ from one region to another. Coal was once the most popular fuel but most coal systems are now obsolete; however, new systems are again being manufactured as a return to coal from oil and gas is being suggested.

--**Fuel oil** is still the least expensive fuel in the Northeast and Northwest sections of the United States and is competitively priced in many other areas as well.

--**Natural gas** offers the convenience of continuous delivery via pipeline without the necessity of storage tanks. In most areas of the country (the major exceptions being the Northeast and Northwest), gas has been the most economical fuel. Liquid petroleum gas is used in many rural areas. It requires on-premises storage tanks and is usually more expensive than natural pipeline gas. In other respects it is similar to natural gas.

--**Electricity** appears to be the fuel of the future. Electric systems are the least expensive to install since they require no furnace, furnace room, ducts, flue or plumbing. They do require, however, a much larger electric service into the house and wiring to each unit. To date, in spite of advertising to the contrary, electric heat costs remain high, except in lower-cost power areas.

--**Solar** is the least developed source of heat to date comes directly from the sun. Solar heat is still in the experimental stages. A variety of solar heating systems are on the market today and appraisers will have to stay current on solar heat developments to appraise a house with solar heating.

Cooling Systems

Until the late 1940's, most cooling was done with fans. In some areas of the West, where the humidity is low even in periods of high heat, a simple system which blows air across wet excelsior or some other water-absorbing material is used to cool the air. Most buildings being currently built have some type of air conditioning system.

--**Window (or sleeve) air conditioning units** are sold by the millions each year. Small 4,000– to 5,000-BTU units usually can be self-installed and plug into a regular duplex outlet. New units gaining popularity are those no longer requiring a sleeve or window mounting. The unit is split into two parts; the compressor hangs or stands on the outside and the fan is hung on the interior wall. Only a small hole in the wall is needed for the connecting tube and wire. The appraiser must determine whether by custom or law air conditioners are classified as real or personal property, and the appraisal report should clearly indicate which case applies.

--**Ducted central air-conditioning systems** may be custom made or pre-wired, pre-charged, factory-assembled packages that are connected at the home site. The condenser portion is set outside the house or on the roof. It is connected by pipe to the evaporator air-handling unit inside the house. The air-handling unit, consisting of the evaporator and a fan, is connected to a system of ducts that distributes cool air to areas of the house to be cooled. If the house has a warm forced-air heating system, the air-conditioning system can use the same fan, filter and duct work. However, the ducts may not be suitable for air conditioning because cooling generally requires double the duct size of heating, and the cooling system works much better if the registers are high on the wall or are the type that direct air steeply upward.

--**Heat pumps** are another device for both heating and cooling. The heat pump is actually a reversible refrigeration unit. In the winter it takes heat from the outside air or ground or well water and distributes it inside. Its efficiency decreases when it is very cold outside and it must be supplemented with resistance heating. In the summer the system cools be extracting heat from the inside of the house like a typical air-conditioning unit. Heat pumps constitute only a small percentage of systems being installed.

Plumbing Systems

The plumbing system is an integral part of any building. The materials used for this system determine its ability to supply adequate clean water and remove wastes over a long period of time. The pipes carrying clean water should work without leaking, making noise, reducing pressure or imparting any color or taste to the water. Brass was used for many years, but is now expensive. Older brass pipes tend to crystallize and become coated inside in areas where the water is corrosive. Galvanized steel is used in some areas. Like brass, it is easy to work and is connected with threaded joints and fittings, but it is easily attacked by corrosive water. Galvanized wrought iron is similar to steel but more resistant to corrosion. Copper and lead are also used. Lead is still used for the pipe from the water main to the house. Plastic is the newest material for pipes. Although plastic piping is gaining acceptance, it is still not permitted in many cities.

FIG. 12-12 PLUMBING SYSTEM

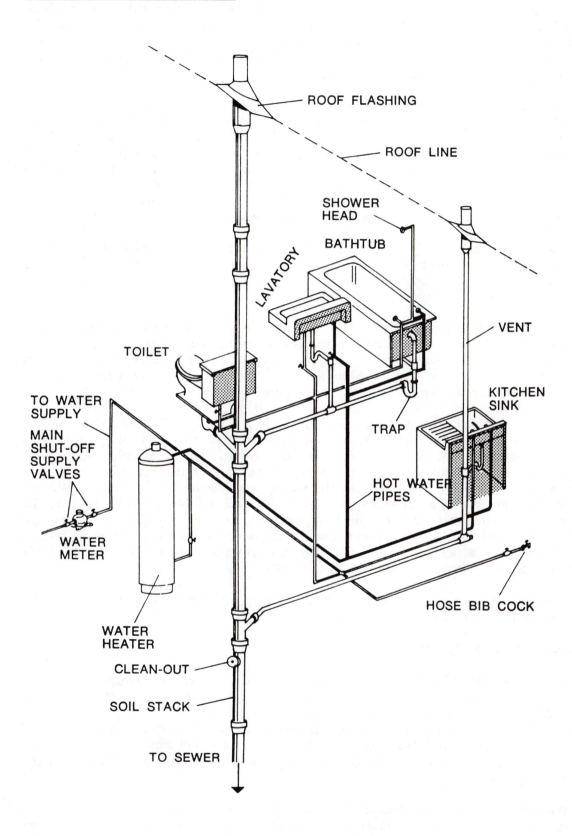

PLUMBING SYSTEM

--**Water pipes** must be strong to withstand the pressure necessary for water to flow through them. Because there is no pressure in a waste drain line, the pipes must be slanted so that waste will flow from each fixture through the main lines into the sewer or sewage disposal system. Pipes for the drainage system are made of cast iron, copper, plastic, tile, brass, lead or fiber. Special fittings are often used, especially on cast iron pipes, to aid the flow of sewage.

--**Standard bathroom fixtures** consist of lavatories (wash basins), bathtubs, showers, and toilets (water closets). The best material for lavatories is cast iron covered with acid-resistant vitreous enamel. Newer ones are made of fiberglass. Bathtubs are the most expensive bathroom fixture. The most common materials are ceramic tile, steel or cast iron covered with vitreous enamel or fiberglass. Standard size is 5 1/2 feet long by 16 inches deep. Many tubs also have a shower unit because they are less expensive to build than a separate tub and shower stall. Separate shower stalls are often prefabricated steel or fiberglass units.

--**Residential toilets** mostly consist of a bowl and a tank that stores sufficient water to create proper flushing action. The toilet can be rated by its self-cleaning properties, its flushing action, the amount of noise during flushing, and the ease of cleaning around the exterior.

--**Kitchen plumbing fixtures** include a single or double sink, generally installed in a counter. The sink drain should have a removable crumb cup or combination crumb cup and stopper. Kitchen sinks may be made of acid-resistant enameled cast iron, enameled steel, stainless steel or Monel metal. A garbage disposal unit and/or a dishwasher may be connected to kitchen plumbing.

--**Bathroom and kitchen fittings** both include a series of faucets, spigots and drains, which require occasional repair or replacement. The most common type of faucet arrangement has two separate valves, one each for hot and cold water. Most faucets now being installed feed into a single spout and a further refinement is a single control valve that controls both the water temperature and volume. A shower should have an automatic diverter control that switches the flow of water back to the tub after each shower so that the next user will not accidentally get wet or scalded. Most modern kitchen sinks have a combination faucet with a swing spout. A separate spray on a flexible tube is also common. Another attachment now available for a kitchen sink provides boiling water instantly.

--**Specialized plumbing fixtures,** such as laundry tubs or a wet bar, may also be found in laundry and family recreation rooms.

Domestic Hot Water System

An adequate supply of hot water is essential. Buildings with inadequate hot water systems suffer from functional obsolescence. The supply is usually generated in a hot water heater, with optional storage tanks as a supplement. The heater may be powered by electricity, gas or oil as a separate unit; or hot water may be supplied from furnace heat. The latter system supplies only a small amount of hot water, which may be exhausted too quickly. Another disadvantage is the need to run the furnace all year.

The recovery rate (the time it takes to heat water) determines the size tank needed. Standard gas hot water tanks range from 30 to 80 gallons. Because the recovery rate of an oil hot water heater is faster than gas or electricity, a 30-gallon tank provides enough hot water. They are not popular, however, because of the initial high cost and installation, especially if no flue or oil storage tank is already available.

In many areas of the country, large amounts of minerals such as calcium, magnesium, sulfates, bicarbonates, iron or sulphur are often found in the water. These minerals react unfavorably with soap, forming a curd-like substance which is difficult to rinse from clothing, hair and skin. A water softening system can be installed to eliminate these mineral deposits.

Electrical System

Most electrical services begins at a "service entrance" which brings power from outside utility wires through an electric meter to a distribution panel. The service entrance may be designed to bring in 30, 60, 100, 150, 200, 300, or 400 amperes of electricity. In smaller and older houses, 30 or 60 ampere service may still be found. A 100-ampere service is the standard today for each dwelling unit that does not have electric heat or central air conditioning. It provides 23,000 watts of power. A typical panel box has 12 to 16 fuses or circuit breakers. In larger units, and where electric heat, central air conditioning or a large number of appliances are used, 150 to 400 ampere service is needed.

--The distribution box has a switch that cuts off all electric service in the house when manually pulled in the event of an emergency. It also must contain either a master fuse or circuit breaker that will automatically disconnect the entire system if the system overloads. A fuse is a piece of wire that will melt when more than the prescribed amount of electricity flows through it. A circuit breaker is a special type of automatic switch that switches off when excess electricity passes through it. The distribution box divides the incoming electric service into separate branch circuits. Each individual circuit must also be protected by a fuse or a circuit breaker. If an overload or short circuit occurs on the line, it automatically shuts off without tripping the main fuse or circuit breaker.

--Wiring comes in a variety of types. The most preferred type of wiring is through rigid steel pipe, which looks like water pipe. It is also the most expensive method. Wires are pulled through the pipe after it is installed. A less expensive system that has code approval in most cities makes use of armored (BX) cable which consists of insulted wires wrapped in heavy paper and encased in a flexible, galvanized steel covering wound in a spiral fashion. Surface raceways made of metal or plastic are sometimes used. Flexible steel conduit is constructed like BX cable except that it is installed without the wire, which is drawn through the conduit after installation.

--Nonmetallic cable is made of wire which is wrapped with a paper tape and then encased in a heavy water and fire resistant fabric. A similar system has cable with a thermoplastic insulation and jacket; the cables are attached to the joists and studs with staples. A now obsolete system involves running two parallel exposed wires from the panel box to outlets and fixtures. The wires are attached to the house with white porcelain insulators, called "knobs." When the wire passes through a wall or joist, it is placed through a white porcelain tube—hence the name "knob and tube wiring." This type of system should be replaced.

FIG. 12-13 ELECTRICAL SYSTEM

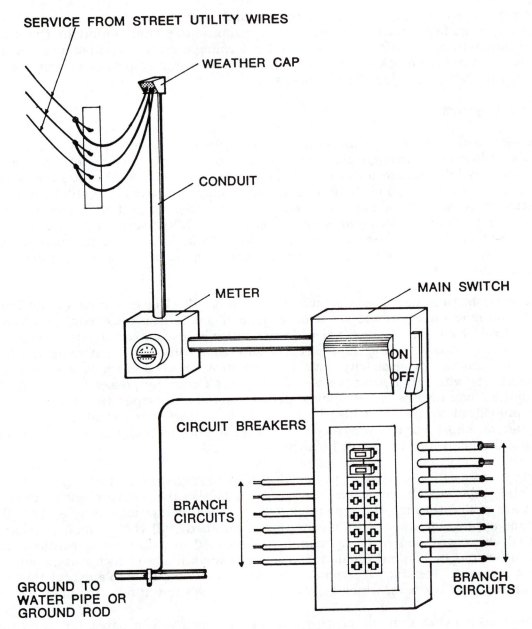

DISTRIBUTION PANEL

Here is the usual relationship between ampere service, number of circuit breakers and maximum number of watts:

Size of Service	No. of Branch Circuits (fuses or circuit breakers)	Maximum No. of Watts
30 ampere	4	6,900
60 ampere	6 to 8	13,800
100 ampere	12 to 16	23,000
150 or more amperes	20 or more	30,000 or more

ELECTRIC SERVICE ENTRANCE

--Telephones and doorbells use low voltage wiring that does not present a safety hazard and therefore can be run loose throughout the walls and along the joists. Intercommunication, central music and burglar alarm systems also use low voltage, hazard-free wiring.

--The duplex receptacle was until 1960 the most common type household outlet used. It accepts a two-prong plug, the type most often found on lamps and small appliances. In 1960 the National Electric Code required that all receptacles be of the grounding type, designed to accept a three-prong plug, to reduce shock hazard. Special waterproof receptacles with caps for outside use and other special purpose outlets are available.

--Wall switches control permanently installed light fixtures and wall outlets. The simplest and most common switch is a two-way snap switch. Three-way switches are used to control a fixture or outlet from different locations, which is useful, for example, for a light in a stairwell.

--Low-voltage switching systems are used for control in some buildings. Instead of the switch directly opening and closing the circuit, it controls a relay, which in turn, operates the switch. The advantage of this system is that many lights and outlets can be controlled from one place.

--Adequate switching arrangements allow one to walk anywhere in a building, turning on a path of light and then being able to turn it off without having to retrace steps or walk in the dark.

Sewers, Septic Tanks and Cesspools

Few will argue the substantial advantage of being connected to a municipal sewer system by a single outlet or separately into the sanitary and storm water disposal system. Freddie Mac and Fannie Mae require that, when available, the municipal sewer system be used. With increasing awareness of the damaging effects of pollution on our environment, rapid improvement and expansion of these systems can be expected in the near future. Health experts estimate that 50 percent of the septic systems now in use are not working properly. Still, it is estimated that almost 50 million people in 15 million homes, especially in the suburbs and rural areas, depend upon a septic system for their waste disposal and that 25 percent of new houses being constructed do not connect to municipal systems.

--A septic system typically consists of a large concrete tank with a capacity of 900 gallons (about 8' by 4' by 4') buried in the ground. One end accepts the waste material from the house drain line. Once inside the tank, the waste tends to separate into three parts. The solid waste materials (only about 1 percent of the total volume) sink to the bottom. The grease (also less than 1 percent of the total volume) rises to the top. The rest is liquid. Bacteria in the tank decompose the solid wastes and grease and a relatively clear liquid flows from the opposite end through the drain line either into a distribution box that directs the liquid into a network of buried perforated pipes called a leaching field or into a seepage pit. From here the liquid runs off into the ground to be absorbed.

FIG. 12-14 SEPTIC SYSTEM

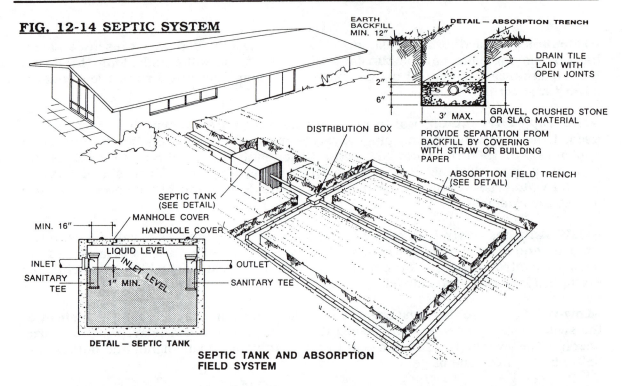

SEPTIC TANK AND ABSORPTION
FIELD SYSTEM

The required capacity of the tank depends upon the size of the house and usage. The size of the leaching field depends on the soil's capacity to absorb water. The rate at which the soil will absorb water can be measured by making a percolation test. A hole at least 12 inches deep is dug in the ground and filled with water. Each hour the depth of the water is measured. Anything less than an inch decrease in depth each 30 minutes is substandard. This test should be carried out in the wettest season of the year and preferably by an expert. Usually the local health department will make the test at no cost or for a nominal charge. Also, it is likely that the local health authorities will have previous knowledge of the individual system.

--Septic tanks must be checked frequently to make sure they are not clogged and that the bacterial action is working properly. Chemicals must be used with care as they can kill bacteria. Often the tank must be pumped out and the cycle started anew.

--A cesspool is similar to a septic system except that instead of a tank there is a covered cistern of stone, brick or concrete. The liquid seeps out through the walls directly into the ground rather than into a leaching field or seepage pit. It is important to learn about a house's particular system, including the location of the clean-out main, which is often buried in an unmarked spot, so that inspections and repairs can be made as required. A properly working system should produce no odor which is one of the first signs of trouble. Learning the location of the clean-out main from the current owner saves a lot of digging and searching if it is buried.

Anyone wishing to gain information on septic systems should find out how often the system has to be pumped out. In many towns the local health officer is very knowledgeable about many systems in the jurisdiction and of problems in a particular neighborhood.

--Septic system problems may sometimes be corrected by simply pumping out the tank. Sometimes new leaching fields are required. Unfortunately, there are situations when the soil absorption rate is poor or the water table is close to the surface and little can be done to make the system function properly.

MISCELLANEOUS SYSTEMS AND EQUIPMENT

A variety of mechanical systems and special equipment is being installed today. Many reflect fads or the special interests of the owner. They include such items as intercommunication and sound systems, burglar and fire alarms, automatic doors, elevators, incinerators, laundry chutes, and central vacuum cleaners. The appraiser must judge each situation to determine how much value these specialized items add. A further consideration in some cases is whether the items are real estate or personal property.

ITEMS REQUIRING IMMEDIATE REPAIR

Except for buildings in an exceptional state of maintenance, there will almost always be items needing repair as of the date of the appraisal. The repair of these normal maintenance items should add more value to the property than the cost. In the cost approach, these items fall under "physical deterioration-curable." The repair list should include conditions observed by the appraiser that constitute a fire or safety hazard. Many clients request that these items be listed separately in the report. Sometimes the appraiser is requested to estimate the cost of each repair (cost to cure). Some of the most commonly found items of immediate repair are:

1. Touching up exterior paint.
2. Minor carpentry repairs to stairs, molding, siding, trim, floors, porches.
3. Redecorating interior rooms.
4. Fixing plumbing leaks and noisy plumbing.
5. Freeing stuck doors and windows.
6. Repairing holes in screens and replacing broken windows or other glass.
7. Re-hanging loose gutters and leaders.
8. Replacing missing roof shingles and tiles.
9. Fixing cracks in pavements.
10. Making minor electrical repairs.
11. Replacing rotted floor boards.
12. Exterminating vermin.
13. Fixing cracked or loose bathroom and kitchen tiles.
14. Repairing septic system.
15. Eliminating all fire and safety hazards.

DEFERRED MAINTENANCE ITEMS

Although the paint, roof, wallpaper, etc., may show some signs of wear and tear, it may not be ready for replacement on the date of the appraisal. The test is whether its repair or replacement will add more value to the property than its cost. For example, if a building has an exterior paint job that is three years old in an area where this type of paint lasts five years, the paint has suffered some depreciation. Repainting, however, probably would not add value to the property equal to its cost if it were done at the end of three years.

The following items normally have to be repaired or replaced before the end of the economic life of the building. They are known as short-lived items:

1 . Interior paint and wallpaper.
2 . Exterior paint.
3 . Floor finishes.
4 . Shades, screens and blinds.
5 . Waterproofing and weather-stripping.
6 . Gutters and leaders.
7 . Storm windows.
8 . Roof covering and flashing.
9 . Hot and cold water pipes.
10 . Plumbing fixtures.
11 . Domestic hot water heater.
12 . Electric service entrance.
13 . Electric wiring.
14 . Electric switches and outlets.
15 . Electric fixtures.
16 . Furnace.
17 . Ducts and radiators.
18 . Air conditioning equipment.
19 . Carpeting.
20 . Kitchen appliances.
21 . Kitchen counters and cabinets.
22 . Well pump.
23 . Water softener system.
24 . Laundry appliances.
25 . Ventilating fans.
26 . Fences and other site improvements.

The appraiser should note any of these or other short-lived items whose condition is better or worse than the overall condition of the building of which they are a part.

Overall Condition of Improvements

This section of the report is substantially completed when all items requiring immediate repair and all deferred maintenance are described. One last step, however, is to report the condition of items that should last the normal economic life of the building. Their condition is affected by abnormal wear and tear, and they can be damaged accidentally. They also may have been poorly made or installed. It would be a very unusual property where all the long-lived items were in exactly the same condition. For example, the clapboard siding may show signs of warping because of a roof leak; the condition may not be bad enough to warrant replacing the siding now. This case is a form of "physical deterioration-incurable."

INTERIOR DESIGN AND LAYOUT (FUNCTIONAL UTILITY)

The perfect residence is one that is the exact size, shape and design to produce the maximum profit. It would be the theoretical highest and best use of the site. Most residences are not the perfect or ideal improvements for their neighborhood. Room sizes, their number and type, and the design and layout differ from the idealized highest and best use. In fact, many things could be improved in the design and layout of a typical building. The appraiser is not on a quest for the perfect building but is trying to identify design elements that adversely affect value. These items constitute "functional obsolescence" in the cost approach.

Since most appraisers have little or no training in design, they tend to rely on their own likes and dislikes as a basis for making design judgments, an inappropriate basis on which to rely. It is better to learn what is generally accepted in the market as good design.

House Zones

A good way to consider the interior layout of a house it to divide it into zones. The private/sleeping zone contains the bedrooms, bathrooms and dressing rooms. The living/social zone consists of the living room, dining room, recreation room, den and enclosed porch. The working/service zone consists of the kitchen, laundry, pantry and other work areas. In addition to these three zones, are circulation areas consisting of halls and stairs plus guest and family entrances (see Fig. 12-15).

The three zones should be separated from one another so that activities in one zone do not interfere with those in another. The private/sleeping zone should be located so that it is insulated from noise in the other two zones, and it should be possible to move from the bedrooms to the bathrooms in this zone without being seen from the other areas of the house. The working/service zone is the nerve center of the house; from here the household activities are directed. From the kitchen, it should be possible to control both guest and family entrances, activities in the private/sleeping zone and living/social zone, plus activities in the porch, patio and backyard areas.

FIG. 12-15 ZONING ONE STORY HOUSE

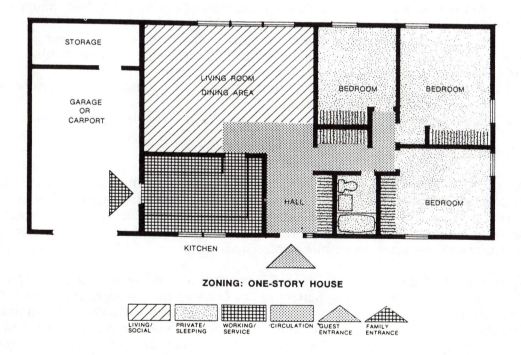

The guest entrance should lead into the center of the house. From here there should be direct access to the living areas, guest closet and guest lavatory. A noise and visibility barrier should exist between the guest entrance and the private/sleeping zone.

Ideally the family entrance should be from the garage, carport, or breezeway into the kitchen or from a circulation area directly connecting to the kitchen. Traffic from this entrance should not have to pass through the work triangle of the kitchen to enter the other rooms of the house. Circulation should be such that one may move from working/service zone to the private/sleeping zone without going through the living/social zone.

If the house has a basement, it may have a separate outside entrance. The inside basement entrance should lead into a circulation area that has access to the private/sleeping zone, the living social zone and both the guest and family entrances, without going through the living room or the kitchen work triangle.

Common Floor Plan Deficiencies

According to a national survey of homeowners, some of the most common floor plan deficiencies include the following items. These will vary depending on the geographic region and the size and value of the residence.

1 . Front door entering directly into the living room.
2 . No front hall closet.
3 . No direct access from front door to kitchen, bath or bedroom without passing through other rooms.
4 . Rear door not convenient to kitchen and difficult to reach from the street, driveway and garage.
5 . No comfortable area in or near the kitchen for family to eat.
6 . A separate dining area or room not easily accessible from the kitchen.
7 . Stairways off a room rather than in a hallway or foyer.
8 . Bedrooms and baths that are visible from the living room or foyer.
9 . Recreation or family room poorly located (not visible from kitchen).
10 . No access to the basement from outside the house.
11 . Walls between bedrooms not soundproof (separation by a bathroom or closet accomplish soundproofing).
12 . Outdoor living areas not accessible and/or not visible from kitchen.

Living Room

Until World War II, the living room was the living center of the house. In the past several decades, the status of the living room has undergone a change. Today, the family room, patio and kitchen are more likely to be the locations for relaxing, socializing and entertaining. As these areas have grown and developed, the size and the importance of the living room has diminished.

The location of the living room may be in the traditional front of the house or, if view or access to outdoor living area is better, in the back or on a side of the house. The room should be positioned to supplement the dining and outdoor entertainment areas in the house. Often one end of the living room is the dining area, so it must have good juxtaposition with the kitchen/service areas as well. The living room should not be a traffic-way between other rooms. The following are some guidelines for judging the size of the living room compared with the rest of the house.

In a three-room house, the living room should have minimum dimensions of 11 by 16 feet, or at least 170 square feet. The recommended dimensions are 12 by 18 feet. If a dining area is at one end of the room, dimensions may go up to 16 by 26 feet or more. A maximum width of 14 feet is recommended for proper furniture arrangements around the room. Where traffic is necessary through the room, a width of 15 or 16 feet could conceivably be used to advantage by routing the traffic outside the conversation circle created by the furniture (see Fig. 12-16).

FIG. 12-16 LIVING ROOM CONVERSATION CIRCLE

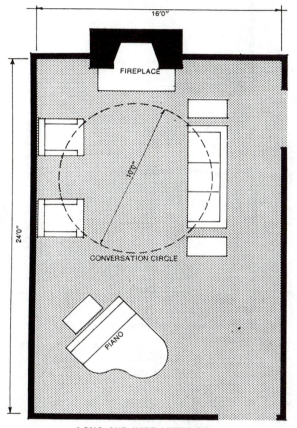

LONG AND WIDE LIVING ROOM

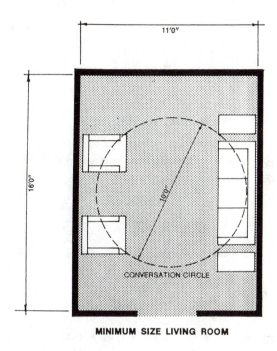

MINIMUM SIZE LIVING ROOM

Kitchen

Traditionally, the kitchen was located at the back of the house. Today it can be located wherever it best fits into the overall design and a current trend is to locate it at the front of the house. The kitchen should not be a main thoroughfare.

The size of the kitchen depends on the space available, the number of people in the family, the kind of equipment desired and what activities other than those directly associated with food preparation are carried on there. The minimum size for a kitchen in a small house is 8 by 10 feet. Better sizes are 10 by 10 and 10 by 12 feet.

Ten percent or more of the cost of a new home is spent on the kitchen. A functional kitchen should have adequate storage space, appliance space, counter and activity space, all arranged for maximum efficiency. The term triangle has become fashionable to describe the essential work zone of the kitchen, since there are three key work areas of use and activity: the refrigerator area, sink/wash/preparation area, and range/serving area. They can be arranged in any logical way, determined by the space available and the personal preference for one particular center over another (see Fig. 12-17).

FIG. 12-17 KITCHEN LAYOUTS

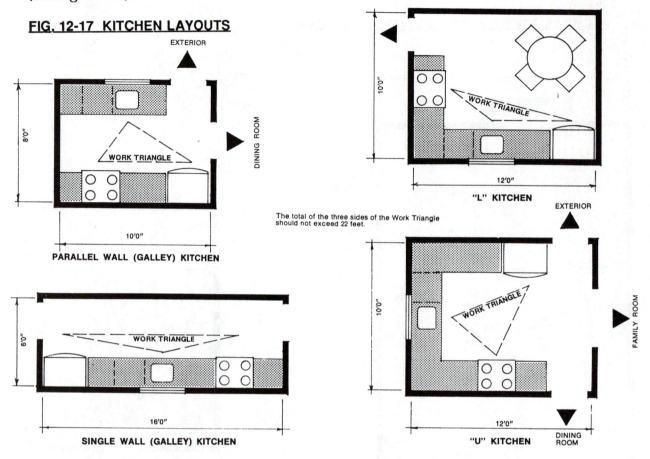

The total of the three sides of the Work Triangle should not exceed 22 feet.

However the kitchen is arranged, work should flow in a normal sequence from one center to another. Ideally, no traffic should move through the triangle in the main kitchen work area. Properly establishing the location of windows and doors will help to ensure a traffic pattern that does not interfere with efficient use of the kitchen. Most building standards require that the window area should equal at least 10% of the floor area of the room. At least one section of a work counter should have a window over it with provision for controlling direct sunlight. Many people prefer to have a window located over the sink. (For reasons of both safety and good housekeeping, the range should never be located under a window.)

Many kitchens suffer from one or more of the following inadequacies (listed in order of most common occurrence):

1. Insufficient base cabinet storage.
2. Insufficient wall cabinet storage.
3. Insufficient counter space.
4. No counter beside the refrigerator.
5. Not enough window area.
6. Poorly placed doors that waste wall space.
7. Traffic through the work triangle.
8. Too little counter space on either side of the sink.
9. No counter beside the range.

10 . Insufficient space in front of cabinets.
11 . Distance between sink, range and refrigerator too great.
12 . Range under a window.

Dining Rooms and Dining Areas

A dining room was included in most pre-World War II homes. Now many houses have dining areas that are part of another room. The traditional space requirements for dining rooms probably no longer apply to many markets. A minimum size dining room is 9 by 11 feet, with 12 by 12 being preferable. In some markets an acceptable alternative to the dining room or area is an extra large "eat-in" kitchen. The appraiser must determine what the market wants and judge if the appraised house meets the requirements.

Bedrooms

The number of bedrooms in a house is an important design consideration. Three bedrooms is most common today. Houses with only two bedrooms are often constructed at the direction of an owner who does not need the third room; however, many markets do not accept only two bedrooms without a substantial discount. A fourth bedroom is appealing to many families, but in many markets the additional price a four-bedroom house brings is not as great as the cost of the extra bedroom. Of course, luxury homes may have five or more bedrooms. One bedroom homes are usually substandard in any market, except for recreational homes.

Two key factors in the location of bedrooms are that they be isolated from the noise generated in the rest of the house, and that one should be able to get from each bedroom to a bathroom without being seen from the living/social zone of the house. The minimum size bedroom for a single bed is 8 by 10 feet; this size is satisfactory only if the layout is good and no space is wasted. The minimum size room for a double bed is 10 by 11-1/2 feet. Some markets expect bedrooms to be more than minimum size; other markets will not pay the extra cost for the larger space. Each bedroom should have at least one closet with a minimum depth of two feet, a width of three feet and a height sufficient to allow five feet clear hanging space.

Bathrooms and Lavatories

Houses with only one bathroom are obsolete in many markets; 1-1/2 baths is becoming a minimum standard, except in low-priced and recreation homes. The older minimum standard for two-story houses of one bath upstairs and a lavatory downstairs is being replaced in many markets with a standard of two baths. The minimum size for a bathroom containing a five-foot tub/shower combination, basin and toilet is 5 by 7 feet. This allows for the toilet to be on the wall opposite the tub rather than between the tub and basin, which is unsatisfactory; it also allows the door to swing in without hitting a fixture (see Fig. 12-18). A bathroom should not be located between two bedrooms with a door leading directly into the bathroom from each bedroom. (This is, however, a common feature of many Victorian homes).

The terminology used to describe bathrooms and lavatories varies around the country. In most areas a full bath consists of a room with a toilet (also known as a water closet), wash basin (also known as a sink, lavatory or vanity) and a tub. A 3/4 bathroom has a toilet, wash basin and stall shower (called a full bath in some areas). A half-bath (also known as a lavatory, or powder room) has a toilet and wash basin.

FIG. 12-18 BATHROOM LAYOUT

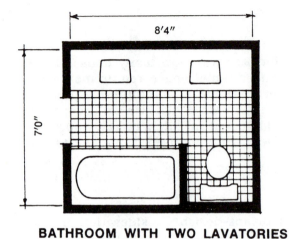

BATHROOM WITH TWO LAVATORIES

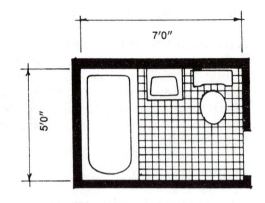

MINIMUM SIZE BATHROOM

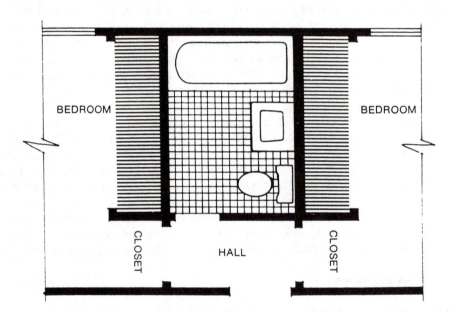

BATHROOM WITH CLOSETS AS SOUND BARRIERS

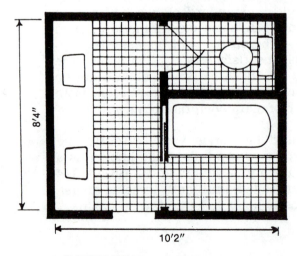

BATHROOM — COMPARTMENTED

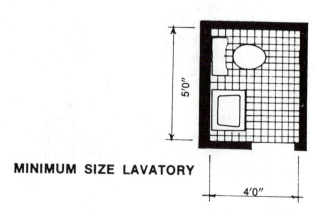

MINIMUM SIZE LAVATORY

The bathroom requires the most heat and the best ventilation of any room in the house. A bathroom or lavatory with or without a window is equally acceptable, but ventilation of an interior bathroom or lavatory is essential. A ventilation fan, ducted to the outside, should be wired to the light switch so that it goes on automatically when the room is in use and turns off automatically when the lights are turned off.

Family and Recreation Rooms

Before World War II attics, dens and finished basements generally were used as additional recreation space. Today the family room is used as a den, study, guest room, nursery, library, TV room, or hobby entertainment center. The key to the successful location of this room is to have it visible from and easily accessible to the kitchen. It also should be accessible to the outdoor living area, such as the backyard or patio. A good size for the recreation room in a small house is 12 by 16 feet. Appraisers should remember that many family or recreation rooms are overimproved or too large for a particular market.

Patios and Porches

In some areas patios are very elaborate and an integral part of the house. They can be described as part of the improvements rather than a site improvement. Porches have been decreasing in popularity and importance for many years except in a few areas of the country. The exceptions seem to be sun and side porches on more expensive homes, the Hawaiian "lanai" (a covered or open porch) and screened-in porches in beach and summer homes. Some styles have special porch features, such as the Victorian wrap-around porch, which will usually add value.

Laundry Rooms and Storage Areas

A growing trend has been to bring the washing machine and clothes dryer out of the basement. These appliances are being installed in the kitchen, a separate laundry or utility room, the garage, or even in hallways or closets on the first or second floors. Anyone who has lived in a house with a basement finds it hard to understand why they are not more universally accepted. A house without a basement may suffer from a lack of adequate storage space, and it will be penalized by the market. Alternate acceptable storage areas are attics, closets, storage rooms, garages, storage sheds, etc.

RENOVATION: REHABILITATION, MODERNIZATION AND REMODELING

Often the appraiser finds that substantial renovations are necessary if the existing improvement is to achieve the highest and best use of the site. These alterations and improvements go beyond the normal curable physical deterioration and functional obsolescence. The owner of the property may have come to a similar conclusion before the appraisal and may already have done some or all of the work.

These substantial changes can be described by the terms rehabilitation, modernization and remodeling. Each term has a specific meaning with which the appraiser should be familiar:

--Rehabilitation. The restoration of a property to satisfactory condition without changing the plan, form or style of a structure. In urban renewal, the restoration to good condition of deteriorated structures, neighborhoods, and public facilities. Neighborhood rehabilitation encompasses structural rehabilitation and in addition may extend to street improvements and a provision of such amenities as parks and playgrounds.

--Modernization. Taking corrective measures to bring a property into conformity with changes in style, whether exterior or interior or additions necessary to meet standards of current demand. It normally involves replacing parts of the structure or mechanical equipment with modern replacements of the same kind.

--Remodeling. Changing the plan, form or style of a structure to correct functional or economical deficiencies.

Rehabilitation

A growing trend in many cities throughout the country is the restoration of older neighborhoods and homes. People are moving back into city neighborhoods, and older homes in center city locations are now attracting young professionals, business people and white-collar workers. Some older homes are not much more than four good walls and sturdy ceilings; more often the interior floors and walls are usable. The woodwork can be restored and although the mechanical systems usually have to be replaced, some parts of the original systems may be usable. The appraisal of this type of property often requires the appraiser to help plan the rehabilitation.

Modernization

Modernization implies replacement or remodeling specifically designed to offset the effect of obsolescence or making additions necessary to meet current design standards. The replacement of old radiators and lighting or plumbing fixtures with new items of fundamentally the same type, is nothing more than improving the condition of the old installation. However, the substitution of convectors for cast-iron radiators, of built-in bathtubs for tubs on legs, or of modern lighting fixtures for old-fashioned types would not necessarily reflect on the physical condition of the items being replaced and therefore would constitute an improvement of the property. These expenditures offset obsolescence and may be classified as modernization. Modernization may cost more than simple renewal but can be economically justified where it offsets the obsolescence inherent in the older equipment.

Modernization usually extends the economic life of property. To be justified, a modernization is done because the owner desires the convenience it creates. The installation of a modern kitchen at a cost of $10,000 may add only $5,000 in value. This is an example of a superadequacy or overimprovement.

Remodeling

Remodeling becomes practical when the use of part of the house can be changed. Common examples are finishing a basement or attic or adding a bathroom to an existing room. Considerable remodeling is often done to suit the needs of a specific owner without much thought given what the market in general expects and will pay for. The expenditure of $6,000 to finish a basement playroom may add only $3,000 to the property value in some markets.

RENOVATION COSTS

It is much more difficult to estimate renovation or rehabilitation costs than that of new construction. Unit-in-place costs for new work, plus an additional allowance for the normally higher cost of repair work, aid in making renovation estimates difficult. Rehabilitation estimates frequently may be based upon actual recent costs for the same or equivalent work performed in the property or in similar properties. Management records may even include bids for specific rehabilitation items that have not been accomplished, such as exterior painting, roof repair, or interior decorating.

The cost of some rehabilitation work may approximate that for similar work in new construction. However, the cost of modernization or remodeling work is almost invariably higher than that for new construction, for several reasons. Although the quantity of materials may be the same as for new work, more labor is involved and the conditions are different. The alteration of a structure usually involves tearing out old work and performing small portions of new work under conditions not conducive to the degree of efficiency attainable on new construction. If the estimate made by the contractor is on a flat-fee basis, the charge may be substantially higher than the cost of identical work in new construction, so the contractor can be protected against complications that may develop as the remodeling progresses. Such unforeseen complications may involve the placement of existing conduits, pipes, and structural load bearing members.

Other costs to be considered are those that may be incurred by the owner rather than the contractor. These include the architect's fee, the owner's cost of supervision and loss of use of the house while the work is being done.

FEASIBILITY OF RENOVATION

Whether rehabilitation, modernization or remodeling is involved, the justification for any renovation program depends on what constitutes the highest and best use of the property. The study that the appraiser gives to this question produces the cost estimates necessary for a program to achieve such use, which in turn provide the basis for a decision as to its economic justification.

If the property is old but in sufficiently sound condition for remodeling, if the neighborhood standards and trends are materially higher than the property's present status, and if the prospective value increase is substantial, a comprehensive program may be feasible. A wide range of potential programs may justify consideration, but there is only one satisfactory way to select the final plan. This is to explore the alternatives, estimate the cost and potential value increases and then be guided by the results of a comparison of the data.

Assume that a brownstone townhouse is available in a neighborhood going through a period of redevelopment. The house can be purchased for $60,000. It is estimated that it will take about $40,000 to rehabilitate the house to meet the minimum code requirements. The estimated value when the rehabilitation is completed is $120,000. Based on these figures, the rehabilitation to meet minimum standards is feasible. A second possibility is to restore the house to its original historical appearance and do a much more elaborate renovation. The estimated cost of this renovation would be $120,000, but the final value would be $240,000.

Renovation Example 1:

Acquisition price		$60,000
Rehabilitation cost		$40,000
Total Cost		$100,000
Estimated value after renovation		$120,000
Estimated profit		$20,000

Renovation Example 2:

Acquisition price		$60,000
Renovation cost		$120,000
Total cost		$180,000
Estimated value after renovation		$240,000
Estimated profit		$60,000

Both the above programs are feasible. However, Example 2 represents the highest and best use of the property, since it produces the maximum profit. In some cases where the profit potential, due to a program of rehabilitation, modernization and modeling is substantial, the "as is" value estimate for the property being appraised should be modified upward. In many cities properties have been purchased at relatively low prices by imaginative investors who have undertaken programs of selective modernization, sometimes involving new exterior ("skin") treatment and other major expenditures. Modernized and attractive properties thus created have become marketable at levels substantially higher than the investments involved. Whether this is practical in any specific situation can be ascertained only by completion of a before-and-after feasibility analysis.

In the final analysis, the appraiser's estimate of a renovation program is part of the process used to arrive at a value estimate for the property. Whether or not the owner actually carries out such a program, the value of the property in its existing state may be influenced by its potential for increased value under a feasible renovation program.

GRAPHIC AIDS

PHOTOGRAPHY

Use of photographs has become an important part of the appraisal report. Out-of-focus, over or under-exposed amateur photos are no long acceptable as part of a professional appraisal report. Instant photography methods are acceptable to some clients. Others require more professional pictures taken with a conventional camera. A 35mm camera is the choice of many experienced appraisers, because of the rectangular shape of the photographs, the versatility of the equipment, the availability of film and low cost for color reproduction. The use of color photographs has become standard.

There is no absolute rule as to what the photographs should include. However, at a minimum, photographs of all sides of the improvements and any major site improvements, plus a shot of the street in both directions showing the subject in the foreground, may be required. When the assignment warrants the extra expense, photographs of construction details and of the interior may also be included.

Many appraisers use 35 mm cameras. The best results at the lowest cost can be obtained in most situations by using 100 speed color film. Try setting your camera at 100th of a second. This setting usually will be fast enough to prevent blurring from the shaking of the camera and will still produce a sufficient depth of field.

PLOT PLAN

A plot plan shows the lot boundaries, important topographical features and the location of the improvements. A well-drawn plot plan is made to scale, with lot dimensions indicated on the boundary lines. In addition to the house and garage or carport, it should show the position of sidewalks, driveways, patios, pools, etc. Any abutting rights-of-way, known easements or apparent encroachments should also be shown. An appraiser is not expected to be a professional draftsperson but the plot plan should be neat and carefully drawn.

SKETCH OF THE BUILDINGS

Often a simple sketch of the exterior walls of the buildings (and garage or carport, if any) or a more complete drawing showing the location of doors, windows and interior walls is included as part of the report. Many appraisers take special pride in their ability to produce professionally drawn sketches. Such drawings are not required for a typical appraisal; a simple, neatly drawn sketch to approximate scale, showing the important dimensions, will usually suffice. The dimensions that appear on the sketch should be the same ones used to calculate the gross living area.

READING A HOUSE PLAN

The appraiser who is appraising a house planned for construction, under construction or being considered for a program of renovation must be able to read the plans that detail the proposed construction. Architects use orthographic projections to picture the proposed work rather than perspective drawings. An orthographic projection permits proportional reduction of the drawing while maintaining the size and spatial relationships of the completed house. Lines drawn parallel in an orthographic projection represents walls that are parallel in the finished house.

A complete set of house plans consists of:

1 . Orthographic projections of each floor and the basement.

2 . Electric plans.

3 . Plumbing plans.

4 . Wall sections.

5. Elevations of all sides.

6 . Plot plan.

7 . Door and window schedules.

8 . Specifications.

The dimensions of an actual house may not appear to agree with those indicated on the house plans. It is impossible to tell from looking at the plans what the actual points of measurement are. An actual measurement read on the tape may be from one inch to more than five inches less than the dimension indicated on the plan. Architects seldom indicate dimensions from one wall surface to another. On drawings of frame houses, they prefer to indicate the dimensions between the surface of the studs of opposite walls or from the center of the opposite wall studs.

When stud-surface-to-stud-surface is used, the actual tape measurements are about one inch less than the indicated dimension line measurement, which is the thickness of the Sheet Rock. When the center of the stud is used as the point of measurement, the tape reading is about five inches less, since half the thickness of the stud is usually two inches plus the thickness of the Sheet rock.

The techniques for dimensioning masonry construction are different from those for frame construction. Dimension lines on masonry construction plans usually run from one masonry surface to another, rather than to the surface of the Sheet Rock or other wall coverings.

To read house plans, it is necessary to know the many symbols architects use to represent the materials, electric switches and outlets, plumbing fixtures and pipes, some of which appear on the following pages.

SUMMARY

The description of the improvements is an important part of the appraisal report. It provides the information used in the three approaches to value. It includes a description of all the improvements to the site as well as a complete description of the residence and any ancillary improvements. Information about all the physical components including their design, quality and condition is included. A list of items requiring immediate repair, plus a list of items that will require repair in the near future, should also be given. When appropriate, any feasible renovations should be specified.

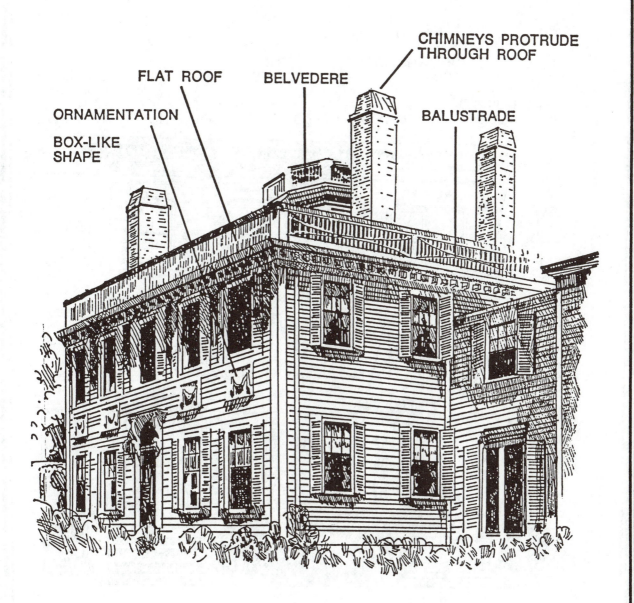

CHIMNEYS PROTRUDE
THROUGH ROOF

FLAT ROOF

BELVEDERE

BALUSTRADE

ORNAMENTATION

BOX-LIKE
SHAPE

Colonial American

FEDERAL (Federal - 101)

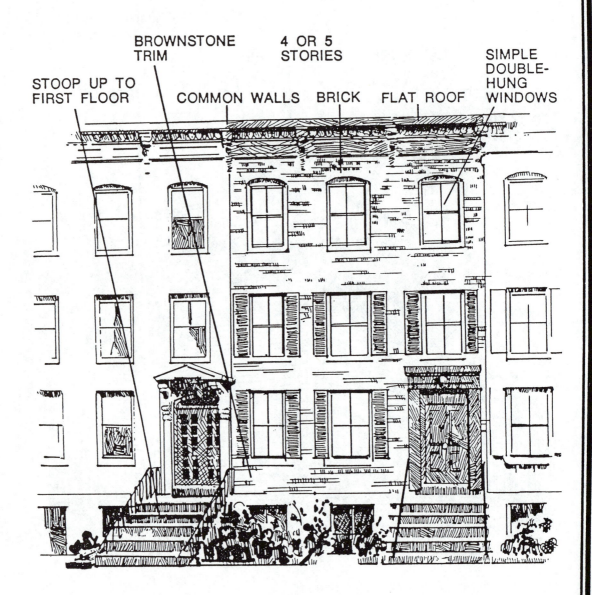

STOOP UP TO
FIRST FLOOR

BROWNSTONE
TRIM

4 OR 5
STORIES

SIMPLE
DOUBLE-
HUNG
WINDOWS

COMMON WALLS   BRICK   FLAT ROOF

Nineteenth Century American

BROWNSTONE OR BRICK ROW HOUSE OR EASTERN TOWNHOUSE (Brown S or Br Row or E Town - 713)

13 Cost Approach

The Cost Approach like the other two approaches to value is based on the assumption that the cost to produce a building plus the cost to acquire and improve the site to make it suitable for building is a good indication of what a property is worth.

Every real estate parcel is different, so that location is a very important component of value. Unlike other commodities where suitable substitutes are easily found, the cost of a property is not as perfect an indication of its value as it is for these other commodities, i.e., automobiles, diamonds, gold, etc.

There are some appraisers and some important buyers of appraisals who do not believe the Cost Approach is useful in residential appraising. The Employee Relocation Council has eliminated it from its required relocation form (see Addenda K). Others (including the author) believe it works well on residences, especially if the reproduction cost is obtained from a computerized cost service and the depreciation is taken from the market by the abstraction process which is explained later in this chapter.

Cost is not necessarily or automatically the equivalent of market value. The procedure for developing the estimated value of the improvements requires the conversion of "cost to construct" figures to market value figures. The process of making such a conversion requires care, caution and skill.

A separate valuation of the improvements is needed for a variety of reasons, and the Cost Approach is one of the ways to obtain it. These reasons include tax purposes (where ad valorem tax laws dictate this separation in value), accounting (where it is used to report the depreciation of buildings) and to obtain the value of the land by the land residual method. The cost approach is especially useful when estimating the value of special purpose properties where there is no market.

STEPS OF THE COST APPROACH

1 . Estimate the value of the site and site improvements (this technique is described elsewhere in this text).

2 . Estimate the Reproduction Cost of the improvements (some appraisers use Replacement Cost; when Replacement Cost is used it should be noted in the comments section).

3 . Estimate the amount of depreciation from all causes and categorize it into the three major types of depreciation: Physical Deterioration, Functional Obsolescence and External Obsolescence.

4 . Deduct the total estimated depreciation from the reproduction or replacement cost of the improvements to derive the amount of value the improvements contribute to the property.

5 . Add together the value of the site, the value contributed by the site improvements and landscaping, and the cost of all the improvements less the applicable depreciation.

ESTIMATE THE VALUE OF THE SITE

The value of the site is normally estimated assuming it is unimproved and ready to be used for its highest and best use.

"In some circumstances, the appraisal of a property may require that the site be considered in terms other than its highest and best use. In appraisal to estimate the use value or legal, non conforming use value of an improved site, an appraiser may need to value the site according to its specified use or the existing improvements, not its highest and best use. In this case, the appraiser should value the site both in terms of its highest and best use and its conditional use."[1]

In the past, the estimate of site value was part of the Cost Approach in the Valuation Process. Now it is considered to be a separate step. It is covered in Chapter 10 Site Valuation in this text.

ESTIMATE THE COST NEW OF THE IMPROVEMENTS

REPRODUCTION COST VERSUS REPLACEMENT COST

Reproduction cost is the dollar amount required to construct an exact duplicate of the subject building, at current prices.

Replacement cost is the cost of creating a structure and other improvements having the same or equivalent utility, using current standards of material and design, based on current prices for labor and materials.

Theoretically, reproduction cost is easier to use but as a matter of practicality, it becomes quite difficult to estimate for older buildings, because identical materials are not always available and construction methods and design are constantly changing. The use of replacement cost provides a practical alternative. It represents the funds required to build an equally desirable substitute building, not necessarily with identical materials or to the same specifications.

For example, reproduction cost for an older house erected with solid brick walls would be computed on the basis of identical construction today. On the other hand, an estimate of replacement cost would not necessarily imply a structure with solid

---

[1]*Appraisal of Real Estate*, 10th Edition, Appraisal Institute, Chicago, IL. 1992

brick walls. Quite possibly current design and construction standards in the neighborhood for a house of this type, style and value would be frame construction with brick veneer walls. Accordingly, by using replacement cost instead of reproduction cost, some of the obsolescence or "inutility" present in the house with solid masonry walls would be eliminated from the estimate before deductions for accrued depreciation are made.

Care must be exercised not to take double depreciation. In the above example, the solid masonry walls have already been treated by using replacement cost of a frame house with brick veneer walls. A penalty should not again be deducted under functional obsolescence.

TYPES OF COSTS

For both reproduction cost and replacement cost estimates, costs can be broken down into direct or hard costs and indirect or soft costs. To these are added the developer's entrepreneurial profit.

Direct (Hard) Costs

These are costs of labor, materials, and contractors and subcontractors overhead and profit. It does not include the profit hoped to be made by the developer (who may or may not be the contractor).

Typically direct costs consist of the following:

1 . Labor.
2 . Materials.
3 . Equipment.
4 . Contractor profit and overhead.
5 . Security during construction.
6 . Temporary construction building.
7 . Temporary fencing and walls.
8 . Utilities used during construction.
9 . Storage of materials during construction.
10. Contractor's performance bond.

Indirect (Soft) Costs

These are all the other costs associated with the construction of a building not included in the direct costs.

Typical indirect (soft) costs consist of the following:

1 . Professional services.
   a. Architect's fees.
   b. Engineer's fees.
   c. Surveyor's fees.
   d. Legal fees and expenses.
   e. Appraisal fees.
2 . Developer's overhead.
3 . Building permits and licenses.
4 . Insurance premiums.
5 . Interest.

6 . Taxes.

7 . Selling expenses (commissions, advertising, promotion).

8 . Carrying costs from time of completion to sale or occupancy.

Entrepreneurial Profit

Many appraisers feel that an additional amount should be added to the direct and indirect cost to represent entrepreneurial profit. Since not all developers make a profit, this figure should represent the typical anticipated developer profit.

ESTIMATING REPRODUCTION OR REPLACEMENT COST

There are three methods for estimating the reproduction or replacement cost of a building:

1 . **Square foot or cubic foot method (comparative-unit method),** in which the cost per square foot or cubic foot of a recently built comparable structure is multiplied by the number of square feet in the subject property.

2 . **Unit-in-place method (segregated cost method),** in which the construction cost per square foot or other appropriate measure of each component part of the subject building (including material, labor, overhead, and builder's profit) is multiplied by the number of square feet or other appropriate measure of that component part in the subject building.

3 . **Quantity survey method,** in which the cost of erecting or installing all of the component parts of a new building are added. Indirect costs (building permit, land survey, overhead expenses such as insurance and payroll taxes, and builder's profit) are totaled, as well as direct costs (site preparation and all phases of building construction, including fixtures).

The quantity survey method is the one generally used by cost estimators, contractors, and builders. Of the three methods, the quantity survey method results in the most accurate cost estimate, since all of the building's components are analyzed. The square foot and unit-in-place methods are generalized cost figures for either comparable building type (square foot method) or specific buildings components (unit-in-place method). Of the two methods, the unit-in-place method is more exact, since it allows for more variables in the subject building.

Square Foot Method

To begin the square foot method of estimating reproduction cost, the appraiser must find the dimensions of the subject building to compute the number of square feet of ground area the building covers. In collecting cost data to use in the square foot method, the appraiser must find the cost of a comparable new building. Since a comparable new building may not be available, the appraiser usually relies on cost manuals for basic construction prices.

A page from a typical cost manual appears in Fig. 13-1. The type of building is specified and construction features are itemized, with utilities (mechanical features) listed separately. If the closest example in the cost manual still has significant differences from the subject building, a cost differential could be added to (or subtracted from) the cost per square foot given in the cost manual. Computer services are available which also produce cost data for appraisers. (Fig. 13-2).

FIG. 13-1 PAGE FROM A COST MANUAL

Square Foot Method
Average Quality
TOWN HOUSES AND DUPLEXES

Average Quality Town Houses and Duplexes are usually constructed to local building code and will exceed the minimum requirements of mortgage insuring agencies. Overall architectural design is simple with attention given only to the front elevation to distinguish one unit from another. The overall quality of materials and workmanship is average.

FOUNDATION . . . . Concrete perimeter foundation with continuous foundation under interior bearing walls, based on a moderate climate. Use Square Foot Adjustments for mild or extreme climate foundations, dividing by number of stories.

FLOOR STRUCTURE . . . . . . Wood structure and subfloor on first and upper story floors. For concrete slab on grade, deduct using Square Foot Adjustment per square foot of slab area.

FLOOR COVER . . . . Floor cover is not included in the basic residence cost. Floor covering includes carpet, hardwood and asphalt or vinyl composition tile or sheet. The floor cover allowance is a weighting of those typically found at this quality, and can be used if floor cover is not itemized.

EXTERIOR WALL . . . . Adequate fenestration using standard grade sash. The basic cost is wood frame with stucco. For other wall types, use percentage adjustments provided below the cost table.

ROOF . . . . Wood structure with lightweight composition shingles or built-up with small rock. Use Square Foot Adjustments for other types of roofing, dividing by number of stories.

INTERIOR FINISH . . . . Interior walls are taped and painted drywall. Ceilings are usually sprayed drywall with some enamel paint in kitchen and bath. Adequate wardrobe type bedroom, guest, and shelved linen closets. Cabinets in kitchen are hardwood veneer or paint grade wood. The cabinet tops are laminated plastic or ceramic tile with splash. Interior doors are stock, hollow core or flat panel, with standard grade hardware.

HEATING/COOLING . . . . . The basic residence cost includes a forced air heating system with adequate output and ductwork. Use Square Foot Adjustments for other types of Heating and/or Cooling.

ENERGY PACKAGE . . . . . . The energy package in the base cost includes those insulation, framing and glazing items typically found in a moderate climate, as outlined in the Introduction to the Square Foot Method. Square Foot Adjustments should be made for deviations from the moderate climate base.

ELECTRICAL . . . . Adequate number of outlets and standard grade fixtures.

PLUMBING . . . . Seven competitively priced white plumbing fixtures and one plumbing rough-in are included in the basic cost. The fixtures can include any of the following: water heater, toilet, lavatory, tub, tub with shower over, tile or fiberglass stall shower, or kitchen sink. Use Lump Sum Adjustments for deviations from seven fixtures and one plumbing rough-in.

BUILT-IN APPLIANCES . . . None are included in the base residence cost. The built-in appliance allowance is a weighting of those typically found at this quality level, and can be used when appliances are not itemized.

PORCHES/BALCONIES . . Similar to the base residence in both quality of materials and workmanship, porches and balconies are priced per square foot of floor area.

BASEMENT, UNFINISHED Costs are inclusive of poured concrete or concrete block walls, concrete slab, floor drains, the necessary columns and beams to support the living area above, and an adequate number of electrical outlets.

BASEMENT, FINISH . . . . . . As an additive cost to an unfinished basement, costs are provided for two degrees of finish: minimal and partitioned. The minimal finish is typical of game rooms and the partitioned finish is somewhat similar in both quality of materials and workmanship to that of the base residence.

GARAGES . . . . Garage costs include a reinforced concrete slab floor, an overhead door and electrical lighting, all of which conform to the residence in both quality and construction.

For Bi-level construction, price as a one story with basement and add partitioned basement finish. For two and one half story residences with a finished upper level, enter the two story cost column at the total floor area of all three levels, and multiply that cost by .956.

page A-142

TOWN HOUSES AND DUPLEXES
Square Foot Costs
Average Quality

FRAME AND STUCCO COSTS PER UNIT:

Sq. Ft. Floor Area	END ROW 1 Story	1-1/2 Story	2 Story	Split level	INSIDE ROW 1 Story	1-1/2 Story	2 Story	Split level
700	$36.79	$32.97	$35.37	$35.92	$34.71	$31.11	$33.31	$33.89
800	35.78	32.06	34.40	34.93	33.75	30.25	32.39	32.95
900	34.91	31.27	33.56	34.08	32.93	29.51	31.60	32.15
1000	34.14	30.59	32.83	33.33	32.21	28.87	30.91	31.45
1100	33.47	29.99	32.18	32.68	31.57	28.29	30.30	30.82
1200	32.86	29.45	31.60	32.09	31.00	27.78	29.75	30.27
1400	31.82	28.51	30.60	31.07	30.01	26.90	28.81	29.30
1600	30.94	27.72	29.75	30.21	29.18	26.16	28.02	28.49
1800	30.19	27.05	29.03	29.47	28.47	25.52	27.33	27.80
2000	29.53	26.46	28.40	28.83	27.85	24.96	26.74	27.19
2200	28.94	25.93	27.84	28.26	27.30	24.47	26.21	26.65
2400	28.42	25.47	27.33	27.75	26.80	24.02	25.74	26.17

FRAME: Plywood/Hardboard, — 2%; Siding/Shingle, + 1%; Masonry Veneer, + 8%;
MASONRY: Common Brick, + 12%; Concrete Block, + 4%

SQUARE FOOT ADJUSTMENTS:

ROOFING: (Divide by number of stories)		HEATING/COOLING:	
Comp. shingle/B.U. rock	(base)	Forced air	(base)
Wood shingle	+ $ .76	Oil fired	+ $ .56
Wood shake	+ .92	Floor or wall furnace	— .96
Concrete tile	+ 2.05	Gravity furnace	— .08
Composition roll	— .49	Electric, radiant	— .05
SUBFLOOR:		Baseboard or panel	— .13
Wood subfloor	(base)	Hot water, baseboard	+ .91
Concrete slab	— $1.69	Warm & cooled air	+ 1.28
FLOOR COVER:		Heat pump, packaged	+ 1.38
Allowance (if not itemized)	+ $1.51	**ENERGY ADJ.:** Moderate climate (base)	
Hardwood	+ 3.82	Mild climate	— $ .91
Carpet	+ 1.48	Extreme climate	+ 1.19
Resilient floor cover	+ 1.39	**FOUNDATION:** (Divide by no. of stories)	
Lt. wt. concrete	+ .53	Moderate climate	(base)
PLASTER INTERIOR:	+ $ .78	Mild climate	— $ .94
LUMP SUM ADJUSTMENTS PER UNIT:		Extreme climate	+ .94
PLUMBING: 7 fixtures + rough-in	(base)	**BUILT-IN APPLIANCES:**	
Per fixture . . . . + or —	$530	Allowance (if not itemized)	+ $1,290
Rough-in . . . . + or —	215	Range & oven	+ 595
FIREPLACES:		Hood & Fan	+ 140
Single, 1 story	$1,100 - $1,575	Dishwasher	+ 385
Single, 2 story	1,450 - 1,950	Garbage disposer	+ 140
Single, 3 story	1,800 - 2,325	Exhaust fan or bath heater .	+ 90
BASEMENT: Outside entrance: $695		Wall air cond., 3/4 ton	+ 465

	End Row				Inside Row			
Unfinished, basement:	200	400	800	1600	200	400	800	1600
Concrete walls	$16.16	$11.91	$ 8.78	$ 6.47	$14.94	$11.01	$ 8.12	$ 5.98
Concrete block walls	14.11	10.40	7.66	5.65	13.05	9.62	7.09	5.22
	Minimal Finish				Partitioned Finish			
Add for finish	$ 3.61	$ 3.26	$ 2.95	$ 2.68	$15.66	$13.51	$11.65	$10.06

PORCH/BALCONY: Exterior stairways per flight: Wood: $555; Cement comp.: $935

Area	Floor Structure: Open Slab	Open Deck W/Steps	Wood Deck	Cement Comp. Deck	Wall Enclosure: Screen Only	Knee Wall W/Glass	Add For Roof	Add For Ceiling
25	$ 3.31	$ 8.22	$10.49	$12.19	$ 6.62	$32.78	$ 5.88	$ 1.79
50	2.83	7.30	9.44	10.97	4.63	22.93	5.32	1.62
100	2.43	6.48	8.51	9.88	3.25	16.04	4.82	1.47
300	1.90	5.36	7.21	8.36	1.85	9.10	4.11	1.25

GARAGE:

	Area	Plywood or Hardboard	Stucco	Siding or Shingle	Masonry Veneer	Common Brick	Concrete Block	Add For Finish
Attached	200	$12.95	$13.24	$13.33	$14.50	$15.54	$13.74	$ 2.58
	400	11.34	11.60	11.67	12.70	13.48	12.01	2.40
Detached	200	$18.47	$18.90	$19.10	$21.70	$23.78	$19.86	$ 3.29
	400	14.10	14.43	14.56	16.30	17.60	15.08	2.75
Built-in	200	$ 9.30	$ 9.57	$ 9.46	$10.31	$11.00	$ 9.67	$ .70
	400	7.90	8.13	8.17	8.71	9.20	8.14	.53

Basement Garages, add lump sum to unfin. bsmt. costs: Single: $ 960, Double: $1,295
Carports: Shed or Flat roof: $5.75, Gable roof: $6.70

RESIDENTIAL COST HANDBOOK
© 1988 - MARSHALL & SWIFT - PRINTED IN U.S.A.

page A-143

FIG. 13-2 COMPUTER PRODUCED COST ESTIMATE

```
                        REPRODUCTION COST



The reproduction cost of the house was obtained by using the
Marshall and Swift cost service.  Information about the suject
house was inputed into an office computer using the Marshall
and Swift software.  The cost calculations were printed on our
printer as shown below:




City, State, ZIP: Bloomville, IL, 60611
Surveyed by     : Henry S. Harrison
Date of Survey  : March 12, 200_

Single Family Residence            Floor Area: 1,888 square feet
Effective Age: 30 years            Quality: Average
Cost as of 3/                      Condition: Average

            Style:  One Story
Heating & Cooling:  Baseboard, Hot Water
   Exterior Wall:   Face Brick
         Roofing:   Composition Shingle
Floor Structure:    Wood Subfloor
    Floor Cover:    Standard Allowance
        Plumbing:   Standard Allowance
      Appliances:   Standard Allowance
  Other Features:   Single Fireplace

                                  Units     Cost      Total
                                  -----     ----      -----
Basic Structure Cost...........   1,888     53.35    100,721
                                  ----------------------------
Garage:
  Attached Garage..............     506     16.15      8,170
                                  ----------------------------
Extras:
  Roofed Porch w/Steps.........     144     13.44      1,935
  Domestic Solar Hot Water Unit.                       3,500
  Subtotal.....................                        5,435
                                  ----------------------------
Replacement Cost New.:.........   1,888     60.55    114,326
                                  ----------------------------
Less Depreciation:
  Physical Depreciation........   <40.0%>             <45,730>
  Functional Depreciation......   <7.9%>              <9,000>
  Locational Depreciation......   <5.0%>              <5,716>
  Subtotal.....................   <52.9%>             <60,446>
Depreciated Cost...............   1,888     28.54     53,880
                                  ----------------------------
Miscellaneous:
  Land.........................                       20,000
  Site Improvements............                        3,000
  Subtotal.....................                       23,000
                                  ----------------------------
Total..........................   1,888     40.72     76,880
                                  ----------------------------
Cost data by MARSHALL and SWIFT
```

Unit-In-Place Method

The unit-in-place method is also called the segregated cost method. It employs unit costs for various building components as they are normally installed.

A unit-in-place cost estimate is made by breaking up a building into components and estimating the cost of the material and labor required to install that unit into the building that is being built, on the date of the appraisal.

Unit-in-place cost estimates are made in terms of standard costs for each of the building components as installed.

FIG. 13-3 ESTIMATE COSTS OF HOUSE CONSTRUCTION COMPONENTS*

Component	Unit	Quantity	Unit Cost	Total
General expense (engineering, plans, survey, site)	sq. ft./GLA	1,442 sq. ft.	$ 2.76	$ 4,000
Foundation	sq. ft./GLA	1,442 sq. ft.	4.44	6,400
Basement	sq. ft./GLA	1.442 sq. ft.	6.64	9,600
Floors	sq. ft./GLA	1,383 sq. ft.	7.52	10,400
Exterior walls & insulation (including windows & exterior doors)	lin.. ft./wall	1,450 lin. ft.	12.96	18,800
Roof	sq. ft./GLA	1,442 sq. ft.	8.32	12,000
Roof dormers	lin. ft. across face	None	-	-
Interior walls, ceilings, doors, cabinets, trim and accessories	sq. ft./GLA	1,442 sq. ft.	13.04	18,800
Stairways	each	2 outside	800.	1,600
Attic finish	sq. ft./fin. area	None	-	-
Heating	sq. ft./GLA	1,442 sq. ft.	4.44	6,400
Cooling				
Electric System	sq. ft./GLA	1,442 sq. ft.	5.56	8,000
Plumbing system	sq. ft./GLA	1,442 sq. ft.	11.08	16,000
Fireplaces & chimneys	each	1 chimney	3,200	3,200
Built-in appliances	each	2	1,200	2,400
Porches	sq. ft./porch	none	-	-
Patios	sq. ft./patio	144 sq. ft.	5.56	800
Other	doors & windows	22	72.72	1,600
Site improvements (not included in land value)	each lump sum	-	2,400	2,400
Garage	sq. ft./garage	460 sq. ft.	17.39	8,000
Indirect costs**	sq. ft./GLA	1,442 sq. ft.	2,052	29,600
TOTAL				$160,000

*These are not actual costs but an illustration of how costs might be approximately allocated in a $160,000 house.

**May be added to each component (rather than shown separately, as in this example).

Quantity Survey Method

This comprehensive method used by many contractors requires preparation of a detailed inventory of all the materials and equipment used to build the house. To this list is applied the cost of each item as of the date of appraisal. Also estimated is the amount of labor in hours needed to install each item, using current labor rates. Finally the indirect costs, overhead and profit items are added to the cost of material, equipment and labor.

An example of a section of a contractor's cost breakdown for a typical house is shown in Fig. 13-4.

FIG. 13-4 SECTION OF CONTRACTOR'S COST BREAKDOWN

Item	Units	Material Price	Total	Hours	Labor Rate	Total	Total Cost
Cabinet work base-finished w/Formica top	16	$ 88	$ 704	14	$14.60	$204.40	$ 908.40
Plumbing 60-gal. hot	1	$1,300	$1,300	30	$30.80	$924.00	$2,224.00

To prepare this breakdown using the quantity survey method, the contractor first lists all the material and equipment and estimates the amount of labor required to install each item. Then the material, equipment and labor are priced out per unit and extended to give the total cost of installing each item.

Except for an unusual appraisal, this type of breakdown is beyond the scope normally required. When such a breakdown is required, the services of a trained cost estimator should be obtained.

Appraisers often use a summary of the contractor's cost breakdown; Fig. 13-4 shows a typical cost breakdown for a house. The specifications and general description of the house used for this example are as follows:

General Description: One-family, one-story, ranch-style, seven rooms (living room, family room, dining room, kitchen, three bedrooms, two full baths), full unfinished basement. No porches. Gross living area: 1,422 square feet. Two-car, attached garage.

General Construction: Concrete footings and foundation walls. Exterior walls: cedar shingles. Roof covering: cedar shingles. Wood, double-hung windows, combination aluminum storm windows and screens, aluminum gutters and down spouts, Batt type insulation. Wood platform framing, plywood subfloors, oak floors, except kitchen (vinyl asbestos) and bathrooms (ceramic tile wainscot).

Mechanical Systems: Plumbing: copper water and waste pipes connected to municipal services in street. Electric 60-gal. domestic hot water heater. One double, stainless steel kitchen sink. Each bathroom has standard water closet, lavatory and tub with shower. Laundry tub in basement and washer/dryer hook-up. Heating: Oil-fired, hot water furnace; two circulators; baseboard radiators. Electrical: 100-ampere service; 16 circuits protected with circuit breakers; BX cable; adequate outlets and features. Built-in Appliances: gas oven and range, hood with exhaust fan in kitchen.

WORK DIVIDED BY SUB-CONTRACTOR

Many contractors use numerous subcontractors who have special expertise in certain areas and can often do the work better and cheaper than a general contractor. Typically, general contractors who use a substantial number of subcontractors figure the cost of a building by breaking it down into components corresponding to the work done by the various subcontractors. Popular cost services also use this technique and call it the segregated cost method. The technique is based on the use of unit prices for the various building components using workable units such as square foot or linear foot or some other appropriate basic unit.

In Fig. 13-5 a typical list of house construction components is given. The cost estimates for these components are made in terms of standardized unit costs for installation. Providing that the units accurately reflect costs, this estimate is a short-cut to an actual quantity survey. The resulting figure should correspond in accuracy with that derived from a quantity survey.

Based on the summary in Fig. 13-5 an appraiser would estimate the reproduction cost new at $160,000. Note that this example is not in itself a complete quantity survey breakdown but represents a recapitulation of the cost estimator's quantity survey analysis.

FIG. 13-5 EXAMPLE OF A COST BREAKDOWN FOR A SINGLE FAMILY HOUSE*

Component	% of Total	Cost
Survey & Financing	1/2	$ 800
Plans & Plan Checking	1/2	800
Site Preparation	1/2	800
Excavation	1	1,600
Footings & Foundation	4	6,400
Basement	6	9,600
Framing	7-1/2	12,000
Interior Walls & Ceiling	3-1/2	5,600
Exterior Siding	3	4,800
Roof Covering & Flashing	5	8,000
Insulation	2	3,200
Fireplaces & Chimneys (no fireplace)	2	3,200
Leaders & Gutters	1	1,600
Exterior & Interior Stairs	1	1,600
Doors, Windows & Shutters	2	3,200
Storm Windows, Doors & Screens	1	1,600
Main Floor Covering (Carpeting)	3	4,800
Kitchen Flooring	1/2	800
Bathroom & Lavatory Floors	1/2	800
Hardware	1/2	800
Water Supply	1	1,600
Waste Disposal	1	1,600
Heating	4	6,400
Cooling (no central air conditioning)	-	-
Domestic Hot Water	1	1,600
Piping	4	6,400
Plumbing Fixtures	3	4,800
Kitchen Cabinets & Counters	3	4,800
Built-In Appliances	1-1/2	2,400
Shower Doors	1/2	800
Bathroom Accessories	1/2	800
Vanities, Medicine Cabinets & Counters	1/2	800
Electric Service	2	3,200
Electric Wires & Outlets	2	3,200
Lighting Fixtures	1	1,600
Painting & Decorating	4	6,400
Porches (none)	-	-
Patios	1/2	800
Finish Grading	1/2	800
Landscaping	1	1,600
Garages & Carports	5	8,000
Clean Up	1/2	800
Interest, Taxes & Insurance	1	1,600
Contractor's Overhead & Temporary Facilities	4	6,400
Professional Services, Permits & Licenses	1	1,600
Selling Expenses, Carrying Costs	5	8,000
Contractor's Profit	7-1/2	12,000
TOTAL COST	100	$160,000

General Quality: House is average quality throughout and meets FHA minimum standards.

The square foot unit cost varies inversely with the size of the house. It reflects the fact that plumbing, heating systems, doors, windows and similar items do not necessarily cost proportionately more in a large house than in a small one. If a similar cost is spread over a larger area, the unit cost is obviously less.

The apparent simplicity of the square foot comparison method can be misleading. Dependable square foot cost figures require the exercise of care and judgment in the process of comparison with similar or standard houses for which actual costs are known. Inaccuracies may result from selection of a square foot cost that is not properly related to the house under appraisal. However, correct application of this procedure will provide estimates of reproduction or replacement cost that are reasonably accurate and entirely acceptable in appraisal practice.

SOURCES OF COST FIGURES

Several reliable sources for obtaining cost data exist.

--Cost Data File. The use of square foot cost estimates involves assembling, analyzing and cataloging data on actual house costs. An appraiser should have available comprehensive current cost information for various types of houses and other improvements, including data on current material and labor costs. A system of grading quality of construction may also be used to refine the data further. This data can often be obtained from local builders, lenders, material suppliers and trade associations.

A file of this kind provides a check against costs of reproducing or replacing an existing residence, as well as against known or projected costs for existing or proposed houses of varying grades of construction. It also provides a check against the probable cost of different components of a house and of the various trades or work involved.

--Cost Services. Several recognized cost reporting services are also available to the appraiser. Some include illustrations of typical structures and provide adjustments to tailor the standard example to differently shaped or equipped residences. Some provide adjustment for individual cities or areas. Some show cubic foot or square foot costs, and some are designed for unit-in-place information.

--Cost Indices. A cost index service reflecting the relative cost of construction over a period of years is also useful. When the actual cost of a residence constructed some years ago is known, application of the index will indicate the present construction cost (provided the actual cost was typical figure). For example, assume that a house cost $53,000 to build in January 1955 and that a 1955 cost index, from a national service, was 284.4. The April 1989 cost index was 863.2. Based upon this data, in 1989 the building cost 3.035 times its January 1955 cost (863.2 ÷ 284.4), or an indicated cost of $160,863.

BUILDING COST ESTIMATES

Building cost estimates should include all materials, equipment and labor. The contractor's overhead and profit, architect's fees and other outside professional services, taxes, insurance, administration and interest on borrowed funds during the period of construction may or may not be included. Some appraisers elect to allocate these costs proportionately across the direct costs; others estimate and report them separately. Some appraisers also add developer's profit.

For example, assume as a benchmark house a two-story, brick residence costs $150,000 to build, exclusive of detached garage or other site improvements. The quality of construction is roughly comparable to that of an average mass-produced home with asphalt shingle roofing, 1/2-inch drywall, good average finish and equipment with combination forced-air heat and air conditioning, plus a dishwasher, disposal and fireplace. Included are three bedrooms, 2-1/2 baths and full basement. This residence contains 1,496 square feet, thus costing approximately $100 per square foot of gross living area.

Assume that the appraiser is preparing a cost estimate for a house roughly comparable to the above example. In contrast to the benchmark house, the house being appraised has a concrete block foundation in lieu of poured concrete, no fireplace and a good grade of wood siding instead of brick exterior walls. The appraiser makes downward adjustments for these differences: $5.00 per sq. ft. GLA for wood siding; $1.00 per sq. ft. GLA for the block foundation; and $3.00 per sq. ft. GLA for lack of fireplace. The adjusted unit cost is now $91.00 per square foot. If indirect costs are not included in these unit cost adjustments, their total may be increased by an additional 15% to 20%.

DEPRECIATION

A simple definition of depreciation is the difference between the cost of an improvement on the date of the appraisal and the value of the improvement.

More formally, it has been defined as:
> A loss of utility and hence value from any cause. An effect caused by deterioration and/or obsolescence. Deterioration or physical depreciation is evidenced by wear and tear, decay, dry rot, cracks, encrustations, or structural defects. Obsolescence is divisible into two parts, functional and external. Functional obsolescence may be due to poor plan, mechanical inadequacy or over adequacy, functional inadequacy or over adequacy due to size, style, age, etc. It is evidenced by conditions within the property. External obsolescence is caused by changes external to the property.

Depreciation begins upon construction of the improvements. They immediately begin to age physically and to suffer from functional obsolescence in their design. Negative environmental forces cause immediate external obsolescence.

When the improvements are constructed, their economic life begins. During this period, they should contribute value to the property. If they are the "perfect improvement", the amount of value they contribute would be their total cost. Since few, if any, perfect improvements are constructed, a difference exists between their total cost and their value which represents some form of depreciation. At the point when an improvement cannot be profitably utilized or when it no longer contributes to the value of the property, it is at the end of its economic life and depreciation has reached 100%.

Generally, if the house is of average condition and design and conforms to the other houses in a neighborhood that is not subject to unusual economic influences, its effective age and chronological age will be about the same. If the house has had better than average maintenance, rehabilitation or modernization, its effective age probably will be less than its chronological age. If it is in poorer condition than typical houses of the same age or has not been modernized or rehabilitated as other similar houses in the neighborhood or if some off-site economic or environmental factor is negatively affecting the value, the effective age will be greater than the chronological age.

TECHNIQUES FOR ESTIMATING ACCRUED DEPRECIATION

Accrued depreciation may be estimated directly through observation and analysis of the components of depreciation affecting the property or through use of a formula based on physical or economic age-life factors. It may also be estimated indirectly by use of the income or market data approaches.

Three techniques are used by the appraiser to measure depreciation:

1. The breakdown method separates charges on the basis of origin for cause of loss (physical deterioration, curable and incurable; functional obsolescence, curable and incurable; and external obsolescence). Each component is estimated separately, using the engineering method or observation techniques.

2. The age-life method is accomplished by estimating the typical economic life of the improvements and their effective age.

3. The abstraction or market method extracts depreciation directly from the market.

THE BREAKDOWN METHOD

The breakdown method is accomplished by dividing depreciation into its three separate components: physical deterioration, functional obsolescence and external (environmental) obsolescence. Physical deterioration and functional obsolescence may be further broken down into curable and incurable types. A grasp of these underlying principles is essential to an overall understanding of depreciation.

--Physical Deterioration-Curable. These are all the items of maintenance that a prudent owner should accomplish on the date of appraisal to maximize the profit (or minimize the loss) if the property is sold. Almost any item of physical deterioration can be corrected at a price. However, to be classified as curable, the cure normally must contribute more value than it costs. Items of normal maintenance usually fall into the category, including paint touch-ups and minor carpentry, plumbing and electric repairs (leaking faucets, squeaking or tight doors and windows, etc.). Interior and exterior painting and redecorating may also be included.

The ultimate test is whether the market will recognize as additional value at least the cost of the repair. Realtors® have long recognized that minor repairs do add value equal to or in excess of their cost and they try to have an owner make these repairs before a house is offered for sale. The measure of physical deterioration-curable is the cost to cure. Many appraisal clients require that an itemized list of the curable items be part of the report together with an estimate of the cost to cure.

--Physical Deterioration-Incurable. As soon as a house is constructed, it begins to age and suffer from wear and tear. Physical deterioration-incurable is based on the physical condition of the components of the house. The total physical life of the house would equal its total economic life if other forms of depreciation were not present. One of the practical problems in estimating the percentage of physical deterioration-incurable is estimating the physical life of the components. There is a tendency to assign too much depreciation to physical deterioration-incurable by using estimates of 50 to 100 years for items such as footings, foundations, framing, wall and ceiling coverings, etc.. Some of these items may last hundreds of years.

To measure physical deterioration-incurable, items are divided into two categories: long-lived and short-lived. Long-lived items, such a footings, foundations, etc. can be depreciated as a group by making an estimate of their effective age and remaining physical life based on their condition. The engineering method, in which items are separately listed and their reproduction cost estimated, can also be used (see Fig. 13.6). By observation, a percentage of depreciation is estimated and extended into a dollar estimate for each component. Indirect costs must be either allocated proportionately to each component or listed separately, and depreciation for them also estimated.

FIG. 13-6 COMPONENT PHYSICAL LIFE (ENGINEERING METHOD)

House Component	Reproduction Cost New		Estimated % Deterioration		Accrued Depreciation
Survey & engineering	$ 800	x	20%	=	$ 160
Foundation	3,200	x	20%	=	640
Plumbing	4,000	x	30%	=	1,200
Electrical system	8,000	x	35%	=	2,800
TOTAL	$160,000				$88,000

Short-lived items are components whose remaining physical life is shorter than the total estimated remaining economic life of the house. Typically they include roof, gutters and down spouts, kitchen cabinets and counters, painting and decorating. Sometimes these items are classified as physical deterioration-curable-deferred.

Again, the technique for estimating depreciation is to make a list of components, estimating the reproduction cost of each as well as a percentage of depreciation, based on the appraiser's observations. These estimates are extended into a dollar estimate for each component and totaled. The process may be shortened by estimating a total reproduction cost of all the short-lived items and using an average percentage of depreciation; this may decrease the accuracy of the estimate.

--Functional Obsolescence-Curable. Most functional obsolescence-curable in residential properties is caused by some kind of deficiency. In other types of properties some superadequacies would also be considered curable but they are rare in residential properties. Typical items that fall into this category are kitchens that need new counters, cabinets, fixtures and floor coverings; inadequate electrical service and hot water systems; and need of an additional bath or powder room where adequate space exists. Again, the test is whether the value added by correcting the obsolescence is greater than the cost to cure as indicated in the market.

The measure of functional obsolescence-curable is the difference between what it would cost on the date of appraisal to reproduce the house with the curable item included and to reproduce the house on the same date without it. Only the excess cost of adding the item to the existing structure above the cost of incorporating the item as part of a total house construction process represents the measure of accrued depreciation. It is neither proper nor logical to deduct accrued depreciation from reproduction cost of an item that has not been included in the reproduction cost estimate for the existing house.

For example, assume that in light of current market expectations, the house being appraised lacks a second bath where room exists to install one. The estimated cost to include this bath as part of the total house construction program as of the date of the appraisal is $8,000. The estimated cost to do it as a separate job as of the same date would be more because it generally costs more to build parts of a house separately as compared to building the whole house at one time. If it would cost $10,000 to build the extra bath as a separate job, the measure of depreciation would be the $2,000 excess cost.

--Functional Obsolescence-Incurable. These items can be divided into two categories: loss in value caused by a deficiency or by an excess or superadequacy. Deficiencies are caused by exterior or interior design that does not meet current market expectations. This can be measured by the rent loss attributable to the deficiency multiplied by the gross monthly rent multiplier applicable to the property (See Fig. 13.7).

FIG. 13-7 ESTIMATING INCURABLE FUNCTIONAL OBSOLESCENCE BY CAPITALIZING RENT LOSS

Monthly rental, House A with 3 bedrooms	$1,140
Monthly rental, House B with 2 bedrooms	1,060
Difference	$ 80
GMRM for neighborhood	130
Difference in value between A and B ($80 monthly rent loss x 130 GMRM)	$10,400

--Functional Obsolescence-Superadequacy. The second type of incurable functional obsolescence is caused by superadequacy. Probably only a small percentage of houses exist that do not have some such obsolescence. The number of superadequacies tends to increase as a house gets older and the occupants improve it with features suited for their individual living style. Superadequacies are not only improvements made after construction but also anything initially built into the house that does not add value at least equal to its cost. For example, a builder elects to install in a new house an intercom system, central air conditioning, stainless steel kitchen sink and vinyl kitchen floor, the cost of which might be $20,000 total. If they only add $16,000 value to the house, the lost $4,000 would be functional obsolescence-superadequacy, assuming no other forms of depreciation existed.

Another example is a master bedroom, 16 by 18 feet, which cost $2,000 more to build than a bedroom 14 by 16 feet. If the extra size only adds $1,200 value, the lost $800 is functional obsolescence, superadequacy (again, assuming there are no other forms of depreciation).

Almost all superadequacies are incurable in houses. (In commercial and investment properties sometimes it pays to remove them because of excess operating costs). For example, a new house suffering from no physical deterioration or external obsolescence has a swimming pool that cost $40,000 to install. It adds only $25,000 value, so $15,000 is functional obsolescence-superadequacy.

Superadequacies are measured in the same manner as deficiencies, by finding a matched pair of sales from the market. If a rent differential can be attributed to the superadequacy, it can be capitalized to indicate the value of the superadequacy. The difference between this value and the cost of the item, less other forms of depreciation, would be classified as functional obsolescence-superadequacy.

--External Obsolescence. Also called locational or environmental obsolescence by some appraisers, it is the loss of value to the improvements caused by factors outside the property boundaries. It is unique to real estate, caused by its fixed location. The value of a house is directly affected by the neighborhood, community and region in which it is located. In analyzing the location and environment of the property, the appraiser must consider government actions, economic forces, employment, transportation, recreation, education services, taxes, etc.

Consideration must also be given to factors in the immediate vicinity that detract from value. Unattractive natural features such as swamps, polluted waterways and obstructed views are examples of items that will detract from value. Poorly maintained non-conforming houses and uncollected junk in nearby yards are indications of possible economic obsolescence.

Although facilities such as fire stations, schools, stores, restaurants, hospitals and gas stations are advantageous to have nearby, they may detract from the value if they are too close to the house. Nearby industry, highways and airports may be another type of nuisance especially if they are unattractive, noisy or smoke and odor-emitting. External obsolescence can also be caused by factors that affect the supply or demand of houses competitive with the house being appraised, such as an unusual number of houses for sale.

The list of factors causing economic obsolescence is almost endless and the appraiser should carefully search for and evaluate anything off the property that detracts from the value of the house.

External obsolescence like functional obsolescence can also be measured by the rent loss attributable to the factor causing the obsolescence. However, a different method is used because part of the rent loss caused by detrimental external factors must be allocated to the land. For example, the market indicated that houses next to gasoline stations rent for $40 less than other houses. The GMRM for the neighborhood is 130. The land-to-improvement ratio in this neighborhood typically is land, 15%, improvements, 85%. Some of the rent loss must be allocated to the land, which in this case is 15%.

FIG. 13-8 ESTIMATING ECONOMIC OBSOLESCENCE USING RENT LOSS METHOD

Total rent loss	$ 40.00
Loss allocated to land ($40 x 15%)	−6.00
Loss allocated to improvement	$ 34.00
Economic obsolescence ($34.00 x GMRM 130)	$ 4,420

External obsolescence can also be calculated by finding matched pairs of sales. The pair must consist of one sale that is affected by the influence causing economic obsolescence and another sale that is not so affected. First, all other differences are adjusted for and any remaining difference is attributed to economic obsolescence. For example, House E is a new, one-story, ranch-style house with a two-car garage. It is two blocks from the local school. House F is very similar to House E except that it has a one-car garage and is next door to the school. House E sold for $192,000. House F sold for $178,000. Two-car garages in this market add $12,000 value to houses in this neighborhood and one-car garages add $4,000 value. Lots in this neighborhood are about 20% of total value of typical property (see Fig. 13-9).

FIG. 13-9 ESTIMATING ECONOMIC OBSOLESCENCE USING MATCHED SALES

Sale price, House E with 2-car garage, away from school	$192,000
Sale price, House F with 1-car garage, next to school	−178,000
Difference	$ 14,000
Difference between value of 2-car garage and 1-car garage	−8,000
Indicated difference in value cased by school	$ 6,000
Value loss allocated to improvements ($6,000 x 80%)	$ 4,800

AGE LIFE METHOD

Definition of Terms

Economic life is the time period over which a house may be profitably utilized. It is the total period of time that the improvements contribute value to the property. As soon as the site alone is worth as much as the site and the improvements combined, the improvements have reached the end of their economic life.

Physical life is the time period during which the house may be expected to remain physically in existence. Since over 90% of the houses ever built in the United States are still in existence and since houses in Europe have lasted hundreds of years, it is almost impossible to forecast the estimated physical life of a house. Caution must be exercised in the use of tables that purport to estimate the total physical life of different types of houses. They are of limited use to the appraiser.

Effective age is how old the house appears to be, based on observation, considering its condition, design and the economic forces that affect its value. To paraphrase an old saying, "If it has the physical condition and design of a 13-year-old house, then for appraisal purposes it should be treated as a 13-year-old house, (effective age - 13 years), even if it is 10 or 20 years old." The chronological age or actual age of the house should be noted in the appraisal (if known) but it normally has little use in the value estimation.

Remaining economic life is the period of time from the date of the appraisal to the end of the house's economic life. It is that period of time the house will continue to contribute value to the property. This is the period the appraiser attempts to estimate. The assumption should not always be that the property will continue to deteriorate at its present rate. Often rehabilitation, modernization or remodeling will extend the life of the property; lack of normal maintenance will shorten the economic life. Changing economic conditions and public tastes will also affect the remaining economic life. The estimate must be based on the assumption there will be no significant changes in the house or neighborhood, and be qualified to recognize that any changes may extend or shorten the remaining economic life.

The relationships between effective age, remaining economic life and total economic life are shown in Fig. 13-10.

FIG. 13-10 LIFE SPAN OF A HOUSE

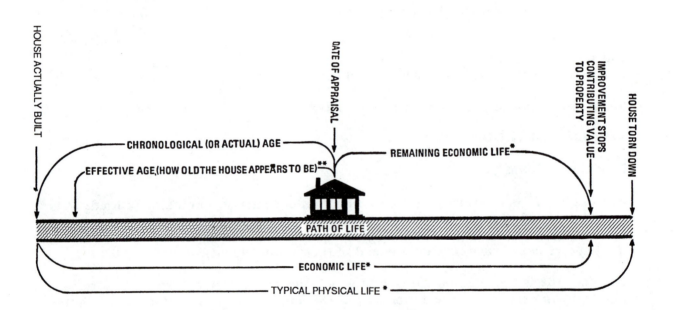

*MAY BE EXTENDED BY REHABILITATION, REMODELING OR MODERNIZATION OR CHANGING CONDITIONS.
**MAY ALSO BE GREATER THAN ACTUAL AGE.

ABSTRACTION METHOD

This method involves the use of market data to obtain an indication of the amount of depreciation existing in the property being appraised. An analysis of current sales indicates the amount of depreciation with which the market has penalized each sale. By analyzing sales of residential properties similar to and in the same neighborhood as that being appraised, the amount and annual rate of depreciation can be calculated. The assumption is that residential properties of similar age, construction, size, condition and location depreciate at the same annual rate.

The following steps are used to analyze the sales of comparable houses to obtain an indication of depreciation:

1. Select recently sold houses that are comparable to the one being appraised and obtain all the data necessary to estimate their reproduction cost.

2. Estimate the value of the site (land) for each comparable. Use the market comparison approach if sales data is available.

3. Deduct the site (land) value from the comparable sales price and obtain an indicated depreciated value of the improvements.

4. Estimate the reproduction cost new of each comparable sale as of the date of the appraisal. Use any of the appropriate techniques described in the first part of this chapter.

5. To obtain the total amount of depreciation indicated for each of the sold properties, subtract the depreciated value of the improvements (Step 3) from the reproduction cost of the improvements (Step 4).

6. Estimate the effective age of the comparable property.

7. To obtain the average annual amount of depreciation indicated by each of the sold properties, divide the total depreciation by the effective age.

8. To obtain the average annual rate of depreciation, divide the annual amount of depreciation by the reproduction cost of the improvements.

9. Convert the rate to a percentage (multiply by 100 and add a percent sign).

The process outlined above should be performed for several comparable sales in the neighborhood. As with the market data approach, the more sales that are used and the closer they are in similarity to the property being appraised, the more accurate the estimate of depreciation will be. Fig. 13-11 is a more specific example. Assume there is a 20-year-old (actual and effective age), two-story colonial style house, with 2,200 sq. ft. of gross living area, including living room, dining room, kitchen, recreation room, four bedrooms and two full baths. This house also a two-car garage with an estimated reproduction cost of $9,900 and site improvements with an estimated cost of $3,600. Lots are estimated to be worth $27,000 from market data available. The estimated reproduction cost of the house is $81.75 per sq. ft. of gross living area. The house sold for $136,500.

FIG. 13-11 ESTIMATING ACCRUED DEPRECIATION BY ABSTRACTION—EXAMPLE A

Step 1:   Select a house that has sold and obtain
the needed data to estimate its
reproduction cost new. Sales Price: $165,000

Step 2:   Estimate the value of the site (land) from
the market. Less site (land) value: -36,000

Step 3: Depreciated value of improvements: $129,000

Step 4: Reproduction cost of comparable sale
as of date of appraisal: $207,000

Step 5: Less depreciated value of improvements   -129,000

Total amount of depreciation indicated
by the market $ 78,000

Step 6: Estimated effective age   13 years

Step 7: $\dfrac{\text{Depreciation (from Step 5)}}{\text{Effective age (from Step 6)}}$ = $\dfrac{\$\ 78,000}{13}$

Average annual amount of depreciation   = $6,000

Step 8: $\dfrac{\text{Annual depreciation (from Step 7)}}{\text{Reproduction cost (from Step 4)}}$ = $\dfrac{\$\ 6,000}{\$207,000}$

Average annual rate of depreciation   =   .0289

Step 9: Average annual percentage of depreciation   =   2.89%
(.0289 x 100)

FIG. 13-12 ESTIMATING ACCRUED DEPRECIATION BY ABSTRACTION—EXAMPLE B

Step 1:	Sales Price	$136,500
Step 2:	Less site (land) value (from market)	-27,000
Step 3:	Depreciated value of the house and other improvements	$109,500
Step 4:	Reproduction cost	
	House (2,200 sq. ft. x $81.75)	179,850
	Garage	9,900
	Site improvements	3,600
	Total Reproduction cost	$193,350
Step 5:	Less depreciated value of improvements	-109,500
	Total depreciation indicated by market	$83,850
Step 6:	Effective age	20 years

Step 7:
$$\frac{\text{Total depreciation}}{\text{Effective age}} = \frac{\$\ 83,850}{20}$$

Annual amount of depreciation = $ 4,192

Step 8:
$$\frac{\text{Annual depreciation}}{\text{Reproduction cost}} = \frac{\$\ 4,192}{\$193,350}$$

Average annual rate of depreciation = .0217

Step 9: Average annual percentage of depreciation (.0217 x 100) = 2.17%

In this example the reproduction or replacement cost of the site improvements, such as stone walls, fences, driveways, landscaping, etc., is difficult to estimate. Under these circumstances an alternate acceptable method is to deduct the estimate value these items contribute to the sale price first and then proceed to abstract the depreciation of the improvements (see Fig. 13-13).

FIG. 13-13 ESTIMATING ACCRUED DEPRECIATION BY ABSTRACTION–EXAMPLE C

Step 1:	Sales Price		$180,000
Step 2:	Site value		45,000
	Contribution of site improvements		13,500
	Value of site and improvements		-$58,500
Step 3:	Depreciated value of the house and other improvements	=	$121,500
Step 4:	Reproduction cost		
	House (3,000 sq. ft. x $87.00)		$261,000
	Garage		18,000
	Total reproduction cost		$279,000
Step 5:	Less depreciated value of improvements		-121,500
	Total of depreciation	=	$157,500
Step 6:	Effective age		15 years
Step 7:	Total depreciation	=	$157,500
	Effective age		15
	Annual amount of depreciation		$ 10,500
Step 8:	Annual depreciation	=	$ 10,500
	Reproduction cost		$279,000
	Average annual rate of depreciation	=	.0376
Step 9:	Average annual percentage of depreciation (.0376 x 100)	=	3.76%

A single type of depreciation can also be calculated by the abstraction method. This is done by first calculating the total depreciation as in the above examples. Then two of the three forms of depreciation (physical, functional and economic) are estimated by observation and subtracted from the total depreciation. What remains is the amount attributed to the remaining form of depreciation.

Total Accrued Depreciation by Abstraction
Less: Physical Deterioration and Functional Obsolescence
Gives: Economic Obsolescence

Total Accrued Depreciation by Abstraction
Less: Functional and Economic Obsolescence
Gives: Physical Deterioration

Total Accrued Depreciation by Abstraction
Less: Physical Deterioration and Economic Obsolescence
Gives: Functional Obsolescence

To estimate Economic Obsolescence, follow this example:

Total depreciation estimated by abstraction	$83,850
Estimated physical deterioration	49,500
Estimated functional obsolescence	21,900
Total physical deterioration and functional obsolescence	-$71,400
Depreciation attributable to economic obsolescence =	$12,450

This technique is limited by the accuracy of the observed estimates of physical deterioration and functional obsolescence. Care must be taken not to attribute to economic obsolescence what is actually an error in estimating physical and functional obsolescence, land value or cost new. The possibility of error is reduced when a number of properties is used.

AGE LIFE METHOD

This method of estimating depreciation is based primarily upon observation. The basis is that the percentage effective age represents of the typical economic life is the same percentage the accumulated depreciation represents of total reproduction cost. Both of these figures are as of the date of the appraisal. This concept can be stated as a formula:

$$\frac{\text{Depreciation}}{\text{Reproduction Cost}} = \frac{\text{Effective Age}}{\text{Typical Economic Life}}$$

An example of this formula is as follows:

$$\frac{20\% \text{ Depreciation}}{100\% \text{ Reproduction Cost}} = \frac{10 \text{ Years Effective Age}}{50 \text{ Years Typical Economic Life}}$$

The formula can also be expressed as follows:

$$\frac{\text{Effective Age}}{\text{Typical Economic Life}} = \text{\% Depreciation of Reproduction Cost}$$

Some appraisers prefer to use the following ratios to estimate the depreciation:

$$\frac{\text{Actual Age}}{\text{Actual Age + Remaining Economic Life}}$$

or

$$\frac{\text{Effective Age}}{\text{Effective Age + Remaining Economic Life}}$$

No matter which technique is used, if the estimates are correct and the assumptions are the same, the estimate of depreciation will be valid.

The age-life method can be used to estimate either depreciation from all causes or a single form of depreciation. Care must be taken to define clearly in the appraisal what is being estimated. The following examples show how the estimates are made.

A house has an estimated typical economic life of 50 years. Its chronological age is 20 years. Its effective age, based on its condition, design, and environment, is 25 years because it is in poor condition and is located near a gasoline service station.

$$\frac{\text{25 years (effective age)}}{\text{50 years (Typical Economic Life)}} = .50 \text{ or } 50\% \text{ depreciated}$$

Another house in the same neighborhood also has an estimated typical economic life of 50 years. Its chronological age is also 20 years. Its effective age, based on its condition, design and environment, is 20 years because it is in average condition and there are not unusual adverse environmental influences.

$$\frac{\text{20 years (Effective Age)}}{\text{50 years (Typical Economic Life)}} = .40 \text{ or } 40\% \text{ depreciated}$$

Still another house in the same neighborhood has an estimated economic life of 60 years. This longer economic life is forecast because it is of superior design and construction. Its chronological age is 20 years. Its effective age, based on its superior construction, modernization and lack of negative environmental influences, is 12 years.

$$\frac{\text{12 years (Effective Age)}}{\text{60 years (Typical Economic Life)}} = .20 \text{ or } 20\% \text{ depreciated}$$

These examples show how three houses in the same neighborhood, all the same chronological age, can suffer from substantially different amounts of depreciation. All of these estimates considered the effect of all three forms of depreciation.

When the estimate of effective age considers only one form of depreciation–say, physical deterioration–then the result is the amount of depreciation caused by physical deterioration. For example, a house has an estimated typical physical life of 75 years. The effective age, based only on the physical condition of the house, is 25 years.

$$\frac{25 \text{ years (Effective Age)}}{75 \text{ years (Typical Economic Life)}} = \frac{.333 \text{ or } 33.3\%}{\text{physical depreciation}}$$

The age-life method is an easy-to-understand, simple-to-use method based primarily upon the appraiser's observations, research and judgment. Therefore, its accuracy is heavily dependent upon the appraiser's knowledge and experience. It is an effective way to estimate the depreciation accumulated to the date of the appraisal but has proved to be a very poor way to estimate the rate of depreciation the property will suffer in the future.

For example, if by the age-life method it is estimated that a 25-year old residence has depreciated at the rate of 2% per year and is now 50% depreciated, it is incorrect to say that the remaining economic life is 25 years. This will only be true if:

1 . The present rate of depreciation continues into the future on a straight line basis.

2 . There are no changes in the forces that affect the value of the property.

3 . There is no modernization, rehabilitation or remodeling.

4 . The property is "normally" maintained through its remaining economic life.

A forecast that is based on a series of assumptions that most likely will not all be true serves a limited purpose. This kind of forecast has been misused by lenders to limit the term of mortgages. If an estimate of remaining economic life is required, it must be made considering all the above factors and it must be noted that any changes may extend or shorten the remaining economic life.

SUMMARY

The cost approach is based on the principle of substitution. It holds that value tends to be set by the cost of a reasonable substitute improvement that could be built without undue delay. The steps of the cost approach are:

1 . Estimate the value of the site (land) in its highest and best use as if vacant.

2 . Estimate the reproduction cost (or replacement cost) new of all the improvements.

3 . Estimate accrued depreciation from all sources.

4 . Deduct the accrued depreciation (from all causes) from the cost new of the improvements to derive the depreciated value of the improvements.

5 . Add the site (land) value to the depreciated value of the improvements to derive an indicated value of the property by the cost approach.

Site (land) value is estimated in its highest and best use as if vacant from data found in the market.

Reproduction cost is the cost of creating a replica of the house and other improvements. Replacement cost is the cost of certain improvements with the same or equivalent utility using current design and materials. Estimating reproduction cost can be done using the quantity survey, unit-in-place or comparative methods.

Accrued depreciation is the difference between reproduction cost new of the improvements and their value as of the date of appraisal. It is the loss of value from all cases, which may be broken down into physical deterioration, functional obsolescence and external obsolescence. There are three principal methods used to measure accrued depreciation. The abstraction method uses sales from the market to indicate the depreciated value of the improvements. The age-life method is based on observation, in which estimates of economic life and effective age are converted into percentages of depreciation. The breakdown method divides depreciation into three categories (physical deterioration, functional obsolescence and external obsolescence). Each one is estimated by whatever technique is most applicable to the property being appraised.

The accuracy of the Cost Approach depends on the appraiser's accuracy in estimating the value of the land, as of the date of the appraisal, reproduction cost new of all the improvements and all forms of depreciation. Without market data to make these estimates, the possibility of significant error is great.

Extreme caution should be practiced when the cost approach is used alone or as the most significant indicator of value. The report should contain valid justification as to why the appraiser has elected to do so.

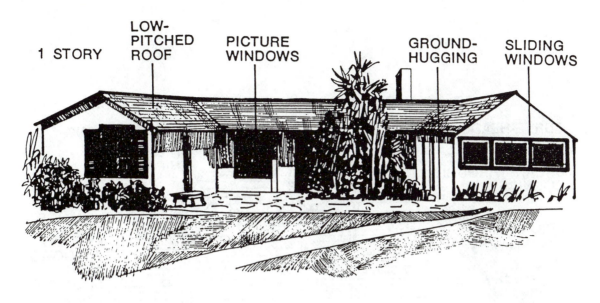

1 STORY   LOW-PITCHED ROOF   PICTURE WINDOWS   GROUND-HUGGING   SLIDING WINDOWS

Post World War II American

CALIFORNIA RANCH (C Ranch - 901)

SMALL, COMPACT SHAPE   1 STORY

Early Twentieth Century American

CALIFORNIA BUNGALOW (Cal Bung - 805)

1½ TO 2½ STORIES

PERFECTLY BALANCED

CURVE-HEADED UPPER WINDOWS THAT BREAK THROUGH CORNICE

FORMAL LOOKING

HIGH, STEEP HIP ROOF

SOME HAVE 2 SYMMETRICAL 1-STORY WINGS

BRICK

FRENCH WINDOWS AND SHUTTERS

French

FRENCH PROVINCIAL (Fr Prov - 302)

14 Sales Comparison Approach

The Sales Comparison Approach, which used to be called the Market Data Approach, involves making a direct comparison between the property being appraised and other properties that have been sold (or listed for sale). All three approaches to value are based on market data, but the cost and income approaches depend on a less direct comparison than does the sales comparison approach.

When carefully collected, analyzed, verified and reconciled, market data usually provides the best indication of market value for a property. The price that a typical buyer pays is often the result of a shopping process, in which many properties are examined and evaluated. Buyers often base their value conclusions primarily on properties that are being offered for sale. Appraisers use this information plus information about properties that have sold and rented.

The principle of substitution states that when several commodities or services with substantially the same utility are available, the one with the lowest price attracts the greatest demand and the widest distribution. It is important to understand how this principle specifically applies to the theoretical framework of the market data approach. In single family residential markets, this means that when a residence is replaceable in the market (which it usually is), its value tends to be set by the cost of acquiring an equally desirable substitute residence. The assumption is that there will be no costly delay encountered in making the substitution. Experienced real estate brokers know that most buyers will accept more than one house in the market in which they are shopping and will accept only a short delay in negotiating the purchase of any specific house.

A popular myth is that one can sell a house at almost any price if one is willing to wait long enough for the one buyer who wants only that particular house and will pay substantially above its market value to obtain it. Houses that are listed substantially above market value generally remain unsold no matter how long they are offered for sale. The principle of substitution provides the basis for the premise that the market value of a house is the value indicated by active and informed buyers in the market for comparable houses offering a similar quality of shelter, amenities and other considerations characteristic of that market.

Individual sales often deviate from the market norm because of individual motivations, knowledge and/or conditions of sale; but in sufficient numbers, they tend to reflect market patterns. When information is available on a sufficient number of comparable sales, offerings and listings in the current market, the resulting pattern is the best indication of market value.

The principle of substitution also applies to income properties. A typical informed buyer compares income properties being offered for sale. The buyer also considers alternate forms of investment. Investment buyers are comparing return of their investment, return on their investment, tax shelter, the burden of management and many other factors.

STEPS IN THE SALES COMPARISON APPROACH

In applying the Sales Comparison Approach, the appraiser takes five steps:

1 . Studies the market and selects the sales and listings of properties most comparable to the residence being appraised. Generally, the most current and similar comparable sales prove to be the best indicators of the value of the subject.

2 . Collects and verifies data on each selected property's selling and listing prices, dates of transaction, physical and locational characteristics and any special conditions.

3 . Analyzes and compares each property with the subject as to time of sale, location, physical characteristics and conditions of sale.

4 . Adjusts the sales or listing price of each comparable for dissimilarities between it and the subject. Adjustments are derived from the market whenever possible, using "matched pairs", regression analysis and other adjustment techniques.

5 . Reconciles the adjusted prices of the comparable properties into an indicated value of the appraised residence.

STUDYING THE MARKET

A market study is made to find those comparable sales and listings that are similar to the property being appraised. Generally, the more current the comparable sale and the more similar it is to the property being appraised, the better it will be as an indicator of the value of the property being appraised. More sales and listings are usually analyzed than are finally used in the appraisal. The best comparables are used in the final calculations and value estimate.

COLLECTING THE DATA

Accuracy of the value indication from the sales comparison approach depends heavily upon the quantity and quality of sales, offerings and listings of competitive properties. Through a sound collection program, a large bank of market data can be accumulated in the appraiser's own files and should be organized to serve the appraiser's needs most effectively. Only some of the data may be immediately pertinent. The remainder may be collected, filed and cross indexed for future use. Records should carry the address, a file number, and any additional salient information. Sales information often is collected and recorded on standardized sheets, or in a computer base.

VERIFYING THE DATA

Each sale used as a comparable in an appraisal report should be personally inspected and the data confirmed with the buyer, seller or broker. The appraiser must be assured of the facts--that is, that all depreciation has been considered, the measurements are correct and the reported price and terms are accurate.

Verification and inspection processes do more than confirm the accuracy of the data gathered. They also provide for exploration of motivating forces involved in a sale, such as: were both buyer and seller acting without financial pressure? Was the sale an "arms-length" transaction, or were the parties related in some way? Were both buyer and seller knowledgeable about the property and market in which the sale took place? Did the seller have a reasonable time to sell and the buyer to buy? Were there any special concessions granted by either party? Was financing typical of the market, or was there a purchase money mortgage, second mortgage, assumed mortgage or other unusual situations? Were there any special sale conditions such as inclusion of personal property in the sale (furniture, above-ground pools, boats, automobiles, sports equipment, etc.)? Was there any special government program involving a subsidy, attractive financing terms or guarantee of payment?

Sometimes an owner sells for less than expected if allowed to occupy the property for a substantial period of time after the transfer of title. Sometimes a sale is the result of an option granted in the past when different market conditions prevailed, resulting in a sales price that may not be typical of the current market. These are only some of the possible conditions that might make the reported sales price different from the market value. Only by personally interviewing the buyer and seller or broker can the appraiser gain knowledge about such conditions.

ANALYZING AND COMPARING THE DATA

Comparison of sales, offers and listings provides a basis for estimating the market value of the property being appraised. When comparable properties are similar to the property being appraised, have sold very recently and have few if any physical, locational and conditions of sale adjustments, such information is helpful to the appraiser in reaching a market value estimate. On most assignments, however, the appraiser recognizes substantial differences between the appraised property and the comparable sales. Two analytical tools used by appraisers are elements of comparison and units of comparison. Each element of comparison (date of sale, physical characteristics, location, and conditions of sale) *must* be considered. Often there is more than one physical characteristic that requires adjustment, the units of comparison provide a means for making these considerations.

ADJUSTING THE COMPARABLES

Once all of the elements of comparison between the comparable sales and property being appraised are described in the appraisal report, they must be analyzed and adjustments must be made to reflect the dollar or percentage value of the dissimilarities noted.

When a comparable sale is better than the subject property, a minus adjustment is made to the comparable sale. When a comparable sale is poorer than the subject property, a plus adjustment is made to the comparable sale.

MATCHED PAIRS OF SALES

In the past, many adjustments were based on nothing more than educated guesses. Good appraisal practice requires that adjustments be supported with data from the market. The best technique is to extract the amount of the adjustment from the market by using *matched pairs*. This is often the only technique acceptable to many sophisticated purchasers of appraisals. It involves the selection of two sales in the market, one with the item for which the adjustment is sought and the other without that item. The theory behind this technique is that if a single item is the only difference between two sales, the difference in sales price can be attributed to that item. Although generally reliable where only one difference is present, the technique may still be use where there are several differences.

The following is an example of an adjustment based on only one difference between matched pairs. Each of the comparable sales used in the following illustrations is assumed to be very similar to the house being appraised and to each other, except as noted. They are also assumed to have sold recently so that no time adjustments are needed.

Comparable Sale 1
1-acre lot
1-car attached garage
Sold recently for $114,000

Comparable Sale 2
1-acre lot
2-car attached garage
Sold recently for $120,000

Difference attributable to extra garage $6,000

The only significant difference between these sales is the garage size. From this information, it appears that the market recognizes a $6,000 difference between one-car and two-car garages. The indicated adjustment for this item is $6,000.

Usually more than one difference exists between two sales. In such cases, adjustments can be made for each of the differences. The final remaining difference in sales price, after all other adjustments have been made, is attributed to the item for which adjustment is being sought. Continuing the above example:

Comparable Sale 3
1-acre lot
1-car attached garage
Next to gasoline service station
Sold recently for $105,000

This sale can be directly paired with Comparable Sale 1. The $9,000 difference in sale price between Comparable Sale 1 and Comparable Sale 3 can be attributed to the gasoline service station.

Comparable Sale 3 can be paired with Comparable Sale 2. There is a $15,000 difference between the sale prices of Comparables 2 and 3 of which $6,000 is caused by the difference in value between a one-car and two-car garage (based on pairing Comparable Sale 1 with Comparable Sale 2).

When there are two or more differences between the matched pairs, the differences may affect the sales in the same or opposite ways. In this example, they both affect the sales in the same way. Comparable Sale 3 is $15,000 less valuable than Comparable Sale 2 because it has a smaller garage and is affected by the gasoline service station next door.

Because it is difficult to tell if the difference affects the sales in the same way or opposite ways just by looking at them, it is necessary to estimate the effect from the market. This is done by designating one comparable sale as the base sale and then first adjusting the other sale for all the differences between it and the base sale, except for the one being sought. When all the adjustments have been made, the remaining difference between the base sale and the other sale can be attributed to the one difference left between them.

Pairing Comparable Sale 2 and Comparable Sale 3 illustrates how this process works.

Comparable 2 (Base)
1-acre lot
2-car attached garage
Sold recently for $120,000

Comparable 3
1-acre lot
1-car attached garage
Adverse influence from nearby gasoline service station
Sold recently for $105,000

Adjustment of Comparable Sale 3 to Base Sale 2 to reflect
difference between 1-car and 2-car garage   +6,000
Adjusted Sales Price 3 $111,000

Abstraction for remaining difference attributable to adverse influence of nearby gasoline service station:

Comparable Sale 2 (Base) $120,000
Adjusted Sales Price 3
Amount attributable to adverse influence

                                                                     -111,000
of location near gasoline service station $ 9,000

This process can be extended still further. Comparable Sale 4 is also similar to the other sales and sold recently for $135,000.

Comparable Sale 4
2-acre lot
2-car garage
Adverse influence from nearby gasoline service station
Sold recently for $135,000

This sale cannot be compared directly with any of the other sales to extract an adjustment for the two-acre lot. In each case, there is at least one other difference:

Comparable 1: 1-acre lot, 1-car garage, away from gasoline service station
Comparable 2: 1-acre lot, away from gasoline service station.
Comparable 3: 1-acre lot, 1-car garage

Even though there is more than one difference in each matched pair, Comparable Sale 4 can be paired with each of the others by first adjusting for the other differences.

Pairing Comparable Sale 4 with Comparable Sale 1 works out as follows:

Comparable Sale 1 (Base)
1-acre lot
1-car garage
Sold recently for $114,000

Comparable Sale 4
2-acre lot
2-car garage
Adverse influence from nearby gasoline service station
Sold recently for $135,000

Adjustment of Comparable Sale 4 to Base Sale 1 to
reflect the difference between 1-car and 2-car garage
(based on comparing 1 with 2) -6,000

Adjustment of Comparable Sale 4 to Base Sale 1 to
reflect adverse influence of gasoline service station
(based on comparing 3 with 1 and 2) +9,000

Adjusted Sales Price of Comparable Sale 4 $138,000

Abstraction for remaining difference attributable to lot size:

Adjusted Sales Price of Comparable Sale 4 $138,000
Sales Price 1 (base) -114,000
Amount attributable to difference between 1-acre
and 2-acre lot $ 24,000

Pairing Comparable Sales 4 and 3 works out as follows:

Comparable Sale 3 (Base)
1-acre lot
1-car attached garage
Adverse influence from nearby gasoline service station
Sold recently for $105,000

Comparable Sale 4
2-acre lot
2-car garage
Adverse influence from nearby gasoline service station
Sold recently for $135,000

Adjustment of Comparable Sale 4 to Base Sale 3 to reflect the difference
between 1-car and 2-car garage
(based on comparing 1 with 2) -6,000

Adjusted Sales Price 4 $129,000

Abstraction for remaining difference attributable to lot size:

Adjusted Sales Price Comparable Sale 4	$129,000
Sales Price 3 (base)	-105,000
Amount attributable to difference between 1-acre and 2-acre lot	$ 24,000

Fig. 14-1 summarizes the data analyzed in the preceding example.

FIG. 14-1 COMPARABLE SALES GRID

Item	Appraised House	Comp Sale 1	Comp Sale 2	Comp Sale 3	Comp Sale 4
Sale Price	-	$114,000	$120,000	$105,000	$135,000
Time of Sale	Date of Appraisal	Recent -0-	Recent -0-	Recent -0-	Recent -0-
Physical Lot Size	1-acre -0-	1-acre -0-	1-acre -0-	1-acre -0-	2-acre -$24,000
Car storage	1-car attached -0-	1-car attached -0-	2-car attached -$6,000	1-car attached -0-	2-car attached -$6,000
Location Adverse influences	none -0-	none -0-	none -0-	Next to a gas tation +$9,000	Next to a gas station +$9,000
Conditions of Sale	none -0-	none -0-	none -0-	none -0-	none -0-
Net Adjustment	-0-	-0-	-$6,000	+$9,000	-$21,000
Indicated value appraised house	-	$114,000	$114,000	$114,000	$114,000

In actual sales analysis, calculations would rarely work out as precisely as in this example, due to two major factors. First, even active, informed markets produce different buyer and seller opinions of the value of each comparison item considered by the appraiser. Thus for each property, there may be a range of prices considered reasonable for its market. Second, the adjustment for one item of difference may already include a partial adjustment for another item of difference.

To illustrate, in the above example, the price per acre may differ for locations near service stations. This may be true in a situation in which the market might require a larger lot to better buffer against the adverse influence, yet not pay more for the extra land. Adjustment for both adverse influence and lot size may overstate the actual difference because an adjustment for location near the service station may already include a partial adjustment for lot size.

The appraiser must be cautious to avoid the conclusion that the apparent procession of the adjustment process provides a more accurate estimate of value. In many situations, that accuracy may be reduced by adding more adjustment factors. Unless aided by properly applied adjustment processes such as regression analysis, the appraiser should generally make the fewest adjustments possible and should reflect the uncertainties of multiple adjustments in the final reconciliation of the value estimate. This is particularly true in making multiple adjustments for physical differences.

Likewise, the appraiser should avoid the temptation to use cost estimates as a basis for market adjustments. While relationships between cost and value contributions of components may exist, they may be supported only by market data. Thus, comparison of market data should be used to support the adjustment used.

REGRESSION ANALYSIS

In recent years, attention has been drawn to methods of analyzing market data through use of regression analysis and other mathematical techniques. Step-wise multiple regression routines, like more traditional methods, are based upon the concept that certain identifiable characteristics of residential markets (called independent variables) may each be studied for their individual and joint contributions to value. Unlike traditional methods, however, the mathematics of analyzing comparable sales is more complex and generally requires more powerful computing equipment.

A major contribution of these newer techniques has been to focus attention on the adjustment process in sales analysis. Where more than one set of matched pairs is used to extract adjustment factors, the possibility of "doubling up" on adjustments exists. This is due to the interdependence or interaction of many comparison elements (often referred to as their "co-linearity"). Traditional comparison methods have generally overlooked these relationships and do not provide a means for measuring interdependence of data.

For example, adjustments made for both square footage of living area and number of bedrooms are not independent. Either variable is likely to include some consideration of the other. Regression techniques (particularly step-wise) can serve to reduce this problem and provide a means of measuring where significant interdependence is present. Regression techniques also permit a measure of reliability and significance of both data used and results produced.

Another reason for the growing use of regression analysis and similar techniques is that they often allow use of more market information and provide a better analysis and understanding of markets for market value estimates than traditional methods. In simple terms, traditional application of the market approach has usually taken one of the mathematical forms listed below.

1 . $Yc = bX$
Where Yc means calculated value, b is a multiplier obtained for a unit of comparison, and X is measured data for the property appraised. Example: the market indicates a price of $82.14 per square foot, and appraised property has 1,738 square feet.

$Yc = (\$82.14)(1,738) = \$142,759.$

2 . Yc = bX + a + b . . .+ n

Where a, b, . . . n are plus and minus adjustment factors. Example: In addition to data already given in example 1, the appraiser considers property appraised to be $4,500 superior as to condition but $2,250 inferior as to location:

Yc = ($82.14) (1,738) + $4,500 - $2,250 = $145,009 or $145,000

3 . Yc = a + b + c + . . . n

Where a is lump sum amount, and b, c . . . n are various adjustment factors. Example: An appraiser estimates a base market value of $142,500 before adjustments (or is dealing with a comparable which sold for that amount) and then considers the condition and location adjustments already mentioned:

Yc = $142,500 + $4,500 - $2,250 = $144,750 or $145,000

4. Yc = X (a + b + . . . n)

Where a,b, . . . n are percentage adjustment factors that are added and subtracted; alternatively each may be applied independently to X, the base for calculations. Example: A property appraised is considered 3% superior as to condition, but 2% inferior as to location to a base of $142,500:

Yc = $142,500 (100%+3%-2%) = $143,925 or $144,000

These basic methods and relationships have other variations in common use. Each should be understood in applying the market data approach to avoid commonly encountered abuses and errors. Particularly important is recognition that the model used for final application of market adjustments must also be used as the model for original extraction of adjustment factors from market data. It is improper to extract adjustment factors using one method and apply them using another.

Where sufficient data for analysis is available in an active market, many appraisers have found that simple linear regression analysis may provide more accurate use of available data and an analysis of more market information than traditional methods. This is particularly true in situations where a simple price-per-square-foot unit of comparison is used. To illustrate, assume that an appraiser has collected sales data for 10 nearby properties which have recently sold, as shown in Fig. 14-2.

FIG. 14-2: COMPARABLE SALES DATA SET FOR SIMPLE REGRESSION ANALYSIS

Sale No.	Sq. Ft. Gross Living Area	Total Sale Price	Sale Price Per Sq. Ft. GLA
1	1, 000	$87, 000	$87. 00
2	1, 100	82, 500	75. 00
3	1, 200	87, 000	72. 50
4	1, 400	87, 000	62. 14
5	1, 500	93, 000	62. 00
6	1, 600	90, 000	56. 25
7	1, 650	96, 000	58. 18
8	1, 750	91, 500	52. 29
9	1, 850	96, 000	51. 89
10	1, 950	94, 500	48. 46

Several situations are found in common practice:

1 . In appraising an 1,100 square foot dwelling, the appraiser might use the mean price of $78.17 per square foot for Sales 1, 2, and 3, as the three prices per square foot do not form an applicable pattern.

2 . In appraising a 1,500 square foot dwelling, the appraiser might use the mean price of $60.13 per square foot for Sales 4, 5, and 6, as the three square foot prices again do not form a regular pattern.

3 . In appraising an 1,800 square foot dwelling, the appraiser might use the mean price of $52.71 per square foot of Sales 7 through 10, as the pattern is once again inconclusive.

4 . In appraising any property for which these sales are considered comparable, it will be extremely difficult through traditional means of analysis to apply more than three or four of the sales in any one sales comparison process. Thus, the concept of market is reduced because of the simple mathematical inadequacies of traditional analysis methods.

Particularly distressing is the tendency of many brokers (and some buyers and sellers) to generalize, based on these 10 sales. One might say, "the market indicates about $60.00 per square foot for properties in this area," because the arithmetic mean of the 10 sales is actually $62.57. Such a generalization is potentially meaningful only for sales near the middle of the group and is severely misleading for those not near the middle.

Often overlooked is the fact that any use of a simple unit of comparison such as price per square foot is an application of simple linear regression analysis. Each of the square foot prices discussed ($78.17, $60.13, $52.71 and $62.57) may be substituted for b in the relationship $Yc = bX$ where X is square footage. A simple linear regression model is implicit with any such use of comparison units. Unfortunately, this application is an oversimplification of a more accurate form of simple linear regression which adds a constant "a" to the equation: $Yc = a+bX$.

Fig. 14-3 illustrates the difficulty of applying the traditional unit of comparison relationship $Yc = bX$ and one of the advantages of the more extensive form $Yc = a +bX$. By plotting the price/square foot relationship, a regular pattern of price increase with an increase in square footage exists.

If the $60 per square foot generalization is used, a 1,500 square foot dwelling would be expected to sell for $90,000. Likewise, a 0 square foot dwelling would be expected to sell for $0. While the latter is ridiculous, this model does establish the slope of the price expectations for any square footage from zero to infinity. However, the traditional method forces a price per square foot slope to pass though the intersection of the X and Y axis (the zero intercept), regardless of the actual relationship of price to square footage.

FIG. 14-3 COMPARISON OF Yc = bX AND Yc = a + bX AS DESCRIPTORS OF RESIDENTIAL SALES DATA

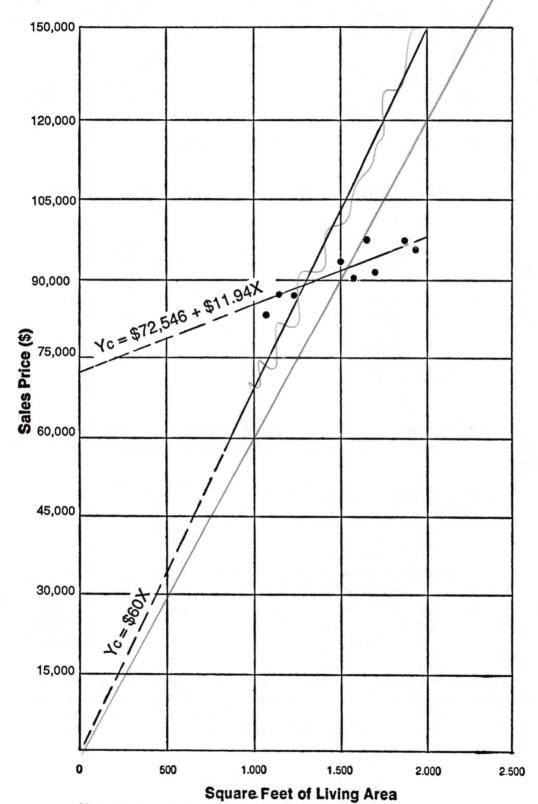

Note: the formula for a straight line is Y = a + bX

This zero intercept fallacy may be overcome by application of the Yc=a+bX relationship which can be calculated by simple linear regression techniques. Figure 14-3 shows that this formula provides a much better explanation of the market data than the traditional method and allows the use of all 10 sales as comparables in this instance. While the mathematics of this calculation can be handled by even simple calculators, it is also possible to approximate the relationships by freehand drawing, on graph paper, once the basic data is plotted.

This same technique also illustrates the hazard of inadvertently "doubling up" on adjustments in the traditional market approach when there is an interdependence of comparison units. Fig. 14-4 includes data for both square footage and bedrooms for each of the 10 comparable sales used in the previous example. Use of both comparison units is common in applying the market approach. However, analysis shows that a high interdependence between square footage and bedrooms is present in this data.

FIG. 14-4 COMPARABLE SALES DATA SET FOR SIMPLE REGRESSION ANALYSIS

Sale No.	Sq. Ft. Living Area	Bedrooms	Sales Price
1	1,000	2	$87,000
2	1,100	2	82,500
3	1,200	2	87,000
4	1,400	2	87,000
5	1,500	3	93,000
6	1,600	3	90,000
7	1,650	3	96,000
8	1,750	4	91,500
9	1,850	4	96,000
10	1,950	4	94,500

Analysis of this data through a step-wise multiple linear regression model produces the following "correlation matrix," which measures the amount of correlation among variables:

Square Feet	Bedrooms	Price
1.00000	.92768	.84687
	1.00000	.81088
		1.00000

These results indicate that over 84% of the price variance among the sales may be explained by square footage and that about 81% is explained by bedroom data. Thus either variable used alone is capable of explaining a great deal about price. The almost 93% correlation between square feet and bedrooms is particularly significant because it indicates a very high level of interaction or interdependence between the two variables.

Other analysis by the multiple regression model produces standard errors of the estimate measures, which indicate the precision of regression estimates. Standard errors were calculated for square footage and bedrooms where each was used as a single independent variable and then for their combined use as joint predictors of value, with the following results:

Independent Variable(s)	Standard Error
1. Square footage only	$2,555
2. Bedrooms only	2,812
3. Square footage and bedrooms	2,709

Use of square footage alone is shown to be a better predictor of value in this instance than either bedrooms alone or a combination of both variables. Bedrooms would seldom be used alone as a unit of comparison in traditional market data methods (except in the paired sales concept), but both bedrooms and square footage would frequently be used.

This example shows that addition of the data regarding bedrooms actually reduces the capability of the units of comparison to predict value because of the high interrelationship between square footage and bedrooms. Without the multiple regression calculation, effects of this interrelationship would possibly be overlooked and a doubling of adjustments would occur. Although the dollar amount here is minimal (due to the simplicity of this example), substantial effects can often be seen in grid analysis techniques, which commonly use numerous independent variables simultaneously.

Simple examples such as these raise at least three questions about contemporary application of the market approach:

1. Can appraisers afford to continue to use only three or four comparables where more market data factually exists and is available?

2. When using only one unit of comparison, can the traditional concept of $Yc=bXa+bX$ continue to be used in favor of the linear regression concept of $Yc=a + bX$ or similar nonlinear relationships?

3. When using more than one unit of comparison, can the appraiser continue to ignore the interdependence of data that is generally present in grid analysis techniques (or to ignore the multiple problems of combining a series of adjustments extracted by the paired sales technique)?

Appraisal methodology is still in transition, but the weaknesses of many traditional methods in the market approach can be overcome by collecting more data and using study methods which analyze larger amounts of data, such as those illustrated.

Although a full exposition of regression analysis is beyond the scope of this discussion, these examples illustrate the complexity of market comparison processes and point out both the basis for common errors and the possibility of overcoming these errors with newer analytical techniques.

OTHER ADJUSTMENT TECHNIQUES

Another commonly used indirect technique for adjusting the comparable is to estimate the cost new, less depreciation, of the item for which adjustment is needed. The accuracy of this technique depends on the relationship of the cost less depreciation estimates and value in terms of market recognition. Depreciation is especially difficult to estimate, because the market may recognize only a small portion of the cost, and substantial functional obsolescence may have to be deducted to obtain the actual value contributed by a specific item.

TYPES OF ADJUSTMENTS

The differences between comparable sales and the subject property can be adjusted for in either dollars or percentages. The manner in which the adjustment is derived for the market determines whether it is expressed as a percentage or a dollar amount.

For residential properties, percentage adjustments are often converted to dollar adjustments to comply with the Freddie Mac and Fannie Mae Guidelines when filling out the URAR, Small Income Property Report and Condominium-PUD Appraisal Report forms. These forms are designed to display the adjustments as dollar amounts either added to or subtracted from the comparable sale prices.

There is no rigid procedure for making adjustments. "Adjustments can be applied in several ways, depending on how the relationship between the properties (i.e., subject and comparable, comparable and subject, or comparable and comparable) is expressed or perceived by the market) This relationship is expressed as an algebraic equation which is solved to determine the amount of adjustment to be made for the differences between the properties.

An appraiser uses logical calculations to make an adjustment, but the mathematics should not control the appraiser's judgment. Using computer and software technology an appraiser can effectively apply mathematical techniques that were prohibitively time-consuming. These techniques can be used to narrow the range of value, but a market value estimate is not determined by a set of precise calculations. Appraisal has a creative aspect in that appraisers use their judgment to analyze and interpret quantitative data."[1]

PERCENTAGE ADJUSTMENTS

Percentages are often used to express the differences between a subject property and a comparable sale especially for time, special conditions and location adjustments. For example, time adjustments are easily expressed as a percentage per month or year. The difference in value between one location and another is also easily expressed as a percentage (i.e., the subject neighborhood is 10% better than the neighborhood where the comparable is located). When necessary, percentages can be converted to dollar adjustments for particular appraisals.

Examples of five possible relationships between Subject and Comparables

1. Subject and comparable are equal: no adjustment is needed.

2. The subject is 10% superior to the comparables: the price of the comparable must be increased to reflect the difference.

This can be expressed as follows when "X" equals the unknown value of the subject and 1.0 equals the known value of the comparables:

$$X = 1.0 + 10\% \text{ (percentage adjustment)} \times 1.0$$
$$= 1.0 (1 + 0.1)$$
$$= 1.1$$

---

[1] *The Appraisal of Real Estate*, The Appraisal Institute, 10th ed., Chicago, IL., 1992.

In effect, we have multiplied the price of the comparable by 1.1 to estimate the value of the subject. The resulting percentage adjustment to the price of the comparable is plus 0.1, or plus 10%.

3. The subject is 10% inferior to the comparables: the price of the comparable must be decreased to reflect the difference.

$$X = 1.0 - 10\% \text{ (percentage adjustment)} \times 1.0$$
$$= 1.0 (1 - 0.1)$$
$$= 0.9$$

In effect, we have multiplied the price of the comparable by 0.9 to estimate the value of the subject. The resulting percentage adjustment to the price of the comparable is minus 0.1 or minus 10%.

4. The comparable is 10% superior to the subject. The price of the comparable must be decreased to reflect the difference.

$$1.0 = X + 10\% \times X$$
$$1.0 = X (1 + 0.1)$$
$$1.0 = X (1.1)$$
$$1 \div 1.1 = X$$
$$0.909 = X$$

Here we divided the price of the comparable by 1.1 to estimate the value of the subject. The percentage adjustment to the price of the comparable is 1.00 minus 0.909, or .091 = 9.% (rounded).

5. The comparable is 10% inferior to the subject. The price of the comparable must be increased to reflect the difference.

$$1.0 = X - 10\% \times X$$
$$1.0 = X(1 - 0.1)$$
$$1.0 = X(0.9)$$
$$1 \div 0.9 = X$$
$$1.111 = X$$

Here we divided the price of the comparable by 0.9 to estimate the value of the subject. The percentage adjustment to price of the comparable is plus 0.111 or 11% (rounded).

The appraiser must be consistent in stating the relationship between the subject and the comparables and this relationship should be stated in a manner that corresponds to the way the market perceives it to be.

DOLLAR ADJUSTMENTS

Many appraisers prefer when possible to compute adjustments in dollars. For example, the appraiser may conclude that the favorable location of a comparable sale resulted in a $50,000 premium paid by the buyer. In analyzing residential properties, the appraiser can frequently use discounting to derive a dollar adjustment for location of properties of similar value. There are many other adjustments especially those for physical characteristics which may be estimated in dollars and which are added or subtracted from the sale price of the comparable.

SEQUENCE OF ADJUSTMENTS

One of the advantages of plus and minus dollar adjustments is that it does not matter what the sequence of the adjustments are. The results will always be the same.

When percentage adjustments are made, the sequence will effect the results. Therefore, the sequence of the adjustments is important.

There is no rigid order in which the appraiser must make the adjustments. The following order is suggested by the Appraisal Institute: [2]

1. Property rights conveyed
This adjustment takes into account differences in legal estate between the subject property and the comparable property. When made first, it is applied directly to the reported sale price.

2. Financing terms
This adjustment converts the transaction price of the comparable into its cash equivalent or modifies it to match the financing terms of the subject property.

3. Conditions of sales
This reflects the difference between the actual sale price of the comparable and its probable sale price if it were currently sold in an arm's-length transaction.

4. Market conditions = time
An adjustment for the difference in the market at the time the comparable sale took place and the date of the appraisal.

5. Location
The location of a property is an important factor in its value. Consider any value differences between the comparable and the subject locations as adjusted.

6. Physical Characteristics
Often, there is more than one adjustment needed for physical characteristics.

SEQUENTIAL PERCENTAGE ADJUSTMENTS

Whatever adjustment is selected to be first is multiplied by the comparable sale price, giving a price that is adjusted for this characteristic. The next adjustment is multiplied by the first adjusted price, not the unadjusted original reported price. This sequence is followed until all of the adjustments have been accounted for.

CUMULATIVE PERCENTAGE ADJUSTMENTS

Cumulative percentage adjustments are obtained by multiplying each of the individual percentage adjustments together. In other words, cumulative percentage adjustments are casually interrelated. A sequence is not required when the adjustments are multiplied by each other as the order of the multiplication does not effect the end result.

---

[2]Ibid.

Up to this point, adjustments have been discussed on the basis of the whole property, resulting in a comparable sales price of the property as a whole to give a direct indication of value for the appraised property. Adjustments on a unit basis may also be applied. A good technique is to work in units, which, for single family residences, is most commonly square feet of gross living area. If this unit is used, the sales price of each comparable is converted into a price per square foot before the adjustments are applied. The adjustments are then made in unit figures. For example, the adjustment for condition might be $2.25 per square foot.

The final value indication would be value per square foot of gross living area. This figure can be converted into an indicated value for the appraised property by multiplying its number of square feet of gross living area by the adjusted value per square foot of each comparable. This procedure could be done at this point or later in the reconciliation.

In the market data approach, each comparable property is analyzed and compared to the property being appraised, based on the elements of comparison. A rating grid may be used to record information about the appraised property and the comparable sales and adjustments for each difference between them.

Each comparable sale is adjusted so that its sale price is converted to an indication of the market value of the appraised property. Therefore, if an element of comparison in a comparable is more valuable than those found in the appraised property, a minus adjustment must be made. For example, the only difference between the appraised property and Comparable Sale 1 is that the first has no porch and the latter has an open porch. This difference contributes $4,500 additional value to the comparable in this market.

	House Being Appraised	Comparable Sale 1
Sales Price		$135,000
Porch	none	- 4,500
Indicated value of appraised property		$130,500

In the following example, the property being appraised has an in-ground swimming pool and the comparable has none. In-ground swimming pools add $12,000 value in this market, making the appraised property superior to the comparable house.

	House Being Appraised	Comparable Sale 1
Sales price		$120,000
In-ground swimming pool	yes	none
		+12,000
Indicated value of appraised property		$132,000

In this example, the comparable was less valuable than the property being appraised so a plus adjustment is made.

RECONCILIATION OF SALES COMPARISON APPROACH

After the best comparable sales have been selected and each one is adjusted to give an indicated value of the appraised property, the indications must be reconciled to produce a final estimate of value via the Sales Comparison Approach. It is not acceptable appraisal practice to use a simple arithmetic mean of the value indications. Averaging small groups of numbers produces a meaningless measure of central tendency and may or may not reflect actual market value.

The accepted procedure is to review each sale and judge its comparability to the property being appraised. Generally, the fewer and smaller the adjustments used on a comparable sale to produce the indicated value estimate, the more weight the sale is given in the final reconciliation. However, consideration should also be given to the basis for the adjustments.

The final value selected is a judgment made by the appraiser based on all the information available. It is not always necessary to select a single figure at this point in the appraisal process. Some appraisers believe that the use of a range is more helpful. The use of such a range to describe market value is becoming more common, most likely as a result of greater awareness of statistical techniques on the part of appraisers.

SUMMARY

The Sales Comparison Approach to value is generally the preferred approach to estimate the market value of residences. However for investment properties, the Income Approach is also given heavy weight. Appraisals that depend primarily upon the cost or income approach have a strong possibility of being subject to substantial error.

The key to the Sales Comparison Approach is market abstraction of adjustments and the use of an appropriate unit of comparison. Typically, in the appraisal of single family houses, the unit of choice is square feet of gross living area.

Each comparable sale is compared with the appraised property. Adjustments are made to the comparable sales price to reflect significant differences between them. Traditionally, the elements of comparison are divided into the four categories: time, location, physical characteristics and conditions of sale. Recently, special conditions and special financing have been added as elements of comparison.

In order to obtain all of the information needed to use a comparable sale, the appraiser should inspect each comparable property and verify the nature of the sale with either the buyer, seller or broker. These are the people who can tell the appraiser about the conditions of sale, special financing and the actual physical condition of the property at the time of sale.

New techniques using more sales are available as alternatives to the above. They do not depend upon adjustments based on limited market information but rather on statistical treatment of many comparable sales.

When the sales comparison approach is based upon a sufficient number of carefully chosen sales similar to the appraised property with appropriate adjustments, the value indication is usually persuasive.

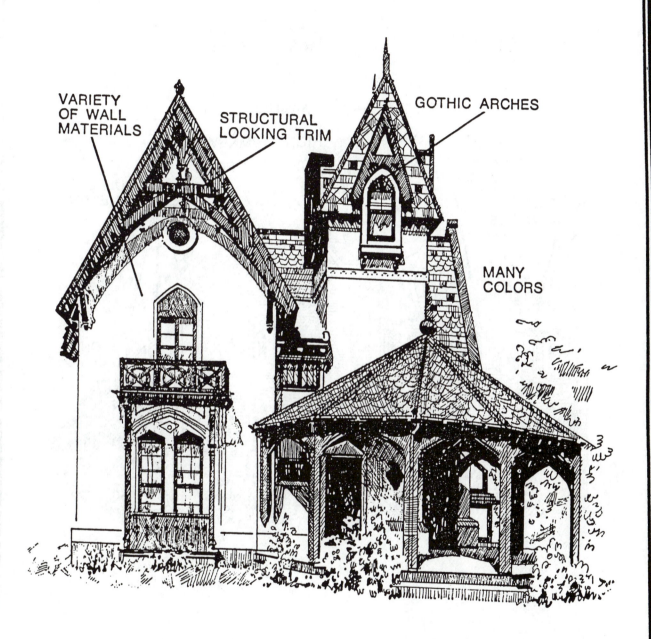

VARIETY
OF WALL
MATERIALS

STRUCTURAL
LOOKING TRIM

GOTHIC ARCHES

MANY
COLORS

Nineteenth Century American

HIGH VICTORIAN GOTHIC (Hi Goth - 705)

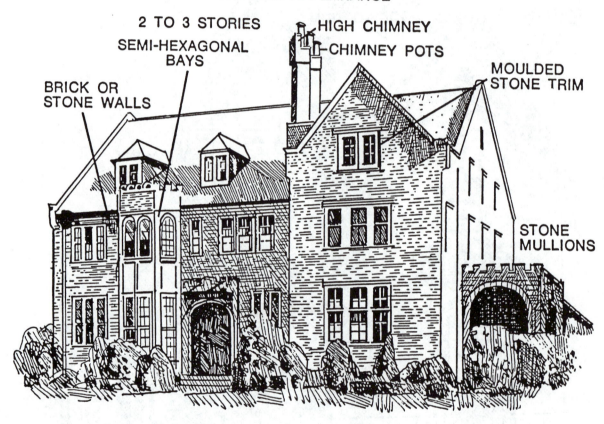

FORT-LIKE APPEARANCE

2 TO 3 STORIES

HIGH CHIMNEY

CHIMNEY POTS

SEMI-HEXAGONAL BAYS

MOULDED STONE TRIM

BRICK OR STONE WALLS

STONE MULLIONS

English

MASONRY TUDOR OR JACOBEAN (Masonry Tudor - 203)

15 The Gross Monthly Rent Multiplier (GMRM) Income Approach

The income approach, applied to single family residences, is also called the Gross Monthly Rent Multiplier (GMRM), Gross Rent Multiplier (GRM) or Gross Income Multiplier (GIM).

The income approach used for single family residences is based on the assumption that there is a direct relationship between what residences sell for and their monthly rent.

By custom, monthly rents are used for single family residences. Usually they are rentals for residences that are unfurnished and do not include utilities.

STEPS OF THE (GMRM) INCOME APPROACH

When sufficient data is available, the appraiser should follow these steps to derive an indication of market value from the (GMRM) income approach:

1 . Calculate the Gross Monthly Rent Multiplier.

   a. Find residences that have recently sold and were rented at the time of sale that are comparable to the property being appraised in the same or similar neighborhoods.

   b. Divide the sales price of each property by this monthly rental to derive a monthly rent multiplier, known as the Gross Monthly Rent Multiplier (GMRM).

   c. Reconcile the multipliers developed above to obtain a single multiplier or a range of multipliers that are applicable to the appraised property. This is not an average; it is a judgment of comparability and applicability.

2 . Estimate the market rent of the residence being appraised.

   a. Find comparable rentals in the neighborhood.

b. Analyze each rental, comparing its features with those of the residence being appraised.

c. Estimate the adjustments required to obtain an indicated market (economic) rent for the residence being appraised.

d. Consider each comparable carefully, with emphasis on the need for adjustments, and formulate an opinion of the market rent of the residence being appraised, based upon the actual rents of the comparables.

3 . Develop an indicated value of the residence being appraised.

a. Multiply the estimated market rent of the residence being appraised by the estimated monthly multiplier (or range of multipliers) to obtain its indicated market value via the income approach.

The multiplier is relied on as an indicator of market value because it tends to express a constant relationship between the gross monthly rental income of a single family residence and its sale price. Practicing appraisers rely on this indicator as a direct application of market data and income information, which expresses the relationship between sale price (or market value) and rental income.

The multiplier is usually a whole number. The number is produced by dividing the monthly rental income into the sale price of a comparable property. For example, if the sale price of a residence were $120,000 and it had been rented for $1,200 a month, $120,000 is divided by $1,200 and the multiplier is found to be 100. The system is used by practicing appraisers because it is straightforward and simple. Its reliability, of course, rests on the dependability of the data used.

Most appraisers believe that no adjustments can or should be made in the development of the multiplier. They feel that if comparable sales are not reasonably similar, they should be dropped from consideration. A few appraisers still feel that under some circumstances adjustments can be made in the data collected, on the same basis as in the market data approach, using the four elements of comparison. This process is not recommended.

LIMITATIONS OF THE GMRM

The multiplier, like any other approach, can produce excellent results if the data used is reliable and appropriate. However, it can be misleading and produce indefensible conclusions if the technique used or the information applied is inappropriate. The situations under which the results are most desirable include:

1 . The properties from which the multiplier is developed have common characteristics (size, age, physical condition, neighborhood, etc.) with the residence being appraised.

2 . The multiplier is extracted from properties for which there is an active market. If there is not an active market (that is, many recent sales), information on which to base a conclusion will be inadequate.

3 . The market information is correct and rentals have been verified. When verification develops significant special conditions or special financing the data should either not be used or given little weight.

CALCULATING A GMRM

The following example illustrates how a GMRM is derived from the market. It is based on using actual sales and dividing them by their actual rentals at the time of the sale, without making any adjustments. The multipliers in Fig. 15-1 range from 106.4 to 112.3 with 110 as most common multiplier. It is the multiplier for properties that appears to be closest to the value of the property being appraised. Therefore, 110 was selected as the appropriate multiplier.

FIG. 15-1 FINDING THE GMRM (WITHOUT ADJUSTMENTS)

Comparable Property	Verified Sale Price	Monthly Rent	Indicate Gross Monthly Rent Multiplier
1	$119,700	$1,125	106.4
2	123,600	1,150	107.5
3	127,500	1,150	110.9
4	128,850	1,200	107.4
5	132,000	1,200	110.0
6	133,500	1,250	106.8
7	133,350	1,200	111.1
8	134,700	1,200	112.3
9	132,000	1,200	110.0
10	133,500	1,200	111.2
11	132,500	1,200	110.4
12	123,600	1,100	112.4

ESTIMATING MARKET RENT OF THE APPRAISED RESIDENCE

The following represent two illustrations that show how to derive the market rent of the residence being appraised from the market. The first is based on the actual rental of the residence being appraised which has been ascertained to be the market rent. The second is based on comparing it with other rental residences and adjusting for any differences. The adjusted comparable rentals are used as indicators of rental value for the residence being appraised.

EXAMPLE ONE - ESTIMATING MARKET RENT WITHOUT ADJUSTMENTS

If the appraised property is rented, the monthly rental can be used as an indication of the market rent. It is not acceptable appraisal practice, however, to use this contract rent without checking it against other rents in the market. In this illustration the appraised property is rented for $1,200 per month. Based on information obtained from the owner and tenant, it appears to be an arms-length arrangement, with both parties believing the rent is what the property should be generating. This is a good indication that the market rent for such a property is $1,200. To check this rental in the market, other rented houses similar to it should be located.

Based on the array shown in Fig. 15-2, and considering the reported rent of the appraised residence, its market rent appears to be about $1,200. Some appraisers would consider this sufficient data on which to base the estimate of market rent. Other appraisers feel it is better to adjust the rental of each of the residences and then make the estimate, especially when the comparables differ to a certain extent from the property being appraised.

FIG. 15-2 ESTIMATING MARKET RENT WITHOUT ADJUSTMENTS

Comparable Property	Monthly Rent
1	$1,185
2	1,200
3	1,215
4	1,200
5	1,200
6	1,170
7	1,230
8	1,200

EXAMPLE TWO - ESTIMATING MARKET RENT WITH ADJUSTMENTS

In this example, the property being appraised has one bathroom, a one-car garage, no central air conditioning and is rented without utilities included. Some comparable rentals have two bathrooms, two-car garages, central air conditioning and/or are rented with utilities included. Adjustments may be needed to reflect the rental differences.

When more than one difference exists, one rental is designated as the base rental which is adjusted for all known differences except the one being sought. Then it is compared with the other rental in the pair and any remaining difference in rent is attributed to the remaining element of comparison. This technique is illustrated in Fig. 15-3.

FIG. 15-3 ESTIMATING MARKET RENT WITH ADJUSTMENTS

Comparable Rental #1 - The same neighborhood and similar to the subject property. It has one bathroom, no central air conditioning, and a one car garage. It was recently rented unfurnished and without utilities for $1,215 per month. There were no reported special conditions.

Comparable Rental #2 - The same neighborhood and similar to the subject property. It has two bathrooms, no central air conditioning, and a one car garage. It was recently rented unfurnished and without utilities for $1,275 per month. There were no reported special conditions.

Comparable Rental #3 - The same neighborhood and similar to the subject property. It has two bathrooms, no central air conditioning, and a two car garage. It was recently rented unfurnished and without utilities for $1,320 per month. There were no reported special conditions.

Comparable Rental #4 - The same neighborhood and similar to the subject property. It has two bathrooms, central air conditioning, and a two car garage. It was recently rented unfurnished and without utilities for $1,395 per month. There were no reported special conditions.

Comparable Rental #5 - The same neighborhood and similar to the subject property. It has one bathroom, no central air conditioning, and a one car garage. It was recently rented unfurnished and with owner-supplied utilities for $1,410 per month. There were no reported special conditions.

Adjustments		Monthly Rent

BATHROOM ADJUSTMENT

Comparable Rental #1 (base) -	one bathroom, one car garage	- $1,215
Comparable Rental #2 -	two bathrooms, one car garage	+ 1,275
Difference attributable to a second bathroom:		$60

GARAGE ADJUSTMENT

Comparable Rental #1 (base) -	one bathroom, one car garage-	$1,215
Comparable Rental #3 -	two bathrooms, two car garage+	1,320
Adjustment to Comparable Rental #3 to reflect difference in number of bathrooms based on Comparable Rentals #1 and #2		−60
Adjusted Comparable Rental #3		$1,260
Monthly rental difference attributed to size of garage: $1,215 [base Comp. #1] - $1,260 [Adjusted Comp. #3]		$45

CENTRAL AIR CONDITIONING ADJUSTMENT

Comparable Rental #1 (base) -	one bathroom, one car garage, no central air conditioning	- $1,215
Comparable Rental #4 -	two bathrooms, two car garage, central air conditioning	+1,395
Adjustment to Comparable Rental #4 to reflect difference in number of bathrooms		-60
Adjustment to Comparable Rental #4 to reflect difference in garage size (based on Comparable Rentals #1 and #3)		−45
Adjusted Comparable Rental #4		$1,290
Difference attributable to central air conditioning:		$75

INCLUSION OF UTILITIES ADJUSTMENT

Comparable Rental #1 (base) -   one bathroom,
                                 one car garage,
                                 no central air,
                                 no utilities   - $1,215

Comparable Rental #5 -   one bathroom,
                                 one car garage,
                                 no central air,
                                 utilities paid by owner   +1410

Difference attributable to inclusion of utilities: $195

Each comparable rental is adjusted to give an indication of the market rental of the appraised property. If an element of comparison in the comparable rental results in a higher rental than what the property being appraised would rent for, a minus adjustment is made. For example, if the only difference is that the appraised property has three bedrooms and a comparable rental has four bedrooms, with the extra bedroom contributing $250 to the monthly rental, then a minus $250 adjustment is made on the comparable rental. These adjustment techniques are identical to those used in the Sales Comparison Approach.

A rating grid may be used to display information about the appraised property and the comparable rentals, along with adjustments for each difference between them (See Fig. 15-4)

FIG. 15-4 COMPARABLE RENTAL GRID

n	Appraised House	Comp. Rental 1	Comp. Rental 2	Comp. Rental 3	Comp. Rental 4	Comp. Rental 5
t		$1215	$1275	$1320	$1395	$1410
hrooms	one	one -0-	two -$60	two -$60	two -$60	one -0-
age Size	one-car	one-car -0-	one-car -0-	two-car -$45	two-car -$45	one-car -0-
tral Air ditioning	no	no	no	no	-$75	no
ities ment	tenant	tenant -0-	tenant -0-	tenant -0-	tenant -0-	owner -$195
adjustment		-0-	-$60	-$105	-$180	-$195
cated rent ppraised house	$1215	$1215	$1215	$1215	$1215	$1215

Actual data would rarely work out this precisely. Often both plus and minus adjustments would be made and the indicated rents for the house being appraised would vary, requiring reconciling into a final indicated rental value.

ESTIMATING THE VALUE OF THE SUBJECT PROPERTY

The third step of the income approach is to estimate the indicated market value of the residence being appraised, which is done by multiplying the estimated market rent of the residence by the GMRM selected. For example, if the GMRM selected were 110, based on market data, and the estimated market rent of the residence being appraised were $1215. per month (unfurnished and without utilities), its indicated market value is calculated as follows:

1. Estimated market rent of house being appraised $1,215

2. Gross Monthly Rent Multiplier   x 110

3. Indicated value of the residence being appraised
    via the income approach $133,650

SUMMARY

This chapter illustrates the use of the GMRM income approach as it applies to the single family residence. It is also referred to as the Gross Monthly Rent Multiplier approach and is considered a reliable approach to estimate market value if the data used is verified and representative of the market.

There are three steps in the GMRM income approach:

1 . The GMRM is selected by finding residences similar to the residence being appraised in the same or nearby neighborhoods that were rented at the time they were sold. The whole number, which is obtained by dividing the sales price by the monthly rent (usually unfurnished and without utilities included), is known as the Gross Monthly Rent Multiplier and expresses the relationship between rental income and market value.

2 . The market rent of the residence being appraised is estimated. Either the actual rent of the residence is used (after confirming that it is typical of the market) or the market rent is estimated by comparing the residence to other rented, comparable properties in the market and adjusting for any significant differences.

3 . The indicated value via the GMRM income approach is obtained by multiplying the GMRM selected in Step 1 by the estimated market rent of the residence being appraised (Step 2).

STEEP, PITCHED ROOF

WHITE CLAPBOARD

SIMPLE BOX SHAPE

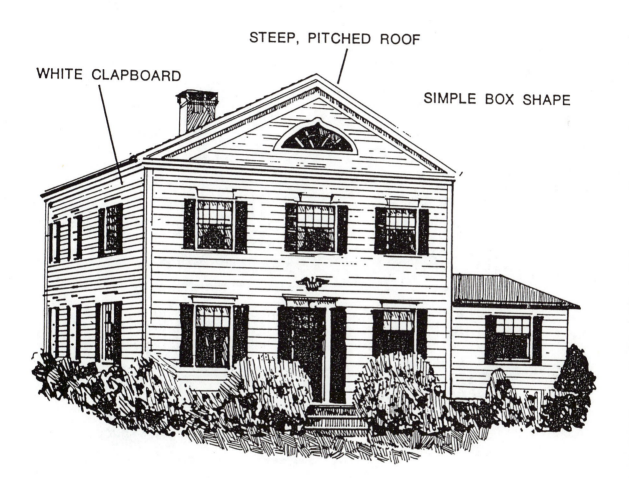

Colonial American

NEW ENGLAND FARM HOUSE (N E Farm - 102)

SHINGLE COVERED
GABLE ROOF

PARTS
RESEMBLE
FURNITURE
LEGS

TOWER OR
TURRET

OPEN
FRONT
PORCH

ROWS OF
SPINDLES

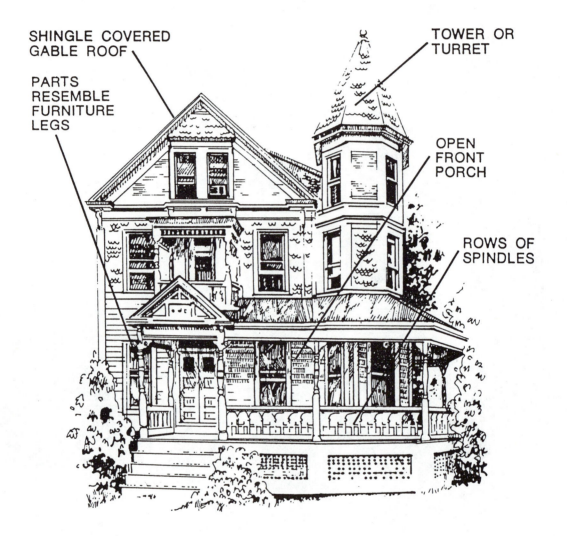

Nineteenth Century American

EASTLAKE (East L - 709)

16 Reconciliation and Final Value Estimate

The purpose of an appraisal is to make a supported objective opinion of value, as of a specific date, of an adequately and accurately described property.

In each step of the appraisal process, the appraiser collects and analyzes data and reconciles it. There is also a final reconciliation. In this process the appraiser considers the quantity and quality of the data collected, analyzed and displayed in the appraisal report.

In addition, the appraiser considers any other related data about which he or she has knowledge, as well as general knowledge of the market and the economy.

In the past, this process was known among appraisers as correlation. Since correlation has a different meaning in statistics and other academic disciplines, it has been replaced by the word reconciliation.

DEFINITION OF THE PROBLEM

Reconciliation starts at the very beginning of an appraisal, with the definition of the appraisal problem, the preliminary survey and the data collection program. The appraiser must ascertain the character and quantity of work to be accomplished and begin to weigh the relative significance and applicability of various data and approaches to the problem.

IDENTIFICATION OF THE REAL ESTATE

The report must provide a positive identification of the residence being appraised. Regardless of the method of identification (street name and number, metes and bounds, etc.) the location and boundaries must be specified. All significant easements, encroachments and rights-of-way must be considered. If there is an owners' association or rights to use nearby facilities are involved, these rights must be completely identified. The appraiser should be sure the identification meets the requirements of the Uniform Standards of Professional Appraisal Practice, which requires a clear and complete description of the property.

IDENTIFICATION OF THE PROPERTY RIGHTS TO BE VALUED

When the property is in fee simple, a plain statement to this effect should be sufficient. If a leasehold or a residence on leased land is involved, the terms of these leases must be described and their effect on the estimated value must be analyzed. Analysis of condominium or cooperative ownership rights requires a survey of the entire project in which the features, both good and bad, of the entire project are related to the ownership interest being appraised. A residence that has time-sharing rights requires other consideration. For example, are the rights to use the property for December and June equal to the rights to use the same property for January and July?

The ownership rights of the property being appraised must be compared to those of comparable sales and offerings. Any differences will require adjustment.

DATE OF VALUE ESTIMATE

In a stable market, the date of valuation and any time adjustments made to comparable sales, rentals, cost estimates and offerings, present few problems. However, in unstable and rapidly changing markets any time differential is reviewed. Time adjustments are often averaged over a period of time when, in reality, the market has been moving both upward and downward during the period. Such adjustments, based on average value changes in a community, may not apply to the neighborhood or the price range of the property being appraised. Large time adjustments, based on one or two matched pairs, may contain substantial error caused by some unknown factor.

USE OF THE APPRAISAL

If the objective of the appraisal is to estimate the market value, the appraiser asks if it accomplishes this objective. Is the potential error in the appraisal within boundaries that are satisfactory to the user of the appraisal? Would more data and better analysis reduce the possibility of potential error? Does the appraisal state the degree of potential error that exists, or is this degree of accuracy misleading?

When the objective of the appraisal is to estimate value other than market value, the data collected and analyzed must be sufficient and proper to produce the required value estimate. For example, if the value estimated is insurable value, have all the items to be excluded such as footings, underground pipes and site work been properly treated?

Finally, the most important question is whether the value estimated is a sufficiently accurate estimate of the defined value.

DEFINITION OF VALUE

It is not satisfactory to put a stock definition of value into an appraisal report without carefully understanding its meaning.

For example, market value may be defined, in part, as the highest price the property will bring or as the most probable selling price. One definition may be more appropriate than the other after an analysis has been made of the data. Insurable value requires a definition that is acceptable in the locale or region for the type of property being appraised. Often a different definition of insurable value exists for residential and commercial properties.

OTHER LIMITING CONDITIONS

For the protection of appraisers and clients it is often appropriate for the appraiser to set forth those other limiting conditions that apply to his or her appraisal assignment, besides the other items included in the definition of the problem which are also considered to be limiting conditions.

PRELIMINARY SURVEY AND APPRAISAL PLAN

DATA NEEDED

A step-by-step review of the preliminary survey and appraisal is made, to determine if all the necessary data has been obtained, and adequate analysis has been provided to arrive at the value estimate. Often, the initial estimate of the data needed to make the appraisal proves to be insufficient to arrive at a satisfactory value estimate. For example, the original plan may call for only the use of comparable sales. However, when the market analysis is made, it may indicate that the shifting market is being affected by the number of competitive listings available. Therefore, information about listings should be used in the market data approach.

Changing building costs and the availability of sites and new, competitive houses may indicate that a detailed application of the cost approach, based on actual costs of available sites and residences currently under construction, will provide a good value indication. The lack of current rentals and information about rented houses that have sold may require the abandonment of an original plan to include an income approach analysis.

As part of the reconciliation process, the data used in each section of the report must be carefully analyzed with emphasis on making a final judgment about whether sufficient data has been collected and which data should be used to make the final value estimate. It is poor practice to have inflexible rules about the type and amount of data used; this decision must be made separately for each appraisal problem.

DATA SOURCES

After the initial data has been collected and analyzed, the data sources should again be reviewed to determine if additional sources may be available. For example, offerings of nearby comparable properties from an MLS may not show as sales because they were sold either by another broker or by the owner after the listing expired. By tracking these particular properties in the sales records of the community, additional useful comparable sales may be found.

Brokers, lenders, and others interviewed for information often supply leads to additional data sources. All data sources should be reviewed to determine if they have been properly used.

PERSONNEL AND TIME REQUIREMENTS

The initial estimate of needed personnel should be reviewed to see if they will be able to obtain all the necessary data within the prescribed time. If additional data is needed, extra personnel or additional time on the part of the original personnel will be required.

Often the time originally allocated to complete an assignment will have to be revised. Only when the special requirements of a specific assignment are known, can a final estimate of the time schedule be made. Other considerations such as new assignments taking priority over existing assignments, unexpected illnesses of personnel, revised requirements of the client and personal needs of the appraiser often make scheduling revisions necessary.

The completion flow chart initially serves as a guide through the appraisal process. It can consist of simple notes on how the appraisal will be made or it may be a formal chart showing the progress of the appraisal on a step-by-step basis. Some appraisers use magnetic boards and movable pieces to plot the progress of each appraisal assignment. Whatever system is used, it should be reviewed to keep track of the progress of the assignment and altered to reflect the updated requirements to complete the assignment.

FEE PROPOSAL AND CONTRACT

It is good practice to have an agreement with each client about what work will be performed, when it is due and how you will be paid. This contract may be verbal or in writing.

DATA COLLECTION AND ANALYSIS

Ongoing decisions must be made on how much data will be collected and whether the quantity and quality are sufficient to complete the appraisal assignment.

GENERAL DATA

It is easy to collect masses of general data about the region, community and neighborhood in which the residence being appraised is located. It is very hard to cull from this mass of data that information which directly describes the environment and explains the forces affecting the value of the property.

This reconciliation is probably one of the most difficult to do properly and one that tends to be downplayed in importance. "Window dressing"–an appraiser's term for unnecessary (merely decorative) figures, charts and displays is not appropriate in a professional appraisal report.

The use of demographic information is a good example. There is little justification for simply presenting population figures. Rather, a comparison of population increase with the availability of housing stock, vacancy rates and a forecast of the rate of growth of new housing is more valuable. Raw figures cannot tell the story. All information pertaining to the region, community and neighborhood must be carefully analyzed and reconciled to produce a meaningful presentation.

Economic data, used to prepare market, financial and economic base analyses and to project future trends, also tends to be available in great masses. A visit to the local Chamber of Commerce will often supply the appraiser with pounds of this type of information. Usually one source, no matter how good, will be insufficient to provide all the needed data. As the data is sorted and analyzed, it must be reconciled into a meaningful analysis that will be useful in making a value estimate of the property being appraised.

SPECIFIC DATA

Information about the property being appraised is obtained at the community record source and at the property site. The goal is to accumulate all of the needed data during one trip to each of these places. This can be accomplished by careful planning and the use of checklists and field note forms. A careful review of the data collected on location is the beginning of the specific data reconciliation.

An appraiser is not expected to be a title searcher. However, it is necessary to acquire enough skill to be able to find and use the needed documents. Title papers are examined to produce a positive description of the property; they also will reveal easements, rights-of-way and any private deed restrictions. Sometimes these items have a substantial effect on the value of the property.

Another item to be checked at the record source is the tax assessment. If possible, the assessor's field card should be examined. It often contains useful descriptive information about the property that may affect the final value estimate.

Zoning information can also be obtained at the municipal record source. A preliminary reconciliation may reveal whether the property conforms or if a reasonable probability of a zoning change exists. An initial reconciliation at the data source can determine whether additional record data pertaining either to the property being appraised or comparable properties is needed. Later, when the data about the community, neighborhood, and property being appraised is reconciled, a more accurate judgment may be made.

Most of the information is usually obtained at the site. The use of checklists or field note forms is helpful. Some clients will provide forms with their special informational requirements. Some clients require a complete list of all items of observed physical deterioration-curable, together with individual estimates of the cost to cure each item.

The final reconciliation of this information determines whether the property has been completely and accurately described and whether there is sufficient information to complete each of the three approaches to value.

HIGHEST AND BEST USE

Estimating the highest and best use starts with an analysis and reconciliation of all the general and specific information collected about the property. It is done in two parts. First the site is analyzed as if vacant, and then taking into consideration any existing improvements. The information is reconciled with the four tests of highest and best use. Zoning information and private restrictions are reconciled to indicate what uses are currently legally permitted. Then the community and neighborhood information is reconciled with economic information to determine if a reasonable probability of change in zoning exists. The information is further reconciled into an estimate of the reasonable and probable permitted legal uses. Next, the physical information about the site is reconciled to estimate which of the reasonable and probable legally permitted uses is also physically possible.

The community, neighborhood and economic data are again reconciled to estimate what uses would result in the production of a profit. Even if the legally permitted use is for a single family residence and such a residence can be built and can produce a profit, this is not sufficient to conclude that the highest and best use is for a single family residence. The type of residence, style, size, design and construction must also be determined.

If after reconciliation of the available information it is estimated that the highest and best use is for something other than a single family residence, this should be stated.

The final step is an estimate of the most profitable use. Again, all the information is reconciled. If additional information is needed, it is gathered and analyzed. Reconciliation produces a decision about what the most potentially profitable, physically and legally permitted use of the site is, assuming it were vacant.

This analysis is then repeated to estimate the highest and best use of the property as improved. The information about the region, community, neighborhood, site and existing improvements is analyzed to estimate what renovation and repairs, if any, could be made to result in a greater potential profit (or smaller loss) by the owner if the property were sold on the date of appraisal. This estimate may range from a simple list of physical and functional curable items through major renovations and proposed additional improvements to the site.

The estimation of highest and best use is based on a thorough analysis and reconciliation of all the data collected. Again, it may be necessary to collect and analyze additional data before final reconciliation as to the highest and best use can be made. For example, the preliminary reconciliation may indicate that some renovation may be needed. At this point additional information about its cost and physical feasibility is necessary before a final determination can be made; the reconciliation process is continued after the needed information is collected and analyzed.

Information about sales of comparative sites and improved properties, comparative rentals and rented properties that have sold is initially reconciled to see if it is sufficient to produce an indicated value by the three approaches to value.

The preliminary reconciliation reviews the sources of cost data which will be used to estimate reproduction or replacement costs. If a cost service is used as one source, a second source should also be developed. The cost data should be subject to a preliminary reconciliation with the description of the improvements to see if material to estimate all of the costs is available.

A decision about the method of estimating depreciation, based on the available data should be made. If the abstraction method is used, comparable sales are analyzed to see if they are sufficient in number and comparable enough to the property being appraised to produce a satisfactory depreciation estimate. If the age-life or breakdown method is used, a preliminary reconciliation is made to determine if sufficient data has been collected.

The income approach depends upon sufficient data on comparable rented residences to estimate both the market rent of the property being appraised and also to develop the GMRM. The rentals used to develop the GMRM must be of properties that have recently sold. The initial reconciliation determines if sufficient usable data has been collected to make these estimates or whether additional rentals and sales are needed. If insufficient data regarding sales of rented properties exists, the income approach may not be usable.

Since the final value estimate of most single family residential appraisals depends heavily on the market data approach, it is necessary to reconcile the comparative sales data continuously during the appraisal process.   Initial reconciliations are needed to see if sufficient comparable sales data, as well as data to make necessary adjustments, has been collected to reflect the differences between the comparable sales selected and the residence being appraised.

It is not good appraisal practice to claim that insufficient data has been found to develop the market data approach unless a thorough search of the market has been conducted.   If sales appear insufficient after the initial reconciliation, the search should begin again.   This expanded search can be over a wider geographic area, wider price range or greater time frame. The process may be repeated several times, each time collecting and reconciling data to determine its usefulness until it is concluded either that sufficient data is collected for the market data approach or that further expansion of the search will not produce any additional useful data.

All of the reconciling done up to this point is of a preliminary nature, with the primary goal being to collect enough useful data to proceed through the three approaches to value.

APPLICATION OF THE THREE APPROACHES

The reconciliation process continues as the collected data is further analyzed for use in each of the approaches.

INCOME APPROACH (GMRM)

The Gross Monthly Rent Multiplier technique used in the appraisal of single family residences includes the following eight steps:

1 . Find residences that have recently sold in the neighborhood that are comparable to the property being appraised, that were rented at the time of sale. All recent sales are reviewed and those most comparable are selected for final use. No fixed number of COMPARABLES is needed. Many appraisers try to find at least 12. If a larger number can be found, they may lend themselves to analysis by statistical techniques (see Appendix E).

2 . Divide the sales price of each comparable by the monthly rental to derive the GMRM. The resulting GMRM figures should be arranged in order to determine if they fall into a useful range and if extremes should be dropped or additional data is needed.

3 . Reconcile the multipliers to obtain a single multiplier or a range of multipliers that is applicable to the appraised property. If a single GMRM is selected, it should not be an average of the multipliers obtained in Step 2. It should be a result of considering how comparable each of the properties that produced a multiplier was to the property being appraised or the result of statistical analysis of the range of multipliers.

4 . Find comparable rentals in the neighborhood.   Comparable rentals are reviewed and selected for final use. Again no fixed number is standard; however, less than three usually is not satisfactory. The reconciliation here emphasizes the

comparability of the rental to the property being appraised and the identification of the existing significant differences for which adjustments are made.

5 . Analyze each of the comparable rentals by comparing them with the corresponding features of the house being appraised. A decision must be made on an item-by-item basis about whether the differences can be adjusted for or if the rental must be rejected. If many rentals are rejected, it may be necessary to go back to the market and expand the search to find additional useful data.

6 . Estimate the required adjustments of each comparable rental property to obtain an indicated rental for the appraised property. All the additional rentals needed to estimate the adjustments are analyzed. Those that will produce indications of the needed adjustments are processed. These adjustments are reconciled with the comparable sales, and data is added or eliminated as required.

7 . Consider each comparable rental carefully, with emphasis on the need for adjustments, and formulate an opinion of the market (economic) rent of the property being appraised, based on the adjusted rentals of the comparables. Often the rentals are adjusted with the aid of a grid. The result is a group of adjusted rentals, each of which is an indication of the market rent of the residence being appraised. These adjusted rentals are individually compared to the property being appraised to estimate which are most comparable. Finally, a decision is made as to the estimated market rent of the property being appraised. This estimate should not be an average but is based on the results of the reconciliation.

8 . Multiply the estimated market rent of the appraised property by the estimated monthly multiplier (or range of multipliers) to obtain an indicated value of the appraised residence via the income approach. This result should not be accepted without another reconciliation of all the data. The appraiser must be satisfied that the data used is of adequate quantity and quality to produce a useful estimate.

INCOME APPROACH (CAPITALIZATION METHOD)

In the appraisal of an investment property, the income capitalization method is usually the most appropriate. The appraiser considers both the quantity and quality of the rental data used to develop the Gross Income Estimate.

Expense and Replacement Reserve estimates are developed from data collected about comparable properties and the subject property.

The rental estimates and expense estimates are reconciled into an estimate of net operating income (NOI).

The final step is to develop an appropriate capitalization rate and then divide the NOI by the capitalization rate for the subject property and market.

COST APPROACH

The reconciliation process is applied to each step of this approach.

1 . Estimate the market value of the site as if vacant and available for development to its highest and best use (see Chapter 8). The estimate of the site value actually requires all of the steps of the market data approach. First, the comparable sites are reconciled, comparing their use with the estimate highest and best use of the

site being appraised. For example, if the site being appraised were best suited for a house in the $80,000 to $100,000 range, sites for houses of similar value would be the best comparables even if the house being appraised were in the $30,000 to $35,000 range and therefore not the highest and best use.

The best comparables are selected and individually compared to the site being appraised. Differences between the comparable sites and the site being appraised are reported. The data is further analyzed for information on which to base adjustments for all the significant differences. A decision is then made about each comparable as to whether it can be adjusted satisfactorily or must be rejected and replaced with a better comparable. If many sales are rejected, it may be necessary to go back to the market and expand the search for more comparable site sales and/or more data on which to base the adjustments.

When the appraiser is satisfied that the assembled data is adequate and all the needed adjustments have been made, the adjusted sales price of each of the comparables is analyzed and a final indicated value of the appraised site is obtained. This estimate is not an average of the adjusted sale price of the comparables; it is based on the results of the reconciliation.

2 . Estimate the reproduction (or replacement) cost new of the improvements. This estimate can be based on data from construction cost services and/or from actual costs of similar residences constructed in the same market. The available data is reconciled to determine which method will be used. Both the description of the improvements and the data being used as a cost basis are analyzed to determine if everything needed to make the cost estimate has been gathered. The cost data is reconciled with the description of the improvements data to produce an estimated reproduction or replacement cost of the residence being appraised.

3 . Estimate the amount of depreciation the improvements have suffered. A decision is made as to which method will be used to estimate the accrued depreciation. When the abstraction method is used, the sales selected from which to abstract the depreciation are analyzed and processed. The range of resulting amounts of depreciation or rates of depreciation are reconciled. Reconciliation considers the comparability of the data from which the amount or rate of depreciation is abstracted. The final reconciliation considers the amount of data used, the degree of variance between the rates and whether additional data is needed to produce a satisfactory estimate of depreciation.

If the age-life method is used, depreciation may be based entirely upon observation. To estimate the typical economic life of a residence, data about the region, community and neighborhood is considered, along with specific data about the residence being appraised. Each of the four great forces that affect the value and life of the residence is considered. This data is then reconciled by the appraiser, who relies heavily on personal knowledge and experience, into an estimate of typical economic life. Finally, the percentage of depreciation is calculated by dividing the effective age by the typical economic life. A final reconciliation of the results determines how good the estimate is and how much weight it will be given in the appraisal process.

The breakdown method of estimating depreciation is done in five steps that correspond to the five types of depreciation identified by this method. First, the physical deterioration-curable is estimated by making a list of all the physical deterioration that is observed. Cost to cure these items is estimated either by the appraiser or by a local contractor who can provide the needed cost information.

Most items of normal maintenance are automatically classified as physical deterioration-curable without actually proving they add value in excess of their cost. However, it may be necessary to obtain market information to justify classifying large items of maintenance as curable. The list of items to be cured and the estimated costs to do the work are reconciled into an estimate of physical deterioration-curable.

Physical deterioration-incurable is divided into two groups. One group is items that are not ready to be cured on the date of the appraisal but will need to be cured before the end of the residence's economic life. A list is prepared together with cost estimates to repair or replace the items. These items are reconciled into an estimate of physical deterioration-incurable (short-lived items). The other group of items includes those that have suffered some deterioration but will not be economically feasible to repair or replace during the remaining typical economic life of the improvements. The estimate is often made based on an engineering breakdown of the components of the residence against which percentage of depreciation estimates are applied to produce a total estimate of the physical deterioration-incurable. This estimate depends heavily on the appraiser's knowledge and judgment. All the data used should be carefully reconciled, and the reliability of the results reported.

Items of functional obsolescence are listed and analyzed to estimate if a cure is possible. If so, it is noted whether the cost to cure is less than the value added. Reconciliation of this information may require the use of additional data to support whether the value added will exceed the cost to cure. Data is also needed to estimate the cost to cure the items as part of a total construction program as well as the cost to do so separately on the date of the appraisal. The reliability of this estimate is considered in the reconciliation.

The loss from functional obsolescence-incurable may be based on comparison of recently sold or rented residences with and without the item or features causing the obsolescence.

The items off the premises that cause a loss in value (economic obsolescence) are listed, measured and estimated.

In the past, the breakdown method was a favorite method of many appraisers. However, it is a very difficult method to use in actual practice because of all the data needed. There is usually a high probability of error.

4 . Deduct the depreciation from the reproduction (or replacement) cost new of the improvements to obtain the depreciated value of the improvements "as is". If depreciation has been estimated by more than one method, the results are reconciled into a depreciation estimate. When sufficient data is available, the abstraction method usually produces the most accurate estimate because it is based directly upon market data. The age-life method usually is based primarily on the appraiser's judgment, supported more heavily by general knowledge than by specific data. Because it is easy to explain, it usually is the best method when insufficient data is available for abstraction method. The results of the breakdown method tend to be deceiving because it is broken into five parts. Because it is not primarily based on the market, there is potential for substantial

error. When used, it should be carefully reconciled to eliminate as much potential error as possible.

When more than one method is used, the results should be compared. Reasons for differences should be sought and the estimates further refined, if possible, to reduce the discrepancies. The final depreciation estimate is deducted from the estimated reproduction or replacement cost to produce the depreciated value of the improvements.

5. Add the site (land) market value obtained in Step 1 to the depreciated value of the improvements to obtain an indicated value of the property. After the estimated value is obtained, it is compared with the values indicated by the other approaches. A wide variance is indicative of possible weaknesses in the data, assumptions, or application of the cost approach or its validity and applicability to the specific appraisal problem.

SALES COMPARISON APPROACH

The reconciliation process is applied to each of the five steps of the market data approach.

1. Find the sales, listings and offerings of properties that are similar to the property being appraised. When a group of sales, listings and offerings has been collected, a preliminary reconciliation is made for the purpose of deciding if enough usable data has been obtained. The setting of arbitrary numbers of sales, listings and offerings to be used--without actually considering the quality of the data--is poor appraisal practice.

2. Verify each sale with the buyer, seller or broker to confirm the selling price, data of transaction, physical and locational characteristics and conditions of sale. The only acceptable way to find out about the conditions of sale that affected a transaction is to interview the buyer, seller or broker. Only these people will know all the terms, motivations and whether the sale was bona fide in nature. The results of the interviews should be reconciled. If information indicates conditions of sale that will be difficult to adjust for, the sale should be rejected and replaced with additional data, if possible, and the reconciliation process repeated.

3. Analyze the important attributes of each comparable and compare the corresponding features of the property being appraised. Use the elements of comparison such as time of sale, location, physical and other characteristics (see Chapter 13). The analysis of the important attributes of each comparable will identify differences between the comparables and the property being appraised. The available data is then reconciled to determine if it will serve as a basis for making the needed adjustments or whether additional data will be needed. The search continues for data until a sufficient number of sales, listings and offerings is found with differences that can be adjusted for.

4. Estimate the adjustments that will be required for the sales price of each comparable to give an indicated value for the appraised property. Adjustments should be supported with data developed from the market, which is reconciled to produce an adjusted sales price for each comparable.

5. Consider each of the comparable sales and the accuracy of any and all adjustments required because of dissimilarities among these sales and the appraised property.

Formulate an opinion of market value for the latter based on the comparable sales which have been analyzed. The reconciliation of the adjusted price of each comparable into a final value estimate for the appraised property is the critical step in the appraisal process because this estimate will most likely be used as the main basis for the final value estimate. The reconciliation process considers the supporting data for each adjustment. When there is a substantial spread in adjusted prices, consideration should be given to expanding the data search and repeating the whole process to obtain better results.

In the final reconciliation of the market data approach, the quantity and quality of all the data is reviewed. Generally, the older the data, the further from the property being appraised and the more physically dissimilar, the less accurate the adjusted price will be. It is particularly difficult to adjust accurately for conditions of sale and economic influences.

Again, the value obtained in the sales comparison approach is compared with value indications derived in the other two approaches. Wide discrepancies in value usually suggest that further collection, refinement and analysis of the pertinent data is needed.

FINAL RECONCILIATION INTO ESTIMATE OF VALUE

The final step in the reconciliation is to check all data for accuracy, reliability and applicability. The purpose and objectives of the report are summarized and the characteristics of the property are reviewed. A decision is made regarding the most appropriate approaches to value and the reliability of each value indication as obtained.

ADVANTAGES AND DISADVANTAGES OF EACH APPROACH

The GMRM income approach is mathematically simple and direct. It is most useful when the subject property is located in a neighborhood where houses are frequently rented. Disadvantages are that the condition of comparables is not always reflected in rent differentials, many quality neighborhoods have few houses that are rented and subsequently sold, and a considerable volume of rental and sales data is necessary to estimate properly the market rent and appropriate multiplier for use in this approach.

The cost approach was traditionally the favorite approach to value for many appraisers. Its advantages are that it is simple to use and usually reliable for new improvements on properties developed to their highest and best use. The disadvantages are the difficulty of accurately estimating accrued depreciation when no sales are available from which to calculate the depreciation by abstraction, and the reproduction cost estimates may not reflect actual prevailing economic and market conditions.

The market data approach is usually the preferred approach in single family residential appraising. The value indication obtained is based on actual market transactions, is easily understood by lay people and is most applicable in court testimony. It is not particularly useful when there is a lack of recent, reliable and highly comparable sales data.

QUANTITY & QUALITY OF DATA

The quantity and quality of the data used as a basis for making the value estimates determines the degree of accuracy of these estimates. The more confidence the appraiser has in the data the more confidence they will have in a value estimate that is made based on the data.

Often the appraiser will have more confidence in the data used in one approach than that used in the other approaches. When this is the case more weight should be given to the approach with the best data.

Generally the larger and more numerous the adjustments are the less confidence the appraiser will have in the adjusted price that results. The accuracy of some data has a greater effect than the accuracy of other data. A difference of a few thousand dollars in an adjustment in the sales comparison approach will usually have a smaller effect on the final value estimated than a percentage difference in estimating a capitalization rate where every percent difference has a significant effect on the final value being estimated.

ROUNDING

Numbers that are estimates indicate to the reader their degree of accuracy by how they are rounded. When the estimated value of a site is reported to be $32,100, the appraiser is saying that their estimate is accurate to the nearest $100. If the estimated value is reported to be $32,000, the appraiser is saying that the estimate is accurate to the nearest $1,000. dollars.

Rounding helps to make an estimate more believable. Clients find it hard to believe that an appraiser can estimate the value of a house to within a hundred dollars or the value of a million dollar commercial property to within a thousand dollars.

There are three different rounding techniques that are commonly used. One rounds every estimate within an appraisal to indicate its degree of accuracy (i.e., reproduction cost, depreciation, individual adjustments, etc.). Some appraisers leave the numbers within each approach unrounded and round only the values indicated by each approach and the final value estimated. Other appraisers round only the final value estimate.

Appraisers should select the rounding technique they feel will best convey their feelings about the accuracy of their estimates. It is less confusing to the client to use the same rounding technique throughout the appraisal report.

APPRAISAL REPORT

The final step of the appraisal process is the preparation of a report of the value estimated. It is poor appraisal practice to give a value estimate without a report that meets at least the minimum reporting requirements.

All the data is reconciled once again to select the material to be displayed in the appraisal report. Reports to be used for condemnation proceedings and other legal proceedings often must be very comprehensive, containing large amounts of the data used to make the value estimate. Photographs, maps, sketches, charts and other graphics are often included to help the reader understand the analysis and reasoning that led the appraiser to the final value estimate. A lender who uses the services of an appraiser on a regular basis may require only a form report that displays the highlights of the data and reasoning used to arrive at the value estimate.

SUMMARY

The accuracy of an appraisal depends on the appraiser's knowledge, experience, and judgment. Equally important are the quantity and quality of the available data that will be reconciled in the final value conclusion. A judgment is made as to the validity and reliability of each of the value indications derived from the three approaches to value. These indications are never merely averaged. To do so is to substitute arithmetic for judgment. Rather, the appraiser reconciles the value indications, analyzes the alternatives and selects from among them that indication of value which will be most defensible and truly representative of the property being appraised.

BALCONY ACROSS FRONT AT SECOND FLOOR

SHINGLE
ROOF

2 STORIES

RAIL SIMPLE
IRON OR WOOD

Nineteenth Century American

MONTEREY (Monterey - 715)

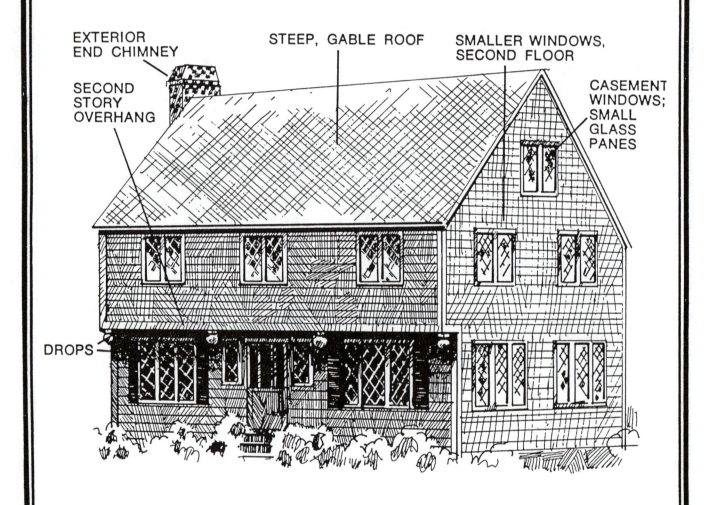

EXTERIOR
END CHIMNEY

SECOND
STORY
OVERHANG

DROPS

STEEP, GABLE ROOF

SMALLER WINDOWS,
SECOND FLOOR

CASEMENT
WINDOWS;
SMALL
GLASS
PANES

Colonial American

GARRISON COLONIAL (Garr Co - 106)

17 Residences & Other Properties Requiring Special Appraisal Techniques

Many appraisal assignments are to appraise properties that require special appraisal techniques. Listed below are the many kinds of residences and other types of properties that are covered in this chapter.

SPECIAL KINDS OF RESIDENCES

- Condominiums
- Cooperatives
- De Minimis PUD
- Colonial Reproductions
- Elderly Housing
- Energy Efficient Homes
- Experimental Houses
- Farm and Ranch Houses
- Historic Houses
- Log Cabins
- Mansions
- Manufactured Houses
- Mobile Homes
- Planned Unit Developments
- Residences on Leased Land
- Second Homes
- Ski Lodges and Homes in Skiing Areas
- Solar Houses
- Timesharing
- Waterfront Houses
- Underground Houses

OTHER TYPES OF PROPERTY

- Hotels, Motels and Inns
- Commercial Buildings
- Industrial Properties
- Storage Buildings
- Agricultural Properties
- Institutional and Government Buildings
- Special Purpose Buildings
- Mixed-Use Buildings

The many types of properties covered briefly in this chapter are only a partial list of properties that often require special appraisal techniques.

When appraising a special type of property, the appraiser must possess the specialized knowledge required to make the appraisal. It is customary for appraisers who lack the necessary knowledge to either turn down the assignment or seek help from someone who possesses it. If the help that is received is substantial, it should be acknowledged in the appraisal report.

CONDOMINIUMS

The biggest change in American home ownership since World War II is the Condominium which did not exist prior to that time.

TYPES OF CONDOMINIUMS

A condominium is a form of ownership that is used for a variety of different types of residences. There are no official categories of the different types of condominiums however, the following is a general breakdown.

- In-town residences with few amenities
- Suburban residences with few amenities
- Suburban residences with recreational facilities
- Resort second homes
- Retirement housing
- Student housing
- Large projects and new towns.

Each of these types of condominiums require different data and different analysis.

The following statements are taken from the Fannie Mae Guidelines:

June 1990 Section 301 Units in Condominium Projects

"A condominium project is one in which individual owners hold title to units in the project along with an undivided interest in the real estate that is designated as the common area for the project.

Appraisals for condominium units must be documented on the Appraisal Report - Individual Condominium or PUD Unit (Form 1073). The appraisal of an individual unit in a condominium project requires the appraiser to analyze the condominium project as well as the individual unit. The appraiser must pay special attention to the location of the project, the location of the individual unit within the project, the project's amenities, and the amount and purpose of the owners' association assessment since the marketability and value of the individual units in a project depend on the marketability and appeal of the project itself."[1]

Condominium is a form of ownership created by special real estate laws passed by state legislatures which permit individual dwelling unit estates to be established within a whole, larger property estate. All 50 states have enacted condominium legislation. These acts vary from state to state but many are similar because they are patterned on a uniform condominium act.

---

[1] *Appraisal and Underwriting Guidelines.* Seller's Guide, Federal National Mortgage Association, Washington, DC., 1990.

Each condominium owner owns the fee to an individual unit and a percentage of the common areas of the land and improvements (entry ways, corridors, elevators, drives, walks and green areas). In some instances owners may have exclusive use of some of the limited common areas, such as basement storage, patios, and parking areas; however, most condominium laws only permit the actual living area to be individually owned.

The location of each individually owned unit must be exact in terms of both the usual horizontal description found in the deed and also a vertical description. The physical horizontal boundaries of individual units for the exterior may be anywhere from the outside of the exterior wall to its inside surface and for the interior may be the wall surface, stud surface or middle of the wall. The vertical boundaries are usually the floors and ceilings within the unit.

The boundaries of the common property are described as they would be for any other type of property. Whatever is within these boundaries and not within an individual unit is common area. The exact boundaries of the common area and the individual units are also shown on a plat (also known as a plot plan) and on the architectural plans, both of which have to be publicly recorded in many states.

A condominium is formed when a master deed is recorded that complies with the requirements of the condominium laws of the state in which it is located. These documents must also establish an owners' association to control the use and maintenance of the common areas. The association (also called a condominium or homeowners' association) is governed by a board of directors, elected by the individual owners. It operates under a set of bylaws recorded by the master deed which in turn must always comply with provisions of the condominium statutes of the state. Usually a 66% or 75% majority of the owners must vote to change the bylaws. It usually takes a 100% vote to change the master deed.

Condominiums can be new units or units in existing buildings that have been converted to condominium ownership. Either new or old, they can take the form of a high-rise, townhouse, small grouping of party-wall units or free-standing unit.

An in-depth study as to what people like and dislike about condominium living has been made by the Urban Land Institute.[2] Among the favorable factors cited were:

1. Building up equity.
2. Lower cost than single family housing.
3. Freedom from house and yard maintenance.
4. Better environment.
5. Recreational facilities.
6. No rent.

People were found to dislike:

1. Living too close together.
2. Noisy or undesirable neighbors and children.
3. Neighbors' pets.
4. Trouble with parking.

[2]Carl Norcross, *Townhouses and Condominiums: Residents' Likes and Dislikes.* Urban Land Institute: Washington, DC., 1973.

5. Poor association management.
6. Poor construction.
7. Dishonest salespeople who sold units.
8. Negligent builders.
9. Renters in other units, rather than owners.
10. Thin party walls.
11. Long identical rows of houses, with poor visual screening between units.

In spite of the problems some condominiums have faced, this form of ownership continues to play an important role in the housing market.

SPECIAL APPRAISAL TECHNIQUES

The appraisal of an entire condominium complex is beyond the scope of this book; the following are considerations for the appraisal of individual condominium units.

The key to these appraisals is use of the market data approach, supported by the income approach if rentals exist of units similar to that being appraised. The cost approach will usually lead to the wrong value estimates. To use it, the costs (both direct and indirect) of the entire project would have to be estimated and then a portion allocated to the unit being appraised.

The best comparables are resales of similar units in the same condominium or similar condominium projects. Because many variables exist in common charges, design, recreational facilities and size, comparable sales from any but the same or very similar complexes will prove to be extremely difficult to adjust accurately. Also, because of the unusual volatility in the market, time adjustments are often difficult to make. The price of new, similar units should be considered but resale prices in some projects are substantially lower than those of comparable new units.

Many lenders (and good appraisal practice) require an analysis of the whole project in order to estimate the value of an individual unit. Special attention should be paid to the common charges and their rate of increase. Similar units in different projects may have different common charges, which affect their value significantly.

COOPERATIVES

New York City is the location of most of the cooperatives in the United States. In the past 10 years, this form of ownership has increased in popularity for a variety of reasons. Probably the most common reason is that in some jurisdictions it is possible to convert a building into cooperative ownership without having to comply with complex cooperative laws.

A cooperative apartment building is owned by a corporation which sells shares to buyers who wish to occupy individual units. Along with the ownership of a cooperative share goes the exclusive right of occupancy for a portion of the space in the building and the nonexclusive right to use other areas of the property.

Technically, a share in a cooperative apartment is not a single family residence but because these shares are bought and sold in a manner similar to condominium units, the public is only vaguely aware of the difference between these ownership forms. Cooperative-owned buildings are financed with one mortgage, whereas condominiums are financed with individual mortgages on individual units. The cooperative corporation owns everything while a condominium association owns nothing.

The share owners (stockholders) of a cooperative elect officers and directors who run the affairs of the corporation. These officers have the power to assess shareholders for operating expenses, and the shareholder's percentage of the monthly payment on the blanket mortgage.

SPECIAL APPRAISAL TECHNIQUES

The best method to use to estimate the value of an individual cooperative unit is to compare it to similar units that have resold in the same building or in a comparable building in a similar location.

In order to compare one sale with another, it is necessary to convert the selling price into the "Effective Selling Price". This is a combination of the selling price plus the unit's percentage share of the underlying blanket mortgage.

Below is an example of two cooperative apartment unit sales whose prices seem similar yet have widely varying effective sales prices:

Sale #1: A three bedroom, two bath unit in a building with 20 units and a $3,200,000 blanket mortgage sold for $80,000.

Sale #2: A three bedroom, 1-1/2 bath unit in a similar building with 30 units and a $6,000,000 blanket mortgage sold for $60,000.

It appears that Sale #2 sold for less than Sale #1; when the effective sales price is calculated it becomes apparent that the opposite is true.

Comparison of Effective Sale Price

Sale #1	Sale Price	$ 80,000
	Share of blanket mortgage ($3,200,000 ÷ 20)	160,000
	Effective Sale Price	$240,000
Sale #2	Sale Price	$ 60,000
	Share of blanket mortgage ($6,000,000 ÷ 30)	200,000
	Effective Sale Price	$260,000

In this example, it is assumed that each unit's percentage of the mortgage is determined by dividing the total number of units into 100. Often it is determined by percentage of total square footage, and therefore varies with the size of the unit to be occupied.

COLONIAL REPRODUCTIONS

Colonial reproductions are a popular group of house styles in most areas. For example, Cape Cod, Massachusetts, is filled with houses that are reproductions of the original Cape Cod style. It has been popular for almost 100 years to copy European styles when building mansions and other large houses. Many of these homes are faithful reproductions of their European ancestors.

In Santa Fe, New Mexico, there are many excellent reproductions of adobe houses constructed with synthetic adobe materials. Other examples of popular reproductions of regional historic styles exist throughout the United States.

Even the builders of tract developments often decorate standard houses with style features from colonial house styles such as bow windows or gambrel roofs.

SPECIAL APPRAISAL TECHNIQUES

Unless the house is an authentic colonial reproduction, the style usually will not significantly affect the value of the house.

DE MINIMIS PUDS

A De Minimis PUD is fee simple ownership of a home with a partial interest in nearby property that is owned together with neighbors. Often the shared property is open space or recreational land.

However, to be classified as De Minimis (a Latin word meaning "of little or no importance"), the joint property must contribute little additional value to the primary residence and any maintenance dues must be insignificant compared to the property value (a few hundred dollars or less per year). The homeowners' association should be loosely constituted and should not have the right to force an owner to pay dues by using special liens.

In contrast, a regular PUD is usually created by formal documents filed in the public land records. Common property does contribute additional value because it is usually a recreational facility or a large tract of vacant land. The homeowners' association is formally constituted with duly elected officers and directors, charges significant dues and has the right to place liens or restrict the use of common property by any owner who does not pay the assessed dues.

SPECIAL APPRAISAL TECHNIQUES

Both Freddie Mac and Fannie Mae allow appraisals of a De Minimis PUD to be done on the URAR, the Single Family Residential Appraisal form.

The commonly owned elements should be described and an opinion rendered that they do not add significant value to the property. The association dues should also be reported.

ELDERLY HOUSING

Elderly housing composes a growing segment of the housing market. One segment of this market is composed of people in the 50 to 65 year old age group. Some of these individuals are still employed, yet they find their housing need changing as their children leave home and they become anxious to be less burdened with the care and cost of a large suburban home. Their preference shifts to smaller houses, townhouses and condominiums, and cooperatives located in affluent neighborhoods, often nearer their place of work and in the city, rather than the suburbs.

New federal regulations uphold the legality of restricting the sale of some property to the elderly without children. However, it is still illegal to restrict sales on the basis of sex, race or religion.

Retirement communities are another form of elderly housing. Here the emphasis is in leisure activities and the accompanying leisure facilities. The ages of these owners tend to be in the 60's and 70's.

Congregate housing facilities is another alternative available to seniors. They tend to consist of relatively small individual apartments with the emphasis being on extensive public areas including a common dining room that provides one or more meals daily. Often the facility also includes a nursing home, and some facilities are marketed together with an extensive health care plan.

SPECIAL APPRAISAL TECHNIQUES

The definition of the problem takes on special importance in the appraisal of housing for the elderly. The type of ownership and special age restrictions (both public and private) must be considered. When the project has special construction and facilities designed for the elderly, it becomes difficult using the market data approach to make the necessary adjustments with sales from outside the project. Housing for the elderly often costs more per square foot than conventional housing. Such factors as higher fire ratings of materials and special equipment may raise the cost. However, housing units for the elderly tend to contain less square footage per unit than conventional housing. Market data from conventional housing is difficult to adjust in appraisals of elderly housing units. The cost approach is useful for newer units in active areas, and the income approach is also used where there are rental units in the same or similar projects.

Housing for the elderly that is subsidized during construction or where the owners or tenants receive government aid, presents unique appraisal problems. The cost and income approaches rarely produce accurate indications of value under these circumstances. Comparable sales with similar special financing history must be found even if it means looking over a wide geographic area.

ENERGY EFFICIENT HOMES

Energy efficient houses are built with extensive insulation--often double the thickness of traditional insulation. They usually are tightly sealed and have small windows. As fuel costs decreased in the 1980s, so did the popularity of this type of house. Now some authorities think the lack of normal ventilation is a health hazard and new concerns about radon have surfaced as well.

SPECIAL APPRAISAL TECHNIQUES

Owners of special energy efficient homes may apply to their lenders for credit for the value of the special energy efficient items. The appraiser may be asked by the lender to complete an **Energy Addendum Residential Appraisal Report** (FHLMC Form 70A). The form provides both a method for reporting special energy efficient items and a way to calculate the value of these items when their value cannot be estimated directly from the market.

EXPERIMENTAL HOUSES

A variety of experimental houses, which use new material such as plastic, fiberglass, foams and other nonconventional building products exist in the United States.

SPECIAL APPRAISAL TECHNIQUES

Most experimental houses lose part of their cost to functional obsolescence because they violate the principle of conformity. The experiment may have been subsidized or have created value-in-use, but often the value-in-use is greater than market value.

Market data is the best evidence of value because the cost approach usually is based on a guess about depreciation and the income approach is rarely applicable. Location is an important consideration as is status and amenity value. For example, an experimental house designed by a nationally-known architect may have more value than one designed by an unknown. In some markets unusual house designs have experienced special market reactions. The flat-roofed, modern or contemporary house appeals to a few buyers but usually not to the market as a whole. The appraiser must take special care to consider such special market reactions.

FARM AND RANCH HOUSES

The recent economic problems of the small farmer increase the need of appraisers to have special skills and experience when appraising farms and ranch houses.

SPECIAL APPRAISAL TECHNIQUES

Freddie Mac and Fannie Mae have special requirements for the appraisal of farms that are used as residences.

The appraisal of rural houses and acreage is based on the market data approach when most of the value is in the improvements, and in the cost approach when most of the value is in the land. For example, if the property being appraised consists of 50 acres of land, with a value of $5,000 per acre, plus a 1,200 square-foot, six-room, one-story, ranch-style house, with a depreciated cost of $15,000, the appraiser should look for comparable land sales and estimate the value of the land and then add $15,000 to arrive at the total value. This produces a more accurate value estimate than using as comparables current sales of houses on small lots and making an adjustment for the excess land.

If the appraisal were of an eight-room, two-story farm house with a value of about $50,000 on two acres of land, it would be best to look for comparable sales of similar farm houses and adjust for land size differences.
A careful highest and best use analysis is essential. Often excess land is present that could be separated from the part of the property that is improved with the house and outbuildings. This land could be valued separately and may have a different highest and best use.

HISTORIC HOUSES

Many houses built before the turn of the century and earlier in the United States are still in habitable condition. Some are considered to be part of the country's national heritage, because of special architectural design or other historic note, and public interest groups have formed in many parts of the country to see that such houses are preserved. When appraising an older house, the appraiser must be aware of whether it has possible historic value.

Houses designated as historic landmarks are governed by special legislation, at either the national or state level or by the local municipality. Such legislation is concerned primarily with the control of the exterior appearance of these structures. There are usually private easements and restrictions controlling the exterior appearance. Most of these regulations provide for an administrative body, which is charged with approving or disapproving any proposed exterior renovation. In the long run, these regulations and restrictions may enhance the value of such properties, although some property owners feel that they limit their ownership freedoms and thereby decrease the value-in-use of their property, and prevent modernization unfairly.

To encourage the preservation of historic homes, special tax legislation has been passed that benefits property owners who give historic easements, which restrict and control exterior and interior renovations. Most states have historic preservation organizations that are qualified to accept historic easements. The National Trust for Historic Preservation operates in the same capacity on a national level. The advantages to the property owner for granting such an historic easement are twofold. According to current Internal Revenue Service regulations, the property owner may be permitted to deduct the value of the easement as a gift for income tax purposes. Also, some communities have special provisions in their property tax laws that lower the property taxes when historic easements have been granted.

SPECIAL APPRAISAL TECHNIQUES

It is difficult to appraise historic houses. Neither the cost approach nor the income approach is applicable. Because market data is scarce in many cases, some appraisers try to apply the cost approach on the theory that historic properties should be appraised as special purpose properties. This is not good appraisal practice. The income approach is difficult to apply since there is rarely a relationship between the rental value of an historic house and its value. This leaves the market data approach, requiring that a much wider area be screened for comparable sales than is normal for non-historic houses.

Two types of comparable sales may be used: non-historic houses in the neighborhood and historic houses wherever they can be found. Location is very important in the value of historic houses. For example, there may be two reasonably similar historic houses in a community. One is in a neighborhood that is part of a redevelopment program. A neighborhood association is being formed, houses are being renovated, exterior appearances are being controlled and the sidewalks and streets are being rebuilt. The other house is in a neighborhood that is reaching the end of its economic life. The exteriors of nearby houses are in need of carpentry repairs and paint, several houses have had serious fires and are in disrepair, the area is primarily tenant-occupied, and many nearby homes are for sale although few are sold. The first house would seem to be more valuable than the latter. A house of major historical importance, however, may be less affected by its neighborhood than a non-historic house in the same neighborhood. But even houses of major historical importance cannot completely escape the effects of their neighborhood.

Estimating the value of historic easements depends on seeking and analyzing relatively scarce market data. It may be possible to find properties granted historic easements where offers were made on the property prior to date the easement was given or where the property was sold and then resold after the easement was granted.

LOG CABINS

The log cabin market has carved itself a unique niche. These homes appear all over the country, usually integrated into an area with few or no other log cabins. Some are authentic reproductions but many are contemporary in design. Most have modern heating and mechanical systems.

SPECIAL APPRAISAL TECHNIQUES

Since there are usually few, if any, sales of log cabins in the same neighborhood as the one being appraised, the appraiser must decide if the Sales Comparison Approach is applicable. It may be justified to seek comparable sales in other similar neighborhoods quite distant from the subject.

Since most log cabins are purchased from a manufacturer, it often is possible to obtain good cost information.

MANSIONS

Mansions or estates used to be vehicles for gracious living for those who could afford the high cost. With many extra rooms for recreation, entertaining, guests and servant quarters, they are usually individually designed to reflect the special tastes of the owner, whose goal is often to enhance family prestige. Some mansions may have historical value.

Now the term mansion is used to describe any large house. In some communities houses as small as 4,000 square feet are called mansions.

SPECIAL APPRAISAL TECHNIQUES

Old-fashioned mansions are still few in number and are sold relatively infrequently.

The highest and best use analysis is an important part of these mansion appraisals. The appraiser must consider whether the land is now best utilized or if there is excess land that can be otherwise developed. Is the main building now suitable as a single family dwelling, or can it be converted into multi-family, institutional or other use?

If the highest and best use of the property continues to be as a single family residence, only the market data approach is meaningful. The cost and income approaches will lead to erroneous conclusions in most cases. If the highest and best use is other than a single family residence, the appraiser should apply generally used appraisal techniques.

When selecting comparable mansion sales, it is often necessary to look into other neighboring communities. The location adjustment is important, but difficult to make. When the gross living area unit value is developed, some type of meaningful range of value may be produced. Often the final value estimate is expressed in terms of a range of values which emphasizes the difficulty of estimating the value of this specialized type of housing.

MANUFACTURED HOUSES

The term manufactured house means that substantial portions of the house were assembled in a factory and then delivered to the site, usually by truck.

Some units are assembled almost totally off the site. There is little difference between a small modular house and a large mobile home. Larger modular houses consist of several segments, which are shipped to the site by rail and/or truck and joined on the site. Prefabricated houses are shells that are factory-built and then shipped to the site for assembly. They usually have less mechanical equipment as part of the package than modular homes.

Modular houses and prefabs are used for a variety of reasons. The construction of single family houses has changed less than almost any other major item manufactured in this country. Theoretically, the efficiency of the assembly line and mass production methods should be applicable to housing, and the manufacturers of modular and prefabricated homes are trying to do this.

Speed of construction is another reason for this system of producing housing units. The on-site assembly of a factory-produced modular or prefabricated home is often as little as a few days.

Another advantage is that the owners of individual lots can see complete model houses. This is not possible if a house is to be constructed from a set of house plans unless the builder has a similar house available for inspection. Also lot owners may also feel more confident they will get a house that is truly similar to the model they have seen when they buy from a large established company rather than buying from a confusing set of plans and specifications.

SPECIAL APPRAISAL TECHNIQUES

Manufactured houses can be appraised in the same manner as conventionally built homes. In most markets, there is little, if any, value difference between these houses and conventionally built houses of the same size, design and quality. The speed of construction, cost differential and other advantages (if they exist) are enjoyed by the original owner, but they usually do not affect the resale value.

MOBILE HOMES

Although not considered real estate in many states, mobile homes account for nearly 10% of all the existing single family residences in the United States. The pre-World War II trailer has evolved into today's mobile home. The most popular size is 12 feet by 60 feet, known as a "12 wide." There are also "14-wides" (which are only permitted in a few states) and "double-wides," which may run from 24 feet by 47 feet to 28 feet by 60 feet. There are also smaller units but they are rarely used for year-round housing. Mobile home owners are insulted when their homes are called "trailers". Once settled on a pad or foundation, a mobile home is rarely moved and experienced mobile home owners claim a unit should never be moved off the original location.

Mobile homes are popular because they offer substantial living space at a cost much below comparable conventional housing. There is a wide choice of mobile homes available in most parts of the country for under $75,000. This is well below the cost of other types of comparable housing. Many mobile home owners are senior citizens, young couples, students and military personnel. Studies show that a typical unit lasts about 15 years, as year-round housing. At that time, the shell still is useful and has some value. Studies also have shown that with average maintenance the typical mobile home depreciates approximately 10% the first year (based on wholesale value) and between 5% and 6% per year thereafter.

SPECIAL APPRAISAL TECHNIQUES

The best way to appraise a mobile home is to use conventional appraisal techniques with the application of all three approaches.

Many mobile home appraisals are made using a valuation book. These books are prepared by national publishers who collect sales data from mobile home dealers all over the country; they are similar to the books car and truck dealers use to appraise used vehicles. They are a useful tool but are not a satisfactory substitute for a well prepared appraisal. The problem with their use is that their figures are derived by averaging sales in many markets. The assumption is that mobile homes can be moved. Surveys show that most mobile homes are not moved when they are sold in place, especially when they are only a few years old. Therefore, like a house, their value is affected by their individual environment, and like a house, they can suffer from economic obsolescence. An appraisal based solely on a valuation book would not reflect the environmental influence.

PLANNED UNIT DEVELOPMENTS

Planned unit developments (PUDs) are a zoning alternative, not a type of housing. Houses built in PUDs can be in fee simple or condominium ownership in the form of single family residences, townhouses or multifamily buildings. PUD developments may also include commercial and industrial uses. In essence the PUD concept permits the grouping of housing units on lots smaller than usually allowed for residential construction. As a trade-off for being allowed to build on smaller lots, the developer sets aside some unused land to be dedicated to the community or to a homeowners' association. PUD developments can provide for more flexible and sensible designs for streets, landscaping and public facilities than are possible in conventional neighborhoods.

The individual single-family residences in PUD are owned in fee simple or as condominiums with joint ownership of open areas; in some areas local law requires that open areas be deeded to the city. Driveways, parking areas, and recreational facilities may also be jointly owned by the residents. An undivided interest in these common areas runs with the title to each property. Consequently, these areas must be inspected as part of the site when individual properties are appraised.

SPECIAL APPRAISAL TECHNIQUES

Freddie Mac and Fannie Mae simplified their requirements for PUD appraisals and now allow them to be made on the URAR form.

The Fannie Mae guidelines require that when the *Uniform Residential Appraisal Report* is used for a PUD the appraiser must provide the following project information:

- If the project has been completed:
  # phases _____,
  # units _____,
  # units sold _____

- If the project is incomplete:
  planned # of phases _____,
  # units _____,
  # units sold _____

- If the project is being developed in phases:
  total units in subject phase _____,
  # of completed units _____,
  # of sold units _____,
  # of rented units _____

- A description of the common elements or recreational facilities

- Owners' association fees per month for the subject unit: $_____

- The utilities that are included in the owners' association fees

- A comment about whether the association fees are reasonable in comparison to those for units in other projects of similar quality and design

- A comment about whether the project appears to be well-maintained

RESIDENCES ON LEASED LAND

With the exception of the state of Hawaii, residences on leased land are relatively scarce.

In Hawaii, residences have long been built on leased land. Leases may be for as long as 99 years or for 50 years or less. To protect the mortgage, some leases provide that the interest of the fee owner is subordinate to the interest of the mortgagee or lender. However, most leases give the mortgagee the right to take over the land rent if the mortgagor defaults. Usually the mortgagee also has the right to find a new mortgagor to continue the lease payments. When the lease expires, the improvements become the property of the landowner, who may extend the lease after modifying it to reflect current market conditions.

SPECIAL APPRAISAL TECHNIQUES

To value a residence on leased land, an appraiser uses the same techniques applied to residences subject to other forms of ownership. The value of the leasehold interest may be estimated by capitalizing the ground rent. An adjustment is usually required to reflect differences between the ground rents and lease terms of the subject property and the comparable properties. Depending on the appraisal problem it may be necessary to estimate the value of both the leased fee interest and the leasehold interest.

SECOND HOMES

Several million houses in the United States are second homes, occupied by their owners on a seasonal basis. Some of these homes are large, expensive mansions, more valuable than many primary homes. Such homes are found in communities like Newport, Rhode Island, and Palm Beach, Florida. However, the majority of second homes tend to be simpler, possibly located near a body of water or other recreation area. Prior to World War II, these houses tended to be developed individually or in small groups. After the war many large corporations went into the second home business, developing large tracts of land and many houses at the same time. Recreational facilities serving the site also were constructed.

SPECIAL APPRAISAL TECHNIQUES

The second home market can be very volatile. Economic and weather conditions, gasoline shortages, and competitive developments may have a greater effect on the value of a second home than on a primary residence. One apparent trend in many areas is that properties on or near water tend to increase in value faster than similar properties without the water amenity.

Resales are better evidence of market value than initial sales, which are often the result of heavy developer promotions. Where recreation homes are rented seasonally, a relationship may exist between rentals and value, which would make it possible to use the income approach. The cost approach may be useful when land is still available and new homes are still being built in the area.

SKI LODGES AND HOMES IN SKIING AREAS

Skiing has grown immensely in the past 25 years. The economy of whole areas and even states (i.e. Vermont, New Hampshire, Colorado and Utah) have been changed by this winter sport. Hundreds of thousands of second homes have been constructed on or near ski slopes.

SPECIAL APPRAISAL TECHNIQUES

It takes special skills to appraise ski homes. The appraiser must be intimately familiar both with the area in which the property is located and the special design and construction of ski homes. Location is critical in some areas. Even a few hundred feet can make a big difference. Prices in some Western ski resorts defy the imagination. There has been a big shake-out recently in the market for these high value lodges. Appraisers should proceed cautiously whenever appraising a ski home.

SOLAR HOUSES

Large tax write-offs, fuel shortages and environmental concerns all helped the proliferation of solar homes in the 1970's. When fuel became cheap and plentiful again and the tax write-offs were eliminated, most solar house construction also stopped.

Solar homes are still considered experimental by many people. The additional costs of design and materials may be offset by future savings, but no conclusive evidence of this possibility now exists. Even if and when successful solar application to housing is made, the results may not apply to many areas of the country.

SPECIAL APPRAISAL TECHNIQUES

The appraiser must first determine if value to be estimated is value-in-use to a special owner or actual market value. In some markets, part or all of the excess costs of a solar house may add value. Some buyers are willing to pay a premium for the privilege of living in a solar house. They want to be part of this housing experiment and feel satisfaction and status is worth the extra cost. They feel that the solar house has a special amenity value.

Resales are scarce. The builder of a solar house may create a house with some functional obsolescence that the market will recognize on resale. The appraiser must be cautious in making the value estimate.

TIMESHARING

The essence of timesharing allows one property to be purchased by several owners, each of whom has the right to use the property for a predetermined period of time. For example, 10 owners may buy a home. Each owner shares the cost of the property equally, and each has the right to use the property five weeks per year. Other devices may be used, but the goal of all of these methods is to allocate the time equally among shareholders or proportionately to what each owner pays.

SPECIAL APPRAISAL TECHNIQUES

The first step of the appraisal process--identifying the rights being appraised--has special significance in this type of appraisal. These rights are divided into the type of ownership and the rights to use the property.

The use rights (which part of the property will be allocated for use by the shareholder) also must be established; these substantially affect value.

The best way to estimate the value of timeshare units is to look for resales in the subject complex or similar complexes. They are better evidence than new sales because the latter are often the result of heavy developer promotions which would not apply to resale properties. The income approach may also be applicable, if some of the units are rented during part of the year. Research into the market may reveal a relationship between the rental value and the resale value of this type of property.

Care must be taken to divide the appraised value between the value of the real estate and the value of the large amount of personal property that is usually included in the price of a timeshare interval. (In some cases, fractional interest in all furnishings including bed linen and kitchen supplies are part of the timeshare sale).

WATERFRONT HOUSES

Waterfront property has probably increased in value at a greater rate than almost any other type of property. Unlike other recreational properties, especially ski homes, waterfront properties have held their value.

There has also been a national trend for commercial property in cities on the water to increase in value. Many city renewal programs are focused on the waterfront of the city. Often these redevelopment programs include residential units.

SPECIAL APPRAISAL TECHNIQUES

A high percentage of the total value is often in the site. Therefore the value of the site is very important. Location within a waterfront neighborhood is very significant. In some neighborhoods a high premium is paid for lots with direct frontage on the water. This is less important in other neighborhoods. Neighborhood location adjustments are often difficult to make.

UNDERGROUND AND BERMED HOMES

People select to build houses into the ground or into a hillside for a variety of reasons ranging from energy savings to protection from nuclear fallout. In the United States, most underground housing is found in the Central Plains states where storm protection and reduced energy costs are important concerns.

Houses built underground benefit from the fact that temperatures below grade are moderate year round. Because the heating and cooling equipment in these houses operates with less power, energy costs are significantly reduced. Earth-covered dwellings of poured concrete and concrete block are usually located on grade or "bermed" (set into a site that is partly or completely excavated).

SPECIAL APPRAISAL TECHNIQUES

Application of the sales comparison approach is difficult because sales of similar houses are scarce. Often the appraiser has no choice but to compare these special houses with houses built with more conventional construction techniques.

HOTELS, MOTELS & INNS

Facilities to house people away from their home range from large metropolitan hotels and convention centers to small inns in outlying areas of the country. In addition to the actual guest rooms, support spaces range from small public areas in an inn to the vast exhibition and meeting areas of large hotels and convention centers. These may also include banquet, entertainment and recreational facilities.

SPECIAL APPRAISAL TECHNIQUES

It takes special knowledge and experience to appraise lodging facilities, whether they be large or small, simple or complex. A highest and best use analysis is especially important. The facility being appraised should be compared to what is the standard up-to-date design for this type of facility.

Many older lodging facilities have unique architectural style and luxury features that are difficult to duplicate in modern facilities. The cost of keeping the facilities up to modern standards has to be weighed against the attraction of the features being preserved. Current life safety laws require that all lodging facilities meet increasingly strict fire, soundproofing and security standards.

Location plays a very important part in the success of all lodging facilities. Changing climate, availability of recreation and amusement attractions, municipal facilities, ease of access and parking are just a few of the factors that have an influence on the success of a facility.

Another important consideration is how much functional obsolescence exists in the facility which may be in the forms of inadequacies, finishes, inefficient equipment just to name a few possibilities.

External obsolescence ranges from over building to a wide variety of factors in the surrounding area.

All three approaches can be used to estimate the value of these properties. The cost of new facilities is an important consideration. However, many new facilities are worth less than their cost because of functional and external obsolescence which is present from the day they open their doors for business.

The sales comparison approach is useful when there are sales of comparable facilities. Making adjustments is often very difficult because of significant differences in physical characteristics, location and other special considerations.

The income approach is often relied upon heavily by the market when these facilities are bought and sold. It is necessary to separate those items of income and expense that should be attributed to the personal property and business portion of the operation rather than to the real estate which is being appraised.

It is important to make it clear in the description section of the appraisal of what is being appraised. Often the client wants the appraisal to include many other items besides the real estate in the appraised value. Few sales of lodging facilities include only the real estate. Therefore, it is important to verify each comparable sale to determine what was included in its reported sale price.

COMMERCIAL BUILDINGS

Included in this category are building uses for retail and wholesale outlets, offices, lending institutions, restaurants and other service businesses. Frequently, two or more commercial uses are combined on a single property.

Current standards of design and structural features are constantly changing. Commercial property developers are constantly looking for ways to make their devel opment more attractive to the public than their older competition. New projects often have to overcome the disadvantage of the superior location of the older competitive buildings. New materials and construction methods make it possible to design and construct buildings that are more efficient than those using old techniques.

SPECIAL APPRAISAL TECHNIQUES

"Some of the specific elements an appraiser describes and considers when doing a commercial appraisal are the column spacing, bay depth, live-load floor capacity, ceiling height, module width, elevator facilities. The work letter (an agreement that is usually part of a lease that specifies the level of interior finish and equipment that the landlord provided the tenant), HVAC adequacy, energy efficiency, public amenities and parking ratios."[3]

The potential existence of hazardous substances and detrimental environmental conditions on or nearby the appraised property should be considered by the appraiser.

All three approaches can be used to estimate the value of commercial properties. The cost of new facilities is an important consideration.   However, many new facilities are worth less than their cost because of their location and of the availability of competitive facilities in the area. In the past, there has been some over-building of commercial properties, especially office buildings.

The sales comparison approach is useful when there are sales of comparable facilities.   Making adjustments is often very difficult because of significant differences in physical characteristics, location and other special considerations.

The income approach is often relied upon heavily by the market when buying and selling retail, commercial and office buildings. It is necessary to separate those items of income and expense that should be attributed to the business fixtures and other items of personal property that belong to the tenant.

It is important to clarify what is being appraised in the Description Section of the appraisal. The appraiser should verify each comparable sale to determine what was included in its reported sale price.

Parking is becoming more and more important to the success of commercial projects. Properties that were thought to have satisfactory parking in the past now may suffer from functional obsolescence because of the better parking being offered by newer competitive properties.

To successfully appraise a commercial property an appraiser must have special knowledge and experience covering the specific type of property being appraised.

INDUSTRIAL PROPERTIES

These properties range from small manufacturing and assembly facilities to giant industrial complexes.

---

[3]**The Appraisal of Real Estate,** American Institute of Real Estate Appraisers, 9th Edition, Chicago, Ill 1987

"Like all properties, an industrial manufacturing property must have a site, buildings, and equipment that function as an operating unit. Inutility is measured against the standard of optimal efficiency for similar properties in the market.

Some industrial properties are designed and equipped to meet the needs of a specific occupant and have limited appeal to others. Buildings used for industries that involve bulky or volatile materials and products have specialized equipment and building designs, so they have few potential users. Buildings used for research and development or for light fabricating and processing are less limited in their appeal.

All industrial buildings are measured in terms of gross building area (GBA). For comparison and measurement in terms of market standards, the GBA can be divided into finished and unfinished categories. The most flexible design for industrial buildings, which will have the greatest appeal on the open market, is embodied in a one-story, square or nearly square structure that complies with all local building codes.

Industrial buildings can be constructed of many types of material, but concrete and steel are used most often. Tilt-up construction, which incorporates concrete walls that are cast horizontally and put in place vertically, is common. The walls are often designed to be load-bearing. Flat roofs supported by steel bar joists are also common. Prefabricated steel buildings are cheaper to build, and their appearance is now considered more acceptable than it was in the past. Plastic skylights can be installed for natural light in lieu of expensive monitor and sawtooth roofs.

Industrial properties must have land-to-building ratios that allow plenty of space for parking, truck maneuvering, yard storage, and expansion. Other locational considerations include reasonable real estate taxes, an available supply of labor, adequate utility service, beneficial zoning, and proximity to supply sources and customers.

Industrial parks are groups of industrial buildings that have similar uses. With landscaping, ample setbacks, building and lot size minimums, and professional architecture, engineering, and management, industrial parks provide an environment that is acceptable to occupants and government land-planning groups.

The combination of old and new industrial space has substantial functional obsolescence when the new construction contributes less than its cost to the value of the whole. The operating layout of industrial space should allow processes to be carried out with maximum efficiency. Typically, receiving functions are performed on one side of the building, shipping functions on the other, and processing or storage functions in the middle. Some industrial buildings include special features such as sprinkler systems, scales, loading dock levelers, refrigeration areas, conveyor systems, process piping (for compressed air, water, and gas), power wiring, and employee lockers and lunch room."[4]

SPECIAL APPRAISAL TECHNIQUES

All three approaches can be used to estimate the value of industrial properties. The cost of new facilities is an important consideration. However, the cost of new facilities is often higher than the value of older competitive facilities which make them uncompetitive with the older but still adequate manufacturing plant.

---

[4]Ibid

The sales comparison approach is useful when there are sales of comparable facilities. Making adjustments is often very difficult because of significant differences in physical characteristics and difficult to determine manufacturing efficiencies.

The income approach is sometimes relied upon by the market when these facilities are bought and sold. However, this information is hard to obtain as many industrial facilities especially the larger ones are owner occupied or owned by related corporations where the reported income and expense figures are not the result of an arms length transaction. It is also necessary to separate those items of income and expense that should be attributed to the industrial equipment and other personal property from real estate which is being appraised.

It is important to make it clear in the description section of the appraisal what is being appraised. Often the client wants the appraisal to include some of the equipment and other items besides the real estate in the appraised value. Few sales of industrial properties include only the real estate. Therefore, it is important to verify each comparable sale to determine what was included in its reported sale price.

The potential existence of hazardous substances and detrimental environmental conditions on or nearby the appraised industrial property should be considered by the appraiser. Often the appraiser seeks expert environmental help when appraising an industrial property.

STORAGE BUILDINGS

"Storage structures range from simple cubicles, known as *mini warehouses*, to huge regional warehouses with one million square feet of area. Functional utility and location have a major impact on the market value of storage buildings; obsolescence usually occurs before the structures deteriorate physically. The functions of warehouses are:

- To store materials in a protected environment.
- To organize materials so that they can be easily inventoried and removed.
- To provide facilities for efficient delivery.
- To provide facilities for efficient access and shipping.

For optimal functional utility, warehouses should have adequate access, open areas, ceiling height, floor load capacity (often 300 pounds or more for heavy-duty industrial storage buildings), humidity and temperature controls, shipping and receiving facilities, fire protection, and protection from the elements.

The primary consideration in warehouse locations is good access. Trucking is the most common means of transporting goods, but certain warehouse operations also need access to rail and water transportation. Operations that depend on trucks to transport goods should be near an arterial highway. The highway's access street or frontage road and the truck maneuvering area at the warehouse loading dock must allow for efficient use of loading facilities at all times. If a warehouse site slopes downward from a frontage road, the loading dock can be constructed at truck-bed level. For rail access, one portion of the site must be long and level.

Forklifts, conveyor belts, and automatically guided-vehicle conveyor systems are used to move materials inside warehouses. Truck docks must be wide enough to accommodate truck widths and the interior servomechanism used to move goods and materials. If electric trucks are used, a battery-charging area should be included. Most storage operations are palletized — i.e., pallets, or portable platforms, are used for moving and storing materials. Therefore, ceiling heights in warehouses should accommodate an ideal number of pallets. Because wide spans provide more flexibility, a square structure generally is the most cost effective.

Office space in warehouses may constitute as little as 1% of the total area, but generally approximately 5% of the total gross building area is used for offices. In distribution facilities, office space may comprise 35% to 50% of the total gross building area. Office space in warehouses should be adequately heated, cooled, and lighted, but its finish is generally utilitarian.

Sprinkler systems are needed in warehouses where flammable goods are stored. The nature of the stored material determines whether the system should be wet or dry, using water or chemicals.

Mini warehouses are usually combined in one- or two-story rectangular structures located near those who will use them. They should be visible, accessible, and surrounded by enough land for parking and maneuvering. The sizes of individual units within mini warehouses vary; they usually include small storage units, which have passage doors, and larger units, which have roll-up truck doors."[5]

SPECIAL APPRAISAL TECHNIQUES

All three approaches can be used to estimate the value of storage buildings. The cost of new facilities is an important consideration. However, the cost of new facilities is often higher than the value of older competitive facilities which make them uncompetitive with the older but still adequate storage facilities.

The sales comparison approach is useful when there are sales of comparable facilities. Making adjustments is often not as difficult as other types of property because location and current design standards are less important. Size is the most important consideration. Access is important but the location of storage facilities is much more flexible that many other types of property. Other physical characteristics should be considered including the number of stories, ceiling heights, weight capacity, etc.

The income approach is sometimes relied upon by the market when these facilities are bought and sold. However, this information is often hard to obtain as many storage facilities are owner occupied or owned by related corporations where the reported income and expense figures are not the result of an arms length transaction.

The potential existence of hazardous substances and detrimental environmental conditions on or nearby the appraised storage facility should be considered by the appraiser. It is important to know what was stored on the property in the past. Often the appraiser seeks expert environmental help when appraising a storage facility.

---

[5]Ibid

AGRICULTURAL PROPERTIES

Appraising agricultural properties takes special knowledge and experience that most appraisers do not possess. However, there is a significant group of appraisers who specialize in agricultural properties.

A special characteristic of agricultural property is the split of value between the land and the improvements. In many agricultural properties the buildings contribute only a small percentage of the total value.

Farms range from the small family farms which grow a variety of food products both for consumption by the family and resale and where often much of the labor is still done by hand to large specialized farming and orchard operations. These large agricultural operations usually require huge amounts of expensive equipment and specialized management knowledge to run.

SPECIAL APPRAISAL TECHNIQUES

A highest and best use study is an important part of a farm property appraisal. Often this study concludes that the highest and best use is no longer farming and that the value to be estimated must be for the alternate highest and best use which may be for residential, commercial, industrial or other type of development.

Other factors that have a significant effect on the value of agricultural property are the availability of water and labor.

The potential existence of hazardous substances and detrimental environmental conditions on or nearby the appraised farm property should be considered by the appraiser. Often the appraiser seeks expert environmental help when appraising an agricultural property.

INSTITUTIONAL & GOVERNMENT BUILDINGS

Institutional and government buildings are types of special purpose buildings characterized by their design and construction for a single purpose. The buildings of our great hospitals and educational facilities are typical institutional buildings. Many government buildings including state and federal legislative houses, courts and post offices are often copies of the Classic Greek style introduced into this country for government buildings by Thomas Jefferson.

These buildings are rarely bought and sold and their income streams are usually impossible to convert into a meaningful Net Operating Income that can be capitalized into a value.

SPECIAL APPRAISAL TECHNIQUES

The cost approach is usually the only approach that is applicable to institutional and government buildings. The value of the site should be estimated assuming that it is vacant and ready to be built upon. The appraiser must determine if its highest and best use is the present institutional or government use or if it is another alternate use.

Cost services have good usable information about the reproduction costs of many types of institutional and government buildings. More direct information may be available from architects, construction companies and from government agencies in charge of their construction.

Physical deterioration of between 1 to 2 percent annually is typical. Functional obsolescence must be deducted carefully. It is not appropriate to compare these buildings to non-government and institutional buildings when estimating functional obsolescence. The same is true for external obsolescence estimates.

The potential existence of hazardous substances and detrimental environmental conditions on or nearby these properties must be considered just as they would be for any other type of property. More appraisers are also requiring an inspection by a trained professional environmental expert to be made as part of these appraisals.

SPECIAL PURPOSE BUILDINGS

In addition to special purpose institutional and government buildings, there are a large number of other single purpose buildings that fall into a special purpose classification. These include churches, synagogues, theaters, other types of auditoriums, sports facilities, transportation facilities, some retail facilities such as automobile dealerships, marinas and amusement parks.

SPECIAL APPRAISAL TECHNIQUES

The cost approach is often the only approach that is applicable to most special purpose buildings. The value of the site should be estimated assuming that it is vacant and ready to be built upon. The appraiser must determine if its highest and best use is the present use or if it is another alternate use.

Cost services have good usable information about many types of special purpose buildings. More direct information may be available from architects, construction companies and from organizations and people in charge of their construction.

Physical deterioration of between 1 to 2% annually is typical. Functional obsolescence must be deducted carefully. It is not appropriate to compare these buildings to non-special purpose buildings when estimating functional obsolescence. Substantial functional obsolescence may occur when the design is replaced by one that is more currently acceptable. The same is true for external obsolescence estimates.

The potential existence of hazardous substances and detrimental environmental conditions on or nearby these properties must be considered just as they would be for any other type of property. More and more appraisers are requiring an inspection by a trained professional environmental expert as part of these appraisals.

MIXED-USE BUILDINGS

Included in this classification are buildings that combine two or more uses. Their popularity increased significantly in the late 1950's and 1960's. This reflected the influence of post World War II developments of shopping centers and later shopping malls which often included other commercial and office uses in addition to retail uses. Large planned cities such as Reston and Columbia contained many different uses.

Mixed-use developments are characterized by the physical and functional integration of their components. They are megastructures built around centrally located shopping galleries or court areas of hotels. Walkways, plazas, escalators, and elevators provide an interconnecting pedestrian thoroughfare with easy access to parking facilities underground, at street level, or aboveground. Because mixed-use developments bring together diverse participants, they require extensive, extraordinarily coherent planning.

SPECIAL APPRAISAL TECHNIQUES

In mixed-use buildings, each type of use creates a number of criteria which must be analyzed separately. The structure should also be considered as a whole to determine its ability to combine uses. Combined uses should be compatible, but minor incompatibilities can be made more congruous with separate entrances, elevators, and equipment. Without separate entrances and elevators, the residential units in upper floors and the office units below would both suffer. Only in a rather large building can the extra expense of such features be justified. A hotel located in an office building should have its own entrance and elevators. In general, security and privacy should characterize a building's residential area; professionalism and prestige should pervade the office portion of the structure.

Mixed-use buildings are an architectural challenge. Traditionally, residential and commercial buildings look different and are easily distinguished from one another. These differences have been diminished, however, by the eclecticism of postmodern architecture.[6]

SUMMARY

Millions of residences are specifically designed and uniquely located to satisfy the special needs of their owners. Others are more conventionally located and designed, yet are special because of their form of ownership. Often these homes combine two or more of these special features.

Besides the traditional ownership form of fee simple, alternative ownership forms widely available include Condominium, Cooperative, De Minimis PUD, Planned Unit Development, Leased Land and Timesharing. Each of these properties presents unique appraisal problems and requires specialized knowledge about how the ownership form works and how it affects the value of the property.

Second homes are usually found in resort areas near skiing, golf and the water. These markets tend to be volatile and are affected by changing weather conditions, availability of gasoline, the health of the economy, and the tax laws. Often only a few hundred feet difference in location can have a significant effect on the value of the property, particularly relative to an amenity like waterfront or the ski slope.

Though housing in general has been slower to change than almost anything purchased by consumers, there are some changes taking place. Manufactured houses and mobile homes are becoming a significant segment of the housing market. Each requires special appraisal skills.

---

[6]Ibid

The demographic profile of the population continues to shift towards older age. This increases the need for housing suitable for senior citizens. Housing for the elderly ranges from condominium projects built like traditional condominiums but limited in availability to owners over a specified age, (often these projects exclude children, which is still permitted by new. Congregate housing not only provides a place to live but also meals, social activities and medical care.

There are many houses that are designed for the special tastes and needs of their owners. This broad category includes energy efficient solar houses, experimental homes and underground homes. Many of these unique residences were designed to save fuel. As fuel has again become cheap and plentiful, market resistance has developed against the extra cost of the fuel saving features.

Mansions and large homes provide space for gracious living for those who can afford them. As the house gets bigger the market gets smaller. What is a mansion in one area may be just another large house in another community.

There are houses that are old, historic, special styles, reproductions or older styles and built of special materials such as log cabins. Each of these present unique appraisal problems and may require special appraisal techniques.. Lodging not only includes homes but also hotels, motels and inns. These facilities range from small inns to large convention centers with their variety of ancillary spaces and services.

Commercial buildings are used for retail, wholesale, offices and many other commercial uses.

Industrial properties range from small manufacturing and assembly plants to giant industrial complexes. These properties are often directly affected by natural economic conditions.

Storage buildings range from small mini warehouses rented to homeowners and small businesses to giant distribution centers.

The appraisal of agricultural properties requires knowledge and experience not possessed by many appraisers. Most of the value is the land and its ability to support crops.

Government and institution buildings often contain design and construction characteristics that would be considered obsolete in other classifications of property yet these buildings suffer little or no functional obsolescence from their excesses. The cost approach is often the only approach to value that is applicable.

Other special purpose buildings include churches, synagogues, theaters, sports facilities and even some retail outlets such as automobile dealerships.

Many properties have more than one use. Mixed-uses in mixed neighborhoods are becoming increasingly common. Often the appraiser must appraise the individual parts and try to fit them together like a jig saw puzzle.

There are other types of properties in addition to those covered in this chapter that require special appraisal techniques. When the appraiser does not have the knowledge and experience required, they must either turn down the assignment or obtain help from a qualified person.

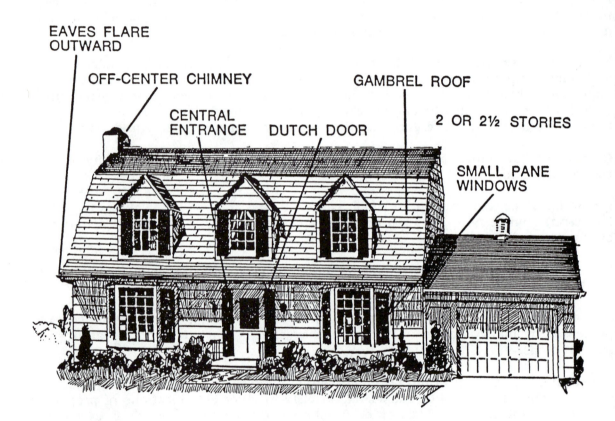

EAVES FLARE
OUTWARD

OFF-CENTER CHIMNEY

GAMBREL ROOF

CENTRAL
ENTRANCE

DUTCH DOOR

2 OR 2½ STORIES

SMALL PANE
WINDOWS

Colonial American

DUTCH COLONIAL (Dutch Co - 108)

18 Income Properties

People buy property for at least three reasons: use, income and amenities. Often it is for a combination of the reasons. The income approach covered in this section will focus on the income motivation and how the appraiser can analyze the income a property produces and use it as an indication of the value of the property.

The income a property produces flows to the owner in a variety of ways:

> Current Cash Flow
> Current Tax Savings
> Deferred Income from Rents
> Deferred Tax Savings from Rent
> Capital Gains from the Sale or Gift of the Property in the Future
> Tax Savings from the Gift or Trade of the Property in the Future

The definition of market value assumes the buyer and seller to be well informed. Therefore it is also assumed that the buyers and sellers consider all of the potential benefits of property ownership.

INCOME CAPITALIZATION

In the income capitalization approach, appraisers measure the present value of the future benefits of property ownership. Income streams and values of property upon resale (reversion) are capitalized (converted) into a present, lump-sum value. Basic to this approach are the formulas:

> Income ÷ Rate = Value
> Income x Factor = Value

The income capitalization approach, like the cost and sales comparison approaches, requires extensive market research. Specific areas that an appraiser investigates for this approach are the property's gross income expectancy, the expected reduction in gross income from lack of full occupancy and collection loss, the expected annual operating expenses, the pattern and duration of the property's income stream, and the anticipated value of the resale or other real property interest reversions. When accurate income and expense estimates are established, the income streams are converted into present value by the process of capitalization. The rates or factors used for capitalization are derived by the investigation of acceptable rates of return for similar properties.

Research and analysis of data for the income capitalization approach are conducted against a background of supply and demand relationships. This background provides information in trends and market anticipation that must be verified for data analysis by the income capitalization approach.

The investor in an apartment building, for example, anticipates an acceptable return on the investment in addition to return of the invested funds. The level of return necessary to attract investment capital fluctuates with changes in the money market and with the levels of return available from alternative investments. The appraiser must be alert to changing investor requirements as revealed by demand in the current market for investment properties, and to changes in the more volatile money markets that may indicate a forthcoming trend.

More books and articles have been written, and more courses and seminars taught on the income approach to value than on any other appraisal subject. It is not the purpose of this chapter to add anything new to this body of literature, but rather, to distill from what is already written, the most practical techniques of using the income approach on a day-to-day basis in an appraisal practice.

TWO SIMPLE STEPS

Many appraisers make the income approach more complex than it need be for the types of property they are appraising. New appraisers should start by using the simple process described below and then, as their assignments become more complex, apply the more advanced techniques when they feel they are necessary.

The two simple steps of the income approach produce an estimate of the anticipated Net Operating Income (NOI) of the property being appraised, which is then converted to a value estimate using the capitalization process.

INCOME ANALYSIS

NET OPERATING INCOME (NOI)

Net operating income is a word developed and used by real estate appraisers. It has special meaning to them and is not regularly used by owners, accountants, tax people, etc. Therefore, whenever you develop the NOI of a property for appraisal purposes, it is important that you define the word in your appraisal report. Net operating income (NOI) is the estimated stabilized anticipated annual net income produced by the property being appraised, after all operating expenses and reserves are deducted, but before mortgage debt service and book depreciation are deducted.

NOI is based on the assumption that the property will be rented at the market rent. It is based on what is projected for the first year after the date of the appraisal.

Estimating the NOI starts by estimating the potential gross income (PGI). It is the anticipated total market rent and other income for the first year after the date of the appraisal.

Anticipated loss due to non-occupancy, turnover and non-payment of rent by tenants (commonly called a "vacancy and collection allowance") is deducted from the PGI. This produces the effective gross income (EGI).

From the projected annual EGI all of the annual projected stabilized expenses are deducted (fixed expenses, operating expenses and reserves). The result is the projected NOI.

To develop the NOI, the appraiser creates a special reconstructed income and expense statement. Information used on this statement is obtained for a variety of sources. The information cannot simply be obtained from the owner, agent, accountant, attorney or tax person though all of these people are potential sources for some of the information that must be assembled in order to create a Reconstructed Operating Statement. This process requires the judgment and expertise of an experienced appraiser.

POTENTIAL GROSS INCOME (PGI)

The estimated total gross rental income is combined with other income available from the property to give the potential gross income (PGI).

The potential gross income estimate is the foundation upon which the income approach is built. A small error in this estimate will be mathematically compounded as it is processed in the income approach and will become a large error in the final value estimate.

It is advisable that the rents being paid by the current tenants also be considered. However, more often than not, the contract rent will not be the current market rent of the property. This is often true because the property was leased prior to the date of the appraisal. In addition, the owner or management of the property may not be typical for this property and their skills or lack of skill will produce a difference between market and contract rent. However, the appraiser should report in the appraisal a rental history including information on the current rents being received. In spite of everything, the actual rents being received for a property should be given serious consideration by the appraiser when estimating the potential gross income.

FIG. 18-1 EXAMPLE OF EXTRACTING A RENTAL ADJUSTMENT FROM THE MARKET

	Monthly Rent
Apartment with two bedrooms, two baths, 1000 sq. ft. with air conditioning	$850
A similar apartment without air conditioning	$825
Indicated adjustment for air conditioning	$ 25

It is not practical or possible to prove every adjustment from data in the market, but an attempt should be made to do so whenever possible. Once a matched pair is developed for an adjustment in a market, it can often be used for more than one appraisal. When an adjustment cannot be supported by market data, the appraiser has no choice but to estimate the adjustment. Large, unsupported market rent adjustments are one of the major contributing factors to the lack of credibility for the Income Approach in appraisal reports.

It is advisable that the rents being paid by the current tenants also be considered. However, more often than not, the contract rent will <u>not</u> be the current market rent of the property. This is often true because the property was leased prior to the date of the appraisal. In addition, the owner or management of the property may not be typical for this property and their skills or lack of skill will produce a difference between market and contract rent. However, the appraiser should report a rental history including information on the current rents being received in the appraisal. In spite of everything, the actual rents being received for a property should be given serious consideration by the appraiser when estimating the potential gross income.

OTHER INCOME[1]

Besides rents from the tenants, there is often other available income to the property owner. Some typical sources of other income are the following:

> Coin-operated washers and dryers
> Other vending machines
> Parking and garage fees
> Advertising signs

VACANCY AND COLLECTION ALLOWANCE

No matter how good a tenant is, there is a potential that some of the rent over a projected ownership period will not be collected. Since the estimate of market rent is based on the assumption that the property is vacant and ready to be rented to a typical tenant, it would not be correct to assume it was rented to a tenant who would never be a credit risk and would remain a tenant throughout the projected period. There is no standard figure for a vacancy and collection allowance. The best way to develop figures is to take properties where you can obtain a rental history over an extended period of time and see what the actual historical results were. Property management companies are good sources of this type of information.

EFFECTIVE GROSS INCOME (EGI)

The Effective Gross Income (EGI) is calculated by deducting from the Potential Gross Income (PGI) the estimate Vacancy and Collection Allowance and adding any projected Other Income.

EXPENSE ANALYSIS (OPERATING EXPENSES)

FIXED EXPENSES

The expenses incurred by the owner of a property are divided into three groups: fixed expenses, operating expenses and reserves. Again, these are special appraisal terms used to classify expenses on the reconstructed operating statement and normally will not be available from any one source. It will be necessary to adjust the information received from a variety of sources before using it.

---

[1]Some appraisers put "other income" after the "vacancy and collection allowance" because their "other income" estimate already includes a collection loss.

Fixed expenses are the property taxes and casualty insurance. They are classified as fixed expenses because they vary little (if at all) with the occupancy of the property.

Property taxes are a matter of public record. A trip to the tax collector's office will develop accurate information about the taxes. If the tax rate has not been set for the community, an estimate is made considering the current taxes and the trend in the community. In many areas, the property tax consists of more than one tax and may include school taxes, sewer taxes, special assessments, etc.

Casualty insurance is normally a combination of fire insurance, boiler insurance, general liability, worker's compensation and flood insurance. It does not include mortgage life insurance. The owner's actual cost is often misleading. Owners sometimes pay for more than one year at a time and they often do not carry the amount or all the kinds of insurance typical owners of the property would carry.

OPERATING EXPENSES (VARIABLE)

These are sometimes called variable expenses and include expenses incurred in a typical year to maintain the property, provide services for the tenants and maintain the income stream. Shown is a list of typical expenses that should be considered when making a reconstructed operating statement. It is recommended that a checklist be used so when you are gathering expense data you will not skip an item that does not appear on the operating statement provided by the owner or the management of the property. This is a list of operating expenses of a composite of many properties:

Management Fees

Utilities
    Electricity
    Gas
    Oil
    Coal
    Telephone
    Water
    Sewer Charges

Rubbish & Garbage Removal

Employee Payroll
    Janitor
    Manager
    Grounds keeper
    Bookkeeper
    Elevator Operator
    Lifeguard
    Engineer
    Security
    Telephone Operator
    Maintenance
    Cleaning
    Other
Payroll Taxes & Employee Benefits
Maintenance and Repairs

Service Contracts
    Sprinkler System
    Elevator
    Intercom & Telephone
    Lawn & Landscaping

Pool Expenses & Supplies

Painting and Decorating

Supplies - office, cleaning & other

Magazines and Newspapers

Snow Removal

Travel and Entertainment

Exterminating

Bank Charges

Legal Fees

Advertising
Accounting Fees
Automobile Expense

Not every property will have all the expenses on this list, and some properties will have other expenses which do not appear on this checklist.

The figures used are not the actual expenses as reported by the owner. It is a forecast of what the expenses would be for the following year, assuming it was a typical year.

For example, for a property that requires fuel oil, you obtain a 5 year history of oil consumption which is

Last year	3,200 gallons
Year before	3,300 gallons
2 years before	3,100 gallons
4 years before	3,100 gallons
5 years before	3,300 gallons

The appraiser forecasts that consumption for a typical year is 3,200 gallons and that the price of fuel next year will be $1.25. Therefore, the forecasted fuel oil expense will be $4,000 ($1.25 x 3,200).

RESERVES (REPLACEMENT ALLOWANCE)

Some expenses vary considerably from year to year and others occur once or twice over a period of many years. A decision must be made as to where in the reconstructed operating statement to include these expenses.   Some of these expenses, such as plumbing repairs, may be included in the maintenance and repair item in the operating expenses. Even though a particular plumbing repair may occur only infrequently, as a group they appear quite regularly; and it is possible to estimate what, as a group, they would be in a typical year.   Those infrequently occurring items that are not included in the operating expenses are included in the reserve section.   For example, if the typical life of a refrigerator was estimated to be 20 years and the cost of a new refrigerator was $1,200, a reserve of $60 for each refrigerator in the property might be established yearly ($1,200 ÷ 20 = $60).

The use of reserves must be carefully explained in the appraisal report because the word reserve implies that the money is being put aside. Most owners do not actually set aside these monies.

Some of the items that are traditionally included in the reserve section of the reconstructed operating statement are listed below:

Kitchen Appliances	Linens and Drapes
Stoves and Ovens	Laundry Equipment
Refrigerators	Dishes and Flatware
Dishwashers	
Garbage Disposals	Short-lived Building Components
Hoods and Vent Fans	Roofs
Microwave Ovens	Boilers
	Elevators
Furniture	Security Systems
Carpeting	Telephone Systems
Air Conditioning	
Grounds Equipment	Pool Equipment

Again, this is a composite list from many types of properties. It is unlikely that any one property will include all of these items. Also, some properties will require reserves for items that are not on this list.

The most common mistake that appraisers make is to include the same item in both the operating expense and the reserve sections of the reconstructed operating statement and to leave out items from both sections which should have been included.

Later in this chapter, the development of capitalization rates will be discussed. Here again the fact that any operating statement used to develop a capitalization rate must include reserves, will be pointed out. If they are left out, an incorrect rate will be developed.

OTHER EXPENSES (NOT INCLUDED)

Some expenses which are a part of an income and expense statement used for tax purposes are not included in the reconstructed operating statement. This is because these items are either reflected in the capitalization rate and to include them as expenses or reserve, would have the effect of including them twice, or they are not considered to be a cost directly related to operating the property. Included in this group are:

Mortgage Interest	Income Tax
Mortgage Amortization	Corporate Taxes
Mortgage Life Insurance	Corporate Directors' Fees
Depreciation	Franchise Taxes

SUMMARY - ESTIMATING NET OPERATING INCOME (NOI)

The first step of the income approach is to estimate the Net Operating Income (NOI) of the property. This is an appraisal technique that is accomplished by making a reconstructed operating statement for the property. This statement uses information gathered by the appraiser from the owner, management, accountant, tax person and a variety of other sources. It usually cannot be obtained from a single source in the format that is required.

The Potential Gross Income (PGI) is estimated using market data and the rental history of the property being appraised. A Vacancy and Collection Allowance is deduced from this figure. Any other income is added, and the result is a projection of what the Effective Gross Income (EGI) of the property would be if it were vacant on the date of the appraisal, and were then rented to a typical tenant in the market at current rental rates.

Next, the typical expenses are projected for the coming year after being divided for clarity in Fixed Expenses, Operating Expenses and Reserves. Other expenses such as interest, amortization, depreciation and expenses, not directly related to the running of the property, are not included.

All of the fixed expenses, operating expenses and reserves are subtracted from the effective gross income (EGI), to produce the net operating income (NOI).

FIG. 18-2 EXAMPLE OF A TYPICAL RECONSTRUCTED OPERATING STATEMENT (12 UNIT APARTMENT HOUSE)

INCOME ANALYSIS

Potential Gross Income

6 two bedroom unit w/o air conditioning @$375/mo.	=	$27,000
(375 x 12 = 4,500 x 6 = 27,000)		
2 two bedroom units w/air conditioning @$400/mo.	=	9,600
(400 x 12 = 4,800 x 2 = 9,600)		
2 three bedroom units w/o air conditioning @$500/mo..	=	12,000
(500 x 12 = 6,000 x 2 = 12,000)		
2 three bedroom units w/air conditioning @$550/mo.	=	13,200
(550 x 12 = 6,600 x 2 = 13,200)		

Total:	$61,800

Other Income

Laundry Machines (Concession)	+1,200
Vending Machines	+ 625

Vacancy and Collection Loss (6%)[2]	-3,818

EFFECTIVE GROSS INCOME	$59,807

OPERATING EXPENSES

Fixed Expenses

Insurance	
(Apartment Package including rents)	2,800
Flood Insurance	300
Property Tax	7,423
School District Tax	4,240

Total Fixed Expenses:	$14,763

Variable (Operating) Expenses

Management Fees	4,040
Utilities	
Electricity (Halls Only)	823
Gas	8,300
Telephone	125
Water	1,600
Sewer Charge	160
Rubbish Removal	385
Employee Payroll	
Part-time Janitor	4,000
Payroll Taxes	120

---

[2]Ibid. 1

Employee Benefits	345
Worker's Compensation Insurance	120
Lawn Care	345
Maintenance Supplies	250
Maintenance & Repairs	1,200
Painting & Decorating	600
Snow Removal	120
Exterminating	240
Legal Fees	150
Accounting	300
Bank Charges	80
Total Operating Expenses:	$23,303

Reserves

Kitchen Appliances	600
Lobby Furniture	100
Carpeting	1,000
Air Conditioning	300
Roof	500
Total Reserves:	$2,500

Total Expenses:	-$40,566

NET OPERATING INCOME PROJECTION: $19,241

CAPITALIZATION

The second step of the Income Approach is to convert the Net Operating Income (NOI) projection to an estimate of the value of the property on the date of the appraisal. This process is called Capitalization and is usually done by dividing the NOI by the capitalization rate.

$$\frac{NOI}{\text{Capitalization Rate}} = \text{Value of Property}$$

Many investors and some appraisers use a capitalization process by which they estimate the value of an investment property by multiplying either the gross income, net income (or some other income figure they rely upon) by a multiplier to produce the value of the property. It is not unusual for investors to say a particular property is worth so many times its current or projected gross rental income.

This multiplier is derived by taking properties one is familiar with and dividing the sale price by the rent or net income. This relationship can be expressed in a formula as follows:

$$\frac{\text{Sales Price}}{\text{Income}} = \text{Rent Multiplier}$$

DIRECT CAPITALIZATION

There are a variety of ways to develop a capitalization rate. The simplest (and best) is to get it directly from the market using data collected in the market. If the above formula converts NOI into value, then the following formula would convert value into a capitalization rate (assuming the NOI is also known).

$$\cdot \frac{NOI}{\text{Value of Property}} = \text{Capitalization Rate}$$

The type of rate developed in this way is called an overall rate. For example, assume there is information available about a property similar to the one being appraised. It shows that the comparable property sold for $185,000 and that it had an NOI of $27,000. Using the above formula, the capitalization rate is taken from this data as follows:

$$\frac{\$27,000 \text{ (N O I)}}{\$185,000 \text{ (Sale Price)}} = .146 \text{ (Capitalization Rate)}$$

Like any other data being used in the appraisal process, the more similar the data source is to the property being appraised the better it is. Also, it is not good practice to develop a rate from just one set of data. Often, the best source of data to develop capitalization rates comes from other appraisals where the property was sold around the date of the appraisal. This is because all the calculations needed to reconstruct the operating statement have already been made. When you receive data about a building that has been sold, you will need to reconstruct its operating statement just as you would if you were appraising the property; otherwise the rate you develop from the property being sold will not work.

Unfortunately, there has been so much emphasis on other more complex, less direct methods of constructing capitalization rates that many appraisers gravitate to these methods rather than taking the time to develop the market data derived from the method explained above.

When rates are developed for a series of properties in a market, it will become apparent that an identifiable pattern develops. Generally, the better the quality of the property, the lower the rate will be.

BAND OF INVESTMENT — MORTGAGE AND EQUITY COMPONENTS[3]

"Because most properties are purchased with debt and equity capital, the overall capitalization rate must satisfy the market return requirements of both investment positions. Lenders must anticipate receiving a competitive interest rate commensurate with the perceived risk of the investment or they will not make funds available. Lenders also require that the principal amount of the loan be repaid through periodic amortization payments. Similarly, equity investors must anticipate receiving a competitive equity cash return commensurate with the perceived risk or they will invest their funds elsewhere.

The capitalization rate for debt is called the *mortgage constant* (R_M). It is the ratio of the annual debt service to the principal amount of the mortgage loan. If the loan is paid off more frequently (e.g., with monthly payments), the mortgage constant is calculated by multiplying each period's payment by the frequency of payment and

---

[3] *The Appraisal of Real Estate*, 10th ed., The Appraisal Institute, Chicago, IL., 1992, pgs. 470-472.

then dividing this amount by the amount of the loan. For example, the annual constant for a monthly payment loan is obtained by multiplying the monthly payment by 12 and dividing the result by the amount of the loan. Of course, the same result can be obtained by multiplying the ratio of monthly payments to the mortgage amount (i.e., the monthly constant) by 12.

The mortgage constant is a function of the interest rate, the frequency of amortization, and the term of the loan. It is the sum of the interest rate and sinking fund factor; when the loan terms are known, the mortgage constant can be found in financial tables. An appraiser must take care to use a table that corresponds to the frequency of amortization (e.g., monthly, quarterly, or annually).

The equity investor also seeks a systematic cash return. The rate used to capitalize equity income is called the *equity capitalization rate* (R_E). It is the ratio of annual pre-tax cash flow to the amount of equity investment. This rate is not simply a rate of return on capital, rather it is a rate of return both on and of capital. The equity capitalization rate may be more or less than the eventual equity yield rate. For appraisal purposes, a property's equity capitalization rate is the anticipated return to the investor, usually for the first year of the holding period.

The overall capitalization rate must satisfy both the mortgage constant requirement of the lender and the pre-tax cash flow requirement of the equity investor. It is a composite rate, weighted in proportion to the total property investment represented by debt and equity. The loan-to-value ratio (M) represents the loan or debt portion of the property investment; the equity ratio is expressed as (1 - M). Typical mortgage terms and conditions may be obtained by surveying lenders active in the market area. Equity capitalization rates are derived from comparable sales by dividing the pre-tax cash flow of each sale by the equity investment. The equity capitalization rate used to capitalize the subject property's pre-tax cash flow ultimately depends on the appraiser's judgment.

When the mortgage constant and equity capitalization rates are known, an overall rate may be derived with the band-of-investment, or weighted-average, technique.

Mortgage component	$M \times R_m$ =	
Equity component	$(1 - M) \times R_E$ =	$\underline{\quad + \quad}$
	R_O =	

To illustrate how the overall capitalization rate is calculated with the band-of-investment technique, assume that the following characteristics describe the subject property.

Available Loan	75% ratio, 13.5% interest, 25 year amortization period, 0.1399 constant (R_m)
Equity capitalization rate	12.0% (derived from comparable sales)

The overall rate is calculated as follows:

$$
\begin{aligned}
R_O &= (0.75 \times 0.1399) + (1 - 0.75)(0.1200) \\
&= 0.1049 + 0.0300 \\
&= 0.1349)
\end{aligned}
$$

Although this technique is frequently used to derive overall capitalization rates, appraisers should be careful when using it for this purpose. The technique is particularly applicable in real estate markets where sufficient market data are available and it can be demonstrated that the equity capitalization rate is the primary investment criterion used by buyers and sellers. A capitalization rate used to estimate market value should be justified and supported by market data, but such data often are not available to derive information for mortgage-equity techniques and are more appropriately used to test market-derived capitalization rates."

BAND OF INVESTMENT — LAND AND BUILDING COMPONENTS[4]

"A band-of-investment formula can also be applied to the physical components of property — i.e., the land or site and the buildings. Just as weighted rates are developed for mortgage and equity in mortgage-equity analysis, weighted rates for the land and buildings can be developed if accurate rates for these components can be estimated independently and the proportion of total property value represented by each component can be identified.

The formula is

$$R_O = L \times R_L + B \times R_B$$

where L = land value as a percentage of total property value, R_L = land capitalization rate, B = building value as a percentage of total property value, and R_B = building capitalization rate.

Assume that the land represents 45% of the value of the property and the building represents the other 55%. The land capitalization rate derived from comparable sales data is 0.1025; the building capitalization rate is 0.1600. The indicated R_O is calculated as follows:

$$
\begin{aligned}
R_O \quad &= \quad (0.45 \times 0.1025) + (0.55) \times 0.1600 \\
&= \quad 0.0461 + 0.0880 \\
&= \quad 0.1341)"
\end{aligned}
$$

THE BUILT-UP METHOD

This method of constructing a capitalization rate separates the rate into its component parts. It would be almost impossible to accurately construct a rate using only this method. However, once some of the components of the rate have been estimated from other sources, they can be assembled and together they can be analyzed and tested for reasonableness by using the built-up method of rate construction.

The two basic components of a capitalization rate consist of the interest rate and capital recovery rate.

[4]Ibid 3

The interest rate is broken down into four parts:

1. Pure Interest - The interest rate of long term United State Government Bonds. It is the safe rate money can earn over a selected period of time. The investor knows, with a high degree of certainty, that at the end of the investment period the invested capital plus any unpaid interest will be 100% returned to the investor.

2. Additional Risk - All other investments, except United States Government Bonds, have a greater degree of risk than the bonds. There is a wide range of risk differences between various available competitive investments. The greater the risk, the higher the amount of interest necessary to entice the investors with capital to take the risk.

3. Burden of Investment Management - It is a simple process to invest in United States Government Bonds. Other investments take more effort. They all require some effort to decide which one to select. The more risky and complex the investment, the more investment management is required. (Investment management is not the same as the fee received for managing real estate, which is an operating expense that is deducted from income as part of the process of determining the net operating income (NOI)).

4. Lack of Liquidity - A United States Government Bond can be sold by making one telephone call, and the proceeds of the sale will be available to the investor within a few days. They are always saleable at anytime the investor wants to sell. Other investments require more time. It may take years to sell some types of real estate, especially when the investor elects to sell in a poor market.

The capital recovery rate, (1.00/number of years to recover the capital), is based on the time a typical investor estimates it will take to recover their capital from the property being appraised.

FIG. 18-3 EXAMPLE OF THE BUILT-UP METHOD OVERALL RATE CALCULATION

An apartment complex has an estimated value of $500,000. At the time of the appraisal, 25 year United States Government Bonds are yielding a safe rate of 9.12% interest.

In the appraiser's judgment, an investor would require 2% for the additional risk of investing in an apartment complex vs. a United States Government Bond.

In addition, a typical investor would require 1.5% to compensate for the effort required to find and place their money in an apartment complex investment vs. a United States Government Bond.

Because it will take time to sell the property should the investor wish to liquidate the investment, the investor seeks an additional 1.5% return to compensate for this lack of liquidity.

The time a typical investor estimates it will take to recover their capital from this type of property is 25 years. Therefore, 4% annually is allocated to capital recovery.

Taking all these factors together, a total interest rate and overall capitalization rate may be constructed as follows:

Safe Interest Rate	.0912
Additional Interest for Risk	.0200
Burden of Money Management	.0150

Lack of Liquidity	.0150
Total Interest Rate	.1412
Capital Recovery Rate	.0400
Overall Capitalization Rate	.1812

MORTGAGE EQUITY CAPITALIZATION (ELLWOOD METHOD)

Some appraisers feel that the Band of Investment method of capitalization rate construction is deficient as it does not take into consideration the length of time of the projected investment or appreciation or depreciation of the property during the investment period. In 1959, L.W. Ellwood, MAI, incorporated these factors along with those already included in the Band of Investment method into one formula that could be used to test or construct an overall capitalization rate. In his book, **Ellwood Tables for Real Estate Appraising and Financing,** he also constructed tables to help the appraiser apply his formula. Another book, Charles B. Akerson's **Study Guide: Course 1-B Capitalization Theory & Techniques,** simplifies and explains the formula and tables Ellwood developed.

[5]The formula Ellwood devised for the construction of an overall rate is:[6]

$$R = Y - MC + \frac{dep}{-app} (SFF)$$

R = Overall Capitalization Rate
Y = Equity Yield Rate
M = Ratio of Mortgage to Value
C = Mortgage Coefficient*
dep = Depreciation in property value for the projection period
app = Appreciation in property value for the projection period
SFF = Sinking-fund factor at Y rate for the ownership projection period

*The appraiser may elect to calculate the mortgage coefficient by using the formula:

$$C = Y + P (SFF) - f$$

P = Percentage of the mortgage that is amortized over the projection period
f = Mortgage constant

With the use of the tables pre-calculated by Ellwood, it is not necessary to calculate "C". It can be looked up on Ellwood's Table "C".

How to Construct A Capitalization Rate Using Ellwood's Mortgage Equity Tables

By carefully following these step-by-step instructions, you can successfully use the Ellwood mortgage equity method of capitalization rate construction for many income properties. It is not necessary that you understand the complex algebra or logic involved in making up the tables.

--Step 1: Collect the following information about the property to be appraised. To do this you must make some estimates based on your knowledge of the property and the market at the time of the appraisal.

---

[5]*Ibid*
[6]*Ibid*

Y (Equity Yield Rate) =

The Equity Yield Rate is the true return on an investment that a typical investor expects to receive over the period of time the investor will keep the property. It includes the loss or gain (most investors plan to sell the properties they buy for more than they purchase them for) made from the sale. Keep in mind that investors know that some of the income they receive for the property will be in the form of tax shelter, and they also consider that the proceeds of the sale may be taxed as a capital gain at the end of the investment period.

The appraiser should consider what yields are available from competitive investments. A good starting place is the yield on tax free bonds. The appraiser considers why an investor selects the property being appraised as an investment rather than invest in tax free bonds. The answer usually will be that they hope to get a higher rate of return.

M (Ratio of Mortgage to Value) =

The ratio of mortgage to value is the percent of the total value of the property that can be financed by a conventional first mortgage that would be available to a typical investor on the property being appraised on the date of the appraisal.

Appraisers should not consider special financing that may be available from the owner or some special source a particular buyer might have (such as a rich relative).

Typical Mortgage Term =

Also, based on the same assumption, determine what the mortgage interest rate will be. When the typical mortgage is not being written at a fixed rate of interest, you may forecast what you estimate a typical investor feels the interest rate will be during the projected holding period. If you conclude you cannot make this projection, you make the mortgage equity method of capitalization rate construction impossible to use for the property you are appraising.

Typical Holding Period =

Some people buy property and never plan to sell it. Rather, they pass it along to their heirs. However, if you study the market in your area, you will find that many investment properties are sold, traded or refinanced in identifiable typical periods of time. You should be familiar with the current tax laws. They will help you estimate how long a prudent investor will hold a property. Generally, the tax law penalizes an investor who sells a property too soon or keeps a property too long. Later, when you use Ellwood's "C" Tables, you will have a choice of 5, 10, 15 or 20 years as typical holding periods. You save yourself a lot of work if your holding period estimate is one of these four figures (enough said).

app or dep (the amount investors believe a property will increase or decrease in value during the holding period).

During my 30 year real estate career, I never met a buyer who thought the property they were buying was going to go down in value during their projected holding period. Many investors, in my experience, are willing to take little or no cash return or immediate tax shelter from a property because they estimate there will be a large capital gain in the future. Most investors in income property believe that the value of the property will continue to rise in the future (people who do not believe this do not buy the property). Many appraisers complain that the mortgage equity capitalization technique tends to produce a rate that is too high. This may be caused by their projecting the rate of appreciation too low.

--Step 2: Determine the appropriate mortgage coefficient. Start by selecting the appropriate "C" table from your Ellwood book.[7] In order to select the appropriate table, you need the following information:

> Projected Amortization Period
> Projected Mortgage Interest Rate
> Projected Holding Period

On the top of each "C" table page is a title "Mortgage Coefficients for Computing Capitalization Rates". Directly under this line, is a line that shows the amortization period and interest rates included in the table on this page. Go through the "C" table until you find the one that matches for the projected amortization period and projected mortgage interest rate you have determined is appropriate for the property being appraised. (See Fig. 18-6- "C Table")

FIG. 18-4 "C" TABLE MORTGAGE COEFFICIENTS FOR COMPUTING CAPITALIZATION RATES

Scope:—

Mortgage Amortization Terms; 10 years to 30 years by 5 year increments.

Mortgage Interest Rates:—3¼% to 12% by ¼% increments.

Income Projection Terms; 5 years to full amortization by 5 year increments.

Equity Yields; 4% to 30% by 1% increments.

To Find Desired Coefficient:—

1. Find Amortization Term in years.

2. Turn to page with desired mortgage interest rate and income projection term.

3. Find desired equity yield rate in *proper projection term bracket*. Move across on this line to column headed by desired mortgage interest rate.

$$Y - MC = r$$

Where:—

$$Y = \text{Equity Yield}$$
$$M = \text{Ratio of Mortgage to Value}$$
$$C = \text{Coefficient from this table}$$
$$r = \text{Basic Capitalization Rate}$$

Note:—Where coefficient is in italics or followed by a minus sign the formula is:

$$Y + MC = r$$

---

[7]L.W. Ellwood, *Ellwood Tables for Real Estate Appraising and Financing*, 4th ed., Ballinger Publishing Co., Cambridge, MA., 1977.

FIG. 18-5 C TABLE - 20 YEAR AMORTIZATION 7 3/4 TO 9%

TABLE C

Mortgage Coefficients for Computing Capitalization Rates.
20 YEARS AMORTIZATION: 7¾% TO 9%

TABLE C

Interest Rate		7¾%	8%	8¼%	8½%	8¾%	9%	$\frac{1}{s\,\overline{n}}$
Annual Requirement (f)		.098520	.100440	.102360	.104160	.106080	.108000	
Installment f/12		.008210	.008370	.008530	.008680	.008840	.009000	

Projection

Balance (b)		.872128	.874844	.877600	.881140	.883981	.886863	+ Dep.
Equity	Yield			Mortgage Coefficients				− App.
4 %	.04	.034911−	.037332−	.039761−	.042215−	.044659−	.047111−	.184627
5 %	.05	.025378−	.027739−	.030208−	.032649−	.035083−	.037525−	.180974
6 %	.06	.015836−	.018237−	.020646−	.023074−	.025498−	.027930−	.177396
7 %	.07	.006284−	.008676−	.011075−	.013491−	.015905−	.018326−	.173890
8 %	.08	.003276	.000893	.001496−	.003899−	.006303−	.008715−	.170456
9 %	.09	.012846	.010472	.008092	.005700	.003305	.000904	.167092
10 %	.10	.022425	.020060	.017688	.015308	.012923	.010531	.163797
11 %	.11	.032012	.029656	.027293	.024925	.022549	.020166	.160570
12 %	.12	.041608	.039260	.036906	.034549	.032182	.029808	.157409
13 %	.13	.051212	.048873	.046528	.044181	.041823	.039458	.154314
14 %	.14	.060824	.058493	.056157	.053821	.051471	.049115	.151283
15 %	.15	.070445	.068122	.065793	.063468	.061127	.058779	.148315
16 %	.16	.080073	.077758	.075438	.073123	.070790	.068451	.145409
17 %	.17	.089709	.087402	.085089	.082785	.080460	.078129	.142563
18 %	.18	.099353	.097053	.094748	.092453	.090136	.087813	.139777
19 %	.19	.109004	.106712	.104414	.102129	.099820	.097505	.137050
20 %	.20	.118663	.116378	.114088	.111812	.109510	.107203	.134379
21 %	.21	.128329	.126051	.123768	.121501	.119207	.116907	.131765
22 %	.22	.138001	.135730	.133454	.131197	.128910	.126617	.129205
23 %	.23	.147681	.145417	.143148	.140899	.138619	.136334	.126700
24 %	.24	.157367	.155110	.152847	.150608	.148335	.146056	.124247
25 %	.25	.167060	.164809	.162554	.160322	.158056	.155785	.121846
26 %	.26	.176760	.174515	.172266	.170043	.167783	.165519	.119496
27 %	.27	.186466	.184227	.181984	.179769	.177516	.175259	.117195
28 %	.28	.196178	.193945	.191709	.189502	.187255	.185004	.114943
29 %	.29	.205896	.203669	.201439	.199240	.196999	.194754	.112739
30 %	.30	.215620	.213399	.211175	.208983	.206749	.204510	.110581

5 Years
n = 5

Balance (b)		.683970	.688381	.692964	.699605	.704573	.709728	+ Dep.
Equity	Yield			Mortgage Coefficients				− App.
4 %	.04	.032197−	.034485−	.036786−	.039139−	.041473−	.043823−	.083290
5 %	.05	.023394−	.025664−	.027949−	.030277−	.032592−	.034922−	.079504
6 %	.06	.014543−	.016798−	.019065−	.021369−	.023666−	.025977−	.075867
7 %	.07	.005646−	.007885−	.010137−	.012418−	.014697−	.016990−	.072377
8 %	.08	.003295	.001070	.001165−	.003423−	.005686−	.007962−	.069020
9 %	.09	.012281	.010070	.007849	.005611	.003365	.001105	.065820
10 %	.10	.021309	.019112	.016905	.014688	.012456	.010213	.062745
11 %	.11	.030379	.028195	.026001	.023804	.021586	.019358	.059801
12 %	.12	.039488	.037317	.035136	.032957	.030754	.028540	.056984
13 %	.13	.048637	.046477	.044308	.042148	.039958	.037758	.054289
14 %	.14	.057823	.055674	.053517	.051374	.049197	.047010	.051713
15 %	.15	.067045	.064907	.062762	.060635	.058470	.056296	.049252
16 %	.16	.076302	.074175	.072040	.069928	.067775	.065614	.046901
17 %	.17	.085592	.083475	.081351	.079254	.077112	.074962	.044656
18 %	.18	.094915	.092808	.090693	.088611	.086479	.084340	.042514
19 %	.19	.104270	.102171	.100066	.097997	.095876	.093747	.040471
20 %	.20	.113654	.111564	.109467	.107412	.105300	.103182	.038522
21 %	.21	.123067	.120985	.118897	.116854	.114751	.112642	.036665
22 %	.22	.132507	.130433	.128353	.126322	.124228	.122129	.034894
23 %	.23	.141974	.139908	.137836	.135815	.133730	.131639	.033208
24 %	.24	.151467	.149407	.147342	.145333	.143256	.141173	.031602
25 %	.25	.160983	.158931	.156873	.154873	.152804	.150729	.030072
26 %	.26	.170523	.168477	.166426	.164436	.162374	.160306	.028616
27 %	.27	.180085	.178045	.176000	.174019	.171964	.169904	.027230
28 %	.28	.189668	.187634	.185595	.183623	.181575	.179521	.025911
29 %	.29	.199272	.197243	.195210	.193246	.191204	.189157	.024657
30 %	.30	.208895	.206871	.204844	.202888	.200851	.198810	.023463

10 Years
n = 10

Next, select the section of the "C" Table that coincides with the project holding period you have determined to be appropriate. There are four sections for each "C" Table (5, 10, 15, 20 years). Each section is identified in the left hand column of the table.

Select from this section of the "C" Table, the mortgage coefficient you will use, by first looking for the proper column with the interest rate you have selected for the first mortgage and the line that represents the equity yield you have estimated an investor will require on the cash invested. (The equity yields are in the second column from the left).

--Step 3: Select the appropriate sinking fund factor from the same section of the "C" Table as was used for Step 2. (The sinking fund factor may also be looked up on the Sinking Fund Table. Select the appropriate line by finding the yield rate in the left column and the appropriate SFF column by finding the projection in the column heading).

Again, the estimated investor's yield on cash invested is found in the second column from the left and the appropriate sinking fund factor is on this same page in the far right hand column. (The estimated investor's yield used here should be the same as that used in Step 2).

--Step 4: Calculate R (Overall Rate) using the formula

$$R = Y - MC + dep$$
$$- app \ (SFF)$$

FIG. 18-6 EXAMPLE OF HOW TO CALCULATE THE OVERALL RATE

The property being appraised is an apartment house. In this market, for this type of investment, investors require a 14% equity yield. Typical financing is 70% of appraised value for 20 years (monthly payments, 100% amortization) at 9% interest. It is projected to appreciate 50% (5% per year average) over the projected 10 year holding period.

$$Y = .14$$
$$M = .70$$
$$C = .047010 \ \{Taken \ from \ "C" \ Table - 20 \ years \ amortization \ 7 \ 3/4 \ to \ 9\% \ (14\% \ yield \ line - 9\% \ interest \ column)\}$$
$$app = .50$$
$$SFF = .051713 \ \{Taken \ from \ C" \ Table - 20 \ years \ amortization \ 7 \ 3/4 \ to \ 9\% \ (14\% \ yield \ line - column)\}$$

First calculate: MC =
$$= .70 \ x \ .047010$$
$$= .032907$$

Next calculate: + dep
$$- app \ (SFF) =$$
$$= -.50 \ x \ .051713$$
$$= -.025857$$

Finally calculate: R = Y -MC + dep
$$- app (SFF)$$

$$R = .14 - .032907 - .025857$$
$$R = .081238$$
$$R = .08 \text{ Rounded}$$

FIG. 18-7 ALTERNATE EXAMPLE

An apartment complex is being appraised. Investors in this market are seeking a 12% equity yield. Typical financing for this type of property is an 80%, 20 year term, 100% amortizing mortgage at 8% annual interest. A typical investor would plan to hold the property 10 years. Because the neighborhood is declining, a typical investor would project the property to decrease in value at the rate of 1% per year (total depreciation 10%).

$$
\begin{array}{ll}
Y & = .12 \\
M & = .80 \\
C & = .037317 \\
dep & = +.10 \\
SFF & = .056984 \\
\end{array}
$$

First calculate: MC =
$$= .80 \times .037317$$
$$= .029854$$

Next calculate: + dep
$$- app (SFF) =$$
$$= +.10 \times .056984$$
$$= +.0056984$$

Finally calculate: R   = Y -MC + dep
$$- app (SFF)$$
$$= .12 - .029854 + .0056984$$
$$= .095844$$
$$= .096 \text{ Rounded}$$

Alternate Method Using "Mortgage Coefficients and Sinking Fund Factors for Computing Capitalization Rates" Table

When the projection period is 10 years, the appreciation rate between 5% and 20%, the interest rate between 9% and 12% and the amortization period 20 years, you can look-up the "Mortgage Coefficient" directly on the "Mortgage Coefficients and Sinking Fund Factors for Imputing Capitalization Tables."

-- **Step 1** and -- **Step 2** are the same as previously described.

--**Step 3:**   From the same "Mortgage Coefficients and Sinking Fund Factors for Computing Capitalization Rates" Table look-up the appropriate sinking fund factor in the last column on the right   select the appropriate line by finding the yield rate in the left column.

FIG. 18-8 (ALTERNATE) MORTGAGE COEFFICIENTS & SINKING FUND FACTORS FOR COMPUTING CAPITALIZATION RATE TABLE

Mortgage Coefficients for Computing Capitalization Rates

Interest Rate

Equity Yield Projection	9%	9 1/4%	9 1/2%	9 3/4%	10%	10 1/4%	10 1/2%	10 3/4%	11%	11 1/4%	11 1/2%	11 3/4%	12%
5%	.034922-	.037267-	.039590-	.041964-	.044313-	.046720-	.049096-	.051486-	.053889-	.056307-	.058739-	.061185-	.063585-
6%	.025977-	.028303-	.030613-	.032667-	.035302-	.037686-	.040047-	.042421-	.044807-	.047207-	.049621-	.052050-	.054438-
7%	.016990-	.019297-	.021595-	.023929-	.026250-	.028613-	.030959-	.033318-	.035688-	.038072-	.040469-	.042879-	.045257-
8%	.007962-	.010251-	.012537-	.014852-	.017160-	.019502-	.021834-	.024178-	.026534-	.028901-	.031282-	.033675-	.036042-
9%	.001105-	.001166-	.003440-	.005737-	.008032-	.010355-	.012673-	.015003-	.017344-	.019696-	.022061-	.024437-	.026796-
10%	.010213	.007957	.005694	.003415	.001131	.001172-	.003477-	.005793-	.008120-	.010458-	.012807-	.015168-	.017517-
11%	.019358	.017118	.014866	.012603	.010331	.008045	.005752	.003449	.001136	.001187-	.003522-	.005868-	.008208-
12%	.028540	.026316	.024073	.021827	.019566	.017297	.015016	.012725	.010425	.008114	.005793	.003462	.001130
13%	.037758	.035548	.033315	.031084	.028833	.026581	.024311	.022033	.019744	.017447	.015139	.012821	.010498
14%	.047010	.044814	.042590	.040374	.038133	.035897	.033638	.031370	.029094	.026809	.024514	.022209	.019894
15%	.056296	.054113	.051897	.049696	.047464	.045243	.042994	.040738	.038473	.036199	.033916	.031624	.029316
16%	.065614	.063443	.061236	.059048	.056825	.054618	.052380	.050134	.047879	.045617	.043345	.041065	.038764
17%	.074962	.072803	.070604	.068429	.066215	.064022	.061793	.059557	.057313	.055061	.052801	.050532	.048238
18%	.084340	.082193	.080002	.077838	.075633	.073453	.017233	.069006	.066772	.064530	.062281	.060023	.057735
19%	.093747	.091611	.089427	.087275	.085078	.082910	.080699	.078481	.076256	.074024	.071785	.069537	.067256
20%	.103182	.101056	.098879	.096738	.094548	.092393	.090190	.087980	.085764	.083541	.081311	.079074	.076798

--Step 4: Calculate R (Overall Rate) using the formula

$$R = Y - MC + dep - app \ (SFF)$$

FIG. 18-9 EXAMPLE OF HOW TO CALCULATE THE OVERALL RATE

The property being appraised is an apartment house. In this market, for this type of investment, investors require a 14% equity yield. Typical financing is 70% of appraised value for 20 years (monthly payments, 100% amortization) at 9% interest. It is projected to appreciate 50% (5% per year average) over the projected 10 year holding period.

Y   =   .14
M   =   .70
C   =   .047010 {(Taken from "C" Table - 20 years amortization 7 3/4 to 9%, (14% yield line - 9% interest column)}
app   =   .50
SFF   =   .051713 {Taken from "Mortgage Coefficients and Sinking Fund Factors for Computing Capitalization Rate Table" (14% yield line)

First calculate: MC   =
= .70 x .047010
= .032907

Next calculate: + dep
- app (SFF) =
= -.50 x .051713
= -.025857

Finally calculate: R = Y -MC + dep
- app (SFF)

R = .14 - .032907 - .025857
R = .081238
R = .08 Rounded

FIG. 18-10 ALTERNATE EXAMPLE

An apartment complex is being appraised. Investors in this market are seeking a 12% equity yield. Typical financing for this type of property is an 80%, 20 year term, 100% amortizing mortgage at 9% annual interest. A typical investor would plan to hold the property 10 years. Because the neighborhood is declining, a typical investor would project the property to decrease in value at the rate of 1% per year (total depreciation 10%).

Y   = .12
M   = .80
C   = .037317
dep   = +.10
SFF   = .056984

First calculate: MC   =
                                 = .80 x .037317
                                 = .029854

Next calculate: + dep
           - app (SFF)   =
                                 = +.10 x .056984
                                 = +.0056984

Finally calculate: R   = Y -MC + dep
                                         - app (SFF)
                                 = .12 - .029854 + .0056984
                                 = .095844
                                 = .096 Rounded

ADVANCED CAPITALIZATION TECHNIQUES

Some appraisers have become serious students of "Ellwood" and other capitalization techniques. Some feel that even the complex "Ellwood" theories do not produce the best results in all instances.

Charles B. Akerson developed procedures that substituted arithmetic formulae for the algebraic equations used by Ellwood. He also incorporated the "J" factor into his formula which provides a tool for the appraiser to incorporate changes in the income stream and property value into the rate calculations.[8]

One of the features that has contributed to the popularity of the "Ellwood" capitalization technique, is the ability to create a graph that displays the results and shows what alternate rates would be when some of the assumptions are changed.

Readers who are interested in these and other advanced capitalization techniques can read about them in the *Appraising of Real Estate*, 10th ed., The Appraisal Institute, 875 North Michigan Avenue, Chicago, IL 60611, 1992. Better still, they should take an advanced capitalization course given by one of the appraisal organizations or colleges.

SUMMARY

The Income Approach is based on the theory that the value of income producing property is determined by the future income the property produces for its owner.

The first step in estimating the value of a property based on its future income stream is to estimate the amount of the income stream to be obtained by the owner in the future. The appraiser starts by estimating the potential gross income (PGI) attributable to the property, assuming it is fully rented at market rent, for the first year from the date of appraisal. Other income from the property is added From this, an estimated income loss from vacancies and uncollected rents is subtracted, and the result is the annual projected effective gross income (EGI).

---

[8]Charles B. Akerson, **Study Guide: Course 1-B Capitalization Theory & Techniques,** American Institute of Real Estate Appraisers, Chicago, IL 1977.

The appraiser subtracts the projected annual fixed expenses, operating expenses and reserves from the effective gross income. The result is the projected annual net operating income (NOI). This term (NOI) is unique to appraising as it does not include deductions for mortgage debt service and book depreciation because they are included as part of the capitalization rate.

The second step uses the projected net operating income to estimate the value of the property by dividing it by a capitalization rate which reflects the ratio between the NOI and the value of the property being appraised.

There are many ways to project an appropriate capitalization rate. The best, most simple and direct way is to abstract an overall rate from the market when market.

The formula for converting NOI into value is:

$$\frac{N \: O \: I}{\text{Capitalization Rate}} = \text{Value}$$

When suitable market data is not available, other techniques must be used. Another popular way to develop an overall capitalization rate is the band of investment method. It is derived by making a weighted average of the rates in the market available to a typical investor, for mortgages, on the property being appraised, with the return on equity invested that a typical investor would expect to receive.

The modified band of investment method is similar to the band of investment method except that is also takes into consideration the length of the mortgage and rate of amortization. Another method is the built-up method of constructing an overall capitalization rate. The rate is divided into its component parts: safe interest rate, risk, burden of money management and lack of liquidity. The appraiser estimates the amount of interest required by a typical investor for each component and adds them together to make an overall capitalization rate.

A more sophisticated direct capitalization method was developed by L.W. Ellwood known as the mortgage equity capitalization method (Ellwood Method). Ellwood devised a formula for the construction of an overall rate.

$$R = Y - MC + dep$$
$$- \: app \: (SFF)$$

His method provides a method for appraisers to use graphs for displaying how the rate changes when some of the assumptions are changed.

There are other methods available for appraisers to estimate the value of a property based on its income, including ones that use multipliers., Internal Rate of Return and Yield Analysis No one method will work for all properties, but all require knowledge and experience to be used properly.

There is now a *General Certification Supplement* available for appraisers who wish to study more about how to use the income stream of a property as an analysis tool. (see advertisement in back of this text) . Covered in the *General Certification Supplement* are Yield Capitalization, Internal Rate of Return and Valuation of Leaseholds and Partial Interests. Each chapter also includes instructions on how to solve problems using the HP12C financial calculator.

REAL OR SIMULATED
ADOBE BRICK

PROJECTING
ROOF BEAMS
(VIGA)

FLAT ROOF

MASSIVE LOOKING

Early Twentieth Century American

PUEBLO OR ADOBE (Pueblo or Adobe - 803)

Addenda

ADDENDA CONTENTS

INCOME PROPERTY
MODEL NARRATIVE APPRAISAL

On the following pages is a Model Narrative appraisal report of a 10 unit rental apartment building. The reported is based on a actual property appraised by Barbara Kaye in Lake Shores, Florida.

The report has been substantially modified for teaching purposes. The location of the subject property and all of the comparable sales and rentals have been fictionalized. The date has been set some time in the near future, 200_

Rarely, if ever, would an appraisal contain data of the same high quality as the fictional data in this report.

Although the appraisal does not give specific dates, the reader should assume all dates are in the same year and that all months indicated in the appraisal are therefore either within one year prior to the date of the appraisal unless otherwise specified.

Again, I wish to thank Barbara Kaye for allowing her work to be published in this text and Richard Chamberlin and my partner Leonard D'Agostino, RM, who collected additional data and photographs for this report. Thanks also to Maura Gianakos, who typed the report on our Wang Word Processor in order to make it look more realistic than it would appear if it were set in type like the rest of this book. Unfortunately during the process, the Wang required 12 service calls and has now been "retired."

This model appraisal is not intended to be an example of a demonstration appraisal applicable for credit towards a designation from an appraisal organization. Each organization has their own specific demonstration appraisal requirements. Demonstration appraisals are a type of examination in which an appraiser shows the examiners his or her knowledge of the appraisal process and the organization's special reporting requirements.

This model appraisal is intended to show the type of work an appraiser would actually do for a client.

PART ONE

INTRODUCTION

REAL ESTATE APPRAISAL

700 DUQUESNE DRIVE
WEST PALM BEACH

OWNER OF RECORD: Etak Trebmal

DATE OF APPRAISAL: December 15, 200_

THIS IS A: 10-Unit rental apartment
                                    building

APPRAISED FOR (CLIENT):   Appraisal student everywhere
                                    100 Main Street
                                    Typical Town, USA 00001

INTENDED USERS: Same as client

INTENDED USE: Educational purposes only

TYPE OF REPORT: Self contained appraisal report

APPRAISED BY: Barbara J. Kaye
                                    315 Whitney Avenue
                                    New Haven, CT 09611
                                    (203) 562-3159

Barbara J. Kaye
315 Whitney Avenue
New Haven, Connecticut 06511
(203) 562-3159

February 25, 200_

Appraisal Students Everywhere
100 Main Street
Typical Town, USA 00001

RE: 700 Duquesne Drive
      West Palm Beach, Florida

Gentlemen:

I herewith submit for your review this appraisal report of the property known as 700 DuQuesne Drive, West Palm Beach, Florida.

The purpose of the appraisal is to estimate the market value of the fee simple estate of the property, as of December 15, 200_, subject to the assumptions, limiting conditions, and certificate included herein.

I personally inspected the property on December 15, 200_, and have gathered and analyzed all the data necessary to arrive at the value conclusion.

The subject site has 100 feet of frontage along Haden Road, an average depth of 210 feet, and contains approximately .48 acre. The site is improved with a two-story, masonry, ten-unit apartment building plus miscellaneous site improvements.

Based upon my investigations and analysis of the real estate market in the area, and after considering all of the pertinent facts as set forth in the body of this report, the estimated market value of the fee, as of December 15, 200_, is:

SIX HUNDRED THOUSAND ($600,000) DOLLARS

Respectfully submitted,

Barbara J. Kaye

Barbara J. Kaye

CERTIFICATION

I, the undersigned, do hereby certify that I have personally inspected the property located at 700 Duquesne Drive, West Palm Beach, Florida

To the best of my knowledge and belief, the statements of fact contained in this report and upon which the opinions herein are based are true and correct, subject to the assumptions and limiting conditions explained in the report.

Employment in and compensation for making this appraisal are in no way contingent upon the value reported, and I certify that I have no interest, either present or contemplated, in the subject property. I have no personal interest or bias with respect to the subject matter of the appraisal report or the parties involved.

This appraisal report identifies all of the limiting conditions affecting the analyses, opinions, and conclusions contained in this report.

The analyses, opinions, and conclusions contained in this report have been developed in accordance with the standards of Professional Appraisal Practice and the Codes of Ethics of the Professional Organizations with which I am affiliated.

No one other than the undersigned prepared the analysis, opinions, or conclusions concerning real estate that are set forth in this appraisal report. I am not currently designated or certified by any appraisal organization.

In my opinion, the subject property has a value representative of market conditions on December 15, 200_ of $600,000.

Barbara J. Kaye
_____
Barbara J. Kaye

A 5

TABLE OF CONTENTS

QUALIFICATIONS OF THE APPRAISER
BARBARA J. KAYE

Business Address: 1985 to Present
                       Vice President and Manager, Appraisal Department
                       Bank of Boston - Connecticut
                       81 West Main Street
                       Waterbury, CT 06702

General Education: Day-Prospect Hill School, New Haven, CT
                       Syracuse University, B.S., Finance and Real Estate

Appraisal Experience: 1976-1985 Commercial Real Estate
                       Appraiser with Henry S. Harrison Appraisal Company,
                       New Haven, CT

Appraisal Education

"Basic Appraisal Principles, Methods and Techniques", given by American
Institute of Real Estate Appraisers, sponsored by University of
Connecticut

"Capitalization Theory and Techniques", given by American Institute of
Real Estate Appraisers, sponsored by the University of Georgia.

Narrative Report Seminar and R-2 Examination, given by Society of Real
Estate Appraisers, sponsored by Connecticut Chapter No. 38, SREA.

"Introduction to Commercial and Investment Real Estate", given by the
National Institute of Real Estate Brokers, sponsored by the Commercial and
Investment Division of N.I.R.E.B.

"Real Estate Construction Costs, Estimating and House Material", given at
the University of Connecticut.

"Case Studies in Real Estate Valuation and Valuation Analysis and Report
Writing", given by American Institute of Real Estate Appraisers, sponsored
by Indiana University.

"Standards of Professional Practice", given by A.I.R.E.A., sponsored by
University of Massachusetts.

Professional and Trade Affiliation
Associate Realtor of the Greater New Haven Board of Realtors

Real Estate Experience
Licensed real estate broker. Actively engaged in the appraisal of
residential, commercial, and industrial properties. Past experience in
real estate sales, management, and leasing.

Court Experience
Qualified as Expert Witness, Superior Court

Articles
What is Actual Cash Value in the Appraisal Journal, American Institute of
Real Estate Appraisers, Chicago, July, 1984.

PHOTOGRAPHS OF THE PROPERTY

Front view looking east from Baden Road (12/15/200_

Partial front and side view looking southeast
from Baden Road (12/15/200_

PHOTOGRAPHS OF THE PROPERTY

A 9

SUMMARY OF SALIENT FACTS & CONCLUSIONS

SUMMARY OF SALIENT FACTS & CONCLUSIONS

Property Address:	700 Duquesne Drive West Palm Beach, Florida
Owner of Record:	Etak Trebmal
Date of Appraisal:	December 15, 200_
Property Rights Appraised:	Fee Simple Estate
Purpose of Appraisal:	Estimate market value of the unencumbered fee simple estate
Land Area:	20,908 sq. ft. or .48 acre
Building Improvement:	Two-story, masonry, apartment building containing ten, one-bedroom units, constructed in 198_ (11 years ago).
Zoning:	RH High Density Multiple Family, 2,000 square feet per unit
Highest and Best Use as if Vacant:	Property is a legal, non-conforming use. Only three units would be allowed if land was unimproved and available for development.
Highest and Best Use as Improved:	Current use as a ten-unit apartment building
Assessment & Taxes:	Assessment: $461,598.00 Tax Liability: $ 7,572.56

Values Indicated:

Cost Approach to Value:	$610,000
Income Approach to Value:	$600,000
Direct Sales Comparison Approach:	$600,000

Final Estimate of Value:	Site	$130,000
	Improvements	$470,000
	Total	$600,000

PART TWO

PREMISES OF THE APPRAISAL

UNDERLYING ASSUMPTIONS AND LIMITING CONDITIONS

This appraisal report has been made with the following general assumptions, and subject to the following limiting conditions.

1. No responsibility is assumed for the legal description or for matters including legal or title considerations. Title to the property is assumed to be good and marketable unless otherwise stated.

2. The property is appraised free and clear of any or all liens or encumbrances unless otherwise stated.

3. Responsible ownership and competent property management are assumed.

4. The information furnished by others is believed to be reliable. However, no warranty is given for its accuracy.

5. All engineering is assumed to be correct. The plot plans and illustrative material in this report are included only to assist the reader in visualizing the property.

6. It is assumed that there are no hidden or unapparent environmental or physical conditions of the property, subsoil, or structures that render it more or less valuable. No responsibility is assumed for such conditions or for arrangiing for engineering environmental studies that may be required to discover them.

7. It is assumed that there is full compliance with all applicable federal, state, and local environmental regulations and laws unless noncompliance is stated, defined, and considered in the appraisal report.

8. It is assumed that all applicable zoning and use regulations and restrictions have been complied with, unless a nonconformity has been stated, defined, and considered in the appraisal report.

9. It is assumed that all required licenses, certificates of occupancy, consents, or other legislative or administrative authority from any local, state, or national government or private entity or organization have been or can be obtained or renewed for any use on which the value estimate contained in this report is based.

10. It is assumed that the utilization of the land and improvements is within the boundaries or property lines of the property described and that there is no encroachment or trespass unless noted in the report.

11. The distribution, if any, of the total valuation in this report between land and improvements applies only under the stated program of utilization. The separate allocations for land and buildings must not be used in conjunction with any other appraisal and are invalid if so used.

12. Possession of this report, or a copy thereof, does not carry with it the right of publication.

13. The appraiser, by reason of this appraisal, is not required to give further consultation, testimony, or be in attendance in court with reference to the property in question unless arrangements have been previously made.

14. Neither all nor any part of the contents of this report (especially any conclusions as to value, the identity of the appraiser, or the firm with which the appraiser is connected) shall be disseminated to the public through advertising, public relations, news, sales, or other media without the prior written consent and approval of the appraiser.

PURPOSE AND USE OF APPRAISAL

The purpose of this appraisal is to create a teaching model to
be used for training appraisers how to make an acceptable
narrative apppraisal of an income producing residential
property.

It is not intended to be an example of a demonstrative appraisal
made by an appraiser for the purpose of obtaining a designation
from an appraisal organization. Such an appraisal would have to
meet the specific requirements for demonstration appraisals as
specified by the organization awarding the designation.

MARKET VALUE DEFINITION AND DATE OF APPRAISAL

The "Market Value" that is estimated in this report is defined as follows:

> "The most probable price in terms of money which a property should bring in competitive and open market under all conditions requisite to a fair sale, the buyer and seller, each acting prudently, knowledgeably and assuming the price is not affected by undue stimulus."

Implicit in this definition is the consummation of a sale as of a specified date and the passing of title from seller to buyer under conditions whereby:

1. buyer and seller are typically motivated.

2. both parties are well informed or well advised, and each acting in what they consider their own best interest.

3. a reasonable time is allowed for exposure in the open market.

4. payment is made in cash or its equivalent.

5. financing is on terms generally available in the community at the specified date and typical for the property type in its locale.

6. the price represents a normal consideration for the property sold unaffected by special financing amounts and/or terms, services, fees, costs, or credits incurred in the transactions.

<u>Date of Value Estimate</u>

December 15, 200_ (this year).

PROPERTY RIGHTS APPRAISED

The property rights being appraised are fee simple.

The following is a definition of Fee Simple:

> "An absolute fee; a fee without limitations to any particular class of heirs or restrictions, but subject to the limitations of eminent domain, escheat, police power, and taxation. An inheritable estate."

PART THREE

PRESENTATION OF DATA

IDENTIFICATION OF THE PROPERTY

The property being appraised is located at 700 Duquesne Drive, in the municipality of West Palm Beach, County of Palm Beach, Florida.

The property is further identified as follows: Municipality 34, Range 43, Township 44, Section 8, Subdivision 6, Block 5, Lot 23.2.

The property being appraised consists of approximately 20,908 square feet of land improved with a two-story, ten-unit apartment building and miscellaneous site improvements.

IDENTIFICATION OF NON REALTY ITEMS

There were no non-realty items included in the appraisal value.

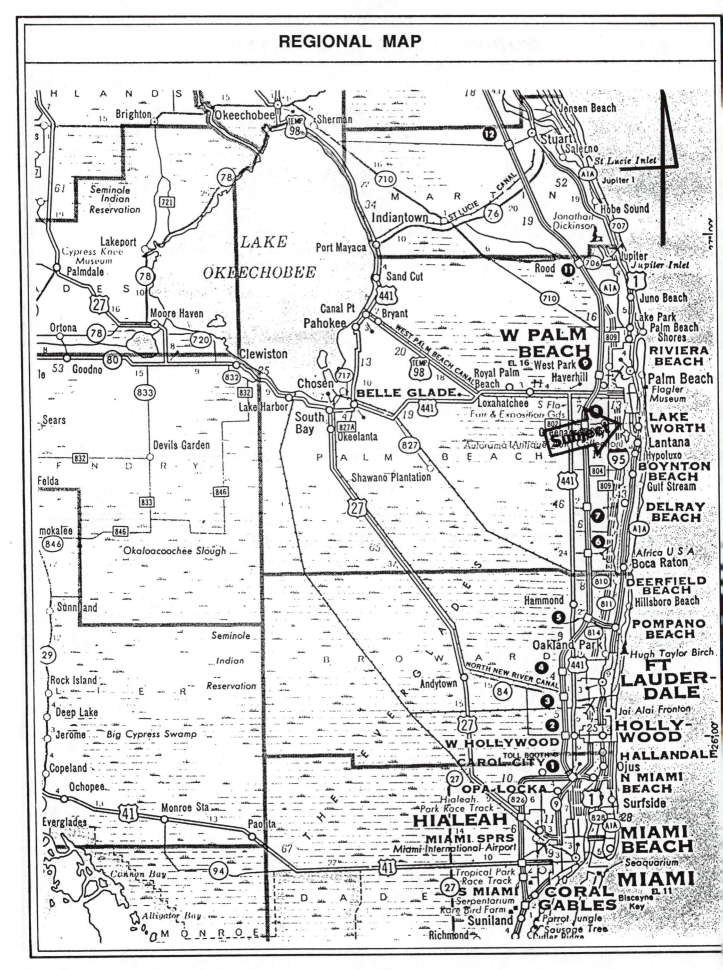

REGIONAL DATA - PALM BEACH COUNTY

Environmental Forces

Geographic Location

Palm Beach County, the largest of Florida's 67 counties, is located along the southeast coast of Florida, situated approximately 40 miles north of Miami. Palm Beach County is bounded to the east by the Atlantic Ocean and 47 miles of sandy beaches, to the north by Martin County, to the northwest by Lake Okeechobee, to the west by undeveloped Hendry County, and to the south by urbanized Broward County.

Climate

The warm climate of Palm Beach County is a major resource. The Gulf Stream flows closer to Palm Beach County than to any other area along the Eastern Seaboard, keeping temperatures at an average 65 degrees in January and 82 degrees in August.

Transportation

The County is served by two major, north/south, limited-access highways: Florida Turnpike (a toll facility) and Interstate 95. Other major, north/south arteries include Federal Highway (U.S. 1), Congress Avenue, Military Trail, and U.S. 441. East/west arteries extend from the Atlantic Ocean to I-95, the Florida Turnpike and to the Everglades area to the west.

Most major commercial bus lines provide passenger and freight service to and from Palm Beach County and have convenient schedules and stations.

The County is serviced by rail for both passengers and freight. Amtrak provides passengers with boarding locations in the county. There is only limited interstate rail passenger traffic. The Florida East Coast Railway and Seaboard Coastline Railroad move major shipments of goods and materials through their Palm Beach County terminals and branch lines.

Servicing the Palm Beaches in air travel is the new Palm Beach International Airport.

REGIONAL DATA - PALM BEACH COUNTY (continued)

Industry

The major industry in the region is tourism, employing 46% of the county's work force between the months of December and April.

Due to the seasonal nature of the major industries - tourism and agriculture - and the cyclical nature of the construction business, the County has made a concerted effort to attract new industry. Most of the recent industrial and residential development has taken place west of the Intracoastal Waterway. The Pratt & Whitney Aircraft Division of United Technologies and IBM are the major employers.

Port of Palm Beach

The Port of Palm Beach is one of Florida's major marine terminals. The Port has become the gateway to the Bahamas and other Atlantic Ocean islands, the Caribbean, and Central and South America, as well as a stopover for cargo destined for Europe and the Middle East.

Education

The Palm Beach County School District is one of the largest in the country and is growing rapidly. There are also many private and parochial schools, colleges, and universities.

Hospitals and Medical Facilities

Palm Beach County offers 14 medical/surgical facilities, including two psychiatric hospitals. All the major communities are equiped with emergency-rescue vehicles and trained paramedics.

Shopping

The Palm Beaches have an array of malls and shopping centers, including the internationally known shopping area on Worth Avenue in Palm Beach.

Social Forces

Population

The 2000 Census Summary of General Population Characteristics showed a total population in Palm Beach County of 1,049,420 persons of which 52.3% were female, and the median age was 40.2 years. The total households was 468,667, with 2.42 persons per household and a total of 340,847 families.

Housing

The 2000 Census Summary of General Housing Characteristics showed a total of 595,664 housing units in Palm Beach County. Of the total housing units, 464,339 were occupied (341,582 owner—occupied and 127,787 tenant—occupied). The rental vacancy rate was 8.9%.

A wide variety of housing opportunities exist in the Palm Beaches. These opportunities vary from single family detached housing to high rise condominium community living.

Rentals are available in a wide range of choice and price. Most rental units include conventional features while others offer several luxury amenities. A lease for six or 12 months is usually required.

Because the Palm Beaches enjoy a very active tourist season (October through April), a lease during this season is usually at rates higher than year—round rates.

Economic Forces

In 2000, the Standard Metropolitan Statistical Area (SMSA) of West Palm/Boca Raton topped the growth list in the state in all business areas (i.e. grocery, restaurant, furniture, cars, department stores).

The median household income, as of December 31, 2000, was $28,642, one of the highest in the state.

Palm Beach County is one of the fastest growing areas in the nation and is an important center for industry, agriculture, international banking, and commerce, with expertise and resources that are highly attractive to investors.

Government Forces

The state and local governments are working closely to provide a healthy and prosperous environment for all Floridians. The State fully supports all activities encouraging the growth of tourism and industry.

Summary

The appraised property is linked to the central business district of West Palm Beach, the largest city in the center of Palm Beach County. A vital cultural climate exists, with resident supported museums, art galleries, symphonies, and theaters.

Downtown West Palm Beach ended the 1990's in the midst of a typical evolution from a retail and social center to a concentrated center for government and financial institutions. The downtown area is now in an extremely enviable position relative to downtown areas throughout Florida and the nation, primarily due to a group of local individuals who are dedicated to the revival of the downtown area as an attractive regional center.

The appraised property is located in the heart of one of the fastest growing areas and one of the most attractive places to live in the nation.

Palm Beach County has a solid and diversified economic base. Considering the recreational and cultural activities available, the climate, the location along the Intercoastal Waterway and Atlantic Ocean, medical and educational facilities, variety and price range of housing, and employment opportunities, it is my opinion that the appraised property will benefit from the strong growth trends in the area.

COMMUNITY MAP

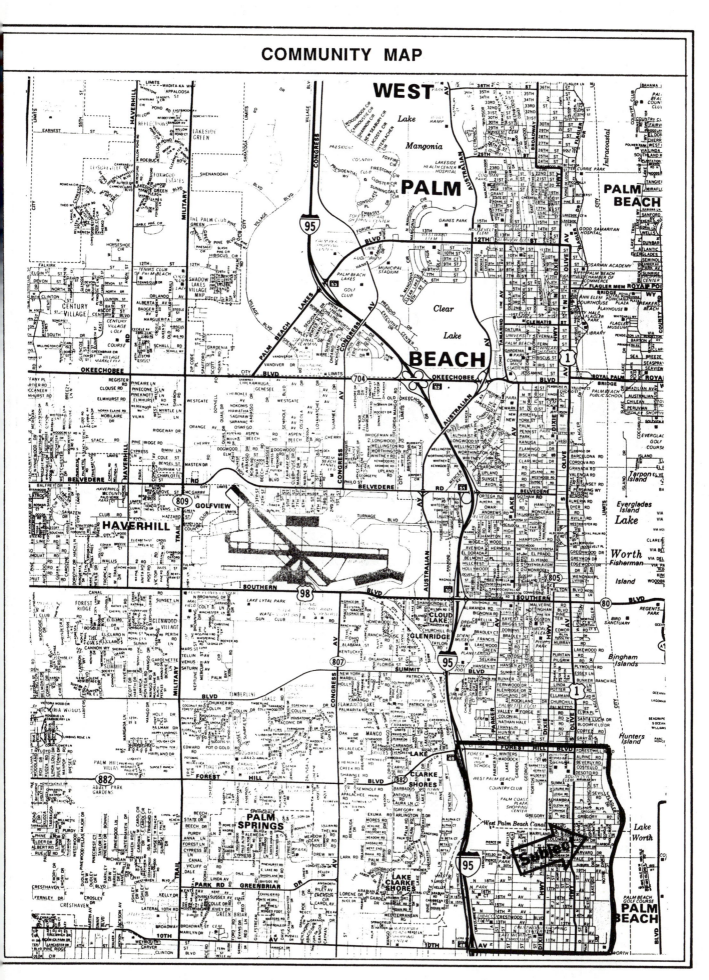

COMMUNITY DATA

West Palm Beach is one of the 37 municipalities comprising Palm Beach County. Greater West Palm Beach Area has a population of 225,000 persons. The influx of people into the community continues at a rate that varies from a 1% to 3% per year population increase.

Industry and Employment
The old airport was surrounded with an industrial area that housed a variety of small industrial and commercial enterprises which benefited from the close proximity to the airport. The rate of unemployment is very low in spite of a substantial increase of available workers.

Air Transportation
The West Palm Beach airport finally outgrew its site and the new airport recently opened. This new facility should substantially increase both the amount of passenger and freight traffic.

Medical Care
There are several well staffed hospitals in the city plus numerous nursing homes.

Education
There are a variety of local and community colleges in the community. The public schools are typical for a large Florida community.

Entertainment
There are ample movie theaters, some regional legitimate theaters, Jai Alai, and a dog track.

Shopping
There are many neighborhood and community shopping areas throughout West Palm Beach and a downtown shopping area. The Palm Coast Plaza shopping center is 1 mile west of the subject property. Worth Avenue in Palm Beach is one of the most famous high price shopping areas in the USA.

Government
The local government is traditional and typical for this area.

Summary
West Palm Beach is virtually 100% built-up, with only a few unimproved parcels remaining. The town benefits from the steady growth of Palm Beach County. The commercial development is competitive with neighboring towns. The appraised property should continue to benefit from continued demand and growth in the area.

NEIGHBORHOOD BOUNDARY MAP

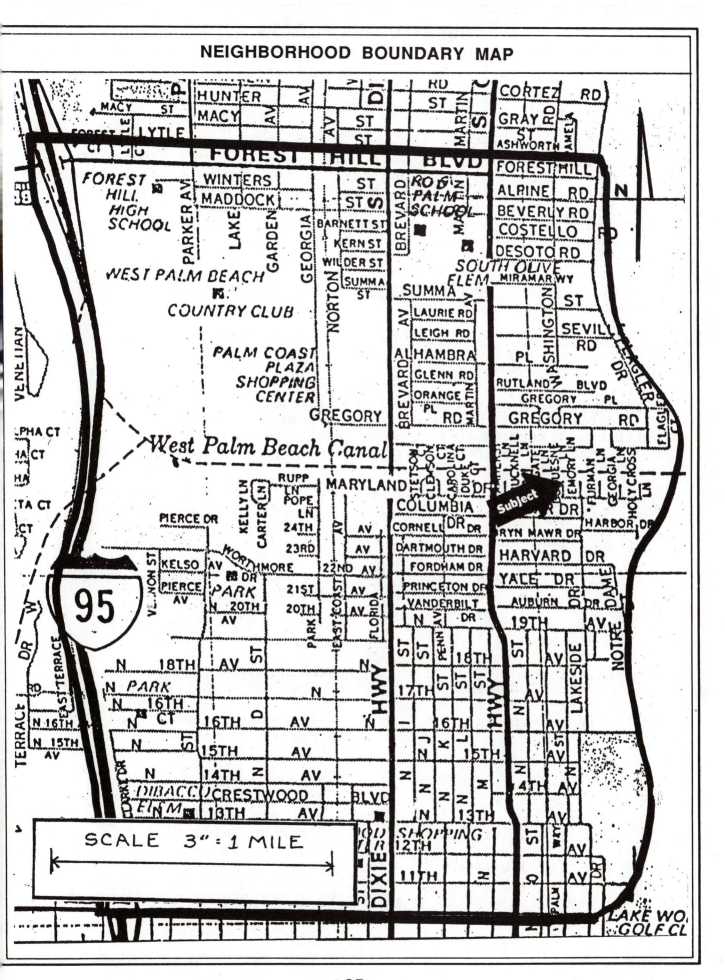

SCALE 3" = 1 MILE

NEIGHBORHOOD DATA

General Description

The subject property is located in West Palm Beach in a
neighborhood known as the West Palm Beach Canal neighborhood.
It is on the east side of Duquesne Drive. It is surrounded with
a mixture of single family and multi-family residential
buildings. Forest Hill Boulevard is the boundary on the north,
Lake Worth on the east, 10th street on the south, and Interstate
Highway 95 on the west.

Proximity to Central Business District: Five miles north of
downtown West Palm Beach.

Percentage Built-up and Trend: Virtually 100% built-up, no new
construction observed in the immediate area. New office and
retail development on Forest Hill Boulevard.

Typical Improvement and Level of Maintenance: Newer (1980 and later)
single family dwellings range in price from $120,000 to $160,000,
exhibiting a very good maintenance level. There are very few
multi-family properties, however, those that do exist also show a high
level of maintenance.

Population Characteristics: Middle income blue and white collar
families; semi-skilled and skilled labor; retirees.

Transportation:

Highway proximity:	Interstate 95 one mile west. U.S. Route 1, 3 blocks West.
Bus:	Cotran - on Forest Hills Boulevard - 2 miles.
Railroad:	Lake Worth - (limited intra state passenger service).
Air Transport:	Palm Beach International Airport - 3 miles.

Schools

Public Grammar:	South Olive Elementary
Public Junior High:	Jefferson Davis Middle
Public High:	Forest Hills High
Parochial Grammar:	Various
Parochial High:	Various
Other:	Palm Beach Junior College and others

Employment Opportunities: Excellent - blue and white collar jobs within five miles of subject property.

Access to Shopping Facilities: Very good - minutes to banks, restaurants, offices and shopping.

Hospitals: Doctor's Hospital on 10th Avenue - 1 mile; plus four other hospitals within ten miles of subject property.

Library: Summit Road - 2 miles.

Recreation: West Palm Beach municipal golf course - 3/4 mile; Palm Beach Auditorium; museums, zoos, beaches, cultural activities.

Conclusion: The subject neighborhood is centrally located within West Palm Beach and the residential properties are well maintained. The rental apartment market is very strong in terms of occupancy and rent levels. Very few new rental properties similar to the appraised property are being developed, indicating continued strong demand. It is reasonable to expect that property values will remain relatively stable, increasing with the general inflationary trends in the country.

ZONING DATA

The appraised property is located in the RM Medium Density zoning district as designated by the Town of West Palm Beach, adopted April 13, 1964, as amended and revised.

This district is designed to provide a minimum area of multiple family, relatively high population density, residential facilities to be located where access from main thoroughfares to such facilities is especially desirable. Certain non-residential uses may be allowed by Special Exception.

<u>Permitted Uses</u>: Two-family dwellings; multiple family dwellings; and single family dwellings.

<u>Permitted Accessory Uses and Structures</u>: Facilities as may be required or useful for the operation of an apartment house, or for the entertainment of guests or tenants, but all such accessory uses shall be conducted within the building or shall be entered only from within the building, and no sign on the exterior of the building shall indicate their presence.

<u>Special Exceptions</u>: Religious, institutional, or public buildings; professional office buildings.

<u>Prohibited Uses</u>: Apartment houses in excess of two stories (20 feet in height); commercial recreational facilities.

<u>Standards for Multi-Family Dwellings</u>:

Minimum Lot Area:	10,000 sq. ft., provided that there shall be at least 2,000 square feet of net lot area for each dwelling unit (approximately 22 units per acre).
Minimum Lot Width:	100 feet
Minimum Front Yard:	25 feet
Minimum Side Yard:	15% of average lot width, but not less than 15 feet.
Minimum Rear Yard:	15% of average lot depth, but not less than 15 feet.
Maximum Lot Coverage:	35%
Minimum Floor Area:	600 sq. ft. per dwelling unit
Minimum Off-Street Parking:	1 1/2 spaces per dwelling unit

The subject property appears to conform with the current zoning requirements and represents a conforming use of the site.

ASSESSMENT AND TAXES DATA

By law, all property in the State of Florida is required to be assessed at 100% of market value. The current assessment for the subject property is as follows:

Land	$ 82,992
Improvements	378,606
Total Assessment	$461,598

Per Unit $46,160

The following 200_ (last year) tax rates and taxes were recorded for the subject property:

Type	Rate	Taxes
General Tax	6.6689	$3,078.35
School Tax	6.9329	3,199.93
Library Tax	.3526	162.76
Municipal Tax	2.3900	1,103.19
Sub-Total (tax rate)	16.3444	$7,544.23
Maintenance Tax (flat per acre)		28.02
Total (Per Unit $757.22)		$7,572.25

Trends

Like most Florida communities, the annual budget of West Palm Beach tends to increase gradually each year. In recent years, the total Grand List has increased at a greater rate than the annual budget, therefore, the tax rates have been decreasing.

Tax Comparables

A study of the assessment and taxes on the four properties used as comparables sales within this report was made and compared to the current assessment and taxes for the appraised property. The taxes of the four comparable properties, located in three different competitive communities, ranged from $392. to $896. per·unit.

The current taxes at the subject property are $757.22 per unit. Considering the location, age and condition of the improvements, and the overall trend in West Palm Beach, the taxes paid at the subject property are similar to the comparable properties.

TAX COMPARABLES

Address	Assessment	General Tax	School Tax	Library Tax	Municipal Tax	Maintenance Tax	Total Annual Taxes	Taxes Unit	% of Taxes to Assessment
825 South St Lake Worth	$416,162	2,613.36	2,226.26	---	1,430.84	---	6,270.46	392	1.5%
2610 Gulfstream Rd West Palm Beach	472,048	4,421.42	2,525.22	166.44	---	56.04	7,169.12	896	1.5%
3713 Davis Rd West Palm Beach	481,340	4,154.38	2,372.68	156.40	---	28.02	6,711.48	838	1.4%
675 Florida Mango Road West Palm Beach	387,578	3,416.38	2,073.44	136.66	---	28.02	5,654.50	472	1.5%
SUBJECT PROPERTY 700 Duquesne Dr. West Palm Beach	461,598	3,078.34	3,200.22	162.76	1,103.22	28.02	7,572.56	758	1.6%

A30

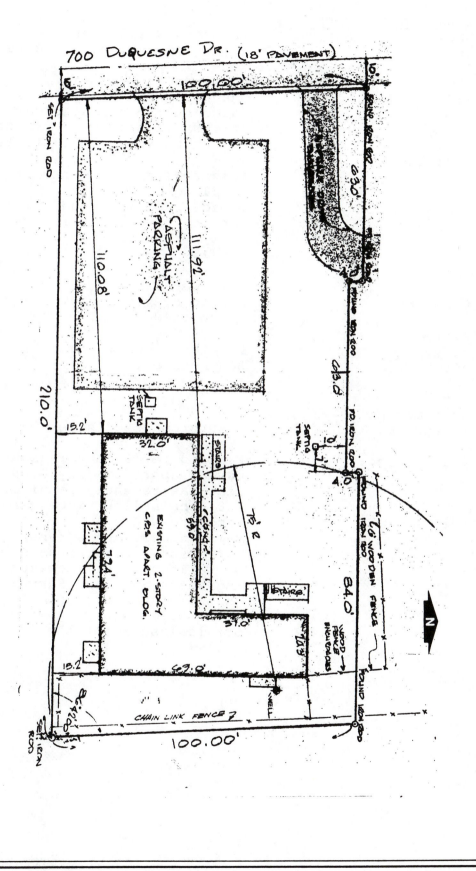

SITE DATA

Physical Characteristics

Dimensions:	100 feet x 210 feet average depth
Total Area:	20,908 sq. ft. or .48 acre
Excess Area:	None
Shape:	Rectangular
Drainage:	Adequate - in heavy rains, a large puddle tends to form in portion of driveway near street.
Topography:	Essentially level at street grade
Corner Influence:	No
View:	Neighboring single-family dwellings
Soil:	Typical Florida sand
Mineral Deposits:	None of any commercial valuee

Utilities

Water:	Well water
Sanitary Sewers:	Septic system, 2,500 gallon tank, drainfield
Storm Sewers:	County
Electricity:	Florida Power & Light
Telephone:	Southern Bell

Site Improvements

Sprinkler system:	Underground sprinkler for yard areas
Driveway & Parking:	Parking for 15 cars; asphalt paved, approximately 5,000 square feet was recently repaird.
Fences:	100' chain link fence - rear yard
Sidewalks:	Concrete walks
Landscaping:	Lawn, trees, and shrubs
Plot Plan:	On facing page; prepared by James D. Carlton, Inc., Registered Engineers and Land Surveyors. This plot has been reduced, therefore, does not reflect the original scale of 1"=20'.

Street Improvements

Paving:	Yes
Sidewalks:	No
Curbing:	No
Lighting:	Yes
Road Surface:	Macadam
Width:	Two lanes
Maintenance by:	Town
Condition:	Good

Easements & Restrictive
Covenants: Asphalt driveway encroaches from
                                    700 Duquesne Drive Road - see
                                    Plot Plan

Nuisances and Hazards: None. There is minimal traffic
                                    on Duquesne Drive basically
                                    generated by residents and their
                                    visitors.

Functional Adequacy: Moderate parking problem as there
                                    are only 1.5 spaces per dwelling
                                    unit.

Relationship of Site to
Surroundings: The compatibility of the
                                    appraised site is good as it is
                                    surrounded by single family and
                                    multi-family residential
                                    dwellings which are considered to
                                    be a positive influence on the
                                    value of the subject property.
                                    The marketability of the site as
                                    compared with other sites in the
                                    area is very competitive.

DESCRIPTION OF THE IMPROVEMENTS

General Description:

Substructure
Foundation: 4" concrete slab on compacted earth, with moistop vapor barrier.

Footings: 12" x 24" concrete

Columns   8' x 16" concrete

Superstructure
Exterior Walls   8" concrete block

Exterior Wall Cover   Stucco

Exterior Doors   Solid wood and metal sliding glass doors

Windows: Double-hung metal with screens

Roof: Mansard style pre-fabricated engineered wood; box trusses with full 6-1/2" batt insulation. Built-up tar and gravel roof cover. Cedar shingles on roof sides.

Second Floor: 3" concrete slab with 12" pre-cast concrete joists

Special Features: Two concrete stairways (13 treads each), two ground floor concrete patios, two extended second floor concrete balconies with aluminum railings, second floor covered concrete walkway/balcony.

Interior

Each apartment consists of a living room, dining area, bedroom, walk-in kitchen, bathroom, and three closets.

Walls & Ceilings: Painted drywall

Floors:
     Kitchen: Vinyl tile
     Bedroom, Living &
     Dining Area: Wall to wall carpet over concrete

Bathroom:	Ceramic tile flooring and wainscot, porcelain tub, shower head, water closet, vanity with sink and mirrored cabinet above.
Kitchen:	Sears two-door refrigerator, Sears self-cleaning oven, stainless steel double sink, Formica counter, ample base and wall cabinets.

Floor Areas:

First Floor:	3,288 square feet
Second Floor:	3,288 square feet
Gross Floor Area:	6,576 square feet

Unit Areas:	10 units contain 625 square feet

Mechanical Equipment

Heating:	Electric; forced air ducted
Air-Conditioning:	Each apartment is centrally air conditioned by a 1.5 ton unit with roof condensors.
Hot Water:	Each apartment has a 30-gallon electric hot water heater.
Plumbing:	Copper tubing - four fixtures per apartment - 40 fixtures
Electric:	400 amps - circuit breakers - 11 meters (including house meter).
Miscellaneous:	Water softener and iron filtering system
Age & Condition:	The actual age of the building is 11 years. The property has received regular maintenance throughout the years and is in average condition. Short-lived items are replaced when needed. The property is in a conditition typical of an 11 year old building in the area.

Deferred Maintenance/
Need Repairs: Stucco covering requires
                                 painting; yard requires some
                                 cleaning up; front portion of
                                 driveway has a drainage problem
                                 after heavy rains.

Functional Utility: The layout, room sizes, closet
                                 space, kitchen size and
                                 equipment, and bathrooms are
                                 all considered average and
                                 acceptable.

                                 There have been septic system
                                 backup problems, although
                                 infrequent. The tanks are
                                 pumped at least once a year.

Effective Age: The overall effective age of a
                                 property is determined by a
                                 variety of factors, including
                                 the quality of construction
                                 (materials and workmanship),
                                 condition, design, and any
                                 external factors affecting
                                 value.

                                 The quality of construction and
                                 design of the appraised
                                 building is rated average and
                                 compares to similar buildings
                                 in the area. Maintenance is
                                 better than average. The
                                 property is a legal,
                                 non-conforming use, having a
                                 density of 20 units per acre as
                                 compared to six units per acre
                                 allowed under current zoning
                                 regulations. The above two
                                 factors tend to reflect a lower
                                 effective age. It is my
                                 opinion that the building has
                                 an effective age of 10 years.

HISTORY OF THE PROPERTY

The appraised site was purchased by Etak Trebmal from Betty and Dorothy Corral on November 19, 1991 for $29,000 (11 years ago). (Official Record Book 2954, Page 350, Warranty Deed.) In 199_ Ms. Trebmal constructed the improvements, which were ready for occupancy in January, 199_ (10 years ago).

In 199 , Ms. Trebmal sold approximately one-half of the parcel (improved with a single family residence) for $104,400. This parcel, known as 720 Duquesne Drive, is not included in this appraisal.

Ms. Trebmal has been renting the apartments year round (as opposed to seasonally). She stated that she does not require a lease, however, she does require a security deposit equal to one month's rent. This property has experienced virtually 100% occupancy over the years. Most of the apartment units have been recarpeted over the last few years, appliances have been reeplaced as needed, and apartments were redecorated at least once every three years. No other major capital improvements have been necessary. Current rentals are being renewed at $675 per month.

Ms. Trebmal owns two other rental buildings and her management performance is rated adequate and competent.

A written offer to purchase the property for $500,000 was made in August, 200_ (last year). However, Ms. Trebmal declined the offer, and stated she would accept an offer of $650,000.

FLOOR PLANS OF TYPICAL APARTMENTS

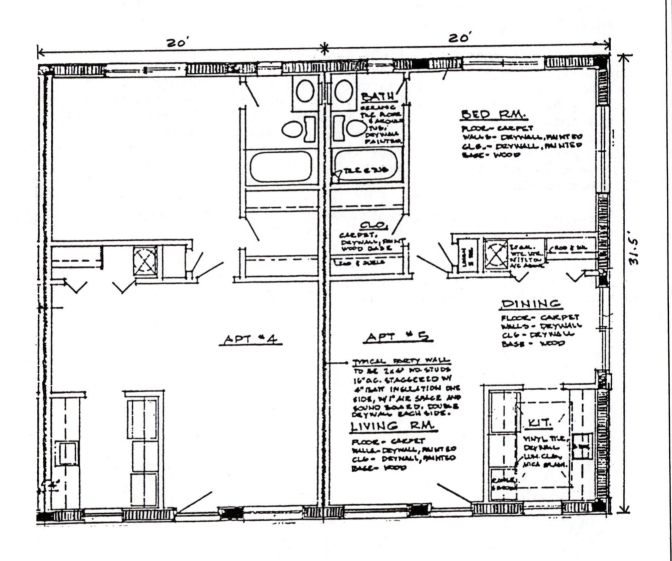

PART FOUR

ANALYSIS OF DATA
AND
CONCLUSIONS

THE APPRAISAL PROCESS

There are three generally recognized approaches to value, which may be used in estimating the value of real estate.

COST APPROACH - That approach in appraisal analysis which is based on the proposition that the informed purchaser would pay no more than the cost of producing a substitute property with the same utility as the subject property. It is particularly applicable when the property being appraised involves relatively new improvements which represent the highest and best use of the land or when relatively unique or specialized improvements are located on the site and for which there exist no comparable properties on the market.

DIRECT SALES COMPARISON APPROACH - That approach in appraisal analysis which is based on the proposition that an informed purchaser would pay no more for a property than the cost of acquiring an existing property with the same utility. This approach is applicable when an active market provides sufficient quantities of reliable data which can be verified from authoritative sources. The Direct Sales Comparison Approach is relatively unreliable in an inactive market or in estimating the value of properties for which no real comparable sales data are available. It is also questionable when sales data cannot be verified with principals to the transaction. Also referred to as the Market Comparison or Market Data Approach.

INCOME APPROACH - That procedure in appraisal analysis which converts anticipated benefits (dollar income or amenitites) to be derived from the ownership of property into a value estimate. The Income Approach is widely applied in appraising income-producing properties. Anticipated future income and/or reversions are discounted to a present worth figure through the capitalization process.

In order to arrive at an estimate of market value for the property being appraised, it is necessary to assemble from the marketplace as much information as is considered pertinent to the appraisal problem. This information is then utilized in the three different appraisal approaches.

After arriving at an indication of value by each of the three approaches, they are reconciled into a single estimate of value based upon the approach which has the highest quantity and quality of data available, and the one in which the market participant typically has the greatest confidence.

HIGHEST AND BEST USE OF THE SITE AS THOUGH VACANT

Real estate is valued in terms of its highest and best use. The highest and best use of the land or site, if vacant and available for use, may be different from the highest and best use of the improved property. This will be true when the improvement is not an appropriate use and yet makes a contribution to total property value in excess of the value of the site.

Highest and best use may be defined as that reasonable and probable use which will support the highest present value as of the date of appraisal. Alternatively, it is the most profitable, likely use to which a property can be put; it may be measured in terms of the present worth of the highest net return that the property can be expected to produce over a stipulated long-run period of time.

The highest and best use is that use from among one or more proposed uses that has been found to be legally permissible, physically possible, appropriately supported, and financially feasible, which is expected to generate the highest rate of net return over a given income-forecast period at the time the decision is made.

The highest and best use of the site if it were vacant and ready to be built upon would be for a 10-unit apartment building.

HIGHEST AND BEST USE OF THE PROPERTY AS IMPROVED

Any determination of highest and best use includes identifying the motivations of probable purchasers. The benefits of an investment property, like the subject property, relates to net income potential and to eventual resale or refinancing. Thus, the highest and best use will be that use which maximizes the net operating income on a long-term basis. This use must meet four criteria:

1.   Physically possible

2.   Legally permissible

3.   Financially feasible

4.   Maximally productive

1.   Physically Possible. The existing improvements are 11 years old, of above average quality construction, and are in good condition. The building can continue to be utilized for rental apartment units, or can be converted to condominiums or a motel.

2.   Legally Permissible. The existing improvements represent a legal, pre-existing, non-conforming use, therefore, current zoning regulations are not applicable. However, a motel would not be allowed in this zoning district.

3.   Financially Feasible. There are two potential highest and best uses: (1) continue as a rental property, (2) convert to condominiums. I have estimated a net operating income for the subject property in the Income Approach section clearly demonstrating that continued use as a rental property is feasible. It is my opinion that conversion to condominiums is not feasible as this thime. From a careful analysis of supply and demand factors in the greater West Palm Beach area, there is currently an over-supply of condominium units. The Board of Realtors estimates there are approximately 10,000 resales on the market, 5,000 new (vacant) units, and 5,000+ planned units. Furthermore, no capital expenditures are necessary for the property to continue as a rental unit. The capital investment costs of conversion for ten units is estimateed at over $100,000. This would include interior and exterior clean up, legal costs, marketing, and a profit for the developer.

4.   Maximally Productive. It is apparent that the current use
     as a rental property is the highest and best use. The
     factors contributing to this conclusion are as follows:

     a.   High intensity, legal, conforming use that would
           prompt the owner to extend the economic (useful) life
           of the improvements via competent management and
           careful maintenance.

     b.   A stable (and increasing) net operating income.

     c.   Tax advantages and inflation hedge.

     d.   The strong demand for rental units, evidenced by the
           high occupancy levels and projected population growth
           of the area.

Thus, the current uses as a ten-unit apartment building
maximizes the net operating income on a long-term basis and
represents the highest and best use.

STEPS OF THE COST APPROACH INCLUDING SITE VALUATION

The following steps including site valuation were followed in order to derive a value indication via the Cost Approach:

1. Estimated the value of the site as though vacant and available to be developed. The value of the site is determined by its potential highest and best use. The value of the site has been estimated using the Sales Comparison Approach as this is the most applicable method of estimating the market value of an unimproved site.

2. Estimated the reproduction cost of the structure on the effective appraisal date.

3. Estimated the amount of accrued depreciation in the structure, categorized by three major types:

    a. physical deterioration
    b. functional obsolescence
    c. external obsolescence

4. Deducted the appropriate estimated depreciation from the reproduction cost of the structure to derive an estimate of the structure's contribution to total value.

5. Added the depreciated reproduction cost of the structure and site improvements to obtain an estimated total present value of all improvements.

6. Added the estimated total present value of all improvements to the estimated site value to arrive at an indication of value for the subject property.

COMPARABLE SITE SALE LOCATION MAP

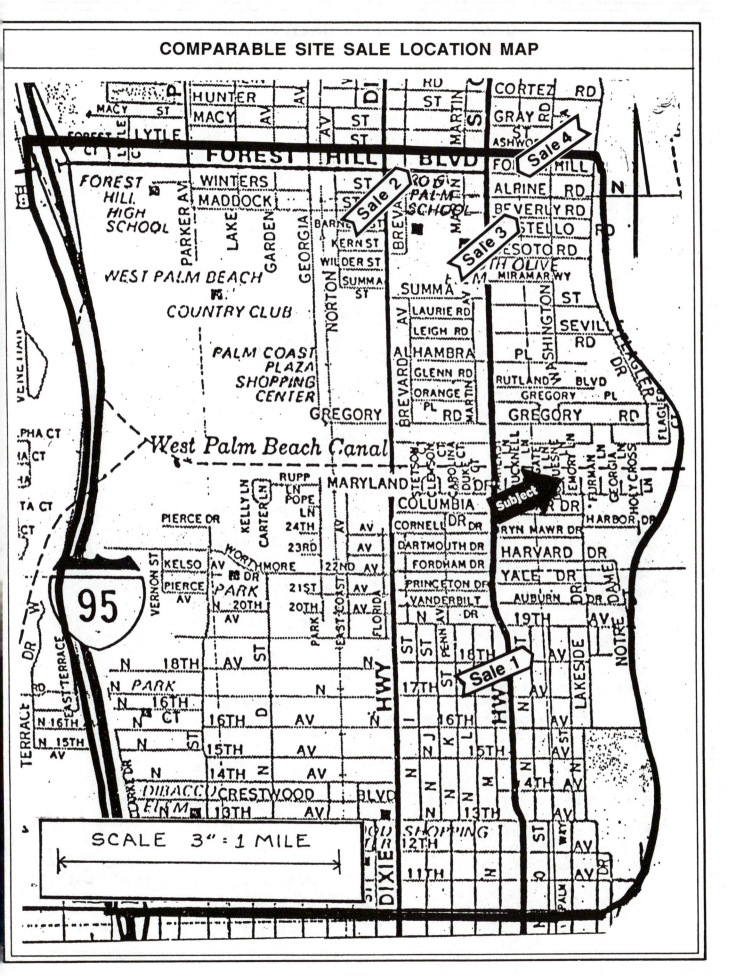

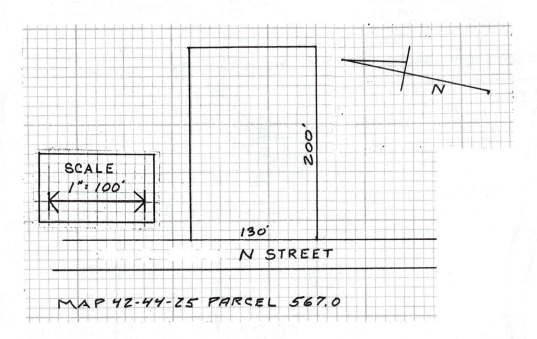

SCALE
1" : 100'

200'

130'

N STREET

MAP 42-44-25 PARCEL 567.0

Address:	1805 N. Street, West Palm Beach, Florida
Location:	1/2 mile southeast of subject
Grantor:	Kurt Coral and Jackie Coral
Grantee:	John McDonnald
Date of Sale:	**May 18, 200_ (this year)**
Sale Price:	$100,000
Date Source/Verification:	Town Records verified by seller
Zoning/Density	RH High density residential 2,000 sq. ft. per unit. Site has room for 8 units
Special Conditions and/or Financing:	None reported
Physical Characteristics:	
Frontage:	130'
Average Depth:	200'
Size:	Almost 1/3 acre
Typography:	Level
Available Utilities:	Electricity, telephone, cable TV
Easements, Encroachments and Restrictions:	None observed
Additional Information:	Small house which needed to be demolished at estimated cost of $4,000
Sale Price per Unit:	Price per unit $13,000 (including demolition cost)

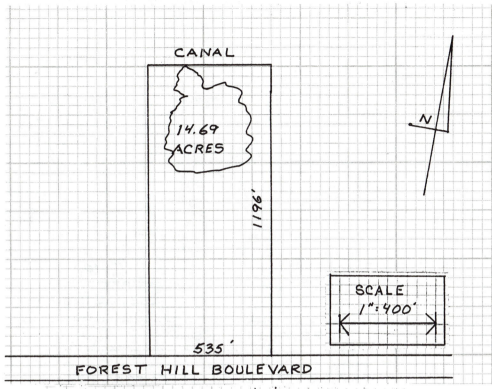

CANAL

14.69 ACRES

1196'

535'

N

SCALE
1":400'

FOREST HILL BOULEVARD

MAP NO 210 44-43-7 PARCELS 135-136

Address:	3760 Forest Hill Boulevard, West Palm Beach, Florida
Location:	1/3 mile northwest of subject
Grantor:	William Glazer and Roz Glazer
Grantee:	Donald Rump, Jr.
Date of Sale:	November 1, 200_ (this year)
Sale Price:	$1,500,000
Data Source/Verification:	Town Records verified by Broker
Zoning/Density:	RM Medium density multiple family 9,000 sq. ft. per unit. Site has room for 71 units
Special Conditions and/or Financing:	None reported
Physical Characteristics:	
Frontage:	535'
Average Depth:	1196'
Size:	14.69 acres (639,896 sq. ft.)
Typography:	Level with fresh water lake
Easements, Encroachments and Restrictions:	None reported
Additional Information:	Lake is suitable for swimming and small boats
Sale Price per Unit:	Per Unit $21,126

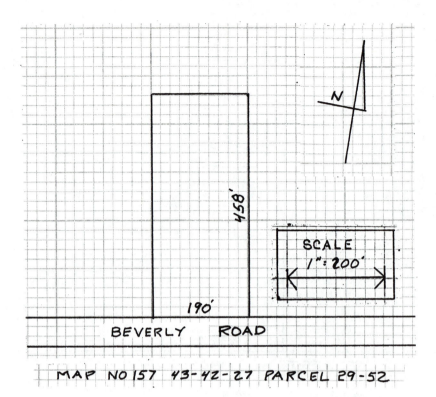

MAP NO 157 43-42-27 PARCEL 29-52

Address:	836 Beverly Road, West Palm Beach, Florida
Location:	1 mile northeast of subject
Grantor:	Diane Ruben and Harvey Ruben
rantee:	Binnick and Assoc.
Date of Sale:	**July 22, 200_ (this year)**
Sale Price:	$$810,000
Data Source/Verification:	Town Records verified by Buyers
Zoning/Density:	RH High density residential, 2,000 sq. ft. per unit. Site has room for 45 units
Special Conditions and/or Financing:	None reported
Physical Characteristics:	
Frontage:	190'
Average Depth:	458'
Size:	2 acres
Typography:	Level with some woods
Available Utilities:	Electricity, telephone, cable TV, municiple water and municiple sewers
Easements, Encroachments and Restrictions:	None reported
Sale Price per Unit:	Per Unit $18,000

COMPARABLE SITE SALE NO. 4

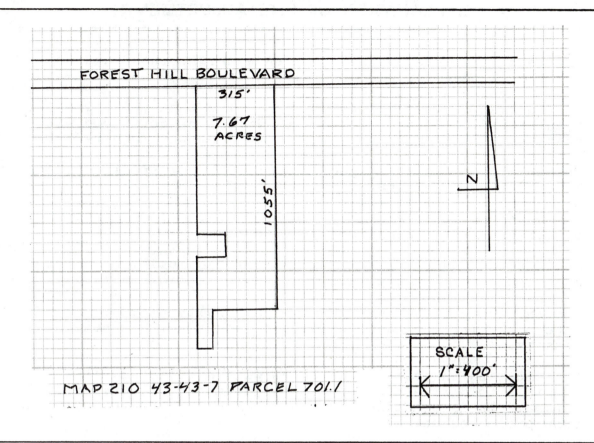

FOREST HILL BOULEVARD

315'

7.67 ACRES

1055'

N

MAP 210 43-43-7 PARCEL 701.1

SCALE
1"=400'

Address:	2469 Forest Hill Boulevard, West Palm Beach, Florida
Location:	1/3 mile west of subject
Grantor:	Samuel Saslafsky
Grantee:	A.H. Minnick
Date of Sale:	**September 13, 200_ (this year)**
Sale Price:	$800,000
Data Source/Verification:	Closing attorney
Zoning/Density:	RM Medium density multiple family 9,000 sq. ft. per unit. Site has room for 37 units
Special Conditions and/or Financing:	None reported
Physical Characteristics:	
Frontage:	315'
Average Depth:	1055'
Size:	7.63 acres
Typography:	Level
Available Utilities:	Electricity, telephone, cable TV, municiple water and municiple sanitary sewers
Easements, Encroachments and Restrictions:	None observed
Additional Information:	Was improved with a 37 one story rental apartment complex
Sale Price per Unit:	Per Unit $21,621

EXPLANATION OF SITE ADJUSTMENTS

All four site sales were in the same neighborhood and no location adjustment was needed.

All four sites were purchased within the past year. There has been significant change of values in the neighborhood within the past year. Therefore, no time adjustment was required.

There were no reported special conditions or special financing. Therefore no adjustments for them were required.

There were some some significant physical characteristic differences which required adjustment.

The subject and comparable site sales had municipal water and municipal sanitary sewers. Comparable #1 did not have either.

The subject property was zoned at a density of 2,000 sq. ft. of site per unit. Comparable Sales #2 and #4 were zoned at a lower density.

By comparing the comparable sales with each other, it was possible to derive the required adjustments directly from the market. The size differences were accounted for by using the unit price per unit.

UTILITY ADJUSTMENT

Sale # 1 and Sale #3 appear to be similar except Sale #3 has municipal water and municipal sewers and Sale #1 has neither.

        Sale #1   Sale price per unit $13,000
        Sale #3   Sale price per unit   18,000

        Difference attributable to
        availability of utilities $ 5,000 per unit

DENSITY ADJUSTMENT

Sale #3 and Sale #4 appear to be similar except for the zoning density. Sale #3 is zoned RH High density residential and Sale #4 is zoned RM Medium density.

        Sale #3   Sale price per unit $18,000
        Sale #4   Sale price per unit   21,621

        Difference attributable to
        difference in zoning density $ 3,621 per unit ($3,500 RD)

SITE SALES ADJUSTMENT GRID

	Subject Property	Site Sale #1	Site Sale #2	Site Sale #3	Site Sale #4
ADDRESS	700 Duquesne Dr	1805 N Street	3760 Forest Hill Road	836 Beverly Rd	2469 Forest Hill Road
COMMUNITY	West Palm Beach,	West Palm Beach,	West Palm Beach,	West Palm Beach,	West Palm Beach,
SALE PRICE		$100,000 Plus $4,000 demolition	$1,500,000	$810,000	$800,000
PERMITTED NO. OF UNITS	10	8	71	45	37
SALE PRICE PER UNIT		$13,000	$21,126	$18,000	$21,621
DATE OF SALE	December 15, 200_ (this year)	May 18, 200_ (this year)	November 1, 200_ (this year)	July 22, 200_ (this year)	September 13, 200_ (this year)
LOCATION	•	Similar -0-	Similar -0-	Similar -0-	Similar -0-
DENSITY	High Density	High Density -0-	Medium Density -$3,500	High Density -0-	Medium Density -$3,500
UTILITIES	No municipal sewers or water•	No municipal sewers or water	Municipal sewers and water -$5,000	Municipal sewers and water -$5,000	Municipal sewers and water -$5,000
SPECIAL CONDITIONS AND FINANCING	None reported	None reported -0-	None reported -0-	None reported -0-	None reported -0-
TOTAL ADJ.		-0-	-$8,500	-$5,000	$8,500
ADJ. SALE PRICE PER PERMITTED UNIT		$13,000	$12,626	$13,000	$13,121

SUMMARY OF SITE VALUE

All four comparable site sales were good indications of the value of the subject site.

Comparable Sale #1 did not have any significant differences from the subject property that could be identified except size. The size difference was handled by using price per permitted unit as the unit of comparison. It sold for $13,000 per unit. This was well supported by the other three sales. Comparable Sale #2 had a small lake. This did not appear to effect its value.

The subject property was zoned for 10 units. Its value was calculated as follows:

    10 units @ $13,000 per unit = $130,000

    Total Estimate Site value $130,000

Estimate of Cost New

I have utilized three of the accepted methods of estimating
replacement cost new:

    1.   Cost-Index Trending
    2.   Segregated Cost Method (Cost Service)
    3.   Quantity Survey Method (Professional Cost Estimator)

Cost-Index Trending

This method involves using a cost index to update a known
historical cost to a current cost estimate. I used the Marshall
Valuation Service, a nationally recognized costing service in
the appraisal field.

The owner stated his total cost to build the appraised apartment
building 11 years ago was approximately $280,000.

The comparable cost multiplier from Marshall Valuation Service,
Section 98, Page 10, Eastern, Class C, January, 199_ is 2.232.
This multiplier is then modified by a monthly correcting factor
from Section 99, Page 44 to bring the multiplier current to
December, 200_.   This factor is 1.009.

Then: 2.232 x 1.009 x $280,000 = $630,584

Segregated Cost Method

This method involves using a cost service to derive a cost
estimate in terms of dollars per square foot based on known
costs of similar structures and adjusted for time and physical
differences. I have the Marshall Valuation Service.
Information about the appraised property was input from my
office terminal via time sharing into the Marshall Valuation
Service computer in California. The cost printout can be found
on the following pages.

This method indicated a replacement cost new of $644,354.

SITE SALES ADJUSTMENT GRID

COST ESTIMATE FOR: Barbara Kaye
PROPERTY OWNER: Etak L. Trebmal
ADDRESS: 700 Duouesne Drive, West Palm Beach, FL
SURVEYED BY: Barbara J. Kaye
DATE OF SURVEY: December 15, 200_

OCCUPANCY: MULTIPLE DWELLING

CLASS: C Masonry   COST RANK: 3.0 Above Average
EFFECTIVE AGE: 10 Years   CONDITION: 4.0 Good
NUMBER OF STORIES: 2.0   AVERAGE STORY HEIGHT: 8.9
FLOOR AREA: 6,576 Sq. Ft.   COST AS OF: 12/0_

COMPONENT	UNITS	COST	REPLACEMENT COST NEW
EXCAVATION & SITE PREPARATION:			
Site Preparation	20,900	0.24	5,016
FOUNDATION			
Column Footings	24	70.76	1,698
FRAME:			
Concrete Frame Members	427	26.50	11,316
FLOOR STRUCTURE:			
Concrete on Ground	3,228	3.84	12,396
Concrete, Elevated Slab	3,228	10.76	34,733
Waterproofing	3,228	0.64	2,066
SUBTOTAL			49,195
FLOOR COVER:			
Carpet and Pad	5,590	3.82	21,354
Tile, Ceramic	460	11.08	5,097
Vinyl Sheet	526	4.10	2,157
SUBTOTAL			28,607
CEILING:			
Gypsum Board, Taped & Painted	6,576	1.68	11,048
INTERIOR CONSTRUCTION:			
Interior Construction, Frame	6,576	17.82	117,184
PLUMBING:			
Plumbing	6,576	7.74	50,898
HEATING AND COOLING:			
Electric	6,576	3.20	21,043
Refrigerated Cooling	6,576	4.60	30,250
SUBTOTAL			51,293
ELECTRICAL:			
Electrical	6,576	5.86	38,535
EXTERIOR WALL:			
Concrete Block	5,283	18.30	96,679
WALL ORNAMENTATION:			
Stucco on Masonry	5,283	2.44	12,891
ROOF STRUCTURE:			
Wood joists, Wood deck	3,288	6.50	21,372
ROOF COVER:			
Wood Shingles	891	3.04	2,709
Insulation	3,288	1.20	3,946
Built-Up Composition	3,288	1.86	6,116
SUBTOTAL			12,770

QUANTITY SURVEY ESTIMATE

Quantity Survey Method

This method is considered the most comprehensive and accurate method of cost estimating. It is a repetition of the contractor's original method of developing a bid figure.

I obtained a cost breakdown from a reputable local general contractor, Steve Martin, of Sharpestimator, Inc. Contractor's Licence No. I0UI0I4. Mr. Martin's summary of his breakdown, as submitted to me, is on the following page.

This method indicated a replacement cost new of $626,800.

QUANTITY SURVEY ESTIMATE

SHARPESTIMATOR, INC
299 PONCE DeLEON
WEST PALM BEACH, FL 33411

OWNER   Etak L. Trebmal
CONTRACTOR   SHARPESTIMATOR, INC.
JOB LOCATION   700 Duouensne Drive, West Palm Beach, FL

1	Earthwork & Exc.	$5,000
2	Soil Poisoning	600
3	Concrete Labor & Mat.	32,000
4	Masonry Labor & Mat.	20,000
5	Metal Windows & Doors	13,000
6	Alum. Rails	9,200
7	Roof Trusses	15,000
8	Roofing & Sheet Metal	16,000
9	Form & Framing Lumber	30,000
10	Millwork	10,000
11	Common Labor	8,000
12	Carpentry Labor	52,000
13	Finished Floors	16,000
14	Cabinets & Vanities	20,000
15	Dry Walls	20,000
16	Stucco	14,000
17	Tile & Marble	8,000
18	Painting	16,000
19	Plumbing	40,000
20	Electric	30,000
21	Finished Hardware	3,000
22	Electric Fixtures	4,000
23	Rough Hardware	2,000
24	A.C. & Heat	30,000
25	Cleaning	2,000
26	Med. Cabinets & Bath Access.	2,000
27	Insulation	4,000
28	Appliances	16,000
29	Septic Tanks	6,000
30	Landscaping	4,000
31	Walks & Drives	18,000
32	Permits	3,000
33	Insurance	4,000
34	Contractors Fee	70,000
35	Arch. Fee	6,000
36	Survey	1,000
37	Supervision	20,000
38	Sprinkler	3,000
39	Precast Conc. & Stairs	48,000
40	Luminous Ceilings	6,000
		————
		$626,800

SUMMARY OF COST NEW

1.	Cost-Index Trending	$630,584
2.	Segregated Cost Method	$644,354
3.	Quantity Survey Method	$626,800

Method 1 was given the least consideration as the historical cost may be not accurate nor typical for the time period, and the national cost index may not apply to the local area.

Method 2 provides a reasonably accurate estimate and supports the general contractor's estimate.

Method 3 is considered an accurate means of replacement cost and, therefore, was given equal weight with Method 2 in arriving at the final estimate. However, it did not include some of the applicable soft costs.

After analyzing all available data, I estimate the reproduction cost new of the subject improvements to be $650,000, including site improvements valued at $25,000. Site improvements include landscaping, sidewalks, paving, and underground sprinkler system.

DEPRECIATION ANALYSIS

Accrued depreciation is a loss in value from the reproduction cost new of the improvements from any cause, as of the date of the appraisal. This loss in value emanates from one or more of three sources: physical deterioration, functional obsolescence, and external obsolescence. Depreciation is a penalty only to the extent that it is recognized as a loss in value by the market.

There are several methods to estimate accrued depreciation. I have applied the breakdown method as it reflects the manner in which an informed buyer would react to the existing conditions of the subject improvements.

A buyer of an income-producing property is concerned with the age and utility of the structure, and the remaining years the real estate can be expected to produce income before major expenditures must be made for modernization.

The existing improvements are 11 years old and have received better than average maintenance. The construction and design are rated above average. I have estimated the effective age to be 10 years.

Due to all the new construction in Palm Beach, it is imperative for owners to maintain their properties in order to compete with the increasing supply of housing and to maximize their income stream.

I have estimated the total economic life to be 50 years (Source: Marshall Valuation Service).

BREAKDOWN METHOD

CURABLE PHYSICAL DETERIORATION

The following items of physical deterioration were observed:

    Exterior needs painting
    Landscaping needs general work
    Driveway has drainage problems during heavy rains

These items are immediately curable at a cost of approximately
$8,000 (Source: Martin Levine, a general contractor). The
$8,000 figure will not be deducted from the final values arrived
at in the Direct Sales Comparison Approach and Income Approach
as the sale and rental comparables all suffer from minor items
of physical deterioration. These items were taken into
consideration in arriving at the final value estimates in each
approach where adjustments were made for condition.

INCURABLE PHYSICAL DETERIORATION

I have estimated all short-lived and long-lived structural
elements that are not practical or currently feasible to
correct.

Short-Lived Components:

	Replacement Cost*	Effective Age	Useful Life	Depreciation %	Depreciation $
Floor Cover	$16,000	2	6	33%	$ 5,280
Roof Cover	12,000	10	15	67%	8,000
Plumbing	40,000	10	30	33%	13,200
Electrical	30,000	10	30	33%	9,900
Heat & Air Conditioning	30,000	10	25	40%	12,000

Total Incurable Physical Deterioration $48,380
Short-Lived Components:

*source: Steve Martin, General Contractor
         Sharpestimator, Inc.

Long-Lived Components

All remaining components are expected to have a remaining
economic life the same as the entire structure.

$$\frac{\text{Effective Age}}{\text{Economic Life}} = \frac{11}{50} = 22\%$$

I applied this percentage to the replacement cost new ($650,000)
less curable items ($8,000) and incurable components ($128,000),
leaving a replacement cost new of $514,000.

    Then: $514,000 x 22% = $113,080

CURABLE FUNCTIONAL OBSOLESCENCE

I observed no defects in design having an adverse effect on value.

INCURABLE FUNCTIONAL OBSOLESCENCE

The subject property has only 1.5 parking spaces per unit. Multi-family dwellings constructed subsequent to 1990 must have 2 1/2 parking spaces per one-bedroom unit. In the Income Approach, I estimated a rent difference of $10.00 per month attributable to better parking. Therefore, this deficiency can be measured by the gross income loss due to poor parking.

The gross annual income loss is calculated as follows:

10 units x $10.00/month x 12 months = $1,200

The gross income multiplier estimated in the Direct Sales Comparison Approach was 7.4.

Thus, $1,200 x 7.4 = $8,880

Utilization of gross income was considered acceptable as the majority of expenses would not be affected by the deficiency.

EXTERNAL OBSOLESCENCE

I observed no negative influence in the neighborhood or community that would have a significant adverse effect on the property's value.

Summary of Depreciation

Physical Deterioration
Physical Curable, Deferred Maintenance	$ 8,000
Physical Incurable, Short-Lived Items	48,380
Physical Incurable, Long-Lived Items	113,080
Sub-Total	$169,460

Functional Obsolescence:
Functional Curable	0
Functional Incurable	$8,880

External Obsolescence	0
Total Accrued Depreciation	$178,340
Rounded to	$178,340

Summary of Cost Approach

Estimated Replacement Cost New - Improvements	$650,000
Less Accrued Depreciation	(178,340)
Depreciated Value of the Improvements (including site improvements)	$481,660
Estimated Land Value	130,000
Value Indicated via the Cost Approach	$601,660
Rounded to	$602,000
VALUE INDICATED BY COST APPROACH	$602,000

STEPS OF THE SALES COMPARISON APPROACH

In this approach the market value is estimated by comparing the subject property to similar properties in the market which have either recently sold or are being offered for sale.

A great number of sales and listings have been examined in the process of making this appraisal. The most comparable sales have been selected for display in this appraisal report.

An attempt was made to verify information about the comparable sales by contacting the buyers, sellers, real estate brokers and closing attorneys. Special attention was given to verify that the transactions were "arm's length" and that any special conditions and special financing were known by the appraiser.

Since this was an apartment building which in this market customarily is priced based on the number of units, it was considered appropriate to select "Number of Units" as the unit of comparison.

Each comparable property was compared to the subject property and adjustments were made significant difference in the elements of comparisons which resulted in an adjusted price of each comparable giving an indication of the value of the subject.

First, I considered whether a time adjustment was needed. All of the Comparable Sales were this year. The market has been very flat during the past year. No data was available to indicate that a time adjustment was required, therefore no time adjustments were made.

No location adjustments were needed as all of the properties were in the same neighborhood and values are similar throughout the neighborhood.

No age or condition adjustments were needed as all the comparable apartments were built about the same time (10 years to 11 years ago) and they all were in average condition.

An adjustment was needed to reflect the special financing of Comparable Sale #3. It was made considering the points saved, lower monthly payment and the convenience of the special financing.

Adjustments were made for the differences in the number of parking spaces per unit and how the units were air conditioned. These adjustments were derived from the market using the matched pair technique.

Finally, the various indicated subject values produced from the analysis of the comparables were reconciled into an indicated value of the subject property via the sales comparison approach.

COMPARABLES SALE LOCATION MAP

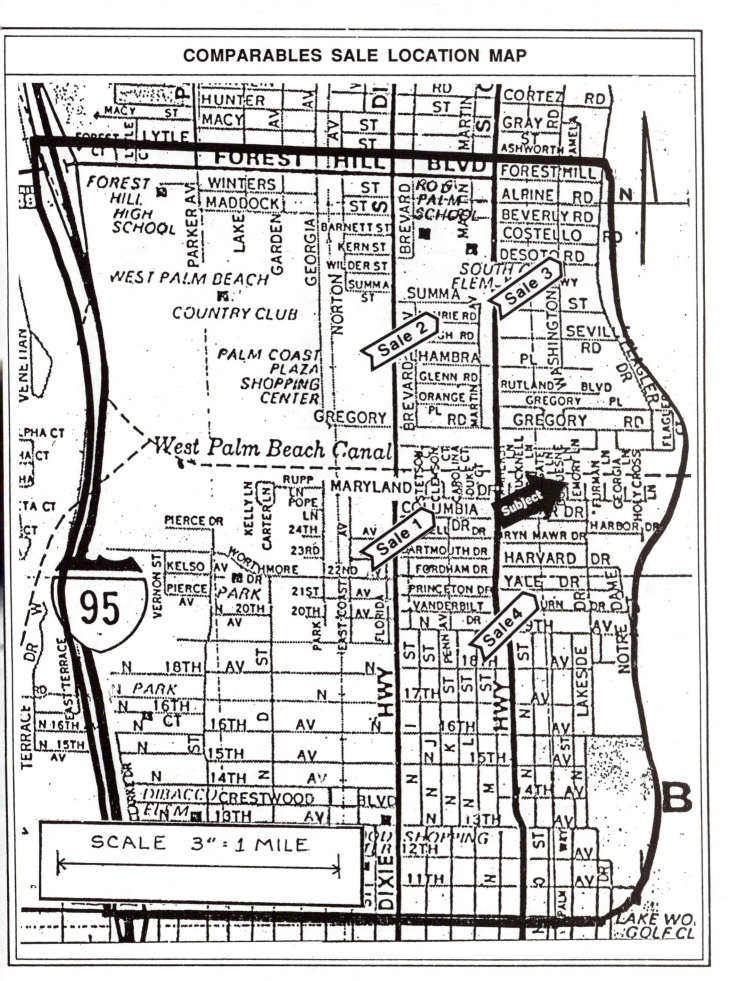

A 63

COMPARABLE SALE NO. 1

Address: 529 Columbia Drive
                                  West Palm Beach, Florida

Grantor: Henry Starin

Grantee: Sttaw Evest

Date of Sale: **April 13, 200_ (this year)**

Sale Price: $960,000

Source of Information: Closing Attorney and Seller

Special Conditions: None reported

Special Financing: None reported

Site Area/Density: 1.2 Acres, 13 units per acre

Location: Six blocks west of subject in
                                  same neighborhood

Description of Improvements

Type of Construction:	One story concrete block building. 13,208 G.B.A.
Year Built:	199_ (11 years ago)
Breakdown of Units:	16 one bedroom apartments, each has one bath. Each apartment is 635 sq. ft.
Description of Interior:	Wall to wall carpeting, typical kitchens & baths, central air conditioning
Condition:	Average
Parking:	16 assigned spaces and 8 guest spaces
Recreation Facilities:	None

Current Rentals:	$660 to $665 per month
Potential Gross Income:	$127,000
Net Operating Income:	$86,822 ($5,426 per apartment)
Overall Capitalization Rate:	.0905
Annual Gross Income Multiplier:	7.52
Sale Price per sq. ft.:	$72.68
Sale Price Per Unit:	$60,000

Address:	376 Gulfstream Road West Palm Beach, FL
Grantor:	L. D'Agostino
Grantee:	Eiluj Nosirrah
Date of Sale:	May 20, 200_ (this year)
Sale Price:	$547,000
Source of Information:	Closing attorney and seller
Special Conditions:	Buyers feel that rents were substantially below market rent. The seller had not raised the rents or visited the property for years prior to the sale
Special Financing:	None reported
Site Area/Density:	1.17 acre, 6.8 units per acre
Location:	Eight blocks north of subject in same neighborhood

Description of Improvements:

Type of Construction: Two story concrete block building. 6,760 sq. ft. G.B.A.

Year Built: **199_ (11 years ago)**

Breakdown of Units: 8 apartments, 8 one bedroom and one bath units, each 650 sq. ft.

Description of Interior: Wall to wall carpeting, typical kitchens & baths, central air conditioning

Condition: Average

Parking: 16 assigned spaces and 8 guest spaces

Recreation Facilities: None

Current Rentals: $775 to $790 per month

Potential Gross Income: $74,880

Net Operating Income: $48,672 ($6,084 per apartment unit)

Overall Capitalization Rate: .0889

Annual Gross Income Multiplier: 7.30

Sale Price per sq. ft. G.B.A.: $80.91

Sale Price per Unit: $68,375

COMPARABLE SALE NO. 3

Address:	47 Desoto Drive West Palm Beach, Florida
Grantor:	Ms. Donna Montagnino
Grantee:	Mr. Richard and Mrs. Jessie Kusmit
Date of Sale:	**September 20, 200_ (this year)**
Sale Price:	$570,000
Source of Information:	Buyer and seller
Special Conditions:	None reported
Special Financing:	Seller took back a $400,000 1st mortgage 8% for 20 years with a balloon payoff at the end of 10 years and no points. The typical mortgage in this market was an 80% mortgage, 20 years at 11% interest with 3 points.
Site Area/Density:	1.17 acre, 6.8 units per acre
Location:	9 blocks north of subject in same neighborhood

Description of Improvements:

Type of Construction: Two two story buildings both concrete block. Total G.B.A. 6,708 sq. ft.

Year Built: 199_ (11 years ago)

Breakdown of Units: 8 apartments:
4 one bedroom & one bath units, each 650 sq. ft.
4 one bedroom & one bath units, each 640 sq. ft.

Description of Interior: Wall to wall carpeting, typical kitchens & baths, central air conditioning

Condition: Average

Parking: 16 assigned spaces and 8 guest spaces

Recreation Facilities: None

Current Rentals: $800 to $825 per month

Potential Gross Income: $77,760

Net Operating Income: $52,876 ($6,690 per apartment)

Overall Capitalization Rate: .0927

Annual Gross Income Multiplier: 7.33

Sale Price per sq. ft. G.B.A.: $84.97

Sale Price per Unit: $71,250

COMPARABLE SALE NO. 4

Address:	16 Yale Drive West Palm Beach, Florida
Grantor:	Roger & Vera Whait
Grantee:	Olive N Court Properties, a Connecticut Partnership
Sale Price:	$738,500
Source of Information:	Realtor who sold property and manages it prior to sale
Special Conditions:	None reported
Special Financing:	New 80% conventional mortgage
Site Area/Density:	1.17 acre, 6.8 units per acre
Location:	Five blocks south of subject in same neighborhood

Description of Improvements:

Type of Construction: One story concrete block
                          building.   Total 10,046 G.B.A.

Year Built: 199_ (10 years ago)

Breakdown of Units: 12 apartments, 12 one bedroom &
                          one bath units, each 644 sq.
                          ft.

Description of Interior: Wall to wall carpeting, typical
                          kitchens & baths, window air
                          conditioning units owned by
                          tenants

Condition: Average

Parking: 24 assigned spaces & 12 guest
                          spaces

Recreation Facilities: None

Current Rentals: $760 to $770 per month

Potential Gross Income: $110,160

Net Operating Income: $71,640 ($5,970 per apartment)

Overall Capitalization Rate: .0970

Annual Gross Income Multiplier: 6.70

Sale Price per sq. ft. G.B.A.: $73.50

Sale Price per Unit: $61,541

EXPLANATION OF ADJUSTMENTS
PARKING ADJUSTMENT

The subject unit is in a high density zone that requires only 2,000 sq. ft. of site per unit. It restricts the available parking to one parking space per unit plus an additional 1/2 parking space for guests. Comparable Sales #2, #3 and #4 are low density zone and there is room for 2 parking spaces per unit plus 1 guest space per unit.

Comparable Sale #1 was similar to Comparable Sale #2 except for the number of parking spaces per unit. (It was not considered proper to also adjust for the density difference as this would be double adjusting for the same difference.)

Comparable Sale #1 (1 1/2 parking spaces per unit)
    Sale price per unit $60,000

Comparable Sale #2 (2 1/2 parking spaces per unut) $68,375

Parking Adjustment (1 1/2 spaces vs. 2 2/1 spaces) $8,000 RD

SPECIAL FINANCING ADJUSTMENT
COMPARABLE SALE #3

Adjustment for 3 points
    $400,000 x .03 = $12,000

Adjustment for below market

Typical Mortgage
    $40,000, 20 yrs, 11% calculates
    to have monthly payments of   4,128.76

Special Financing
    $400,000 20 yrs (10 year balloon)
    8% calculates to have monthly
    payments of   3,345.76

Monthly Savings   783.00

Present Value of $783 per month for
    10 years at 11% market interest rate $56,842.00

Adjustment for saving 3 points   12,000.00

Estimated total dollars saved by
    special financing $68,842

I have also considered the convenience of having
a purchase money mortgage and then estimated the
appropriate financing adjustment to be $70,000
or $8,750 per apartment unit ($70,000 / 8).

AIR CONDITIONING ADJUSTMENT

The subject property has central air conditioning. Some of the
comparable sales do not. Below is how an adjustment was
estimated from the market data available to make an appropriate
per unit air conditioning adjustment.

Comparable Sale #2 and Comparable Sale #4 were similar except
for the number of units and the air conditioning. In Comparable
Sale #2 each unit had a central air conditioning owned by the
landlord. In Comparable Sale #4 window units were owned by the
tenants.

The appropriate air conditioning adjustment was estimated as
follows:

Comparable Sale #2 (central air conditioning)
    Sale price per unit $ 64,125

Comparable Sale #4 (no central air conditioning)
    Sale price per unit   61,541

Air Conditioning Adj. $ 2,584
                                                 ($2,500 RD)

ANALYSIS AND ADJUSTMENT OF SALES DATA

The four sales analyzed in detail on the preceding pages were chosen among many recent apartment building sales. These four sales required the fewest adjustments for difference with respect to the appraised property.

The analysis of these sales produced the following ranges:

G.I.M.	7.30	to	7.52
O.A.R.	.0889	to	.0970
Sale Price/Square Foot	$72.68	to	$84.97
Adjusted Sale Price/Unit	$54,500	to	$60,375

The use of a G.I.M. (Gross Income Multiplier) is valid only for types of properties that are reasonably consistent in net-to-gross income operating ratio and sell with sufficient frequency in the market to produce a descernible pattern.

The G.I.M. is closely related to market action. Its principal advantage is that the reflection of income is direct. Therefore, differences in age, condition, location, and physical characteristics do not require adjustment as these factors have been resolved by the free action of the rental market.

I have given about equal weight to all four sales and selected 7.4 as the gross income multiplier for the subject property.

The potential gross income estimated in the Income Approach was $39,600.

Then: $81,000 x 7.4 = $599,400 rounded to $600,000

The development of an O.A.R. (Overall Capitalization Rate) will be utilized in the Income Approach.

The sale price per square foot ranged fom $72.68 to $84.97. I selected $80.00 for the subject property.

Then: 6,576 sq. ft. x $80.00 = $526,000

This was not considered to be a very good indicator of value as it did not consider the significant adjustments that were made for parking and special financing.

COMPARABLE SALE ADJUSTMENT GRID

COMPARABLE SALES ADJUSTMENT GRID

(All adjustments made on basis of number of apartments unit of comparison)

	Appraised Property	Comparable Sale #1	Comparable Sale #2	Comparable Sale #3	Comparable Sale #4
ADDRESS	700 Duquesne Dr West Palm Beach	529 Columbia Dr W Palm Beach	376 Gulfstream Rd W Palm Beach	47 Desoto Dr W Palm Beach	16 Yale Dr W Palm Beach
SALE PRICE	No sale pending	$960,000	$547,000	$570,000	$738,500
NUMBER OF APARTMENTS	10	16	8	8	12
SALE PRICE PER APARTMENT	---	$60,000	$68,375	$71,250	$61,541
DATE OF SALE	12/16/0_ (This Year)	04/13/0_ (This Year)	05/20/0_ (This Year)	09/20/0_ (This Year)	06/08/0_ (This Year)
SPECIAL FINANCING	None	None -0-	None -0-	Purchase money mortgage -8,750	None -0-
SPECIAL CONDITIONS	None	None -0-	None -0-	None -0-	None -0-
CONDITION	Average	Same -0-	Same -0-	Same -0-	Same -0-
LOCATION	West Palm Beach Canal	Same -0-	Same -0-	Same -0-	Same -0-
PARKING	1 1/2 spaces per apt. unit	1 1/2 spaces per apt -0-	2 1/2 spaces per apt -$8,000	2 1.2 spaces per apt -$8,000	2 1/2 spaces per apt -$8,000
AIR CONDITIONING	Central	Central -0-	Central -0-	Central -0-	Central -0-
					Tenant owned window units +$2,500
TOTAL ADJ.	---	-0-	-$8,000	-$16,750	-$5,500
ADJ SALE PRICE PER APT UNIT	---	$60,000	$60,375	$54,500	$56,041

SUMMARY OF SALES COMPARISON APPROACH

The best indication of the value of the subject is the sale price per unit. The following adjustment grid displays each sale and how they were adjusted for special financing, parking and air conditioning. No adjustments were needed for time or location.

The four adjusted sales prices ranged from $54,500 to $60,375. Comparable Sale #1 was most similar to the subject and in fact required no adjustments. $60,000 per unit was selected as the indicated value of the subject property.

Then: $60,000 x 10 units = $600,000.

This is well supported by the $600,000 value indicated by the gross income multiplier.

VALUE INDICATED VIA DIRECT SALES COMPARISON APPROACH $600,000

INCOME APPROACH

This type of property is typically purchased as an investment. Therefore, the earning power of the property is an important element affecting its value. An investor who purchases this property is essentially trading his or her present dollars for an income stream of future dollars plus the return of their investment at some date in the future.

STEPS OF THE INCOME APPROACH

The steps of the Income Approach using direct capitalization are summarized as follows:

1.   Estimate the Potential Gross Income (P.G.I.) of the property.

2.   Add any additional income from sources other than rent.

3.   Subtract the typical annual amount of income that will not be collected because of vacancies and collection problems.

4.   The result is the Effective Gross Income (E.G.I.).

5.   Subtract from the E.G.I., operating expenses, fixed expenses and reserves for the replacement of short lived items.

6.   The result is the Net Operating Income (N.O.I.).

7.   Develop a direct capitalization rate by dividing the known N.O.I.'s of properties that have sold that are comparable to the subject property by the selling price of the Comparable Sale. Reconcile them into one rate appropriate for the subject property.

8.   Divide the N.O.I. of the property being appraised by the appropriate capitalization rate which gives an indicated value of the property via the Income Approach.

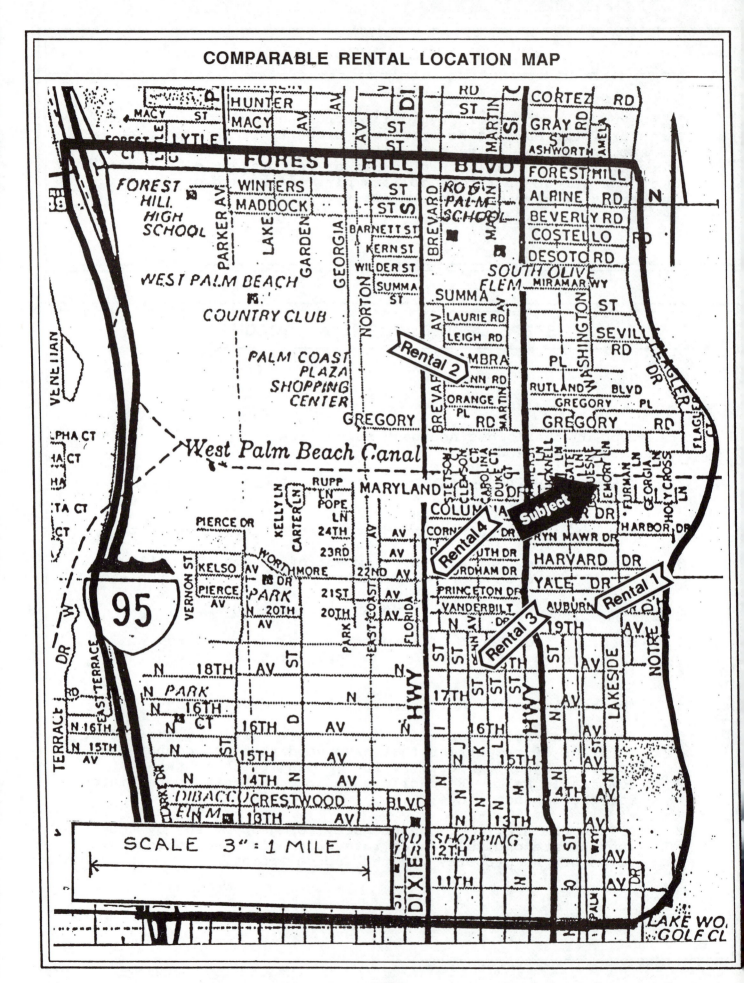

COMPARABLE RENTAL NO. 1

Address:	Auburn Road West Palm Beach, Florida
Location:	Seven blocks south of the subject in the same neighborhood
Source of information:	Exchange Court Properties
Number of units:	12 units each with one bedroom and one bath
Year built/Condition:	199_ (10 **years ago**) / **Average**
Type of construction:	Two story concrete block building, central air conditioning
Parking:	1.5 cars per apartment unit
Apartment sizes:	625 to 650 sq. ft.
Vacancy history:	Usually full. One unit available for January rental
Current rents:	$550 to $575 no utilities or furniture
Monthly Rent per sq. ft.:	$.88 to $.92
Remarks:	View of Lake Worth from side

Address:	165 Glen Road West Palm Beach, Florida
Location:	Six blocks south of the subject in the same neighborhood
Source of information:	Jancie Franklin
Number of units:	12 units each with one bedroom and one bath
Year built/Condition:	199_ (12 years ago) / Average
Type of construction:	Two story concrete block building, central air condition
Parking:	1.5 cars per apartment unit
Apartment sizes:	625 to 660 sq. ft.
Vacancy history:	Usually full
Current rents:	$575 no utilities or furniture
Monthly rent per sq. ft.:	$.88
Remarks:	None

COMPARABLE RENTAL NO. 3

Address:	156 18th St. corner of K St. West Palm Beach, Florida
Location:	Nine blocks southwest of the subject in the same neighborhood
Source of information:	James Dew
Number of units:	20 units each with one bedroom and one bath
Year built/Condition:	199_ (11 years ago) / Average
Type of construction:	Two story concrete block building
Parking:	1.5 cars per apartment unit
Apartment sizes:	640 to 660 sq. ft.
Vacancy history:	Approximately 3%
Current rents:	$625 to $650 no utilities or furniture
Monthly rent per sq. ft.:	$.98 to $1.02
Remarks:	There are two tennis courts and a swimming pool on the site

COMPARABLE RENTAL NO. 4

Address:	Sherwood Villas 1755 Fordham Drive West Palm Beach, Florida
Location:	Five blocks southwest of the subject in the same neighborhood
Source of information:	Captain Edward Fink
Number of units:	36 units each with one bedroom and one bath
Year built/Condition:	199_ (12 years ago) / Average
Type of construction:	Concrete block buildings
Parking:	1.5 cars per apartment unit
Apartment sizes:	625 to 675 sq. ft.
Vacancy history:	Approximately 4%
Current rents:	$550 to $575 no utilities or furniture
Monthly rent per sq. ft.:	$.81 to $.96
Remarks:	Coin operated laundry facilities on the premises

EXPLANATION OF ADJUSTMENTS

RENTAL ADJUSTMENT FOR POOL AND COURTS

The subject unit does not have a swimming pool or tennis courts. Comparable Rental No. 3 has a swimming pool and two tennis courts. An appropriate adjustment for a swimming pool and tennis courts was estimated by comparing Comparable Rental No. 3 with Comparable Rental No. 2. The only significant difference between these apartment units were the availability of a swimming pool and two tennis courts.

Monthly Rental Comparable Rental No. 2
    (no swimming pool or tennis court) $575 to $600

Monthly Rental Comparable Rental No. 3
    (swimming pool and two tennis courts) $625 to $650

Estimated rental difference attributable
to availability of swimming pool and
tennis courts $50

AIR CONDITIONING ADJUSTMENT

The subject property has central air conditioning. Some of the comparable sales do not. Below is how an adjustment was estimated from the market data available to make an appropriate per unit air conditioning adjustment.

Comparable Sale #2 and Comparable Sale #4 were similar except for the number of units and the air conditioning. In Comparable Sale #2 each unit had a central air conditioning owned by the landlord. In Comparable Sale #4 window units were owned by the tenants.

The appropriate air conditioning adjustment was estimated as follows:

Comparable Sale #2 (central air conditioning)
    Sale price per unit $ 64,125

Comparable Sale #4 (no central air conditioning)
    (Sale price per unit   61,541

Air Conditioning Adj. $ 2,584
                               ($2,500 RD)

PARKING ADJUSTMENT

The subject unit is in a high density zone that requires only 2,000 sq. ft. of site per unit. It restricts the available parking to one parking space per unit plus an additional 1/2 parking space for guests. Comparable Sales #2, #3 and #4 are low density zone and there is room for 2 parking spaces per unit plus 1 guest space per unit.

Comparable Sale #1 was similar to Comparable Sale #2 except for the number of parking spaces per unit. (It was not considered proper to also adjust for the density difference as this would be double adjusting for the same difference.)

Comparable Sale #1 (1 1/2 parking spaces per unit)
    Sale price per unit $60,000

Comparable Sale #2 (2 1/2 parking spaces per unut)   <u>$68,375</u>

Parking Adjustment (1 1/2 spaces vs. 2 2/1 spaces) $8,000 RD

COMPARABLE SALE #3

SPECIAL FINANCING ADJUSTMENT

Adjustment for 3 points
    $400,000 x .03 = $12,000

Adjustment for below market

Typical Mortgage
    $40,000, 20 yrs, 11% calculates
    to have monthly payments of   4,128.76

Special Financing
    $400,000 20 yrs (10 year balloon)
    8% calculates to have monthly
    payments of   <u>3,345.76</u>

Monthly Savings   783.00

Present Value of $783 per month for
    10 years at 11% market interest rate $56,842.00

Adjustment for saving 3 points   <u>12,000.00</u>

Estimated total dollars saved by
    special financing $68,842

I have also considered the convenience of having a purchase money mortgage and then estimated the appropriate financing adjustment to be $70,000 or $8,750 per apartment unit ($70,000 / 8).

ANALYSIS OF COMPARABLE RENTALS

Because there are many one bedroom rental apartments in this market, I was able to obtain comparable rentals that required few adjustments. They all were current rentals so no time adjustment was required. They are all in the same neighborhood so no location adjustments were needed. The only significant difference in physical characteristics between them was that Comparable Rental No. 3 had a swimming pool and two tennis courts. Using the matched pair technique, an adjustment of $50 per unit was estimated for the tennis courts and a swimming pool.

The rentals ranged from $560 to $725 per month without utilities or furniture. The units that rented for $600 or more either had parking for 2.5 cars per apartment unit or a swimming pool and tennis courts.

The rental range for apartments similar to the subject with 1.5 parking spaces per unit and without a swimming pool or tennis courts was $560 to $575.

The owner reported that she was getting $675 per month from each tenant on the anniversary of their renewal. This was confirmed by the rental data to be market rent.

ESTIMATE OF POTENTIAL GROSS INCOME

The first step is to estimate the potential gross income from all sources assuming the property is under competent management.

The following rental information has been obtained from four apartment properties judged to be comparable and competitive with the appraised property. Common to all the rentals is that tenants pay for all utilities except cold water.

First, the rentals of the four comparable sales were considered. Added to these were the rentals of four other apartment buildings in the neighborhood which had not been recently sold. All these rentals were adjusted and reconciled into estimated market rentals of the subject units which when totaled produce the estimated potential gross income.

EXPLANATION OF EXPENSES

In estimating the anticipated expenses for the appraised property, I have analyzed the actual expenses furnished to me and operating statements for similar properties in the area.

Vacancy &
Collection
Loss
The appraised property has experienced a vacancy level similar to comparable buildings in the area of 1% to 3%. It is my opinion that with competent management, the current rental rates can be maintained in line with the strong occupancy levels and development trends in the market area without experiencing undue vacancy and collection losses. A vacancy and collection loss factor of 3% has been utilized.

Real Estate
Taxes
Current taxes are $7,572.56 and have been gradually increasing over the past four years. Based upon comparable properties and my tax analysis, I have stabilized this expense at $7,700 per year.

Insurance
The cost for insurance at the subject property was $1,000. In comparison to similar buildings, this figure falls within an acceptable range.

Management
A survey of local real estate managers revealed management fees range from 4% to 5% of gross income collected. Based upon the comparable properties, the current management fee of 4% is reasonable and acceptable.

Water/Septic
Actual costs have been utilized and include salt for the water softener and annual pumping of the septic tank.

Electricity
The actual charge for electricity was $288. This figure has been increased somewhat to $300 in the stabilized operating statement.

Trash Removal
The actual cost (contract) was $1,200. This fee is not expected to increase during the next year.

Grounds	The actual cost of maintaining the grounds was $160 per month. This cost appears reasonable and in line with other such known costs at similar developments.
Maintenance & Repairs	Items included in this category include interior and exterior maintenance of the property, supplies, subcontractor's fees, and painting and redecorating. It has been estimated that the subject property will require an average annual maintenance expense of $3,000 or approximately $300 per unit.
Miscellaneous	This category includes any minor interior operating costs such as exterminating or petty cash items. Amounts in this category may vary considerably relative to management practices. However, an amount of $600 per year has been estimated for a property of this size.
Replacement Allowance	It is customary in this locale to account for replacing short-lived items. Based on the replacement costs arrived at in the Cost Approach and the following life expectancies, this expense has been estimated as follows:

Item	$\dfrac{\text{Cost}}{\text{Life Expectancy}}$	=	Allowance
Appliances	$\dfrac{\$16,000}{10 \text{ yrs.}}$		$1,600
Carpeting	$\dfrac{\$16,000}{6 \text{ yrs.}}$		$2,660
Roof	$\dfrac{\$12,000}{15 \text{ yrs.}}$		$ 800
Heat and A/C	$\dfrac{\$30,000}{25 \text{ yrs.}}$		$1,200
Total Replacement Allowance			$6,266

RECONSTRUCTED OPERATING STATEMENT

Potential Gross Income (10 units x $675/mo. x 12) = $81,000

Less Vacancy & Collection Loss (3%)   (2,430)

Effective Gross Income $78,570

Less Operating Expenses:

Fixed:			
Real Estate Taxes	$ 7,700		
Insurance	1,000		
Sub-Total		$ 8,700	
Variable:			
Management (4% of E.G.I.)	$ 3,143		
Water/Septic	400		
Electricity	300		
Trash Removal	1,200		
Grounds Maintenance	1,200		
Maintenance & Repairs	3,000		
Miscellaneous	600		
Sub-Total		$ 9,843	
Replacement Allow.(Reserves)	$ 6,266		
Sub-Total		$ 6,266	

Total Operating Expenses   32%
(operating expense ratio = 32% of E.G.I.) $24,809

Net Operating Income $53,761

Capitalization Process

The final step in the Income Approach is to capitalize the net operating income into an indication of value. Two methods are available: direct capitalization and yield capitalization.

The major difference between direct capitalization and yield capitalization is that the former does not make an allocation between return on and return of capital. However, a satisfactory rate of return is implicit in the rates derived from the market data.

Direct capitalization converts one year's income into a value indication either by dividing the income by a capitalization rate of multiplying it by a factor derived from the market.

I have derived an overall capitalization rate from the comparable market sales used in the Sales Comparison Approach. A replacement allowance has been deducted as an operating expense for each sale.

Comparable Sale	1	2	3	4
Sale Price	$960,000	$513,000	$510,000	$738,500
Net Oper. Income	$ 86,822	$48,672	$ 52,876	$ 71,640
Indicated O.A.R.	.0905	.0889	.0927	.0970

Most weight was given to Comparable Sale #1 as it had the same parking ratio and central air conditioning. The other Comparable Sales required adjustments for those items. Comparable Sale #3 also required adjustment for special financing. I selected an overall capitalization rate of .09 for the subject property.

Value = Net Operating Income
           Overall Capitaization Rate

Value = $53,761   = $597,344
            .09

A Gross Income Multiplier has also been utilized in this appraisal report. This multiplier was developed in the Direct Sales Comparison Approach to be 7.4. The potential gross income is $81,000, thus:

7.4 x $81,000 = $599,400

As previously explained good income and expense data was available. The final estimate by the Income Approach was $598,000.

RECONCILIATION AND FINAL VALUE ESTIMATE

Value Indicated via Cost Approach $602,000

Value Indicated via Direct Sales
     Comparison Approach $600,000

Value Indicated via Income Approach $598,000

Reconcilation is the step in the valuation process in which the relative significance, applicability, and defensibility of each value indication is weighed. The final conclusion of value is based upon the appropriateness, accuracy, and quality of evidence contained in the appraisal.

The appraised property is improved with an 11 year old, ten unit, rental apartment building in good condition. The property is located in a well established, residential neighborhood, within convenient distance from employment, education, recreation, and shopping facilities. The economic and demographic data of the community has been carefully analyzed. Considering the projected population growth and per-capita income, it is reasonable to expect continued high occupancy levels and the ability of the subject proeprty to command competitive rental rates.

The existing improvements are a legal use. It has been concluded that the highest and best use of the property is the continued use as a ten-unit rental apartment building.

The comparable data found in this appraisal was chosen from a large quantity of data. Data was considered in addition to the data displayed in the report.

All three approaches to value have been developed in this appraisal report. The Cost Approach indicated a value of $602,000, the Direct Sales Comparison indicated a value of $600,000, and Income Approaches indicated a value of $598,000. Although there are no great differences to resolve among the value indications, greater confidence has been placed in the Income and Direct Sales Comparison Approaches.

The major weaknesses of the Cost Approach were (1) the lack of multi-family land sales having a similar density of development when compared to the appraised site, and (2) the difficulty in estimating accrued depreciation of an 11-year old building. Therefore, this approach was used as a guide and check on the values estimated by the other two approaches.

The Direct Sales Comparison Approach was considered appropriate and accurate. The comparable sales were judged to be valid and reliable indicators of market value. The quantity of evidence provided by each comparable was sufficient. The few adjustments that were made were derived from the market. These sales reflect the actions of typical buyers for this type of property and, therefore, led to a logical and well documented conclusion of value.

The Income Approach is considered to be the most applicable method for estimating market value as the subject property is income-producing. The quality of the comparable rental data was particularly good and resulted in a reliable gross income estimate. A reconstructed operating statement was developed based upon expense data obtained from the subject property and from similar properties. The final step was to convert the net operating income into an estimate of value. This process is known as capitalization. Most investment properties in this market are financed with conventional 20 year mortgages at market rates of interest. Typical mortgages are 75% to 80% of the value of the property. With this type of homogeneous financing, direct capitalization gives the best indication of the value of a property being appraised.

As a result of my appraisal and analysis, giving most weight to the Income and Direct Sales Comparison Approaches, and considering all other available facts and circumstances pertinent to an estimate of value, it is my opinion that the estimated market value of the appraised property, as of December 15, 200_ ,is:

SIX HUNDRED THOUSAND ($600,000) DOLLARS

PART FIVE

ADDENDA

SUGGESTED READING

BOOKS AND PAMPHLETS

American Institute of Real Estate Appraisers, Chicago, IL:

-*Appraising the Single Family Residence* by George Bloom and Henry S. Harrison, 1980.

-*The Appraisal of Real Estate*, 9th Edition, 1988.

-*The Condominium Appraisal Report in Communicating the Appraisal* by Arlen Mills, 1988.

-*Historic Properties: Preservation and The Valuation Process*, 1982.

-*The Narrative Report in Communicating the Appraisal Series*, 1988.

-*The Uniform Residential Appraisal Report in Communicating the Appraisal* by Arlen Mills, 1988.

-*Valuing the Time Share Property* by Kathleen Conroy, 1981.

Harrison, Henry S.:

-*Environmental Manual* with the National Association of Environmental Risk Auditors, The H^2 Company, New Haven, CT, 1990.

-*Environmental Risk Screening* with the National Association of Environmental Risk Auditors, The H^2 Company, New Haven, CT, 1990.

-*Harrisons' Illustrated Dictionary of Real Estate Appraisal*, Collegiate Companies, New Haven, CT, 1986.

-*Houses, The Illustrated Guide to Construction, Design and Systems*, rev. ed., Realtors National Marketing Institute, Chicago, IL, 1976.

-*Houses Cook Book* with Ruth D. Lambert, Forms and Worms, Inc., New Haven, CT, 1988.

-*Homebuying* with Margery B. Leonard, Realtors National Marketing Institute, Chicago, IL, 1980.

-Illustrated Guide Freddie Mac - Fannie Mae Series, The H^2 Company, New Haven, CT,
  Single Family Residential Appraisal Report   *1988*
  Small Income Properties   *1990*
  Individual Condominium Unit   *1988*

-*Review Appraiser's Handbook*, The H^2 Company, New Haven, CT, 1990.

Laurenti, Luigi. Property Values and Race: *Studies in Seven Cities.* Berkeley, CA University of California Press, 1960.

O'Flaherty, John D. "An Appraiser's Dilemma: The Cost Approach Value," The Real Estate Appraiser, January-February, 1969.

Smith, Halbert C. *Real Estate Appraisal.* Columbus, Ohio: Grid Publishing, 1976.

Building Cost Manuals

Boeckh Building Valuation Manual, Milwaukee: American Appraisal Co., 3 vols.
Vol. 1 - *Residential and Agricultural*; Vol. 2 - *Commercial*;
Vol. 3 - *Industrial and Institutional*. Includes wide variety of building models. Built up from unit-in-place costs converted to cost per square foot of floor or ground area. Boeckh Building Cost Modifier is published bimonthly for updating with current modifiers.

Building Construction Cost Data. Duxbury, Mass.: Robert Snow Means Co., annual.
Lists average unit prices on many building construction items for use in engineering estimates. Components arranged according to uniform system adopted by the American Institute of Architects, Associated General Constractors, and Construction Specification Institute.

Dodge Building Cost Calculator & Valuation Guide. New York: McGraw-Hill Information Systems Co.
(looseleaf service, quarterly supplements).
Lists building costs for common types and sizes of buildings.
Local cost modifiers and historical local cost index tables included. Formerly Dow Building Cost Calculator.

Marshall Valuation Service. 1617 Beverly Boulevard, Los Angeles, CA 90026:
Marshall and Swift Publication Co.
(looseleaf service, monthly supplements).
Cost Data for determining replacement costs of buildings and other improvements in the United States and Canada. Includes current cost multipliers and local modifiers.

Residential Cost Handbook. 1617 Beverly Boulevard, Los Angeles, CA 90026:
Marshall and Swift Publication Co.
(looseleaf service, quarterly supplements).
Presents square-foot method and segregated-cost method. Local modifiers and cost-trend modifiers included.

Mathematics & Statistics

Today, appraising all types of properties requires the use of a wide variety of mathematical techniques ranging from simple arithmetic through the use of algebraic formulas and the statistical techniques of stepwise multiple regression analyses. Often adding, subtracting, multiplying and dividing can be done with pencil and paper or a simple calculator. More sophisticated calculators are helpful for solving algebraic formulas and some linear regression analysis. Computers are required for almost all stepwise multiple regression analysis. The use of statistics is rapidly becoming an effective tool with which to make and support the value of all types of property and to better understand available data.

BASIC ARITHMETIC

Data is the information that is collected in the market and analyzed in the appraisal process to produce an estimate of value. Types of data include building dimensions, population figures, reproduction costs, rentals and sales among many others. The numbers that represent this data can be processed to produce other numbers or results. There are four basis arithmetic operations known as addition, subtraction, multiplication and division.

Addition is the process of adding two or more numbers together to produce the *sum* of the numbers. The symbol for addition is a plus sign (+).

   Example: $120 + $135 + $130 = $385.

Subtraction is the process of deducting one number from another to produce the *difference* between the numbers. The symbol for subtraction is a minus sign (-).

   Example: 93 inches − 10 inches = 83 inches

Multiplication is the process of multiplying one number, the *multiplicand*, by another number, the *multiplier*, to produce a result which is called the product. The multiplier is also sometimes known as a *coefficient*. The symbols for multiplication are a times sign (x) or a period (•). In algebra it is also a sign to multiply when one number is inside a bracket and the other is outside the bracket.

> Example: $4 \times 5 = 20$
> $6 • 7 = 42$
> $8(9) = 72$

In the above examples 4 could be called the coefficient of 5; 6 the coefficient of 7; and 8 the coefficient of 9.

When a series of different multiplicands are multiplied by the same multiplier, that multiplier is also known as a *constant*.

> Example: $6 \times 7 = 42$
> $6 \times 8 = 48$
> $6 \times 14 = 84$

In this example, 6 can be called a multiplier, coefficient or constant. In algebra the symbol for a constant is "k."

When a series of numbers is multiplied by each other, the results are the same no matter in what sequence the numbers are multiplied.

> Example: $6 • 4 • 8 = 192$
> $8 \times 6 \times 4 = 192$
> $6(8) \times 4 = 192$

Division is the process of dividing one number, the *dividend*, by another number, the *divisor*, to produce a result which is called a *quotient*. The symbol for division is (÷) or a line placed under the dividend and over the divisor.

> Example: $18 \div 9 = 2$
> $\dfrac{20}{5} = 4$

In the above examples, 18 and 20 are the dividends and 9 and 5 are the divisors and 2 and 4 are the quotients. The number 20 is also known as the *numerator* and 5 the *denominator* when the numbers are shown as a fraction. Therefore, the value of a fraction is found by dividing the numerator by the denominator.

RULES FOR PROCESSING NUMBERS

- In addition and multiplication the order of the numbers does not affect the results.
- In subtraction the order of the numbers does make a difference in the results.
- In division the sequence of the numbers may affect the results.
- When a series of operations is performed, the ones within brackets (grouping symbols) are done first.

> Example: $2 (4 + 6) \times (6 - 2) =$
> $2 (10) \times (4) =$
> $20 \times 4 = 80$

- When there are brackets within brackets, the innermost operations are done first.

$$\text{Example:} \quad 2\left[(8 + 2) + (6 - 3)\right] =$$
$$2\left[(10) + (3)\right] =$$
$$2\left[13\right] = 26$$

- When there are no grouping symbols, all the multiplication and division operations are performed before the addition and subtraction operations.

$$\text{Example:} \quad 4 \times 5 \div 2 \times 10 + 12 =$$
$$20 \div 2 \times 10 + 12 =$$
$$10 \times 10 + 12 =$$
$$100 + 12 = 112$$
$$\text{or}$$
$$3 \times 6 + 9 \div 3 - 10 =$$
$$18 + 3 - 10 = 11$$

There are many more rules that apply to the addition, subtraction, multiplication and division operations that cover what to do when the signs are different, how to use absolute numbers, fractions, etc. These are beyond the scope of this introductory material.

RATIOS

Ratios are the result of dividing one number by another number. The three different ways to express a ratio are as a whole number (integer), decimal figure or fraction.

Example: In a community school there is a ratio of 58 students to 2 teachers.

The ratio of 58 to 2 is $58 \div 2 = 29$

The ratio of 2 to 58 is $2 \div 58 = .0345$ (rounded)

The ratio of 2 to 58 is $\dfrac{2}{58} = \dfrac{1}{29}$

PERCENTAGES

Percentages are ratios multiplied by 100 (or expressed on a base of 100).

Continuing the above example:

$\dfrac{2}{58} = .0345 \times 100 = 3.45\%$ of a teacher for each student.

RATES

Rates are percentages expressed in terms of a time period. $8.00 interest per year on $100 principal = 8% interest per year; $.50 interest per month on $100 = .005 or 1/2% interest per month.

DECIMALS

Decimals are added, subtracted, multiplied and divided similar to the way whole numbers (integers) are with some additional rules being applied. When decimals are added and subtracted, the number of places to the right of the decimal point is equal to the largest number of places in any of the numbers being added or subtracted.

Example:
$$
\begin{array}{r}
242.071 \\
+ \quad 63.12 \\
+ \quad 4.2 \\
+ \quad 2.7983 \\
\hline
312.1893
\end{array}
$$

$$
\begin{array}{r}
621.0037 \\
- \quad 11.02 \\
\hline
609.9837
\end{array}
$$

When decimals are multiplied, the number of places to the right of the decimal point is the total number of places to the right of the decimal point in the numbers being multiplied.

Example: $3.23 \times 7.459 = 24.09257$
$17.31 \times 6.9 \times 41.27 = 4929.24753$

This does not mean the number cannot be rounded in the appraisal process.

When decimals are divided, the decimal points in the dividend (numerator) and divisor (denominator) are moved to the right to make the divisor a whole number (integer); the decimal point is moved the same number of places and in the same direction in both numbers.

Example: $896.487 \div 57.31 =$

$$57.31 \, \overline{)896.487}$$

$$5731 \, \overline{)89648.7} \quad \overset{15.64 \text{ (rd.)}}{}$$

ALGEBRA

The same rules that apply to basic arithmetic apply to algebra. The main difference is that in algebra letters and symbols are used together with numbers.

Algebra makes use of equations to solve problems. An equation is a statement of fact that a number or group of quantities on one side of an equal sign is equal to another quantity or group of quantities on the opposite side of the equal sign.

Example: $6 + 10 = 16$
$12 - 8 = 3 + 1$
$44 + (5 + 4) = 53$
$15 + (6 \times 5) = 25 + (5 \times 4)$

$$\frac{200}{20} = 10$$

$$\sqrt{36} = 3 \times 2$$

$$(\frac{12}{3} + 1)(11 - 1) = (7 \times 8) - 6$$

The most important rule in solving equations is that with every change in the statement of the equation the integrity or accuracy of the equation must always be maintained. One side of the equation must always equal the other side.

There are three laws or rules that illustrate the application of symbols.

1. The commutative laws state that as with regular addition the sum of two or more symbols is the same no matter in what order they are added together.

Example: $2 + 4 + 10 = 10 + 4 + 2$
$16 = 16$
or
$X + Y + Z = Y + Z + X$

The commutative laws state that as with regular multiplication the product of two or more symbols is the same no matter in what order they are multiplied by each other.

Example: $8 \times 12 \times 5 = 12 \times 5 \times 8$
$480 = 480$
or
$X \cdot Y \cdot Z = Z \cdot X \cdot Y$

2. The associative laws state that as with regular addition and multiplication when brackets are used the operations within the brackets are always performed first. When two or more brackets are used, the operation within the innermost bracket is performed first and then each outer one is performed successively.

Example: $5 \cdot (6 + 3) + 12 - 10 =$
$5 \cdot (9) + 12 - 10 \quad =$
$45 + 12 - 10 \quad\quad = 47$
or
$18 + [(5 \cdot 9) - (18 - 3) + (4 \times 5)] =$
$18 + [(45) - (15) + (20)] \quad =$
$18 + [50] \quad\quad =$
$18 + 50 \quad\quad\quad = 68$
or
$X + (Y + Z) = (X + Y) + Z$
or
$X \cdot (Y \cdot Z) = (X \cdot Y) \cdot Z$

3. The distributive law states that the number or symbol outside the bracket is actually multiplied by each number or symbol within the bracket.

Example: $8 (4 + 12) =$
Can be solved:
$$= 8(16)$$
$$= 8 \cdot 16$$
$$= 128$$

but according to the distributive law may also be solved:

$$8 (4 + 12) = 32 + 96 = 128$$

or using symbols:

$$X (Y + Z) = XY + XZ$$

(Each symbol within the bracket is multiplied by the symbol outside the bracket).

In algebra in order to solve equations it is necessary to simplify them.   The commutative, associative and distributive laws are used for this process.

Example of simplification using the commutative law:

$$10 + (2Y + 3Y + 6Y) = 10 + 11Y$$

Example of simplification using the associative law:

$$(7 + 8X) + 3X = 7 + (3X + 8X)$$

This same equation can be simplified using the distributive law:

$$(7 + 8X) + 3X = 7 + (8 + 3)X$$
$$= 7 + 11X$$

Equations are mathematical expressions which relate one group of numbers and symbols to another group of numbers and symbols.

$$3X = 4Y$$

If we know that X equals 4, we can solve the equation to find that Y equals 3:

$$3X = 4Y$$
$$3 \cdot 4 = 4Y$$
$$12 = 4Y$$
$$3 = Y$$

The key to solving algebraic equations is the assertion that two different combinations of numbers and symbols called *groups* or *quantities* are equal to each other.   This fact is usually shown in the equation by the use of an equal sign.   Groups or quantities are made up of constants, coefficients and variables.

The following are examples of some different types of algebraic equations.   In them the variables are unknowns and are represented by letters of the alphabet.

Reflective equation: $X = Y$
Symmetric equation: if $X = Y$ then $Y = X$
Transitive equation: if $X = Y$ and $Y = b$ then $X = b$

Another key to solving algebraic equations is the axiom that both sides of an equation will remain equal after equal amounts are added, subtracted, multiplied by or divided into both sides of the equation.

Example of adding equal amounts to both sides of an equation:

$$X + 15 = 21$$

Add 8 to both sides

$$X + 23 = 29$$

Example of subtracting equal amounts to both sides of an equation:

$$X + 15 = 21$$

Subtract 10 from both sides

$$X + 5 = 11$$

Example of multiplying both sides of an equation by equal amounts:

$$X + 15 = 21$$

Multiply both sides by 7

$$7(X + 15) = 147$$

Example of dividing both sides of an equation by equal amounts:

$$X + 15 = 21$$

Divide both sides by 7

$$\frac{X + 15}{7} = \frac{21}{7}$$

Another key to solving algebraic equations is that any term may be transposed from one side of an equation to the other side and the sides will remain equal provided that the sign of the transposed term is changed (+ to -, or - to +, or x to +, or + to x).

Example of moving a plus term in an equation to the other side of the equation:

$$9X + 2 = 29$$

Move the + 2 to the other side: $9X + \cancel{2} + (-\cancel{2}) = 29 + (-2)$

$$9X = 29 - 2$$

(The effect is the same as dividing both sides by 3.)

Example of moving a minus term in an equation to the other side of the equation:

$$9X - 2 = 25$$

Move the - 2 to the other side: $9X - \cancel{2} + (+\cancel{2}) = 25 + (+2)$

$$9X = 25 + 2$$

(the effect is the same as adding + 2 to both sides)

Example of moving a multiplier in an equation to the other side of the equation:

$$3(9X) = 81$$

Move the multiplier 3 to the other side: $\dfrac{\cancel{3}(9X)}{\cancel{3}} = \dfrac{81}{3}$

$$9X = \frac{81}{3}$$

(The effect is the same as subtracting - 2 from both sides.)

Example of moving a divisor in an equation to the other side of the equation:

$$\frac{9X}{3} = 9$$

Move the divisor 3 to the other side: $\cancel{3} \cdot \dfrac{9X}{\cancel{3}} = 9 \cdot 3$

$$9X = 3(9)$$

(The effect is the same as multiplying both sides by 3.)

NOTE: In all of the above transposition examples the value of X is 3.

The purpose of this algebra review is to demonstrate the skills needed to solve simple equations of the type encountered by appraisers. Here is an example of how to use the previously explained techniques to solve an equation.

Example: Find the value of X when

$$13X - 6X + 12 = -6X + 3X + 32$$

Step 1: Collect like terms.

$$7X + 12 = -3X + 32$$

Step 2: Clear the negative terms by adding equal amounts to both sides.

$$
\begin{array}{rcr}
7X + 12 &=& -3X + 32 \\
+3X & & +3X \\
\hline
10X + 12 &=& 32
\end{array}
$$

Step 3: Clear the equation by adding or substituting equal numbers to both sides.

$$
\begin{array}{rcr}
10X + 12 &=& 32 \\
- 12 & & -12 \\
\hline
10X &=& 20
\end{array}
$$

Step 4: Divide each side of the equation by equal numbers to find the value of the unknown letter (X).

$$10X = 20$$
$$\frac{10X}{10} = \frac{20}{10}$$
$$X = 2$$

This algebra review provides a basis upon which to proceed to statistics, which is a quantitative tool used to analyze data.

BASIC STATISTICS

An appraisal, according to one popular definition, is a supportable estimate of a defined value. In the language of statistics, a *population* is a complete data set or all the data in a certain group. Using statistics enables an appraiser (or any investigator) to derive and evaluate conclusions about a population from sample data. A sample is only part of the population and conclusions about a population based on a sample may be erroneous.

When they can be measured, observations about a population are called *quantitative*. The numerical value of a quantitative observation is a *variate*.

Observations about a population that cannot be measured is called *qualitative*. Those are *attributes*. A typical population of attributes would be house types, i.e., one-story houses, two-story houses, split levels, etc. It is usually easy to display or tell about a population of attributes. It is hard to display or tell about a population of variates because there are many different ones.

For appraisal purposes one of the most useful functions of statistics is to forecast what some variate in a population will be or do. A variate is one factor in a population. It is called *discrete* when it can assume only a limited number of values on a measuring scale and *continuous* when it can assume an infinite number of values on a measuring scale.

A continuous variate can become an unlimited number of values.

One of the problems in statistics is to describe a population in universally understandable terms. This is a very difficult thing to do. How does one describe all the houses in a community that have sold in the past year without an individual description of each sale?

One way is to use a single number to describe the whole population. This is called a *parameter*.

One parameter that is used to describe a population is an *aggregate*. It is a sum of all the variates. It is possible to describe all the house sales in a community in any given year by the total dollar amount of all the sales. This is written in statistical language as:

$A = \sum X$
where
A = aggregate
$\sum$ = sigma = sum of
X = variate

Three other commonly used parameters are the mean, median or mode.

The *mean*, which is denoted by the symbol μ, is commonly called the average. It is obtained by dividing the sum of all the variates in the population by the number of variates.

The mean is by far the most commonly used parameter. In real estate appraising, some common uses of the mean are average sale price, average number of days for sale, average apartment rent and average cost per square foot. What is usually meant by each of the statements (unless specifically stated otherwise) is the mean sale price, days for sale, apartment rent or cost per square foot.

The problem with the use of the mean to describe these and other populations is that it can be distorted by extreme variates. For example, on the following page is a grouping of 36 house sales in a neighborhood. The "average" (or mean) price in this example — $43,494 — does not give a fully accurate picture of the population of houses that have been sold.

The *median* is also used to describe a population or at least the average variate in the population. The median divides the variates of a population into equal halves. To compute the median of a population, the variates are arranged in numerical order as are the 36 sale prices in the example. If the total number of variates is odd, the median is the middle variate. If the total number of variates is even as it is in this example, the median is the arithmetic mean of the two middle variates.

In the example of the 36 house sales the middle two variates are $43,900 and $43,900. The mean of these two variates is $43,900 ($43,900 + $43,900 = $87,800 + 2 = $43,900) which is the median of the 36 sales.

$ 36,000
37,300
38,000
38,600
39,000
39,500
39,900
39,900
41,000
41,000
42,000
42,800
42,900
43,000
43,500
43,600
43,700
43,900   ←median = Md. = $43,900
43,900
43,900
44,000
44,900
45,000 ⎫
45,000 ⎬ mode = Mo = $45,000
45,000 ⎪
45,000 ⎭
45,300
45,500
45,500
46,900
46,900
48,300
48,500
48,600
48,600
49,400
―――――――
$1,565,800

A = Sum of the variates
N = Number of variates = 36

$$\text{Mean} = \overline{X} = \frac{A}{N} = \frac{\$1,565,800}{36} = \$43,494$$

Here is an example of an odd number of variates:

Monthly Rent
$180
$180
$190
$200 ←——— Middle variate (the median)
$210
$215
$220

Like the median and mean, the *mode* is another parameter that describes the typical variate of a population. The mode is the most frequently appearing variate or attribute in a population. The following is an example of a population of monthly rentals showing the mode:

$170
$175
$180
$180
$185
$190 ⎫
$190 ⎬   The most frequent variate is the mode.
$190 ⎭
$195
$200

Below is another example showing a population of types of condominium apartments available in a 9-unit complex:

efficiency
efficiency
efficiency
town house ⎫
town house ⎪
town house ⎬   The most frequent attribute is the mode.
town house ⎪
town house ⎭
multi-bedroom

In the example of 36 houses, four of them sold for $45,000. This is the most frequent sale price and therefore is the mode. Sometimes two houses of different price may be of the same frequency in the sample or population. Both prices would be modes and the sample would be said to be bi-modal.

One of the problems that must be solved by the appraiser using statistics is to select the appropriate parameter to describe the population being used. In the previous example, the following choices can be used to describe the 36 variates in the group of house sales:

ΣX = $1,565,800 = sum of all the sales
$\overline{X}$ = $ 43,494 = the mean of all the sales
Md = $ 43,900 = the median of the sales
Mo = $ 45,000 = the mode of the sales

The mean is often selected to describe the sample or population because it is the most commonly used and most people are familiar with it.

MEASURES OF VARIATION

The parameters of mean, median and mode all are used to describe central tendencies of the population. Other sets of parameters are used to provide more information about the population being described. They measure the disparity among values of the various variates comprising the population. These parameters, called *measures of variation* or *dispersion*, are designed to indicate the degree of uniformity among the variates.

One way to measure the disparity between the variates is known as the *range* which is denoted by R. The range is the difference between the highest and lowest variate. The formula is: R = Maximum variate – minimum variate.

Using the figures in the example of the 36 house sales:
R = $49,400 to $36,000
R = $13,400

The range as a measure of variation is of limited usefulness since it considers only the highest and lowest values and neglects the variation in the remaining values. It also does not lend itself to further statistical treatment.

AVERAGE DEVIATION

Another parameter used to measure deviations between the variates is the *average deviation* which is also known as the average absolute deviation because plus or minus signs are ignored. It is a measure of how much the actual values of the population or sample deviate from the mean or the average. It is the mean of the sum of the absolute differences of each of the variates from the mean of the variates.

Using traditional statistical formula and symbols, the calculations of the average deviation of the 36 sales are :

$$\text{A.D. (ungrouped data)} = \frac{\Sigma|X-\overline{X}|}{n}$$

$$\text{A.D. (grouped data)} = \frac{\Sigma f|X-\overline{X}|}{n}$$

where
A.D. = average deviation
Σ = sum of
f = frequency
X = observed value
$|\ |$ = ignore the + or – signs
n = number of observations in sample (N = population)
$\overline{X}$ = means of sample (σ = population)

$$\text{Mean} = \frac{\$1,565,800}{36} = \$43,494$$

$$\text{Average deviation from the mean} = \frac{\$96,048}{36} = \$2,668$$

Sale Price	Absolute deviation between each variate and the mean sale price
$ 36,000	$ 7,494
37,300	6,194
38,000	5,494
38,600	4,894
39,000	4,494
39,500	3,994
39,900	3,594
39,900	3,594
41,000	2,494
41,000	2,494
42,000	1,494
42,800	694
42,900	594
43,000	494
43,500	6
43,600	106
43,700	206
43,900	406
43,900	406
43,900	406
44,000	506
44,900	1,406
45,000	1,506
45,000	1,506
45,000	1,506
45,000	1,506
45,300	1,806
45,500	2,006
45,500	2,006
46,900	3,406
46,900	3,406
48,300	4,806
48,500	5,006
48,600	5,106
48,600	5,106
49,400	5,906
$1,565,800	**$96,048**
Total of the sale prices	Total deviation from the mean

X	$|X-\overline{X}|$	f	$f|X-\overline{X}|$
$36,000	$7,494	1	$ 7,494
37,300	6,194	1	6,194
38,000	5,494	1	5,494
38,600	4,894	1	4,894
39,000	4,494	1	4,494
39,500	3,994	1	3,994
39,900	3,594	2	7,188
41,000	2,494	2	4,988
42,000	1,494	1	1,494
42,800	694	1	694
42,900	594	1	594
43,000	494	1	494
43,500	6	1	6
43,600	106	1	106
43,700	206	1	206
43,900	406	3	1,218
44,000	506	1	506
44,900	1,406	1	1,406
45,000	1,506	4	6,024
45,300	1,806	1	1,806
45,500	2,006	2	4,012
46,900	3,406	2	6,812
48,300	4,806	1	4,806
48,500	5,006	1	5,006
48,600	5,106	2	10,212
49,400	5,906	1	5,906
		36	$96,048

Mean = $43,494

$$\text{A.D.} = \frac{\Sigma f|X-\overline{X}|}{n} = \frac{\$96,048}{36} = \$2,668$$

This indicates that on the average the individual values in the sample population deviate from the mean $2,668 or about 6%. This is a fairly tight fit and suggests that the mean is an acceptable descriptive representation of this sample.

Like the range, the average deviation does not lend itself to further statistical calculations.

STANDARD DEVIATION

The *standard deviation* provides a way of describing a sample or a population that lends itself to further mathematical treatment. In particular, it permits application of rules of probability to draw inferences of populations from samples.

In this method, the square of the difference between each observation and the mean of the observations is used as a calculation step. This serves to magnify the effects of extreme variance from the mean.

In the illustration, the mean sales price is $43,494. Therefore, the measure of deviation for a $41,000 sale would be $2,494 squared or $6,220,036.

When the standard deviation of a *whole* population is being calculated, it is symbolized by a sigma (σ). The standard deviation of a population is the square root of the sum of the squared differences between each observation's value and the mean of all of the observations in the population divided by the number of observations in the population.

When the standard deviation of a *sample* of a population is being calculated, it is symbolized by the letter "s." The formula for a standard deviation of a sample is the square root of the sum of the squared differences between each observation's value and the mean of all the observations in the sample divided by the number of observations in the sample minus 1.

The reason the number 1 is subtracted from the number of observations in a sample is to adjust for one degree of freedom which is lost when the mean is calculated. A set of data originally has as many *degrees of freedom* as there are observations. Each time a statistic is calculated directly from the data, a degree of freedom is lost.

The formula for calculating the standard deviation for a sample:

$$s = \sqrt{\frac{\Sigma (X-\overline{X})^2}{n-1}} \text{ or } \sqrt{\frac{\Sigma f(X-\overline{X})^2}{n-1}}$$

The formula for calculating the standard deviation for a population is:

$$\sigma = \sqrt{\frac{\Sigma(X-\overline{X})^2}{N}}$$

In real estate appraising, samples are usually used.

The standard deviation is an important way to describe the variance of a population or sample. It tells how representative of the whole sample or population the mean is by explaining a standard variance. With the availability of electronic calculators, it can be calculated easily.

When used for this purpose, the standard deviation can indicate what percent of the sample of the population may be expected to fall within selected ranges or *confidence intervals* .

Approximately 68.2% of the sample or population will generally fall within plus or minus one standard deviation from the mean if the data meets certain tests of *distribution normalcy*. Many types of real estate data are commonly found to be normally distributed, or normal distributions can be approximated by appropriate sampling techniques.

In this example, 68.2% of the house sales in the population are expected to be between $40,080 and $46,908 ($43,494 – $3,414 and $43,494 + $3,414) if the data is normally distributed. Approximately 95% of the sales should fall within three standard deviations from the mean.

STANDARD DEVIATION FOR 36 HOUSE SALES

X	f	$(X-\overline{X})$	$(X-\overline{X})^2$	$f(X-\overline{X})^2$
$36,000	1	$7,494	$56,160,036	$ 56,160,036
37,300	1	6,194	38,365,636	38,365,636
38,000	1	5,494	30,184,036	30,184,036
38,600	1	4,894	23,951,236	23,951,236
39,000	1	4,494	20,196,036	20,196,036
39,500	1	3,994	15,952,036	15,952,036
39,900	2	3,594	12,916,836	25,833,672
41,000	2	2,494	6,220,036	12,440,072
42,000	1	1,494	2,232,036	2,232,036
42,800	1	694	481,636	481,636
42,900	1	594	352,836	352,836
43,000	1	494	244,036	244,036
43,500	1	6	36	36
43,600	1	106	11,236	11,236
43,700	1	206	42,436	42,436
43,900	3	406	164,836	494,508
44,000	1	506	256,036	256,036
44,900	1	1,406	1,976,836	1,976,836
45,000	4	1,506	2,268,036	9,072,144
45,300	1	1,806	3,261,636	3,261,636
45,500	2	2,006	4,024,036	8,048,072
46,900	2	3,406	11,600,836	23,201,672
48,300	1	4,806	23,097,636	23,097,636
48,500	1	5,006	25,060,036	25,060,036
48,600	2	5,106	26,071,236	52,142,472
49,400	1	5,906	34,880,836	34,880,836
				$407,938,896

$$s = \sqrt{\frac{\sum f(X-\overline{X})^2}{n-1}}$$

$$s = \sqrt{\frac{\$407,938,896}{36-1}}$$

Mean: $43,494

$$s = \sqrt{\$11,655,397}$$

$$s = \quad \$3,414$$

STATISTICAL INFERENCE

This technique which is useful to forecast actions is based on the assumption that past actions in the market are a valid basis for forecasting present or future actions in the market. In this example, past sale prices are used to estimate current sale prices. This technique can also be used to forecast rentals, costs, depreciation, etc., using rules of probability.

The *normal curve* plots a normal distribution and is a technique used to illustrate a distribution of data. Where original data may not be normally distributed, repeated random samples may be drawn with results which approximate a normal distribution. Sales are often treated as though they were normally distributed in competitive, open market situations. The normal curve is often graphed in a form known as a bell curve.

A major characteristic of a bell curve is that it is symmetrical. Both halves have exactly the same shape and contain the same number of observations. The mean, median and mode are the same value and this value is the midpoint (apex) of the curve.

Figure A illustrates a bell curve and shows that 68.2% of the observations will fall within the range of the mean plus or minus one standard deviation, 95.44% within plus or minus two standard deviations and 99.74% plus or minus three standard deviations. It depicts an analysis of the probable population distribution for the 36 sales, assuming a normal distribution.

FIGURE A. BELL CURVE

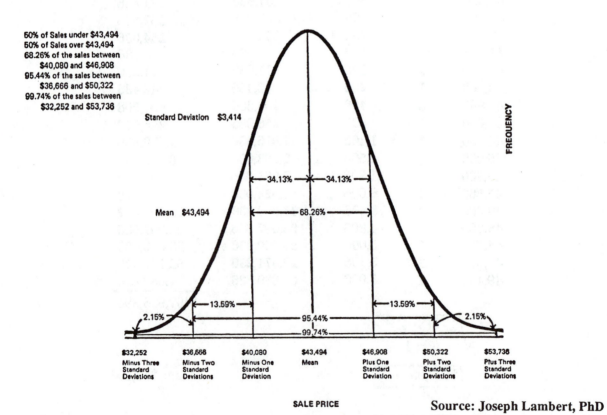

Source: Joseph Lambert, PhD

The ranges for 1, 2 and 3 standard deviations are shown. One can also calculate the percent of a population that will fall within any given distance from the mean.

Continuing the example, it is possible to calculate the percentage of sales that will fall within any specified ranges. For example, $2,500 plus the mean of $43,494 ($40,994) or minus the mean ($45,994) may be estimated by calculating the Z value using the following formula:

Z = the deviation of X from the mean measured in standard
deviations

$$Z = \frac{X - \text{mean}}{\text{Standard deviation}}$$

$$Z = \frac{\$45,994 - \$43,494}{\$3,414} = \frac{\$2,500}{\$3,414} = .7323$$

This shows that $45,994 deviates from the mean $43,494 (or $40,994 deviates from the mean $43,494) by .7323 standard deviations.

FIGURE B.   AREAS UNDER THE NORMAL CURVE

Areas under the normal curve

z	.00	.01	.02	.03	.04	.05	.06	.07	.08	.09
0.0	.0000	.0040	.0080	.0120	.0160	.0199	.0239	.0279	.0319	.0359
0.1	.0398	.0438	.0478	.0517	.0557	.0596	.0636	.0675	.0714	.0753
0.2	.0793	.0832	.0871	.0910	.0948	.0987	.1026	.1064	.1103	.1141
0.3	.1179	.1217	.1255	.1293	.1331	.1368	.1406	.1443	.1480	.1517
0.4	.1554	.1591	.1628	.1664	.1700	.1736	.1772	.1808	.1844	.1879
0.5	.1915	.1950	.1985	.2019	.2054	.2088	.2123	.2157	.2190	.2224
0.6	.2257	.2291	.2324	.2357	.2389	.2422	.2454	.2486	.2517	.2549
0.7	.2580	.2611	.2642	.2673	.2704	.2734	.2764	.2794	.2823	.2852
0.8	.2881	.2910	.2939	.2967	.2995	.3023	.3051	.3078	.3106	.3133
0.9	.3159	.3186	.3212	.3238	.3264	.3289	.3315	.3340	.3365	.3389
1.0	.3413	.3438	.3461	.3485	.3508	.3531	.3554	.3577	.3599	.3621
1.1	.3643	.3665	.3686	.3708	.3729	.3749	.3770	.3790	.3810	.3830
1.2	.3849	.3869	.3888	.3907	.3925	.3944	.3962	.3980	.3997	.4015
1.3	.4032	.4049	.4066	.4082	.4099	.4115	.4131	.4147	.4162	.4177
1.4	.4192	.4207	.4222	.4236	.4251	.4265	.4279	.4292	.4306	.4319
1.5	.4332	.4345	.4357	.4370	.4382	.4394	.4406	.4418	.4429	.4441
1.6	.4452	.4463	.4474	.4484	.4495	.4505	.4515	.4525	.4535	.4545
1.7	.4554	.4564	.4573	.4582	.4591	.4599	.4608	.4616	.4625	.4633
1.8	.4641	.4649	.4656	.4664	.4671	.4678	.4686	.4693	.4699	.4706
1.9	.4713	.4719	.4726	.4732	.4738	.4744	.4750	.4756	.4761	.4767
2.0	.4772	.4778	.4783	.4788	.4793	.4798	.4803	.4808	.4812	.4817
2.1	.4821	.4826	.4830	.4834	.4838	.4842	.4846	.4850	.4854	.4857
2.2	.4861	.4864	.4868	.4871	.4875	.4878	.4881	.4884	.4887	.4890
2.3	.4893	.4896	.4898	.4901	.4904	.4906	.4909	.4911	.4913	.4916
2.4	.4918	.4920	.4922	.4925	.4927	.4929	.4931	.4932	.4934	.4936
2.5	.4938	.4940	.4941	.4943	.4945	.4946	.4948	.4949	.4951	.4952
2.6	.4953	.4955	.4956	.4957	.4959	.4960	.4961	.4962	.4963	.4964
2.7	.4965	.4966	.4967	.4968	.4969	.4970	.4971	.4972	.4973	.4974
2.8	.4974	.4975	.4976	.4977	.4977	.4978	.4979	.4979	.4980	.4981
2.9	.4981	.4982	.4982	.4983	.4984	.4984	.4985	.4985	.4986	.4986
3.0	.4987	.4987	.4987	.4988	.4988	.4989	.4989	.4989	.4990	.4990

The .7323 can be interpreted from the table by first finding .7 under the Z column and then looking across the top of the page for the next digits. Accordingly, 26.73% of the sales are shown to fall between $43,494 and $45,994 or between $43,994 and $40,994 and 53.46% of the sales will be between $45,994 and $40,994.

REGRESSION ANALYSIS

SIMPLE LINEAR REGRESSION ANALYSIS

Trying to estimate the most probable sale price of a property in the market is the goal of many appraisers. It is seldom sufficient to take a sample of sales and then calculate the standard deviation and base the estimate upon these results. The range of values is usually too great at the confidence level required to be directly useful. Appraisers long ago discovered that the accuracy of the estimate could be substantially increased by considering one or more characteristics of each sale property in addition to the sale prices of individual properties.

Looking again at the 36 sales in the original example, there appears to be a relationship between sale price and the number of square feet of living area as seen below.

COMPARABLE SALES DATA FOR SIMPLE REGRESSION ANALYSIS

Sale No.	GLA/Sq. Ft.	Sale Price	Price per Sq. Ft. of GLA
1	1,321	$38,000	$28.77
2	1,372	$44,000	$32.07
3	1,394	$39,000	$27.98
4	1,403	$37,300	$26.59
5	1,457	$42,900	$29.44
6	1,472	$43,700	$29.69
7	1,475	$42,000	$28.47
8	1,479	$42,800	$28.94
9	1,503	$36,000	$23.95
10	1,512	$38,600	$25.53
11	1,515	$41,000	$27.06
12	1,535	$39,500	$25.73
13	1,535	$43,900	$28.60
14	1,577	$45,500	$28.85
15	1,613	$45,000	$27.90
16	1,640	$39,900	$24.33
17	1,666	$45,500	$27.31
18	1,681	$39,900	$23.74
19	1,697	$43,600	$25.69
20	1,703	$43,500	$25.54
21	1,706	$44,900	$26.32
22	1,709	$45,300	$26.51
23	1,709	$46,900	$27.44
24	1,720	$46,900	$27.27
25	1,732	$41,000	$23.67
26	1,749	$48,600	$27.79
27	1,771	$48,600	$27.44
28	1,777	$43,000	$24.20
29	1,939	$43,900	$22.64
30	1,939	$45,000	$23.21
31	1,939	$45,000	$23.21
32	1,939	$45,000	$23.21
33	1,939	$48,300	$24.91
34	1,940	$43,900	$22.63
35	2,014	$49,400	$24.53
36	2,065	$48,500	$23.49

In traditional appraisals, it is likely that an appraiser would use only those sales which have approximately the same square footage as the appraised property and essentially ignore the others.

Note the appraiser's dilemma in appraising a 1,375 square foot dwelling. Sales 1, 2 and 3 are reported as $28.77, $32.07 and $27.98 per square foot respectively. Other sales may give a clue to the right answer, but Sales 5 and 6 do little to resolve the conflict. Adjustments will likely have to be made for other differences.

Sales 1 through 3 indicate a range of $27.98 to $32.07 per square foot or when applied to the appraised property's 1,375 square feet, an indicated value range of $38,473 to $44,096. (These would be rounded in practice.) However, the remaining market information cannot effectively be applied to the analysis in traditional appraising except to generally reinforce the appraiser's judgement.

Simple linear regression provides a technique in which more market data may be applied to this analysis. For application in the simple linear regression formula, $Y_c = a + bX$, the 36 sales were analyzed by calculator and produced the following:

a = $24,630
b = $11.29
r = .6598 (simple correlation coefficient)

Thus, for the 1,375 square foot property appraised:

Y_c= $24,630 + $11.29 (1,375)
Y_c = $40,154
        (or $29.20 per square foot)

The calculated regression line and a plot of the 36 sales is shown in Figure C. Also shown is another statistical measure called the *standard error of the estimate* which allows construction of confidence intervals about the regression line.

Calculations in this example produce a standard error estimate of $2,603. When applied to property appraised, the appraiser may now state that the 36 sales in this market support an estimate of about $40,150 for the appraised property (based only upon comparison of square footage). Further, at a 68% confidence level, the market price should lie between $40,150 ± $2,603 (or $37,547 to $42,753). At a 95% confidence level, price should lie between $40,150 ± (2) ($2,603) or $34,944 to $45,356.

Although other statistical measures such as the *standard error of the forecast* may be used, this analysis is generally considered sufficient and reasonably representative of most single family market situations. It should also be noted that a more refined analysis of this data is possible, but this example illustrates the simple application of a regression technique.

FIGURE C   PLOT OF SALES.   REGRESSION LINE AND STANDARD ERROR — 36 SALES

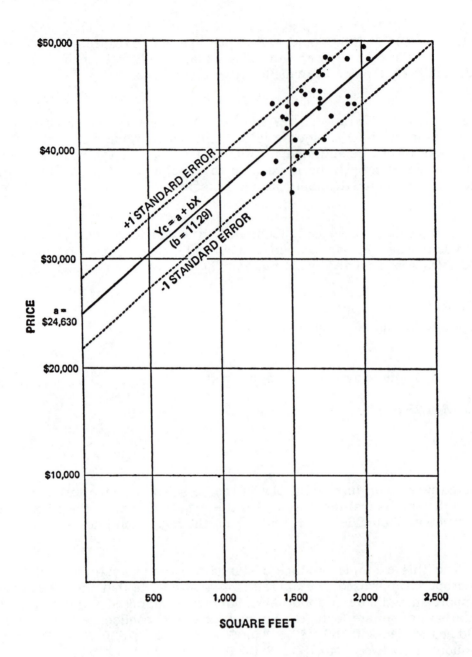

COMPOUND INTEREST TABLES

The Foundation of Capitalization

"To understand the income approach, the appraiser must understand the arithmetic of compound interest. The reason this branch of arithmetic has remained a mystery, shunned by many people, is not because it is complex or hard to understand. Rather, it is because manual application is a tedious, time-consuming and mentally exhausting process."

This statement by "Pete" L. W. Ellwood in his classic book <u>Ellwood Tables for Real Estate Appraising and Financing</u>[6] was written when the electronic calculator was a novelty and the financial calculator had not yet been invented.

He went on the add *"The critical factors in the income approach by any technique are amount, time and investment yield...The appraiser cannot make an intelligent selection of technique unless he knows exactly what the assumptions are and how they effect his result.*

Moreover, he cannot do a professional job with integrity unless he believes the assumptions implicit in the technique he selects. Otherwise, the appraiser will not be the result of his own judgment applied to pertinent facts. Instead it will be the product of a formula which may not be plausible in the light of relevant facts."

The invention of the financial calculator has compounded the problem Ellwood wrote about. Today, many untrained appraisers attempt to make income property appraisals without a clear understanding of the basics of the capitalization technique. They punch numbers into the *six functions of a dollar* keys of their financial calculator and in an instant, out pops a number which they hope leads them to the correct value of the property.

The following pages have two examples of Compound Interest Tables which present the six standard functions of a dollar. One shows 8% annual interest and the other 8% monthly interest.

Examples are given for the type of problems which can be solved with each of the six standard functions by using the table. These are followed by examples of how the same problems can be solved by using a financial calculator. I used a Hewlett Packard Hp 12c calculator for the calculations. A different financial calculator might produce a slightly different result.

Following the Ellwood tables is a chart prepared by my wife, Ruth D. Lambert, when she was taking the SREA 201 course many years ago in Richmond, KY. It has been helpful to many students and hopefully, you will find it helpful too.

---

[6]L.W. Ellwood, *Ellwood Tables for Real Estate Appraising and Financing*, 4th ed., Ballinger Publishing Co., Cambridge, MA., 1977.

8% ANNUAL COMPOUND INTEREST TABLE

EFFECTIVE RATE = 8%   BASE = 1.08

YEARS	1 AMOUNT OF 1 AT COMPOUND INTEREST $S^n = (1+i)^n$	2 ACCUMULATION OF 1 PER PERIOD $S_{\overline{n}} = \frac{S^n - 1}{i}$	3 SINKING FUND FACTOR $1/S_{\overline{n}} = \frac{i}{S^n - 1}$	4 PRES. VALUE REVERSION OF 1 $V^n = \frac{1}{S^n}$	5 PRESENT VALUE ORD. ANNUITY 1 PER PERIOD $a_{\overline{n}} = \frac{1 - V^n}{i}$	6 INSTALMENT TO AMORTIZE 1 $1/a_{\overline{n}} = \frac{i}{1 - V^n}$	n YEARS
1	1.080000	1.000000	1.000000	.925926	.925926	1.080000	1
2	1.166400	2.080000	.480769	.857339	1.783265	.560769	2
3	1.259712	3.246400	.308034	.793832	2.577097	.388034	3
4	1.360489	4.506112	.221921	.735030	3.312127	.301921	4
5	1.469328	5.866601	.170456	.680583	3.992710	.250456	5
6	1.586874	7.335929	.136315	.630170	4.622880	.216315	6
7	1.713824	8.922803	.112072	.583490	5.206370	.192072	7
8	1.850930	10.636628	.094015	.540269	5.746639	.174015	8
9	1.999005	12.487558	.080080	.500249	6.246888	.160080	9
10	2.158925	14.486562	.069029	.463193	6.710081	.149029	10
11	2.331639	16.645487	.060076	.428883	7.138964	.140076	11
12	2.518170	18.977126	.052695	.397114	7.536078	.132695	12
13	2.719624	21.495297	.046522	.367698	7.903776	.126522	13
14	2.937194	24.214920	.041297	.340461	8.244237	.121297	14
15	3.172169	27.152114	.036830	.315242	8.559479	.116830	15
16	3.425943	30.324283	.032977	.291890	8.851369	.112977	16
17	3.700018	33.750226	.029629	.270269	9.121638	.109629	17
18	3.996019	37.450244	.026702	.250249	9.371887	.106702	18
19	4.315701	41.446263	.024128	.231712	9.603599	.104128	19
20	4.660957	45.761964	.021852	.214548	9.818147	.101852	20
21	5.033834	50.422921	.019832	.198656	10.016803	.099832	21
22	5.436540	55.456755	.018032	.183941	10.200744	.098032	22
23	5.871464	60.893296	.016422	.170315	10.371059	.096422	23
24	6.341181	66.764759	.014978	.157699	10.528758	.094978	24
25	6.848475	73.105940	.013679	.146018	10.674776	.093679	25
26	7.396353	79.954415	.012507	.135202	10.809978	.092507	26
27	7.988061	87.350768	.011448	.125187	10.935165	.091448	27
28	8.627106	95.338830	.010489	.115914	11.051078	.090489	28
29	9.317275	103.965936	.009619	.107328	11.158406	.089619	29
30	10.062657	113.283211	.008827	.099377	11.257783	.088827	30
31	10.867669	123.345868	.008107	.092016	11.349799	.088107	31
32	11.737083	134.213537	.007451	.085200	11.434999	.087451	32
33	12.676050	145.950620	.006852	.078889	11.513888	.086852	33
34	13.690134	158.626670	.006304	.073045	11.586934	.086304	34
35	14.785344	172.316804	.005803	.067635	11.654568	.085803	35
36	15.968172	187.102148	.005345	.062625	11.717193	.085345	36
37	17.245626	203.070320	.004924	.057986	11.775179	.084924	37
38	18.625276	220.315945	.004539	.053690	11.828869	.084539	38
39	20.115298	238.941221	.004185	.049713	11.878582	.084185	39
40	21.724521	259.056519	.003860	.046031	11.924613	.083860	40
41	23.462483	280.781040	.003561	.042621	11.967235	.083561	41
42	25.339482	304.243523	.003287	.039464	12.006699	.083287	42
43	27.366640	329.583005	.003034	.036541	12.043240	.083034	43
44	29.555972	356.949646	.002802	.033834	12.077074	.082802	44
45	31.920449	386.505617	.002587	.031328	12.108401	.082587	45
46	34.474085	418.426067	.002390	.029007	12.137409	.082390	46
47	37.232012	452.900152	.002208	.026859	12.164267	.082208	47
48	40.210573	490.132164	.002040	.024869	12.189136	.082040	48
49	43.427419	530.342737	.001886	.023027	12.212163	.081886	49
50	46.901613	573.770156	.001743	.021321	12.233485	.081743	50
51	50.653742	620.671769	.001611	.019742	12.253227	.081611	51
52	54.706041	671.325510	.001490	.018280	12.271506	.081490	52
53	59.082524	726.031551	.001377	.016925	12.288432	.081377	53
54	63.809126	785.114075	.001274	.015672	12.304103	.081274	54
55	68.913856	848.923201	.001178	.014511	12.318614	.081178	55
56	74.426965	917.837058	.001090	.013436	12.332050	.081090	56
57	80.381122	992.264022	.001008	.012441	12.344491	.081008	57
58	86.811612	1072.645144	.000932	.011519	12.356010	.080932	58
59	93.756540	1159.456755	.000862	.010666	12.366676	.080862	59
60	101.257064	1253.213296	.000798	.009876	12.376552	.080798	60

8% MONTHLY COMPOUND INTEREST TABLE

EFFECTIVE RATE = 2/3%   BASE = 1.00666666+

MONTHS	1 AMOUNT OF 1 AT COMPOUND INTEREST $S^n = (1+i)^n$	2 ACCUMULATION OF 1 PER PERIOD $S_{\overline{n}|} = \frac{S^n - 1}{i}$	3 SINKING FUND FACTOR $1/S_{\overline{n}|} = \frac{i}{S^n - 1}$	4 PRES. VALUE REVERSION OF 1 $v^n = \frac{1}{S^n}$	5 PRESENT VALUE ORD. ANNUITY 1 PER PERIOD $a_{\overline{n}|} = \frac{1 - v^n}{i}$	6 INSTALMENT TO AMORTIZE 1 $1/a_{\overline{n}|} = \frac{i}{1 - v^n}$	n MONTHS
1	1.006667	1.000000	1.000000	.993377	.993377	1.006667	1
2	1.013378	2.006667	.498339	.986799	1.980176	.505006	2
3	1.020134	3.020044	.331121	.980264	2.960440	.337788	3
4	1.026935	4.040178	.247514	.973772	3.934212	.254181	4
5	1.033781	5.067113	.197351	.967323	4.901535	.204018	5
6	1.040673	6.100893	.163910	.960917	5.862452	.170577	6
7	1.047610	7.141566	.140025	.954553	6.817005	.146692	7
8	1.054595	8.189176	.122112	.948232	7.765237	.128779	8
9	1.061625	9.243771	.108181	.941952	8.707189	.114848	9
10	1.068703	10.305396	.097037	.935714	9.642903	.103704	10
11	1.075827	11.374099	.087919	.929517	10.572420	.094586	11
YEARS							
1	1.083000	12.449926	.080322	.923361	11.495782	.086989	12
2	1.172888	25.933190	.038561	.852596	22.110544	.045228	24
3	1.270237	40.535558	.024670	.787255	31.911805	.031337	36
4	1.375666	56.349915	.017746	.726921	40.961913	.024413	48
5	1.489846	73.476856	.013610	.671210	49.318433	.020277	60
6	1.613502	92.025325	.010867	.619770	57.034522	.017534	72
7	1.747422	112.113308	.008920	.572272	64.159261	.015587	84
8	1.892457	133.868583	.007470	.528414	70.737970	.014137	96
9	2.049530	157.429536	.006352	.487917	76.812497	.013019	108
10	2.219640	182.946036	.005466	.450523	82.421481	.012133	120
11	2.403869	210.580392	.004749	.415996	87.600600	.011416	132
12	2.603389	240.508387	.004158	.384115	92.382799	.010825	144
13	2.819469	272.920391	.003664	.354677	96.798498	.010331	156
14	3.053484	308.022575	.003247	.327495	100.875783	.009914	168
15	3.306921	346.038223	.002890	.302396	104.640592	.009557	180
16	3.581394	387.209151	.002583	.279221	108.116871	.009250	192
17	3.878648	431.797246	.002316	.257822	111.326733	.008983	204
18	4.200574	480.086130	.002083	.238063	114.290596	.008750	216
19	4.549220	532.382969	.001878	.219818	117.027313	.008545	228
20	4.926803	589.020419	.001698	.202971	119.554291	.008365	240
21	5.335725	650.358749	.001538	.187416	121.887606	.008205	252
22	5.778588	716.788131	.001395	.173053	124.042099	.008062	264
23	6.258207	788.731119	.001268	.159790	126.031475	.007935	276
24	6.777636	866.645339	.001154	.147544	127.868388	.007821	288
25	7.340176	951.026401	.001051	.136237	129.564522	.007718	300
26	7.949407	1042.411050	.000959	.125796	131.130667	.007626	312
27	8.609204	1141.380579	.000876	.116155	132.576785	.007543	324
28	9.323764	1248.564531	.000801	.107253	133.912075	.007468	336
29	10.097631	1364.644698	.000733	.099033	135.145030	.007400	348
30	10.935730	1490.359462	.000671	.091443	136.283493	.007338	360
31	11.843390	1626.508488	.000615	.084435	137.334707	.007282	372
32	12.826386	1773.957818	.000564	.077964	138.305356	.007231	384
33	13.890969	1933.645368	.000517	.071989	139.201617	.007184	396
34	15.043913	2106.586907	.000475	.066472	140.029189	.007142	408
35	16.292550	2293.882508	.000436	.061378	140.793337	.007103	420
36	17.644824	2496.723552	.000401	.056674	141.498922	.007068	432
37	19.109335	2716.400303	.000368	.052330	142.150433	.007035	444
38	20.695401	2954.310116	.000338	.048320	142.752012	.007005	456
39	22.413109	3211.966325	.000311	.044617	143.307487	.006978	468
40	24.273386	3491.007874	.000286	.041197	143.820391	.006953	480
41	26.288065	3793.209733	.000264	.038040	144.293988	.006931	492
42	28.469961	4120.494198	.000243	.035125	144.731288	.006910	504
43	30.832954	4474.943112	.000223	.032433	145.135074	.006890	516
44	33.392074	4858.811111	.000206	.029947	145.507915	.006873	528
45	36.163600	5274.539965	.000190	.027652	145.852182	.006857	540
46	39.165161	5724.774109	.000175	.025533	146.170065	.006842	552
47	42.415850	6212.377465	.000161	.023576	146.463585	.006828	564
48	45.936345	6740.451660	.000148	.021769	146.734611	.006815	576
49	49.749039	7312.355752	.000137	.020101	146.984865	.006804	588
50	53.878184	7931.727602	.000126	.018560	147.215941	.006793	600

COMPOUND INTEREST TABLES

Column #1 AMOUNT OF 1 AT COMPOUND INTEREST

Formula: $S^n(1+i)^n$

    S = Value at end of period of time

    n = Number of periods

    i = Rate of interest per period

Description: The amount to which an investment or deposit of one dollar will grow in a given number of time periods, including the accumulation of interest at the effective rate per period. This factor is commonly known as the *Future Worth of One Dollar with Interest*.

Relationship of Tables: Reciprocal of Column 4

Problem: $1,000 is deposited in a savings account that pays 8% annual interest that is compounded <u>monthly</u>. All the interest is left in the account for 10 years. At the end of the 10 years how much as the account has grown to?

Example of calculation using the 8% annual interest table:

    $1,000 x 2.219640 = $2,219.40

Example of calculation using a financial calculator:

    Enter into the "n" key (10 x 12) = 120
    Enter into the "i" key (.08/12) = .666667
    Enter into the "pv" key = $1,000
    "fv" key produces the results of $2,219.40

Problem: $1,000 is deposited in a savings account that pays 8% annual interest that is compounded <u>annually</u>. All the interest is left in the account for 10 years. At the end of the 10 years how much as the account has grown to?

Example of calculation using the 8% annual interest table:

    $1,000 x 2.158925 = $2,158.93

Example of calculation using a financial calculator:

    Enter into the "n" key = 10
    Enter into the "i" key = 8
    Enter into the "pv" key $1,000
    "fv" key produces the results of $2,158.93

COMPOUND INTEREST TABLES

Column #2 ACCUMULATION OF 1 PER PERIOD

Formula: $\quad S\overline{\underset{n}{\rceil}} = \dfrac{S^{n} - 1}{i}$

    S = Value at end of period of time
    n = Number of periods
    i = Rate of interest per period

Description: The total accumulation of principle and interest of a series of deposits or installments of 1 dollar per period for a given number of periods with interest at the effective rate per period.   This factor is commonly known as the *Future Worth of One Dollar per Period with Interest.*

Relationship of Tables: Reciprocal of Column 3

Problem: $1000 per year is deposited in a savings account that pays 8% annual interest that is compounded <u>annually</u>.   All the interest is left in the account for 10 years.   At the end of the 10 years how much as the account has grown to?

Example of calculation using the 8% annual interest table:

    $1000 x 14.486562 = $14,486.56

Example of calculation using a financial calculator:

    Enter into the "n" key = 10
    Enter into the "i" key = 8
    Enter into the "pmt" key = $1000
    "fv" key produces the results of $14,486.56

(If HP 12c calculator is used the payment is entered as a "-".)

Problem: $100 is deposited monthly in a savings account that pays 8% annual interest compounded <u>monthly</u>. All the interest is left in the account for 10 years. At the end of the 10 years how much as the account has grown to?

Example of calculation using the 8% monthly table:

    $100 x 182.946036 = $18,294.60

Example of calculation using a financial calculator:

    Enter into the "n" key (10 x 12) = 120
    Enter into the "i" key (8/12) = .6666678
    Enter into the "pmt" key = $100
    "fv" key produces the results of $18,294.60

(If HP 12c calculator is used the payment is entered as a "-".)

COMPOUND INTEREST TABLES

Column #3 SINKING FUND FACTOR

Formula: $1/S_{\overline{n}|} = \dfrac{i}{s^n - 1}$

$1/S_{\overline{n}|}$ = Sinking Fund Factor

S = Value at end of period of time
n = Number of periods
i = Rate of interest per period

Description: The level periodic investment or deposit required to accumulate one dollar in a given number of periods including the accumulation of interest at the effective rate. This is commonly known as the *"Sinking Fund Factor"*

Relationship of Tables: Reciprocal of Column 2

Problem: How much will be needed to be deposited annually at the end of each year for 15 years to accumulate $100,000 for a child's college education at an annually compounded interest rate of 8%?

Example of calculation using the 8% annual interest table:

   $100,000 x .036830 = $3,683.30

Example of calculation using a financial calculator:

   Enter into the "n" key = 15
   Enter into the "i" key = 8
   Enter into the "fv" key = $100,000
   "pmt" key produces the results of $3,682.95*

(If a HP 12c calculator is used the payment shows as a "-".)

   *Sometimes a financial calculator will produce a slightly
   different answer than a compound interest table.*

Problem: How much will it take per month invested in an IRA for a 35 year old person accumulate $1,000,000 in 30 years to retire at age 65 assuming an 8% compounded monthly interest rate?

Example of calculation using the 8% monthly table:

   $1,000,000 x .000671 = $671.00

Example of calculation using a financial calculator:

   Enter into the "n" key (30 x 12) = 360
   Enter into the "i" key (8/12) = .666667
   Enter into the "fv" key = $1,000,000
   "pmt" key produces the results of = $670.98

(If a HP 12c calculator is used the payment shows as a '-".)

COMPOUND INTEREST TABLES

Column #4   PRESENT VALUE REVERSION OF 1

Formula: $V^n = \dfrac{1}{S^n}$

V = Present value of a single payment to be received in the future.

n = Number of periods

i = Rate of interest per period

Description: The present value of one dollar to be collected at a given future time when discounted at the effective interest rate for the number of periods from now to the date of collection. This is called the *Reversion Factor*.

Relationship of Tables: Reciprocal of Column 1

Problem: $100,000 will be received 10 years in the future. The applicable discount interest rate is 8 % compounded annually. What is its present value of the $100,000?

Example of calculation using the 8% annual interest table:

$100,000 x .463193 = $46,319.30

Example of calculation using a financial calculator:

Enter into the "n" key = 10

Enter into the "i" key = 8

Enter into the "fv" key = $100,000

"pv" key produces the results of = $46,319.35 *

(The present value payment shows on a HP 12c as a "-".)

Sometimes a financial calculator will produce a slightly different answer than a compound interest table.

COMPOUND INTEREST TABLES

Column #5 PRESENT VALUE ORDINARY ANNUITY
1 PER PERIOD

Formula: $\quad a_{\overline{n}|} = \dfrac{1 - V^n}{i}$

$a_{\overline{n}|}$ = Level annuity factor

V = Present value of a series of payments to be received in the future.

n = Number of periods

i = Rate of interest per period

Description: The present value of a series of future install-ments or payments of one dollar per period for a given number of periods when discounted at the effective interest rate. This factor is commonly known as the *Inwood Ordinary Annuity Coeffi-cient.*

Relationship of Tables: Reciprocal of Column 6

Problem: A person offers to buy your property and pay you $1000 per month at the end of each month for 20 years. The current interest rate is 8% per year. What is the cash equivalent amount you are being offered for the property?

Example of calculation using the 8% interest monthly table:

$1000 x 119.554291 = $119,554.29

Example of calculation using a financial calculator:

Enter into the "n" key (20 x 12) = 240

Enter into the "i" key (8/12) = .6666678

Enter into the "pmt" key = $1000

"pv" key produces the results of $119,554.29

(If HP 12c calculator is used the payment is entered as a "-".)

COMPOUND INTEREST TABLES

Column #6 INSTALLMENT TO AMORTIZE 1

Formula: $$1/a_{\overline{n}\rceil} = \frac{i}{1 - v^n}$$

$a_{\overline{n}\rceil}$ = Level annuity factor

V = Present value of a series of payments to be received in the future.

n = Number of periods

i = Rate of interest per period

Description: The level periodic installment which will pay interest and provide full amortization or recapture of an investment of one dollar in a given number of periods with interest at a given rate per period. Its most common application is as the periodic mortgage installment per dollar, and is in fact the *Ordinary Annuity which has a Present Value of One Dollar.*

Relationship of Tables: Reciprocal of Column 5

Problem: What is the level monthly payment of amortization and interest of a $100,000, 20 year, 8% mortgage?

Example of calculation using the 8% interest monthly table:

$100,000 x .008365 = $836.50

Example of calculation using a financial calculator:

Enter into the "n" key (20 x 12) = 240

Enter into the "i" key (8/12) = .666667

Enter into the "pv" key = $100,000

"pmt" key produces the results of = $836.44[*]

(If a HP 12c calculator is used the payment shows as a "-".)

Sometimes a financial calculator will produce a slightly different answer than a compound interest table.

RULES FOR USING SIX FUNCTIONS OF A DOLLAR TABLES AND THEIR RELATIONSHIP TO EACH OTHER

	1 AMOUNT OF 1 AT COMPOUND INTEREST	2 ACCUMULATION OF 1 PER PERIOD	3 SINKING FUND FACTOR	4 PRES. VALUE REVERSION OF 1	5 PRESENT VALUE ORD. ANNUITY 1 PER PERIOD	6 INSTALMENT TO AMORTIZE 1
	$S^n = (1+i)^n$	$S_{\overline{n}|} = \dfrac{S^n - 1}{i}$	$1/S_{\overline{n}|} = \dfrac{i}{S^n - 1}$	$V^n = \dfrac{1}{S^n}$	$a_{\overline{n}|} = \dfrac{1 - V^n}{i}$	$1/a_{\overline{n}|} = \dfrac{i}{1 - V^n}$
Formula	Amount of 1 at Compound Interest	Accumulation of 1 Per Period	Sinking Fund Factor	Present Value of Reversion of 1	Present Value Ordinary Annuity 1 Per Period	Installment to Amortize 1
When Payment Made and Withdrawn	Made at begining withdrawn at end of period	Made at End of Period & Withdrawn at End of Period				
How to Convert to Beginning of Period	If investment is withdrawn at B.O.P. then use E.O.P. from period before	Next highest factor -1 or E.O.P. x Base Factor	or E.O.P. Factor Base	or E.O.P. x Base Factor	Next lowest Factor-1 or E.O.P. x Base Factor	or E.O.P. Factor Base
How to Expand the Table	Multiply Factors	Add one Factor from Col.2 to a 2nd factor from Col. 2 times the Col. 1 factor opposite the 1st factor.	Cannot be extended directly. Use Col. 2 divided into 1 (1 + Col. 2 factor)	Multiply Factors	Add one Factor from Col. 5 to a 2nd factor from Col. 5 times the Col. 4 factor opposite the 1st factor.	Cannot be extended directly. Use Col. 5 divided into 1 (1 + Col. 5 factor)
Lay-Person's Description of Each Function	How much a deposit made now will grow to at compound interest.	How much a series of regular periodic deposits will grow to at compount interest.	How much must be deposited on a regular basis earning compound interest to accumulate a future sum.	How much a lump sum to be received in the future is worth now.	How much a series of regular payments to be received in the future is worth now.	What are the regular level payments of interest & amortization needed to pay-off a mortgage.
Relationship of Table	Reciprocal of Col. 4	Reciprocal of Col. 3	Reciprocal of Col. 2	Reciprocal of Col. 1	Reciprocal of Col. 6	Reciprocal of Col. 5
How to Handle a Deferred Payment	Use the factor for the number of years the money is actually on deposit.	Use the factor for the number of of periods the payments are actually made.	Use the factor for the number of years the money is actually left on deposit.	From the factor for the period when the payment is to be received substract the factor for the years from now the valuation is to be made.	Subtract the factor for the year before the annuity period starts from the factor for the year the annuity period ends.	Divide Col. 5 factor as per method to the left into 1.

Chart prepared by Ruth D. Lambert, President of Forms and Worms, Inc. May be reprinted and distributed as needed.

SUMMARY

The Income Approach is based on the proven theory that the value of income-producing property is determined by the future income the property produces for its owner.

The first step in estimating the value of a property based on its future income stream is to estimate the amount of the income stream to be obtained by the owner in the future.

The appraiser starts by estimating the potential gross income (PGI) attributable to the property, assuming it is fully rented at market rent, for the first year from the date of appraisal. From this, an estimated income loss from vacancies and

SUMMARY

Appraising simple single family residences requires sound knowledge of mathematical techniques. They range from adding and subtracting a series of comparable sales adjustments to plotting the results of a market study and applying some statistical tests to the results. The URAR and other Fannie Mae and Freddie Mac forms ask for information in terms of ranges. The cost approach requires addition, subtraction, multiplication and division of a wide variety of cost and depreciation numbers.

The income approach is an important part of the appraisal of any property which produces an income stream. To understand and use it requires extensive use of mathematical techniques. These include applying the advanced capitalization techniques needed to be a general certified appraiser. A certified appraiser also needs to understand and be able to work with algebraic equations.

In addition to basic arithmetic and statistics, this chapter also has information on performing a simple Linear Regression Analysis and Multiple Regression Analysis.

This chapter will not make a mathematical expert out of anyone who does not already possess the necessary skills. Its goal is consistent with the overall purpose of the book. It will remind you of things you have already learned. When you answer the practice questions, you will be able to better access your level of mathematical skills. Based on the number of questions you get correct, you can then decide what additional mathematical instruction you might need in order to pass which ever examination you select.

The chapter concludes with the Compound Interest Tables which illustrate the six functions of a dollar. They are the foundation of understanding capitalization. If this is new information to you, it is a signal that you may not have sufficient appraisal education to pass either the Residential or General license or any certification examination.

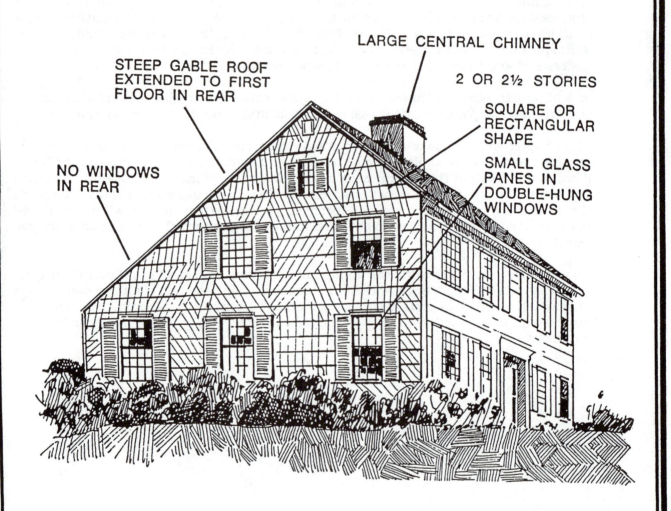

LARGE CENTRAL CHIMNEY

STEEP GABLE ROOF
EXTENDED TO FIRST
FLOOR IN REAR

2 OR 2½ STORIES

SQUARE OR
RECTANGULAR
SHAPE

NO WINDOWS
IN REAR

SMALL GLASS
PANES IN
DOUBLE-HUNG
WINDOWS

Colonial American

SALT BOX COLONIAL OR CATSLIDE (IN SOUTH)
(Salt Box or Catslide - 109)

ADDENDA CONTENTS

STUDENT WORKBOOK

Appraisal Software

Some time ago, we included a demonstration disk of "Know the Neighborhood—Appraisal Edition" on a CD-Rom in *REV*. Since then, many appraisers have found it to be a reliable and useful service for up-to-the-minute data right at their desktop.

"Know the Neighborhood" provides a vast amount of material for appraisers to use every day, which is packed into the CD-Rom they provide. The 4 million comparable sales—all less than 1 year old, which makes them perfect for FHA appraisals—are the key to this program's popularity, but it also offers street maps and census tracts for the whole USA with detailed data about everything from schools to fire protection for *every neighborhood.*

---

4 million comparable sales, all less than 1 year old

What you really must see to believe is the elegant ways this information can be displayed graphically and in text, for inclusion in your appraisal reports.

eNeighborhoods Inc. which markets "Know the Neighborhood— Appraisal Edition" —is so confident that you will like the program once you try it that they offer a trial subscription *at no risk to you.*

Sign up, and you'll get their complete CD-Rom—not a demo disk—which you may use as many times as you wish for a full month. If you do not want to continue your subscription, you just return the CD-Rom within 30 days and 100% of your money will be promptly refunded— *no questions ask*ed. Your refund is also guaranteed by *REV Magazine.*

SAVE TIME IN THE FIELD

With "Know the Neighborhood" you know before you inspect the subject property exactly where you can find reasonable comparable sales. Therefore, it is usually possible to select and photograph your comparables *before returning to your office.* You end up making just one trip to the site, as opposed to two. (We recommend taking a few extra pictures so that you have some leeway and can reject any sales which

you find upon later analysis do not meet your needs.)

CONVENIENT AND USEFUL

Appraisers who use the program regularly find that it is the simplest way to access neighborhood sales and other key data they need, and produce high quality exhibits for their reports.

Order the CD-Rom using the special introductory order form below, at a 50% discount. *Try it for a full month, and see how it works for you.* If you don't like it, simply return it within 30 days and you will get 100% of your money back — no hassles, no arguments.

TERRIFIC DATA SOURCE

We think you'll find that you've got an indispensable new data source right in your office. It amazes me whenever I use my CD-Rom that they can get so much information into such a small, compact and convenient format. They certainly had nothing like this when I was appraising. As for *how* they do it, you'd have to ask our 19 year old son, H Alex!

HSH

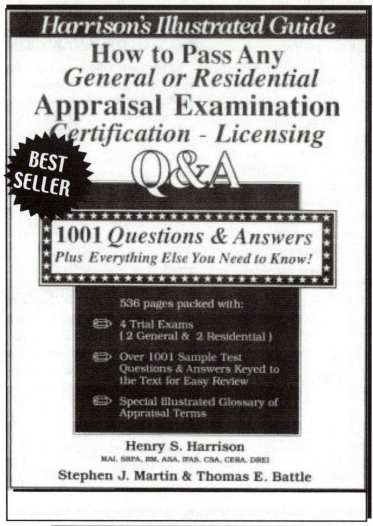

I hope you enjoy using this new *Appraising Residences and Income Properties* **CD-ROM.** This CD contains the complete text and all the illustrations in both the textbook and the student workbook. We have tried the CD on a wide variety of computers:. IBM PCs, clones and Macintosh systems. The *System Requirements* below tell you what computer configurations work best.

This CD-ROM incorporates the latest technology available and a copy of *Adobe Acrobat Reader Software. What is special about this software is its ability to let you search for any entry on the CD-ROM.* To use the CD-ROM, *you must first Install the version on this CD-ROM of Adobe Acrobat Reader Software* on your computer following the instructions below (and-in the *Read Me* file on the CD-ROM).

Note: *Most of the problems students have using the ARIP CD-ROM are caused by their failure to install the version of Adobe Acrobat Reader Software that is on the ARIP CD-ROM —wrongly thinking the one they already have on their computer will work.*

If you have a problem, and have trouble finding someone locally to help you, I will try my best to help. Contact me by FAX at (203) 562-5481, by e-mail at henryhsq@aol.com or write to me at: 315 Whitney Avenue, New Haven, CT 06511. (You may call the telephone number on the disk, but most likely you will get my voicemail, as I no longer have a secretary.)

Once you have installed the *Adobe Acrobat Reader Software,* you can begin to use the textbook and workbook portion of the CD-ROM, by clicking on the cover pictures. The first screen also shows a *Search* button. Click on it, and a box appears for you to type the term you are looking for.

For example, if you were looking for <u>Highest</u> <u>and</u> <u>Best</u> <u>Use</u>, you would type that phrase in the *Search* box. (The program will automatically ignore upper and lower case, unless you specify otherwise.) You will then get a list of chapter references where the term appeared, in order of importance (according to the computer!). Since "Highest and Best Use" is itself a chapter heading, this reference will appear first, and have a solid circle to the left, to indicate its importance. When you click on any item in the list, you are automatically taken to the *first page* of the chapter where it appears. Also, following such a search, every time "Highest and Best Use" appears in the text it will be highlighted. To view additional citings of the same item, flip through the pages looking for the highlighted words.

You may elect to read the material *on screen.* You should check your operating system instructions to be sure you know how to make your screen the full window size so you can read it more comfortably. In addition, anything that you see on screen may be printed on your printer.

SYSTEM REQUIREMENTS

This CD-ROM is designed to run on many modern computers. However, because it contains many graphics and a complex search program, it may not run on minimum configurations or computers with an old operating system or a slow processor.

IBM PCs and Clones
For IBM PCs or clones it is desirable to have Windows 98 and at least 16MB of memory. (It will run on some Windows 3.1 and NT systems too; for non-Windows 98 systems, see the software installation instructions in the *Read Me* file on the CD-ROM.) More memory will make the program run better (on some systems it will run with as little as 8MB of memory.) If you find you are getting *out of memory* messages you need to do one of three things:

1. Reset the minimum and maximum memory allocation (see your system manual).
2. Install a RAM Doubler program (they are very inexpensive and well worth the money).
3. Install additional memory in your computer. This will make all your programs run better.

Macintosh
For Apple Macintosh owners, it is desirable to have MacOS 9.2 or higher and at least 16MB of memory. More memory will make the program run better. If you find you are getting *out of memory* messages you need to do one of three things described above.

INSTALLATION INSTRUCTIONS

This CD-ROM uses *Adobe Acrobat Reader* as its foundation. It is a state of the art CD-ROM program that includes a multi-level search capability. Even if you already have Adobe Acrobat Reader installed on your computer, you should re-install it from this CD; not all versions of the software include the *Search* capabilities.

IBM PC & Clone Computers

Install the Adobe Acrobat Reader on the ARIP CD-ROM even if you have another version of the program already installed on your computer. (If you are not using Windows 98 or newer or Windows NT, refer to the alternate Windows installation instructions in the *Read Me* file on the CD-ROM.)

Insert the CD ROM into your CD ROM drive.
1. Select "My Computer" (by pointing and double clicking).
2. Select "Aripcd" (by pointing and double clicking).
3. Select "Acroread" (by pointing and double clicking).
4. Select "Win98" (by pointing and double clicking).
5. Select "setup" (by pointing and double clicking).
6. Select "yes" (by pointing and double clicking) to the question "This will install Acrobat Reader Search. Do you wish to continue?"
7. Follow the on-screen instructions to install the Adobe Acrobat Reader software.
8. Restart your computer.

How to run the ARIP Program:
Insert the CD-ROM into your CD-ROM drive.
1. Select "My Computer" (by pointing and double clicking).
2. Select the "ARIP pdf" Icon (by pointing and double clicking).

When the main menu appears, adjust your window size (follow the instructions in your operating system manual). You may now start using the program by double clicking on either of the book covers, one of the six addenda subject boxes, the word "Search" or the "?" icon (to get more help on how to use the program).

Apple Macintosh Computers

Insert the CD-ROM into your CD-ROM drive and wait for the Icon to appear on your screen. Open it by pointing and double clicking on it.

Install the Adobe Acrobat Program on the ARIP CD-ROM.
1. Select "acroread " folder (Open it by pointing and double clicking).
2. Select "Mac" folder (Open it by pointing and double clicking).
3. Select "Readers" folder (Open it by pointing and double clicking).
4. Select "Reader 301" Icon (Open it by pointing and double clicking).
5. Follow the instructions on the screens that appear.
6. Restart your computer after you successfully install the Adobe Acrobat Reader software.

How to run the ARIP Program:

Insert the CD ROM into your CD ROM drive.
Select the "ARIP.pdf" Icon (by pointing and double clicking).

When the main menu appears, adjust your window size (follow the instructions in your operating system manual). You may now start using the program by double clicking on either of the book covers, one of the six addenda subject boxes, the word "Search" or the "?" icon (to get more help on how to use the program).